Handbook of Parenting

Volume 4
Social Conditions and Applied Parenting

Handbook of Parenting

Second Edition

Volume 4
Social Conditions and Applied Parenting

Edited by

Marc H. Bornstein

National Institute of Child Health and Human Development

 LAWRENCE ERLBAUM ASSOCIATES, PUBLISHERS
2002   Mahwah, New Jersey   London

KH

Editor:	Bill Webber
Editorial Assistant:	Erica Kica
Cover Design:	Kathryn Houghtaling Lacey
Textbook Production Manager:	Paul Smolenski
Full-Service Compositor:	TechBooks
Text and Cover Printer:	Hamilton Printing Company

This book was typeset in 10/11.5 pt. Times, Italic, Bold, Bold Italic.
The heads were typeset in Helvetica, Italic, Bold, Bold Italic.

Lawrence Erlbaum Associates, Inc., Publishers
10 Industrial Avenue
Mahwah, New Jersey 07430

Library of Congress Cataloging-in-Publication Data

Handbook of parenting / edited by Marc H. Bornstein.—2nd ed.
    p. cm.
    Includes bibliographical references and indexes.
    Contents: v. 1. Children and parenting—v. 2. Biology and ecology of parenting—v. 3. Being
and becoming a parent—v. 4. Social conditions and applied parenting—v. 5. practical issues
in parenting.
    ISBN 0-8058-3778-7 (hc : v. 1 : alk. paper)—ISBN 0-8058-3779-5 (hc : v. 2 : alk. paper)—
ISBN 0-8058-3780-9 (hc : v. 3 : alk. paper)—ISBN 0-8058-3781-7 (hc : v. 4 : alk. paper)—
ISBN 0-8058-3782-5 (hc : v. 5 : alk. paper)
    1. Parenting. 2. Parents. I. Bornstein, Marc H.

HQ755.8.H357 2002
649′.1—dc21   2001058458

Printed in the United States of America
10 9 8 7 6 5 4 3 2

10/19/06

For *Marian* and *Harold Sackrowitz*

Contents of Volume 4:
Social Conditions and Applied Parenting

PART I: SOCIAL CONDITIONS OF PARENTING

Preface

This new edition of the *Handbook of Parenting* appears at a time that is momentous in the history of parenting. The family generally, and parenting specifically, are today in a greater state of flux, question, and redefinition than perhaps ever before. We are witnessing the emergence of striking permutations on the theme of parenting: blended families, lesbian and gay parents, teen versus fifties first-time moms and dads. One cannot but be awed on the biological front by technology that now renders postmenopausal women capable of childbearing and with the possibility of designing babies. Similarly, on the sociological front, single parenthood is a modern-day fact of life, adult–child dependency is on the rise, and parents are ever less certain of their roles, even in the face of rising environmental and institutional demands that they take increasing responsibility for their offspring. The *Handbook of Parenting* is concerned with all facets of parenting.

Despite the fact that most people become parents and everyone who has ever lived has had parents, parenting remains a most mystifying subject. Who is ultimately responsible for parenting? Does parenting come naturally, or must we learn how to parent? How do parents conceive of parenting? Of childhood? What does it mean to parent a preterm baby, twins, or a child with a disability? To be a younger or an older parent, or one who is divorced, disabled, or drug abusing? What do theories in psychology (psychoanalysis, personality theory, and behavior genetics, for example) contribute to our understanding of parenting? What are the goals parents have for themselves? For their children? What are the functions of parents' beliefs? Of parents' behaviors? What accounts for parents' believing or behaving in similar ways? What accounts for all the attitudes and actions of parents that differ? How do children influence their parents? How do personality, knowledge, and world view affect parenting? How do social status, culture, and history shape parenthood? How can parents effectively relate to schools, daycare, their children's pediatricians?

These are some of the questions addressed in this second edition of the *Handbook of Parenting* . . . for this is a book on *how to parent* as much as it is one on *what being a parent is all about*.

Put succinctly, parents create people. It is the entrusted and abiding task of parents to prepare their offspring for the physical, psychosocial, and economic conditions in which they will eventually fare and, it is hoped, flourish. Amidst the many influences on child development, parents are the "final common pathway" to children's development and stature, adjustment and success. Human social inquiry—at least since Athenian interest in Spartan childrearing practices—has always, as a matter of course, included reports of parenting. Yet Freud opined that childrearing is one of three "impossible professions"—the other two being governing nations and psychoanalysis. And one encounters as many views as the number of people one asks about the relative merits of being an at-home or a working mother, about whether daycare, family care, or parent care is best for a child, about whether good parenting reflects intuition or experience.

The *Handbook of Parenting* concerns itself with different types of parents—mothers and fathers, single, adolescent, and adoptive parents; with basic characteristics of parenting—behaviors, knowledge, beliefs, and expectations about parenting; with forces that shape parenting—employment, social status, culture, environment, and history; with problems faced by parents—handicaps, marital difficulties, drug addiction; and with practical concerns of parenting—how to promote children's health, foster social adjustment and cognitive competence, and interact with school, legal, and public officials. Contributors to the *Handbook of Parenting* have worked in different ways toward understanding all these diverse aspects of parenting, and all look to the most recent research and thinking in the field to shed light on many topics every parent wonders about.

Parenthood is a job whose primary object of attention and action is the child. But parenting also has consequences for parents. Parenthood is giving and responsibility, but parenting has its own intrinsic pleasures, privileges, and profits as well as frustrations, fears, and failures. Parenthood can enhance psychological development, self-confidence, and sense of well-being, and parenthood also affords opportunities to confront new challenges and to test and display diverse competencies. Parents can derive considerable and continuing pleasure in their relationships and activities with their children. But parenting is also fraught with small and large stresses and disappointments. The transition to parenting is formidable; the onrush of new stages of parenthood is relentless. In the final analysis, however, parents receive a great deal "in kind" for the hard work of parenting—they are often recipients of unconditional love, they gain skills, and they even pretend to immortality. This edition of the *Handbook of Parenting* presents the many positives that accompany parenting and offers solutions for the many challenges.

The *Handbook of Parenting* encompasses the broad themes of who are parents, whom parents parent, the scope of parenting and its many effects, the determinants of parenting, and the nature, structure, and meaning of parenthood for parents. This second edition of the *Handbook of Parenting* is divided into five volumes, each with two parts:

Volume 1 concerns CHILDREN AND PARENTING. Parenthood is, perhaps first and foremost, a functional status in the life cycle: Parents issue as well as protect, care for, and represent their progeny. But human development is too subtle, dynamic, and intricate to admit that parental caregiving alone determines the developmental course and outcome of ontogeny. Volume 1 of the *Handbook of Parenting* begins with chapters concerned with how children influence parenting. The origins of parenting are, of course, complex, but certain factors are of obvious importance. First, children affect parenting: Notable are their more obvious characteristics, like age or developmental stage; but more subtle ones, like gender, physical state, temperament, mental ability, and other individual-differences factors, are also instrumental. The chapters in Part I, on Parenting Children and Older People, discuss the unique rewards and special demands of parenting children of different ages—infants, toddlers, youngsters in middle childhood, and adolescents—as well as the modern notion of parent–child relationships in adulthood and later years. The chapters in Part II, on Parenting Children of Varying Status, discuss the common matters of parenting siblings and girls versus boys as well as more unique situations of parenting twins, adopted and foster children, and children with special needs, such as those born preterm, with mental retardation, or aggressive and withdrawn disorders.

Volume 2 concerns the BIOLOGY AND ECOLOGY OF PARENTING. For parenting to be understood as a whole, psychophysiological and sociological determinants of parenting need to be brought into the picture. Volume 2 of the *Handbook* relates parenting to its biological roots and sets parenting within its ecological framework. Some aspects of parenting are influenced by the biological makeup of human beings, and the chapters in Part I, on the Biology of Parenting, examine the evolution of parenting, hormonal and psychobiological determinants of parenting in nonhumans and in human beings, parenting in primates, and intuitive universals in human parenting. A deep understanding of what it means to parent also depends on the ecologies in which parenting takes place. Beyond the nuclear family, parents are embedded in, influence, and are themselves affected by larger social systems. The chapters in Part II, on the Social Ecology of Parenting, examine employment status and parenting, the socioeconomic, cultural, environmental, and historical contexts of parenting, and provide an overarching developmental contextual perspective on parenting.

Volume 3 concerns BEING AND BECOMING A PARENT. A large cast of characters is responsible for parenting, each has her or his own customs and agenda, and the psychological makeups and social interests of those individuals are revealing of what parenting is. Chapters in Part I, on The Parent, show how rich and multifaceted is the constellation of children's caregivers. Considered successively are mothers, fathers, coparenting, single parenthood, grandparenthood, adolescent parenthood, nonparental caregiving, sibling caregivers, parenting in divorced and remarried families, lesbian and gay parents, and the role of contemporary reproductive technologies in parenting. Parenting also draws on transient and enduring physical, personality, and intellectual characteristics of the individual. The chapters in Part II, on Becoming and Being a Parent, consider the transition to parenting, stages of parental development, personality and parenting, parents' knowledge of, beliefs in, cognitions about, attributions for, and attitudes toward childrearing, as well as relations between psychoanalysis and parenthood. Such parental cognitions serve many functions: They generate and shape parental behaviors, mediate the effectiveness of parenting, and help to organize parenting.

Volume 4 concerns SOCIAL CONDITIONS AND APPLIED PARENTING. Parenting is not uniform in all communities, groups, or cultures; rather, parenting is subject to wide variation. Volume 4 of the *Handbook* describes socially defined groups of parents and social conditions that promote variation in parenting. The chapters in Part I, on Social Conditions of Parenting, include ethnic and minority parenting in general and parenting among Latino, African American, and Asian populations, in particular, as well as parents in poverty and parenting and social networks. Parents are ordinarily the most consistent and caring people in the lives of children. In everyday life, however, parenting does not always go right or well. Information, education, and support programs can remedy these ills. The chapters in Part II, on Applied Issues in Parenting, explore parenting competence, maternal deprivation, marital relationships and conflict, parenting with a sensory or physical disability, parental psychopathology, substance-abusing parents, parental child maltreatment, and parent education.

Volume 5 concerns PRACTICAL ISSUES IN PARENTING. Parents meet the biological, physical, and health requirements of children. Parents interact with children socially. Parents stimulate children to engage and understand the environment and to enter the world of learning. Parents provision, organize, and arrange children's home and local environments and the media to which children are exposed. Parents also manage child development vis-à-vis childcare, school, the worlds of medicine and law, as well as other social institutions through their active citizenship. Volume 5 of the *Handbook* describes the nuts and bolts of parenting as well as the promotion of positive parenting practices. The chapters in Part I, on Practical Parenting, review the ethics of parenting, parenting and attachment, child compliance, the development of children's self-regulation, children's prosocial and moral development, socialization and children's values, maximizing children's cognitive abilities, parenting talented children, play in parent–child interactions, everyday stresses and parenting, parents and children's peer relationships, and health promotion. Such caregiving principles and practices have direct effects on children. Parents indirectly influence children as well, for example, through their relationships with each other and their local or larger community. The chapters in Part II, on Parents and Social Institutions, explore parents and their children's childcare, schools, media, and doctors and delve into relations between parenthood and the law and public policy.

Each chapter in the second edition of the *Handbook of Parenting* addresses a different but central topic in parenting; each is rooted in current thinking and theory as well as in classical and modern research in that topic; each has been written to be read and absorbed in a single sitting. Each chapter in this new *Handbook* follows a standard organization, including an introduction to the chapter as a whole, followed by historical considerations of the topic, a discussion of central issues and theory, a review of classical and modern research, forecasts of future directions of theory and research, and a set of conclusions. Of course, each chapter considers the contributors' own convictions and research, but contributions to this new edition of the *Handbook of Parenting* present all major points of view and central lines of inquiry and interpret them broadly. The *Handbook of Parenting* is intended to be both comprehensive and state of the art. To assert that parenting is complex is to understate the obvious. As the expanded scope of this second edition of the *Handbook of Parenting* amply shows, parenting is naturally and closely allied with many other fields.

The *Handbook of Parenting* is concerned with child outcomes of parenting but also with the nature and dimensions of variations in parenting per se. Beyond an impressive range of information, readers will find *passim* critical discussions of typologies of parenting (e.g., authoritarian–autocratic, indulgent–permissive, indifferent–uninvolved, authoritative–reciprocal), theories of parenting (e.g., ecological, psychoanalytic, behavior genetic, ethological, behavioral, sociobiological), conditions of parenting (e.g., mother versus father, cross cultural, situation-by-age-by-style), recurrent themes in parenting studies (e.g., attachment, transaction, systems), and even aphorisms (e.g., "A child should have strict discipline in order to develop a fine, strong character," "The child is father to the man").

In the course of editing this new edition of the *Handbook*, I set about to extract central messages and critical perspectives expressed in each chapter, fully intending to construct a comprehensive Introduction to these volumes. In the end, I took away two significant impressions from my own efforts and the texts of my many collaborators in this work. First, my notes cumulated to a monograph on parenting . . . clearly inappropriate for an Introduction. Second, when all was written and done, I found the chorus of contributors to this new edition of the *Handbook* more eloquent and compelling than one lone voice could ever be. Each chapter in the *Handbook of Parenting* begins with an articulate and persuasive Introduction that lays out, in a clarity, expressiveness, and force (I frankly envy), the meanings and implications of that contribution and that perspective to parenting. In lieu of one Introduction, readers are urged to browse the many Introductions that will lead their way into the *Handbook of Parenting*.

Once upon a time, parenting was a seemingly simple thing: Mothers mothered; Fathers fathered. Today, parenting has many motives, many meanings, and many manifestations. Contemporary parenting is viewed as immensely time consuming and effortful. The perfect mother or father or family is a figment of past imagination. Modern society recognizes "subdivisions" of the call: genetic mother, gestational mother, biological mother, birth mother, social mother. For some, the individual sacrifices that mark parenting arise for the sole and selfish purpose of passing one's genes on to succeeding generations. For others, a second child is conceived to save the life of a first child. A multitude of factors influence the unrelenting advance of events and decisions that surround parenting—biopsychological, dyadic, contextual, historical. Recognizing this complexity is important to informing people's thinking about parenting, especially information-hungry parents themselves. This second edition of the *Handbook of Parenting* explores all these motives, meanings, and manifestations of parenting.

Each day more than three fourths of a million adults around the world experience the rewards and the challenges as well as the joys and the heartaches of becoming parents. The human race succeeds because of parenting. From the start, parenting is a "24/7" job. Parenting formally begins during or before pregnancy and can continue throughout the lifespan: Practically speaking for most, *once a parent, always a parent*. But parenting is a subject about which people hold strong opinions and about which too little solid information or considered reflection exists. Parenting has never come with a *Handbook* . . . until now.

ACKNOWLEDGMENTS

I would like to express my sincere gratitude to the staffs at Lawrence Erlbaum Associates, Publishers, and TechBooks who perfectly parented production of the *Handbook of Parenting*: Victoria Danahy, Susan Detwiler, Sheila Johnston, Arthur M. Lizza, Paul Smolenski, and Christopher Thornton.

—Marc H. Bornstein

Contents of Volume 1:
Children and Parenting

Contents of Volume 2:
Biology and Ecology of Parenting

PART II: SOCIAL ECOLOGY OF PARENTING

Contents of Volume 3:
Being and Becoming a Parent

Contents of Volume 5:
Practical Issues in Parenting

About the Authors in Volume 4

SANDRA T. AZAR is an Associate Professor at the Frances L. Hiatt School of Psychology, Clark University, where she has served as Director of the Clinical Psychology Training Program. She received her B.A. from Wheaton College and M.A. and Ph.D. from the University of Rochester. She was also an Assistant Professor at Concordia University in Montreal, she has been a Liberal Arts Fellow at Harvard Law School, and she received an NIMH FIRST Award grant. Azar is a member of the American Psychological Association and the Association for the Advancement of Behavior Therapy. She has published on cognitive theory, research, and treatment in child abuse and neglect, as well as on legal issues in this area. She has conducted workshops at the federal level on the treatment needs of abusive and neglectful parents and definitional issues.

* * *

MARGO A. CANDELARIA is a graduate student in the Applied Developmental Psychology at the University of Maryland, Baltimore County. She received her B.A. from The Pennsylvania State University and her M.A. from the University of Maryland, Baltimore County. A member of the American Psychological Association, Candelaria has clinical experience working in the fields of early intervention and parent education with infants and young children and their families, particularly with children and families at risk. She has been associated with the Public Policy Office of the American Psychological Association. Her research interests include factors that influence parental involvement in intervention programs and program evaluation.

* * *

VIVIAN J. CARLSON is a postdoctoral Fellow at the University of Connecticut. She was educated at Tufts University and the University of Connecticut. Her career has focused on home-based developmental therapy with the families of infants, toddlers, and preschoolers with special needs, and includes experience in early intervention, public preschool, and Head Start programs. Her research investigates the cultural patterning of everyday experiences among European American and Puerto Rican mothers and infants.

* * *

RUTH CHAO is an Assistant Professor in the Department of Psychology at the University of California, Riverside. She received her B.A. from the University of California, Irvine, and her Ph.D. from the University of California, Los Angeles. Chao was also an Assistant Professor in the Department of Child and Families Studies at Syracuse University. Her research interests include sociocultural perspectives on parenting and the family focusing on Asian immigrants. She studies the effects of parental control, warmth, and involvement in school on adolescent school performance and behavioral adjustment. This research also includes studies of the language acculturation of Asian immigrant families across time and its effects on adolescent's adjustment.

* * *

MONCRIEFF COCHRAN is Professor of Human Development and Family Studies in the College of Human Ecology at Cornell University. Cochran received his A.B. from Harvard College and M.A. and Ph.D. from the University of Michigan. His research interests address environmental systems affecting parent and child development, and his program development activities involve empowerment-oriented family support and early care and education programs based on that research. The content of his research and program development work includes childcare, home-school relations, the social networks of parents and children, and the empowerment process. Cochran is coauthor of *Extending Families: The Social Networks of Parents and their Children* and *Child Care that Works*. He has edited the *International Handbook of Child Care Policies* and *Programs and Empowerment and Family Support*.

* * *

CYNTHIA GARCÍA COLL is Professor of Education, Psychology and Pediatrics, Chair of the Education Department, and the Mittlemann Family Director for the Center for the Study of Human Development at Brown University. She received her Ph.D. from Harvard University. García Coll is a Fellow of the American Psychological Association. She has published articles on the sociocultural and biological influences on early childhood development and teenage pregnancy and served on the editorial boards of *Child Development*, *Development and Psychopathology*, and *Infant Behavior and Development*. She is a member of the Committee on Racial and Ethnic Issues for the Society for Research on Child Development, on whose Executive Committee she serves. García Coll has coedited several books: *The Psychosocial Development of Puerto Rican Women*; *Puerto Rican Women and Children: Issues in Health, Growth and Development*; and *Mothering Against the Odds: Diverse Voices of Contemporary Mothers*.

* * *

SUNITA DUGGAL is a licensed psychologist in the Section on Developmental Psychopathology at the National Institute of Mental Health in Bethesda, MD, and in private practice. She received her education at Williams College (B.A.) and the University of Minnesota (M.A. and Ph.D.). She completed a postdoctoral internship at Western Psychiatric Institute and Clinic in Pittsburgh. She is a member of the American Psychological Association and is on the ethics committee of the Maryland Psychological Association. Her research interests include the role of parent–child relationships in the development of psychopathology and the development of sex differences in internalizing problems such as depressive and anxiety disorders.

* * *

GREG J. DUNCAN is Professor of Education and Social Policy and a Faculty Associate in the Institute for Policy Research at Northwestern University. He is director of the Northwestern University/University of Chicago Joint Center for Poverty Research. Duncan received a Ph.D. from the University of Michigan. Duncan was a Research Scientist at the University of Michigan's Institute for Social Research, and he directed the Panel Study of Income Dynamics. Duncan's research has focused on economic mobility both within and across generations, how economic conditions in families and neighborhoods affect child development, and how welfare reform affects families and children. He is the author of *Years of Poverty, Years of Plenty* and is coeditor of *Consequences of Growing Up Poor* and *Neighborhood Poverty*.

* * *

JOHN M. GOTTMAN is Professor of Psychology at the University of Washington. He received his M.S. at Massachusetts Institute of Technology and his M.A. and Ph.D. at the University of Wisconsin. Gottman was Professor of Psychology at the University of Illinois. He is a Fellow of the American Psychological Association and the author of *Seven Principles to Making Marriage Work*, *The Marriage Clinic: A Scientifically Based Marital Therapy*, *Metaemotion: How Families Communicate Emotionally*, *The Heart of Parenting*, and *What Predicts Divorce*.

* * *

REUT GRUBER is a Visiting Fellow in the Section on Developmental Psychopathology at the National Institute of Mental Health in Bethesda, MD. She received her Ph.D. at Tel-Aviv University in Israel. Her research interests include the study of ADHD, development of children at risk for psychopathology, sleep in normal and special populations, and sex differences in emotional and social development.

* * *

JOHN H. GRYCH is Assistant Professor in the Department of Psychology at Marquette University. He received his B.A. at the University of Wisconsin-Madison and Ph.D. at the University of Illinois at Urbana-Champaign and was a postdoctoral Fellow at the University of Wisconsin-Madison. He is a member of the Society for Research in Child Development and the American Psychological Association and has served on the editorial board of the *Journal of Family Psychology*. His interests include the effects of family processes, such as interparental conflict, domestic violence, and divorce, on children's development, children's perceptions of family interactions, and the links between marital and parental functioning. Grych is coeditor of *Interparental Conflict and Child Development: Theory, Research, and Applications*.

* * *

ROBIN L. HARWOOD is an Associate Professor in the School of Family Studies at the University of Connecticut. She received her Ph.D. from Yale University. Previously, she was at the University of New Orleans. She received a FIRST Award from NIH. Her research interests are in the study of culture, mother–infant interactions, and attachment outcomes among middle-socioeconomic Puerto Rican and European American families. She is currently an associate editor for the *Journal of Developmental and Behavioral Pediatrics* and is a member of the Society for Research in Child Development, the American Psychological Association, and the American Anthropological Association. She is the author of *Culture And Attachment: Perceptions of The Child in Context*.

* * *

CATHERINE A. LESESNE is a Behavioral Scientist at the Centers for Disease Control and Prevention, working in early child development and attention-deficit/hyperactivity disorder. Lesesne was educated at the University of South Carolina (B.A. and M.P.H.) and is currently a graduate student at Georgia State University in the Community Psychology doctoral program. She has been an ASPH Public Health System Fellow and, professionally, is interested in the design, implementation, and evaluation of intervention and prevention programs targeting abnormal child development and adolescent behavior.

* * *

BIRGIT LEYENDECKER is a Research Fellow at the Ruhr-University in Bochum, Germany. She was educated at the Universities of Marburg and Osnabrueck. Her main interests are sociocultural issues and migration. During her time as a Fogarty Fellow at the National Institute of Child Health and Human Development, she was involved in a study on migrant families from Central America. Currently, she is Co-Investigator of a study funded by NIH, examining group differences in childrearing beliefs and practices among Turkish immigrants in Germany and Puerto Rican immigrants in Connecticut.

* * *

KATHERINE A. MAGNUSON is currently a graduate student in Northwestern University's Human Development and Social Policy Doctoral Program. Magnuson received her B.A. from Brown University. She is a Joint Center for Poverty Research graduate Fellow, and her research focuses on how socioeconomic status affects family functioning and child development.

* * *

LINDA C. MAYES is the Arnold Gesell Associate Professor of Child Psychiatry, Pediatrics, and Psychology in the Yale Child Study Center. Mayes holds an NIH Career Development Award and oversees a behavioral and psychophysiology laboratory at the Child Study Center. Trained as a child and adult psychoanalyst and as a pediatrician, neonatologist, and developmentalist, Mayes' work integrates theoretical perspectives from developmental psychology, neuroscience, and child psychiatry. Her theoretical and empirical writings are published in the child psychiatric, developmental psychology, and pediatric literature.

* * *

HARRIETTE PIPES McADOO is University Distinguished Professor of Family and Child Ecology, Michigan State University. She received her B.A. and M.A. from Michigan State University and her Ph.D. from the University of Michigan, and she has done postdoctoral study at Harvard University. She formerly taught at Howard University in the School of Social Work, where she was Acting Dean. She was Visiting Lecturer at the Smith College School of Social Work, the University of Washington, and the University of Minnesota. She has served as Director of the Groves Conference on Marriage and the Family, as National Adviser to the White House Conference on Families, and as President of the National Council on Family Relations. She has been a member of the Governing Council of the Society for Research in Child Development and is a lifetime member of the National Association of Black Psychologists. McAdoo was honored with the Marie Peters Award for Outstanding Scholarship, Leadership, and Service in the Area of Ethnic Minority Families and the Helms Award. She is a Fellow of the Institute of Children, Youth, and Families at Michigan State University. She has published on racial attitudes and self-esteem in young children, Black mobility patterns, coping strategies of single mothers, and professional Kenyan and Zimbabwean women. She edited *Family Ethnicity: Strength in Diversity* and *Black Families,* coedited *Services to Young Families: Program Review and Policy Recommendations* and *Black Children: Social, Educational, and Parental Environments*, and coauthored *Women and Children: Alone and in Poverty.*

* * *

KATHRYN P. MEADOW-ORLANS is Professor Emerita in the Department of Educational Foundations and Research at Gallaudet University, where she also served as a Senior Research Scientist in the Gallaudet Research Institute. She received a B.A. from Denison University, M.S. from the University of Chicago, and Ph.D. from the University of California, Berkeley. She was Adjunct Professor of Sociology, Department of Psychiatry, the University of California, San Francisco. She is a member of the Society for Research in Child Development, the American Sociological Association, and the District of Columbia Sociological Society (past President). She was honored by the American Psychiatric Association as "A Pioneer in Deafness and Mental Health" and with the publication of *The Deaf Child in the Family and at School: Essays in Honor of Kathryn P. Meadow-Orlans.* Meadow-Orlans is author of *Deafness and Child Development*, coauthor of *Sound and Sign, Childhood Deafness and Mental Health*, and coeditor of *Educational and Developmental Aspects of Deafness.*

* * *

AMY M. MILLER is a postdoctoral Fellow at the National Institute of Child Health and Human Development. She holds a Ph.D. from the University of Connecticut School of Family Studies and was also educated at the University of New Orleans. Her research interests include the cultural coherence between parents' beliefs and behaviors, the intergenerational construction of parenting beliefs and values, and the adaptation of parenting beliefs, values, and behaviors in the face of rapid societal change or migration.

* * *

STARR NIEGO is a Developmental Psychologist who specializes in designing, implementing, and evaluating education and health promotion programs, particularly for at-risk youth. She received her B.A. from Williams College and M.A. and Ph.D. from Cornell University. Most recently, she was a Senior Research Associate at Sociometrics, where she directed the Program Archive on Sexuality, Health and Adolescence (PASHA), a collection of effective teen pregnancy and STD/HIV/AIDS prevention programs.

* * *

LEE M. PACHTER is Associate Professor of Pediatrics and Anthropology and Head of the Division of General Pediatrics at the University of Connecticut School of Medicine. He is the Director of the pediatric inpatient unit and the sickle cell service at Saint Francis Hospital and Medical Center in Hartford, CT. He is Associate Editor of the *Journal of Developmental and Behavioral Pediatrics* and is on the Editorial Board of *Ambulatory Pediatrics: The Journal of the Ambulatory Pediatric Association*. He is a Fellow of the American Academy of Pediatrics and the Society for Applied Anthropology. His research interests include the study of minority child behavior and development, perceptions of racism in children, community level influences on child health and development, social pediatrics, ethnomedicine, and cross-cultural communication in the medical setting.

* * *

RUTH PEROU is a Research Psychologist at the Centers for Disease Control and Prevention. She received her doctorate degree in Applied Developmental Psychology from the University of Miami in Coral Gables, Florida. At the CDC, she is part of the Child Development Studies Team in the Developmental Disabilities Branch. Currently, she is working on developmental disabilities, attention-deficit/hyperactivity disorder, and *Legacy for Children*™, a research project designed to examine the potential for improvement in child developmental outcomes.

* * *

MICHAEL RUTTER is Professor of Developmental Psychopathology at the Institute of Psychiatry, Kings College, University of London. He trained in medicine at the University of Birmingham, England, with post-graduate training in neurology, pediatrics, and psychiatry in the United Kingdom, and then training in child development at Albert Einstein College of Medicine, New York. He was Director of the Medical Research Council Child Psychiatry Research Unit and also the Social, Genetic and Developmental Psychiatry Research Centre in London. His research interests span a wide field, but with a particular focus on the developmental interplay between nature and nurture and on the use of natural experiments to test causal hypotheses about genetic and environmental mediation of risk in relation to normal and abnormal psychological development. He is the recipient of numerous international awards and honors and was elected a Fellow of the Royal Society in 1987. He was President of the Society for Research in Child Development and the International Society for Research into Child and Adolescent Psychopathology. His books include *Maternal Deprivation Reassessed* and *Developing Minds: Challenges and Continuity Across the Lifespan*.

* * *

D. CAMILLE SMITH is a Behavioral Scientist at the Centers for Disease Control in Atlanta. Smith was educated at Florida State University, George Washington University, and the University of Washington. Her research interests include the study of improving child developmental outcomes through programs designed to influence parenting behavior. Her professional experience includes statewide program planning and administration for young children with disabilities, university-based teaching in infant and child psychology, and direct service delivery with children and families. Smith has served as a member of the CDC Children's Health Initiative, CDC Child Care Working Group, the PA Governor's Commission for Children and Families, as well as numerous planning projects designed to improve the well-being of children and families.

* * *

DOUGLAS M. TETI is Professor of Psychology in the Department of Psychology at the University of Maryland, Baltimore County (UMBC). He received his B.S. from St. Joseph's College, his M.S. from Villanova University, and his Ph.D. from the University of Vermont. He was a postdoctoral Fellow at the University of Utah. He is a member of the Society for Research in Child Development, the American Psychological Association, and the International Society for Infant Studies. Teti's research includes the assessment, caregiving antecedents, and developmental sequelae of early attachments, intervention with clinically depressed mothers of infants, the development and significance of early sibling relationships, and parental, familial, and psychosocial predictors of parent–infant outcomes among families with preterm infants. He has served on the editorial boards of *Child Development, Developmental Psychology*, and *Early Education and Development* and is Associate Editor of *Developmental Psychology*. He is editor of the forthcoming *Handbook of Research Methods in Developmental Psychology* and coauthor of *Development in Infancy*.

* * *

SEAN D. TRUMAN is a Post Doctoral Fellow at the Yale Child Study Center. Truman received his B.A. from Reed College and his Ph.D. in Clinical Psychology from the University of Connecticut. His research interests include the study of parenting in high-risk families, including the ways in which maternal substance abuse, exposure to trauma, and social disruption affect outcomes in children. Truman has also worked to develop and implement Welfare to Work programs in Connecticut.

* * *

VIVIAN TSENG is Assistant Professor of Psychology at California State University, Northridge. She received her Ph.D. in Psychology at New York University and her B.A. in Psychology and Asian American Studies at the University of California, Los Angeles. She is a member of the Society for Research in Child Development, Society for Research on Adolescence, and the Society for Community Research and Action. She is founding chair of the SCRA Students of Color Interest Group and a member of the SCRA Mentoring Task Force. Her research examines cultural and immigration processes in the social development and adaptation of adolescents, young adults, and their families in U.S. society. She is also interested in prevention and promotion frameworks for enhancing the adaptation of children and families.

* * *

CAROLYN ZAHN-WAXLER is a Research Psychologist in the Intramural Research Program of the National Institute of Mental Health in Bethesda, MD. She is the Head of the Section on Developmental Psychopathology. She obtained her B.A. from the University of Wisconsin and M.A. and Ph.D. from the Institute of Child Development at the University of Minnesota. She is a Fellow of the American Psychological Association and of the American Psychological Society. She has been a member of the Governing Council for the Society for Research in Child Development, and she served as President of Division 7 of the APA in 1997. Her developmental research interests include the study of empathy, affective, and behavioral problems, gender differences in psychopathology, emotion regulation, and socialization of emotion. She served as editor of *Developmental Psychology,* Senior Editor for the American Psychological Association–Oxford University Press *Encyclopedia of Psychology, and* Associate Editor for the *Annual Review of Psychology*. She is the author of *Altruism and Aggression: Biological and Social Origins* and coauthor of *A Century of Developmental Theory*.

* * *

BEVERLY J. WILSON is Assistant Professor in the Department of Graduate Psychology at Seattle Pacific University. She received her B.A. and M.A. from California State University-Fresno and Ph.D. from the University of Washington. Wilson was previously at Oregon State University. She is a member of the Society for Research in Child Development, the American Psychological Association, and American Association on Mental Retardation. Her research interests include the peer relationship difficulties and conduct problems of children in the early elementary-school years and the role of emotions and families in children's development.

* * *

Handbook of Parenting

Volume 4
Social Conditions and Applied Parenting

PART I

SOCIAL CONDITIONS
OF PARENTING

1

Ethnic and Minority Parenting

Cynthia García Coll
Brown University
Lee M. Pachter
University of Connecticut

Marvin is a 7-year-old African American boy who is disruptive in the classroom and aggressive toward younger children on the playground. He has been evaluated at school and has been given the diagnosis of attention deficit/hyperactivity disorder (ADHD) and recommended that he be placed on medication to help control his behavior. He is being reared by his mother and grandmother in public housing project where drug related violence occurs frequently. The family's disciplinary practices include spanking and withholding meals, which are described as necessary given the potentially high price of misbehavior around the project. Teachers and school officials are frustrated by the family's apparent dismissal of Marvin's school behavioral issues as "nothing to worry about" and defend their disciplinary measures as "getting him ready for the real world." The mother refuses to put Marvin on any medication that would "control" his behavior or "make him a zombie."

Rosa is a 4-year-old girl who recently immigrated with her family from the Dominican Republic. She and her 5-year-old sister sleep in the parents' bedroom, often sharing the same bed with the parents. A church member was concerned when Rosa drew a picture of herself sleeping next to her father as part of a Sunday school project and spoke with the parents. Rosa's parents were angry and did not understand the church member's concerns. The family questioned whether they really belonged in the church after all, even though worship and church community had always been important to them.

Linda, a 27-year-old recent immigrant from Puerto Rico, brings her 14-month-old infant into the clinic for a checkup. The doctor asks her how she thinks the baby is doing, and she says fine. When the doctor expresses concern that the baby is not yet walking, he tells Linda that she really should be keeping a closer watch on the child's development so that he does not fall behind and gives Linda the impression that she is a "bad mother" for not being concerned about this issue. The doctor also notices that the baby has an ear infection and prescribes an antibiotic that he states is new and very good for ear infections. Linda goes to the pharmacy to pick up the medication but finds out that her insurance does not cover that particular antibiotic and the cost is $95, which she cannot afford. She decides to treat the ear infection with warm olive oil applied to the ear canal, which her mother gave to her as a child and which always made her earaches better.

INTRODUCTION

Do ethnic and minority groups differ from the majority and from each other in respect to parenting practices and processes? What explains the similarities and differences among groups? How do differences in parenting relate to developmental outcomes in these populations?

Although the responses to these questions vary given the particular group under study and the particular aspect of parenting under scrutiny, increasing our understanding of ethnic and minority parenting in the United States is crucial for a variety of reasons. Most of the extant literature on "normative" aspects of parenting is based on middle–socioeconomic status (SES), Anglo, United States based samples. The limitations of that particular research strategy are clearly exemplified by recent research showing that certain aspects of parenting (i.e., expected educational attainment and authoritative style) are not only distributed differently in different ethnic and minority groups, but the same parenting behaviors can be associated with positive developmental outcomes in some groups but not in others (e.g., Brody and Flor, 1998; Okagaki and Frensch, 1998; Steinberg, Dornbush, and Brown, 1992). Thus, studying parenting among ethnic and minority groups in the United States informs our understanding of normative parenting process and their associations with developmental outcomes in general.

A second reason is that there are some unique conditions under which ethnic and minority parents have to operate. For example, a potential issue for ethnic and minority parents is the discontinuity between their cultural and social capital with that of mainstream culture and institutions. The work by Delgado-Gaitán (1991) and Moll (1994) exemplifies the struggle that discontinuities between home and school create on the day-to-day interactions with their children's schools for some minority parents. This sociocultural discontinuity might not be present or might be smaller in magnitude for European American, middle-SES parents.

Another source of discontinuity stems from the particular social location that ethnic and minority groups occupy in the social stratification system in the United States and that is constantly reinforced by mainstream institutions, policies, and practices (Baca-Zinn and Wells, 2000). Elsewhere we have elaborated on theoretical frameworks that delineate the particular mechanisms (i.e. racism, discrimination, prejudice and oppression, among others) that operate in our society as a social stratification system (García Coll et al., 1996; García Coll, 2000; Pachter, 2000). The discontinuities observed between majority and minority parenting is not only a matter of cultural, socioeconomic, or racial and ethnic differences, it is also a function of the portrayal of these differences as deficits and the real consequences for these families in terms of opportunities, resources, and rewards.

These unique conditions place specific demands on ethnic and minority parents that need to be addressed in our understanding of parenting processes in these populations. For example, there is growing attention to the specific strategies that ethnic and minority parents use to deal with racial socialization (Hughes and Chen, 1999). In addition, studying parenting within different contextual demands can increase our understanding of parenting processes in general as a function of environmental input by providing variability in environmental conditions and allowing for testing associations that are not observed under more uniform contexts.

Finally, a more pragmatic reason underscoring the importance of understanding ethnic and minority parenting is the fact that the United States is going through a major demographic shift. In 1970, the minority population (Hispanics, non-Hispanic African Americans, Asians, and Native Americans) represented 16% of the population. In 1998, this percentage increased to 27%, and it is estimated that by the year 2050 these groups will account for about half of the United States population (Figure 1.1; Council of Economic Advisors, 1998). The rise in minority population is a function of immigration as well as differential fertility rates in different groups.

There are also differences in the age distribution of these populations (Figure 1.2). Minority populations in general are younger than the European American population. In 1997, school-age

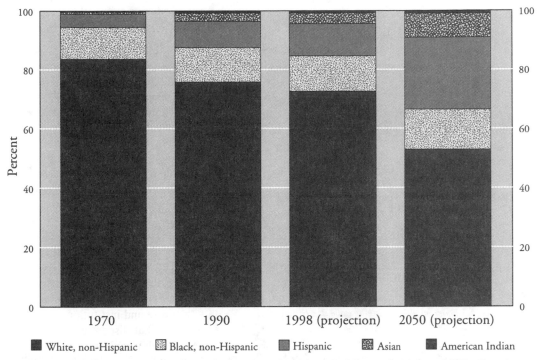

FIGURE 1.1. Racial/ethnic composition of the population. From: Council of Economic Advisors (1998), *Changing America: Indicators of Social and Economic Well-being by Race and Hispanic Origin.*

children (ages 5–17) were more ethnically diverse than the population as a whole. All these data point to the increasing heterogeneity and diversity of the United States population.

Thus, the study of parenting among ethnic and minority families is important not only for scholarly reasons pertaining to our understanding of parenting in general or within particular groups. As minority and ethnic children become the majority of the youth population in the United States, scholarly work in parenting among these populations is necessary to inform public policy, practice, and effective intervention on these children's behalf.

This chapter begins with an historic overview of the extant research with ethnic and minority parents from a theoretical perspective, followed by an elaboration of the unique issues faced by these families in the United States, and thus the need and importance for research with these particular populations. We conclude with implications for policy and practice and for future research.

HISTORICAL OVERVIEW OF ETHNIC AND MINORITY RESEARCH

The literature on ethnic and minority parenting in the United States displays a prevalence of deficit models (García Coll et al., 1996; McLoyd and Randolph, 1985; see also Demo, Allen, and Fine, 2000). Historically, parenting practices of ethnic and minority families have been conceptualized as those of "the other" group, which then are compared to the "standard" (defined as those displayed by Caucasian, middle-SES, northern European, American parents). Moreover, the differences observed between the groups are interpreted in terms of deficits, and not necessarily as adaptive strategies responsive to unique environmental and historical demands. For example, early studies of African American, Puerto Rican, and Mexican Americans depicted their parenting practices as pathogenic and dysfunctional (e.g., Lewis, 1965; Moynihan, 1965; Rubel, 1966). Most of these studies were based

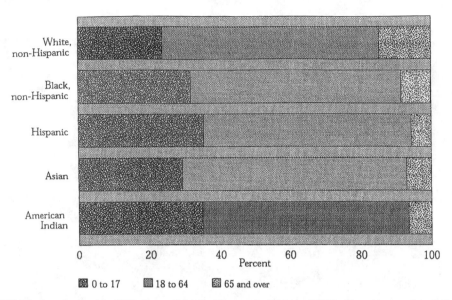

FIGURE 1.2. Age distribution, 1997. From: Council of Economic Advisors (1998), *Changing America: Indicators of Social and Economic Well-being by Race and Hispanic Origin.*

on low-income and typically problem-ridden families, but their findings were quickly generalized and accepted as descriptive of the family life of all families within the particular ethnic or minority group (Taylor, 2000).

This particular approach to the "scientific" work on parenting in ethnic and minority groups reflects the dominant paradigms of assimilation and modernization prevalent toward immigrants, former slaves, and indigenous populations in the United States (Baca-Zinn and Wells, 2000). This particular theoretical and empirical approach assumes that there is a universal way to parent or at least a uniformly good one in the United States. Since the inception of child development as a field in the nineteenth century, the field has responded to society's needs to establish certain childrearing practices as optimal. In other words, the need for scientific data to inform the effectiveness or superiority of some childrearing practices over others has motivated historically the research in this area. Parenting and the shaping of parenting were seen by social scientists and others as a way to improve developmental outcome in our society and to promote the integration of those considered the "others" into an American way of life. As such, the field of child development responded to societal needs and pressures as it has in many other aspects of its endeavors (e.g., as designing interventions to promote various aspects of development).

In contrast, several approaches to the study of ethnic and minority parenting represent a deviation from the deficit model that has dominated most of the field until now (e.g., Arnold, 1995; Stevenson, Chen, and Uttal, 1990). There has been a shift away from a social pathological perspective to one emphasizing the resilience and adaptiveness of families under a variety of social and economic conditions (Harrison, Wilson, Pine, Chan, and Buriel, 1990; Ishii Kuntz, 2000; Ogbu, 1981; Taylor, 2000). The particular contextual forces that impinge on minority and ethnic families are increasingly acknowledged, measured, and documented. Moreover, conducting studies that do not compare across groups but examine variability within groups emphasizes the heterogeneity within ethnic and minority groups. The work by McLoyd (1990) and McLoyd, Jayaratne, Ceballo, and Borquex (1994) exemplifies how variability in parenting strategies reflects the way that families react to the multiple stresses of poverty. Similarly, Jarret (1995, 1997) identified family behavioral patterns of community bridging between the African American community and with the majority culture as a means of providing social mobility opportunities for youth living in neighborhoods with few resources (i.e., inadequate schools, housing, and municipal services) and many risks (i.e., crime, drugs, gangs, violence, etc.).

Unlike mainstream models of parenting. (e.g., Belsky, 1984) theoretical models that are designed particularly to understand minority and ethnic parenting tend to place in a prominent position the impact of the larger sociocultural context on parenting practices (García Coll, 2000; Harrison et al., 1990; McAdoo, 1978; McLoyd, 1990; Ogbu, 1981). These theoretical models include particular sources of stresses for ethnic and minority parents such as those stemming from poverty, segregation, and racism. For example, Boykin and Toms (1985) presented a conceptual framework of African American child socialization wherein parents have to pay attention to three distinct, but overlapping, cultural orientations: African American, mainstream, and minority. If we could extend such a framework to other ethnic and minority parents, we could expect that contradictions, inconsistencies, and surely complexity will be part of being a parent within these three cultural orientations.

In conclusion, both empirically and theoretically, we have seen a paradigm shift in the study of minority and ethnic parenting. Earlier theoretical and empirical work projected a deficit view wherein childrearing practices of ethnic and minority parents were seen as deficient and in need of intervention. More recent theoretical and empirical work reflects an analysis wherein parenting practices are seen as adaptive responses to circumstances such as the stresses associated with poverty and racism, alongside unique culturally defined and sustained patterns of behaviors and beliefs.

CENTRAL ISSUES IN THE STUDY OF ETHNIC AND MINORITY PARENTING

Our primary theoretical orientation is that the overall goal of parenting across any ethnic, minority, or cultural group is to assure children's successful navigation through life. Although the roles and functions of parenthood do not end here, for the purpose of this chapter the discussion of parenting emphasizes the roles parents play in the lives of infants, children, adolescents, and young adults.

A major proponent of this theoretical orientation is LeVine (1977), who has argued that biological and cultural evolution created "standardized strategies" for infant and childhood survival and that these strategies reflect the particular environmental milieu. Likewise, there are standardized goals for parenting based on the need to promote the successful transition of one's children from the complete dependency of early years to the relative self-sufficiency as an adult. These universal goals include assuring the physical safety of one's children, providing an environment that allows for the successful progression through developmental stages, and teaching and modeling normative social values.

Within this framework, most goals of parenting may be seen as universal, but how these goals are accomplished might differ. Because parenting behaviors respond to immediate contextual demands and reflect long-term goals and values aspirations for children, differences in parenting styles among ethnic and minority groups as well as between these groups and the mainstream majority culture are based on the adaptation of parenting to these contextual issues (Bornstein, 1995). The goals, or ends, of parenting are relatively similar; the means may vary based on context. Specific contexts that are particular to many ethnic and minority parents include ethnocultural (being from a different cultural heritage from the majority, with different customs of parenting and childrearing), economic (many ethnic and minority families live under economic hardship), and social (the influence of being "the other").

An ecological model for the understanding of minority child development has been proposed (García Coll et al., 1996) as well as models for minority parenting (e.g., Boykin and Toms, 1985; García Coll, 2000; Harrison et al., 1990). What we propose here is that a truly integrative model of minority parenting would distinguish between the independent effects of cultural orientation, social class, and minority status on parenting, and at the same time acknowledge the complex interrelations among these factors. Culture, class, and minority status account for issues that are specific to minority populations as well as issues that are also salient in the majority group but

TABLE 1.1
Contextual Variables and Ethnic and Minority Parenting

Variables Specific to Ethnic and Minority Parenting	Variables Relevant to All Parents but Might Have Differential Effects on Ethnic, Minority, and non-Minority Parenting
Race, ethnicity	Social class
Racism, prejudice, and discrimination	Proximal environments
Migration	Cultural traditions and histories
Acculturation	Family factors
	Child factors

have differential effects in minority groups (Table 1.1). Examples of the former group include social mechanism variables such as racism, prejudice, discrimination, and segregation, and adaptive variables such as successful adaptation to migration and acculturation. Factors that may have a differential effect on ethnic and minority as compared to mainstream populations include, social class, environment (e.g., neighborhoods, schools, and health care), cultural traditions and histories, family factors (e.g., structure, individual roles, and family values), and child characteristics. Differences in parenting approach and style are in part adaptive responses to these factors.

These contextual variables clearly overlap and influence each other. For example, migration and acculturation modify cultural traditions; racism and discrimination become part of cultural histories and influence social class determination. Family composition is influenced by culture, economics, and class. Proximal environments are affected by social class, migration, and cultural traditions. Despite these interrelations, the primary effects of culture, class, and minority status should be examined separately.

Cultural Factors

Elsewhere in this *Handbook* (see Harkness and Super, in Vol. 2) the role of cultural beliefs and practices are discussed in detail. Cultural traditions can influence parenting through the influence of family structure, residency patterns, childrearing practices, and beliefs and attitudes about the roles of children at different ages and stages. These traditions are carried on to a greater or lesser extent within each family based on level of acculturation, residency location (e.g., living in an ethnic neighborhood or in a predominantly majority community), family residency pattern (closeness and involvement of older and more traditional relatives), as well as the utility or fit of specific cultural practices vis-à-vis the environment that the family is living in. Culture is adaptive, and beliefs, attitudes, and practices are molded to fit within the present context.

Acculturation is the process through which cultural adaptation and change occurs. During this process, families combine ethnic, minority, and dominant culture parenting values. The outcome of cultural contact in pluralistic societies is based on attitudes of both the host and minority groups (e.g., the degree to which maintaining one's cultural identity is important, the degree to which relationships with other groups in society are valued, and so forth). Berry (1997) describes four potential outcomes or "strategies" of cultural contact based on host and minority group attitudes and values—integration, assimilation, separation and segregation, or marginalization.

The process of acculturation is dynamic and occurs over time within the context of family life and broader social experiences (Sluzki, 1979; Zuniga, 1992). Although acculturation is an ongoing process, discontinuities may be expected due to family relocation, economic and social constraints, formation or disruption of important relationships, or traumatic experiences. Acculturation and adaptation to a new culture may include several stages: initial joy, relief, and idealization of the new culture; disillusionment associated with adjustment; and gradual acceptance of the positive and negative aspects of the new culture (Arredondo-Dowd, 1981). Children who are enrolled in schools or adults who are employed are generally exposed to greater acculturation opportunities and demands. This can result in uneven acculturation levels among family members, incurring disagreement and conflict about family values and parenting behaviors (Szapocznik and Hernandez, 1988; Zuniga, 1992).

Traditionally, acculturation has been conceptualized as a process of learning about a new culture and deciding what aspects are to be retained or sacrificed from the culture of origin (Lin, Masuda, and Tazuma, 1982). More recent views of acculturation emphasize the multidirectional and multidimensional nature of the process, acknowledging that cultural contact affects, modifies, and changes the host group as well as the minority group. Also, the process of individual and group change occurs along multiple dimensions (e.g., ethnic pride, loyalty, language, retention of traditions, and so forth). Degree of cultural retention or change differs among these dimensions; it is not an "all or nothing" phenomenon. Because of the multidimensional nature of cultural change, those individuals and families who have the ability to retain real social, psychological, and attitudinal linkage with their original culture while being able to live with a sense of ease and competency in the host culture (i.e., are "bicultural") may be seen as having the best adjustment to the multicultural context of modern life (Szapocznik, Kurtines, and Fernandez, 1980).

In support of these speculations, several studies have shown the effects of acculturation style on the family system. Rueschenberg and Buriel (1989) indicate that as families of Mexican descent became acculturated, they became increasingly involved with formal social support services outside the family while the basic internal family system remained the same. Level of acculturation was significantly related to four of the five external family system variables: independence, achievement orientation, intellectual and cultural orientation, and active recreational orientation. In contrast, acculturation level was not related to any internal family system values: cohesion, expressiveness, conflict, organization, and control. Similarly, familial obligations of Mexican Americans and the perception of family support does not change (Sabogal, Marin, Otero-Sabogal, VanOss Marin, and Perez-Stable, 1987). These studies support the notion that these families do not "assimilate" per se, but become bicultural, maintaining some aspects of functioning of the traditional family and adopting new important values and behavioral patterns.

Although acculturation is related to immigration, it is conceptually distinct. Immigration is defined by mobility in terms of physical location; acculturation refers to one's psychological adaptation to a different cultural environment. The process of acculturation is important not only for immigrants but also for any individual who for historic, economic, political, linguistic, and/or religious reasons is exposed or expected to adapt to a new cultural environment. Thus, we can hypothesize that the process of acculturation can be experienced as much by a recent immigrant family from southeast Asia as it may be by a middle-SES African American child whose family moves from an African American to a predominantly White community (Tatum, 1987, 1997). Similarly, Native Americans who may or may not have been subjected to mandatory migration and resettlement on reservations experience the acculturation process and its attendant stressful aspects.

Within this global conceptualization of acculturation, ethnic and minority children are expected to transcend their own cultural background and to incorporate aspects of the dominant culture, not necessarily due to migration, but on account of their ethnic or racial group's relative status in society. Young children's expectations and opportunities for acculturation are in large part mediated by their parents and by the extended family system (Caudill, 1973; García Coll, Meyer, and Brillon, 1995; McGoldrick, Pearce, and Giordano, 1996), as well as other agents in the child's environment (e.g., peers and daycare providers). Family acculturation level and style might have an impact on parenting style by influencing developmental expectations, mother–infant interaction, feeding and caregiving practices, and the role of the extended family. These areas may be fertile ground for conflict or confusion regarding the appropriateness of caregiving practices between less acculturated and more acculturated family members. For example, Perez-Febles (1992) found that level of acculturation and maternal education were the strongest predictors of patterns of mother–infant interaction among Hispanic mothers and their 6- to 12-month-old infants. Other studies show that effects of acculturation on maternal behaviors may be minimal after controlling for other sociodemogaphic variables such as family SES, mother's education level, age, and number of hours mother works per week (Bornstein and Cote, in press).

During the preschool years, the family's acculturation level and attitudes toward the outside culture continue to influence the caregiving environment directly, as well as influencing important decisions such as daycare or preschool experiences. As the children grow older, they are exposed to daycare centers, school, church, and other community settings. In these settings, children, and consequently their families, learn about the dominant cultural values and behaviors, and may be expected to adapt to unfamiliar cultural norms (e.g., being on the winning team, expressing emotions, and being self-reliant). For example, an African American mother might prefer to leave her children with extended family while she is at work because the kinship network is seen as a natural way to cope with maternal absence. This well-intentioned, culturally appropriate decision might, however, put the child at an educational and social disadvantage relative to other children of similar age who have the benefit of important preschool experiences that may ease the transition into early school years.

During school age and into adolescence, the family's acculturation level and attitude toward the outside culture interact with the child's own acculturation and attitudes. The issue of acculturation disparity is extremely important and relevant during these stages (Szapocznik et al., 1980). During adolescence, children become real active agents and determinants of their own acculturation status. Thus, the family's as well as the child's acculturation level and attitudes toward the dominant culture (and any disparity between the two) are critical influences on the development of the child's self-concept, racial and ethnic identity, and sex role. Acculturation also affects school performance, academic success and achievement, and career goals and expectations (Ogbu, 1987). Finally, degree and attitude toward acculturation can also be very influential in the development of important relationships, including peer and sibling relationships as well as conflicts with parents.

Regarding parenting acculturation, parents determine, to some extent, the aspects of parenting (e.g., disciplinary practices and educational expectations) they uphold and those they relinquish in favor of the dominant culture parental values, attitudes, and practices. For example, the parenting attitudes of Hispanic women born in the United States more closely resemble those of American-born African American women than the attitudes of recently immigrated Hispanic women when socioeconomic status is controlled (Rauh, Wasserman, and Brunelli, 1990). Similarly, Chinese mothers demonstrate comparable use of reasoning in response to common childrearing problems as European American mothers, which may reflect an acculturation influence because reasoning with children might not be a common practice in Chinese families (Kelly and Tseng, 1992). Gutierrez, Sameroff, and Karrer (1988), in examining the relative contribution of socioeconomic status and level of acculturation, found that more acculturated Mexican American, higher SES mothers were more perspectivistic about child development (e.g., child development seen as a more dynamic, multiply determined process) than less acculturated mothers of comparable SES. However, among mothers of lower SES, the degree of acculturation did not significantly influence attitudes about child development.

The experience of acculturation for ethnic and minority parents can be positive, negative, or mixed. For example, learning a new language and behavioral competencies can present new areas for personal mastery and socioeconomic mobility. However, the process might also precipitate feelings of confusion, guilt, loss, and alienation from significant others as well as the culture of origin. In particular, parents may experience acculturative stress given that they bear the primary responsibility for rearing their children, fostering developmental success, and inculcating a sense of cultural identity. The far-reaching effects of this acculturation process are captured in Burnam, Telles, Hough, and Escovar (1987, p. 107): "The psychosocial adaptation which is acculturation involves more than becoming knowledgeable of the language, norms, and values of the new culture; it can be a fundamental change which includes relearning the meaning of symbols, readjusting to a new system of values and relinquishing some old customs, beliefs, and behaviors." From a more personal perspective, the words of Jerry Valdez, a 14-year-old Jemez Pueblo Indian, illustrate the potential conflict and challenge inherent in acculturation:

> *For me, to live in both these worlds is hard. I want to live my traditional ways, to be out in the wilderness. I want to be at home living with my grandparents, picking up my ways. But I have to go to school in order to survive in this world. Yes, I want to live traditionally. But we as Indians have to survive in one way or the other. I love my tradition so much that I would give up my education in order to live in my world. But to many people, my world is just a dream and nothing but a dream.*

The concept of acculturation highlights the variation and individual differences within any given group. These distinctions are critical if we are to move beyond stereotypes, platitudes, and superficial generalizations.

Social Position Factors

These factors pertain to social stratification, a social process that creates a hierachy of positions that are unequal with regard to power, property, social evaluation of status, and/or psychic gratification (Tumin, 1967). In the United States, social stratification occurs primarily along lines of race, ethnicity, and class, although other factors such as gender and age are also important.

Social stratification creates unequal distribution of resources. This process is mediated through social mechanisms such as racism, prejudice, and discrimination, along with other factors. The end product of this process includes residential segregation. Segregation fosters the unequal distribution of resources to promote optimal environments for parenting, such as housing stock, disposable income, quality daycare, preschools and schools, commerce, quality health care, and jobs (Pachter, 2000).

Although the tendency is to view the environmental contexts described above as inhibiting to parenting and child development, a balanced view allows for the possibility of positive or promoting influences counteracting these conditions so as not to stereotype and fall prey to the deficit view of ethnic and minority contexts described above. Parents and families who live in segregated and disadvantaged communities nevertheless may have other individual, family, and community level resources that may act to buffer the effects of economic or material disenfranchisement. For example, living in a neighborhood with a shared cultural identity may offer members a level of social cohesion and support that is not seen in other contexts. Barnes (1991) contended that a sense of belonging to an ethnic community may help neutralize some effects of living in a racist society by helping to reject negative messages, or transforming them so that they have less negative impact. Conversely, minority families who live in middle-SES European American communities may not have the same burden of low economic and material capital, but may suffer the consequences of racism, prejudice, and discrimination on a more constant and regular basis (and without the social support seen in ethnic communities) (Tatum, 1987, 1997).

This concept of social cohesion is one component of what some term *social capital*. Social capital is defined as the features of social organization that facilitate cooperation for mutual benefit (Coleman, 1990). It includes mechanisms such as interpersonal trust among individuals, community participation, norms of reciprocity, and availability of civil organizations. Social capital is an ecological, community-level construct. It is a characteristic of places, not individuals. Communities with a high degree of social capital, as exemplified perhaps through availability of social organizations that promote cultural and ethnic awareness and pride, early child development centers, childcare options, houses of worship, block watch groups, block associations and other civic associations could be seen as providing a promoting context for parenting and child development. A study of 343 neighborhood clusters in Chicago demonstrated that collective efficacy (i.e., social cohesion among neighbors combined with a willingness to intervene on behalf of the common good) is negatively correlated with violence even after individual characteristics (e.g., SES, home ownership, and age) and prior violence were controlled for (Sampson, Raudenbush, and Earls, 1997).

The promoting effects of social capital may occur in the face of economic disenfranchisement and may buffer some of its effects. In social contexts such as predominantly European American suburbs, minority families may not have a large amount of social capital at their disposal. In this case, low social capital may moderate the positive effects of a higher level of material resources that the middle- or upper-SES minority family may have at their disposal. To date, little empirical research has been conducted on the concept of social capital, particularly with regard to its potential effects on parenting resources and outcomes.

Minority Status

Independent of culture and class, being a minority in a society has its unique potential implications for parenting. The psychological effects of living in a society that has certain assumptions, prejudices, and behaviors toward "the other" in all aspects of daily life has not been adequately studied vis-à-vis parenting per se (Daniel and Daniel, 1999), but one investigation demonstrated its effects on child development. In a comparative study of the psychological adjustment of South African Black and African American children, it was found that African American children had greater prevalence of psychological symptoms as determined by the Behavioral Problems Index (Babarin, 1999). The African American and South African samples were similar with regard to race, family structure, and poverty level. The major difference is that in the U.S. African Americans are minorities, whereas in South Africa, Black Africans are not. This study shows that minority status per se has effects on child behavior. Similarly controlled studies regarding parenting issues need to occur.

Protecting children from the devastating effects of racism, prejudice, and discrimination is another important issue for ethnic and minority parents. Unlike socioeconomic status, racism is a stressor that is specific to minority families. Little research has been conducted on the effects of racism on parenting practices or styles. Since parents are the prime socializing agent for young children, their attitudes and responses to prejudice and discrimination will have great effects on their children's behavioral and developmental outcomes, including psychological attributes such as self-esteem, response to stress, academic performance, and social competency and attitudes. On one hand, minority parents need to impart to their children the philosophy that hard work and living a "good" life will result in rewards (i.e., meritocracy); on the other hand, they need to prepare their children for the facts that discrimination and prejudice may likely influence outcomes as well.

Attributing negative outcomes to racism and discrimination may be a psychologically protective mechanism for minorities (Neighbors, Jackson, Broman, and Thompson, 1996). Crocker and Major (1989) hypothesize that by attributing negative feedback or situations to racial discrimination (against a group), individual self-esteem would be protected. Others have alternatively proposed that minimizing perceptions of discrimination may be psychologically beneficial (Ruggiero and Taylor, 1997). Proponents of this view distinguish between *performance state self-esteem* (which may be protected by attributing failure to racial discrimination) and *social state self esteem* (which is protected by minimizing the effects of racial discrimination).

In a study of psychological adjustment in a sample of low-income African American children, parents with high external racial attribution scores reported that their children had more problem behaviors, particularly peer conflict and social withdrawal (Christian and Barbarin, 2001). This finding was contrary to the researcher's a priori hypothesis, which was that high parental racial attribution would be associated with better child behavioral profiles by improving parental function and reducing self-blame, which might be passed on to the child, resulting in greater self-esteem.

Teaching children about racism and discrimination is a component of the racial socialization process. Racial socialization has been defined as "messages and practices that are relevant to and provide information concerning the nature of race status" (Thorton, Chatters, Taylor, and Allen, 1990). The nature and content of racial socialization can include components such as group identity, intergroup relations, and social position and stratification. Hughes and Chen (1999) break down the content areas of racial socialization messages into the following domains: cultural socialization (teaching about heritage, history, customs, and traditions), preparation for bias (promotion of an awareness of prejudice and discrimination), socialization of mistrust (warning children to be wary of interacting with individuals from outside the racial or ethnic group, relaying a sense of distrust), and egalitarian socialization (promoting an appreciation of all peoples and groups). According to Hughes and Chen, racial socialization messages that parents give to children can be either deliberate or unintended, verbal and nonverbal, proactive or reactive. It is also a bidirectional and synergistic process that is modified by both giver and receiver (Hughes and Chen, 1999).

There is a wide range of individual differences among ethnic and minority parents on the relative importance they assign to racial issues in the socialization process (Thorton et al., 1990). For example, Spencer (1985) found that a sample of southern African American parents was equally divided on whether they considered it important to teach children about race. In a study by Thorton et al. (1990), two out of three African American parents indicated that they acted to racially socialize their children. Among the most frequent examples of racial socialization messages were those emphasizing racial pride (e.g., "never be ashamed of your color"), African American heritage and tradition, acceptance of racial background, positive self-image, the presence of racial restrictions and blocked opportunities (e.g., "Blacks do not have the opportunities that Whites have"), and the fundamental equality of African American and White people. Racial socialization messages also change as the child's age and developmental level progresses. In a study of African American parent–child communication, Hughes and Chen (1997) found that messages regarding promotion of mistrust and preparation for bias were more common with parents of children 9 to 14 years old than with parents of those 4 to 8 years old, whereas the frequency of the parents' cultural socialization messages did not vary with the age of the child.

The importance of the racial and ethnic socialization process for parenting is underscored by observations that this process emerges as a component of socialization for families across diverse socioeconomic backgrounds (Branch and Newcombe, 1986; Hale-Benson, 1982; Marshall, 1995; Renne, 1970; Tatum, 1987, 1997; Thorton et al., 1990). As with the process of acculturation, racial socialization represents another source of variability in the parenting process of ethnic and minority parents. Differences noted among ethnic and minority families in these processes have profound influences on critical aspects of child development. For example, Bowman and Howard (1985) found that the manner in which parents oriented their children toward racial barriers was associated with children's motivation, achievement, and prospects for upward mobility. Emphasis on ethnic pride, self-development, awareness of racial barriers, and egalitarianism were associated with positive outcomes. In discussing the possible influences on school performance in minority children, Ogbu (1991) argued that African American parents might be exposing their children to ambivalent and contradictory beliefs and attitudes toward schooling. On one hand, parents stress the importance of getting a good education in order to secure good employment; on the other hand, as part of racial and ethnic socialization, they also teach their children that U.S. society does not reward African Americans and Whites equally for similar school credentials or educational accomplishments. In Ogbu's analysis, these messages actually contribute to the disengagement found among minority youth toward school. Marshall (1995) found that among middle-income African American children, those who received more ethnic socialization from parents had poorer school performance. The fact that this study was conducted with middle-income African American families whose children attended predominantly White schools speaks to the importance of context. Spencer (1983, 1985) argued that achieving group identity is difficult without consistent messages from important socializing agents such as parents, relatives, and teachers.

There are little empirical data regarding racial socialization in diverse ethnic groups. Most of the studies have been conducted in African American families, with a few notable exceptions (Quintana and Vera, 1999). Phinney and Chavira (1995) studied ethnic and racial socialization in Japanese American, African American, and Mexican American teen–parent dyads and found significant differences. For example, African American and Japanese American parents more frequently discussed the theme of adaptation to the overall society more than Mexican American parents. Compared to the other groups, African American parents more frequently discussed prejudice as a problem. This finding was also seen in a study of urban African American and Hispanic (Puerto Rican, Dominican, and Mexican Americans) parents (Hughes, in press). In this study, African American parents reported more frequent racial socialization, particularly with regard to discussion about racial discrimination and bias.

It is clear that the central issues for ethnic and minority parents reflect a complex combination of group, individual, and contextually derived processes. Group processes are embodied in the traditional childrearing formulations on which parents draw according to their own ethnic background. Individual processes are reflected in acculturative effects that incorporate the impact of migration and the nature of contact with the dominant culture. Finally, contextually derived processes include sources of oppression derived from their ethnic and minority status inclusive of chronic poverty and the derivatives of racism.

Our analysis suggests that parenting style and practice are an adaptation to a specific niche. For ethnic and minority parents' that niche includes being of a specific ethnocultural heritage, being of a specific social class, and being "the other." These are factors that may have combined effects, but also need to be considered independently because each creates specific contexts for each individual parent and family. For example, does an African American middle-SES parent who lives in a European American suburb and participates in community groups and activities have more in common with a European American parent within the same suburb, or with an African American parent with Afrocentric orientation living in the inner city? Does an English-speaking, blue-collar Puerto Rican parent who has lived in the United States her whole life have more in common with a recently migrated Spanish speaking mother, or with a blue-collar European American mother? These examples are not presented to promote stereotypes; they exemplify the multivariate relations among minority status (race), culture, and class.

A study of parental perceptions of normal child development shows the complexity of these relations (Pachter and Dworkin, 1997). Two hundred and fifty-five mothers from minority (Puerto Rican, African American, and West Indian/Caribbean) and majority (European American) cultural groups were given a questionnaire asking for their perceptions of the normal ages of attainment of typical developmental milestones during the first three years of life. Results demonstrated significant perceptual differences among ethnic groups. For example, when asked "at what age should children be able to sleep throughout the night without awakening," Puerto Rican mothers responded with a mean age of 10.5 months, African American mothers with 8.4 months, and West Indian/Caribbean mothers 6.7 months, whereas European American mothers gave a mean of 5.7 months. One possible explanation for these differences is that infant–parent cosleeping is more common with African American and Puerto Rican families. Cosleeping places the infant and mother in closer proximity, allowing the mothers to be more aware of the infant's sleep–wake cycle than if the infant was sleeping in another room, which is the normative style in European American households. In addition to cultural practices, socioeconomic conditions may influence sleeping practices (cosleeping due to increased household density in low-SES families). In this case, cultural practices and environmental conditions secondary to social class may have independent as well as combined effects on parental perceptions. One should not assume that "it's all cultural," or "it's all due to poverty."

In summary, minority parenting practices, as well as minority child developmental competencies, need to be viewed from the perspective of contextual adaptation. The specific circumstances that are pertinent to minority families include socioeconomic conditions and social class, cultural styles, neighborhood and community influences, and intergroup macrosystem-level mechanisms such as racism, prejudice, discrimination, and oppression (García Coll et al., 1996). Because of these unique conditions, parenting process, competency, and outcome should be evaluated vis-à-vis the goodness of fit between the parenting practice and the context in which it occurs.

IMPLICATIONS FOR PRACTICE, POLICY, AND RESEARCH

Although our extant knowledge of ethnic and minority parenting has limitations, many lessons emerge with clear implications for practice, policy, and research (García Coll and Magnuson, 1999; Jarret, 1995).

Practice

For practitioners working with ethnic and minority parents who are recent immigrants, strong in their own culture's capital or with strong ethnic identity and/or poor, there are certain principles that can be derived from this body of theoretical and empirical research that could guide interventions and practice. One is the critical importance of the larger sociocultural and socioeconomic context in family life. The fact that the context of ethnic and minority families reflects structural (poverty and racism) and cultural dimensions (i.e., that importance of extended kinship) that are unique and might be foreign to us deserve particular attention.

One refers to the attention that we have to pay to our own position in those structural and cultural continua. We have to be particularly cognizant of possible stereotypes that we bring due to our unfamiliarity of such families or our own class and cultural biases. There is no way that we as human beings cannot react to certain childrearing practices with disbelief and disapproval, even if we try not to. Most of us have been socialized to a particular sociocultural milieu, and as good members of that particular segment of society we adhere to certain patterns of beliefs and behaviors. All the sensitivity training cannot erase completely our own worldviews, and these can blind us to the strengths or differences that permeate family life in ethnic and minority groups, and vice versa.

In addition, our perceived position in the hierarchy of class, culture, and race may get in the way of our well-intended interventions. Cross-cultural relationships have to be cognizant of the historical understanding of groups' relations and the "real" consequences for current interactions (García Coll, Cook-Nobles, and Surrey, 1995). Cultural mistrust might make our recommendations or models ineffective with some individuals and not with others. Awareness of our own and the families' constructions of our mutual groups, inclusive of class, race, ethnicity, and gender, is crucial in the delivery of effective services.

The second implication from considering the larger contextual influences on ethnic and minority parenting would reflect our current theoretical and empirical understanding of the etiology of childrearing beliefs, goals, and practices. We and others have elaborated how family functioning responds to many sources of influence other than internal ones (i.e., Boykin and Toms, 1985; García Coll et al., 1996; García Coll, 2000). Understanding parenting within these families without taking into consideration neighborhood characteristics (i.e., violence), extended family involvement, economic stresses, perceived racism, and/or cultural constructions of family functioning can undermine our intervention strategies.

On the cultural side, for example, Towsend (in press) described two models of father involvement: distributive (where father's involvement is expected to be there throughout the lifetime of the child) versus concentrative (where father's involvement is seen as critical and necessary perhaps when children are young, but he is not expected to be involved thereafter, or only minimally). In each of these models, fathers assume rather different places in childrearing as a function of the life stage of the father and the child. Variability in dimensions like this can have clear implications for who is involved in decision making around parenting, and ignorance of such patterns can undermine family functioning and the effectiveness of interventions.

Similarly Jarret's (1995) work on family strategies and McLoyd's (1990) work on coping with poverty reflect adaptations of family life in response to larger contextual demands. Jarret (1995) proposed strategies that youth-serving programs can consider based on lessons from qualitative research with African American families: recognize the role of surrogate parents, foster alliances between parents in the same neighborhoods, promote a clear understanding of safe and dangerous niches within the neighborhood, and promote parent–staff relationships.

The final implication of our extant knowledge on ethnic and minority parenting for practice is the increasing recognition of the enormous variability observed within ethnic and minority families (see Demo et al., 2000). Issues of acculturation, generation, recency of migration, social class, and national origin are all sources of variability within these groups (e.g., Delgado-Gaitán, 1994). For example, acculturation has been a clear source of variability when we look at Latino, Asian

American, and Native American individuals, and other research with ethnic and minority parents identifies acculturation as a source of variability for family structure, family roles, parental goals in development, adaptations to extrafamilial stresses and demands, childrearing practices, intergenerational conflict, and the like (Buriel and de Ment, 1997; Delgado-Gaitán, 1994; Gutierrez and Sameroff, 1990; Rueschenberg and Buriel, 1989).

For practice, issues of adherence to mainstream developmental goals, knowledge of how to negotiate institutional systems on behalf of your child, and where a family stands on an assimilation continuum ("Are your traditional practices and values extremely important or do you want your children to assimilate?") are major dimensions that practitioners need to be aware and constantly assess in their work with these families. The use of this knowledge can lead to effective interventions with families that otherwise erroneously seem apathetic and noncompliant to our services (Delgado-Gaitán, 1991, 1992).

Policy

One of the major issues for public policy in the United States is the role of government agencies and interventions in family life. This becomes a particularly sensitive issue in dealing with ethnic and minority parenting when differences in the meaning and consequences of parenting behavior can arise. Historically, as discussed previously in this chapter, public policy and consequent practice has been for the most part remediative and espoused a deficit model, congruent with most of the extant research literature (García Coll and Magnuson, 1999). But how do we incorporate more contemporary research and theory with these families into public policy?

One way would be to use more recent research and theoretical work that points out the unique sources of stress and unique adaptations of ethnic and minority families to inform public policies. How would policies be shaped accordingly? Perhaps all interventions will need to employ a multiprong approach acknowledging the varied influences on ethnic and minority parenting. For example, parent education programs would have to address simultaneously—if not a priori—structural variables that constitute sources of stress. Neighborhood-level interventions as well as parental formal education and occupation interventions would be critical components of parenting programs. Interventions on behalf of the children would not only target the child, but the family as a system, embedded in a larger socioeconomic and cultural context.

Another way to implement lessons from contemporary analyses of ethnic and minority parenting would be to take seriously the notion of variability among ethnic and minority families. Issues of acculturation, or response to stresses associated with poverty and coping with racism, could be core to the design, implementation, and execution of public policies. For example, the work of Delgado-Gaitán (1991, 1992, 1994) has clear implications for school policies. Differences in generation status as a proxy for acculturation would be clearly taken into account when working with ethnic and minority parents. Outreach programs that target ethnic and minority parents would need to be designed to be flexible in their strategies depending on the generation, acculturation level, and recency of migration of the family. The success of strategies for promoting family involvement depends on the family's fund of knowledge (Moll, 1994) or the essential information and strategies that families have and use to promote their well-being.

Research

Finally, there is a need for multimethod studies (both qualitative and quantitative) that go beyond group comparisons or examining intragroup variability. We need to push the field beyond descriptive comparisons or analyses to specifying the processes underlying differences and similarities.

As a field, we need to stop studying parenting out of context and inferring contextual explanations out of nominal group membership. For example, parenting strategies of African American families differ if they live in predominantly European American, middle-SES communities or in danger-ous neighborhoods (Jarret, 1995, 1997; Tatum, 1987, 1997). Categorizations of African American families (and of any other ethnic and minority group) as parents need to be able to indicate the environmental conditions within which parents operate.

Moreover, recent research and theory has acknowledged the importance of dissecting the effects of culture and ethnicity, poverty and social class, and minority status while appreciating the interrelations among these variables. More studies need to use multivariate statistical models inclusive of path analyses as an approach to determining primary and secondary effects of these interrelated factors. These more complex analytic strategies will reflect more accurately the complexity of day to day life in these families. Another approach to disentangling social class from ethnic and minority membership is represented by studies of middle-SES ethnic and minority families (i.e., Cote and Bornstein, 2000; Harwood, Schoelmerich, Ventura-Cook, Schulze, and Wilson, 1996; McAdoo, 1981; Tatum, 1987). These studies elucidate how some aspects of parenting remain and other change as a function of social class membership. Another approach is represented by those studies that try to disentangle social class effects or group membership from acculturation effects (Gutierrez et al., 1988; Rueschenberg and Buriel, 1989).

Research instruments such as scales, surveys, and questionnaires should be tested for validity and reliability in minority groups (Marín and VanOss Marín, 1991; Pachter, Sheehan, and Cloutier, 2000; Pachter and Harwood, 1996). It is common practice that research instruments are developed and psychometrically tested on individuals and study samples that do not include minorities. The use of these instruments in studies of minority populations are then suboptimal for various reasons. At a basic level, the theoretical construct being measured may have different meanings in different groups (i.e., lack of conceptual equivalency; Berry, 1969). Second, specific items or questions contained within the instrument may be interpreted differently by members of different groups. Also, interpretation of response categories may differ (measurement equivalency). Finally, in instruments with subscales, the factors (or latent variables) that these subscales are based on may be conceptualized differently in different groups (Pachter and Harwood, 1996).

For example, the Parental Health Belief Scale is a questionnaire instrument that measures parental health locus of control for their children's health (Tinsley and Holtgrave, 1989). The initial instru-ment, which was tested and validated on 88 low- and middle-income European American and African American mothers, was divided into three subscales: Internality, Chance, and Powerful Others (the first subscale relating to an internal locus of control, the second and third relating to components of and external locus of control). Because of concerns whether these structural factors tapped into cul-turally salient values and conceptualizations in Puerto Rican culture, another group of researchers administered the survey to 420 mainland Puerto Rican mothers and subjected the results to ex-ploratory and confirmatory factor analysis, as well as item analysis (Pachter, Sheehan, and Cloutier, 2000). Results showed that an alternative four factor structure (External/Luck, External/Others, External/Professional, and Internal) had a better fit than the original structure. In addition, this subscale structure better fit conceptually with traditional, normative Puerto Rican cultural values (e.g., respeto, collectivism, and fatalism).

If validity and reliability of commonly used instruments have not been tested in specific popula-tions during the initial testing process, it becomes the responsibility of the researcher to reanalyze the instrument within the specific demographic group under study to assure conceptual and measure-ment equivalency at the level of the question or item (through item analysis), the subscale structure (through factor reanalysis), as well as the instrument as a whole.

Finally, research on ethnic and minority families needs to be integrated into normative views of parenting in general. We need meta-analyses of research based on both mainstream and minority and ethnic parents to start reflecting both commonalties and differences, the universal ways of achieving parental goals, and which are more context specific. We also need to revise theoretical assumptions and conclusions of research based on European middle-SES families in light of the research on ethnic and minority families. Knowledge should no longer be segregated.

CONCLUSIONS

Increasing our understanding of ethnic and minority parenting in the United States is crucial for a variety of reasons. Most of the extant literature on "normative" aspects of parenting is based on middle-SES, Anglo-European, North American samples. There are also unique conditions under which ethnic and minority parents have to operate, inclusive of the discontinuity between their cultural and social capital with that of mainstream culture and institutions and the particular social location that ethnic and minority groups occupy in the social stratification system in the United States. These unique conditions place specific demands on ethnic and minority parents that need to be addressed in our understanding of parenting processes in these populations. Finally, as minority and ethnic children become the majority of the youth population in the United States, scholarly work in parenting among these populations is necessary to inform public policy, practice, and effective intervention on these children's behalf.

Historically, the literature on ethnic and minority parenting in the United States displays a prevalence of deficit models, whereby parenting practices of ethnic and minority families have been conceptualized as those of "the other" group, which then are compared to the "standard" (defined as those displayed by Caucasian, middle-income, Northern European, American parents). In contrast, several approaches to the study of ethnic and minority parenting represent a deviation from the deficit model that has dominated most of the field until now, shifting away from a social pathological perspective to one emphasizing the resilience and adaptiveness of families under a variety of social and economic conditions. Within these frameworks, most goals of parenting may be seen as universal, but how these goals are accomplished may vary based on context. Specific contexts that are particular to many ethnic and minority parents include ethnocultural (being from a different cultural heritage from the majority, with different customs of parenting and childrearing), economic (many ethnic and minority families live under economic hardship), and social (the influence of being "the other").

It is clear that the central issues for ethnic and minority parents reflect a complex combination of group, individual, and contextually derived processes. Group processes are embodied in the traditional childrearing formulations on which parents draw according to their own ethnic background. Individual processes are reflected in acculturative effects that incorporate the impact of migration and the nature of contact with the dominant culture. Finally, contextually derived processes include sources of oppression derived from their ethnic and minority status inclusive of chronic poverty and the derivatives of racism. These are factors that may have combined effects, but also need to be considered independently because each creates specific contexts for each individual parent and family.

Although our extant knowledge of ethnic and minority parenting has limitations, many lessons emerge with clear implications for practice, policy, and research. One is the critical importance of the larger sociocultural and socioeconomic context in family life. The facts that the context of ethnic and minority families reflects structural (poverty and racism) and cultural dimensions (i.e., the importance of extended kinship) that are unique and might be foreign to us deserve particular attention. Another refers to the attention that we have to pay to our own position in those structural and cultural continua. We have to be particularly cognizant of possible stereotypes that we bring due to our unfamiliarity of such families or our own class and cultural biases. Awareness of our own and the families' constructions of our mutual groups, inclusive of class, race, ethnicity, and gender is crucial in the delivery of effective services. Issues of acculturation, generation, recency of migration, social class, and national origin are all sources of variability within these groups Perhaps all interventions will need to employ a multiprong approach acknowledging the multiple influences on ethnic and minority parenting. These issues could be core to the design, implementation, and execution of public policies.

Finally, there is a need for multimethod studies (both qualitative and quantitative) that go beyond group comparisons or examining intragroup variability. We need to push the field beyond descriptive comparisons or analyses to specifying the processes underlying differences and similarities. We need to study why different families have different outcomes despite being in the same environments.

Research on ethnic and minority families needs to be integrated into normative views of parenting in general. We need meta-analyses of research based on both mainstream and minority and ethnic parents to start reflecting both commonalties and differences, the universal ways of achieving parental goals, and which are more context specific. We also need to revise theoretical assumptions and conclusions of research based on European middle-SES families in light of the research on ethnic and minority families. The needs are many; the time is now.

ACKNOWLEDGMENT

Thanks to Wanda Hunter for helping on the preparation of this manuscript.

REFERENCES

Arnold, M. S. (1995). Exploding myths: African-American families at promise. In B. B. Swandner and S. Lubeck (Eds.), *Children and families at promise* (pp. 143–162). Albany: State University of New York Press.

Arredondo-Dowd, P. (1981). Personal loss and grief as a result of immigration. *Personnel and Guidance Journal, 59*, 376–378.

Babarin, O. A. (1999). Social risks and psychological adjustment: A comparison of African-American and South African children. *Child Development, 70*, 1348–1359.

Baca-Zinn, M., and Wells, B. (2000). Diversity within Latino families: New lessons for family social science. In D. H. Demo, K. R. Allen, and M. A. Fine (Eds.), *Handbook of family diversity* (pp. 252–273). New York: Oxford University Press.

Barnes, E. J. (1991). The black community as the source of positive self concept for black children: A theoretical perspective. In R. L. Jones (Ed.), *Black psychology* (3rd ed., pp. 667–692). Berkeley, CA: Cobb and Henry.

Belsky, J. (1984). The determinants of parenting: A process model. *Child Development, 55*, 83–96.

Berry, J. W. (1969). On cross-cultural comparability. *International Journal of Psychology, 4*, 207–229.

Berry, J. W. (1997). Immigration, acculturation, and adaptation. *Applied Psychology: An International Review, 46*, 5–68.

Bornstein, M. C. (1995). Form and function: Implications for studies of culture and human development. In G. M. Breakwell, S. Hammond, and C. Fife-Schaw (Eds.), *Research methods in psychology*. Thousand Oaks, CA: Sage.

Bornstein, M. H., and Cote, L. R. (in press). Mother–infant interaction and acculturation I: behavioral comparisons in Japanese American and South American families. *International Journal of Behavioral Development*, xx–xx.

Bowman, P. J., and Howard, C. (1985). Race-related socialization, motivation and academic achievement: a study of Black youths in three-generation families. *Journal of the American Academy of Child Psychiatry, 24*, 134–141.

Boykin, A. W., and Toms, F. D. (1985). Black child socialization: A conceptual framework. In H. P. McAdoo and J. L. McAdoo (Eds.), *Black children: Social, educational, and parental environments* (pp. 33–52). Newbury Park, CA: Sage.

Branch, C. W., and Newcombe, N. (1986). Racial attitude development among young Black children as a function of parental attitudes: A longitudinal and cross-sectional study. *Child Development, 57*, 712–721.

Brody, G. H., and Flor, D. L. (1998). Maternal resources, parenting practices, and child competence in rural, single-parent African-American families. *Child Development, 69*, 803–816.

Buriel, R., and De Ment, T. (1997). Immigration and sociocultural change in Mexican, Chinese, and Vietnamese American families. In A. Booth, A. C. Crouter, and N. Landale (Eds.), *Immigration and the family* (pp. 167–199). Mahwah, NJ: Lawrence Erlbaum Associates.

Burnam, M. A., Telles, C. A., Hough, R. L., and Escovar, J. I. (1987). Measurement of acculturation in the community population of Mexican-Americans. *Hispanic Journal of Behavioral Sciences, 9*, 105–130.

Caudill, W. A. (1973). The influence of social structure an culture on human behavior in modern Japan. *Journal of Nervous and Mental Disease, 157*, 240–257.

Christian, M. D., and Barbarin, O. A. (2001). Cultural resources and psychological adjustment of African-American children: effects of spirituality and racial attribution. *Journal of Black Psychology, 27*, 43–63.

Coleman, J. S. (1990). *The foundations of social theory*. Cambridge, MA: Harvard University Press.

Cote, L. R., and Bornstein, M. H. (2000). Social and didactic parenting behaviors and beliefs among Japanese American and South American mothers of infants. *Infancy, 3*, 363–374.

Council of Economic Advisors. (1998). *Changing America: Indicators of social and economic well-being by race and Hispanic origin* [online]. Available: http://www.whitehouse.gov/WH/EOP/CEA/html/publications.html

Crocker, J., and Major, B. (1989). Social stigma and self esteem: The self protective properties of stigma. *Psychological Review, 96*, 608–630.

Daniel, J. L., and Daniel, J. E. (1999). African American childrearing: The concept of a hot stove. In T. J. Socha and R. C. Diggs (Eds.), *Communication, race, and family: Exploring communication in black, white, and biracial families* (pp. 25–43). Mahwah, NJ: Lawrence Erlbaum Associates.

Delgado-Gaitán, C. (1991, November). Involving parents in the schools: A process of empowerment. *American Journal of Education*, 20–46.

Delgado-Gaitán, C. (1992). School matters in the Mexican-American home. *American Educational Research Journal, 29*, 495–513.

Delgato-Gaitán, C. (1994). Socializing young children in Mexican-American families: An Intergenerational Perspective. In P. M. Greenfield and R. R. Cocking (Eds.), *Cross-cultural roots of minority child development*. Hillsdale, NJ: Lawrence Erlbaum Associates.

Demo, D. H., Allen, K. R., and Fine, M. A. (Eds.). (2000). *Handbook of family diversity*. New York: Oxford University Press.

García Coll, C. T. Are numbers enough? Parenting among Latino families in the United States. Paper presented at Latinos in the 21st century: Mapping the research agenda, Cambridge, MA, April 6–8, 2000.

García Coll, C. T., Cook-Nobles, R., and Surrey, J. L. (1995). Diversity at the core: Implications for relational theory. *Stone Center Working Papers Series, 75*, 1–12.

García Coll, C. T., Lamberty, G., Jenkins, R., McAdoo, H. P., Crnic, K., Wasik, B. H., and Vazquez García H. (1996). An integrative model for the study of developmental competencies in minority children. *Child Development, 67*, 1891–1914.

García Coll, C. T., and Magnuson, K. (1999). Theory and research with children of color: Implications for social policy. In H. Fitzgerald (Ed.), *Children of color: Research, health, and policy issues* (pp. 219–255). New York: Garland.

García Coll, C. T., Meyer, E. C., and Brillon, L. (1995). Ethnic and minority parents. In M. H. Bornstein (Ed.), *Handbook of parenting* (Vol. 2, pp. 189–209). Mahwah, NJ: Lawrence Earlbaum Associates.

Gutierrez, J., and Sameroff, A. (1990). Determinants of complexity in Mexican-American mothers' conceptions of child development. *Child Development, 61*, 384–394.

Gutierrez, J., Sameroff, A. J., and Karrer, B. M. (1988). Acculturation and SES effects on Mexican American parent's concepts of development. *Child Development, 59*, 250–255.

Hale-Benson, J. E. (1982). *Black children: Their roots, culture and learning styles*. Baltimore: John Hopkins University Press.

Harrison, A. O., Wilson, M. N., Pine, C. J., Chan, S. Q., and Buriel, R. (1990). Family ecologies of ethnic minority children. *Child Development, 61*, 347–362.

Harwood, R. L., Schoelmerich, A., Ventura-Cook, E., Schulze, P. A., and Wilson, S. P. (1996). Culture and class influences on Anglo and Puerto Rican mothers' beliefs regarding long-term socialization goals and child behavior. *Child Development, 67*, 2446–2461.

Hughes, D. (in press). Correlates of African American and Latino parents' messages to children about ethnicity and race: A comparative study of racial socialization.

Hughes, D., and Chen, L. (1997). When and what parents tell children about race: An examination of race-related socialization among African American families. *Applied Developmental Science, 1*, 200–214.

Hughes, D., and Chen, L. (1999). The nature of parents' race-related communications to Children: A developmental perspective. In L. Balter and C. S. Tamis-Lemonda (Eds.), *Child psychology: A handbook of contemporary issues* (pp. 467–490). Philadelphia: Psychology Press.

Ishi-Kunta, M. (2000). Diversity within Asian American families. In D. H. Demo, K. R. Allen, and M. A. Fine (Eds.), *Handbook of family diversity* (pp. 274–292). New York: Oxford University Press.

Jarret, R. L. (1995). Growing up poor: The family experiences of socially mobile youth in low-income African-American neighborhoods. *Journal of Adolescent Research, 10*, 111–135.

Jarret, R. L. (1997). African American family and parenting strategies in impoverished neighborhoods. *Qualitative Sociology, 20*, 275–288.

Kelly, M. L., and Tseng, H. (1992). Cultural differences in child rearing: A comparison of immigrant Chinese and Caucasian American mothers. *Journal of Cross-Cultural Psychology, 23*, 444–455.

LeVine, R. A. (1977). Childrearing as cultural adaptation. In P. H. Leiderman, S. R. Tulkin, and A. H. Rosenfeld (Eds.), *Culture and infancy* (pp. 15–27). London: Academic Press.

Lewis, O. (1965). *La vida*. New York: Vintage.

Lin, K. M., Masuda, M., and Tazuma, L. (1982). Adaptational problems of Vietnamese refugees: III Case studies in clinic and field: Adaptive and maladaptive. *Psychiatry Journal of the University of Ottawa, 7*, 173–183.

Marín, G., and VanOss Marín, B. (1991). *Research with Hispanic populations*. Newbury Park, CA: Sage.

Marshall, S. (1995). Ethnic socialization of African American children: Implications for parenting, identity development, and academic achievement. *Journal of Youth and Adolescence, 24*, 377–396.

McAdoo, H. P. (1978). Minority families. In J. Stevens (Ed.), *Mother/child, father/child: relationships* (pp. 177–195). Washington, DC: National Association for the Education of Young Children.

McAdoo, H. P. (1981). Upward mobility and parenting in middle-income Black families. *Journal of Black Psychology, 8*, 1–22.

McGoldrick, M., Pearce, J. K., and Giordano, J. (Eds.). (1996). *Ethnicity and family therapy*. New York: Guilford.

McLoyd, V. C. (1990). The impact of economic hardship on Black families and children: Psychological distress, parenting, and socioemotional development. *Child Development, 61*, 311–346.

McLoyd, V. C., Jayaratne, T. E., Ceballo, R., and Borquex, J. (1994). Unemployment and work interruption among African American single mothers: Effects on parenting and adolescent socioeconomical functioning. *Child Development, 65*, 562–589.

McLoyd, V. C., and Randolph, S. (1985). Secular trends in the study of Afro-American history and research in child development. *Monographs of the Society for Research in Child Development, 50* (Serial No. 211).

Moll, L. S. (1994). Literacy research in community and classrooms: A sociocultural approach. In R. B. Rudell, M. R. Rudell et al. (Eds.), *Theoretical models and processes of reading* (pp. 179–207). Newark: International Reading Association.

Moynihan, D. (1965). *The Negro family: The case for national action.* Washington, DC: U.S. Department of Labor, Office of Policy Planning and Research.

Neighbors, H. W., Jackson, J. S., Broman, C., and Thompson, E. (1996). Racism and the mental health of African-Americans: The role of self and system blame. *Ethnicity and Disease, 6*, 167–175.

Ogbu, J. U. (1981). Origins of human competence: A cultural ecological perspective. *Child Development, 52*, 413–429.

Ogbu, J. U. (1987). Variability in minority school performance: A problem in search of an explanation. *Anthropology and Education Quarterly, 18*, 312–334.

Ogbu, J. U. (1991). Minority coping responses and school experience. *Journal of Psychohistory, 18*, 433–457.

Okagaki, L., and Frensch, P. A. (1998). Parenting and children's school achievement: A multiethnic perspective. *American Educational Research Journal, 35*, 123–144.

Pachter, L. M. (2000, June). *Social stratification and child health status.* Paper presented at the second annual meeting of Child Health Services Researchers, held in conjunction with the agency for Health Care Research & Quality (AHRQ) annual meeting, Los Angeles. http://www.ahcpr.gov/research/chsr2soc.htm

Pachter, L. M., and Dworkin P. H. (1997). Maternal expectations about normal child development in 4 cultural groups. *Archives of Pediatrics and Adolescent Medicine, 151*, 1144–1150.

Pachter, L. M., and Harwood, R. L. (1996). Culture and child behavior and psychosocial development. *Journal of Developmental and Behavioral Pediatrics, 17*, 191–198.

Pachter, L. M., Sheehan, J., and Cloutier, M. M. (2000). Factor and subscale structure of a parental health locus of control instrument (Parental Health Beliefs Scales) for use in a mainland United States Puerto Rican community. *Social Science and Medicine, 50*, 715–721.

Perez-Febles, A. M. (1992). *Acculturation and interactional styles of Latina mothers and their infants.* Unpublished honors thesis, Brown University, Providence, RI.

Phinney, J. S., and Chavira, V. (1995). Parental ethnic socialization and adolescent coping with problems related to ethnicity. *Journal of Research on Adolescence, 5*, 31–53.

Quintana, S. M., and Vera, E. M. (1999). Mexican American children's ethnic identity, understanding of ethnic prejudice, and parental ethnic socialization. *Hispanic Journal of Behavioral Sciences, 21*, 387–404.

Rauh, V. A., Wasserman, G. A., and Brunelli, S. A. (1990). Determinants of maternal child-rearing attitudes. *Journal of the American Academy of Child and Adolescent Psychiatry, 29*, 375–381.

Renne, K. (1970). Correlates of dissatisfaction in marriage. *Journal of Marriage and the Family, 32*, 54–67.

Rubel, A. J. (1966). *Across the tracks: Mexican American in a Texas city.* Austin: University of Texas Press.

Rueschenberg, E., and Buriel, R. (1989). Mexican American family functioning and acculturation: A family perspective. *Hispanic Journal of Behavioral Sciences, 11*, 232–244.

Ruggiero, K. M., and Taylor, D. M. (1997). Why minority group members perceive or do not perceive the discrimination that confronts them: The role of self-esteem and perceived control. *Journal of Personality and Social Psychology, 72*, 373–389.

Sabogal, F., Marin, G., Ortero-Sabogal, R., VanOss Marín, B., and Perez-Stable, E. J. (1987). Hispanic familism and acculturation: What changes and what doesn't. *Hispanic Journal of Behavioral Sciences, 9*, 397–412.

Sampson, R. J., Raudenbush, S. W., and Earls, F. (1997). Neighborhoods and violent crime: A multilevel study of collective efficacy. *Science, 277*, 918–924.

Sluzki, D. (1979). Migration and family conflict. *Family Process, 18*, 379–390.

Spencer, M. B. (1983). Children's cultural values and parental child rearing strategies. *Developmental Review, 3*, 351–370.

Spencer, M. B. (1985). Cultural cognition and social cognition as identity correlates of Black children's personal–social development. In M. W. Spencer, G. K. Brookins, and W. R. Allen (Eds.), *Beginnings: The social and affective development of Black children.* Hillsdale, NJ: Lawrence Earlbaum Associates.

Steinberg, L., Dornbusch, S. M., and Brown, B. B. (1992). Ethnic differences in adolescent achievement: An ecological perspective. *American Psychologist, 47*, 723–729.

Stevenson, H., Chen, C., and Uttal, D. H. (1990). Beliefs and achievement: A study of Black, White, and Hispanic children. *Child Development, 61*, 508–523.

Szapocznik, J., and Hernandez, R. (1988). The Cuban-American family. In C. H. Mindel, R. W. Habenstein, and R. Wright (Eds.), *Ethnic families in America.* New York: Elsevier.

Szapocznik, J., Kurtines, W. M., and Fernandez, T. (1980). Bicultural involvement and adjustment in Hispanic-American youths. *International Journal of Intercultural Relations, 4*, 353–365.

Tatum, B. (1987). *Assimilation blues: Black families in a white community.* Northampton, MA: Hazel-Maxwell.

Tatum, B. (1997). Out there stranded? Black families in white communities. In H. P. McAdoo (Ed.), *Black families* (3rd ed.). Thousand Oaks, CA: Sage.

Taylor, R. L. (2000). Racial, ethnic, and cultural diversities in families. In D. H. Demo, K. R. Allen, and M. A. Fine (Eds.), *Handbook of family diversity* (pp. 232–251). New York: Oxford University Press.

Thorton, M. C., Chatters, L. M., Taylor, R. H., and Allen, W. R. (1990). Sociodemographic and environmental correlates of racial socialization by Black parents. *Child Development, 61*, 401–409.

Tinsley, B. J., and Holtgrave, D. R. (1989). Maternal health locus of control beliefs, utilization of childhood preventive health services, and infant health. *Journal of Developmental and Behavioral Pediatrics, 10*, 236–241.

Townsend, N. (in press). Concentration and distribution: Father involvement in two cultural contexts. In C. Tamis-Lemonda and N. Cabrera (Eds.), *The handbook of father involvement: Multidisciplinary perspectives*. Mahwah, NJ: Lawrence Earlbaum Associates.

Tumin, M. M. (1967). *Social stratification*. Englewood Cliff, NJ: Prentice-Hall.

Zuniga, M. E. (1992). Families with Latino roots. In E. W. Lynch, and M. J. Hanson (Eds.), *Developing cross-cultural competence: A guide for working with young children and their families* (pp. 151–179). Baltimore: Brookes.

2

Parenting Among Latino Families in the U.S.

Robin Harwood
University of Connecticut
Birgit Leyendecker
Ruhr University
Vivian Carlson
Marysol Asencio
Amy Miller
University of Connecticut

INTRODUCTION

The United States is entering a time of unprecedented ethnic diversity, one which Hernandez (1997, p. 159) calls an era of "revolutionary demographic transformations . . . in the nature of childhood." In particular, between 1900 and 1970, European Americans accounted for 85% to 89% of the U.S. child population. By 1995, this proportion had fallen to 69%, and is projected to decline still further to 42% by 2050. Also by that date, Latino children are expected to be the largest minority group, comprising 28% of the U.S. child population; early returns from the 2000 census indicate that Latinos have already edged out African Americans as the largest U.S. minority population (12.5% as compared to 12.3% of the population). Latinos, an umbrella term used to refer to people who have their origins in Mexico, Central or South America, and the Spanish-speaking Caribbean, are one of the fastest growing minority groups within the United States. Between 1990 and 2000, the Latino population grew by 58%, compared to a single-digit growth rate in the nation among non-Latino groups. The 2000 census counted 35.3 million Latinos living in the United States, or roughly one out of every eight Americans. Given the relative youth of the Latino population (over 70% are under age 40), and assuming a continuation of current migratory and fertility trends, this number is expected to rise to one in four by 2050 (United States Census Bureau, 1992, 1993, 2001).[1]

Aside from their youth and rapid growth, one characteristic often noted regarding the Latino population in the United States is their relative poverty. In particular, Latinos in 1991, compared to non-Latinos, had higher unemployment (11.3% versus 7.5%), lower median family incomes ($23,900 versus $37,000), and were more likely to be living below the poverty line (27%

---

[1]Due to the large number of undocumented immigrants, even census counts act as conservative estimates of the actual Latino population within the United States.

versus 10%), in metropolitan areas (90.4% versus 76.2%), and in inner cities (51.5% versus 29.3%, U.S. Census Bureau, 1993). These demographic trends have contributed to research emphasizing social ills among Latinos, such as substance abuse, teen pregnancy, and juvenile delinquency. In addition, Lewis's ethnographic work (1965) examining a Puerto Rican family living in what he termed "the culture of poverty" has had a lingering impact on the field, inasmuch as it reinforced perceived links between being poor and being Latino, and being poor and living in a "tangle of pathology." Although the "culture of poverty" has been widely repudiated among scholars, the literature provides stark evidence of a continued bias toward problem-focused research in studies of Latino children, youth, and families. Of 900 articles written since 1989, roughly 75% to 80% of those specific to adolescence were identified with terms relating to teen pregnancy, substance use, juvenile delinquency, and psychopathology. Among articles focused on infancy and childhood, nearly half dealt with problem behaviors. As researchers have suggested, there is a serious need for studies which examine normative growth, development, and resilience among a group of people that is projected to become one fourth of the U.S. population by 2050 (Fisher, Jackson, and Villarruel, 1998; García Coll, 1990; García Coll, Meyer, and Brillon, 1995). Given this need, we have decided to limit our inquiry in this chapter to those studies which pertain to normative processes.

In this chapter, we will: (1) address theoretical considerations relevant to the study of parenting among Latinos, including within-group heterogeneity, the individualism–sociocentrism construct, and definitions of culture, (2) examine central issues in parenting among Latinos, including childrearing beliefs and values, particularly *respeto* and *familismo*; parent–child interactions in early childhood; acculturation and ethnic identity, including intergenerational maintenance of culture and socialization for ethnic pride; and the possible role of culture and parenting with regard to academic achievement among Latino adolescents, (3) explore practical implications of an understanding of Latino culture for practitioners who serve Latino families, and (4) suggest future directions for research on parenting among Latino families in the United States.

THEORETICAL CONSIDERATIONS IN THE STUDY OF PARENTING AMONG LATINOS IN THE UNITED STATES

In this section, important theoretical issues with regard to the study of parenting among Latinos in the United States will be examined. In particular, issues related to the conceptualization of culture will be explored. First, it is necessary to consider the fact that Latinos are not a single, homogeneous group. Second, broad constructs that have been used to contrast Latino with European American culture (individualism and sociocentrism) will be examined. Finally, questions regarding what constitutes a "culture" will be looked at.

Within-Group Heterogeneity

Using ethnicity as a variable for examining group differences can create false impressions of internal homogeneity and thus carries the risk of reinforcing stereotypes (Phinney, 1996; Roosa, Morgan-Lopez, Cree, and Specter, in press; Vega, 1990; Wolf, 1994). This danger is particularly evident with Latinos. The term *Latino* is itself a label of convenience used to refer to people who have their origins in Mexico, Central or South America, and the Spanish-speaking Caribbean (Cauce and Rodríguez, in press). Although this label represents a group of people who share a history of colonization by Spain, it is important to keep in mind that "Latinos" are a diverse people with diverse reasons for being in the United States.

First, Latinos differ by their place of origin. In 2000, the largest percentage (66.1%) claimed Mexican heritage, followed by Puerto Rican (9%) and Cuban (4%, U.S. Census Bureau,

2001).[2] The remaining 21% of Latinos represent all Central and South American countries, as well as the remainder of the Spanish-speaking Caribbean. Thus, some 20 countries of origin are represented by the broad term *Latino*. Second, Latinos differ substantially among themselves with regard to the historical and personal circumstances of their arrival in the United States. Many Latinos in the Southwest were "acquired" as citizens due to the annexation of a large portion of Mexico in 1848. In 1917, Puerto Ricans became U.S. citizens nearly two decades after the island was won from Spain in 1898. Among both Mexicans and Puerto Ricans, several waves of migration can be identified based on periods of economic unrest in the homeland or renewed labor opportunities in the United States. In Cuba, internal revolution resulted in the exodus of members of the elite classes following Castro's takeover in 1959; three distinct phases of migration from Cuba have been identified since then (Cauce and Rodríguez, in press). Among Central and South Americans, migrants have included people fleeing homelands ravaged by war and poverty as well as educated professionals seeking employment opportunities. Latinos thus vary widely in terms of their historical and personal reasons for being in the United States, including those who are citizens by virtue of conquest, political refugees seeking asylum, both documented and undocumented laborers attempting to find jobs, family members seeking to be reunited with loved ones, students pursuing higher education, and professionals in search of employment opportunities.

A third and related source of internal diversity among Latinos is socioeconomic status. Although 27% of Latinos in the United States live below the poverty line, the majority do not. Within-group differences also arise on this index, with Cubans having the lowest (11%) and Puerto Ricans the highest (30%) poverty rate. In terms of educational attainment, internal diversity is also present, with 70% of Cubans, 64% of Puerto Ricans and Central Americans, but only 50% of Mexicans over the age of 25 having finished high school (U.S. Census Bureau, 1999). Although a great deal of attention has been focused on Latinos as a high-risk group living in poverty, it is important to keep in mind that the majority of Latinos are in this country legally, complete high school, obtain employment, and live above the poverty line. An almost exclusive focus on low–socioeconomic status (SES) Latino groups in the research literature not only makes it difficult to disentangle culture from SES as a source of influence on behavior (Betancourt and Regeser López, 1993; García Coll, 1990), but also perpetuates the "stereotypic view that ethnic families are monolithic... and generally 'different' than the 'normative middle-class white families,' as well as the unsupported assumption that with educational and occupational mobility, ethnic minorities will become indistinguishable from white middle-class families" (Fisher et al., 1998, p. 1151). It is thus crucial to highlight and be sensitive to diversity among Latinos with regard to socioeconomic status.

A fourth source of diversity is level of acculturation. Approximately 38% of Latinos in the United States were not born here (U.S. Census Bureau, 1993). Among these, researchers differentiate between the first or immigrant generation (generally, those who migrated after the age of 12), and what is called the 1.5 generation (people who were not born in the United States but migrated here with their families as children). Second-generation Latinos are comprised of individuals who were born here but whose parents were not, whereas the third generation has parents who were born in the United States but grandparents who were not. Each of these generational groups is likely to have had different opportunities for exposure to both the culture of origin and U.S. culture.

Moreover, the differential geographical distribution of Latinos across the United States creates different local environments for the relative preservation of the culture of origin. For example, in 1990, 70% of U.S. Latinos lived in just four states (California, Texas, New York, and Florida). However, the states with the highest concentration of Latinos were New Mexico (38.2% of total

---

[2] Although Puerto Ricans are U.S. citizens who travel freely between the island and the mainland, the census counts Puerto Ricans living on the island in a separate category from Puerto Ricans on the mainland. Some 3.5 million Puerto Ricans living on the island are thus not included in the official count of "Latinos in the U.S." On the island itself, one out of every four Puerto Ricans is estimated to have undergone some sort of migratory experience to the mainland (Lucca Irizarry and Pacheco, 1992).

population), California (25.8%), Texas (25.5%), and Arizona (18.8%; U.S. Census Bureau, 1993). This differential distribution suggests the existence of ethnic enclaves in which cultural preservation is more likely to occur across generations. In addition, individuals differ among themselves with regard to family and personal experiences that have led them to either strengthen or attenuate ties to Latino culture within their own lives.

Given these various sources of diversity, it is imperative to become more sensitive to the fact that "Latinos" are in fact a heterogeneous group of people differing among themselves in terms of their country of origin, historical and personal reasons for being in the United States, socioeconomic status, and level of acculturation (Cauce and Rodríguez, in press; Roosa et al., in press). As Wolf (1994, p. 7) observed, we must "recognize that ethnicities come in many varieties and to call a social entity an 'ethnic' group is merely the beginning of the inquiry."

Individualism and Sociocentrism

The constructs of egocentrism/independence/individualism versus sociocentrism/interdependence/collectivism have proven to be robust and useful heuristics for understanding broad cultural differences. Briefly, American culture is often described as "individualistic" in that it conceives of the individual as an "independent, self-contained, autonomous entity who (a) comprises a unique configuration of internal attributes . . . and (b) behaves primarily as a consequence of those internal attributes" (Markus and Kitayama, 1991, p. 224). This construal of the self is described as a key component of the beliefs and practices that organize perceptions of and interactions with children in America, thus constituting a primary aspect of the cultural context of childhood in this country (Harwood, Miller, and Lucca Irizarry, 1995; Kessen, 1979; Rogoff, Mistry, Göncü, and Mosier, 1993).

In contrast, many other cultures are described as "sociocentric" or "interdependent" in that they emphasize the fundamental connectedness of human beings to one another: "Experiencing interdependence entails seeing oneself as part of an encompassing social relationship and recognizing that one's behavior is determined, contingent on, and, to a large extent organized by what the actor perceives to be the thoughts, feelings, and actions of *others* in the relationship" (Markus and Kitayama, 1991, p. 227). This emphasis on interdependence is depicted as a key component of beliefs and practices that organize perceptions of and interactions with children in a variety of non-Western cultures, thus constituting a primary aspect of the cultural context of childhood in these countries (Greenfield, 1994; Kagitçibasi, 1997; Triandis, 1995).

Researchers have cautioned against using terms such as *individualism* or *sociocentrism* to create or reinforce a false sense of within-group homogeneity (Killen and Wainryb, 2000). Indeed, diversity among Latino families includes not only country of origin, circumstances for being in the United States, socioeconomic status, and acculturation, but also individual variation in beliefs and practices regarding parenting and childrearing (Harwood, Handwerker, Schölmerich, and Leyendecker, in press; Harwood, Schölmerich, and Schulze, 2000). At this point, substantial evidence exists documenting the tendency for Latinos, when compared to European Americans, to adhere to childrearing beliefs and values which are consonant with a more sociocentric perspective (Cauce and Rodríguez, 2000); however, statistical tendencies by no means obviate individual variation. One challenge to research on parenting among U.S. Latinos is therefore to examine both shared beliefs and sources of heterogeneity. That is, it is important to acknowledge the ways in which Latinos as a group may adhere to normative models of parenting and child development which differ from those of the European American cultural majority. On the other hand, it is equally important to investigate internal sources of variation that may lead Latinos to differ among themselves in this regard.

What Constitutes a "Culture"?

One of the problems for research in this domain has been to define what constitutes a "cultural unit." The tendency to equate "culture" with ethnic or national group membership runs the risk of perpetuating group stereotypes by treating large, diverse groups of people as "all of the same kind." The challenge is to find a way of conceptualizing culture that recognizes group differences without reifying them. For a fuller treatment of theoretical approaches to the study of culture and ethnicity, Harkness and Super (in Vol. 2 of this *Handbook*) and García Coll and Pachter (in Vol. 4 of this *Handbook*). For our purposes in this chapter, we elaborate briefly on a perspective articulated by Harwood, Handwerker et al. (in press), which locates culture not in the group but in the contextualized individual; culture is viewed not as an entity equivalent to group membership labels but as a shifting continuum of shared commonality among individuals. In particular, definitions of culture as shared discourse or shared scripts for the understanding of self and other, or as shared norms for social interaction imply a relatively fluid definition of what constitutes a cultural community (Strauss and Quinn, 1997). A person may simultaneously be a member of multiple groups, each with its own particular "morally enforceable conceptual scheme instantiated in practice" (Shweder, 1996). For example, a person may share a common ethnic heritage with other Latinos, but she may also share practices and discourse relevant to a cultural community of ivy-educated psychologists, of middle-SES New England suburbanites, and of avid Red Sox fans.

Conversely, any identifiable social group is comprised of individuals who also participate in multiple other social groups. For example, the Latino cultural center on a college campus may contain members who are also active in the local gay and lesbian community, whereas other members of this Latino community may participate in conservative religious groups that decry homosexuality. Any identifiable social group thus carries within it, by definition, elements of diversity. According to this approach, a cultural community may be viewed not as a bounded, static entity, but as a group of individuals who coconstruct a shared reality in one or more domains of life and who involve themselves in discourse and activities appropriate to an agreed-on level of commonality. What is of primary interest then is not the ultimately arbitrary boundary we draw to define the cultural community in question, but instead what we can learn about the extent to which specific types of discourse are indeed shared among those we have chosen to include as members of the same cultural community (Harwood, Handwerker et al., in press; Harwood, Schölmerich, and Schulze, 2000).

CENTRAL ISSUES IN PARENTING AMONG LATINOS IN THE UNITED STATES

Childrearing Beliefs and Values

Given this view of culture as levels of shared discourse and practice among contextualized individuals who participate in multiple groups, what can we learn about the childrearing beliefs and values of United States parents who share an ethnic heritage as Latinos? What commonalities do we find, and what seem to be some sources of within-group variation? The primary threads of commonality among diverse groups of Latino parents regarding childrearing beliefs and values reflect the individualism–sociocentrism dimension described above. In particular, *respeto* and *familismo* emerge as especially important themes among U.S. Latinos, taken as a group.

Respeto. Harwood et al. (1995) refer to a concept which they believe captures much of the Puerto Rican cultural construct of *respeto*, and which they call "Proper Demeanor." This construct emerged in open-ended interviews with 60 lower- and middle-SES Puerto Rican mothers of 12- to 18-month-old infants, living both on the island and the mainland. According to Harwood et al. (1995, p. 98), "Proper Demeanor implicitly assumes appropriate relatednes (both intimate and nonintimate) . . . . [It] is intrinsically contextual; it involves, by definition, knowing the level of courtesy and decorum required in a given situation in relation to other people of a particular age, sex, and social status. The cardinal rule governing Proper Demeanor in Puerto Rico is *respeto*, or respect, which will manifest itself differently in different contexts."

Qualitative studies of first and second generation Mexican American families living in both California and Texas found that parents' descriptions of desirable qualities for their children frequently focused on being respectful and obedient (Arcia and Johnson, 1998; Azmitia and Brown, in press; Delgado and Ford, 1998). Gonzalez-Ramos, Zayas, and Cohen (1998) found similar results when they asked 80 lower SES Puerto Rican mothers of preschoolers living in New York City to rank order 13 qualities; honest, respectful/obedient, and responsible were ranked the highest, whereas assertive and creative were ranked relatively low.

The mothers sampled in these studies were largely of lower-SES or blue collar origin. It is thus possible that the emphasis on respectfulness among these mothers represents not culture but socioeconomic circumstances. In particular, Kohn (1977) documented that lower SES and blue-collar parents, compared to middle-SES parents, are more likely to emphasize conformity to authority and less likely to emphasize autonomy and personal initiative. Of interest, then, is whether a relatively greater emphasis on Proper Demeanor or respectfulness is obtained among Latinos even when controlling for SES.

Harwood and her colleagues (Harwood, 1992; Harwood and Miller, 1991; Harwood et al., 1995; Harwood, Schölmerich, Ventura-Cook, Schulze, and Wilson, 1996) attempted to address systematically the long-standing confounds between SES and culture. They found that Proper Demeanor and a construct they call "Self-Maximization" (self-confidence, independence, and the development of personal skills and talents) have served, across socioeconomic status and on both the island and the mainland, to organize Puerto Rican and European American mothers' beliefs regarding desirable long-term socialization goals and child behavior. In particular, the constructs of Self-Maximization and Proper Demeanor have been related to mothers': (1) perceptions of attachment behavior (Harwood and Miller, 1991; Harwood, 1992; Harwood et al., 1995), (2) long-term socialization goals and perceptions of desirable and undesirable child behavior (Harwood et al., 1996), (3) interactions with their infants in everyday settings (Harwood, Schölmerich, Schulze, and Gonzalez, 1999; Harwood, Miller, Carlson, and Leyendecker, in press), (4) organization of infants' social contacts (Miller and Harwood, 2001), and (5) beliefs and practices regarding the attainment of developmental milestones (Schulze, Harwood, and Schölmerich, 2001; Schulze, Harwood, Schölmerich, and Leyendecker, 2001).

Other studies have presented similar findings regarding Proper Demeanor or *respeto* as it may influence attitudes toward independence and autonomy among Latino families. Bulcroft, Carmody, and Bulcroft (1996) used a nationally representative sample to examine patterns of parental independence giving among 1,729 families across the United States with children between the ages of 12 and 18. They found that, compared to European American families, Latino families exerted higher degrees of direct control over the adolescents' behavior, both within the family and outside of it. Fuligni (1998) obtained similar results in a study of 998 sixth-, eighth-, and tenth-grade students in California, representing four different ethnic backgrounds and three different generations (immigrant, second, and third). The author concluded that "adolescents with non-European backgrounds held some beliefs and expectations consistent with a greater respect for parental authority and less of an emphasis on individual autonomy" (Fuligni, 1998, p. 790). Moreover, there were generational differences in adolescents' beliefs about the acceptability of disagreeing with parents and expectations for behavioral autonomy, and generational differences seemed to explain the ethnic differences. These results highlight the need for research that carefully examines the effects of acculturation on beliefs and values related to respect and autonomy.

A final aspect of childrearing beliefs and values regarding respect and cooperation among Latinos comes from studies examining attitudes toward competitiveness. In particular, in a program of research extending back over 20 years, Knight and his colleagues (Knight, Cota, and Bernal, 1993; Knight, Dubro, and Chao, 1985; Knight and Kagan, 1977) demonstrated a greater tendency for Mexican American children, compared to European American children, to choose cooperative rather than competitive solutions to resource allocation tasks. Flannagan (1996) provided supporting evidence for a deemphasis on competition among Latino families. In a qualitative study of talk about interpersonal relationships among 36 Latino and European American middle-SES mothers and their kindergarten-age children, it was found that child–peer comparisons were discussed less frequently among the Latino mother–child dyads. The author interpreted this result as an indication that Latino families may discourage competition and confrontation.

The literature thus supports a high valuing of *respeto* among Latino families in the United States. Moreover, these findings may obtain to some extent among Latinos from a variety of diverse backgrounds, including country of origin and socioeconomic status. However, the majority of studies on this topic have been designed as between-group comparisons using Latino and European American samples and have found that, on average, Latinos place more emphasis on respectfulness or proper demeanor than do European Americans. Nevertheless, statistical tendencies do not obviate individual variation, nor do such studies take into account variation among groups of Latinos.

A few studies address the issue of within-group heterogeneity. Although Harwood et al. (1996) found that Latinos in general placed more emphasis on proper demeanor than did European Americans, there were nonetheless within-group socioeconomic differences, with lower-SES Puerto Rican mothers placing even greater emphasis on this dimension than middle-SES Puerto Rican mothers. Moreover, in an examination of long-term socialization goals among 106 middle-class Puerto Rican and European American mothers, Harwood, Handwerker et al. (in press) found that a sizable minority of middle-SES Puerto Rican mothers showed a patterning of goals that was more similar to those of the European American mothers than to their island peers. Finally, in a study of beliefs and practices related to feeding among 60 middle-SES Puerto Rican and European American mothers, Harwood et al. (in press) found that Puerto Rican mothers who had spent time in the mainland United States, who were more highly educated, and who were not Catholic were more likely to show patterns of beliefs and behaviors more similar to those of their European American counterparts than other middle-SES island Puerto Rican mothers.

It thus appears that in general Latinos place greater emphasis than do European Americans on proper demeanor and respectfulness, but there is nonetheless significant within-group variation which remains relatively unexplored. In particular, variations by country of origin, socioeconomic status, level of acculturation, and personal circumstances related to migration remain underexamined.

Familismo.   As Vega (1990) notes, a depiction of Latinos as relatively more family oriented than European Americans has emerged as a consistent theme in numerous studies. Cortés (1995, p. 249) defined *familismo* as "a belief system [that] refers to feelings of loyalty, reciprocity, and solidarity towards members of the family, as well as to the notion of the family as an extension of self." Baca Zinn (1994) outlined four types of familism: demographic, structural, normative, and behavioral. Demographic familism examines variables such as family size, structural familism considers multigenerational households or extended family systems; normative familism is concerned with the value that people place on family solidarity and support, and behavioral familism refers to the amount of contact among extended family members (Cauce and Rodríguez, in press).

Several studies have found that, compared to European Americans, U.S. Latinos have larger and more cohesive social networks, comprised of a higher proportion of extended family members (García, 1993; MacPhee, Fritz, and Miller-Heyl, 1996; Miller and Harwood, 2001; Miller-Loncar, Erwin, Landry, Smith, and Swank, 1998; Schaffer and Wagner, 1996; Zambrana, Silva-Palacios, and Powell, 1992). Social network differences by ethnicity have been noted among children as well. Levitt, Guacci-Franco, and Levitt (1993) investigated social networks among 333 young people, including 112 Latinos, representing three age points from elementary school to high school and a wide range of socioeconomic backgrounds. They found that extended families were more salient for Latino than European American children. Similarly, a study of 88 Mexican American and European American children from one- and two-parent homes found that children from intact Mexican American families reported the most, and children from intact European American families the fewest, social network members (Gamble and Dalla, 1997).

Other researchers have provided evidence that Latino youth, compared to their European American peers, are more likely to turn to family members for advice, to report more positive attitudes toward their parents, to express greater levels of satisfaction with family life, and to feel a greater duty to respect and assist their parents (Fuligni, Tseng, and Lam, 1999; Suárez-Orozco and Suárez-Orozco, 1995; Zayas, 1994). However, within-group variability has also been found on these dimensions, with seasonally migrant compared to seasonally nonmigrant youth reflecting stronger preferences for family consultation (Morrison, Laughlin, San Miguel, Smith, and Widaman, 1997), more socioeconomically disadvantaged youngsters demonstrating a greater need for active parental interaction in decision making (Lamborn, Dornbusch, and Steinberg, 1996), and first-generation compared to later generation adolescents reporting more positive attitudes toward their parents (Suárez-Orozco and Suárez-Orozco, 1995).

Familism has been associated with a variety of positive outcomes among Latinos. Harrison, Wilson, Pine, Chan, and Buriel (1990, p. 351) describe the extended family as "a problem-solving and stress-coping system that addresses, adapts, and commits available family resources to normal and nonnormal transitional and crisis situations." Indeed, family support among Latinos has been linked to good prenatal outcomes as indexed by infant birth weight (Sherraden and Barrera, 1996), breastfeeding among immigrant women (Thiel de Bocanegra, 1998), grandmother support for childcare (Burnette, 1999; Contreras, López, Rivera-Mosquera, Raymond-Smith, and Rothstein, 1999; Fuller, Holloway, and Liang, 1996; Kontos, Howes, Shinn, and Galinsky, 1997; Way and Leadbeater, 1999), quality of parenting (de Leon Siantz and Smith, 1994; de Siantz, 1990; Uno, Florsheim, and Uchino, 1998), and positive school and social outcomes in middle childhood (Franco and Levitt, 1998; Levitt, Guacci-Franco, and Levitt, 1994). However, Contreras, Narang, Ikhlas, and Teichman (in press) offered evidence that outcomes may vary according to the nature of the support offered. In a study of grandmother and partner support among 60 adolescent Puerto Rican mothers, Contreras et al. (in press) found that whereas the availability of family members to meet a variety of social needs was related to more positive maternal behaviors, greater childcare assistance from the grandmother had the opposite effect. It thus appears important that future research distinguish among possible components of familism, such as emotional support versus tangible assistance.

A few studies have examined the impact of acculturation on *familismo* among Latinos, with mixed results. Although some studies have indicated that high educational attainment, generational status, and exposure to American cultural norms lead Latinos away from traditional values (Cortés, 1995; Procidano and Rogler, 1989), other researchers have suggested that certain aspects of familism may maintain importance into the second and third generations. For example, Fuligni et al. (1999) investigated family attitudes among 820 high school students representing first-, second-, and third- or more generation youth from a variety of countries, including Mexico, Central, and South America. They found that attitudes emphasizing family obligation and duty remained high among Latino youth into the second and third generations. Similarly, Gil and Vega (1996) studied 885 Cuban and Nicaraguan middle school students and one of their parents in Dade County, Florida; although family cohesion deteriorated as a function of acculturation, familism as a value remained high.

Together, these findings point to the significance of *familismo* among United States Latinos across a wide range of countries of origin and socioeconomic backgrounds. However, these studies also suggest that familism is a complex, multidimensional phenomenon that needs more systematic study. For example, we know little regarding the ways in which specific types and components of *familismo* may or may not attenuate with exposure to United States culture. The importance of studying acculturation's impact on familism is evident in work by Contreras et al. (1999), who examined associations between grandmother involvement and adjustment among 61 Puerto Rican adolescent mothers. They found that greater grandmother support was related to less symptomatology and parenting stress among low-acculturated mothers, but to greater symptomatology and stress among more highly acculturated mothers. Results such as these highlight the necessity of investigating the ways in which exposure to U.S. culture modifies or fails to modify different aspects of familism among Latinos. In addition, a more nuanced approach which takes into account different types and components of familism is in order.

Parent–Child Interactions in Infancy and Early Childhood

Gallimore, Goldenberg, and Weisner (1993) suggested that ecological and cultural effects are mediated through activity settings of the daily routine, which provide opportunities for children to learn and develop through modeling, joint production, apprenticeship, and other forms of mediated social learning. They identified several activity setting variables that must be considered, including: (1) cultural beliefs and expectations, (2) personnel present during an activity, (3) characteristics of the activities themselves, and (4) scripts for conduct.

Beliefs and expectations.   Despite within-group heterogeneity, Latino parents in the United States have been shown to place relatively greater emphasis in their structuring of parent–child interactions on behaviors associated with sociocentrism than their European American counterparts. Specifically, group differences have been found regarding parents' developmental beliefs, including expectations for participation in family life as well as for the attainment of milestones. In an in-depth, qualitative examination of ten immigrant and second-generation Mexican American families in southern California, Delgado-Gaitan (1993) found that children were expected to participate in household responsibilities at a relatively early age. Along these lines, Schulze, Harwood, Schölmerich, and Leyendecker (2001) found that, compared to European American mothers in Connecticut, middle-SES island Puerto Rican mothers placed more emphasis on instrumental independence, or the ability to perform tasks without an adult's help, and less emphasis on aspects of autonomy related to self-esteem. Azmitia, Cooper, García, and Dunbar (1996) looked at 72 lower-SES European and Mexican American families in central California and also found that the Latino parents had higher expectations for self-reliance with regard to the completion of household chores and everyday tasks.

In contrast, other studies investigating middle- and lower-SES Puerto Rican mothers' age expectations regarding the attainment of developmental milestones have found that, compared to European American mothers, Puerto Rican mothers expect their infants to achieve specific social and self-care milestones, such as self-feeding, at a later age (Pachter and Dworkin, 1997; Schulze, Harwood, and Schölmerich, 2000). Similarly, Savage and Gauvain (1998) examined low-income Mexican American and European American parents of school-age children in southern California, and found that Latino parents reported older ages than European American parents for when their children were or would be able to participate in specific decisions regarding after-school activities and personal care. Although apparently contradictory, we believe these findings point to a greater emphasis among Latino families on interdependence, both in terms of expectations that the child contribute more to the household at an earlier age, but assert his or her own agency at a later age.

Who is present?   When considering children's early interactions, it is important to take into account the people that make up their social world. Latino infants and children appear more likely than Anglo children to have active contact with multiple extended family members. Although immigrant families may share their living quarters with friends and relatives for economic reasons, families appear to continue patterns of mutual support even after they have the financial resources to live as a nuclear family (García, 1993; Zambrana et al., 1992).

Along these same lines, Leyendecker, Lamb, Schölmerich, and Fricke (1997) found that 3-month-old Costa Rican firstborn infants of middle- to upper-middle-SES families did not differ from lower-SES families with respect to the relative amount of time they spent in dyadic compared to multiparty situations. In both samples, while infants were awake, they were exclusively with their mothers for almost 50% of the total 12-hour observation time, whereas a parallel study of a middle-class European American sample in Washington, D.C., revealed that mothers and their infants were by themselves for more than two thirds of the infants' waking time. Moreover, Latino children have been found to be more likely to be taken care of by grandmothers and other (predominantly female) relatives rather than by unrelated caregivers (Leyendecker, Lamb, Schölmerich, and Fracasso, 1995; Miller and Harwood, 2001). Sibling caregiving as well as play in mixed-age groups, as opposed to organized mother–child play groups, may also be more common among some Latino families (Farver and Howes, 1993).

Finally, Rogoff and her colleagues (Chavajay and Rogoff, 1999; Rogoff, Mistry, Göncü, and Mosier, 1993) have provided evidence that Mayan caregivers and their toddlers are more likely to attend simultaneously to spontaneously occurring competing events than U.S. caregivers and their toddlers, who are more likely to alternate their attention between competing events. They interpret these findings as reflecting, in part, greater experience with multiparty versus dyadic settings among the Mayan families.

Everyday activities and scripts for conduct.   Several studies have found distinctive patterns among Latino families in the organization of infants' activities and parent–child interactions. In a diary study of infants' everyday lives, Leyendecker et al. (1995) found that, unlike middle-SES European American families, infants from immigrant Central American families were more likely to follow their families' routines closely. That is, the European American families had established special schedules for feeding, napping, and night sleep that included a tripartite morning–noon–evening pattern, as well as night sleep in their own bedrooms. In contrast, the Central American infants followed their parents' daily routines more closely and were more likely to cosleep with their parents. Feeding thus appeared to be a more social activity that was most likely to take place with other family members.

Despite findings that Latino children spend more time in multiparty settings than their European American peers, research on parent–child interactions among Latinos has followed the traditional research paradigm of primarily focusing on dyadic mother–child interactions. Investigations of mother–child interactions in Latino families have generally drawn comparisons with European American families and have found similarities as well as important differences. Studies looking at maternal responsiveness to infant distress and nondistress signals have not found any overall differences (Leyendecker, Lamb, Fracasso, Schölmerich, and Larson, 1997; Richman, Miller, and LeVine, 1992). However, studies that have examined other aspects of maternal interaction have found that Latina mothers are more likely than European American mothers to structure their child's behavior directly through positioning, restraining, and signalling (Bornstein et al., 1992; Harwood, Schölmarch, Schulze, and Gonzalez, 1999) and to use more physical control strategies when interacting with their infants (Carlson and Harwood, 2000; Fracasso, Busch-Rossnagel, and Fisher, 1994). Similarly, in a study examining feeding practices among 60 middle-SES island Puerto Rican and European American mothers in Connecticut, Harwood et al. (in press) found that Puerto Rican mothers were more likely to signal their 12-month-old infants' attention and to maintain greater direct control over the feeding task by preferring spoon- or bottle-feeding to self-feeding, and by holding the infants on their laps rather than placing them in a high chair.

With regard to interactions during teaching, findings are more mixed and highlight the importance of examining teaching behaviors in culturally salient contexts (Harwood et al., 1999; Kermani and Janes, 1999; Planos, Zayas, and Busch-Rossnagel, 1995). Group differences have been found more consistently with regard to play. In particular, several studies have found that, in contrast to European American mothers, Latina mothers are more likely during play settings to: (1) engage in didactic interactions geared at teaching something to the child, (2) use toys as part of social interaction within the context of pretend play, (3) spend more time attempting to redirect the infant's attention to a new activity, and (4) spend less time sitting back and watching the child explore toys on his or her own (Bornstein, Haynes, Pascual, Painter, and Galperín, 1999; Cote and Bornstein, 2000; Farver and Howes, 1993; Harwood et al., 1999).

A less child-centered approach among Latinos was also evident in a study by Eisenberg (1999) of emotion talk among 80 middle- and lower SES European and Mexican American mothers and their 4-year-old children living in the San Antonio area. Compared to the European American dyads, Mexican American dyads spent proportionately less time talking about the child's emotions and more time talking about the mothers' and others' emotions. This hypothesis is supported in a recent study by Leyendecker, Harwood, Lamb, and Schölmerich (2000), which found that, when describing and evaluating everyday situations, immigrant Central American parents were more likely than middle-SES European American parents in Washington, D.C., to attribute the desirability or undesirability of these situations to the child's own appropriate and cooperative behavior. Together, these findings suggest that there is a tendency for Latino families to place greater emphasis on the child's obligations to the family and the larger group, and less emphasis on centering interactions around the child's own wishes, thoughts, and desires.

Fathers and gender socialization.   As Roopnarine and Ahmeduzzaman (1993, p. 97) observe, "Traditional views of Latino fathers portray them as distant, avoiding intimacy, obsessed with machismo, and as inspiring fear in children." In Latino cultures, the male gender role has often been characterized by the so-called machismo complex, a poorly defined set of characteristics associated with masculinity which may include, but is not limited to: violent or aggressive behavior; having large numbers of sexual partners, both premarital and extramarital; fathering many children in and out of marriage as a sign of virility; avoiding any work labeled feminine, such as childrearing or housecleaning; placing an emphasis on respect and honor; having absolute authority within the family; and venerating one's mother (Andrade, 1992; DeYoung and Zigler, 1994; Gutmann, 1994; Ingoldsby, 1991; Zaitchik and Mosher, 1993). Scholars have taken a variety of positions regarding the link between machismo and Latino culture, from believing that machismo is a persistent Latin American male characteristic that permeates the entire culture, to the view that it is nothing more than a stereotypic myth (Asencio, 1999; Gaines, Ríos, and Buriel, 1997). Unfortunately, despite its popularity as a concept, little empirical research has been done examining the actual existence of machismo among either Latinos or non-Latinos.

However, the few studies that have directly examined the role of fathers in childrearing among Latino families have found little support for these stereotypic views of Latino masculinity. For example, in their study of middle- to lower-SES mainland Puerto Rican fathers, Roopnarine and Ahmeduzzaman (1993) found that Puerto Rican fathers estimated they spent about 2.7 hours per day as primary caregivers for their preschool-age children, roughly 37% of the time that mothers estimated they spent as primary caregivers. This is similar to the proportion of time (33%) that European American fathers estimated they spent as primary caregivers. Caldera, Fitzpatrick, and Wampler (in press) similarly found that, unlike the stereotypic image of Latino fathers as domineering, the California fathers in their study appeared to have more egalitarian views of themselves and to take partial responsibility for the care of their children. Finally, in a study of Mexican American mothers' and fathers' questions to their preschool-age children during play, Tenenbaum and Leaper (1997) found that fathers' attitudes toward gender equality acted as a significant moderator in their use of questions. In particular, fathers with more egalitarian gender attitudes were more likely to ask their children questions during a feminine-stereotyped play setting. These findings imply that gender attitudes vary among Latino fathers as they do among European American fathers, thus providing further evidence against stereotypic images of Latino fathers. Clearly, research that examines gender roles among Latino families from a normative perspective that eschews stereotypes and takes within-group variation seriously is needed.

Acculturation and Ethnic Identity Among Latino Parents and Children

Nearly 40% of Latinos in the United States today were not born in this country. Figures such as these reflect the salience of issues related to acculturation when studying U.S. Latino parents and their children. Acculturation has been defined as "the process through which immigrants and their offspring acquire the values, behavioral norms, and attitudes of the host society" (Cortés, Rogler, and Malgady, 1994, p. 708). Standardized, validated acculturation scales that have been widely used with Latinos in the United States include: (1) the Acculturation Rating Scale for Mexican Americans, or the ARSMA and ARSMA II (Cuéllar, Arnold, and Maldonado, 1995; Cuéllar, Harris, and Jasso, 1980), (2) the Biculturalism Involvement Questionnaire, initially validated with Cuban Americans (Szapocznik, Kurtines, and Fernandez, 1980), and (3) two scales designed specifically for use with

Puerto Ricans: the American and Puerto Rican Cultural Involvement Scales (Cortés et al., 1994), and the Psychological Acculturation Scale (Tropp, Erkut, Alarcón, García Coll, and Vázquez, 1994).

Recently, researchers have begun to emphasize the need to broaden our examination of acculturation and the migratory experience (Cortés et al., 1994; García Coll et al., 1996; Phinney, 1996; Rogler, 1994). In particular:

(1) Past investigations have tended to view migration from a deficit perspective, viewing it as a stressor on families and examining its relation to mental health outcomes (García Coll et al., 1995; Rumbaut, 1997). Normative processes of cultural change either within or across generations have seldom been studied.

(2) Most attempts to measure acculturation have focused narrowly on linguistic competence, with little attention given to the impact of migration on the actual content of parents' beliefs and practices (Betancourt and Regeser Lopéz, 1993; Cortés et al., 1994; García Coll et al., 1995; Gonzales, Knight, Morgan-Lopez, Saenz, and Sirolli, in press).

(3) We know relatively little regarding the ways in which specific aspects of the migratory experience, such as country of origin, circumstances of migration, and socioeconomic status, may relate to parents' adoption of the host country's beliefs and practices; acculturation as a complex social process that unfolds over time remains understudied (Gonzales et al., in press; Rogler, 1994).

(4) Finally, most past research has tended to assume what Rogler, Cortés, and Malgady (1991) call a "bipolar" view of ethnic identity, in which "the adoption of the new culture occurs at the expense of a corresponding rejection of the culture of origin" (Cortés et al., 1994, p. 718). The development of a bicultural identity among parents and their children, as well as the delineation of processes involving selective rather than wholesale cultural change, remain underexamined. As Wolf (1982, p. 361) notes, "It is an error to envisage the migrant as the protagonist of a homogeneously integrated culture that he either retains or yields up as a whole."

According to Phinney (1990, p. 501), "the term *ethnic identity* has sometimes been used virtually synonymously with *acculturation*, but the two terms should be distinguished . . . . ethnic identity may be thought of as an aspect of acculturation, in which the concern is with individuals and the focus is on how they relate to their own group as a subgroup of the larger society." As Phinney (1996) points out, ethnicity is a complex multidimensional construct. In particular, she identifies three key aspects of ethnicity: (1) maintenance of cultural norms and values, (2) strength, salience, and meaning of ethnic identity or belonging, and (3) experiences and attitudes associated with minority status.

Maintenance of cultural norms and values across generations. One key issue involves the extent to which Latino parents maintain traditional beliefs and attitudes following migration, and also the extent to which their children adopt these traditional attitudes versus those of the host culture. Only a few studies have explicitly examined intergenerational differences among Latinos in the maintenance of cultural norms and values, such as *respeto* and *familismo*. The findings from these studies point to the complexity of the topic. In their study of 200 New York Puerto Rican husband–wife intergenerational pairs (that is, 200 parents and their married children), Rogler and his colleagues (Procidano and Rogler, 1989; Rogler and Santana Cooney, 1984) found that the value orientation of familism diminished intergenerationally according to educational upward mobility; however, intergenerational interactions and supportive patterns between parents and children remained strong and stable. Similarly, Rueschenberg and Buriel (1989) examined 45 Mexican American families in Los Angeles county varying in generational status. They found that, although level of acculturation was significantly related to four of five variables external to the family system (such as achievement orientation), it was not related to any of five internal family system variables (such as cohesiveness and authority of parents), suggesting that the basic internal organization of the family, including the role of parental authority, remained relatively unchanged during the acculturation process. Two additional studies (Delgado-Gaitin, 1993; Phinney, Ong, and Madden, 2000) have found that immigrant Mexican

American parents and their children in southern California were very comparable in their values regarding *familismo* and *respeto*. Findings such as these highlight the complexity of the process of intergenerational change, yet suggest that Latino children may retain many of their immigrant parents' central values.

As Fisher et al. (1998) point out, there is increasing evidence that the transmission of culture across generations is individual and dynamic. That is, the content and significance of culture across time depends on a variety of social network, individual, and family demographic variables (Portes and Rumbaut, 1990). In general, it seems safe to say that maintenance of cultural norms and values across generations of Latinos within the United States is an understudied phenomenon. A common tendency among many studies of Latino families to mix generational status within the same sample makes conclusions on this topic particularly difficult to draw and underlines the importance of more carefully controlled investigations of this domain.

Strength, salience, and meaning of ethnic identity. A second aspect of ethnic identity is its strength, salience, and meaning. Parents' own sense of ethnic identity can have a direct impact on how they choose to socialize their children, and there is some evidence that biculturalism itself may serve a positive role for both parents and children. For example, Gutierrez and Sameroff (1990) found, in their study of 60 middle-SES Mexican American and Anglo-American mothers, that a bicultural subgroup of highly acculturated Mexican American mothers were the most likely to offer responses to vignettes of family incidents that took into account multiple perspectives of the actors. The authors interpret these findings as suggesting that biculturalism has a positive effect on an individual's cognitive capacities.

Recognition of the protective role that ethnic pride or identity may play has given rise to several studies examining the role of parental socialization on the development of ethnic identity in Latino children and adolescents. In particular, Knight and his colleagues (Knight, Bernal, Garza, Cota, and Ocampo, 1993; Knight, Cota, and Bernal, 1993; Ocampa, Knight, and Bernal, 1997) examined family socialization practices and the development of ethnic identity among Mexican American children in the Southwest. Mothers' greater comfort and knowledge of Mexican culture, as well as generation of migration of the fathers' family, led children to develop a greater sense of ethnic identity. Quintana, Castañeda-English, and Ybarra (1999) similarly found that ethnic socialization was strongly predictive of ethnic identity achievement among a group of 43 Mexican American high schoolers in central Texas.

Experiences and attitudes associated with minority status. Research regarding the way Latino parents help their children cope with negative experiences related to minority status is sparse (Phinney and Chavira, 1995; Spencer and Markstrom-Adams, 1990). Gil, Vega, and Dimas (1994) found that family or ethnic pride mediates the impact of acculturative stress among both foreign- and U.S.-born Latino adolescents. Because a strong ethnic identity is often hypothesized to act as a psychological resource for coping with prejudice and discrimination (Padilla, 1994), a few researchers have examined family socialization variables that may relate to the child's ability to deal with negative experiences associated with minority status.

Quintana and Vera (1999) investigated ethnic identity, understanding of ethnic prejudice, and parental ethnic socialization among 47 Mexican American grade school children. They found that parental socialization about ethnic discrimination was associated with the development of ethnic knowledge among children. Similarly, Phinney and Chavira (1995) studied ethnic identity, self-esteem, and parental ethnic socialization among 60 minority adolescents (age 16–18) in the Los Angeles area. Results indicated that adolescents who either ignored or used a more proactive style of coping with discrimination and stereotypes had higher self-esteem, and also had parents who were more likely to discuss discrimination with them. Finally, Ruggiero, Taylor, and Lambert (1996) examined 329 mothers from Miami, including 142 Latinos, regarding the importance they placed on heritage culture maintenance and on their experiences with ethnic discrimination. They found a negative correlation between the amount of discrimination mothers perceived for themselves person-ally and the importance they assigned to maintaining Latino culture in their homes and communities. Together, these findings are consistent with the hypothesis that parents who maintain a strong ethnic identity and discuss issues related to ethnicity and minority status openly with their children appear to provide both themselves and their children with an important buffer against negative experiences associated with minority status.

Parenting and Academic Achievement among Latinos

In 1997, only 63% of Latino compared to 88% of European American adults age 25 to 29 had completed high school (U.S. Census Bureau, 1998). Further examination of these statistics indicate differences among Latinos with regard to country of origin and generational status. Specifically, 70% of Cubans, 64% of Puerto Ricans, 64% of Central and South Americans, and 50% of Mexicans age 25 or older had completed high school, compared to 84% of European Americans (U.S. Census Bureau, 1999). Statistics such as these have given rise to a considerable number of studies attempting to understand why Latino adolescents drop out of school at a higher rate than European Americans. Okagaki and Frensch (1998) identify at least five potential causes: (1) motivational differences in individuals' desires to improve their lives, (2) differences in parent education and socioeconomic status, (3) differences in parental expectations for children's achievement, (4) incongruence between cultural practices at home and at school, and (5) societal oppression. For our purposes here, we will group these explanations into two categories, those which maintain that Latino parents hold beliefs and/or values that may work against their children's school success, and those which maintain that societal discrimination rather than parental socialization has led to high dropout rates among Latino adolescents.

Parental beliefs, attitudes, and values. Several studies have refuted the notion that Latino parents place less value on education than do European American parents. For example, Stevenson, Chen, and Uttal (1990) investigated beliefs and achievement in a representative sample of 2,973 chil-dren attending public and private elementary schools in the Chicago metropolitan area; a subsample of mothers of 968 of the children was included. Minority children and mothers, including Latinos, placed greater emphasis on and concern about education than did European Americans. Other studies have similarly found that Latino parents emphasize effort and the importance of education (Azmitia et al., 1996; Bempechat, Graham, and Jiminez, 1999; Fuligni, 1997; Hernandez, Vargas-Lew, and Martinez, 1994; Pérez Granados and Callanan, 1997), and seek involvement in their children's school life (Cooper, 1990; López, Rodríguez, and Sánchez, 1995; Sánchez and López, 1999).

With regard to parents' sense of their own efficacy in this domain, Stevenson et al. (1990) found that, although Latino mothers in their sample were eager to help their children with school, they believed that their help was less likely to contribute to the child's achievement than was the case with either African American or European American mothers. Similarly, Okagaki, Frensch, and Gordon (1995) examined educational expectations and parental efficacy among 82 fourth- and fifth-grade Mexican American children and their parents in northern California. Although parents of low achievers reported helping their children as frequently as did parents of high achievers, the parents of high achievers were more convinced that their help was effective. The influence of generational and socioeconomic status on findings such as these remains underexamined.

With regard to the cultural mismatch hypothesis, which posits that the cultural values and practices of Latino families are incongruent with those of United States schools, findings are mixed. Okagaki and Sternberg (1993) offer evidence that first generation Latino parents perceive being obedient, a quality related to *respeto* in children, as a behavior that will facilitate their children's school success. A few researchers have suggested that a greater emphasis on obedience among Latino families may actually inhibit the school performance of Latino children and adolescents (Steinberg, Dornbusch, and Brown, 1992).

However, Suárez-Orozco and Suárez-Orozco (1994, p. 142) reject this notion, maintaining that it "is based on an erroneous juxtaposition of independence training as a sine qua non (requirement) for achievement motivation." They concluded that the problems facing Latinos in U.S. schools have less to do with culture and parental socialization than with immigration, resettlement, resulting minority status, and the poverty, segregation, and discrimination that accompany these processes (Suárez-Orozco and Suárez-Orozco, 1995). Other researchers have similarly concluded that school dropout may reflect the fact that Latino adolescents, particularly low-income youth living in inner cities, may perceive discrimination toward themselves as minorities and believe that finishing school will not bring them increased opportunities (Okagaki, Frensch, and Dodson, 1996; Steinberg et al., 1992; Valdés, 1997). As Ogbu (1991) observes, young people who, based on their personal experiences, believe that racial barriers will affect their occupational status regardless of whether they finish high school may be less motivated to persevere academically.

IMPLICATIONS FOR PRACTITIONERS WHO SERVE LATINO PARENTS

Only recently have the findings of normative research among Latino families begun to have an impact on the provision of services to Latino parents and their children. Service providers and programs have moved from a simple translation approach, through deficit-based programs, to an emerging understanding of the need for individualized exploration of the cultural context of the Latino families they serve. An understanding of culture as interactive and ever changing is gradually overcoming the stereotypic approaches to culture as a static set of facts to be learned about particular groups. Articles addressing these issues are emerging in the literature aimed at medical, mental health, education, and therapeutic practitioners.

Medicine and Mental Health

Zayas (1994) challenged the medical community to abandon deficit models of Latino family functioning and begin to attend to adaptive strategies and socialization goals of minority parents. Several other authors have also begun to investigate normative socialization patterns and family interactions among Latinos to better inform health care service providers and intervention programs (Cousins, Power, and Olvera-Ezzell, 1993; Elder et al., 1998; Lees and Tinsley, 1998; Niska, Lia-Hoagberg, and Snyder, 1997; Rehm, 1999).

The mental health literature includes a variety of examples of normative research based on the everyday experiences and cultural contexts of participants. Bernal, Bonilla, and Bellido (1995) present a framework for adapting mental health treatment services to reflect the unique cultural context of Latino families. This framework defines the culturally sensitive elements of clinical interventions and provides examples of effective adaptations for use with Latino participants. Garrison, Roy, and Azar (1999) similarly present a school-based model that requires consideration of the cultural values and immigration experiences of Latino parents and their children. Finally, Malgady, Rogler, and Constantino (1990) have developed "cuento therapy," which adapts island-based Puerto Rican folktales to the host society and uses them to model desirable behaviors and promote positive outcomes with Puerto Rican adolescents.

In addition to adapting services to reflect Latino cultural values, mental health professionals have begun to address the issue of cultural validity in the measures used to diagnose and evaluate treatment outcomes among the families they serve. Some studies focus on adapting current standardized assessment methods to better reflect Latino family values and experiences (e.g., Canino and Guarnaccia, 1997; French, 1993), whereas others use an ethnographic perspective to develop new assessment concepts based upon the actual experiences and beliefs of Latino families (Dumka, Gonzales, Wood, and Formoso, 1998; Guarnaccia, Parra, Deschamps, and Milstein, 1992; Guarnaccia, Rivera, Franco, and Neighbors, 1996).

A few examples of staff training programs designed to enhance cultural competency skills among mental health professionals serving Latino families are also found in the current literature (Inclan, 1990; Kiselica, 1991; Zayas, Evans, Mejia, and Rodriguez, 1997; Zayas and Solari, 1994). The core component of such training programs is the development of a basic understanding of essential elements of Latino culture, such as emphases on *respeto* and *familismo*. These fundamentals are then used to promote understanding of key interactive adaptations likely to enhance the effectiveness of treatments offered to Latino parents and children. The inherent dangers of generating stereotypic overgeneralizations using this approach are decried by Martinez (1994). Active negotiation skills useful in resolving cultural issues and differences between care providers and Latino parents are addressed in only the most recent contributions to the staff training literature (e.g., Zayas et al., 1997).

Education

Education literature pertaining to Latino families primarily focuses on issues and approaches to involving parents in classroom programs, special education, and school psychology or counseling services. Professionals working within the special education system, birth through age 21, are required by federal legislative mandate to actively collaborate with parents in assessing, planning, and programming for their special needs children. Early childhood educators who seek program accreditation from the National Association for the Education of Young Children are also required to demonstrate active collaboration with all parents, including seeking to understand family goals and showing respect for cultural differences when present. Most teacher training programs have responded to these requirements by moving away from the deficit model of cultural difference; however, many continue to use overgeneralizations and stereotypic information regarding Latino culture. This situation is exacerbated by the serious shortage of Latino educators available within the U.S. education and higher education systems.

An investigation of Latino family classroom and home literacy involvement has found that middle-SES European Americans and lower-SES Latino families do not differ in terms of knowledge of their child's classroom, nor the value they place on home literacy activities (McCarthey, 1997). Others find that culturally sensitive literacy and preschool programs combining home and school participation for Latino families are associated with higher achievement and motivation and lower grade retention among participating children (Morrow and Young, 1997; Quintero, 1999; Reynolds, 1989; Reynolds, Mavorgenes, Bezruczko, and Hagemann, 1996). Mexican American families' support of child education has been found to include the family's physical resources, emotional climate, and interpersonal interactions that place a high value on education (Delgado-Gaitan, 1992).

The role of school psychologists in relation to Latino families is particularly important given the frequent use of school psychologists as home–school liaisons as well as diagnosticians who help determine eligibility for special educational services. Knowledge of cultural values, beliefs, and practices is essential to the successful fulfillment of such roles among Latino families. Henning-Stout (1996) and Thomas (1992) issue pleas for school psychologists to actively seek understanding of Latino migrant families in sociocultural context, including attention to the potential trauma involved in the migratory experience. These authors call on school psychologists to assume the role of community advocate and emphasize the need for basic research investigating such issues as acculturation, learning needs, and mental health correlates of the migratory experience. The need to promote cultural tolerance among classroom teachers and children is also highlighted. The ultimate goal of effective school psychology services with this population is the support and mentoring of migrant children through our educational system and into the ranks of the school psychology profession (Henning-Stout, 1996).

Although the special education literature has begun to address issues of cultural reciprocity as a result of the mandate to engage in active collaboration with parents (Harry, Rueda, and Kalyanpur, 1999; Kalyanpur and Harry, 1997), relatively few investigations specifically address the concerns of Latino families. Few articles include ethnographic information regarding Latino perceptions of special education issues from the family's perspective. Harry (1992) presented compelling qualitative evidence of the multiple theoretical and practical barriers to effective participation experienced by Puerto Rican families in the special education system. The medical model of disability, the reliance on formal, written communication, and the hierarchical and decontextualized nature of school district interactions were found to result in mistrust and withdrawal on the part of participating families.

Other qualitative studies have explored Latino parents' construction of meaning systems regarding their child with special needs (Skinner, Bailey, Correa, and Rodriguez, 1999; Skinner, Rodriguez, and Bailey, 1999). This work promoted the use of narrative, content, and cultural model analyses to demonstrate the interactive, changing, and interpretive role of culture in the everyday lives of Latino parents. Examining the ways in which 150 Latino mothers used cultural beliefs to construct meanings of self in relation to disability, the authors found that most mothers viewed their special needs child as a source of positive transformations in their lives (Skinner, Bailey et al., 1999). An investigation of 250 parents' religious interpretations of disability leads to the emergence of three models: disability as a fact of nature, unrelated to God; disability as a positive message from God; and disability as a punishment from God. Fifty-five percent of Latino parents interpreted disability as a sign or message from God, but only 3% saw it as a punishment (Skinner, Rodriguez et al., 1999). Clinicians who understand the implications of such interpretations and possess the skills to explore such meanings with families will greatly enhance their effectiveness in setting appropriate goals and designing collaborative interventions.

Parent Education

Parent training programs have a particularly strong history of using behavioral standards derived from research among middle-SES European Americans as goals for all parents (Smith, Pevou, and Lesesne, in Vol. 4 of this *Handbook*). Parenting practices that deviate from these standards are often defined as deficits without attention to cultural influences on parenting behavior (Forehand and Kotchick, 1996). Challenges to this tradition, in the form of parenting programs developed specifically to meet the needs of particular minority populations, have emerged gradually (Dumka, Graza, Roosa, and Stoerzinger, 1997; Johnson and Walker, 1991; Zegarra, 1998). In a review of Latino parenting interventions, Dumka, Lopez, and JacobsCarter (in press) found no program that was designed so that the course of the upcoming intervention could be changed based on parents' expressed needs at the outset. However, Zayas and Rojas Flores (in press) offer preliminary evidence of the efficacy of using combined etic (standardized across cultures) and emic (indigenous) approaches in the development of a culturally appropriate Latino parenting program.

In a review of the efficacy of culturally sensitive parent education programs, Gorman and Balter (1997) called for the inclusion of qualitative research. The issue of measurement adequacy using scales based upon middle-SES European American validation samples has received limited attention in the literature. Common outcome measures of family interaction, parenting, and home environments in early childhood have been found to have mixed patterns of prediction for Latinos in comparison to European American families (Knight, Tein, Prost, and Gonzales, in press; Knight, Tein, Shell, and Roosa, 1992; Knight, Virdin, and Roosa, 1994; Sugland et al., 1995). Although some subscales seem equivalent across ethnicities, others appear less valid in predicting Latino child outcomes. Sugland et al. (1995) concluded that standardized measures of the home environment may fail to capture some aspects of the home that are important to the development of minority children. Nonetheless, other researchers continue to publish program efficacy data for Latino families based on these measures.

Summary

This overview of trends in service provision to Latino families reveals several areas of concern common to all disciplines. First, a paradigm shift from deficit or risk prevention programs to positive programs designed to actively enhance existing family and community strengths is of the utmost importance (Roth and Brooks-Gunn, 2000). In addition, an active program of recruitment into various human service professions among Latino children, youth, and adults must be undertaken in order to provide highly skilled, bicultural professionals to meet the needs of future generations of Latino parents and their children. While working toward the goal of increasing available bicultural professionals, the current labor force of service providers must be educated in the skills necessary to appropriately serve Latino children, youth, and families.

This final and most immediate goal requires comprehensive efforts to move beyond stereotypic staff training models that treat culture as a static set of facts and attempt to acquaint professionals with generic "differences" between Anglo and Latino culture. The ultimate goal of more appropriate training is to produce professionals capable of establishing respectful, collaborative, and effective cross-cultural relationships with individual Latino children, youth, and families. Such a program must first establish a sophisticated understanding of culture as shared knowledge used in social interactions and interpretations of the world. One staff training model (Carlson and Harwood, 1999) addresses these issues as they pertain to early education and intervention professionals who work directly with parents from diverse cultural backgrounds. This model explores culturally varied parenting practices and respectful, collaborative negotiation techniques useful in establishing mutually agreed on, and individualized intervention goals and practices. The mutual benefits of culturally reciprocal and respectful relationships with this rapidly growing segment of our population are too important to be delayed or ignored.

FUTURE DIRECTIONS IN RESEARCH ON PARENTING AMONG LATINOS IN THE UNITED STATES

Strickland (2000, p. 332) asked, "How do we avoid using psychology, both overtly and more subtly, to label and punish those who are different from ourselves?" First, it is imperative that future research on Latino parents recognize the diversity which characterizes this group of people who share what is essentially a label of convenience, but which includes individuals from some 20 countries of origin, with widely differing reasons for being in the United States, a full range of socioeconomic status, and varying levels of acculturation. Research studies which state that "the sample consisted of 60 Latino mothers, the majority of whom were Mexican, 40% of whom were 1st generation, and 75% of whom were lower class," and then go on to contrast "the Latino parents" with European American parents, need to become a thing of the past. Instead, research that takes seriously within-group variation is sorely needed. As a first step, population samples need to: (1) be specific with regard to country of origin (e.g., El Salvadorans rather than a mixed group of Central Americans), (2) control carefully for the effects of SES, (3) control carefully for differences according to generational status, and (4) take seriously the potential effects of acculturation on parents' beliefs and practices. In addition, it is important to recognize the various personal and historical circumstances that have brought different groups of Latino families to the United States. On a related note, the study of culture itself needs to move beyond a simple equation of ethnic group with culture. Although it is important to recognize the power of ethnicity in parents' lives, it is nonetheless true that ethnic group membership does not perfectly predict a parent's beliefs and practices. More careful delineation of sources of influence on within-group heterogeneity is necessary (Harwood, Handwerker et al., in press).

Second, there continues to be a need for normative research that is based on participants' own indigenous meaning systems (Harwood et al., 1995). This is particularly important for Latino parents, many of whom are first generation immigrants from a variety of different countries. Mixed evidence has been found regarding the equivalence for Latinos of parenting and family interaction measures that have been created using middle-SES European American populations (Bradley, Mundfrom, Whiteside, Casey, and Barrett, 1994; Knight et al., 1992; Knight, Virdin, and Roosa, 1994). Moreover, research is needed on normative processes of growth and development among Latino families and children. The preponderance of problem-focused research using inner-city samples not only perpetuates negative stereotypes, but also limits our understanding of normative development among what is projected to become a quarter of the United States population by 2050.

Third, it is important to examine the effects of acculturation on childrearing beliefs and practices among Latinos from a perspective that acknowledges that it is a bicultural, socially embedded process that unfolds over time (Gonzales et al., in press). The use of measures that examine changes in specific parenting variables rather than global measures of linguistic competence will enable us to move forward in our understanding of acculturation's effect on parenting among Latinos (Betancourt and Regeser López, 1993).

CONCLUSIONS

Despite considerable within-group heterogeneity, there appears to be a general tendency for Latino parents in the United States to adhere to childrearing beliefs and practices that emphasize key cultural values such as *respeto* and *familismo*. However, the impact on these beliefs and practices of variables such as socioeconomic status and acculturation remains underexamined.

As Strickland (2000, p. 336) observed, "Excluded from our theories, ignored by our methods, and punished by our conclusions, the others, especially women and minorities, have often turned away from us, knowing that our idiosyncratic notions of psychological need and normality do not represent them.... We must expand our boundaries by remembering that our theories and methods were designed to be replaced.... We cannot continue to push our notions of normality and psychological well-being without regard and respect for the dignity of every individual and the contributions of every culture." These would seem to be wise words of warning as we stand at the start of the twentyfirst century, poised to continue our efforts to understand parenting and normative development in all its diverse complexity.

ACKNOWLEDGMENTS

We thank the National Institutes of Child Health and Human Development for support (grant no. HD32800), and Marc Bornstein, Cynthia García Coll, and Joan Miller for assistance and support of this work over the years. We gratefully acknowledge several colleagues who read and commented on earlier versions of this manuscript: Andrew Fuligni, Andres Gil, Lynn Okagaki, Jean Phinney, Lloyd Rogler, and Carola Suárez-Orozco. In addition, we are indebted to the participants of the 2000 Kent State Psychology Forum on Latino Children and Families in the United States for the many ideas discussed and shared during a productive and enjoyable week: Margarita Azmitia, Yvonne Caldera, Ana Mari Cauce, Josefina Contreras, Larry Dumka, Nancy Gonzales, George Knight, Lisseth Rojas-Flores, Mark Roosa, and Luis Zayas. Finally, we thank Maris Faulkner and Becky Shields for their gracious assistance with the preparation of this manuscript.

REFERENCES

Andrade, A. R. (1992). Machismo: A universal malady. *Journal of American Culture*, 5, 33–41.

Arcia, E., and Johnson, A. (1998). When respect means to obey: Immigrant Mexican mothers' values for their children. *Journal of Child and Family Studies*, 7, 79–95.

Asencio, M. W. (1999). Machos and sluts: Gender, sexuality, and violence among a cohort of Puerto Rican adolescents. *Medical Anthropology Quarterly*, 13, 107–126.

Azmitia, M., and Brown, J. R. (in press). Continuity and change in Latino immigrant parents' beliefs about 'the path of life'. To appear in J. M. Contreras, K. A. Kerns, and A. M. Neal-Barnett (Eds.), *Latino children and families in the United States*. Westport, CT: Greenwood.

Azmitia, M., Cooper, C. R., García, E. E., and Dunbar, N. D. (1996). The ecology of family guidance in low-income Mexican-American and European American families. *Social Development*, 5, 1–23.

40 Harwood et al.

Baca Zinn, M. (1994). Adaptation and continuity in Mexican-origin families. In R. L. Taylor (Ed.), *Minority families in the United States: A multicultural perspective.* Englewood Cliffs, NJ: Prentice-Hall.

Bempechat, J., Graham, S., and Jiminez, N. (1999). The socialization of achievement in poor and minority students. *Journal of Cross-Cultural Psychology, 30,* 139–158.

Bernal, G., Bonilla, J., and Bellido, C. (1995). Ecological validity and cultural sensitivity for outcome research: Issues for the cultural adaptation and development of psychosocial treatments with Hispanics. *Journal of Abnormal Child Psychology, 23,* 67–82.

Betancourt, H., and Regeser López, S. R. (1993). The study of culture, ethnicity, and race in American psychology. *American Psychologist, 48,* 629–637.

Bornstein, M. H., Haynes, O. M., Pascual, L., Painter, K. M., and Galperín, C. (1999). Play in two societies: Pervasiveness of process, specificity of structure. *Child Development, 70,* 317–331.

Bornstein, M. H., Tal, J., Rahn, C., Galperín, C. Z., Pêcheux, M.-G., Lamour, M., Toda, S., Azuma, H., Ogino, M., and Tamis-LeMonda, C. S. (1992). Functional analysis of the contents of maternal speech to infants of 5 and 13 months in four cultures: Argentina, France, Japan, and the United States. *Developmental Psychology, 28,* 593–603.

Bradley, R. H., Mundfrom, D. J., Whiteside, L., Casey, P. H., and Barrett, K. (1994). A factor analytic study of the infant-toddler and early childhood versions of the HOME inventory administered to white, black, and Hispanic American parents of children born preterm. *Child Development, 65,* 880–888.

Bulcroft, R. A., Carmody, D. C., and Bulcroft, K. A. (1996). Patterns of parental independence giving to adolescents: Variations by race, age, and gender of child. *Journal of Marriage and the Family, 58,* 866–883.

Burnette, D. (1999). Social relationships of Latino grandparent caregivers: A role theory perspective. *The Gerontologist, 39,* 49–58.

Caldera, Y., Fitzpatrick, J., and Wampler, K. (in press). Co-parenting in Mexican American families: Mothers' and fathers' perceptions. To appear in J. M. Contreras, K. A. Kerns, and A. M. Neal-Barnett (Eds.), *Latino children and families in the United States.* Westport, CT: Greenwood.

Canino, G., and Guarnaccia, P. (1997). Methodological challenges in the assessment of Hispanic children and adolescents. *Applied Developmental Science, 1,* 124–134.

Carlson, V. J., and Harwood, R. L. (1999). Understanding and negotiating cultural differences concerning early developmental competence: The six raisin solution. *Zero to Three, 20,* 19–24.

Cauce, A. M., and Rodríguez, M. D. (in press). Latino families: Myths and realities. To appear in J. M. Contreras, K. A. Kerns, and A. M. Neal-Barnett (Eds.), *Latino children and families in the United States.* Westport, CT: Greenwood.

Chavajay, P., and Rogoff, B. (1999). Cultural variation in management of attention by children and their caregivers. *Developmental Psychology, 35,* 1079–1090.

Contreras, J. M., López, I. R., Rivera-Mosquera, E. T., Raymond-Smith, L., and Rothstein, K. (1999). Social support and adjustment among Puerto Rican adolescent mothers: The moderating effect of acculturation. *Journal of Family Psychology, 13,* 228–243.

Contreras, J. M., Narang, D., Ikhlas, M., and Teichmann, J. (in press). Parenting among Latino mothers. To appear in J. M. Contreras, K. A. Kerns, and A. M. Neal-Barnett (Eds.), *Latino children and families in the United States.* Westport, CT: Greenwood.

Cooper, A. M. (1990). Fallacy of a single model for school achievement: Considerations for ethnicity. *Sociological Perspectives, 33,* 159–184.

Cortés, D. E. (1995). Variations in familism in two generations of Puerto Ricans. *Hispanic Journal of Behavioral Sciences, 17,* 249–255.

Cortés, D. E., Rogler, L. H., and Malgady, R. G. (1994). Biculturality among Puerto Rican adults in the United States. *American Journal of Community Psychology, 22,* 707–721.

Cote, L. R., and Bornstein, M. H. (2000). Social and didactic parenting behaviors and beliefs among Japanese American and South American–U.S. mothers of infants. *Infancy, 1,* 363–374.

Cousins, J. G., Power, T. G., and Olvera-Ezzell, N. (1993). Mexican-American mothers' socialization strategies: Effects of education, acculturation, and health locus of control. *Journal of Experimental Child Psychology, 55,* 258–276.

Cuéllar, I., Arnold, B., and Maldonado, R. (1995). Acculturation rating scale for Mexican Americans-II: A revision of the original ARSMA scale. *Hispanic Journal of Behavioral Sciences, 17,* 275–304.

Cuéllar, I., Harris, L. C., and Jasso, R. (1980). An acculturation scale for Mexican American normal and clinical populations. *Hispanic Journal of Behavioral Sciences, 2,* 199–217.

De Leon Siantz, M. L., and Smith, M. S. (1994). Parental factors correlated with developmental outcome in the migrant Head Start child. *Early Childhood Research Quarterly, 9,* 481–503.

Delgado, B. M., and Ford, L. (1998). Parental perceptions of child development among low-income Mexican American families. *Journal of Child and Family Studies, 7,* 469–481.

Delgado-Gaitan, C. (1992). School matters in the Mexican-American home: Socializing children to education. *American Educational Research Journal, 29,* 495–513.

Delgado-Gaitan, C. (1993). Parenting in two generations of Mexican American families. *International Journal of Behavioral Development, 16,* 409–427.

De Siantz, M. L. (1990). Maternal acceptance/rejection of Mexican migrant mothers. *Psychology of Women Quarterly*, *14*, 245–254.

DeYoung, Y., and Zigler, E. F. (1994). Machismo in two cultures: Relations to punitive childrearing practices. *American Journal of Orthopsychiatry*, *64*, 386–395.

Dumka, L. E., Gonzales, N. A., Wood, J. L., and Formoso, D. (1998). Using qualitative methods to develop contextually relevant measures and preventive interventions: An illustration. *American Journal of Community Psychology*, *26*, 605–637.

Dumka, L. E., Graza, C. A., Roosa, M. W., and Stoerzinger, H. D. (1997). Recruitment and retention of high-risk families into a preventive parent training intervention. *Journal of Primary Prevention*, *18*, 25.

Dumka, L. E., Lopez, V., and JacobsCarter, S. (in press). Parenting interventions adapted for Latino families: Progress and prospects. To appear in J. M. Contreras, K. A. Kerns, and A. M. Neal-Barnett (Eds.), *Latino children and families in the United States*. Westport, CT: Greenwood.

Eisenberg, A. R. (1999). Emotion talk among Mexican American and Anglo American mothers and children from two social classes. *Merrill-Palmer Quarterly*, *45*, 267–284.

Elder, J. P., Broyles, S. L., McKenzie, T. L., Sallis, J. F., Berry, C. C., Davis, T. B., Hoy, P. L., and Nader, P. R. (1998). Direct home observations of the prompting of physical activity in sedentary and active Mexican- and Anglo-American children. *Developmental and Behavioral Pediatrics*, *19*, 26–30.

Farver, J. M., and Howes, C. (1993). Cultural differences in American and Mexican mother–child pretend play. *Merrill-Palmer Quarterly*, *39*, 344–358.

Fisher, C. B., Jackson, J. F., and Villarruel, F. A. (1998). The study of African American and Latin American children and youth. In W. Damon (Series Ed.), *Handbook of child psychology: Vol. 1. Theoretical models of human development* (5th ed., pp. 1145–1207). New York: Wiley.

Flannagan, D. (1996). Mothers' and kindergarteners' talk about interpersonal relationships. *Merrill-Palmer Quarterly*, *42*, 519–536.

Forehand, R., and Kotchick, B. A. (1996). Cultural diversity: A wake-up call for parent training. *Behavior Therapy*, *27*, 187–206.

Fracasso, M. P., Busch-Rossnagel, N. A., and Fisher, C. B. (1994). The relationship of maternal behavior and acculturation to the quality of attachment in Hispanic infants living in New York City. *Hispanic Journal of Behavioral Sciences*, *16*, 143–154.

Franco, N., and Levitt, M. J. (1998). The social ecology of middle childhood: Family support, friendship quality, and self-esteem. *Family Relations*, *47*, 315–321.

French, L. A. (1993). Adapting projective tests for minority children. *Psychological Reports*, *72*, 15–18.

Fuligni, A. J. (1997). The academic achievement of adolescents from immigrant families: The roles of family background, attitudes, and behavior. *Child Development*, *68*, 351–363.

Fuligni, A. J. (1998). Authority, autonomy, and parent–adolescent conflict and cohestion: A study of adolescents from Mexican, Chinese, Filipino, and European backgrounds. *Developmental Psychology*, *34*, 782–792.

Fuligni, A. J., Tseng, V., and Lam, M. (1999). Attitudes toward family obligations among American adolescents with Asian, Latin American, and European family backgrounds. *Child Development*, *70*, 1030–1044.

Fuller, B., Holloway, S. D., and Liang, X. (1996). Family selection of child-care centers: The influence of household support, ethnicity, and parental practices. *Child Development*, *67*, 3320–3337.

Gaines, S. O., Ríos, D. I., and Buriel, R. (1997). Familism and personal relationship processes among Latina/Latino couples. In S. O. Gaines (Ed.), *Culture, ethnicity and personal relationship processes* (pp. 41–66). New York: Routledge.

Gallimore, R., Goldenberg, C. N., and Weisner, T. S. (1993). The social construction and subjective reality of activity settings: Implications for a community psychology. *American Journal of Community Psychology*, *21*, 537–558.

Gamble, W. C., and Dalla, R. L. (1997). Young children's perceptions of their social worlds in single- and two-parent, Euro- and Mexican-American families. *Journal of Social and Personal Relationships*, *14*, 357–372.

García, C. (1993). What do we mean by extended family? A closer look at Hispanic multigenerational families. *Journal of Cross-Cultural Gerontology*, *8*, 137–146.

García Coll, C. T. (1990). Developmental outcome of minority infants: A process-oriented look into our beginnings. *Child Development*, *61*, 270–289.

García Coll, C., Lamberty, G., Jenkins, R., McAdoo, H. P., Crnic, K., Wasik, B. H., Vázquez García, H. (1996). An integrative model for the study of developmental competencies in minority children. *Child Development*, *67*, 1891–1914.

García Coll, C., Meyer, E. C., and Brillon, L. (1995). Ethnic and minority parenting. In M. H. Bornstein (Ed.), *Handbook of parenting: Vol. 2. Biology and ecology of parenting* (pp. 189–209). Mahwah, NJ: Lawrence Erlbaum Associates.

Garrison, E. G., Roy, I. S., and Azar, V. (1999). Responding to the mental health needs of Latino children and families through school-based services. *Clinical Psychology Review*, *19*, 199–219.

Gil, A. G., and Vega, W. A. (1996). Two different worlds: Acculturation stress and adaptation among Cuban and Nicaraguan families. *Journal of Social and Personal Relationships*, *13*, 435–456.

Gil, A. G., Vega, W. A., and Dimas, J. M. (1994). Acculturative stress and personal adjustment among Hispanic adolescent boys. *Journal of Community Psychology*, *22*, 43–54.

Gonzales, N. A., Knight, G. P., Morgan-Lopez, A., Saenz, D., and Sirolli, A. (in press). Acculturation and the mental health of Latino youths: An integration and critique of the literature. To appear in J. M. Contreras, K. A. Kerns, and A. M. Neal-Barnett (Eds.), *Latino children and families in the United States*. Westport, CT: Greenwood.

Gonzalez-Ramos, G., Zayas, L. H., and Cohen, E. V. (1998). Child-rearing values of low-income, urban Puerto Rican mothers of preschool children. *Professional Psychology: Research and Practice, 29*, 377–382.

Gorman, J. C., and Balter, L. (1997). Culturally sensitive parent education: A critical review of quantitative research. *Review of Educational Research, 67*, 339–369.

Greenfield, P. M. (1994). Independence and interdependence as developmental scripts: Implications for theory, research, and practice. In P. M. Greenfield and R. R. Cocking (Eds.), *Cross-cultural roots of minority development* (pp. 1–37). Hillsdale, NJ: Lawrence Erlbaum Associates.

Guarnaccia, P. J., Parra, P., Deschamps, A., and Milstein, G. (1992). Si Dios quiere: Hispanic families' experiences of caring for a seriously mentally ill family member. *Culture, Medicine, and Psychiatry, 16*, 187–215.

Guarnaccia, P. J., Rivera, M., Franco, F., and Neighbors, C. (1996). The experiences of ataques de nervios: Towards an anthropology of emotions in Puerto Rico. *Culture, Medicine, and Psychiatry, 20*, 343–367.

Gutierrez, J., and Sameroff, A. (1990). Determinants of complexity in Mexican-American and Anglo-American mothers' conceptions of child development. *Child Development, 61*, 384–394.

Gutmann, M. C. (1994). The meaning of macho: Changing Mexican identities. *Masculinities, 2*, 21–33.

Harrison, A. O., Wilson, M. N., Pine, C. J., Chan, S. Q., and Buriel, R. (1990). Family ecologies of minority children. *Child Development, 61*, 347–362.

Harry, B. (1992). An ethnographic study of cross-cultural communication with Puerto Rican-American families in the special education system. *American Educational Research Journal, 29*, 471–494.

Harry, B., Rueda, R., and Kalyanpur, M. (1999). Cultural reciprocity in sociocultural perspective: Adapting the normalization principle for family collaboration. *Exceptional Children, 66*, 123–136.

Harwood, R. L. (1992). The influence of culturally derived values on Anglo and Puerto Rican mothers' perceptions of attachment behavior. *Child Development, 63*, 822–839.

Harwood, R. L., Handwerker, W. P., Schölmerich, A., and Leyendecker, B. (in press). Ethnic category labels and the contextualized individual: An exploration of the individualism/sociocentrism debate. To appear in *Parenting: Science and Practice*.

Harwood, R. L., and Miller, J. G. (1991). Perceptions of attachment behavior: A comparison of Anglo and Puerto Rican mothers. *Merrill-Palmer Quarterly, 37*, 583–599.

Harwood, R. L., Miller, A. M., Carlson, V. J., and Leyendecker, B. (in press). Parenting beliefs and practices among middle-class Puerto Rican mother-infant pairs. To appear in J. M. Contreras, K. A. Kerns, and A. M. Neal-Barnett (Eds.), *Latino children and families in the United States*. Westport, CT: Greenwood.

Harwood, R. L., Miller, J. G., and Lucca Irizarry, N. (1995). *Culture and attachment: Perceptions of the child in context*. New York: Guilford.

Harwood, R. L., Schölmerich, A., and Schulze, P. A. (2000). Homogeneity and heterogeneity in cultural belief systems. In S. Harkness, C. Raeff, and C. M. Super (Eds.), *Variability in the social construction of the child, New directions for child Development, no. 87* (pp. 41–57). San Francisco: Jossey-Bass.

Harwood, R. L., Schölmerich, A., Schulze, P. A., and Gonzalez, Z. (1999). Cultural differences in maternal beliefs and behaviors: A study of middle-class Anglo and Puerto Rican mother–infant pairs in four everyday situations. *Child Development, 70*, 1005–1016.

Harwood, R. L., Schölmerich, A., Ventura-Cook, E., Schulze, P. A., and Wilson, S. P. (1996). Culture and class influences on Anglo and Puerto Rican mothers' beliefs regarding long-term socialization goals and child behavior. *Child Development, 67*, 2446–2461.

Henning-Stout, M. (1996). Qué podemos hacer?: Roles for school psychologists with Mexican and Latino migrant children and families. *School Psychology Review, 25*, 152–164.

Hernandez, A., Vargas-Lew, L., and Martinez, C. L. (1994). Intergenerational academic aspirations of Mexican-American females: An examination of mother, daughter, and grandmother triads. *Hispanic Journal of Behavioral Sciences, 16*, 195–204.

Hernandez, D. J. (1997). Child development and the social demography of childhood. *Child Development, 68*, 149–169.

Inclan, J. (1990). Understanding Hispanic families: A curriculum outline. *Journal of Strategic and Systematic Therapies, 9*, 64–72.

Ingoldsby, B. B. (1991). The Latin American family: Familism vs. Machismo. *Journal of Comparative Family Studies, 22*, 57–62.

Johnson, D. L., and Walker, T. (1991). A follow-up evaluation of the Houston parent–child development center: School performance. *Journal of Early Intervention, 15*, 226–236.

Kagitçibasi, C. (1997). Individualism and collectivism. In J. W. Berry, M. H. Segall, and C. Kagitçibasi (Eds.), *Handbook of cross-cultural psychology: Vol. 3. Social behavior and applications* (2nd ed., pp. 1–49). Boston: Allyn and Bacon.

Kalyanpur, M., and Harry, B. (1997). A posture of reciprocity: A practical approach to collaboration between professionals and parents of culturally diverse backgrounds. *Journal of Child and Family Studies, 6*, 485–509.

Kermani, H., and Janes, H. A. (1999). Adjustment across task in maternal scaffolding in low-income Latino immigrant families. *Hispanic Journal of Behavioral Sciences, 21*, 134–153.

Kessen, W. (1979). The American child and other cultural inventions. *American Psychologist, 34*, 815–820.

Killen, M., and Wainryb, C. (2000). Independence and interdependence in diverse cultural contexts. In S. Harkness, C. Raeff, and C. M. Super (Eds.), *Variability in the social construction of the child* (pp. 5–20). San Francisco: Jossey-Bass.

Kiselica, M. S. (1991). Reflections on a multicultural internship experience. *Journal of Counseling and Development, 70*, 126–130.

Knight, G. P., Bernal, M. E., Garza, C. A., Cota, M. K., and Ocampo, K. A. (1993). Family socialization and the ethnic identity of Mexican-American children. *Journal of Cross-Cultural Psychology, 24*, 99–114.

Knight, G. P., Cota, M. K., and Bernal, M. E. (1993). The socialization of cooperative, competitive, and individualistic preferences among Mexican American children: The mediating role of ethnic identity. *Hispanic Journal of Behavioral Sciences, 15*, 291–309.

Knight, G. P., Dubro, A. F., and Chao, C. (1985). Information processing and the development of cooperative, competitive, and individualistic social values. *Developmental Psychology, 21*, 37–45.

Knight, G. P., and Kagan, S. (1977). Development of prosocial and competitive behaviors among Anglo American and Mexican American children. *Child Development, 48*, 1385–1394.

Knight, G. P., Tein, J.-Y., Prost, J., and Gonzales, N. (in press). Measurement equivalence and research on Latino children and families: The importance of culturally informed theory. To appear in J. M. Contreras, K. A. Kerns, and A. M. Neal-Barnett (Eds.), *Latino children and families in the United States*. Westport, CT: Greenwood.

Knight, G. P., Tein, J. Y., Shell, R., and Roosa, M. (1992). The cross-ethnic equivalence of parenting and family interaction measures among Hispanic and Anglo-American families. *Child Development, 63*, 1392–1403.

Knight, G. P., Virdin, L. M., and Roosa, M. (1994). Socialization and family correlates of mental health outcomes among Hispanic and Anglo American children: Consideration of cross-ethnic scalar equivalence. *Child Development, 65*, 212–224.

Kohn, M. L. (1977). *Class and conformity: A study in values*. Chicago: University of Chicago Press.

Kontos, S., Howes, C., Shinn, M., and Galinsky, E. (1997). Children's experiences in family child care and relative care as a function of family income and ethnicity. *Merrill-Palmer Quarterly, 43*, 386–403.

Lamborn, S. D., Dornbusch, S. M., and Steinberg, L. (1996). Ethnicity and community context as moderators of the relations between family decision making and adolescent adjustment. *Child Development, 67*, 283–301.

Lees, N. B., and Tinsley, B. J. (1998). Patterns of parental socialization of the preventive health behavior of young Mexican origin children. *Journal of Applied Developmental Psychology, 19*, 503–525.

Levitt, M. J., Guacci-Franco, N., and Levitt, J. L. (1993). Convoys of social support in childhood and early adolescence: Structure and function. *Developmental Psychology, 29*, 811–818.

Levitt, M. J., Guacci-Franco, N., and Levitt, J. L. (1994). Social support and achievement in childhood and early adolescence: A multicultural study. *Journal of Applied Developmental Psychology, 15*, 207–222.

Lewis, O. (1965). *La vida*. New York: Vintage.

Leyendecker, B., Harwood, R. L., Lamb, M. E., and Schölmerich, A. (in press). *Mothers' socialization goals and evaluations of desirable and undesirable everyday situations in two diverse cultural niches*. To appear in International Journal of Behavioral Development.

Leyendecker, B., Lamb, M. E., Fracasso, M. P., Schölmerich, A., and Larson, C. (1997). Playful interaction and the antecedents of attachment: A longitudinal study of Central American and Euro-American mothers and infants. *Merrill-Palmer Quarterly, 43*, 24–47.

Leyendecker, B., Lamb, M. E., Schölmerich, A., and Fracasso, M. P. (1995). The social worlds of 8- and 12- month-old infants: Early experiences in two subcultural contexts. *Social Development, 4*, 194–208.

López, L. C., Rodríguez, R. F., and Sánchez, V. V. (1995). The relationship between parental education and school involvement of Mexican-American parents. *Psychological Reports, 77*, 1203–1207.

Lucca Irizarry, N., and Pacheco, A. M. Intercultural encounters of Puerto Rican migrants. *Environment and Behavior, 24*, 226–238.

MacPhee, D., Fritz, J., and Miller-Heyl, J. (1996). Ethnic variations in personal social networks and parenting. *Child Development, 67*, 3278–3295.

Malgady, R., Rogler, L., and Constantino, G. (1990). Culturally sensitive psychotherapy for Puerto Rican children and adolescents: A program of treatment outcome research. *Journal of Consulting and Clinical Psychology, 58*, 704–712.

Markus, H. R., and Kitayama, S. (1991). Culture and the self: Implications for cognition, emotion, and motivation. *Psychological Review, 98*, 224–253.

Martinez, K. J. (1994). Cultural sensitivity in family therapy gone awry. *Hispanic Journal of Behavioral Sciences, 16*, 75–89.

McCarthey, S. J. (1997). Making the invisible more visible: Home literacy practices of middle-class and working-class families. *Early Child Development and Care, 127–128*, 179–189.

Miller, A. M., and Harwood, R. L. (2001). Long-term socialization goals and the construction of infants' social networks among middle-class Anglo and Puerto Rican mothers. *International Journal of Behavioral Development, 25*, 450–457.

Miller-Loncar, C. L., Erwin, L. J., Landry, S. H., Smith, K. E., and Swank, P. R. (1998). Characteristics of social support networks of low socioeconomic status African American, Anglo American, and Mexican American mothers of full-term and preterm infants. *Journal of Community Psychology, 26*, 131–143.

Morrison, G. M., Laughlin, J., San Miguel, S., Smith, D. C., and Widaman, K. (1997). Sources of support for school-related issues: Choices of Hispanic adolescents varying in migrant status. *Journal of Youth and Adolescence, 26*, 233–252.

Morrow, L. M., and Young, J. (1997). A family literacy program connecting school and home: Effects on attitude, motivation, and literacy achievement. *Journal of Educational Psychology, 89*, 736–742.

Niska, K. J., Lia-Hoagberg, B., and Snyder, M. (1997). Parental concerns of Mexican American first-time mothers and fathers. *Public Health Nursing, 14*, 111–117.

Ocampo, K. A., Knight, G. P., and Bernal, M. E. (1997). The development of cognitive abilities and social identities in children: The case of ethnic identity. *International Journal of Behavioral Development, 21*, 479–500.

Ogbu, J. U. (1991). Minority coping responses and school experience. *The Journal of Psychohistory, 18*, 433–456.

Okagaki, L., and Frensch, P. (1998). Parenting and children's school achievement: A multiethnic perspective. *American Educational Research Journal, 35*, 123–144.

Okagaki, L., Frensch, P. A., and Dodson, N. E. (1996). Mexican American children's perceptions of self and school achievement. *Hispanic Journal of Behavioral Sciences, 18*, 469–484.

Okagaki, L., Frensch, P. A., and Gordon, E. W. (1995). Encouraging school achievement in Mexican american children. *Hispanic Journal of Behavioral Sciences, 17*, 160–179.

Okagaki, L., and Sternberg, R. J. (1993). Parental beliefs and children's school performance. *Child Development, 64*, 36–56.

Pachter, L. M., and Dworkin, P. H. (1997). Maternal expectations about normal child development in four cultural groups. *Archives of Pediatrics and Adolescent Medicine, 151*, 1144–1150.

Padilla, A. M. (1994). Bicultural development: A theoretical and empirical examination. In R. G. Malgady and O. Rodriguez (Eds.), *Theoretical and conceptual issues in Hispanic mental health* (pp. 19–51). Malabar, FL: Krieger.

Pérez Granados, D. R., and Callanan, M. A. (1997). Parents and siblings as early resources for young children's learning in Mexican-descent families. *Hispanic Journal of Behavior Sciences, 19*, 3–33.

Phinney, J. S. (1990). Ethnic identity in adolescents and adults: Review of research. *Psychological Bulletin, 108*, 499–514.

Phinney, J. S. (1996). When we talk about American ethnic groups, what do we mean? *American Psychologist, 51*, 918–927.

Phinney, J. S., and Chavira, V. (1995). Parental ethnic socialization and adolescent coping with problems related to ethnicity. *Journal of Research on Adolescence, 5*, 31–53.

Phinney, J. S., Ong, A., and Madden, T. (2000). Cultural values and intergenerational value discrepancies in immigrant and non-immigrant families. *Child Development, 71*, 528–539.

Planos, R., Zayas, L. H., and Busch-Rossnagel, N. A. (1995). Acculturation and teaching behaviors of Dominican and Puerto Rican mothers. *Hispanic Journal of Behavioral Sciences, 17*, 225–236.

Portes, A., and Rumbaut, R. G. (1990). *Immigrant America: A portrait*. Berkeley: University of California Press.

Procidano, M., and Rogler, L. H. (1989). Homogamous assortative mating among Puerto Rican families: Intergenerational processes and the migration experience. *Behavior Genetics, 19*, 343–354.

Quintana, S. M., Castañeda-English, P., and Ybarra, V. C. (1999). Role of perspective-taking abilities and ethnic socialization in development of adolescent ethnic identity. *Journal of Research on Adolescence, 9*, 161–184.

Quintana, S. M., and Vera, E. M. (1999). Mexican American children's ethnic identity, understanding of ethnic prejudice, and parental ethnic socialization. *Hispanic Journal of Behavioral Sciences, 21*, 387–404.

Quintero, E. (1999). The new faces of Head Start: Learning from culturally diverse families. *Early Education and Development, 10*, 475–497.

Rehm, R. S. (1999). Religious faith in Mexican-American families dealing with chronic childhood illness. *Journal of Nursing Scholarship, 31*, 33–38.

Reynolds, A. J. (1989). A structural model of first-grade outcomes for an urban, low socioeconomic status, minority population. *Journal of Educational Psychology, 81*, 594–603.

Reynolds, R. J., Mavorgenes, N. A., Bezruczko, N., and Hagemann, M. (1996). Cognitive and family-support mediators of preschool effectiveness: A confirmatory analysis. *Child Development, 67*, 1119–1140.

Richman, A. L., Miller, P. M., and LeVine, R. (1992). Cultural and educational variations in maternal responsiveness. *Developmental Psychology, 28*, 614–621.

Rogler, L. H. (1994). International migrations: A framework for directing research. *American Psychologist, 49*, 701–708.

Rogler, L. H., Cortés, D. E., and Malgady, R. G. (1991). Acculturation and mental health status among Hispanics. *American Psychologist, 46*, 585–597.

Rogler, L. H., and Santana Cooney, R. (1984). *Puerto Rican families in New York City: Intergenerational processes*. Maplewood, NJ: Waterfront.

Rogoff, B., Mistry, J., Göncü, A., and Mosier, C. (1993). *Guided participation in cultural activity by toddlers and caregivers. Monographs of the Society for Research in Child Development, 58* (Serial No. 236).

Roopnarine, J. L., and Ahmeduzzaman, M. (1993). Puerto Rican fathers' involvement with their preschool-age children. *Hispanic Journal of Behavioral Sciences, 15*, 96–107.

Roosa, M. W., Morgan-Lopez, A., Cree, W., and Specter, M. (in press, 2000). *Ethnic culture, poverty, and context: Sources of influence on Latino families and children.* To appear in J. M. Contreras, K. A. Kerns, and A. M. Neal-Barnett (Eds.), *Latino children and families in the United States.* Westport, CT: Greenwood.

Roth, J., and Brooks-Gunn, J. (2000). What do adolescents need for healthy development? Implications for youth policy. *Social Policy Report, 14,* 3–19.

Rueschenberg, E., and Buriel, R. (1989). Mexican American family functioning and acculturation: A family systems perspective. *Hispanic Journal of Behavioral Sciences, 11,* 232–244.

Ruggiero, K. M., Taylor, D. M., and Lambert, W. E. (1996). A model of heritage culture maintenance: The role of discrimination. *International Journal of Intercultural Relations, 20,* 47–67.

Rumbaut, R. G. (1997). Paradoxes (and orthodoxies) of assimilation. *Sociological Perspectives, 40,* 483–511.

Sánchez, V. V., and López, L. C. (1999). Parents' involvement with schools in a Mexican border town. *Psychological Reports, 84,* 1031–1033.

Savage, S. L., and Gauvain, M. (1998). Parental beliefs and children's everyday planning in European American and Latino families. *Journal of Applied Developmental Psychology, 19,* 319–340.

Schaffer, D. M., and Wagner, R. M. (1996). Mexican American and Anglo single mothers: The influence of ethnicity, generation, and socioeconomic status on social support networks. *Hispanic Journal of Behavioral Sciences, 17,* 74–86.

Schulze, P. A., Harwood, R. L., and Schölmerich, A. (2001). *Feeding practices and expectations among middle-class Anglo and Puerto Rican mothers of 12-month-old infants. Journal of Cross-Cultural Psychology, 32,* 397–406.

Schulze, P. A., Harwood, R. L., Schölmerich, A., and Leyendecker, B. (2001). *The cultural structuring of universal developmental tasks.* Manuscript under review.

Sherraden, M. S., and Barrera, R. E. (1996, May). Maternal support and cultural influences among Mexican immigrant mothers. *Families in Society: The Journal of Contemporary Human Services,* 298–313.

Shweder, R. A. (1996). True ethnography: The lore, the law, and the lure. In R. Jessor, A. Colby, and R. A. Shweder (Eds.), *Ethnography and human development: Context and meaning in social inquiry.* Chicago: University of Chicago Press.

Skinner, D., Bailey, D. B., Correa, V., and Rodriquez, P. (1999). Narrating self and disability: Latino mothers' construction of identities vis-à-vis their child with special needs. *Exceptional Children, 65,* 481–495.

Skinner, D., Rodriguez, P., and Bailey, D. B. (1999). Qualitative analysis of Latino parents' religious interpretations of their child's disability. *Journal of Early Intervention, 22,* 271–285.

Spencer, M. B., and Markstrom-Adams, C. (1990). Identity processes among racial and ethnic minority children in America. *Child Development, 61,* 290–310.

Steinberg, L., Dornbusch, S. M., and Brown, B. B. (1992). Ethnic differences in adolescent achievement: An ecological perspective. *American Psychologist, 47,* 723–729.

Stevenson, H. W., Chen, C., and Uttal, D. H. (1990). Beliefs and achievement: A study of black, white, and Hispanic children. *Child Development, 61,* 508–523.

Strauss, C., and Quinn, N. (1997). *A cognitive theory of cultural meaning.* New York: Cambridge University Press.

Strickland, B. R. (2000). Misassumptions, misadventures, and the misuse of psychology. *American Psychologist, 55,* 331–338.

Suárez-Orozco, C., and Suárez-Orozco, M. (1994). The cultural psychology of Hispanic immigrants. In T. Weaver (Vol. Ed.), *Handbook of Hispanic cultures in the United States: Anthropology.* Houston, TX: Arte Público.

Suárez-Orozco, C., and Suárez-Orozco, M. (1995). *Transformations: Migration, family life, and achievement motivation among Latino adolescents.* Stanford, CA: Stanford University Press.

Sugland, B. W., Zaslow, M., Smith, J. R., Brooks-Gunn, J., Coates, D., Blumenthal, C., Moore, K. A., Griffin, T., and Bradley, R. (1995). The early childhood HOME Inventory and HOME-Short Form in differing racial/ethnic groups. *Journal of Family Issues, 16,* 632–663.

Szapocznik, J., Kurtines, W. M., and Fernandez, T. (1980). Bicultural involvement and adjustment in Hispanic-American youths. *International Journal of Intercultural Relations, 4,* 353–365.

Tenenbaum, H. R., and Leaper, C. (1997). Mothers' and fathers' questions to their child in Mexican-descent families: Moderators of cognitive demand during play. *Hispanic Journal of Behavioral Sciences, 19,* 318–322.

Thiel de Bocanegra, H. (1998). Breast-feeding in immigrant women: The role of social support and acculturation. *Hispanic Journal of Behavioral Sciences, 20,* 448–467.

Thomas, T. N. (1992). Psychoeducational adjustment of English-speaking Caribbean and Central American immigrant children in the United States. *School Psychology Review, 21,* 566–576.

Triandis, H. C. (1995). *Individualism and collectivism.* Boulder, CO: Westview.

Tropp, L. R., Erkut, S., Alarcón, O., García Coll, C., and Vázquez, H. (1994). *Toward a theoretical model of psychological acculturation* (Working Papers Series No. 268). Wellesley, MA: Wellesley College, Center for Research on Women.

Uno, D., Florsheim, P., and Uchino, B. N. (1998). Psychosocial mechanisms underlying quality of parenting among Mexican-American and white adolescent mothers. *Journal of Youth and Adolescence, 27,* 585–605.

U.S. Census Bureau. (1992). *General population characteristics: United States* (Current Population Reports, CP-1-1). Washington, DC: U.S. Department of Commerce.

U.S. Census Bureau. (1993). *Hispanic Americans today* (Current Population Reports, P23–183). Washington, DC: Government Printing Office.

U.S. Census Bureau. (1998). (Current Population Reports, P20-513). Washington, DC: U.S. Department of Commerce.

U.S. Census Bureau. (1999). *Current population survey, Ethnic and Hispanic statistics branch, Population Division* [online]. Available: http://www.census.gov/population/socdemo/ hispanic/cps99/tab05-2.txt

U.S. Census Bureau. (2001). Overview of race and hispanic origin: Census 2000 brief [online CENBR/01-1]. Available: http://www.census.gov/population/www/cen2000/briefs.html

Valdés, G. (1997). Dual-language immersion programs: A cautionary note concerning the education of language-minority students. *Harvard Educational Review, 67,* 391–429.

Vega, W. (1990). Hispanic families in the 1980s: A decade of research. *Journal of Marriage and the family, 52,* 1015–1024.

Way, N., and Leadbeater, B. J. (1999). Pathways toward educational achievement among African American and Puerto Rican adolescent mothers: Reexamining the role of social support from families. *Development and Psychopathology, 11,* 349–364.

Wolf, E. R. (1982). *Europe and the people without history.* Berkeley: University of California Press.

Wolf, E. R. (1994). Perilous ideas: Race, culture, people. *Current Anthropology, 35,* 1–11.

Zaitchik, M. C., and Mosher, D. L. (1993). Criminal justice implications of the macho personality. *Criminal Justice and Behavior, 20,* 227–239.

Zambrana, R. E., Silva-Palacios, V., and Powell, D. (1992). Parenting concerns, family support systems, and life problems in Mexican-origin women: A comparison by nativity. *Journal of Community Psychology, 20,* 276–288.

Zayas, L. H. (1994). Hispanic family ecology and early childhood socialization: Health care implications. *Family Systems Medicine, 12,* 315–325.

Zayas, L. H., Evans, M. E. E., Mejia, L., and Rodriguez, O. (1997). Cultural-competency training for staff serving Hispanic families with a child in psychiatric crisis. *Journal of Contemporary Human Services, 78,* 405–412.

Zayas, L. H., and Rojas Flores, L. (in press). Learning from Latino parents: Combining etic and emic approaches to designing interventions. To appear in J. M. Contreras, K. A. Kerns, and A. M. Neal-Barnett (Eds.), *Latino children and families in the United States.* Westport, CT: Greenwood.

Zayas, L. H., and Solari, F. (1994). Early childhood socialization in Hispanic families: Context, culture, and practice implications. *Professional Psychology, 25,* 200–206.

Zegarra, G. (1998). Educando á la familia Latina: Ideas for making parent education programs accessible to the Latino community. *Family and Conciliation Courts Review, 36,* 281–293.

3

African American Parenting

Harriette P. McAdoo
Michigan State University

INTRODUCTION

Parenting is a source of comfort for us and at the same time a source of frustration for many of us. All of us expect that parenting will come naturally and we are not prepared for the tasks that are ahead. We basically respond to children as we were responded to by our own parents. This may be good and also not as good as we desire. It is important to be aware of many of the pitfalls that parents face as they attempt to rear children to be functioning adults.

Parents of color face many of the same developmental tasks that all parents face. They, however, must surmount additional tasks to ensure that their children will survive and grow up to be functioning adults, secure within their own group and able to work with those of other groups. Parents of color have more difficult times facing the many tasks that they have as parents. They are all but ignored by the popular press, except in negative manners, and their special issues are often not addressed.

African American families and children can be fully understood only in relation to the interaction of their race, social class, culture, and ethnicity (Garcìa Coll et al., 1996). African American parenting will be examined in the context of these variables. The interactions of these factors have resulted in a wide array of types and diversity of life experiences. The variety of family settings, family interaction patterns, and socioeconomic environments has resulted in diverse family arrangements. The families have evolved into many segments that do not fit the monolithic view of African American families that is too often presented in the lay and research literature.

There is a need to understand the economic situations, cultural patterns, and socialization practices of African American families. Significant changes have occurred in the lives of African Americans. Major policy changes at the federal and local levels have truncated government programs that have contributed to the vulnerability of these families. Some African Americans have benefitted from earlier government programs and have been upwardly mobile. Many others have fallen deeper into despair.

HISTORICAL CONSIDERATIONS IN AFRICAN AMERICAN PARENTING

There are many issues that lie within the historical consideration of parenting by African Americans. All of these issues lie within the context of experiences with discrimination that had the vestiges of enslavement. These two elements have had an impact on the resources that are available to these parents, the high level of single parenting, and the approaches that are used to enable African American children to cope with Euro-oriented media and schools.

The continuation of racism in the everyday life of African Americans has lead to continued economic and geographic isolation. These have been built on a historical context that is unrelenting. The isolation has lead to one of the most crucial elements that affect African Americans, their lessened economic status, and the lack of resources that are available. This also leads to the growing number of babies being born to women outside of marriage.

Unrelenting Racism and Discrimination

Unfortunately, the one fact of life that parents of color have to face is that their children will have to contend with devaluation of their own worth and their future potentials in school and in their careers. At one point it was expected that racism would lessen. But experience has shown that full integration of schools and neighborhoods has not occurred. There may be legal access available, but there are serious, deep reservoirs of devaluation of anything that is African based. There are more sophisticated ways now of handling exclusion or isolation of African Americans. Even when parents who are highly educated, have sufficient resources from professional positions, and middle-class orientations, they encounter subtle discrimination throughout their lives.

This context of parenting is difficult and calls upon a full range of actions and messages from parents. They must first protect their child from racism from outside the groups and also from within their ethnic group. But parents cannot overprotect children, for children must be prepared to cope with racism their entire lives. They will have to develop the Du Bois (1899) "double conscious" in which the child must view the world through African American eyes and also view the world through European American eyes. The ability to "code switch" in situations enables children to understand that certain behaviors are acceptable only in specific situations. This skill at being bicultural is essential. Only when they are able to do this, and to make necessary adjustments with wariness and caution, will children be able to effectively function in the complexities of the multicultural world.

Even if one were to find a way of waving a magic wand and eliminating racism, there would still exist gaps in African America families. Some form of "catch up" would have to be made. Affirmative action plans, with all of their difficulties, were one attempt to level the playing field. There was much progress made, but it has about come to a standstill because of concern of European Americans that African Americans were being given priorities.

It has been established that the group that has benefitted the most from affirmative action hiring policies has been European American women (Guy-Sheftall, 1993; Ladson-Billings, 2000). There is also the argument that because of the differences in family structures—more European American families have two-parent families—these women who earn incomes also support households in which other European Americans live. Therefore, more than women benefit from these policies, but men, women, and children all benefit from these civil rights policies. The attitudes toward African Americans have remained rather negative, and the opportunities have not been as open for African Americans as they have been for other groups in North America, such as Asian American or even Hispanics.

Legacies of Enslavement

The historical past of many African American families is substantially different from all of the other immigrant groups that have come to the United States. These groups were escaping oppression or were seeking new freedoms and economic possibilities. In contrast, Africans were brought against their wills. They built the foundations of many American cities and vast pools of family wealth exist today because of the centuries of free African labor.

The enslavement experience within the Americas brought loss of control, violent uprootings, and great suffering. Brutal experiences shaped the ideological forces that lead to modern day families, with their strengths and weaknesses (Wilkinson, 1997). Billingsley (1968) has observed that the legacy of enslavement and the caste-like system of segregation left many African Americans in an inferior status, both psychological and in the reality of their existence.

To cope with enslavement and its aftermath, family members have felt the importance of maintaining communal family traditions, that result in more matriarchal family systems (Prince, 1997). Many of the strengths that have facilitated families to cope with adversities are still in action today (Dodson, 1997; Sudarkasa, 1993, 1997). Among the cultural legacies that are African derived and have been transmitted and altered in the United States have been the communal traditions of shared childcare, spirituality, and oral traditions (Boykin, 1986; Jones, 1991). The importance of coresidential extended families and their support systems has been cited as one of the major survival systems of African American families (Billingsley, 1968; Hatchett, Cochran, and Jackson, 1991; Hill, 1997; McAdoo, 1992). There are many family similarities for many of those who are in the African Diaspora: Brazilian, Caribbean, and American families (Herskovitz, 1941).

CENTRAL ISSUES OF AFRICAN AMERICAN PARENTING

The central issues that face African American parents are: (1) the lack of adequate financial resources, (2) the roles of education, (3) the high proportion of single parents, (4) grandparents as primary parent, and (5) the task of racially socializing their children. These are issues and tasks that are held in addition to all of the many tasks that all parents must perform. These issues require special effort and approaches that most other parents do not have to handle.

Family Finances and Resources

African Americans at the present time are no longer essential to the economic survival of the Unites States as they were during enslavement. Nor are they as essential as they were during the period of industrial growth or during the two world wars in terms of cheap skilled labor. As the nation has moved into a global economy, with greater emphasis on technology and offshore production, there is less need for large numbers of low-skilled and less-educated people in the workforce (McAdoo, 1997) here on shore, while much cheaper labor can be found.

Most important is the growing disparity of African American and European American incomes that are the result of economic restructuring, discrimination, and impoverishment (Hatchett, 1991; McAdoo, 1997). Many economic gains were made during the 1970s, immediately after the civil rights movement. But during the 1980s, progress slowed for many African American households.

The worth of American families refers to what you own minus what you owe. The University of Michigan Panel Survey of Income Dynamics, which tracts 7,056 families every five years, has established that the net worth of the average African American household shrank from 1984 to 1999. The overall European American experienced a boom and households grew 9%, from $63,400 to $83,700. The average African American household net worth shrank by 17%, from $4,000 to $7,000 (Despeignes, 2000).

In the 1990s, these households began experiencing increases that were greater than that of the general population (Wellner, 2000). The percentage of African Americans with middle incomes has increased over the past three decades. In 1998, 41% of African American householders had middle incomes of $25,000 to $75,000. At the same time European American declined by 7%, and Hispanics also declined.

An extra bonus has been the economic boom of the 1990s, for the southern region of the country had the greatest boom, where for the first time in decades, more African Americans moved south than north. A recovery has also started in the Rust Belt region, where African Americans were disproportionately hit when many of the manufacturers left the country. Positive education trends have helped the transition of middle-income and stable working class (Wellner, 2000).

Welfare reform is suspected to have played a part. The changes in welfare rules phased out approximately 14 million Americans on public assistance. About 36% of these were African American, and welfare caseloads have fallen to around 6 million (Despeignes, 2000). Being off of welfare is no guarantee of equal treatment. For example, a 1999 study of home purchases and refinance activity showed that African Americans were twice as likely to be rejected for conventional mortgages. Although the number of mortgage applications by European American (51.6%) and African Americans (49.7%) rose by roughly the same rate from 1995 to 1998, the number of loans to African Americans grew by 22%, whereas loans to European Americans increased 48% (Lach, 1999).

The resources that parents depend on more than their salaries and net worths, is on their wealth. In 1999, for every wealth dollar that the average European American householder held, the average African American householder held barely nine cents. African American's had lower house values and few stock holdings (Wellner, 2000). For this reason, in spite of the increase of some people, many African American families have not been able to accumulate the wealth of middle–socioeconomic status (SES) groups. The major wealth of European American families comes from intergenerational transfers in the form of inheritance and gifts. Each generation of African American middle-SES families must create the climb the economic ladder again, whereas European American families start at a higher level (McAdoo, 1998). This has a profound impact on the parenting by African American adults (Despeignes, 2000). There are few resources within the family to help younger couples with childhood expenses, new houses, or college expenses. There is no cushion available within the family.

Roles of Education

For generations of African Americans, education has held a special position, for it held the key to freedom and opportunity for boys and girls (Hines, 1996). Schools have been segregated, and, even if now legally integrated because of the civil rights conflicts, they are probably as racially isolated as before because of European American flight to supposedly safer suburbs. Yet these "safe" suburbs are the places where many school shootings have occurred. Quality education has been kept from African Americans for many years, under a segregated system, and then under a separate-but-equal period. Even now schools in the inner city are inferior to those in suburban areas. Only now the blame is placed on the negligence of parents, rather than upon the systematic forms of inferiority of the quality of education. School systems have worked around the legal rights of persons into a continuation of more of the same, which has resulted in a two-tier educational system, one that is good and one that is inferior.

Children bring to school in the early years a chain of experiences, both positive and negative, that undoubtably lead to positive outcomes in adulthood (Luster and McAdoo, 1996; Werner and Smith, 1992). Parent's socialization practices toward educational attainment influence what children bring to school. Parenting practices influence how well their children acquire school-related skills and other behaviors that are likely to affect achievement and attainment. Parents who place a high value on education tend to have children with higher attainment in school and in their later careers (Eastman, 1988; Seginer, 1983). But the parents' actions while at home are more important than the amount of time that children spend in school (Luster and McAdoo, 1996). Low-income African American children who attended a preschool, as adults were found to have higher achievement and fewer pregnancies (Schweinhart and Weikart, 1980). Many African Americans want their children to reach higher educational and occupational status than they themselves attained. The parenting approaches and higher expectations are essential, especially in the long run.

Single Parenting

Two thirds of African American babies are born to unmarried mothers (DeParle, 1994). Bumpass (1993) has suggested that African American children have only a one-in-five chance of growing up with two parents until the age of 16. African American children are finding that there are not the resources available for them, as they would if they were from homes with two married parents.

Unlike the typical stereotype of African American women, the majority of these births were not to adolescent mothers (Weinraub, Horvath, and Gringlas, in Vol. 3 of this *Handbook*). The Children's Defense Fund data indicate that the majority of babies born to unmarried African American women are born to women who are over 20 years of age (Edelman, 1997; McAdoo, 1995). These are women who have been previously married and have since divorced or who have never been married. But it is accurate that the birth of babies to unmarried teenage mothers is very problematic, with long-term consequences, and laden with predicted financial, educational, and social challenges. This number now includes a few women of middle-SES status who have been unable to find a husband and have decided that they are in a position of rearing a child without husbands. Although one third of unmarried males have continued interactions, of some form, with the child (McAdoo, 1995).

The Center on Budget and Policy Priorities (1999) found that the poorest 20% of female-headed households with children fell from 1994 to 1977. Poverty is present for 65% of single mother–child units, but only 18% of married couples (Ingrassia, 1993). Yet having children without the benefit of marriage occurs across all economic levels. Those African American women who are poor have more children without benefit of wedlock, 65%, double the number of European Americans. Among well-to-do African American women, with incomes of $75,000 and up, 22% have children out of wedlock (Ingrassia, 1993). This is almost 10 times the European American rate.

The sex ratio imbalance or lack of sufficient eligible males is overlooked by those who are in positions of formulating national policies and social service programs. There are many more women than men who are available and eligible to marry and rear children. Even if all men married who were available, there would still be many women who would be left without mates. So the problem of African American children growing up without fathers cannot be solved only by getting men married off.

In fact, Darity and Meyers (1991) have stated there are four key different sex ratios within African American communities: (1) the ratio of unmarried males to unmarried females, (2) the ratio of men to women who are of marriageable age, (3) the ratio of employed males to females, and (4) the ratio of unmarried males who are in the labor market, or in schools, to the unmarried females. It goes without saying that there are more women who need husbands than there are men available, thus marginalizing the male.

The marginalization of African American males contributes to the stresses that lead to the high level of divorce in these families. The level of divorce is much higher than in families not of color (Hetherington and Stanley-Hagan, in Vol. 3 of this *Handbook*). There should be an awareness of the situations of women and their children. The parenting roles that African American women have played, in Africa, during enslavement, and now into contemporary times, shows a continuation of the dependence on the extended consanguial relationships of the mothers, not the conjugal relationship found within European and European American families (Tucker and Mitchell-Kernan, 1997). This points to a major difference between African American families and mainstream American families.

The roles of males in adolescent childbearing is often ignored. Adolescents, however, are at a higher risk because of inconsistent use of contraceptives (Elster and Lamb, 1986). However, it tends not to be an adolescent issue, for the majority of the fathers of children born to adolescents are in fact older than 20 years of age (Edelman, 1997; Scott-Jones, 1993). Yet African American males are, more often than European American males, under the criminal justice system. Almost 10% of men between the ages of 25 and 29 are incarcerated (Tucker, 2000). The early years of early adulthood ought to represent the passage into responsibility, careers, and starting families. The criminal justice system has been shown to incarcerate disproportionately all over the country. This does not lend to responsible behavior in other aspects of their lives, including parenting.

The number of African American children who are born out of wedlock are the result of many factors: the heavy economic and psychological isolation of the African American male, but it is less so for the females. African American females may get jobs, but they are at such a low level that African American women earn at the bottom of the race–gender ladder. There are major tensions between African American men and women in relation to sex role expectations in their roles in parenting. For these reasons mothers depend on relatives rather than on marriage partners.

For the majority of African families, with the exception of some upwardly mobile families, not as many differences are made between differential socialization of their children. The situations of African American males often must be given special consideration. The life situations of African American males are more precarious than those of non–African Americans. The incarceration rate is higher, the educational levels are lower, their part of the conception of out of wedlock children, and their economic status is lower. To these must be added the general stereotypes that abound in the literature and newspapers about the urban, dangerous, and probably criminal African American male. Their social climates are infected with racism, sexism, and class bias that have not been overcome, despite valiant efforts (Scott-Jones, 1993).

Grandparents as Primary Parents

The percentage of elderly in the African American population is expected to nearly double, from 8% to 15% in the period from 1990 to 2050 (U.S. Census Bureau, 1993). Grandparents tend not to live with their children and grandchildren. African Americans accept, but they do not welcome, early grandparenthood (Hill, 1999). African Americans have lost many of the traditional extended family resources and have not yet found or been able to obtain help from other sources. Elderly grandparents do not naturally select to have the full-time care of their grandchildren (Burton, 1992). Many have anticipated that they would have more time for their own interests and hobbies. Grandparents who are parenting full-time are at a place and time where their own personal and health needs should be addressed (Smith and Drew, in Vol. 3 of this *Handbook*). When resources are limited, grandparents may tend to take care of their grandchildren and not their own needs. The funds that are available for food, medicine, and housing may instead be used for their grandchildren's school supplies, food, and clothing. There are many stressors on African American grandparents who were at the point in their lives where they are becoming dependent on others.

African American grandparents had generally been pictured as providing gifts and comfort and as a temporary childcare provider (Bengtson and Robertson, 1985; Sands and Goldberg-Glen, 2000). In African American families there was a greater tendency for grandparents to assume more childcare and possibly take over for the parents (Burton and Dilworth-Anderson, 1991; George and Dickerson, 1995). But grandparents who are African American reported less stress than those who were European American (Puchno, 1999).

More African American children are being orphaned or being left alone because of the trauma of death of the parents, alcohol or drug use, HIV/AIDS, and imprisonment (Minkler and Roe, 1996; Ruiz, 2000). Traditionally this has usually meant that the children would be absorbed within the extended family. But the incidence of children being left alone has taken on different dimensions now, as so many children are involved. More grandparents were African American than European American (9% versus 5%) primary parent (Casper and Bryson, 1998).

The "off-time" parenting may have negative effects on the lives of the grandparents (Burton, Dilworth-Anderson, and Merriwether-deVries, 1995). But when things become difficult, grandparents are usually the persons who step in to assist them (Bowers and Myers, 1999). This is often a last resort option that occurs after the grandchildren's home situation has deteriorated (McAdoo, 1990). Many African American grandparents feel overwhelmed and unable to keep up with their grandchildren's activities (Burton and Merriwether-deVries, 1992). They often feel very tired.

Grandchildren who live with their grandparents are most likely to be poor, to receive public assistance, and are more likely to be without health insurance (Casper and Bryson, 1998). However, many grandparents do work outside of the home and thus need child care during working hours. Younger African American grandparents have been found to be associated with stress when they had low family cohesion and lack of support from other family members (Sands and Goldberg-Glen, 2000). African American grandparents attribute symptoms due to the stress of caring for grandchildren (Kelley, 1993; Minkler, Fuller-Thomson, Miller, and Driver, 1997; Strawbridge, Wallhagen, Shema, and Kaplan, 1997). Child card services, medical services for age-related illnesses, and generally "time-outs" are often unavailable.

Racial Socialization

One of the most important parenting decisions that must be made by African American parents is that of racial socialization. This socialization takes the form of the socialization messages that are passed on and actions that are taken by the parents. Different racial strategies given or used with their children (Frazier, 1963). The social context of the parenting will determine the ethnic identity that the child acquires (Murray and Mandara, 2001).

The majority of parents are aware of their responsibility to teach their children about race. Racial socialization is the process by which the family shapes their children's attitudes about race and shows the child how the child fits into the context of race in their society (Murray and Mandara, 2001; Phinney and Rotheram, 1987). Historically, African Americans have understood the importance of training their children in the race appropriate manner when confronting a European American person. The approaches of imparting attitudes toward race and the appropriate actions to take, or not to take, are many. For example, children can be taught to ignore slights, be assertive in responding to them, or be militant in the presence of racism.

Racial socialization messages are used by parents that are associated with the significance that parents place on issues regarding race (Boykin and Toms, 1985). African Americans have been found to perceive that race is more important than class considerations in terms of influencing their life changes and social status (Durant and Sparrow, 1997; Feagin, 1989; Mydral, 1964). Whenever parents come in contact with European Americans, they must establish once again their status and position. European Americans are considered to be stable and middle socioeconomic status, but they seem not to make the same assumptions about African American families.

African American parents emphasize ethnic pride and awareness of racial barriers. Some parents are active with their children in African American culture events, such as Kwanza, an African festival of harvest (December 26–January 1), or Juneteenth, a celebration of the end of enslavement, when the people in Texas were told that they had been freed for several months (Bowman and Howard, 1985; Hill, 1999). All of these celebrations instill pride and a knowledge of their race history.

Children overhear parents' conversations about race, they notice how they react to persons of other races, and they receive direct instructions from their parents (Murray and Mandela, 2001). There is no monolithic African American experience (Boykin and Toms, 1985). Parents may behave proactively or teach their children to deal with race issues. Or they may behave actively and openly discuss race and discrimination. Or they may be reactive by taking a defensive stance on racial issues. (Bowman and Howard, 1985; Boykin and Toms, 1985; Murray and Mandara, 2000; Stevenson, 1995). They receive further messages at school from their peers. They begin to internalize stereotypes, prejudices, and racism from all of these sources.

Some African American parents feel that it is essential to teach their children about race, whereas others feel it is insignificant (Tatum, 1997). These actions flow from not acknowledging race to an overemphasis on the race issue. Peters (1997) has observed that children should be taught an awareness of racism and not to expect fair play to always be given by European American children. This will shelter them from being hurt and instill pride. The children should be taught that it is their (European American's) problem, but you have to deal with it.

Many parents do not talk about race with their children. They feel that society will teach the child eventually. Others believe that to discuss race will make the child feel inferior. Those parents do not teach anything about race. Their attitude is if the concept of race is not talked about, it will never hurt their children.

Some African American parents have a reduced sense of closeness with the African American community. They feel that one must work hard and be a good citizen, and race is not discussed with children. Peters (1997) stated that this type of humanistic parenting does not prepare children to negotiate effectively within their own community and the larger society.

Sometimes African American's show acceptance of negative stereotypes (Demo and Hughes, 1990): discussed several racial socialization classifications. If a cautious or defensive attitude is adopted, parents will pass on their own prejudices, such as European Americans have power and should be kept at a distance. When children are reared in this atmosphere and they become adults, they may become alienated from their own community.

The approach that parents use depends on their own attitudes about their racial identity (Murray and Mandara, 2000; McAdoo, 1985). This is defined by the degree an individual understands and identifies with being African American (Martin and Hall, 1992). Attitudes are also held about the physical features of the hair texture, shapes and size of the lips, and complexion of skin. These attitudes are communicated to the children in various ways. Hatchett et al. (1991) found that 61% of the African American children receive socialization messages of one type or other, only 39% were told nothing about being African American. No messages about how to deal with European Americans were given to 52%.

Children focus on characteristics, such as skin color, to group people (Asher and Allen, 1969; Williams and Morland, 1976). Children exist in a world in the early years in which membership into categories is unconditional (Murray and Mandara, 2001). The process that children go through, regardless of race, is similar for the first approximately 5 years of their lives. Then there is a convergence that is more difficult for children of color than for those who are not of color. At the same time, the messages that children are given are different across racial groups.

Race awareness occurs at about 2 to 3 years of age. Gender and race categories are quickly formed by children. No meaning is placed on being in one or another group; they just know that some people are dark and others are lighter.

At about age 3 to 4, all children begin to racially identify with a particular group. They know that their mother or best friend is like them or different from them. At first, no meaning is placed on these differences. Then, almost immediately, the messages of their environment seep in and they form a preference for one over the other racial group.

At first all children prefer "Whiteness" over "Blackness". A subtle form of devaluation occurs with the present "color caste" that continues in many forms to this day. The preference for "Whiteness" over "Blackness" by the media, television, and books has caused many problems with the development of the racial attitudes and preferences of African American children and adults (Cohen, 1972; Cross,1985; McDonald,1970). This preference has been found to result in mental distress (Fulmore, Taylor, Ham, and Lyles, 1994; Guthrie, 1976). Originally it was felt that this preference was a rejection of themselves, but research has shown that African American children are able to discriminate between their racial preference (European American oriented) and their self-esteem (African American oriented). Thus, their racial attitudes can be modified (McAdoo, 1985).

Children who are European American remain in this position, it is reinforced in the media and in power situations, the schools, and their environments. Children of color still have to change, develop, and have a own-group orientation. This is done between the ages of 5 and about 8 years. It is not until the age of 9 that African American children become comfortable with their own racial identification. African American children must overlook the Whiteness orientation of their environments. The process of seeing their racial group in a positive manner takes a great deal of work and input from many elements. It is as if children say: "I know that it may be easier to be White. But I am Black and I feel good about being Black." Despite pressures to remain "White oriented," the children are able to develop an identity that allows them to take pride in their own racial group.

PRACTICAL INFORMATION ABOUT AFRICAN AMERICAN PARENTING

The experience of racism has many evolving negative experiences on the life of parents. Racism and discrimination confront all parents of color to some extent. Children need to be prepared to cope with it, and parents may face it directly on their jobs. Racism at work is exacerbated by the threat of economic loss that accompanies the work context (Morgan, Beale, Mattis, Stovall, and White, 2000). Those who base their self-concept on racial group membership might be more sensitive to racist attitudes or actions. Theorists, researchers, and family therapists have much to gain by understanding the particular threat that racism presents in various contexts of the families' experiences, the domains of self esteem. The unmitigating pressure of race will always be an element in their lives, but the involvement within the friend and family extended kinship patterns may be a mediating factor on their stress. Perceived closeness to other African Americans has been found to moderate the impact of racism at work on physical health and longevity (Morgan et al., 2000). It is very important to highlight the positive coping strategies of these support networks.

The practical information that could be gained from these data is that African American parents should be alert to the many sources of devaluation that they and their children experience. It is not going to go away, but will supercede lifelong issues that must be coped with. Racism must be transcended in order for parents and children to form good, functional families. In spite of the high levels of incarceration, lower income, and poor schools, African American parents are producing children who have all the attributes that are desired. Whether or not African American families exist in two-parent or single-parent units, with grandparents, or in some other diverse format, African American parenting will proceed in presenting competent children who will grow into competent adults.

FUTURE THEORY AND RESEARCH
IN AFRICAN AMERICAN PARENTING

Writings on future theory and research will have to widen the lens and be open to the diversity of families and children that now exist. We must transcend stereotypical projections of parenting and family life to see that there are many forms of parenting within African American families. Although not all are succeeding, concentration should be placed on those who do succeed despite any of their hardships. There appear to be more funds available to study pathological and problem centered families, but by studying those families with special concerns, we are focusing on the difficulties and not on the strengths of these families. We will need to document those strengths in the parenting in African American families in order to build more realistic guidelines for parents as they work with their children to become adults. We need to examine whether the role of spirituality has any special impact upon their lives. Churches within the African American communities have been the source of much strength and childrearing practices and advice in the past, but the roles of the churches are changing under present day pressures on families and on churches themselves. More African Americans are getting away from traditional churches, because of moves to suburbia and more mobility.

CONCLUSIONS

Guidelines for the growth and direction of parenting guidelines will have to be responsive to the new directions in which African American families are finding themselves. We need to see if the fast evolving lifestyle of young parents will have a negative impact upon parenting. Will African American coping strategies be useful in the new settings in the future? Focusing only on what is now known is to miss the many changes that technological advances are bringing into families' lives. Will African American parenting be stagnant or will it evolve into more dynamic ways that are really beyond our abilities to see? We do know that the future direction in research and theory will continue, and we must be prepared and open to the many changes that are evolving in parenting if African American and other families of color.

REFERENCES

Asher, S., and Allen, V. (1969). Racial preference and social comparison processes. *Journal of Social Issues, 25,* 157–165.

Bengtson, V. L., and Robertson, J. (1985). *Grandparenthood.* Beverly Hills, CA: Sage.

Billingsley, A. (1968). *Black families in white America.* Englewood Cliffs, NJ: Prentice-Hall.

Bowers, B., and Myers, B. (1999). Grandmothers providing care for grandchildren: Consequences of various levels of caregiving. *Family Relations, 48,* 303–311.

Bowman, P., and Howard, C. (1985). Race-related socialization, motivation, and academic achievement: A study of black youths in three-generation families. *Journal of the American Academy of Child Psychiatry, 24,* 134–141.

Boykin, A. W. (1986). The triple quandary and the schooling of Afro-American children. In U. Neisser (Ed.), *The school achievement of minority children: New perspectives* (pp. 57–92). Hillsdale, NJ: Lawrence Erlbaum Associates.

Boykin, A. W., and Toms, F. (1985). Black child socialization: A conceptual framework. In H. McAdoo and J. McAdoo (Eds.), *Black children: Social, educational, and parental environment* (pp. 35–51). Newbury Park, CA: Sage.

Bumpass, L. (1993, August 30). Quoted by Ingrassia, M. A world without fathers: The struggle to save the black family (Special Report). *Newsweek,* 16–29.

Burton, L. M. (1992). Black grandparents rearing children of drug-addicted parents: Stressors, outcomes, and social service needs. *The Gerontologist, 32,* 744–751.

Burton, L. M., and Dilworth-Anderson, P. (1991). The intergenerational family roles of aged black Americans. *Marriage and Family Review, 16,* 311–330.

Burton, L. M., Dilworth-Anderson, P., and Merriwether-deVries, C. (1995). Context and surrogate parenting among contemporary grandparents. *Marriage and Family Review, 20,* 349–366.

Burton, L. M., and Merriwether-deVries, C. (1992). Challenges and rewards: African American grandparents as surrogate parents. *Generations, 16,* 51–54.

Casper, L. M., and Bryson, K. R. (1998). *Co-resident grandparents and their grandchildren: Grandparent maintained families* (Population Division Working Paper No. 26). Washington, DC: U.S. Bureau of the Census.

Center on Budget and Policy Priorities. (2000, February 1). Quoted by Despeignes, P. Blacks see wealth shrink amid national boom. *Detroit News,* pp. A1, A6.

Cohen, R. (1972). *The color of man.* New York: Bantam Pathfinder.

Cross, W. E. (1985). Black identity. Rediscovering the distinction between personal identity and reference group orientation. In M. B. Spencer, G. K. Brookins, and W. R. Allen (Eds.), *Beginnings: The social and affective development of black children* (pp. 152–172). Hillsdale, NJ: Lawrence Erlbaum Associates.

Darity, W., and Myers, S. (1991, May). *Sex ratios, marriageability, and the marginalization of black males.* Paper presented at the biennial meeting of the Society for Research in Child Development, Seattle, WA.

Demo, D. H., and Hughes, M. (1990). Socialization and racial identity among black Americans. *Social Psychology Quarterly, 53,* 364–374.

DeParle, J. (1994, March 22). Clinton target: Teenage pregnancy. *New York Times,* p. A10.

Despeignes, P. (February 1, 2000). Blacks see wealth shrink amid a national boom. *Detroit News,* pp. A1, A6.

Dodson, J. E. (1997). Conceptualizations of African American families. In H. P. McAdoo (Ed.), *Black families* (3rd ed., pp. 67–82). Thousand Oaks, CA: Sage.

Du Bois, W. E. B. (1899). *The Philadelphia Negro.* New York: Schocken.

Durant, T., and Sparrow, K. (1997). Race and class consciousness among lower- and middle-class blacks. *Journal of Black Studies, 27,* 334–351.

Eastman, G. (1988). *Family involvement in education.* Madison, WI: Department of Public Instruction.

Edelman, M. W. (1997). An advocacy agenda for black families and children. In H. P. McAdoo (Ed.), *Black families* (3rd ed., pp. 323–332). Thousand Oaks, CA: Sage.

Elster, A., and Lamb, M. (Eds.). (1986). *Adolescent fatherhood.* Hillsdale, NJ: Lawrence Erlbaum Associates.

Feagin, J. R. (1989). *Racial and ethnic relations* (3rd ed.). Englewood Cliffs, NJ: Prentice-Hall.

Frazier, E. F. (1963). *The Negro church in America.* New York: Schocken.

Fulmore, C., Taylor, T., Ham, D., and Lyles, B. (1994). Psychological consequences of internalized racism. *Psych Discourse, 24,* 12–15.

Garcìa Coll, C., Lamberty, G., Jenkins, R., McAdoo, H. P., Crnic, K., Wasik, B. H., and Vasquez Garcia, H. (1996). An integrative model for the study of developmental competencies in minority children. *Child Development, 67,* 1891–1914.

George, S. M., and Dickerson, B. J. (1995). The role of the grandmother in poor single-mother families and households. In B. J. Dickerson (Ed.), *African American single mothers: Understanding their lives and families* (pp. 146–163). Thousand Oaks, CA: Sage.

Guthrie, R. (1976). *Even the rat was white.* New York: Harper & Row.

Guy-Sheftall, B. (1993, April). *Black feminist perspectives on the academy.* Paper presented at the annual meeting of the American Educational Research Association, Atlanta, GA.

Hatchett, S. J. (1991). Women and men. In J. Jackson (Ed.), *Life in black America* (pp. 84–104). Newbury Park, CA: Sage.

Hatchett, S. J., Cochran, D. L., and Jackson, J. S. (1991). Family life. In J. S. Jackson (Ed.), *Life in black America* (pp. 46–83). Newbury Park, CA: Sage.

Herskovits, M. (1941). *The myth of the Negro past.* New York: Harper & Row.

Hill, R. (1997). *The strengths of African American families: Twenty-five years later.* Washington, DC: R & B.

Hill, S. (1999). *African American children: Socialization and development in families.* Thousand Oaks, CA: Sage.

Hines, D. (1996). *Culture, consciousness, and community. Speak truth to power: Black professional class in United States history.* New York: Carlson.

Ingrassia, M. (1993, August 30). A world without fathers: The struggle to save the black family (Special Report). *Newsweek,* 16–29.

Jones, J. (1991). Racism: A cultural analysis of the problem. In R. L. Jones (Ed.), *Black psychology* (3rd ed., pp. 609–635). Berkeley, CA: Cobb & Henry.

Kelley, S. J. (1993). Caregiver stress in grandparents raising grandchildren. *Image: Journal of nursing scholarship, 25,* 331–337.

Lach, J. (1999, November). Lending inequities. *American Demographics,* pp. 11–12.

Ladson-Billings, G. (2000). Racialized discourses and ethnic eistemologies. In N. Denzin and Y. Lincoln (Eds.), *Handbook of qualitative research* (2nd ed., pp. 257–277). Thousand Oaks, CA: Sage.

Luster, T., and McAdoo, H. P. (1996). Family and child influences on educational attainment: A secondary analysis of the High/Scope Perry Preschool data. *Developmental Psychology, 32,* 26–39.

Martin, J. K., and Hall, G. C. (1992). Thinking black, thinking internal, thinking feminist. *Journal of Counseling Psychology, 39,* 509–514.

McAdoo, H. P. (1990). A portrait of African-American families in the United States. In S. Rix (Ed.), *The American woman 1990–1991: A status report* (pp. 71–93). New York: Norton.

McAdoo, H. P. (1992). Upward mobility and parenting in middle-income black families. In A. Burlew, W. Banks, H. P. McAdoo, and D. Azibo (Eds.), *African American psychology: Theory, research, and practice* (pp. 63–86). Newbury Park, CA: Sage.

McAdoo, H. P. (1995). African-American families: Strength and realities. In H. McCubbin, E. Thompson, A. Thompson, and J. Futrell (Eds.), *Resiliency in ethnic minority families: African-American families* (pp. 17–30). Thousand Oaks, CA: Sage.

McAdoo, H. P. (1997). *Black families* (3rd ed.). Thousand Oaks, CA: Sage.

McAdoo, H. P. (1998). African American families. In C. H. Mendel, R. W. Habenstein, and R. Wright, Jr. (Eds.), *Ethnic families in America: Patterns and variations* (pp. 361–381). New York: Prentice-Hall.

McAdoo, J. L. (1985). Modification of racial attitudes and preferences in young black children. In H. P. McAdoo and J. L. McAdoo (Eds.), *Black children: Social, educational, and parental environments* (pp. 342–256). Beverly Hills, CA: Sage.

McDonald, M. (1970). *Not by the color of their skin.* New York: International Universities Press.

Minkler, M., Fuller-Thomson, E., Miller, D., and Driver, D. (1997). Depression in grandparents raising grandchildren. *Archives of Family Medicine, 6,* 445–452.

Minkler, M., and Roe, K. M. (1996). Grandparents as surrogate parents. *Generation, 20,* 34–38.

Morgan, L., Beale, R., Mattis, J., Stovall, E., and White, D. (2000, Winter). The combined impact of racism at work, non-racial work stress, and financial stress on black women's psychological well-being. *African American Research Perspectives,* 41–50.

Murray, C., and Mandara, J. (2001). Racial identity in African American children: Cognitive and experimental antecedents. In H. P. McAdoo (Ed.), *Black children.* Thousand Oaks, CA: Sage.

Mydral, G. (1964). *An American dilemma.* New York: McGraw-Hill.

Peters, M. F. (1997). Racial socialization of young black children. In H. P. McAdoo and J. L. McAdoo (Eds.), *Black children* (pp. 159–173). Beverly Hills, CA: Sage.

Phinney, J., and Rotheram, M. (1987). *Children's ethnic socialization.* Newbury Park, CA: Sage.

Prince, K. (1997). Black family and black liberation. *Psych Discourse, 28,* 4–7.

Puchno, R. (1999). Raising grandchildren: The experiences of black and white grandmothers. *The Gerontologist, 39,* 209–221.

Ruiz, D. (2000). Guardians and caretakers: African American grandmothers as primary caregivers in intergenerational families. *African American Research Perspectives,* 1–12.

Sands, R. G., and Goldberg-Glen, R. S. (2000). Factors associated with stress among grandparents raising their grandchildren. *Family Relations, 49,* 97–105.

Schweinhart, L. J., and Weikart, D. P. (1980). *Young children grow up: The effects of the Perry Preschool program on youths through age 15.* Ypsilanti, MI: High/Scope Press.

Scott-Jones, D. (1993, November). Adolescent childbearing: Whose problem? What can we do? *Kappan Special Report,* K2–K12.

Seginer, R. (1983). Parents' educational expectations and children's academic achievements. A literature review. *Merrill-Palmer Quarterly, 29,* 1–23.

Stevenson, H. C. (1995). Relationship of adolescent perceptions of racial socialization to racial identity. *Journal of Black Psychologists, 21,* 49–70.

Strawbridge, W. J., Wallhagen, M. I., Shema, S. J., and Kaplan, G. A. (1997). New burdens or more of the same? Comparing grandparent, spouse, and adult–child caregivers. *The Gerontologist, 37,* 505–510.

Sudarkasa, N. (1993). Female-headed African American households: Some neglected dimensions. In H. P. McAdoo (Ed.), *Family ethnicity: Strength in diversity* (pp. 81–89). Newbury Park, CA: Sage.

Sudarkasa, N. (1997). African American Families and Family Values. In H. P. McAdoo (Ed.), *Black families* (3rd ed., pp. 9–40). Thousand Oaks, CA: Sage.

Tatum, B. D. (1997). Out there stranded: Black families in white communities. In H. P. McAdoo (Ed.), *Black families* (3rd ed., pp. 214–233). Thousand Oaks, CA: Sage.

Tucker, C. (2000, October 3). Injustices for Blacks ignored. *Lansing State Journal,* p. A4.

Tucker, M. B., and Mitchell-Kernan, C. (1997, Winter). Understanding marital decline among African Americans. *African American Research Perspectives,* 40–45.

U.S. Census Bureau. (1993). *We the American elderly.* Washington, DC: U.S. Department of Commerce, Economics and Statistical Administration.

Wellner, A. S. (2000). The money in the middle. *American Demographics, 22,* 56–64.

Werner, E., and Smith, R. (1992). *Overcoming the odd: High-risk children from birth to adulthood.* Ithaca, NY: Cornell University Press.

Wilkinson, D. (1997). American Families of African Descent. In M. DeGenova (Ed.), *Families in cultural context: Strengths and challenges in diversity* (pp. 335–360). London: Mayfield.

Williams, J., and Morland, J. (1976). *Race, color, and the young child.* Chapel Hill: University of North Carolina Press.

4

Parenting of Asians

Ruth Chao
University of California, Riverside
Vivian Tseng
California State University, Northridge

INTRODUCTION

Recognition of the importance of culture in understanding parenting has included a keen interest in many Asian countries and societies. However, some clarification of the designation of "Asia" or "Asian" is necessary in light of the vast amount of variation that exists across different cultures and societies within Asia. For the purposes of this chapter, geographically speaking, "Asia" represents countries in the regions of East Asia (China, Japan, and Korea), South Asia (India, Pakistan, Nepal, Bangladesh, and Sri Lanka), and Southeast Asia (Vietnam, Laos, and Cambodia), in addition to countries such as the Philippines and Thailand and also other countries or regions in Asia that have rarely been included in studies of parenting (Singapore, Malaysia, Burma, and Indonesia). Depending on one's sociopolitical perspective, "China" may also be an oversimplification, because a number of countries may or may not be represented in this designation, including the People's Republic of China (P.R.C.), Taiwan, and Hong Kong (although Hong Kong is now part of the P.R.C.). Similarly, Asian countries such as India are comprised of extensive regional, ethnic, linguistic, and religious distinctions. This chapter will reveal some of this diversity, although more attention is paid to East Asians, especially Chinese, due to the greater amount of research conducted with this group, including Chinese immigrants in the United States.

The immigration of Chinese and other Asians to countries such as the United States has helped to create substantial populations of Asians in these receiving countries. For instance, between 1980 and 1988, Asians made up 40% to 47% of the total U.S. immigrants (Min, 1995). However, this proportion had gone down to 27% in 1999 due to the increasing number of Mexican and other Latino immigrants (U.S. Census Bureau, 2000). Also, between 1965 and 1999, the number of Asian Americans soared from 1 million to over 10.9 million, constituting 4% of the total population (U.S. Census Bureau, 2000). In the next 20 years their numbers will more than double to over 20 million, the majority of whom will continue to be immigrants and their children. These recent Asian immigrants comprise distinct, cultural groups by bringing with them their own beliefs, practices, and norms. Thus, the Asian immigrant parents in the United States may be important to examine not only with respect to parents in Asia, but also with respect to parents of European descent in the United States. This chapter will incorporate the parenting research conducted on Asians both in Asia and in the United States. In addition, other countries that have substantial numbers of immigrants from Asia will also be included, although there are only a few studies.

The first of our central themes for Asian parenting, that of "family as center," the importance of family, and family interdependence captures some points of commonality across Asian societies. However, each society or group has different notions of the family and of the roles, responsibilities, and membership for defining families that also reflect their diversity or uniqueness. A range of indigenous notions or terms for describing the central importance of family is provided across a number of Asian societies. Also, shifts or transformations in these views of the family are recognized that further capture the diversity of Asian parenting. Another salient theme in Asian parenting that has generated some debate has been control and strictness. Some early and comparative research stressed the restrictiveness and harshness of Asian parental control. Other research though has attempted to provide further elaborations or distinctions of the parental control of Asians that provide a more in-depth understanding of its cultural meaning for Asians. Ultimately, cultural differences in the meaning of parental control for Asians are also addressed in studies examining the effects that parental control may have on children's development and well-being. Finally, the third theme focuses on the societal and parental importance placed on educational achievement. Because a great deal of attention has been given to the school success of Asians in the United States, a number of the studies reviewed in this chapter focus on Asian Americans. In this theme, parental concern over the educational achievement of children is described in a number of ways—through examining parental beliefs regarding children's development and learning, their educational expectations, and the type of support or involvement that parents provide for their children's education and schooling.

While the majority of research on Asian parenting is relatively recent, the chapter begins by addressing our topic from a sociohistorical perspective. We trace Confucian and Buddhist views of childhood and their influences on Asian parenting historically and in the modern era, with Japan as an example. Then we also provide some of the classic research on Asian parenting. The three central themes we have identified above are then discussed. These emphases include the centrality of the family and family interdependence, the use of parental control and strictness, and fostering educational achievement in children each have their own major section. Finally, some suggestions for future research are presented followed by our conclusions.

HISTORICAL CONSIDERATIONS INFLUENCING ASIAN PARENTING

Historical, Religious, and Philosophical Perspectives of Childhood

Many of the historical sources of childrearing can be found in historical perspectives of childhood that encompass the meanings accorded childhood as a distinct period in the life course and perspectives on children's basic in-born nature and their process of development. Beliefs about childhood have direct implications for childrearing, specifically in shaping how parents regard and treat children in order to foster or protect them from their own basic nature and how they should help children develop and grow. The historical roots of childhood and childrearing, emphasized in China, Japan, Korea, and Vietnam, have often been traced to Confucian sources, particularly Mencius, and Buddhist influences that spread throughout many regions of Asia (Boocock, 1991; Chao, 2000a; Kojima, 1986). Although these sources represent only a few of the many historical perspectives of childrearing in Asia, these examples are some of the more widely recognized accounts provided by researchers and historians.

Throughout most of Asia, Confucian views regarding the nature of the child have been captured in analogies such as "children are like white paper," indicating their innocence, lack of knowledge, and innate goodness. According to Boocock (1991), the notion of children's innocence and innate goodness is also consistent with Buddhism as it developed in Japan. Both Confucian and Buddhist influences suggest that children can only be corrupted by the adult world, not by their own nature. That is, children are regarded as naturally good unless tainted by their environments. Childhood also has been regarded as an important and even revered period in the life course, particularly in Japan (Chen, 1996). Some societies view childhood as an inevitable but not negative state, or simply as a period that must be grown out of. In Japan, however, childhood is seen as having merit or virtue of its own (Chen, 1996). Researchers have even typified Japanese childhood as a cherished and highly romanticized period of life that is continuously recapitulated throughout adulthood in images of leisure, relaxation, and enjoyment, especially in advertisements for travel agencies (Lebra, 1994).

This cherished and special quality of children is captured in folk proverbs or popular sayings such as "There is no treasure that surpasses a child." This specialness also extends to notions about children being divine or sacred, reflected in the folk proverb, "Until seven, children are with the gods." Young children were believed to be closer to the spiritual than the human world because of their physical vulnerability or increased chances of mortality. According to Hara and Minagawa (1996, p. 14), children before age 7 were for many centuries believed to "develop not only in the hands of parents, family, and neighbors, but also under the protection of super-natural beings." Because of their relationship to the spiritual world, very young children were afforded special religious recognition, such as acting as mediators between the spiritual and earthly worlds or walking at the head of religious processions, indicating their closeness to the gods (Boocock, 1991; Hara and Minagawa, 1996). Hara and Minagawa also argue that such traditional beliefs are the foundation for parental indulgence, and even respect and awe for young children before age 7.

There is also some evidence that such notions of children's pureness or divinity are espoused in regions and societies in Asia that extend beyond East Asia. Minturn and Hitchcock (1963) provide similar descriptions of Rajputs in India. Children are not only considered pure, they are also considered holy in that "God resides in them" (Minturn and Hitchcock, 1963, p. 311). They are considered to be without sin and unable to distinguish between good and evil. Mothers in their study commented that children remain in this state of purity until they begin to eat solid food. Mothers also reiterated the expression that "children are born with their hands shut because they are sent from God fully equipped and do not want anything from the world" (Minturn and Hitchcock, 1963, p. 311).

These views about the importance of childhood and the nature of the child are linked to views about how children develop and parents' roles in fostering that development. The importance placed on the parental role is evident in "plant cultivation" metaphors espoused in many Japanese writings about childhood (Chen, 1996). In fact, Chen points out that in Japanese, the word for cultivating a person is the same as that for cultivating plants. The development of children is analogous to the cultivation of a tree that first begins with the seedling. As the tree grows, the grower's care is needed in the trimming of its branches and leaves to enable it to grow in the right direction. However, care must also be taken to let the plant's own "inner tendencies" unfold before such shaping is initiated. Shaping should not be started too early. The parent is essential in starting the child off in the "correct" direction, by providing the proper education, as the child is ready. Chen points out that the plant metaphor is apparent today in principles involving the education or schooling of children, though plant cultivation images are not explicitly invoked in parenting or by parents.

Childhood in the Modern Era: Change and Continuity in Japan

Japan is a compelling example of an Asian country that has undergone rapid economic growth and demographic transformations and yet retained some of its traditional folk beliefs. Japan, now has the lowest infant mortality rate of any modern society and, during the decade following World War II, the most rapid and unprecedented declines in fertility (Cherlin, 1994). Japanese men and women also marry later than previous generations and even later than couples from some countries in the West (Tsuya, 1994). Also, just as in countries in the West, birth rates for women over 30 have increased dramatically in Japan (Cherlin, 1994). Social shifts in Japan have also been noted in the number of children considered desirable. Between 1945 and 1971, the ideal number was three, whereas in

1973, over 47% of wives considered two children ideal, and 40.7% considered three children ideal. Finally, Hara and Minagawa (1996) argued that contacts and relationships with extended family or relatives have changed in Japan, with over 75% of people over the age of 65 living with one of their children and his or her family in 1971, and less than 40% doing so today.

These changes in Japan have also spurred childrearing views that reflect not only Western influences, but also traditional notions of childhood. Hara and Minagawa (1996) summarized three primary contemporary, social views of children. The first is that children are regarded as important human resources for the future of society. The second is based on humanistic and Western views emphasizing human rights for children. A third view is based on the traditional notion, mentioned above, emphasizing devotion and tolerance toward babies and children. Children are still the focal point of families. Children have also become a national priority in the development of private and federal programs devoted to their well-being.

Despite major demographic changes, Hara and Minagawa (1996) argue that many traditional folk beliefs are still practiced today. Even with government initiatives to conduct research on and eradicate the influence of "superstition," some folk beliefs have actually increased since World War II. As part of the views of children "being a gift from the gods," couples still turn to the supernatural when they are expecting a child. In the fifth month of pregnancy, parents visit a shrine or temple to pray for a healthy pregnancy and safe delivery. In the first month after the baby is born, parents again visit the shrine to report the birth of the baby and to thank the gods. Hara and Minagawa argue that these are more than just rituals practiced without belief in their impact on children's development. They provide additional evidence of the saliency of folk beliefs of childrearing in modern Japan. One popular book on childrearing, *Japanese Ways of Childrearing* (Matsuda, 1964), was written by a famous pediatrician who extolled the virtues of some traditional folk beliefs. Hara and Minagawa believe that this book had such a significant impact because a medical authority advocated and incorporated folk beliefs about childrearing into a modern framework.

The popular Japanese metaphor, "river crossing," also reflects traditional folk beliefs for childrearing (Chen, 1996). This metaphor broadly reflects the Japanese view of children's development and the type of assistance parents should provide to help their children "cross the river." In Western societies, such metaphors often imply that the parent is on the other side of the bridge urging the child to cross. In Japanese society, Chen explains adults provide assistance by being on the *same* side of the bridge as the child and walking them through to the other side, representing the adult world. This assistance suggests a dynamic process of socialization involving the interactive experiences of both parent and child. Japanese parents feel that this assistance necessitates the physical presence of the parent because of the potential risk and particularly the loneliness that is entailed in bridge crossing. According to Chen, Japanese are very concerned about children's feelings of loneliness and being left alone. Chen believes that the extensive physical closeness of Japanese mothers with their babies reflects parents' preoccupation with keeping the child from feeling lonely. In particular, the practices of cosleeping and cobathing are examples of what Chen identifies as another important metaphor involving the "loneliness-prone child."

Classical studies of Asian parenting incorporated an important integration and demonstration of these historical, religious, and philosophical perspectives. Through much of the early ethnographic studies on parenting provided by anthropologists, research on parenting in different regions of Asia became very prominent.

CLASSIC RESEARCH IN ASIAN PARENTING

The study of culture and parenting gained prominence through the work of anthropologists such as Benedict (1934) and Mead (1928). Mead, in particular, placed socialization as one of the central aspects of studying and understanding culture. In the mid-1950s, the study of culture and parenting became more explicitly comparative as Whiting, Child, and Lambert (1966) conducted their research of childrearing in six cultures, including several Asian groups: the Rajputs of Khalapur, India (Minturn and Hitchcock, 1963), the Tairans of Okinawa, Japan (Maretzki and Maretzki, 1963), and the Ilocanos of Tarong, the Philippines (Nydegger and Nydegger, 1963). Across most of the cultures, responsibility training was an important goal, but cultural beliefs about the development or timing of training varied. For example, Taira adults believe that before age 6, children "do not have sense," and so parents do not begin to seriously train their children until that age (Minturn and Hitchcock, 1963, p. 480). Similarly, Tarong parents believe children begin to acquire "sense," or the ability to benefit from instruction, at age 4 and should have it by age 6 (Nydegger and Nydegger, 1963, p 840). Compared to the Taira and Tarong parents, Rajputs do not have discrete stages for childhood, and children's transition from infancy to middle childhood is a gradual one from child as observer to participant in village life. Similarly to the other groups, Rajputs believe that children cannot be directly trained until they have learned speech so young children learn best by imitation and observation rather than by direct instruction. Whiting and Edwards (1988) later followed up the Six Culture Project with a volume on *Children of Different Worlds*, to which they had added several additional sites to the data collected from the original samples. In this later volume, they present evidence of both transcultural similarities in childrearing as well as cultural forces that "modulate" development and particular behaviors in children. This ethnographic work conducted by anthropologists and a handful of psychologists represented the first large-scale, systematic comparison of child training and its influences on children within different cultures.

At about the same time in the 1950s, Hsu (1953) published his comparative work *Americans and Chinese*. Weaving together ethnographic observations, anecdotes, and literature, Hsu portrayed differences between the two societies, often linking them back to the structure of the family and parenting goals and practices. Decades before the study of independence–interdependence or collectivism–individualism came into popularity, Hsu contrasted the emphasis placed on individualism within American families to that of filial piety and children's obligations to their parents within Chinese families. Whereas "in America, the child learns to see the world strictly on an individual basis," "the Chinese child learns to see the world as a network of relationships" (Hsu, 1953, p. 88). Preceding much of the literature on parental control, Hsu noted the great importance placed on parental authority among Chinese parents and linked it to the Confucian philosophies regarding filial piety and respecting parents. He also noted the sociohistorical differences in approaches to schooling across the two cultures, though spending less time than recent scholars have on the role of Chinese and European American parenting on children's education.

During the late 1950s and early 1960s, Wolf (1972) collected ethnographic observations that examined the roles of mothers versus fathers within rural Taiwanese families. According to Wolf (1970), Chinese mothers and fathers played very different and complementary roles in child training. She and other scholars emphasized that, traditionally, fathers' principal duties were to provide economic support, moral instruction, and a suitable inheritance for their sons. Emphasis was not placed on developing warm emotional relationships with children; instead, part of a father's role was as a disciplinarian who should "*not* encourage or tolerate emotional indulgence" (Jankowiak, 1992, p. 347). In contrast and complement, the role of a Chinese mother was to provide a "secure and loving environment within the home" (Jankowiak, 1992, p. 347). Mothers, then, often developed very intense, emotional relationships with their children that were not seen between fathers and children.

Other research by Solomon (1971) on Chinese fathers pointed out that fathers were not without a deep, warm sentiment for their children. Although fathers were expected to assume the role of a strict disciplinarian, they nonetheless, felt a compassion and love toward their children. Solomon stressed that fathers' expressions of their sentiments were constrained by their traditional parenting role. He provides a historical basis for his descriptions of father–child relations in a Qing dynasty quote that explained that "a father loved his child with all his heart, but he would not express it" (1971, p. 60). Solomon also argued that Chinese mothers and fathers provided important complementary roles for their children to develop into responsible and ethical individuals.

During roughly the same period, other American scholars were pioneering work with other Asian societies. Lynch (1984), an anthropologist and sociologist, was developing his research on cultural values within Philippine society. Although he was not explicitly interested in parenting nor socialization, his early writings on smooth interpersonal relations (SIR) noted the emphasis on interdependence among Filipinos and its manifestation in culturally indigenous concepts such as *pakikisama*, *hiya*, and *utang na loob* for parenting (described below). Anthropologist Seymour (1999) similarly studied the importance placed on interdependence and family obligations among mothers within rural and urban families in Bhubaneswar, India. Both bodies of work are evident in the scholarship on family interdependence across diverse Asian cultures discussed next.

INTERDEPENDENCE IN ASIAN FAMILIES

Perhaps the most often cited characteristic of Asian parenting is the strong emphasis on interdependence among family members. Typically, researchers contrast Asian and Asian American emphases on interdependence with European and European American emphases on independence. Interdependent construals of the self stress persons in relation to others within harmonious relationships, whereas independent construals stress individualism and persons as separate or unique from others (Markus and Kitayama, 1991). In Asian parenting, the strong emphasis on interdependence has "important implications for what is responded to, emphasized, and sanctioned in the socialization process and for the character of social relations" (Greenfield, 1994, p. 4).

Interdependence orientations depend on the reference group, and within Asian cultures, children are socialized to view the family as the focal reference group for interdependence. The family is so prominent in Asian cultures that some scholars have asserted that "the family is considered the proto- type for all relationships," including educational, political, economic, and religious ones (Ho, 1996; Javillonar, 1979; Kim and Choi, 1994). Similarly, Rhee, Uleman, and Lee (1996) have found that delineating kin versus nonkin reference groups is important for contrasting cultures along the re- lated concepts of collectivism and individualism. Collectivistic cultures emphasize interdependent relationships and prioritizing of the in-group's goals over personal ones. Individualistic cultures, in contrast, emphasize independence and prioritizing personal goals over those of the in-group. Their findings indicated that Koreans were more collectivistic (interdependently oriented) and less indi- vidualistic (independently oriented) than were European Americans *in relation to their families*. In relation to nonkin or general others, Koreans either did not differ from European Americans or were actually less collectivistic and more individualistic. These findings generally were obtained across several established measures of collectivism and individualism, including Triandis's (1991) Self-Behaviors, Attitudes Scales, and Parent's Behavior Scale and Hui's (1988) Individualism– Collectivism (INDCOL) Scale.

Asian parenting beliefs are shaped by a cultural emphasis on interdependence among family mem- bers. Chao's (1995) comparisons of childrearing beliefs among immigrant Chinese and European American mothers provided a contrast between parenting for interdependent versus independent goals. Both groups of mothers stressed the importance of loving the child. However, Chinese moth- ers emphasized the importance of love for fostering a close, enduring parent–child relationship, whereas European American mothers emphasized the importance of love for fostering the child's self-esteem. Both groups of mothers stressed the same quality, but Chinese mothers were motivated toward relational goals and European American mothers were motivated toward individual goals. Moreover the Chinese mothers' interdependence goals were focused principally on harmonious relationships within the family.

Even with infants and toddlers, Asian and Asian American parents are oriented toward in- terdependence. For example, Japanese mothers are more likely to engage in social interactions, emphasizing physical and verbal interpersonal exchanges with their infants than are European American mothers (Bornstein, Azuma, Tamis-LeMonda, and Ogino, 1990). In addition, mothers in Japan and Japanese mothers in the United States actually engage in more social than didactic interactions, the latter of which involves encouraging attention toward objects, properties, or events, rather than people (Bornstein et al., 1992; Bornstein and Cote, 2000; Cote and Bornstein, 2000). In another study of Japanese mothers' verbal interactions with their 2-year-old children, Clancy (1986) found that these mothers strongly engaged in what she labeled "empathy training." Such training was achieved by these mothers through (1) directing their children's attention to fulfilling the wishes of others, (2) expressing their own feelings to their children in the hopes that their children will feel the same, and (3) fostering the abillity to anticipate the needs of others by instructing or telling children what others are thinking and feeling. Clancy also points out, in another study by Matsumori (1981) of interactions with 3- to 6-year-old children, that Japanese mothers often used directives that appealed to social norms, particularly those reflecting the intimacy of the mother–child relationship.

Scholars have often noted this emphasis on family interdependence within Asian cultures, but they have rarely examined the sociocultural roots of interdependence for different Asian groups. Below, we contrast some of these sociocultural roots among diverse Asian groups and the insights they lend for understanding different meanings or manifestations of family interdependence.

Sociocultural Roots of Family Interdependence

Very little attention has been directed at understanding the underlying cultural principles for defining family interdependence across different Asian cultures. Where does family interdependence arise from in different Asian cultures? How do the sociocultural roots of interdependence shape parenting within each culture? In Confucian-based societies in East Asia and parts of Southeast Asia, filial piety has been identified as a set of unifying principles underlying parenting and specifically, notions of family interdependence. In countries such as India or the Philippines, such sociocultural roots may be more difficult to define. This may be due, in part, to greater difficulties in identifying unified cultural principles in these countries that have vast regional or island differences and that have been influenced by extensive colonization.

East Asians and Vietnamese.   Over several centuries, Confucian philosophy regarding filial piety has shaped parenting within China and its neighboring societies, particularly Japan, Korea, and Vietnam (Ho, 1994; Sung, 1995; Zhou and Bankston, 1998). Ho (1996, p. 155) has written extensively about filial piety and describes it as "a guiding principle governing general Chinese patterns of socialization, as well as specific rules of intergenerational conduct." Filial piety traditionally entails a rigid system of age veneration and patriarchy. Parents and elders wield greater authority and should be treated with respect and obedience, and children often continue to seek their parents' advice and guidance throughout their adulthood. Respecting and honoring elders extends beyond those who are living to those who are already dead, in the form of ancestor worship, and to those who are not yet born, in the continuation of the family line. In this patriarchal system, fathers also wield greater decision-making power than do mothers. In caregiving, fathers play a lesser role during infancy and increasingly assume the role of disciplinarian as the child matures (Ho and Kang, 1984). Traditionally, sons are reared to be the caregivers of their elder parents, whereas daughters are reared "for someone else's family" (Wolf, 1970). Among contemporary families, however, Jankowiak (1992) has found that Chinese parents in the P. R. C. maintain extensive contact with their daughters, even perhaps more than with their sons. Despite a similar patriarchal structure, Zhou (1998) suggests that Vietnamese mothers possess a larger share of power than that found in many East Asian families by managing the family finances and playing the role of *noi-tuong*, or "home minister."

Within East Asian and Vietnamese families, filial piety strongly influences parenting around family interdependence, specifically in how parents admonish and teach children to behave or orient themselves toward their parents and even ancestors. Ho's and Lee's (1974) and Sung's (1995) measures of filial piety identify a number of prescripts for children's filial behavior. These include treating parents with great respect, being obedient, caring for parents materially and emotionally, providing for family continuity, performing ancestral worship duties, bringing honor and glory to the family, making sacrifices for the family, and seeking parental advice and guidance. These pre-scripts stress particular filial behaviors as well as ways children should regard their parents more generally. Simply caring for parents' material needs is not sufficients. Children should have strong, positive regard, respect, and warmth for them (Cheung, Lee, and Chan, 1994; Sung, 1995). Filial duties not only extend to one's parents, but also to one's overall family in terms of respecting and honoring the family and the family name. Thus, filial piety emphasizes family interdependence in that children's actions do not simply have ramifications for themselves. Instead, their actions can potentially bring honor and pride or, conversely, shame and loss of face to the entire family (Cheung et al., 1994).

Asian Indians.   In contrast to the larger volume of research on filial piety among East Asians, less work has examined parenting among South Asians. Similar to East Asian and Vietnamese families, fathers in India are traditionally the heads of the household within a patriarchal system (Ranganath and Ranganath, 1997). Mothers spend the most time caring for children, but fathers' relationships with their children are marked by greater physical distance and high levels of deference. Similar to research on Confucian-based societies, parenting work on Indian families indicates that family interdependence is of utmost importance, but this work does not extensively explicate the social, cultural, or historical roots that have shaped this emphasis on family interdependence. For example, Seymour's (1999, p. 71) ethnographic work on families in India (in Bhubaneswar) found that the "principal value . . . children must learn is interdependence—the understanding that they are one of many, are not unique individuals." This early socialization toward interdependence has similar elements to that of filial piety, stressing obedience, sacrifice, harmony, and identification with the family (Ranganath and Ranganath, 1997).

Gupta (1979) indicated that the emphasis on family interdependence throughout India may be guided by the main text of Hindu law, *Mitakshara*, which specifies common ownership of property among a joint household, consisting of brothers and their respective spouses and children and also their elderly parents. Seymour's (1999) ethnographic analysis describes how joint households in India might bring family interdependence to the forefront of parenting. A large proportion of adults' verbal interactions with infants and young children is spent teaching them the numerous terms for nuclear and joint household members, including parents, older versus younger sisters and brothers, and relatives on their father's versus mother's side of the family. Children, too, are often addressed by their kinship, gender, and birth order rather than by their personal names, which might place undue emphasis on their individuality.

Filipinos.   In contrast to families from East Asia, Vietnam, and parts of India, Filipino culture does not as rigidly emphasize patriarchal authority and age stratification. Children take on their fathers' surnames, but lineage is traced through both parents (Yu and Liu, 1980). Husbands and wives share financial and family decision making (Javillonar, 1979). This is consistent with a Filipino creationist legend that both man and woman emerged simultaneously from a large bamboo tube (Agbayani-Siewert and Revilla, 1995).

Although unifying cultural principles are often difficult to determine for Filipinos, researchers have found that family interdependence is important. When asked what it means to them to be Filipino, Filipino youths in the United States often respond in ways that centered on the family. They cite the importance of spending time with family, emphasizing the needs and well-being of the family, and providing emotional and instrumental support for family members. As with families from India, however, the cultural or historical roots for this emphasis on family interdependence in Filipino families are less clear. Lynch (1981) offered one interpretation when he related family support and cooperation to the more general cultural value of smooth interpersonal relationships. SIR specifies that the interests or desires of individuals should be sacrificed for the good of others, especially the family. Family relationships should be guided by parental authority, sacrifice, and obligation, and family members should not bring shame or *hiya* to the entire family (Agbayani-Siewert and Revilla, 1995; Ranganath and Ranganath, 1997). SIR also includes *pakikisama*, which means going along with others to maintain harmony, even if it contradicts personal desires or needs (Agbayani-Siewert and Revilla, 1995).

Although SIR is a culturally specific value for Filipinos and filial piety for East Asians, there are similarities in the parental expectations of family interdependence within these cultures. Structurally, age veneration and patriarchy might be more salient among East Asian, Vietnamese, and Indian families than in Filipino families, but Filipino parents still have strong expectations for parental authority and children's obligations to their families. For example, adolescents' self-reports show that both East Asians and Filipinos place greater importance on parental authority and children's family obligations than do European Americans (Fuligni, 1998; Fuligni, Tseng, and Lam, 1999). This section has contrasted some of the sociocultural roots of family interdependence across different Asian societies; the next section examines the similarities in how interdependence is structured in Asian families.

Role Relationships and Reciprocity

Despite differences in the sociocultural roots of family interdependence across Asian societies, commonalities in parenting can be found in the particular roles through which authority and responsibility are conferred among family members. Family members fulfill different roles within an overall family system of reciprocity, defined by caring and mutual obligation. Parents and other elders hold considerable authority and responsibility, and are to be treated with great respect by their children. For example, Chinese mothers hold the primary responsibility for their children's early training and are expected to provide immense devotion and sacrifice for this training (Chao, 1994; Wu and Tsong, 1985). Children, in turn, are expected to fulfill obligations and responsibilities to their families. Similarly, Filipino families are guided by the concept of *utang na loob*, which translates literally as "internal debt" (Almirol, 1982). Just as children can expect to receive support and assistance from other family members, they are also expected to fulfill responsibilities to the family.

Parental authority, respect, and caring. Family roles in most Asian societies are structured largely by age (Javillonar, 1979; Yee, Huang, and Lew, 1998). Parents as well as other elders (i.e., grandparents, aunts, uncles, older siblings, and cousins) wield greater authority than do younger family members (Javillonar, 1979). They are expected to be highly involved, responsible for decision making, and caring for children throughout their lives. Parents should provide advice and guidance even after the child becomes an adult and moves out of the household (Yu and Liu, 1980). Children, in turn, are expected to consult with parents and other family members on important decisions. For example, Gibson's ethnography of Punjabi Sikhs (1988) noted that even adult men consult with their parents and siblings before making decisions on issues ranging from mate selection to business transactions.

Cross-cultural research often finds that Asian American parents place greater importance on parental authority than do European American parents (see section below on parental control), but there are different interpretations as to the expression or extent of parental authority, particularly in Chinese families. Ho (1996, p. 161) argued that filial piety is associated with authoritarian moralism, defined as "overcontrol, overprotection, and harshness; placement of emphasis on proper behavior; and neglect, even inhibition of the expressing of opinions, of independence, and of self-mastery." Other research, however, seems to indicate that contemporary Asian parents, or at least mothers, do not appear to endorse absolute parental authority or control. In qualitative interviews and focus groups, immigrant Chinese mothers reported that they prefer to guide their children rather than impose absolute control (Chao, 1995; Gorman, 1998). They often have particular expectations and desires for their children's behavior, but they also explain the reasoning behind their requests and expectations and allow their children to "make up their own minds" (Gorman, 1998, p. 78). Children are thus encouraged to make their own decisions, but to do so interdependently by taking the welfare and wishes of family members into account (Chao, 1995). These findings, however, are limited to Chinese mothers, and Chinese fathers' expectations of parental authority or control rarely have been assessed in similar qualitative ways. Given the traditional role of fathers as disciplinarians who are more emotionally distant, it is possible that more absolute forms of parental authority or control may be more appropriate for describing fathering.

Interpretations of Asian parenting emphasizing the harsh, stifling nature of parental authority also may reflect independence-oriented cultural frameworks. In contrast, Asian cultural frameworks that emphasize interdependence suggest that parental authority reflects parents' caring for their children within a highly interdependent family system. These distinct cultural frameworks for parenting goals are reflected in Chao's (1995) findings that both immigrant Chinese and European American mothers emphasized loving the child as their first priority. However, Chinese mothers emphasized the importance of love for fostering close, enduring parent–child relationships, whereas European American mothers emphasized the importance of love for fostering children's self-esteem or positive feelings about themselves as individuals. Both groups of mothers stressed the same value, but Chinese mothers were motivated toward relational goals, and European American mothers were motivated toward individual goals.

Based on both survey data and qualitative interviews, East Asians report that love and affection are among the most important aspects of filial piety and childrearing (Chao, 1995; Sung, 1995). Indeed, Chao's immigrant Chinese mothers asserted that parental love and sacrifice were critical for developing loving and harmonious family relationships. As with parental authority, parental respect may be best understood in terms of the emotional qualities defining family relationships. In a factor analysis of filial piety items, Sung (1995) found that respect loads on the same factor with items such as "family harmony" and "love and affection," reflecting the emotional aspects of filial piety rather than behavioral aspects. Sung (1995, p. 245) described parental respect within East Asian cultures as "deference, courtesy, esteem, and earnest and sincere consideration," such that respect involves an emotional component of fostering harmonious and loving relationships.

Children's obligations to their parents and families. Similar to the greater endorsement of parental authority among Asian and Asian American parents, studies find that they also have stronger expectations for their children's family obligations than do European American parents (Fuligni, Tseng, and Chan, 1999; Phinney, Ong, and Madden, 2000). Throughout childhood and adulthood, Asian children are socialized to believe they should respect and follow the guidance of their parents as well as fulfill a range of financial, instrumental, and caregiving obligations to their families. Although the specific obligations and their relative importance vary somewhat across the child's developmental stage, gender, and socioeconomic status, the common, underlying theme is the emphasis on reciprocity in role relationships and the importance of "repaying" parents for their sacrifices and caring. In a study of Filipino Cebuano families, a woman described her family's reciprocal financial obligations in the following way (Yu and Liu, 1980, pp. 213–214):

> My father lives on what my brother Manuel [can afford to] give him. Every fifteenth of the month, when Manuel receives his share of the fishing earnings, my father gets a certain amount. The other [siblings], Manang Auring, Opring, and Proceso, also contribute a little amount of money to support my old father. He supported us by fishing. Now it is our turn to support him. We would feel ashamed if we as children abandon him. Especially those of us who live near him have an obligation to support him.

Developmental stage. Few systematic studies have examined longitudinally parents' changing expectations of their children's obligations (Jose, Huntsinger, Huntsinger, and Liaw, 2000). There are some suggestions, however, that parents' expectations for their children's responsibilities may increase at about 5 to 6 years of age (Ho, 1986). Seymour's (1988) work on responsibility among families from Bhubaneswar, India, suggested that children begin to take on chores at about 3 to 5 years of age, but the dramatic increase in chores does not begin until age 6. Similarly, Wolf (1985) and Suzuki (1988) found that Chinese mothers' expectancies for when children should begin to take care of themselves and perform chores was also at about age 5 to 6.

During childhood and adolescence, children are expected to assist the family in day-to-day chores as well as strive toward long-term goals of economic and social betterment, usually through educational and occupational achievements (Santos, 1997). Parental expectations for their children's obligations to the family continue well into children's adulthood. Yu and Liu (1980) also reported that it is not uncommon for Filipino Cebu parents to visit their children on payday to collect money to support themselves. In addition to financial support, children who are not married are expected to live with or near their parents to maintain family closeness and support (Feldman, Mont-Reynaud, and Rosenthal, 1992; Fuligni, Tseng, and Lam, 1999). In Japan, for example, almost 80% of unmarried young adults live with their parents (Kinoshita and Keifer, 1992, in Silver, 1998). Similarly, Filipinos in Almirol's (1982, p. 302) study reported that it was "good" and "practical" to live with their parents even if they could afford to live on their own.

Gender and socioeconomic differences: Obligation attitudes and behaviors.   Although gender and socioeconomic comparisons of children's obligations to their families have been assessed in somewhat different ways, most studies confirm that there are no gender differences, and in some studies, no socioeconomic differences. Ho (1993) is one exception. Ho's (1993) Filial Piety Scale (FPS) contains wide-ranging beliefs about filial piety, but the vast majority of the items in the scale pertain to expectations of filial obligations by adult respondents. He found among Chinese in Hong Kong and Taiwan that women endorsed filial piety more than did men, and those with lower socioeconomic backgrounds endorsed filial piety more than did those with higher socioeconomic backgrounds. However, using the FPS, Zhang and Bond (1998) did not find gender differences after accounting for various personality constructs. Studies of late adolescents and young adults in the United States also did not find gender differences among Asian Americans on the FPS (Lin, 1999).

Fuligni, Tseng, and Lam (1999) and Phinney et al., (2000) have developed measures of "family obligation" that specifically assess expectations for children to assist and respect their parents, and support or live near them in their old age. Fuligni and colleagues did not find gender or socioeconomic differences on three separate measures of attitudes of family obligation (i.e., current assistance, respect for family, and future support). Phinney, Ong, and Madden also did not find gender differences on their measure of family obligation attitudes.

Although gender differences in attitudes regarding children's obligations are not consistently found, it is nevertheless possible that gender differences do exist in the extent to which girls and boys carry out or fulfill their obligations. Indeed, Seymour's research on obligation behavior or practices suggests that parents rely more heavily on girls than boys to fulfill family obligations, at least within the home. Her work on responsibility among families in Bhubaneswar, India (1988), found that girls performed at least twice as many chores as did boys, with the gender difference being the greatest in low socioeconomic households. She argued that mothers, particularly those with few financial means who work outside the home, relied more heavily on their daughters than sons to fulfill the responsibilities that they were unable to do themselves. Similarly, Fuligni and his colleagues (1999) found that Chinese American girls spent more time each day fulfilling their obligations than did boys, but girls did not differ from boys in the number of different behaviors that they performed. These gender differences in family obligations are confined to responsibilities within the home. Parents may have different expectations for their sons' and daughters' obligation behaviors outside the home, such as in educational and occupational endeavors that would bring support or honor to their families.

Seymour also finds that children's obligation behaviors are heavily influenced by socioeconomic status and, more specifically, mothers' employment. As mentioned above, Seymour's (1988) study of families from Bhubaneswar, India, found that mothers with lower socioeconomic status were more likely to work outside the home. These mothers relied quite heavily on their children to perform the chores and childcare duties that would otherwise have fallen to the mothers. In contrast, children in higher socioeconomic households performed fewer chores but were more likely to attend school and fulfill their family obligations by concentrating on schoolwork. Many lower status children were unable to attend school because their labor was needed at home.

Cases of Change and Continuity

Given the rapid changes in the last century, increasing interest has been paid to examining change and continuity in the family interdependence of Asians in the diaspora. Two aspects of change include how urbanization in Asian countries and how migration to and settlement in Western Hemisphere countries have influenced parenting by altering family structure and children's obligation behaviors.

Urbanization.   One area of concern in Asian countries is how urbanization and social change are affecting beliefs that undergird family interdependence. In Ho and Kang's (1984) study of intergenerational changes in Hong Kong, few differences between mother and grandmother pairs in childrearing attitudes and practices emerged, but there were more consistent, substantial differences between father and grandfather pairs. Fathers placed less emphasis on filial piety and were more involved in infant caregiving than were their own fathers.

Seymour's (1988, 1999) ethnographic studies of childrearing in India examined how urbanization can bring about transitions in parenting by altering family structure. In her research in Bhubaneswar, India, she contrasted an older, more rural section called Old Town and a newer, more urban section called New Capital. New Capital families appeared to be living in smaller, more nuclear households that had arisen as families moved to this new area to take advantage of occupational opportunities. Despite this change in family structure, however, Seymour found there was also continuity such that families were still ideologically, if not always structurally, joint. For example, several New Capital households had extended family members living with them, but were not entire joint households. These households included a few nieces or nephews because they wanted to attend the better schools in Bhubaneswar, or an uncle because he wanted to be closer to the doctors in this urban area. Because of shifts away from joint households, the caregiving of children by a myriad of elders had also changed. In Old Town, childcare was provided principally by grandmothers, aunts, and older sisters over one third of the time, and only about one tenth of the time in New Capital. In the smaller more nuclear households of New Capital, grandmothers were still involved in caregiving, but the role of older sisters and aunts had diminished. Instead, New Capital mothers and to some extent fathers took on a larger role in caregiving than did their counterparts in Old Town.

Immigration and settlement: Intergenerational differences.   Changes among Asian immigrants in Western Hemisphere countries are evident in intergenerational differences between parents and adolescents. A few studies and much anecdotal evidence of Asian immigrants in the United States suggest that parents and adolescents often disagree about their expectations regarding family obligation. Fuligni, Tseng, and Lam (1999) and Phinney et al. (2000) confirm these parent–adolescent differences: Parents placed greater importance on family obligation than did their children, particularly in regard to treating parents with respect. These findings may not be surprising given the greater emphasis placed on independence and egalitarianism among many families in the United States.

Some clarification is needed as to whether these differences are due to acculturation challenges faced by immigrant families (i.e., the more accelerated acculturation of adolescents compared to their parents) or to normative disagreements between all parents and adolescents. There is some evidence of normative disagreement: Fuligni, Tseng, and Lam (1999) and Phinney and her colleagues (2000) found parent–adolescent differences in beliefs about family obligation among European American families, and not just among Asian immigrant families. In addition to normative disagreements, Phinney and her colleagues also found evidence of acculturation effects. Among immigrant families, there was greater disagreement among those with U.S.-born adolescents than those with foreign-born adolescents. That is, immigrant parents and their U.S.-born children disagree to a larger degree than do immigrant parents and immigrant children. Future research needs to examine the acculturation of family obligation expectations and practices by examining changes in expectations over time. As foreign- and U.S.-born adolescents become parents themselves, their expectations for their children's family obligations might shift to more mainstream views of the family in the United States.

Settlement into a new society can also alter the traditional roles between parents and children, particularly in caring for elderly immigrant parents (see Yee et al., 1998). Kim, Kim, and Hurh (1991), for example, reviewed how socioeconomic conditions for Korean immigrants in the United States strain traditional filial piety prescripts of caring for and respecting elderly parents. In some cases, elderly immigrant parents lose their social status as they become reliant on their children and grandchildren to negotiate the new host society. They often are not accorded the traditional levels of authority and respect, and their children may no longer seek their guidance in important family decisions. Instead, some elderly parents feel "neglected, slighted, and humiliated in their children's home" (Kim, Kim, and Hurh, 1991, p. 239).

The socioeconomic challenges of settling into a new society can also affect the ability of immigrants to fulfill their filial duties to their elderly parents. Kauh (1997), for example, found that 40% of Korean adults in the United States felt that they couldn't carry out their filial obligations because of time constraints. Many Korean immigrants report declines in occupational status from pre- to postmigration (Kim and Kim, 1998). In the United States, they often experience underemployment such that their occupations in the United States are not commensurate with their education. Barringer and Cho (1989) reported that this downward occupational mobility occurs initially and generally improves over time in the United States. These socioeconomic challenges may initially be too great to allow for continuity in filial obligations to elderly parents. Future research will need to assess whether obligations to elderly parents rebound along with an upswing in mobility over time in the United States or whether obligations continue to decline due to acculturation to Western independence orientations.

Change and continuity in Asian families and their emphasis on interdependence are also noted in the research on parental control and authority. Early research on the parental control of Asians has suggested almost absolute indulgence of very young children, with more harsh strictness applied when children reached school age. Similarly, some comparative research suggests strong restrictiveness in Asian parenting. However, other recent research suggests that such descriptions of Asian parenting may be somewhat limited.

PARENTAL CONTROL IN ASIAN FAMILIES

One of the more prominent and controversial aspects of Asian parenting has been concern over their strictness or what some have labeled as "excessive" control. A Chinese researcher, Ho (1986), has in fact described the parental control of Chinese as harsh strictness due to their primary concerns over children's "impulse control." Although many comparative studies (across societies or across ethnic-immigrant groups within societies) have also characterized the parenting of Asians as "restrictive" or "domineering," other research relies on indigenous concepts of Asian parenting. This research makes important distinctions in the control of Asian parents that raise questions about whether the labels of "restrictive" or "domineering" are entirely accurate. This research provides support for cultural arguments that the meaning of control may differ for Asian and Asian American parents compared to European and European American parents. Support for the different meanings of control can also be found in research examining the effects of parenting on child outcomes.

Early Research on Parental Control

In his review of Chinese parenting, Ho (1986) first described the Chinese parental concern over what he, as a clinical psychologist, referred to as "impulse control." Interestingly, although Ho never explicitly defined what he meant by impulse control, he did describe how Chinese parents are stricter with their children when they reach school age compared to when they are infants. Among Chinese, childrearing of infants and toddlers consists of immediate gratification of their needs and a great deal of indulgence with almost no demands or expectations. A fairly abrupt shift, however, toward greater harshness or strictness begins when the child reaches the age of 6, or "the age of understanding." Before then, children are not yet considered capable of understanding things, so parents do not hold them responsible for their actions or behaviors. This parental indulgence of young children has also been reported for parents in Japan (Lanham and Gerrick, 1996), Korea (Kim, Kim, and Rue, 1997), all of Southeast Asia (including Vietnam, Cambodia, and Laos, Morrow, 1989), and India (Joshi, and MacLean, 1997; Kakar, 1978). In fact, researchers have argued that Japanese parents are less authoritarian, more lenient, and more permissive of young children's exploratory behaviors than American mothers (Conroy, Hess, Azuma, and Kashiwagi, 1980; Lanham and Garrick, 1996).

Some researchers clarify though that these depictions of total indulgence of young children are not completely accurate among contemporary Asian parents (Ho and Kang, 1984; Seymour, 1999; Wu, 1996). Ho and Kang (1984) and Wu (1996) have found that more recent generations of Chinese parents believe that children are capable of understanding before the traditional distinction of age 6. Ho and Kang attribute this change to increases in education and a concomitant awareness of children's early development and abilities. Wu has argued, in response to concerns among officials in People's Republic of China over "spoiling" of single or only-children, that parents are actually demanding even more of children at younger ages than parents of previous generations. Likewise, in her ethnographic study of families from Bhubaneswar, India, Seymour (1999) argued that indulgence is not the norm. Children are taught very early that their needs do not always come first and that they must submit to the authority of others in order to foster family coherence and harmony.

According to Ho (1986, 1996), parental control of children's impulses around sex and aggression are especially prominent among Chinese. Ho pointed out that regardless of the traditional leniency given to children before age 6, Chinese parents often begin disciplining children as early as $2\frac{1}{2}$ years of age around any displays of aggression or sexual interest. Chinese concerns over aggression are based on their beliefs that quarreling among children would lead to parents being drawn into such conflicts, thereby disrupting family relations and harmony (Wolf, 1970).

This control of children's aggression is not found, however, among Japanese parents. Although Japanese parents also strongly disapprove of aggression among children, they believe that expression of aggression is a natural developmental challenge that young children must experience in order to learn how to handle their emotions and resolve conflicts with others (Osterweil and Nagano-Nakamura, 1992; Tobin, Wu, and Davidson, 1987). These beliefs are very clearly demonstrated in studies of Japanese preschools. Japanese parents and teachers tend to take a very hands-off approach to children's conflicts, even those that involve physical aggression, because they believe that children need to experience and resolve these conflicts on their own (Lanham and Garrick, 1996; Lewis, 1988; Tobin et al., 1987). In contrast to Chinese parents' more authority-driven approach to aggression, Japanese teachers and parents de-emphasize their authority role and appeal more to the social or interpersonal consequences of the child's actions. Although such de-emphasis of parental authority may be apparent with Japanese socialization around aggression, Japanese parents will rely on their authority for socialization around what Clancy (1986) has referred to as "empathy training." Clancy (1986) has found in verbal interactions of Japanese mothers, that even with their 2-year-old children, mothers will often use forceful directives such as statements of obligation and prohibition, instructions, as well as indirect imperatives such as, posing questions to children.

Comparative Research on Parental Control

Other research involving cross-societal or cross-ethnic comparisons with European Americans and Australians has found that Asians and also Asian Americans are more restrictive in their parenting. Chinese in Hong Kong, Taiwan, and the United States are higher on restrictive control and hostility, and lower on encouragement of autonomy than parents of European descent in the United States and Australia (Chiu, 1987; Feldman and Rosenthal, 1990; Feldman and Rosenthal, 1991; Fuligni, 1998; Kelley and Tseng, 1992; Kriger and Kroes, 1972; Law, 1973; Lin and Fu, 1990; Rosenthal and Feldman, 1991; Rosenthal and Feldman, 1992; Stewart, Bond, Deeds, and Chung, 1999). The greater control among Asian parents may be specific to definitions of control as "restrictive."

However, based on observational data of parent–child interactions during a counting game, Jose et al. (2000) have also found that both immigrant Chinese in the U.S. and Taiwanese parents were more directive than European American parents, but that they were equally warm. Using other types of control (i.e., Moos' Family Environment Scales of rule setting and order keeping and a subscale of parental decision making), Chiu, Feldman, and Rosenthal (1992) found that Hong Kong Chinese were lower on all the scales than European Americans and Australians, and first- and second-generation Chinese immigrants in the United States and Australia.

Studies show that other Asian groups also tend to demonstrate higher levels of restrictive control than groups of European descent. Japanese parents were more controlling and likely to report scolding or speaking angrily toward their children than European American and German parents (Trommsdorff, 1985; Winata and Power, 1989). Vietnamese parents in Australia were also more controlling, intrusive, and less encouraging of autonomy than Australians of European descent (Herz and Gullone, 1999). Compared to their European-descent counterparts in the U.S. and Australia, Chinese Americans, Hong Kong Chinese, and Asian Americans overall were also higher on the authoritarian parenting style, which involved high parental control (Chao, 1994; Chao, 2000b; Chao, 2001; Dornbusch, Ritter, Liederman, Roberts, and Fraleigh, 1987; Herz and Gullone, 1999; Leung, Lau, and Lam, 1998; Steinberg, Lamborn, Dornbusch, and Darling, 1992).

Distinctions in Parental Control

Whereas much of the literature on the parental control of Asians and Asian Americans primarily involved cross-societal or cross-ethnic comparisons, other studies have provided examinations within specific Asian groups, focusing on differences (1) between fathers and mothers, (2) between sons and daughters, and (3) across social class or socioeconomic status. Another important goal of some studies has been to examine parental control in its sociocultural context to provide a more culturally based or in-depth understanding of control. This research has primarily involved different methodological approaches. These approaches not only include qualitative and ethnographic research, but also survey-based research that attempts to derive culturally relevant constructs for defining and measuring parental control.

Differences within Asian groups. Parenting differences purported between Asian fathers and mothers have been based on the traditional adage, "strict father, kind mother"—wherein fathers exert high degrees of authoritarian control and mothers manifest high degrees of warmth. The traditional role of fathers as authority figures also implies that fathers do not typically display much closeness and affection toward children. This traditional distinction is mostly supported in research involving East Asians, but not in the research involving different Asian immigrant groups in the United States. In studies of Chinese from the P.R.C., Taiwan, and Hong Kong, mothers in all three countries were more warm and less restrictive than fathers, but they were also more demanding (Berndt, Cheung, Lau, Hau and Lew, 1993; Shek, 1998). Shek (2000) has also found with Hong Kong Chinese that adolescents not only reported less communication with fathers, they also reported more negative communication with fathers. A study of Japanese adolescents found that they perceived their fathers and mothers to be similar on "conformity demands," but that mothers were perceived as being more supportive than fathers (Trommsdorff and Iwawaki, 1989). Studies of Asian immigrants in the United States, though, found that Chinese, Korean, and Vietnamese fathers and mothers were similar in their levels of authoritarian parenting, control, and warmth (Chao and Kim, 2000; Kim, 1996; Nguyen and Williams, 1989).

Though not specific to parental control per se, another question researchers have addressed is whether fathers and mothers each have unique contributions to the child's development. A study conducted by Chen, Dong, and Zhou (1997) of Chinese in Beijing provides some indication that Chinese fathers' parenting styles have effects on child outcomes above and beyond the effects of mothers' parenting styles. In another study of 11- to 12-year-old Chinese children from Shanghai, the P.R.C., Chen, Liu, and Li (2000) found that father's indulgence and sometimes their warmth, above and beyond their control, over two years was associated with different child outcomes (e.g., leadership, social skills, and academic achievement) than mother's parenting. Specifically, mother's warmth, above and beyond her control and indulgence, was positively associated with the child's self-worth and negatively with feelings of loneliness and depression. According to these researchers, the traditional role of the father as the authority figure is to assure that children achieve academically and socially, whereas mothers serve as an emotional support, and so their parenting is likely to affect children's emotional well-being and perceptions of the self. Studies of Asian fathers are especially needed to determine whether fathers today are as strict and harsh as traditional notions imply.

In one of the few studies on Asian fathers, specifically Chinese fathers in P.R.C. (the inner Mongolian region), Jankowiak (1992) found that among the college educated, greater importance is now being given to intimate father–child relations. Newer attitudes are apparent stressing that fathers should demonstrate care and affection toward their children rather than the traditional style of aloofness. Jankowiak attributes much of this change to a new urban infrastructure that includes (1) women working outside the home, (2) smaller domestic space consisting of one-room apartments which place fathers and children in constant close proximity, and (3) new folk notions promoting fatherly involvement. Jankowiak also found that even though mothers are generally more involved in the caretaking of children, fathers are more involved with their children regarding their education once children enter middle school. In another study by Sun and Roopnarine (1996) involving Chinese parents from Taiwan, mothers were more involved in childcare responsibilities of their infants than fathers were, but mothers and fathers were similar in their displays of affection to infants.

Studies examining *gender differences* of the child find that parents exert more control over sons than daughters. Xie's (1998) study of Chinese students (ages 9 through 12) in Beijing assessed the child's and parent's reports of parental control and found that both reported more control for sons than daughters. Similarly, Trommsdorff and Iwawaki (1989) found that Japanese adolescents reported more "negative sanctions" for sons than daughters. Additional studies yield mixed findings when sons' and daughters' reports of their mothers and fathers are compared. Based on adults' retrospective reports of their parents, Berndt et al. (1993) found that Chinese daughters from Hong Kong, P.R.C., and Taiwan perceived their fathers to be less restrictive and more warm than sons did. Similarly, Chen, Liu, and Li (2000) found in their study with 12-year-old Chinese children from Shanghai, the P.R.C., that daughters reported less control from their fathers than sons did. In contrast, Shek (1998) found for Hong Kong Chinese that daughters perceived their mothers to be more demanding but less harsh than did sons, and no differences were found for fathers. Studies of Korean parenting also yield mixed findings. Based on adolescents' reports, Rohner and Pettengill (1985) found that Korean daughters found their fathers to be more restrictive or controlling than sons did, but Rohner, Hahn, and Rohner (1980) found no differences among Korean immigrants in the United States in sons' and daughters' reports of their mothers' and fathers' control.

Studies examining socioeconomic (SES) differences in parental control and even in other areas of parenting for Asians are quite limited. Studies comparing mean levels of parenting indicate a greater restrictiveness among lower SES parents than among higher SES parents (Chauhan, 1980; Li et al., 2000). Chauhan assessed childrearing attitudes of Asian parents and found that low-SES parents emphasized dominance and conformity, but also attitudes of loving the child more than middle- and high-SES parents. Another study by Li et al. of childrearing behaviors of mothers of young children (under age 7) in the region of Yunnan, the P.R.C., found that lower education in mothers was associated with less teaching and playing with children, but more corporal punishment. Finally, studies including Asian Americans seem to indicate some SES differences in mean levels but not in the effects of parenting on child outcomes. A study conducted by Rohner, Hahn, and Rohner (1980) focusing only on differences in mean levels found that among Korean Americans, children from middle-SES families perceive their mothers as less rejecting than children from lower-SES families. A few studies that have specifically examined the effects of parental control and parenting style on child and adolescent outcomes seem to indicate that these effects for Asian Americans are similar across socioeconomic status (Radziszewska, Richardson, Dent, and Flay, 1996; Steinberg, Mounts, Lamborn, and Dornbusch, 1991).

Different types of parental control and their meanings. Some studies have examined distinctions in the types of control used among specific Asian groups based on more indigenous notions of control. These indigenous notions reflect different meanings for parental control than the meanings implied by "restrictive" or "domineering." Researchers have also found that control may have different meanings for parents of Asian and European descent, such that parental control may be associated with warmth and caring in Asian families.

Fung (1999) described a range of control and discipline techniques that she labeled as "shaming" in her recent ethnographic study of parents of preschool-age children. Different Asian societies, including Taiwan, were described as "shame cultures," in that children from these cultures were "taught to be aware of what others think of them" (p. 181). Parental socialization of shame in children involved explicit techniques such as using gestures and labels of shame (e.g., "shame on you"), and implicit techniques such as reminding the child that other people were watching or seeing them, and comparing the child to other well-behaved children. Parents' own descriptions of how they disciplined children involved what Fung labeled "opportunity education." Parents would use specific events in children's direct experiences, such as pointing out another misbehaving child and explaining why such behavior is not allowed. Parents in Taiwan believe that children should be introduced earlier to notions of shame than do parents in the United States, and their children acquire shame-related terms earlier than do U.S. children. Fung (1999) and other researchers (Miller, Fung, and Mintz, 1996; Miller, Wiley, Fung, and Liang, 1997) also described how Chinese parents often used personal storytelling, in which a past event involving the child was invoked in order to convey the transgression the child committed and to shame them.

Another indigenous notion of parental control for Chinese has been described by Chao (1994) as *guan*, which, when translated, literally means "to govern." *Guan* also has a very positive connotation among Chinese, because it can mean "to care for" or "to love" as well as "to govern." Therefore, parental care, concern, and involvement are synonymous with a firm control and governance of the child. Chao (2000a) has described the control practices of Chinese parents as a more "preventative" approach to child misbehavior. These preventative approaches have been richly described by Tobin et al. (1987) in their study of preschools in the P.R.C., Japan, and the United States. Teachers in China would continuously monitor and correct children's behaviors by appraising whether children were meeting the teacher's expectations or standards, by comparing children to each other on these appraisals and making very clear what they expected from the child. Control and governance of children were also regarded as the role responsibilities or requirements of parents as well as teachers. Without *guan*, parents would be viewed as negligent and uncaring. Based on this notion of control, or *guan*, Chao (1994) derived and tested an alternative conceptualization for the parenting style of immigrant Chinese that she labeled as *chiao shun*, or "training." She demonstrated that even after controlling for mothers' levels of authoritarian and authoritative parenting, styles originally derived by Baurmind (1971), training was still more important or endorsed more by Chinese mothers than European American mothers. This study provides some support for the argument that parental control may have different meanings for Asians and Asian Americans, specifically Chinese immigrants, than it does for Europeans and European Americans.

There are also studies that have provided empirical support for the different meanings of parental control among Asians by demonstrating positive associations between dimensions of parental control and warmth. These associations reflect the positive connotations that Asian parents have for control that are not found among European-descent parents. For example, Nomura, Noguchi, Saito, and Tezuka (1995) found that parents' ratings of family cohesion or closeness were positively correlated with their control among Japanese, but negatively correlated among Americans. These positive connotations for control and governance should also be reflected in children's perceptions of their parents' control—that is, how children interpret such control. If Asian children feel or perceive that parents' control and governance reflect their care and concern, then this provides additional evidence of the differential, positive meaning of control for Asians.

Indeed, there appears to be support for the positive interpretation of parental control among Asian adolescents. Stewart et al. (1998) conducted a study of Hong Kong Chinese in late adolescence in which they derived a measure for assessing *guan*. They also included a measure of control that combined aspects of strictness (e.g., "My parent is strict" and "... is restrictive") with aspects of hostility (e.g., "I am afraid of my parent" and "My parent becomes angry"). Interestingly, they found that *guan* was strongly and positively associated with warmth. They also found that *guan* was only weakly associated with restrictive or hostile control. Thus, the concept of *guan* may overlap somewhat with restrictive control, but it is also distinct from restriction or domination of children per se. Additionally, *guan* appears to have positive connotations for Chinese adolescents, as it was positively associated with their perceptions of parental warmth.

Studies that have assessed control in terms of the degree to which parents place demands on children and attempt to direct their behaviors have also found similar positive associations with warmth among Asian adolescents. In North America and Germany, parental control was found to be associated with perceived parental hostility and rejection (Rohner and Rohner, 1978; Trommsdorff, 1985; Trommsdorff and Iwawki, 1989), but in Japan and Korea the same behaviors of parental control were associated with perceived parental warmth and acceptance (Kornadt, 1987; Rohner and Pettengill, 1985; Trommsdorff and Iwawki, 1989). Trommsdorff (1985, p. 238), in fact, stressed that "Japanese adolescents even feel *rejected* by their parents when they experience only little control and a broader range of autonomy." These studies provide support for the culturally based arguments that Asian children seem to perceive their parents' control as very positive, important, and necessary.

However, Lau and Cheung (1987) and Lau, Lew, Hau, Cheung, and Berndt (1990) argue that a more domineering or restrictive control may have negative associations with parental warmth among Asians as it does among Europeans and European Americans. In a study of Chinese from Beijing, Lau et al. (1990) derived their own measure of "domineering control" (i.e., the degree to which parents restricted children's autonomy, were strict, kept them in awe, and were angry with them). Their measure of control appears to combine aspects of control, such as strictness, with aspects of harshness or hostility. They primarily found that both sons and daughters who perceived their mothers and fathers as more domineering also perceived them as less warm. This domineering control was also negatively associated with family harmony by both sons and daughters. In another study of parents in Hong Kong, Lau and Cheung (1987) distinguished what they labeled "family-based" control from a domineering control based on the functions that each type served, or in other words, the purpose of control. If the function of domineering control is to dominate and subjugate children, the function of the family-based control is to maintain the harmony and integrity of the family unit. Based on Moos' Family Environment Scale (FES), they found that the "organizational control" subscale, assessing their notion of "family-based" control, was positively correlated with warmth, whereas the "domineering control" subscale was negatively associated with warmth. Thus, for Chinese and perhaps for other Asian groups, control may be perceived very positively by both children and parents unless it includes aspects of harshness or hostility.

Examination of the effects of parental control on child and adolescent outcomes may provide another window onto the cultural meaning of parental control. For Asians, do different types of control have different consequences in that more indigenous notions of control have positive effects on child outcomes, whereas, as Lau and Cheung (1987) have argued, more domineering or restrictive types of control do not? Are there different consequences for the parental control of groups of Asian descent versus those of European descent?

Effects of Parental Control

With regards to the first question, the effects of control on child well-being for Asians appear to depend on the way control is defined such that indigenous notions have positive effects and a domineering control primarily has negative effects among groups of Asian and European descent. Most of this research though has focused on either Asian Americans in general, or specifically on Chinese in the United States, Hong Kong, and the P.R.C., and has relied heavily on correlational analyses without examining effects over time using longitudinal studies.

Parental control defined as domineering or overprotective was generally associated with negative outcomes for children of Asian and European descent. Herz and Gullone (1999) found that control (defined as "overprotection") was negatively associated with adolescents' self-esteem for both adolescents of Vietnamese and European descent in Australia. The magnitude of these associations also did not differ across the two groups. Similarly, Cheung and Lau (1985) found that Hong Kong Chinese adolescents with parents high on Moos's domineering control were also low on self-esteem. Stewart et al.'s (1998) study of young Chinese women (nursing students) in Hong Kong also demonstrated that their mother's restrictive control was negatively associated with adolescent's self-esteem, relationship harmony, and perceived health, but not with their life satisfaction, and their father's restrictive control was unrelated to these adolescent outcomes. In another study by Stewart, Bond, Zaman, McBride-Chang, Rao, Ho, and Fielding (1999) of young Pakistani women (also nursing students), domineering control was negatively associated with perceived health, life satisfaction, and relationship harmony.

In contrast, parental control defined more indigenously for Asians has been associated with positive child outcomes. In their study of Hong Kong Chinese, Stewart et al. (1998) found that control defined as *guan* was positively associated with adolescents' health and life satisfaction, and except for the outcome of health, was found for both mothers and fathers. Stewart, Bond, Zaman, McBridge-Chang, Rao, Ho, and Fielding (1999) also found with Pakistani young women that Chao's (1994) "training" parenting style, which is based on the notion of *guan*, was positively associated with relationship harmony. This positive effect was found even after accounting for the effects of parental warmth and domineering control. Based on factor analyses in which their items for warmth loaded positively on the same factor with the training items, they also found that this combined warmth–training dimension was positively related to all four of their outcomes, specified previously. Zhengyuan et al. (1991) found that control defined as parental emphasis on child compliance was positively associated with traditionally desired characteristics such as self-control, tolerance of frustration, and being hardworking, in addition to independence, self-confidence, and positive attitudes toward others. More research is needed to examine the effects of different types or definitions of parental control for different Asian groups. The effects of parenting style though have been examined somewhat more extensively among Asians in the United States.

Research on parenting style

Studies examining the effects of parenting style on children's development provide further evidence for the cultural arguments made above by examining the composite effects of parental control and warmth. Parenting style may actually have different effects for Asians or Asian Americans than it does for Europeans or European Americans. This could be demonstrated in two ways. First, based on within-group examinations, the pattern of associations between control and child outcomes for some Asian groups may be somewhat different from the associations found for groups of European descent.

Likewise, examinations across groups in the magnitude of associations found between control and child outcomes may indicate that some types of control have more positive effects for Asians than for their counterparts of European descent.

Much of the research on parenting style has been based on Baumrind's (1971) original conceptualizations involving initially three typologies—authoritative, authoritarian, and permissive. These typologies were primarily based on assessments of parents' control or demandingness and warmth or responsiveness, with a third dimension recognized as involving reasoning or democratic give-and-take with the child. Authoritative parents are described by high levels of demandingness, responsiveness, and democratic reasoning; whereas authoritarian parents are described by high levels of control but low levels of warmth or responsiveness and democratic reasoning. Chao (1994) has demonstrated that these parenting style typologies may not be culturally relevant or meaningful to Asians and Asian Americans due to the different meanings they ascribe to parental control and warmth. That is, there are qualitative distinctions in how both these dimensions are defined or conceptualized and measured for Asians. Often measures of parental control or demandingness involve a restrictiveness or domination of the child that does not capture the essential features of parental control for Asians, described above. Likewise, measures of warmth or responsiveness typically include an emotional and physical "demonstrativeness" (e.g., praising the child, and hugging and kissing the child, respectively) that does not capture the primary features of responsiveness for Asian parents. The responsiveness of Asian parents can be more accurately described as involvement and support, through their prioritizing of the caregiving and education of their children. These distinctions in both the dimensions of control and warmth were then incorporated in an alternative parenting style for Chinese training, previously discussed.

In examinations of the effects of parenting style on child outcomes, consistent results across studies have not been found for Asian Americans as they have for European Americans. For European Americans, researchers have consistently found that the authoritative style has positive effects on child well-being, whereas the authoritarian style has negative effects (Dornbusch et al., 1987; Lamborn, Dornbusch, and Steinberg, 1996; Steinberg, Lamborn, Darling, Mounts, and Dornbusch, 1994). For Asian Americans, however, the authoritative style was unrelated to adolescent's school performance, whereas the authoritarian style was negatively related (Dornbusch et al., 1987). Steinberg et al. (1994) though found that, in tests across ethnic groups, the effects of authoritarian parenting were less negative and the effects of authoritative less positive among Asian Americans than European Americans.

Studies conducted on Asians in the United States have attempted to examine specific subgroup distinctions involving ethnicity and generational status. In a study of immigrant Chinese parents in the United States, Chao (2001) and Chao and Tran (2001) used Steinberg et al.'s measures of parenting style. Among first- and second-generation Chinese adolescents, parenting style (authoritative relative to authoritarian) was not predictive of their school grades, but was predictive of the grades of European Americans. That is, for European Americans only, authoritative parenting predicted higher school grades than did authoritarian parenting. Also, the effects of authoritative parenting on school effort were significant and positive for European Americans and second-generation Chinese, but not for first-generation Chinese. Thus, first-generation Chinese adolescents from authoritative homes were not better off in school than those from authoritarian homes. The effects for second-generation Chinese primarily ranked between those of first-generation Chinese and those of European Americans, indicating that they may be more similar to European Americans than first-generation Chinese are. This is consistent with a cultural explanation, because first-generation immigrants have had more exposure to Chinese society and culture than second-generation immigrants who have spent all their lives in the United States. In testing for differences in these effects across the groups, the effects of authoritative parenting (relative to authoritarian) on school grades and effort were also more positive for European Americans than for both first- and second-generation Chinese.

In examining the effects of parenting style another way, Chao and Tran (2001) broke down the parenting style typologies into their separate dimensions of parental control and warmth in order to examine their interactive effects. Consistent with the above findings, the influence of control depended on warmth for European Americans but not Chinese Americans. Specifically, for European Americans, parental control had increasingly more positive effects on school grades and school effort at higher levels of parental warmth. This interaction was not found for both first- and second-generation Chinese immigrants. These interactive effects were also more pronounced among European Americans than first generation Chinese, providing further evidence for cultural arguments that the meaning of parenting may differ for Chinese immigrants. Another study on Korean immigrants in the United States also found that parenting style was unrelated to adolescents' school performance (Kim, 1996).

Studies of Chinese in Hong Kong have found either no effects for parenting style, or the effects that were found were in the opposite direction as those found for European American adolescents. Using the same measure of parenting style by Dornbusch et al. (1987), Leung et al. (1998) found that the authoritative style was unrelated to the grades of Hong Kong Chinese but positively related to the grades of Americans and Australians of European descent. More surprisingly, the authoritarian style was positively related to the grades of Chinese adolescents and was unrelated to the grades of European Americans. Using parents' reports of their parenting, McBride-Chang and Chang (1998) found that both the authoritative and authoritarian styles were unrelated to adolescents' achievement test scores. Surprisingly, they also found parents who were more authoritative were less encouraging of their adolescent's autonomy. Thus, even with outcomes other than school performance, the effects of parenting style for Chinese are not consistent with what has been found for European Americans.

In contrast to these studies of Hong Kong Chinese, Chen et al. (1997) found that the authoritative style of both mothers and fathers was positively related to children's school achievement and social competence, and the authoritarian style of both parents was negatively related to these outcomes. However, this study involved much younger children (6 and 7 years old) than the studies conducted in Hong Kong, which may account for the different findings. The different findings between these studies may also be due to geographical distinctions in parenting style. Studies have found that parents from Hong Kong were more authoritarian and controlling than those from Beijing and Taiwan (Berndt et al., 1993; Lai, Zhang, and Wang; 2000). Further studies must be conducted to determine whether there are differences in the effects of parenting style among Chinese from large urban regions in the P.R.C., Hong Kong, and Taiwan.

In summary, Asian parents have been found to be relatively more restrictive in their parenting compared to parents from other societies or ethnic groups. Parental control though may not have the same meanings or the same negative effects on children's development for parents of Asian descent as it does for parents of European descent. Although restrictive control appears to have negative effects for Asians, parenting style, specifically authoritarian parenting, does not always have negative effects, and in some studies the effects are actually positive. These findings provide additional demonstration that there are important cultural distinctions in the meaning of parental control for Asians. Another concern, though, of Asian parenting involves their emphasis on educational achievement, which also has important cultural distinctions.

EDUCATIONAL ACHIEVEMENT IN ASIANS

One the more prevalent impressions held by the media, the larger public, and researchers has been Asian educational achievement. In the United States, this picture of school success has served to promote stereotypic views of Asian Americans as the "model minority." As a group, Asian Americans do indeed have higher grades during mid to late elementary school (Okagaki and Frensch, 1998), grade point averages in middle school, high school, and college (Fuligni, 1997; Hao and Bonstead-Bruns, 1998; Kao, 1995; Sue and Abe, 1988), higher scores on the Scholastic Aptitude Test (SAT, Reglin and Adams, 1990; Sue and Abe, 1998), and higher scores on other standardized achievement tests (Kao, 1995; Mau, 1997; Peng and Wright, 1994). In addition, higher rates of completion of high school and enrollment in college have also been reported for Asian Americans compared to all ethnic groups, including European Americans (O'Hare and Felt, 1991; Suzuki, 1988). Cheung (1982) reported that although Asian students had parents with less education and family income than European Americans students, they had higher grade point averages in college and completed more years of schooling. However, great disparities have been reported in achievement across different ethnic subgroups with Chinese, Japanese, Koreans, and South Asians performing better than Southeast Asians, Filipinos, and Pacific Islanders (Bradby and Owings, 1992; Kao, 1995; Olsen, 1988; Wong, 1990). Studies have also found that Asian Americans apply more effort to their schoolwork and spend more time in activities such as private tutoring, after-school study groups, and music and language lessons, which may enhance their education (Chen and Stevenson, 1995; Huang and Waxman, 1995; Kao, 1995; Peng and Wright, 1994; Yao, 1985). They also spend less time on activities that may compete with their studies, such as holding a part-time job and performing household chores, and are less involved in dating (Chen and Stevenson, 1995; Kao, 1995; Lee, 1994, 1996; Reglin and Adams, 1990). When students' time use, attitudes and values for education, and educational aspirations are accounted for, differences in the academic performance of Asian American and European American students are no longer apparent (Chen and Stevenson, 1995; Kao, 1995).

International comparisons of academic achievement have also revealed the school success of students in Asia. Stevenson and Lee (1990) compared students from Taipei (Taiwan) and Sendai (Japan) with American students in the United States (in Minneapolis, Minnesota) on tests of reading, vocabulary, comprehension, and math. They have shown that Chinese children obtained the highest scores on all sections of the reading test at Grade 1 and on the vocabulary and comprehension sections at Grade 5. In mathematics, the Chinese and Japanese both scored higher than the Americans on word problems involving application of mathematical principles and on items requiring only calculation. Stevenson and Lee (1990) also reported that these students spent more time studying and engaging in educationally related activities than students in the United States.

Regardless of the conclusions drawn by the media or by researchers regarding the educational success of Asians, one thing that is rather clear is parental concern in many Asian societies over children's educational achievement. Children's schooling is regarded as the primary responsibility of Asian parents. In fact, for many Asians, their efficacy in parenting is judged by how well their children do in school (Chao, 1995, 1996; Tu, 1985; Wu and Tseng, 1985). Tu has emphasized that a successful Confucian father is defined by the scholarly achievements and cultural attainments of his family. The importance placed on educational achievement for Asian parents is reflected in broader cultural folk beliefs and attitudes about child development and learning, in their educational expectations and aspirations, and in their involvement in their children's schooling.

Cultural Folk Beliefs and Attitudes

Folk beliefs regarding child development and learning. Cultural folk beliefs of children's development and learning have shaped how parents regard children's schooling and education. Notions about how children learn and the timing of children's learning are based on "cultivation" perspectives discussed above (see section on historical perspectives), which are espoused throughout many parts of Asia, particularly East Asia (Chen, 1996; Kojima, 1986). This perspective places a great deal of importance on the parental role. The education of children is analogous to the cultivation of a tree that first begins with the seedling and necessitates the grower's care in the trimming of its branches and leaves as the tree grows. In order to keep the child on the morally right course, early educational intervention is regarded as essential. However, as Kojima (1986) clarifies, early does not mean earliest, but rather when children are ready.

Li (1997, in press) also examined historical and contemporary cultural notions of learning for Chinese that are very similar to "cultivation" perspective discussed above. As Li explained, folk notions of learning date back several thousand years to Confucian philosophies emphasizing human malleability and self-improvement as a moral purpose. Li also clarified that the goals of learning are not only to seek inner self-cultivation and virtue (*neisheng*), but also to give back this learning to society in the form of "meritorious service" (*waiwang*).

Li (in press) conducted a study of Chinese college seniors from the eastern region of the P.R.C. in which they performed a sorting task for common learning terms. Based on cluster analyses for determining students' categorizations, Li found two superordinate-level categories, "desirable approaches" and "undesirable approaches." Many more words were generated for the desirable than the undesirable, indicating that, for educated Chinese, a heavier emphasis is placed on positive than negative models of learning. The most strongly emphasized category under desirable approaches involved "seeking knowledge," the idea that learners should assume primary responsibility for their own learning. This category included the Chinese notion of *hao-xue-xin*, literally translated as "heart and mind for wanting to learn." Li explains that this notion is a common folk term used to describe one's desire to learn, or a passion for learning, which is somewhat distinct from the term *achievement motivation*, used in the United States. Also under the category of "seeking knowledge" was the idea of learning as a "life-long pursuit," and a combination of related ideas involving diligence, hardship, steadfastness, and single-minded concentration. Jose et al. (2000) have also found with parents of preschool children that personality traits such as persistence, neatness, concentration, and precision were also endorsed more by both Chinese immigrants in the U.S. and Chinese in Taiwan than European American parents.

These cultural notions of cultivation and learning among Asians emphasize education both broadly defined as well as specific to schooling. Cultivation through schooling is still regarded as the primary avenue for social mobility. However, it is also important for "building character," or qualities such as being hardworking, self-disciplined, persevering, and moral. Many of the cultural beliefs and views about children's development and learning espoused throughout parts of Asia are distinctly linked to views about education and the importance of children's schooling.

Cultural and parental attitudes regarding the importance of effort. Researchers have examined parental and cultural attitudes regarding the importance of effort in school. As Li (in press) explained, Confucian philosophies have stressed the importance of human malleability and values for self-improvement with effort being the route to self-improvement. There are also a number of folk tales reiterating the importance of effort in attaining educational achievement (Hess, Chih-Mei, and McDevitt, 1987; Li, 2000a).

Hess, Chih-Mei, and McDevitt (1987) conducted a study on parents' causal explanations of their children's performance in math among Chinese parents from the P.R.C. and parents of Chinese and European descent from the United States. They found that all three groups put more weight on effort than on other causes (i.e., ability, school training, home training, and luck). For the P.R.C. parents, however, lack of effort was the predominant cause of low performance, and relatively little weight was attributed to the other causes. The Chinese American parents were similar to the P.R.C. parents, but gave slightly less weight to effort and more to lack of natural ability and poor school and home training than the P.R.C. parents. European American parents placed more equal weight on all five causes than did the Chinese groups. Research on Asian Americans, Chinese from Taiwan, and Japanese have also found that parents' beliefs in the importance of effort are associated with their children's beliefs in effort and academic achievement (Chen and Stevenson, 1995; Huang, 1997).

Parental Expectations and Aspirations for Education

Asian parents also have very high expectations and aspirations for their children's education. Asian Americans, compared to other groups, including European Americans, tend to have higher parental expectations for educational attainment, the school grades they consider acceptable, and the amount of effort or work they believe their children can accomplish (Chao, 1996; Chen and Stevenson, 1995; Fuligni, 1997; Hao and Bonsted-Bruns, 1998; Kao, 1995; Lee, 1987; Okagaki and Frensch, 1998; Yao, 1985). Furthermore, studies across a range of Asian American ethnic subgroups have found that parental expectations explain a large portion of children's high educational expectations, even more so than socioeconomic and other demographic factors (Goyette and Xie, 1999; Kim, Rendon, and Valdez, 1998; Lee, 1987).

Asian American parents also value education more for their children's future than do parents of other ethnic groups (Chao, 1996; Chen and Stevenson, 1995; Steinberg, Dornbusch, and Brown, 1992; Yao, 1985). In a study by Steinberg, Dornbusch, and Brown (1992) involving high school students from Asian American, African American, Hispanic American, and European American backgrounds, all students reported that their parents believed in the value of education for their future success. However, Asian American parents, more than any other ethnic group, also believed in the negative repercussions of not getting a good education—the idea that one could not be successful without a good education.

Important differences across ethnic subgroups of Asian Americans have also been found. A study by Fuligni (1997) compared adolescents of East Asian (i.e., Chinese, Japanese, and Koreans), Filipino, Latino, and European backgrounds on different measures of parental educational expectations. East Asian and Filipino parents had similar values for academic success (e.g., doing well in school by getting "A" grades) and educational aspirations (i.e., educational attainment level), but on another indicator of parental expectations (e.g., disappointment over not getting high grades on tests), East Asian parents were higher than Filipino parents. Other studies based on the National Educational Longitudinal data have found differing results, depending on the ethnic and immigrant groups that were included (Blair and Qian, 1998; Fuligni, 1997; Hao and Bonstead-Bruns, 1998; Kao, 1995; Kim, Rendon, and Valdez, 1998). Specifically, when aggregated across generations of immigrants, Kim and colleagues found that Asian Indians, and Blair and Q-ia-n found that Chinese, had the highest expectations (although the latter study did not include Asian Indians). Among recent generations of immigrants, Hao and Bonstead-Bruns (1998) found that Koreans had the highest levels of parental expectations across all ethnic subgroups.

Despite differences in mean levels of parental expectations across ethnic subgroups of Asian Americans, their effects on children's academic achievement appear to be positive for all groups. For Asian Americans, overall, parental expectations for educational attainment were positively associated with the academic achievement of students in elementary school and middle school (Okagaki and Frensch, 1998; Peng and Wright, 1994). For different ethnic subgroups (i.e., Chinese and Filipinos) Blair and Qian (1998) found parental expectations for educational attainment had positive effects on the educational performance of high school students even after accounting for other socioeconomic and parenting factors. Finally, Mau (1997) found positive effects for both U.S.-born and immigrant Asians, even after controlling for socioeconomic status, parental involvement in school, and students' effort. The findings though for parental involvement in school are not quite as consistent as they are for parental expectations.

Parental Involvement in School

The findings for both differences in mean levels and effects of parental involvement in school are not consistent for Asian Americans, largely because of differences due to the age of the child and the type of parental involvement studied. In a summary of the literature, Keith et al. (1993) identified four general types of parental involvement: (1) parents' expectations for children's school achievement (previously discussed), (2) participation in school activities and programs (e.g., involvement in PTA), (3) discussions between parents and children about school, and (4) a home structure that supports learning (e.g., family rules about homework). Epstein (1987) has also reported types of parental support that include the above as well as providing children with practice activities and an enriching environment (e.g., reading to the child, visiting the library, and exposing children to parents' own educational activities).

Descriptive studies. More descriptive or ethnographic studies have found that Asian American parents provide types of support for children's schooling and education that may not be tapped in typical assessments of parental involvement. These include teaching basic school-readiness skills before children entered school, assigning extra homework during their early elementary school years, purchasing extra workbooks or textbooks, arranging for a desk or study area, enrolling children in academically related activities such as private tutoring, supplementary study classes, music and language lessons, saving money for children's college education, and structuring and monitoring children's after-school time (Chao, 1996; Hieshima and Schneider, 1994; Mordkowitz and Ginsburg, 1987; Schneider and Lee, 1990; Shoho, 1994; Yao, 1985). Many of these studies, though, relied on parents' or college-age students' retrospective reports of parental involvement when they or their children were much younger.

Surprisingly though, as Leong, Chao, and Hardin (2000) have pointed out, Asian Americans are less likely to be involved in their children's later schooling than European Americans, especially by the time their children are in high school. For instance, Rosenthal and Feldman compared first- and second-generation Chinese immigrants from the United States and Australia and groups of European descent from both countries, and found that first-generation Chinese reported less parental involvement than second-generation Chinese and adolescents of European descent, and second-generation Chinese reported less than both groups of European descent. In another study involving comparisons of Asian American, Hispanic, African American, and European American adolescents, Steinberg, Dornbusch, and Brown (1992) found that Asian American parents were the least involved in their adolescents' schooling. However, these findings may be due to how parental involvement was assessed, as well as to the child's age. In both studies, assessment of parental involvement involved a global scale that included helping children with homework, participating in school programs and sports activities, and discussing school courses.

Clarifications of findings due to child's age and types of involvement. These types of involvement reflect a more hands-on or direct participation in the child's schooling that may not be as salient for Asian American parents with their older children. Rather, some types of direct support may be more salient for Asian parents during children's early elementary or preschool years as opposed to later high school years. Indeed, studies have shown that East Asian parents exert a more intensive educational socialization during the child's early school years, with this socialization decreasing as children become older (Chao, 1996; Choi, Bempechat, and Ginsburg, 1994; Shoho, 1994). For example, Huntsinger and her colleagues (1997, 1998, 2000) found that Chinese American parents, and to a lesser degree Chinese parents from Taiwan, were more likely than their European American counterparts to teach their 4- to 5-year-old children mathematics and reading. They did so by employing focused, directed methods such as vocabulary flashcards, extra homework, and math programs rather than informal, play-oriented methods such as spontaneously bringing up math or reading in everyday experiences. Furthermore, the focused or formal teaching method predicted higher levels of achievement during these early elementary school years. In light of the argument put forth by many early childhood educators, that teaching academics to young children is dangerous to their social development, Huntsinger, Jose, and Larson (1998) also examined whether parents' formal teaching methods are related to later problems in children's social adjustment, and no effects were found. Thus, in the child's early years, Asian American parents are providing much more formal and direct types of support.

At later years, Asian American parents may be offering a range of indirect types of support. In four studies involving eighth-grade students from the National Educational Longitudinal Survey from 1988 (NELS: 88), a variety of aspects of parental involvement in school was assessed. Asian Americans generally scored lower than European Americans on some measures of parental involvement, including discussions about school, helping with homework, and participating in school, whereas they scored higher than European Americans on helping prepare for ACT and SAT tests, planning for college, and providing a home structure and resources such as a place to study, a personal computer, and savings for college (Ho and Willms, 1996; Kao, 1995; Mau, 1997; Peng and Wright, 1994). Thus, by the time their children reach middle school, Asian American parents are not providing direct support for children's homework nor are they participating in school. Instead, they are already beginning to prepare for the child's eventual entrance to college as they continue to provide structure in the home. This pattern of change in the parental involvement of Asian Americans as their children reach high school may explain some of the negative effects found for parental involvement on school achievement that are described next.

Examinations of the effects of parental involvement in school.   Several studies examining the effects of parental involvement in school on child and adolescent school achievement also suggest that these effects vary according to how parental involvement is defined. Even with elementary school children, Okagaki and Frensch (1998) found that Epstein's distinction of an "educationally enriching environment" (e.g., parents and children reading nonschool material) was unrelated to the school grades of Asian Americans, but helping with homework was negatively related. With adolescents, studies using the NELS: 88 data have found a lack of association and some negative associations for Asian Americans. Kao (1995) found that discussions about school, providing educational resources in the home, and enrolling adolescents in outside classes were unrelated to the school performance of Asian Americans but were positively related to the school performance of European Americans. Peng and Wright (1994) reported similar findings, except that for European Americans helping with homework was negatively related to adolescents' school achievement. Mau (1997), however, found that for Asian Americans helping with schoolwork and participating in school were negatively related to adolescents' school performance, whereas discussions about school were unrelated. For European Americans, primarily positive associations were found. Additionally, Mau found differences across generations of Asian immigrants such that the effects of parental involvement on school performance were more negative for U.S.-born adolescents than for foreign-born adolescents. In examining the effects of parental involvement for different ethnic subgroups, studies have found that parents' provision of educational material in the home (i.e., an encyclopedia and atlas, a dictionary, typewriter, computer, calculator, and many books) had positive effects on adolescents' school performance for both Chinese Americans and Filipino Americans (Blair and Qian, 1998; Kim, Rendon, and Valadez, 1998).

The negative associations found among some Asian American groups underscore the necessity for longitudinal studies that account for prior school performance. Longitudinal studies are needed to determine whether parental involvement is influenced by adolescents' prior school performance. That is, by the time their children are in high school, some Asian American parents may only become involved with their children's schooling when they are experiencing difficulties. However, a study by Steinberg, Lamborn, Dornbusch, and Darling (1992) found that even after accounting for adolescents' prior school performance, parental involvement had no effect on the school performance of Asian Americans, although for the overall sample it had a positive effect. As mentioned above though, their assessment of parental involvement relied on a global scale. Longitudinal studies are still needed that examine different aspects of parental involvement in school across different ethnic subgroups and generations of Asian immigrants.

FUTURE DIRECTIONS FOR RESEARCH
ON THE PARENTING OF ASIANS

Research on Asian parenting has increased dramatically in the past two decades, but much research is still needed. In particular, the emphasis on identifying and assessing indigenous cultural notions of parenting, such as the research on parental control, involving Fung's (1999) descriptions of "shaming" and the notion of *guan*, represent substantial steps forward in conceptualizing Asian parenting. Studies must attempt to derive measures for such indigenous concepts because they shed light on important aspects of parenting that may not have been captured in studies relying on parenting constructs typically used with samples involving those of European descent. Indigenous concepts of Asian parenting allow us to understand the limitations and complexities of our typical constructs and measures of parenting as applied to Asians as well as to families of European descent. What may be most critical in understanding the parenting of different Asian groups is to determine how different assessments of a particular domain of parenting affect child well-being. Studying the effects of parenting on child outcomes, especially how the effects vary across time, can inform us about the consequences of such cultural differences in parenting for children. The research on Asian American parental involvement in school seems to indicate that whereas there appear to be negative effects for parental involvement, these effects depend on the type of involvement and the age of the child, in addition to the longitudinal association between these variables. Direct types of parental involvement among Asian Americans seem to have negative effects on adolescents' school performance. However, these negative effects may disappear once preexisting levels of school performance are accounted for. Such a longitudinal study would provide support for arguments that Asian American parents are not directly involved with the schooling of their older children, and they only become involved with their schooling if they are having difficulties. In addition, research has predominantly involved East Asians, and further research is needed on the parenting of South and Southeast Asians.

Descriptive studies on cultural differences in parenting overwhelmingly demonstrate the importance of family and family interdependence within Asian families. In extending research beyond descriptive differences in independence and interdependence across nations in the Eastern and Western hemispheres, further research is needed to examine the bases underlying these differences. For example, research has rarely explored the sociohistorical or ecological roots for the strong abiding theme of interdependence across Asian societies, despite their vast differences in religion, language, geography, climate, and economic conditions. What role does family interdependence serve? Are there sociohistorical or ecological similarities for which parents are preparing their children to meet? While discussing the similarities in family interdependence across Asian societies, we have tried to describe the different cultural roots for the particular expression or manifestation of interdependence. These subgroup differences require further study into why different Asian societies would develop somewhat dissimilar views on parenting.

Research on changes in parenting due to urbanization and migration are interesting because they begin to tap into some of the ways in which ecological changes can affect the parenting of Asians from different regions in Asia and of immigrants from these regions. Further research, however, needs to systematically assess the particular elements of ecological or acculturative change that affect parenting themes, styles, and practices. For example, does the emphasis placed on education erode across successive generations of Asians in the United States? If so, are those declines due simply to cross-cultural contact of values or do later generations of Asians simply find additional, noneducational avenues to mobility in the United States?

CONCLUSIONS

Although the parenting of Asians is extremely diverse, there are also important commonalities or overarching themes that can be identified for describing their parental concerns or goals. Even with important forces of change, there may be some degree of continuity in parenting among some Asian groups or societies, with Japan provided as one example. While Japan has experienced impressive economic growth and demographic transformations, many traditional Confucian and Buddhist perspectives of childhood and the parenting role have been infused into contemporary Japanese parenting, resulting in some continuity across time and across generations of Japanese parents. Likewise, such broad themes as the importance of the family and family interdependence can be identified across many Asian subgroups or societies. However, different notions or ideas of the importance of the family for East Asians, Asian Indians, and Filipinos have been described in this chapter. These different notions of the family can be more fully understood in terms of the sociocultural roots or principles underlying the family and family relations—the precepts of filial piety in East Asian societies, principles of *Mitakshara* specifying joint household structure in some Hindi societies in

India, and notions of *pakikisama*, stressing family harmony over personal desires or needs among some Filipino societies. Each set of principles prescribes its own structure for how family roles are defined, even though each also incorporates the importance of reciprocity among family members and parental authority and respect. Another broad commonality that can be identified as a concern of Asian parents is their control or use of control, although perhaps this theme may be more salient to the eyes of many Americans, especially European Americans, than it is to Asians in Asia and the United States.

According to some researchers, parental control seems to be very limited or nonexistent with very young children, before they reach the "age of reasoning," especially among Japanese. However, among more current generations of Asian parents, especially those that are well educated, parental expectations of children at earlier ages appear to be increasing. Perhaps also, comparative studies, as opposed to within-culture studies, have contributed to the impression that parents of Asian descent are quite controlling relative to parents of European descent. On the other hand, within-culture or within-group studies of Asians have attempted to examine traditional distinctions between fathers and mothers or between daughter's and son's perceptions of parenting, and to a very limited degree, distinctions across social class. Many within-culture studies have also attempted to provide a more in-depth understanding of parental control by relying on more indigenous notions of control. What may be summarized from this research is that different definitions or notions of control seem to have different associations with child and adolescent outcomes. Whereas restrictive or domineering distinctions of control, especially when incorporated with hostility and rejection, have primarily negative effects on Asian children's well-being, control defined in terms of guidance and structure, and also in terms of indigenous notions such as *guan*, have positive effects on Asian children's well-being.

In addition, an important cultural argument for the different meanings of control between families of Asian descent and European descent has also been demonstrated by examining whether the effects of control on child and adolescent outcomes differ across these groups. Indeed, there is some evidence, especially in studies focusing on parenting style (involving combinations of control and warmth), that the effects do differ. For example, in studies conducted on Chinese in the United States and Hong Kong, the beneficial effects for authoritative parenting do not seem to be found among families of Chinese descent, but they are found among families of European descent. Additionally, in a study of Hong Kong Chinese, it was the authoritarian style that had beneficial effects on adolescents' school performance. Such different patterns in the effects of parenting style found among families of Asian-descent, as compared to families of European descent, seem to indicate that applying these parenting style typologies to Asian families may be problematic. These typologies may not be capturing the types of control and warmth that are used and endorsed by these families.

Another area that has certainly drawn a great deal of attention in the United States to the parenting of families of Asian descent is their concern for children's educational achievement. Many cultural distinctions can be drawn between families of Asian descent and families of European descent in the different beliefs and attitudes toward learning and education, different expectations for educational achievement, and ways of engaging in and supporting children's education and schooling. Both the age of the child and the type of educational support or involvement offered by parents must be considered when describing families of Asian descent. Parents of Asian descent try to offer more direct, instructional support to children's education and schooling very early on, when the child is young. By the time their children enter high school, this type of support would not only be considered unnecessary, it would also be regarded as inappropriate because children at this age are already supposed to have the skills to succeed or apply themselves in school. Although cross-sectional studies of Asian American adolescents' school performance indicate negative associations, especially with direct types of parental involvement (e.g., helping with homework), such associations may be indicative of preexisting school problems among adolescents rather than the consequences of parental involvement per se. With longitudinal data, researchers may be able to determine whether adolescents' difficulties in school are actually driving parents' involvement at a later point in time, rather than parental involvement influencing adolescents' school performance over time. If so, such a demonstration would indicate that Asian American parents may become involved in their older children's schooling only when these children are experiencing difficulties. Considerations of both the child's age, type of involvement, and the association over time between school performance and parental involvement need to be addressed in future studies. In addition, studies are particularly needed that capture change across the age of the child in addition to change across generations of parents.

REFERENCES

Agbayani-Siewert, P., and Revilla, L. (1995). Filipino Americans. In P. G. Min (Ed.), *Asian Americans* (pp. 134–168). Thousand Oaks, CA: Sage.

Almirol, E. B. (1982). Rights and obligations in Filipino American families. *Journal of Comparative Family Studies, 13*, 291–305.

Baumrind, D. (1971). Current patterns of parental authority, *Developmental Psychology Monographs, 4*(Part 2).

Benedict, R. (1934). *Patterns of cultures*. Cambridge, MA: Houghton Mifflin.

Berndt, T., Cheung, P., Lau, S., Hau, K., and Lew, W. (1993). Perceptions of parenting in Mainland China, Taiwan, and Hong Kong: Sex differences and societal differences. *Developmental Psychology, 29*, 156–164.

Barringer, H. R., and Cho, S. N. (1989). *Koreans in the United States: A fact book*. Honolulu: University of Hawaii, Center for Korean Studies.

Blair, S. L., and Qian, Z. (1998). Family and Asian students' educational performance: A consideration of diversity. *Journal of Family Issues, 19*, 355–374.

Boocock, S. S. (1991). Childhood and childcare in Japan and the United States: A comparative analysis. In P. A. Adler and P. Adler (Series Eds.) and N. Mandell (Vol. Ed.), *Sociological studies of child development: Vol. 4. Perspectives on and of children* (pp. 51–88). Greenwich, CT: JAI.

Bornstein, M. H., and Cote, L. (2000). Mother–infant interaction and acculturation I: Behavioral comparisons in Japanese American and South American families. *International Journal of Behavioral Development, XX*, xx–xx.

Bornstein, M. H., Tamis-LeMonda, C. S., Tal, J., Ludemann, P., Toda, S., Rahn, C. W., Pecheux, M. G., Azuma, H., and Vardi, D. (1992). Maternal responsiveness to infants in three societies: The United States, France, and Japan. *Child Development, 63*, 808–821.

Bornstein, M. H., Toda, S., Azuma, H., Tamis-LeMonda, C. S., and Ogino, M. (1990). Mother and infant activity and interaction in Japan and in the United States: II. A comparative microanalysis of naturalistic exchanges focused on the organization of infant attention. *International Journal of Behavioral Development, 13*, 289–308.

Bradby, D., and Owings, J. (1992). Language characterstics and academic achievement: A look at Asian and Hispanic eighth graders in NELS: 88 (Statistical Analysis Report NCES 92-479). Washington, DC: U.S. Department of Education, National Center for Education Statistics.

Chao, R. (1996). Chinese and European Americans mothers' beliefs about the role of parenting in children's school success. *Journal of Cross-cultural Psychology, 27*, 403–423.

Chao, R. K. (1994). Beyond parental control and authoritarian parenting style: Understanding Chinese parenting through the cultural notion of training. *Child Development, 65*, 1111–1119.

Chao, R. K. (1995). Chinese and European American cultural models of the self reflected in mothers' childrearing beliefs. *Ethos, 23*, 328–354.

Chao, R. K. (2000a). Cultural explanations for the role of parenting in the school success of Asian American children. In R. W. Taylor and M. C. Wang (Eds.), *Resilience across contexts: Family, work, culture, and community* (pp. 333–363). Mahwah, NJ: Lawrence Erlbaum Associates.

Chao, R. K. (2000b). The parenting of immigrant Chinese and European American mothers: Relations between parenting styles, socialization goals, and parental practices. *Journal of Applied Developmental Psychology, 21*, 233–248.

Chao, R. K. (2001). Extending the research on the consequences of parenting style for Chinese Americans and European Americans. *Child Development, 72*, 1832–1843.

Chao, R. K., and Kim, K. (2000). Parenting differences among immigrant Chinese fathers and mothers in the United States. *Journal of Psychology in Chinese Societies, 1*, 71–91.

Chao, R. K., and Tran, P. (2001). *The interactive effects of parental control and warmth for different ethnic groups*. Manuscript under review.

Chauhan, N. S. (1980). "Parenting" on dimensions of economic well-being, culture, and education. *Asian Journal of Psychology and Education, 6*, 17–22.

Chen, C. S., and Stevenson, H. W. (1995). Motivation and mathematics achievement: A comparative study of Asian-American, Caucasian-American, and East Asian high school students. *Child Development, 66*, 1215–1234.

Chen, S. J. (1996). Positive childishness: Images of childhood in Japan. In C. P. Hwang, M. E. Lamb, and I. E. Sigel (Eds.), *Images of childhood* (pp. 113–128). Mahwah, NJ: Lawrence Erlbaum Associates.

Chen, X., Dong, Q., and Zhou, H. (1997). Authoritative and authoritarian parenting practices and social and school performance in Chinese children. *International Journal of Behavioral Development, 21*, 855–873.

Chen, X., Liu, M., and Li, D. (2000). Parental warmth, central, and indulgence and their relations to adjustment in Chinese children: A longitudinal Study. *Journal of Family Psychology, 14*, 401–409.

Cherlin, A. (1994). The Japanese family in comparative perspective. In L. J. Cho and M. Yada (Eds.), *Tradition and change in the Asian family* (pp. 421–434). Honolulu, HI: East-West Center.

Cheung, C. (1982). Student perceptions of parental practices and effort: A comparison of Chinese, Anglo, and Hispanic students. *Dissertation Abstracts International, 43*, 1811–1812.

Cheung, C., Lee, J., and Chan, C. (1994). Explicating filial piety in relation to family cohesion. *Journal of Social Behavior and Personality, 9*, 565–580.

Cheung, P. C., and Lau, S. (1985). Self-esteem and its relationship to the family and school social environments among Chinese adolescents. *Youth and Society, 16*, 438–456.

Chiu, L. H. (1987). Childrearing attitudes of Chinese, Chinese-American, and Anglo-American mothers. *Journal of Social Psychology, 128*, 411–413.

Chiu, M. L., Feldman, S. S., and Rosenthal, D. A. (1992). The influence of immigration on parental behavior and adolescent distress in Chinese families residing in two Western nations. *Journal of Research on Adolescence, 2*, 205–239.

Choi, E., Bempechat, J., and Ginsburg, H. (1994). Educational socialization in Korean American children: A longitudinal study. *Journal of Applied Developmental Psychology, 15*, 313–318.

Clancy, P. M. (1986). The acquisition of communicative style in Japanese. In B. B. Schieffelin and E. Ochs (Eds.), Language socialization across cultures (pp. 213–250). New York: Cambridge University Press.

Conroy, M., Hess, R. D., Azuma, H., and Kashiwagi, K. (1980). Maternal strategies for regulating children's behavior in Japanese and American families. *Journal of Cross-Cultural Psychology, 11*, 153–172.

Cote, L., and Bornstein, M. H. (2000). Mother–infant interaction and acculturation II: Behavioral coherence and correspondence in Japanese American and South American families. *International Journal of Behavioral Development, XX*, xx–xx.

Dornbusch, S., Ritter, P., Leiderman, P., Roberts, D., and Fraleigh, M. (1987). The relation of parenting style to adolescent school performance, *Child Development, 58*, 1244–1257.

Epstein, J. (1987). Parent involvement: What research says to administrators. *Education and Urban Society, 19*, 119–136.

Feldman, S. S., Mont-Reynaud, R., and Rosenthal, D. A. (1992). When East moves West: The acculturation of values of Chinese adolescents in the U.S. and Australia. *Journal of Research on Adolescence, 2*, 147–173.

Feldman, S. S., and Rosenthal, D. A. (1990). The acculturation of autonomy expectations in Chinese high schoolers residing in two Western nations. *International Journal of Psychology, 25*, 259–281.

Feldman, S. S., and Rosenthal, D. A. (1991). Age expectations of behavioral autonomy in Hong Kong, Australian, and American youth: The influence of family variables, and adolescents' values. *International Journal of Psychology, 26*, 1–23.

Fuligni, A. J. (1997). The academic achievement of adolescents from immigrant families: The roles of family background, attitudes, and behavior. *Child Development, 68*, 351–363.

Fuligni, A. J. (1998). Authority, autonomy, and parent–adolescent conflict and cohesion: A study of adolescents from Mexican, Chinese, Filipino, and European backgrounds. *Developmental Psychology, 34*, 782–792.

Fuligni, A. J., Tseng, V., and Lam, M. (1999). Attitudes towards family obligations among American adolescents with Asian, Latin American, and European backgrounds. *Child Development, 70*, 1030–1044.

Fung, H. (1999). Becoming a moral child: The socialization of shame among young Chinese children. *Ethos, 27*, 180–209.

Gibson, M. A. (1988). *Accommodation without assimilation*. Ithaca, NY: Cornell University Press.

Gorman, J. C. (1998). Parenting attitudes and practices of immigrant Chinese mothers of adolescents. *Family Relations, 47*, 73–80.

Goyette, K., and Xie, Y. (1999). Educational expectations of Asian American youths: Determinants and ethnic differences. *Sociology of Education, 72*, 22–36.

Greenfield, P. M. (1994). Independence and interdependence as developmental scripts: Implications for theory, research, and practice. In P. M. Greenfield and R. R. Cocking (Eds.), *Cross-cultural roots of minority child development* (pp. 1–37). Hillsdale, NJ: Lawrence Erlbaum Associates.

Gupta, G. R. (1979). The family in India: The joint family. In M. S. Das and P. D. Bardis (Eds.), *The Family in Asia* (pp. 72–88). London: Allen and Unwin.

Hao, L., and Bonstead-Bruns, M. (1998). Parent–child differences in educational expectations and the academic achievement of immigrant and native students. *Sociology of Education, 71*, 175–198.

Hara, H., and Minagawa, M. (1996). From productive dependents to precious guests: Historical changes in Japanese children. In D. W. Schwalb and B. J. Schwalb (Eds.), *Japanese childrearing: Two generations of scholarship* (pp. 9–30). New York: Guilford.

Herz, L., and Gullone, E. (1999). The relationship between self-esteem and parenting style: A cross-cultural comparison of Australian and Vietnamese Australian adolescents. *Journal of Cross-Cultural Psychology, 30*, 742–761.

Hess, R. D., Chih-Mei, C., and McDevitt, T. M. (1987). Cultural variations in family beliefs about children's performance in mathematics: Comparisons among People's Republic of Chinese, Chinese American, and Caucasian American families. *Journal of Educational Psychology, 79*, 179–188.

Hieshima, J., and Schneider, B. (1994). Intergenerational effects on the cultural and cognitive socialization of third- and fourth-generation Japanese Americans. *Journal of Applied Developmental Psychology, 15*, 319–327.

Ho, D. Y. F. (1986). Chinese patterns of socialization: A critical review. In M. H. Bond (Ed.), *The psychology of Chinese people* (pp. 1–37). Hong Kong: Oxford University Press.

Ho, D. Y. F. (1993). Relational orientation in Asian social psychology. In U. Kim and J. W. Berry (Eds.), *Indigenous psychologies: Research and experience in cultural context* (pp. 240–259). Thousand Oaks, CA: Sage.

Ho, D. Y. F. (1994). Cognitive socialization in Confucian heritage cultures. In P. Greenfield and R. Cocking (Eds.), *Cross-cultural roots of minority child development* (pp. 285–314). Hillsdale, NJ: Lawrence Erlbaum Associates.

Ho, D. Y. F. (1996). Filial piety and its psychological consequences. In M. H. Bond (Ed.), *The handbook of chinese psychology* (pp. 155–165). Hong Kong: Oxford University Press.

Ho, D. Y. F., and Kang, T. K. (1984). Intergenerational comparisons of childrearing attitudes and practices in Hong Kong. *Developmental Psychology, 20*, 1004–1016.

Ho, D. Y. F., and Lee, L. Y. (1974). Authoritarianism and attitude toward filial piety in Chinese teachers. *Journal of Social Psychology, 92*, 305–306.

Ho, E. S. C., and Willms, J. D. (1996). The effects of parental involvement on eighth grade achievement. *Sociology of Education, 69*, 126–141.

Hsu, F. L. K. (1953). *Americans and Chinese*. Honolulu, University Press of Hawaii.

Huang, D. (1997). The role of parental expectation, effort and self-efficacy in the achievement of high- and low-track high school students in Taiwan. University of Southern California. *Dissertion Abstracts International, 57*, (9-A).

Huang, S. L., and Waxman, H. C. (1995). Motivation and learning-environment differences between Asian-American and White middle school students in mathematics. *Journal of Research and Development in Education, 28*, 208–219.

Hui, C. H. (1988). Measurement of individualism–collectivism. *Journal of Research on Personality, 22*, 17–36.

Huntsinger, C. S., Jose, P. E., and Larson, S. L. (1998). Do parent practices to encourage academic competence influence the social adjustment of young European American and Chinese American children? *Developmental Psychology, 34*, 747–756.

Huntsinger, C. S., Jose, P. E., Larson, S. L., and Krieg, D. S. (2000). Mathematics, vocabulary, and reading development in Chinese American and European American children over the primary school years. *Journal of Educational Psychology, 92*, 1–15.

Huntsinger, C. S., Jose, P. E., Liaw, F. R., and Ching, W. D. (1997). Cultural differences in early mathematics learning: A comparison of Euro-American, Chinese-American, and Taiwan-Chinese families. *International Journal of Behavioral Development, 21*, 371–388.

Jankowiak, W. (1992). Father–child relations in urban China. In B. S. Hewlett (Ed.), *Father–child relations: Cultural and biosocial contexts* (pp. 345–363). New York: De Gruyter.

Javillonar, G. V. (1979). The Filipino family. In M. S. Das and P. D. Bardis (Eds.), *The family in Asia* (pp. 344–380). London: Allen and Unwin.

Jose, P. E., Huntsinger, C. S., Huntsinger, P. R., and Liaw, F. (2000). Parental values and practices relevant to young children's social development in Taiwan and the U.S. *Journal of Cross-Cultural Psychology, 31*, 677–702.

Joshi, M. S., and MacLean, M. (1997). Maternal expectations of child development in India, Japan, and England. *Journal of Cross-Cultural Psychology, 28*, 219–234.

Kakar, S. (1978). *The inner world: A psychoanalytic study of childhood and society in India*. New Delhi, India: Oxford University Press.

Kao, G. (1995). Asian Americans as model minorities? A look at their academic performance. *American Journal of Education, 103*, 121–159.

Kauh, T. (1997). Intergenerational relations: Older Korean-Americans' experiences. *Journal of Cross-Cultural Gerontology, 12*, 245–271.

Keith, T. Z., Keith, P. B., Troutman, G. C., Bickley, P. G., Trivette, P. S., and Singh, K. (1993). Does parental involvement affect eighth-grade student achievement? Structural analysis of national data. *School Psychology Review, 22*, 474–496.

Kelley, M. L., and Tseng, H. M. (1992). Cultural differences in child rearing: A comparison of immigrant Chinese and Caucasian American mothers. *Journal of Cross-Cultural Psychology, 23*, 444–455.

Kim, C. K., and Kim, S. (1998). Family and work roles of Korean immigrants in the United States. In H. I. McCubbin, E. A. Thompson, A. I. Thompson, and J. E. Fromer (Eds.), *Resiliency in Native American and immigrant families* (pp. 225–274). Thousand Oaks, CA: Sage.

Kim, H., Rendon, L., and Valadez, J. (1998). Student characteristics, school characteristics, and educational aspirations of six Asian American ethnic groups. *Journal of Multicultural Counseling and Development, 26*, 166–176.

Kim, K. C., Kim, S., and Hurh, W. M. (1991). Filial piety and intergenerational relationship in Korean immigrant families. *International Journal of Aging and Human Development, 33*, 233–245.

Kim, S. (1996). The effects of parenting style, cultural conflict, and peer relations on academic achievement and psychosocial adjustment among Korean immigrant adolescents. *Dissertation Abstracts International, 57,* 578.

Kim, U., and Choi, S. (1994). Individualism, collectivism, and child development: A Korean perspective. In P. M. Greenfield and R. R. Cocking (Eds.), *Cross-cultural roots of minority child development* (pp. 1–37). Hillsdale, NJ: Lawrence Erlbaum Associates.

Kim, W. J., Kim, L. I., and Rue, D. S. (1997). Korean American children. In G. Johnson-Powell and J. Yamamoto (Eds.), *Transcultural child development: Psychological assessment and treatment* (pp. 183–207). New York: Wiley.

Kojima, H. (1986). Japanese concepts of child development from the mid-17th to mid-19th century. *International Journal of Behavioral Development, 9,* 315–329.

Kornadt, H. J. (1987). The aggression motive and personality development: Japan and Germany. In F. Halish and J. Kuhl (Eds.), *Motivation, intention and volition.* Berlin: Springer-Verlag.

Kriger, S. F., and Kroes, W. H. (1972). Childrearing attitudes of Chinese, Jewish, and Protestant mothers. *Journal of Social Psychology, 86,* 205–210.

Lai, A. C., Zhang, Z. X., and Wang, W. Z. (2000). Maternal childrearing practices in Hong Kong and Beijing Chinese families: A comparative study. *International Journal of Psychology, 35,* 60–66.

Lamborn, S. D., Dornbusch, S. M., and Steinberg, L. (1996). Ethnicity and community context as moderators of the relations between family decision making and adolescent adjustment. *Child Development, 67,* 283–301.

Lanham, B. B., and Garrick, R. J. (1996). Adult to child in Japan: Interaction and relations. In D. W. Schwalb and B. J. Schwalb (Eds.), *Japanese childrearing: Two generations of scholarship* (pp. 97–124). New York: Guilford.

Lau, S., and Cheung, P. C. (1987). Relationships between Chinese adolescents' perception of parental control and organization and their perception of parental warmth. *Developmental Psychology, 23,* 726–729.

Lau, S., Lew, W. J. F., Hau, K. T., Cheung, P. C., and Berndt, T. J. (1990). Relations among perceived parental control, warmth, indulgence, and family harmony of Chinese in mainland China. *Developmental Psychology, 26,* 674–677.

Law, T. T. (1973). Differential childrearing practices among Chinese American mothers. *Dissertation Abstracts International, 34,* 4406-A.

Lebra, T. S. (1994). Mother and child in Japanese socialization: A Japan–U.S. comparison. In P. M. Greenfield and R. R. Cocking (Eds.), *Cross-cultural roots of minority child development* (pp. 259–274). Hilldale, NJ: Lawrence Erlbaum Associates.

Lee, S. J. (1994). Behind the model minority stereotype: Voices of high- and low-achieving Asian American students. *Anthropology and Education Quarterly, 25,* 413–429.

Lee, S. J. (1996). *Unraveling the model minority stereotype: Listening to Asian American youth.* New York: Teacher's College Press.

Lee, T. (1987). The relationships of achievement, instruction, and family background to elementary school science achievement in the Republic of China. Ohio State University, *Dissertation Abstracts International, 48,* (5-A): p. 1164–1165.

Leong, F. T. L., Chao, R. K., and Hardin, E. E. (2000). Asian American adolescents: A research review to dispel the model minority myth. In R. Montemayor (Ed.), *Advances in adolescent development* (Vol. 9.). Thousand Oaks CA: Sage.

Leung, K., Lau, S., and Lam, W. L. (1998). Parenting styles and achievement: A cross-cultural study. *Merril-Palmer Quarterly, 44,* 157–172.

Lewis, C. (1988). Cooperation and control in Japanese nursery schools. In G. Handel (Ed.), *Childhood socialization* (pp. 125–142). Hawthorne, NY: De Gruyter.

Li, J. (1997). The Chinese heart and mind for wanting to learn (hao-xue-xin): A culturally based learning model. Doctoral dissertation. Harvard University, Cambridge, MA.

Li, J. (in press). Chinese conceptualization of learning. *Ethos.*

Li, Y., Liu, J., Liu, F., Gui, G., Anme, T., and Ushijima, H. (2000). Maternal children behaviors and correlates in rural minority areas of Yannan, China. *Developmental and Behavioral Pediatrics, 21,* 114–1222.

Lin, C. C., and Fu, V. R. (1990). A comparison of childrearing practices among Chinese, immigrant Chinese, and Caucasian-American parents. *Child Development, 61,* 429–433.

Lin, E. C. (1999). Family obligations, parent–adolescent relationships, and psychological functioning among Asian American college students. *Dissertation Abstracts International,* DAI-B 60/05, 2344.

Lynch, F. (1981). Social acceptance reconsidered. In A. A. Yengoyan and P. Q. Makil (Eds.), *Philippine society and the individual: Selected essays of Frank Lynch, 1949–1976* (pp. 23–92). Ann Arbor, MI: University of Michigan, Center for South and Southeast Asian Studies.

Maretzki, T. W., and Maretzki, H. (1963). Taira: An Okinawan village. In B. Whiting (Ed.), *Six cultures: Studies of child rearing* (pp. 363–540). New York: Wiley.

Markus, H. R., and Kitayama, S. (1991). Culture and self: Implications for cognition, emotion, and motivation. *Psychological Review, 98,* 224–253.

Matsuda, M. (1964). Nihon-shiki ikuji-hoh [Japanese ways of childrearing]. Tokyo: Kohdansha.

Matsumori, A. (1981). Hahoya no Kodomo e no gengo ni yoru Koodoo Kisei–yookyuu hyoogen no nichibei hikaku. In F. C. Peng (Ed.), *Gengo shuutoku no Shosoo* [Aspects of language acquisition] (pp. 320–339). Hiroshima: Bunka Hyoron.

Mau, W. (1997). Parental influences on the high school students' academic achievement: A comparison of Asian immigrants, Asian Americans, and White Americans. *Psychology in the Schools, 34,* 267–277.

McBride-Chang, C., and Chang, L. (1998). Adolescent–parent relations in Hong Kong: Parenting styles, emotional autonomy, and school achievement. *Journal of Genetic Psychology, 159,* 421–436.

Mead, M. (1928). *Coming of age in samoa.* New York: Morrow Quill.

Miller, P. J., Fung, H., and Mintz, J. (1996). Self-construction through narrative practices: A Chinese and American comparison of early socialization. *Ethos, 24,* 237–280.

Miller, P. J., Wiley, A. R., Fung, H., and Liang, C. H. (1997). Personal storytelling as a medium of socialization in Chinese and American families. *Child Development, 68,* 557–568.

Min, P. G. (1995). Introduction in P. G. Min (Ed.), *Asian Americans: Contemporary trends and issues* (pp. 1–9). Thousand Oaks, CA: Sage.

Minturn, L., and Hitchcock, J. T. (1963). The Rajputs of Khalapur, India. In B. Whiting (Ed.), *Six cultures: Studies of child rearing* (pp. 203–362). New York: Wiley.

Mordkowitz, E., and Ginsburg, H. (1987). Early academic socialization of successful Asian-American college students. *The Quarterly Newsletter of the Laboratory of Comparative Human Cognition, 9,* 85–91.

Morrow, R. D. (1989). Southeast Asian child rearing practices: Implications for child and youth care workers. *Child and Youth Quarterly, 18,* 273–287.

Nguyen, N. A., and Williams, H. L. (1989). Transition from east to west: Vietnamese adolescents and their parents. *Journal of the American Academy of Child and Adolescent Psychiatry, 28,* 505–515.

Nomura, N., Noguchi, Y., Saito, S., and Tezuka, I. (1995). Family characteristics and dynamics in Japan and the United States: A preliminary report from the family environment scale. *International Journal of Interlectural Relations, 19,* 59–86.

Nydegger, W. F., and Nydegger, C. (1963). Tarong: An Ilocos barrio in the Philippines. In B. Whiting (Ed.), *Six cultures: Studies of child rearing* (pp. 693–868). New York: Wiley.

O'Hare, W. P., and Felt, J. C. (1991). *Asian Americans: America's fastest growing minority group.* Washington, DC: Population Reference Bureau.

Okagaki, L. F., and Frensch, P. A. (1998). Parenting and children's school achievement: A multiethnic perspective. *American Educational Research Journal, 35,* 123–144.

Olsen, L. (1988). *Crossing the schoolhouse border: Immigrant students and the California public schools* (A California Tomorrow Policy Research Report). San Francisco: California Tomorrow.

Osterweil, Z., and Nagano-Nakamura, K. N. (1992). Maternal view on aggression: Japan and Israel. *Aggressive Behavior, 18,* 263–270.

Peng, S. S., and Wright, D. (1994). Explanation of academic achievement of Asian American students. *Journal of Educational Research, 87,* 346–352.

Phinney, J. S., Ong, A., and Madden, T. (2000). Cultural values and intergenerational value discrepancies in immigrant and non-immigrant families. *Child Development, 71,* 528–539.

Radziszewska, B., Richardson, J. L., Dent, C. W., and Flay, B. R. (1996). Parenting style and adolescent depressive symptoms, smoking, and academic achievement: Ethnic, gender, and SES differences. *Journal of Behavioral Medicine, 19,* 289–305.

Ranganath, V. M., and Ranganath, V. K. (1997). Asian Indian children. In G. Johnson-Powell and J. Yamamoto (Eds.), *Transcultural child development: Psychological assessment and treatment* (pp. 103–125). New York: Wiley.

Reglin, G. L., and Adams, D. R. (1990). Why Asian-American high school students have higher grade point averages and SAT scores than other high school students. *High School Journal, 73,* 143–149.

Rhee, E., Uleman, J. S., and Lee, H. K. (1996). Variations in collectivism and individualism by ingroup and culture: Confirmatory factor analyses. *Journal of Personality and Social Psychology, 71,* 1037–1054.

Rohner, R. P., Hahn, B. C., and Rohner, E. C. (1980). Social class differences in perceived parental acceptance–rejection and self-evaluations among Korean American children. *Behavioral Science Research, 1,* 55–66.

Rohner, R. P., and Pettengill, S. M. (1985). Perceived parental acceptance–rejection and parental control among Korean adolescents. *Child Development, 56,* 524–528.

Rohner, R. P., and Rohner, E. C. (1978). Unpublished research data. University of Connecticut, Center for the Study of Parental Acceptance and Rejection.

Rosenthal, D. A., and Feldman. S. S. (1991). The influence of perceived family and personal factors on self-reported school performance of Chinese and western high school students. *Journal of Research on Adolescence, 1,* 135–154.

Rosenthal, D. A., and Feldman. S. S. (1992). The relationship between parenting behavior and ethnic identity in Chinese-American and Chinese-Australian adolescents. *International Journal of Psychology, 27,* 19–31.

Santos, R. A. (1997). Filipino American children. In G. Johnson-Powell and J. Yamamoto (Eds.), *Transcultural child development: Psychological assessment and treatment* (pp. 126–142). New York: Wiley.

Schneider, B., and Lee, Y. (1990). A model of academic success: The school and home environment of East Asian students. *Anthropology and Education Quarterly, 21,* 358–377.

Seymour, S. (1988). Expressions of responsibility among Indian children: Some precursors of adult status and sex roles. *Ethos, 16,* 355–370.

Seymour, S. (1999). *Women, family, and child care in India: A world in transition*. New York: Cambridge University Press.

Shek, D. (1998). Adolescents' perceptions of paternal and maternal parenting styles in a Chinese context. *Journal of Psychology, 132*, 527–537.

Shek, D. (2000). Differences between fathers and mothers in the treatment of, and relationship with, their teenage children: Perception of Chinese adolescents. *Adolescence, 35*, 137.

Shoho, A. (1994). A historical comparison of parental involvement of three generations of Japanese Americans (Isseis, Niseis, Sanseis) in the education of their children. *Journal of Applied Developmental Psychology, 15*, 305–311.

Silver, C. B. (1998). Cross-cultural perspective on attitudes toward family responsibility and well-being in later years. In J. Lomrang (Ed.), *Handbook of aging and mental health: An integrative approach* (pp. 383–412). New York: Plenum.

Steinberg, L., Dornbusch, S. M., and Brown, B. B., (1992). Ethnic differences in adolescent achievement: An ecological perspective. *American Psychologist, 6*, 723–729.

Steinberg, L., Lamborn, S. D., Darling, N., Mounts, N. S., and Dornbusch, S. M. (1994). Over-time changes in adjustment and competence among adolescents from authoritative, authoritarian, indulgent, and neglectful families. *Child Development, 65*, 754–770.

Steinberg, L., Lamborn, S. D., Dornbusch, S. M., and Darling, N. (1992). Impact of parenting practices on adolescent achievement: Authoritative parenting, school involvement, and encouragement to succeed. *Child Development, 63*, 1266–1281.

Steinberg, L., Mounts, N. S., Lamborn, S. D., and Dornbusch, S. M. (1991). Authoritative parenting and adolescent adjustment across varied ecological niches. *Journal of Research on Adolescence, 1*, 19–36.

Stevenson, H. W., and Lee, S. Y. (1990). Contexts of achievement. *Monographs of the Society for Research in Child Development, 55*(Serial No. 221).

Stewart, S. M., Bond, M. H., Deeds, O., and Chung, S. F. (1999). Intergenerational patterns of values and autonomy expectations in cultures of relatedness and separateness. *Journal of Cross-Cultural Psychology, 30*, 575–593.

Stewart, S. M., Bond, M. H., Zaman, R. M., Mc-Bride-Chang, C., Rao, N., Ho, L. M., and Fielding, R. (1999). Functional parenting in Pakistan. *International Journal of Behavioral Development, 23*, 747–770.

Stewart, S. M., Rao, N., Bond, M. H., McBride-Chang, C., Fielding, R., and Kennard, B. D. (1998). Chinese dimensions of parenting: Broadening Western predictors and outcomes. *International Journal of Psychology, 33*, 345–358.

Sue, S., and Abe, J. (1988). *Predictors of academic achievement among Asian-American and White students* (Report No. 88–11). College Board Report.

Sun, L. C., and Roopnarine, J. (1996). Mother–infant, father–infant interaction and involvement in childcare and household labor among Taiwanese families. *Infant Behavior and Development, 19*, 121–129.

Sung, K. (1995). Measures and dimensions of filial piety in Korea. *The Gerontologist, 35*, 240–247.

Suzuki, B. (1988, April). *Asian Americans in higher education: Impact of changing demographics and other social forces*. Paper presented at the meetings of the National Symposium on the Changing Demographics of Higher Education, New York.

Tobin, J., Wu, D. Y. H., and Davidson, D. (1987). Preschool in three cultures. New Haven, CT: Yale University Press.

Triandis, H. C. (1991). *Manual of instruments for the study of allocentrism or collectivism and idiocentrism or individualism*. Unpublished manuscript, University of Illinois, Champagne–Urbana.

Trommsdorf, G. (1985). Some comparative aspects of socialization in Japan and Germany. In I. R. Lagunes and Y. H. Poortinga (Eds.), *From a different perspective: Studies of behavior across cultures* (pp. 231–240). Lisse Netherlands: Swets and Zeitlinger.

Trommsdorff, G., and Iwawaki, S. (1989). Students' perceptions of socialization and gender role in Japan and Germany. *International Journal of Behavioral Development, 12*, 485–493.

Tsuya, N. O. (1994). Changing attitudes towards marriage and the family in Japan. In L. J. Cho and M. Yada (Eds.), *Tradition and change in the Asian family* (pp. 91–120). Honolulu, HI: East-West Center.

U.S. Census Bureau. (August, 2000). *Foreign-born population in the U.S.* (Current Population Reports, P20-519). Washington, DC: Author.

Whiting, B. B., and Edwards, C. P. (1988). *Children of different worlds: The formation of social behavior*. Cambridge, MA: Harvard University Press.

Whiting, J. W., Child, I. L., and Lambert, W. W. (1966). *Field guide for a study of socialization*. New York: John Wiley Press.

Winata, H. K., and Power, T. G. (1989). Childrearing and compliance: Japanese and American families in Houston. *Journal of Cross-Cultural Psychology, 20*, 333–356.

Wolf, M. (1970). Child training and the Chinese family. In M. Freedman (Ed.), *Family and kinship in Chinese societies* (pp. 221–246). Palo Alto, CA: Stanford University Press.

Wolf, M. (1972). *Women and the family in rural Taiwan*. Stanford, CA: Stanford University Press.

Wong, M. G. (1990). The education of white, Chinese, Filipino, and Japanese students: A look at "high school and beyond." *Sociological Perspectives, 33*, 355–374.

Wu, D. Y. H. (1996). Parental control: Psychocultural interpretations of Chinese patterns of socialization. In S. Lau (Ed.), *Growing up the Chinese way* (pp. 1–68). Hong Kong: Chinese University of Hong Kong Press.

Wu, D. Y. H., and Tseng, W. S. (1985). Child training in Chinese culture. In W. S. Tseng and D. Wu (Eds.), *Chinese culture and mental health* (pp. 113–134). Orlando, FL: Academic Press.

Xie, Q. (1998). Perceptions of childrearing practices by Chinese parents and their only children, and their relations to children's school achievement. *Dissertation Abstracts International, 58*, 3425.

Yao, E. L. (1985). A comparison of family characteristics of Asian American and Anglo American high achievers. *International Journal of Comparative Sociology, 26*, 198–208.

Yee, B. W. K., Huang, L. N., and Lew, A. (1998). Families: Life-span socialization in a cultural context. In L. C. Lee and N. W. S. Zane (Eds.), *Handbook of Asian American Psychology*. Thousand Oaks, CA: Sage.

Yu, E., and Liu, W. T. (1980). *Fertility and kinship in the Philippines*. Notre Dame, IN: University of Notre Dame Press.

Zhang, J., and Bond, M. H. (1998). Personality and filial piety among college students in two Chinese societies. *Journal of Cross-Cultural Psychology, 29*, 402–417.

Zhengyuan, X., Jian-Xian, S., Wen, W. C., Chang-Min, L., Mussen, P., and Fang, C. Z. (1991). Family socialization and children's behavior and personality development in China. *Journal of Genetic Psychology, 152*, 239–253.

Zhou, M., and Bankston, C. L. (1998). *Growing up American: How Vietnamese children adapt to life in the United States*. New York: Russell Sage Foundation.

5

Parents in Poverty

Katherine A. Magnuson
Greg J. Duncan
Northwestern University

INTRODUCTION

Challenging even in circumstances of middle-income families, successful parenting is extraordinarily difficult when either family or neighborhood economic resources are inadequate. In this chapter we review the conceptual and empirical linkages between poverty and parenting, focusing mostly on the economic dimension of poverty at the family rather than the neighborhood level, and almost exclusively on the United States.

Poverty has been defined as a state of lacking "a usual or socially acceptable amount of money or material possessions" (Encyclopedia Britannica, 2001). Income in general and poverty in particular, although correlated, are distinct from the more conventional education and occupational status markers of family socioeconomic status. Because of the importance of this distinction, we begin our chapter with a primer on poverty measurement and trends.

Research on parenting in poverty has been driven largely by a desire to understand why poor children, compared with more affluent children, are at greater risk of poor school achievement, behavior problems, and poor health. The strength and consistency of these associations are striking. Brooks-Gunn and Duncan (1997) summarized the higher risks for poor relative to nonpoor children as follows: 1.7 times for low birth weight, 2.0 times for having a short hospital stay, 2.0 times for grade repetition and high school dropout, 1.4 times for learning disability, 1.3 times for a parent-reported emotional or behavior problem, 3.1 times for a teenage out-of-wedlock birth, 6.8 times for reported cases of child abuse and neglect, and 2.2 times for experiencing violent crime.

These associations say little about the processes by which poverty affects children. Identifying causal pathways is important not only for the greater understanding of how poverty affects children, but also because it can lead to policy and program interventions to improve the life chances of poor children. Ecological models of child development (e.g., Bronfenbrenner, 1979; Sameroff and Fiese, 1990) argue that children's developmental pathways are determined by their interactions with their environment, so research on the pathways through which income affects children have focused largely on the most immediate, family-based environments. Parenting, defined both narrowly as micro interactions and more broadly as gatekeeping activities, was one of the first pathways that researchers thought might link economic hardship to child well-being, and it remains one of the most explored.

Most of the research that we review has been conducted in the United States. Given the pervasive influence of culture on parenting practices but with little comparative international or cross-cultural work on parents in poverty, it is difficult to conjecture whether the processes we highlight operate outside of the United States. Consequently, we limit our discussion of the effects of poverty on parenting to the U.S. context, but see great value in comparative studies, and studies in diverse cultural contexts, that address whether parents' responses to poverty differ across cultures.

After our primer on poverty, we identify issues at the center of the study of parenting in poverty. Next we discuss the methodological challenges of this type of research and present a selective review of relevant research on parenting in poverty. We conclude the chapter with our suggestions for future research directions.

A PRIMER ON POVERTY

Social scientists disagree on how poverty should be conceived and measured. Townsend (1992, p. 10) defined poverty as income insufficient to enable individuals to "play the roles, participate in the relationships, and follow the customary behavior which is expected of them by virtue of their membership of society" and directed his research toward determining income levels that correspond to low scores on a "deprivation index." Other researchers (e.g., Mack and Lansley, 1985) defined poverty directly in terms of deprivation indicators such as access to a telephone and appliances or wearing new rather than used clothing, without regard to income. Still others used income (e.g., O'Higgins and Jenkins, 1990), but defined poverty thresholds by some fraction (e.g., 50%) of a country's median income. This income-based definition finesses the difficult task of developing the definitive list of deprivation indicators and adjusts the poverty line to keep pace with changes in the general living standards of the population.

In contrast to these approaches, the official U.S. definition of poverty is based solely on a comparison of a household's total household income with a threshold level of income that varies with family size and inflation. Total household income consists of cash income from work, welfare, relatives, and all other sources received by all household members during the previous calendar year.

In recognition of the fact that a household's need for income increases with the number of household members, the poverty threshold, or poverty line, is adjusted for differing family sizes. In 1999, the respective thresholds for two-, three-, and four-person families were $11,214, $13,290, and $17,029 (U.S. Bureau of the Census, 2000a). Households with incomes below these thresholds are considered poor, whereas households with incomes above—even one dollar above—are not counted as poor. A household's poverty status is assumed to apply to each household member. Official U.S. thresholds are adjusted each year for inflation, but not for changes in living standards of the general population.

Proposed refinements to the official definition include distinguishing between households well below the poverty line (e.g., income less that half the poverty threshold), closer but still under that line, and just above it ("near poor"); including "near-cash" resources such as food stamps in the definition of income; adjusting the threshold for work-related and medical expenses; and changing the accounting period from one year to a longer or shorter period, depending on the intended use of the poverty measure (Citro and Michael, 1995).

According to opinion polls, official poverty thresholds are lower than the amounts of money—typically around $20,000—judged by Americans as necessary to "get along in their community," to "live decently" or to avoid hardship (Vaughn, 1993). The official thresholds are also lower than the amount of money identified by social scientists as necessary to make ends meet. A detailed

FIGURE 5.1. Child poverty trends by race and ethnicity. .... All African American children; _ _ _ All Hispanic children; _____ All young children; ▮▮▮▮▮ All children; __ __ _ All European American children.

ethnographic study of family budgets by Edin and Lein (1995) identified $16,500 as the approximate income level that enables a thrifty three-person family to live without severe hardship.

To focus on poverty among parents, we present in Figure 5.1 historical data on the fraction of children living in families with incomes below the official poverty line (U.S. Bureau of the Census, 2000b). After economic growth and social program expenditures produced a precipitous decline during the 1960s, the overall poverty rate for children climbed during the 1970s and has fluctuated with macroeconomic conditions since then. As of 1999, some 16.9% of U.S. children were poor, a figure that is several percentage points lower than in the early 1990s, but still higher than 25 years before.

In the United States, poverty is not evenly distributed among ethnic or racial groups, nor among families within these groups. A considerably higher percentage of African American, Hispanic, and Native American than European American children are poor, although the recent declines in poverty rates have been sharper for African American than other children. Poverty rates are consistently higher for families with younger than older children.

Demographic studies of these poverty trends identify the following as important determinants: macroeconomic conditions, the rise in the number of single-parent families (who are twice as likely to be poor as two-parent families; Weinraub, Horvath, and Gringlas, in Vol. 3 of this *Handbook*), stagnating wages for low-skill workers, and inflation-adjusted drops in welfare benefits. The secular increase in poverty over the last 2 decades would have been even higher had parental schooling levels and the benefits from the earned income tax credit not increased as much and had family sizes not fallen as much as they did (Eggebeen and Lichter, 1991; Lichter and Eggebeen, 1993).

Also noteworthy is that poverty is not synonymous with unemployment or joblessness. Many poor families contain working adults. In 1996, about 5 million children lived in a "working poor" family, defined as a family with an income below the poverty line and either: (1) two parents who work the equivalent of a full-time job or (2) a single parent who works at least 20 hours per week. About half of children in poor, married-couple families and one third of poor children in single-mother families fit this definition of "working poor" (Werthheimer, 1999).

Ironically, the United States now has both more poor *and* more affluent children than most other Western countries. If we define poverty in relative terms (i.e., family-size-adjusted income less than half of a country's median income), then the 20.3% rate of relative poverty for U.S. children is highest among Western countries and several times as high as that of most continental European and Scandinavian countries. Only the United Kingdom and Italy are within five percentage points of the U.S. poverty rate. An analogous definition of "affluence" (i.e., family-size-adjusted income greater than twice a country's median income) produces rates of affluence that are twice as high in the United States as in many other countries. Only the United Kingdom has higher rates of affluent families with children than the United States.

How persistent is poverty? Popular perceptions of the permanence of poverty are widespread. We speak easily of "the poor" as if they were an ever present and unchanging group. Indeed, the way we conceptualize the "poverty problem" or the "underclass problem" seems to presume the permanent existence of well-defined economic groups within American society.

As can be seen in Figure 5.1, comparative cross-sectional evidence from the 1980s and 1990s shows that roughly one in five children was poor in any two consecutive Census Bureau survey "snapshots" and that poverty rates rarely change by as much as a single percentage point from one year to the next. This fact, plus census data showing that poor children in adjacent years shared similar characteristics (e.g., about half live in mother-only families), is consistent with the inference that there is very little change in who is poor from year to year and that poor families with children have little hope of economic improvement. However, the same evidence is just as consistent with 100% turnover—or any other percentage one might pick—provided that equal numbers of people with similar characteristics fall into and climb out of poverty between the adjacent years under study.

In fact, longitudinal data have always revealed a great deal of turnover among the poor, as events like unemployment and divorce push families into poverty, and reemployment, marriage and career gains pull them out (Duncan et al., 1984). More than one fourth of the individuals living in poverty in a given year report incomes above poverty in the next, and considerably less than one half of those who experience poverty remain persistently poor over many years. A clear majority of poverty spells are short (60% last less than 3 years). A substantial but small subset of poor families experience longer-run poverty (14% of poverty spells last 8 or more years; Bane and Ellwood, 1986). As with all poverty, persistent poverty is not evenly distributed among ethnic groups. Long-term poverty rates for minority children are especially high, with nearly one fourth of African American children living in persistent poverty (U.S. Department of Health and Human Services, 1997).

Economic mobility from one generation to the next is also surprisingly high. Using nationally representative data from the Panel Study of Income Dynamics, Corcoran (1995) found that most children who experienced poverty did not live in poverty as young adults. In fact, only 1 in 10 European American children and 1 in 4 African American children who were reared in poverty remained poor in early adulthood. However, the odds of being poor in adulthood are still much higher for children who grow up in poverty than for children who do not. African American children reared in poverty are 2.5 times more likely to be poor as adults than African American children who grow up in nonpoor households, and European American children reared in poverty are 7.5 times more likely to be poor as adults than children reared in nonpoor households. Corcoran also found that children who spent more than half of their childhood in poverty were likely to cycle in and out of poverty as adults. Over 45% of African Americans and 24% of European Americans reared in persistently poor homes reported at least 1 year of adult incomes below the poverty line.

Neighborhood-based poverty is distinct from family-level poverty. Using census tracts (geographic areas defined to approximate neighborhoods and typically containing 3,000 to 5,000 individuals), Kasarda (1993) estimated that the fraction of poor urban families living in high-poverty neighborhoods (i.e., with 40% or more of residents in households with incomes below the poverty line) nearly doubled between 1970 and 1990, from 16.5% to 28.2%. Surprisingly, most poor families do not live in high-poverty urban neighborhoods. The most recent data, from the 1990 census, show that only 14.5% of all poor children live in high-poverty urban neighborhoods (Jargowsky, 1997). More than one fourth of all poor children lived outside metropolitan areas altogether, and one third lived in urban neighborhoods with poverty rates below 20%.

The combination of family and neighborhood poverty is more prevalent among African American than either Hispanic or, especially, European American children. Some 27% of poor African American children lived in high-poverty urban neighborhoods, as compared with 20% of Hispanic and only 3% of European American children (Jargowsky, 1997). Parents face the double challenge of raising children with few resources in the context of a neighborhood plagued by poverty and its accompanying risks (McAdoo, in Vol. 4 of this *Handbook*).

The pervasiveness of family stressors caused by low family economic resources is best conveyed in qualitative rather than quantitative data. An ethnographic study conducted as part of an evaluation of New Hope, an antipoverty program in Milwaukee, Wisconsin, provided a rich description of poor families' lives and parental struggles to provide for and care for their children. Howard (2000) used data from the New Hope Ethnographic study to explore the associations between employment, social support, and parental well-being. We draw on Howard's work to present two cases that illustrate the stresses and strains that often permeate the lives of low-income parents.

Samantha (a pseudonym) is a 25-year-old African American single mother of four children, two boys ages 2 and 4, and two girls, ages 10 and 12. Samantha has never been married, and her children's fathers are not involved in their lives. Samantha has primarily supported her children through the welfare system. She left welfare for work only a year before the ethnography began. Despite having a General Education Development (GED) degree, Samantha has only found work at low-wage jobs, which she had found very boring. Within an 18-month period she worked at a fast-food restaurant, a dry cleaner, and a video store. Although she was hired for full-time jobs, her unpredictable schedule seldom totaled more than 30 hours a week. In addition, Samantha had problems getting along with managers and coworkers.

Although the minimum wage jobs she has held have helped to pay her household bills, she found the jobs were not accommodating to her parenting obligations. The managers did not give her enough notice about her work schedule, which made it difficult to plan for family appointments and arrange childcare. Samantha knows that there are better jobs available if she can increase her education, but her efforts to take college-level courses have failed because of the associated expenses and a lack of affordable and reliable childcare. Samantha's only informal source of emotional and instrumental support is her mother, who has assisted Samantha by watching her children and offering financial assistance. However, Samantha's mother has financial concerns of her own, and giving Samantha money often means that she is unable to pay her own bills.

All of Samantha's money is used to pay for the basic expenses of her household. After paying for rent, phone service, electricity, food, gas, and childcare, she has no money left over. Not only does she live from check to check, but also she is unable to buy herself new shoes. She told the fieldworker that she has been wearing the same pair of shoes for 3 years. In addition, she can't afford to buy the children the boots and winter clothes that they need.

The financial strain associated with low wage jobs makes managing to pay her household expenses is emotionally taxing. As Samantha described:

> I'm just like, I'm tired and stressed out. If I come off the wrong way just know that I am stressed. But I'm not stupid. If I didn't have as much stress on me, man I probably could get far in life. But right now I can't see past to make sure that bills are paid (Howard, 2000, p. 111).

The constant inability to give her children want they want and need often makes Samantha feel inadequate and helpless. She describes that she often feels "run over by people and never getting ahead." Samantha admits that her high levels of stress and feelings of helplessness affect her parenting. She describes that working hard and being so worried about money often results in her having little patience with her children. She finds herself exhausted, and unable to respond warmly to her children's demands on her time and energy. She said that she started to hate her children and no longer enjoys being at home with them.

Rose is a 25-year-old single African American mother of two boys, ages 4 and 6. Rose lives with her children, her boyfriend, Doug, and her stepfather. Rose works part-time at a temporary nursing agency as she had for the four years prior to the ethnographic study. She describes this work as unpredictable and sporadic, and boring. She rarely works more than 30 hours a week and averages 15 to 20 hours of work a week. The short-term job placements may provide a week or two or full-time work, but that solid week may be followed by a week with only 12 hours of work. She earns $8.50 an hour, and even though the pay is above minimum wage, her earnings are well short of her needed income.

The temporary nature of the work is part of the reason that she has irregular and few work hours, but her difficulties in finding transportation and childcare also create problems. Many job placements are virtually inaccessible by public transportation, so if Rose can't find a ride or borrow a car she usually declines the job placement. Rose also can only accept jobs that allow her to get her children off to school at 8 a.m., which means that she is not able to accept placements for first-shift jobs. However, working second shift jobs means that she has to arrange for someone to care for her children until ten or eleven at night.

Rose relies on her family, especially her cousins, for childcare, but Rose feels that they are not trustworthy, and her feelings were justified when one cousin was convicted of attempted murder, and the murder was committed when her cousin was supposed to be caring for Rose's children. Other cousins are only willing to watch her children if they are able to borrow her car. If Rose's car is not running or they have other means of transportation, they are unwilling to watch her children. Other family members are sometimes able to watch her children, but this usually depends on their schedules, and Rose finds it exhausting to find someone to watch her boys.

Despite the inconsistent nature of the temporary placements, Rose appreciates the flexibility that her work gives her to attend to the needs of her children. For example, if they are ill she has the ability to stay home with them, but if she were employed by a nursing facility she would be unable to do this.

Rose is under constant financial pressure. She is behind on her household bills, suffers from food shortages, and cannot afford formal childcare for her boys or to maintain a reliable car. With the difficulty in getting to work and finding childcare, Rose often feels that she is more stressed by trying to work than by not trying. Spending so much energy just to get her children what they need makes Rose feel helpless about her situation.

Rose has relied on traditional welfare services to help provide her family with health insurance and food, but she describes the formal services as frustrating, confusing, and highly unpredictable. She has been turned away from the welfare office being told that she earned too much money to receive food stamps, only to find that she was eligible several months later despite the fact that she was working more hours and earning more money than before.

The struggles of Samantha and Rose illustrate only some of the pressures and strain that low-income parents face. However, their stories are not extraordinary, and the themes echoed in their stories are heard among the other families in the New Hope ethnography as well as other ethnographies (e.g., Edin and Lein, 1997; Newman, 1999). Poor parents hope to support their children through employment, but find that unpredictable work schedules and low wages as well as difficulties arranging for childcare and finding transportation make work an exhausting endeavor. Low-wage jobs often involve tedious or boring work, offering little reward other than pay. In addition, being unable to meet household expenses leaves poor parents feeling frustrated, helpless, and depressed. Perhaps most remarkable about these stories is that despite the difficulties these parents face, they continue the daily struggle to provide for their children.

CENTRAL QUESTIONS IN THE STUDY OF PARENTS IN POVERTY

We turn now to the questions that are central to understanding parents in poverty. We briefly discuss why these questions are important and provide a theoretical explanation of relevant issues. To the extent that research allows, we also summarize current thinking about the issues raised by these questions.

How Does Family Economic Stress Affect Parents and Parenting?

A long line of research (reviewed in McLoyd, 1990) has found that low-income parents, as compared with middle-class parents, are more likely to use an authoritarian and punitive parenting style and less likely to either support their children or provide them with stimulating learning experiences in the home. They are more likely to use physical punishment and other forms of power-assertive discipline, and less likely to ask children about their wishes, reward children for positive behavior, or be responsive to children's expressed needs. In the extreme, these behaviors may lead to child abuse or neglect, and poor parents are more likely than more advantaged parents to abuse their children (Azar, in Vol. 4 of this *Handbook*).

Recent theoretical models of parenting that have been developed for low-income populations (e.g., Chase-Lansdale and Pittman, in press; McLoyd, 1990) include an explicit role for both family economic resources and mental health. These constructs are included because each of these characteristics may have a direct effect on childrearing. A family's economic resources may constrain the quality and quantity of goods such as childcare or books that parents can purchase for their child's benefit. Poverty and economic insecurity take a toll on a parent's mental health, and this may be an important cause of low-income parents' nonsupportive parenting. As described by Zahn-Waxler, Duggal, and Gruber (in Vol. 4 of this *Handbook*) depression and other forms of psychological distress can profoundly affect parents' interactions with their children.

How Does Low-Wage Maternal Employment Affect Mothers and Parenting?

Recent reforms to U.S. welfare policies have changed the life situations of many low-income mothers and children. Until 1996, welfare benefits were an entitlement available to all low-income mothers who met the income-based eligibility criteria. With the passing of the 1996 Personal Responsibility and Work Opportunity Reconciliation Act, cash benefits to low-income mothers have become a temporary safety net contingent on demonstrated work efforts. Legislation now requires that most mothers work or participate in a work-training program in order to receive financial support.

Many former welfare recipients have already moved into the workforce. Between 1993 and 1999, welfare caseloads dropped by 50%, with eight states reducing caseloads by over 70% (Administration on Children and Families, 2000). Not all mothers transitioning off welfare enter into the workforce, but studies have found that many women do (Corcoran, Danziger, Kalil, and Seefeldt, 2000). Yet despite employment, few former welfare recipients find jobs that pay enough to lift their families out of poverty. Thus they transition from welfare to the ranks of the working poor (Wertheimer, 1999). In large part because of these changes in social welfare policies, social scientists have renewed their efforts to understand the effect of low-wage parental employment on parenting and child well-being.

Researchers have suggested several reasons why low-wage work may negatively affect parenting. Developmental scientists have argued that the labor force participation of women, and the concomitant time away from their young children, may harm their relationship with their children and lead to the children's social maladjustment (e.g., Belsky and Rovine, 1988). Nonmaternal childcare may compromise the amount and quality of attention and stimulation in the early years of children's lives, leading to poor cognitive development (e.g., Greenstein, 1995). Job role strain and the stress of working may have a negative effect on mothers' parenting (e.g., Hoffman, 1984). Finally, features of work, such as inflexible work hours, a lack of control over day-to-day tasks, and repetitious and boring duties may have a detrimental affect on parental cognitive skills, such as intellectual flexibility, or other personal characteristics, such as self-direction, and ultimately on parenting practices (Kohn 1963, 1969; Parcel and Menaghan, 1994, 1997; Whitbeck et al., 1997).

At the same time, there are several reasons to think that parenting may benefit from maternal employment (Vandell and Ramanan, 1992). The socioemotional benefits that poor parents may derive from even low-wage work might include increased self-esteem, personal efficacy, and a sense of hope. These increases in parental mental health may in turn improve parenting practices and family relationships (Desai, Chase-Lansdale, and Michael, 1989). In addition, low-wage work may not raise a family out of poverty, but it could still provide the family with greater economic resources than social welfare programs. Consequently, a transition from welfare to work may enable a parent to meet more of her or his children's basic needs as well as to provide them with more toys and varied educational or cultural experiences (Beyer, 1995).

Maternal employment has been a rich area of research for the past 20 years. However, the bulk of research has led to more calls for research than to firm conclusions (Harvey, 1999). Part of the disparity in hypotheses and findings is due to the fact that employment means very different things to different working parents. Some parents work full-time, full-year in low-wage jobs that fail to lift their families out of poverty. In other cases, work is intermittent, combined with welfare support, or several family members, including older children, hold multiple low-wage jobs, all contributing to family income. In addition, the characteristics of jobs, such as the flexibility of work hours and the challenging nature of job tasks, may vary widely.

Do Poor Parents Have Different Goals for or Views of Children's Development?

Another potential source of a disparity between poor and nonpoor parents is rooted in parenting beliefs and values, as well as parents' understanding of children's development. Many studies using diverse samples and outcome measures have found differences in socialization goals and understanding of children's development among parents from different socioeconomic strata. But research on parents' cognitions has been conceptually diverse, and very little effort has been directed toward understanding the extent to which income or socioeconomic status influences parenting values, goals, and beliefs. Despite researchers' relative neglect of this area, debate in the public arena on this topic remains prominent.

Early research on differences in parents' cognitions focused on particular parenting values that differed by broad socioeconomic classes (Hoff, Laursen, and Tardiff, in Vol. 2 of this *Handbook*). One of the most often cited differences thought to affect childrearing is that lower-class parents value conformity in their children, whereas parents in a higher social class value self-direction (Gecas, 1979). Recent attention has also been focused on understanding differences between lower-class and middle-class parents in goals as manifested in discrete parent–child interactions. Prior research has suggested that lower-class parents, and particularly lower-class parents of color, may be more likely to use parent-centered discipline strategies intended to result in short-term compliance. In contrast, middle-class parents may use child-centered discipline strategies intended to teach the child a lesson, satisfy a child's emotional needs, or foster positive familial relations (for a review see Kelley, Power, and Wimbush, 1992; McLoyd and Wilson, 1992). Finally, lower-class parents appear to have a less complex understanding of children's behavior and development compared with more advantaged parents (Sameroff and Feil, 1985).

Complicating this research are the facts that important parental values and beliefs (e.g., academic achievement) do not differ by social class (Kelley et al., 1992) and that social class is only one of many potential influences on a parent's belief system (Sigel and McGillicuddy-De Lisi, in Vol. 3 of this *Handbook*). In addition, class differences in values have declined over time, suggesting that values may be a less important source of differences in parenting practices than once thought (e.g., Alwin, 1984; Hoff et al., in Vol. 2 of this *Handbook*; Wright and Wright, 1976), especially given that the association between a parent's cognitions and behaviors has been found to be modest and inconsistent (Sigel, 1992).

Perhaps most important, using social class as a basis for comparison provides few insights about processes unless class is broken down into its component parts and processes of influence are investigated for each of the dimensions—education, income, and occupation (Belsky, Hertzog, and Rovine, 1986). But for all the recent attention directed toward better understanding the links between beliefs and behaviors, we know precious little about the processes and contextual or parental characteristics that determine parent's goals, values, and beliefs. As McLoyd and Wilson (1992) and Brody, Flor, and Gibson (1999) suggested, differences in cognition may result from or complement psychological distress associated with economic strain. Likewise, Dix (1992) argues that parent-centered discipline strategies are more likely to be used by parents when they are in stressful situations. Finally, as we will discuss later in the chapter, Ogbu (1981) and others suggested these differences might be the result of adaptive responses to rearing children in a dangerous environment.

How Does Poverty Affect Fathers' Parenting?

The role of married, coresident fathers has long been the subject of research on families in poverty. The seminal works of Elder (1974; Liker and Elder, 1983), Conger and colleagues (1990), and Brody and colleagues (1994) have all demonstrated that job loss and economic strain negatively affect fathers' mental health, as well as decrease the warmth and increase the hostility of coparent relations. Consequently, poor mental health and more hostile coparent relations may compromise the quality of father–child relations and other aspects of parenting (Conger et al., 1992; Conger et al., 1993; Elder and Caspi, 1988; Whitbeck et al., 1997).

Although married fathers have played a central role in our understanding of parenting and family functioning in intact poor families, nonmarried fathers have been largely overlooked in descriptions of parenting among low-income populations. The majority of research on parenting in low-income single parent families has focused almost solely on the children's primary caretakers—mothers. Nearly one third of all infants in the United States today were born to unmarried parents. The proportions are even higher among poor and minority populations, 40% among Hispanics, and 70% among African Americans (Ventura et al., 1995). Whereas in the western European countries, the vast majority of unmarried fathers are living with the mother when their child is born, in the United States only about 40% to 45% of unwed parents follow this pattern (Bumpass and Lu, 2000; McLanahan, Garfinkel, Reichman, and Teitler, 2001).

Despite the fact that many children of single mothers do not live with their fathers, we do know that some of these fathers are not absent from their children's lives (Hardy, Duggan, Masnyk, and Pearson, 1989; Mott, 1990). For example, using data from the National Longitudinal Survey of Youth, Mott (1990) found that among children who had never lived with their fathers, over 25% saw their fathers at least weekly. Consequently, the challenge is to understand the nature of children's involvement and relationships with noncustodial fathers and father figures, as well as the antecedents and consequences of these relationships.

Most existing research has sought to link the extent of paternal involvement or the quality of father–child relationships to children's well-being (e.g., Black, Dubowitz, and Starr, 2000; Coley, 1998; Furstenberg and Harris, 1993). In a meta-analysis of previous studies, Amato and Gilbreth (1999) found that the frequency of fathers' visits had no discernable impact on their children's academic or social well-being. However, the authors concluded that fathers' financial support, as well as a higher quality father–child relationships, and a positive parenting style on the part of the fathers does have a small effect on children's academic and social well-being. Although this generalization is not specific to lower income populations, studies on low-income populations support these findings (Furstenberg and Harris, 1993; Greene and Moore, 2000).

All in all, we still know very little about the antecedents of parenting among nonresident fathers, especially low-income fathers. Nonresident fathers are underrepresented in most of our national surveys. Garfinkel, McLanahan, and Hanson (1998) estimate that about one third of the "missing fathers" are not included in prominent national surveys and about two thirds of this group do not provide accurate reports of their parental status. What we do know comes mainly from large-scale quantitative studies that have linked fathers' demographic characteristics to their financial support or the frequency of their visits with their children. Characteristics associated with higher levels of nonresidential paternal involvement include geographic proximity, whether the father has additional children, as well as the father's financial resources, employment, and education (Cooksey and Craig, 1998; Danziger and Radin, 1990; Greene and Moore, 2000; Seltzer, 1991). These findings are suggestive of factors that are important in understanding parenting among never married populations, but none of these studies has been able to look at a broad range of theoretically important determinants of fathers' parenting among never-married fathers.

What Are Important Sources of Variation Among Low-Income Parenting Practices?

Past research on low-income parenting has often used a comparative framework in which parenting styles or particular behaviors of low-income parents are contrasted with those of more-affluent parents. This approach has generated important insights and information, but it has been criticized for its deficit orientation and inattention to individual differences in parenting among disadvantaged populations.

Critics of comparative frameworks (Huston, McLoyd, and Garcìa Coll, 1994; Kelley et al., 1992; Spencer, 1990) have argued that they do not provide information about the extent or sources of variation in parenting among low-income populations. On average, low-income parents may be less responsive or provide less stimulating home learning environments, but substantial proportions of poor parents are just as warm as their middle-class counterparts and provide comparably stimulating home environments. Consequently, understanding the characteristics or circumstances that promote positive parenting among low-income populations may prove as important as understanding the risks that poverty might pose (McLoyd, 1990).

Social support, including emotional and instrumental support, may buffer some of the negative effects of economic hardship on parenting behavior (McLoyd, 1997). Low-income mothers who report sources of social support are less likely than other low-income mothers to display harsh and punitive parenting (Hashima and Amato, 1994; Stevens, 1998). Family, friends, and intimate relationships may help to alleviate the stress associated with economic hardship by offering parents affection, companionship, an opportunity to talk things over, as well as more concrete types of help with financial obligations and childcare tasks (Simons, Beaman, Conger, and Chao, 1993). In addition, social networks may provide parents with information and suggestions about managing their households and childrearing (Cochran and Niego, in Vol. 4 of this *Handbook*; Jackson, Gyamfi, Brooks-Gunn, and Blake, 1998).

Poor families are a heterogeneous group, and several characteristics of parents may promote positive parenting and predict variations in patterns of childrearing. For example, strong religious beliefs and higher educational attainment have been associated with less controlling discipline (Brody, Stoneman, and Flor, 1996; Kelley et al., 1992). Higher education has also been associated with more stimulating home learning environments (Parcel and Menaghan, 1994). Other potential sources of variation include maternal age, feelings of maternal self-efficacy, intergenerational coresidence and relationships, and children's temperamental difficulty (Brody, Flor, and Gibson, 1999; Raver and Leadbetter, 1999; Wakschlag, Chase-Lansdale, and Brooks-Gunn, 1996).

Critics have also argued that a comparative approach tends to consider the behavior of middle-class parents to be the standard of normative parenting and characterize the differences of low-income parents as deficits. They suggest that, before such comparisons are made, a more in-ductive approach is necessary to identify and describe important dimensions, patterns, and styles of parenting among low-income families. Underlying this critique is the argument that parenting among low-income populations is qualitatively different from parenting in middle-class samples. For example, recent research (Brody and Flor, 1998; McGroder, 2000) suggests that high levels of warmth and displays of affection often accompany harsh or punitive parenting among low-income populations, and that therefore the typically negative behaviors are interpreted as parental involvement and concern rather than harsh or rejecting.

Summary

The current issues involving parents in poverty that we have chosen to highlight center on basic questions about the processes by which poverty affects parenting, as well as how these processes may differ by characteristics and contextual circumstances of families. We recommend that research continue on both fronts. If we hope to explain aggregate differences in parenting practices between poor and nonpoor parents we need to continue to refine our understanding of the pathways by which poverty affects parents. However, we must also continue to appreciate the heterogeneous nature of the characteristics and circumstances of poor families and parents, especially with regard to socialization goals, parenting knowledge, employment, social support, and family structure.

RESEARCH ON PARENTS IN POVERTY

We begin our review of research on parents in poverty with a discussion of the methodological challenges such research entails. Next we center our discussion of the relevant empirical studies on several important topics: (1) psychological distress and parenting, (2) home learning environments, (3) interventions, and (4) neighborhood poverty. We provide a representative, but not exhaustive, discussion of these literatures, highlighting the seminal works as well as recent studies, and pointing to both the strengths and limitations of our knowledge.

Methodological Challenges

Developmental research on families and children in poverty has grown exponentially in recent years (see Brooks-Gunn and Duncan, 1997; Chase-Lansdale and Brooks-Gunn, 1995; McLoyd, 1998). Earlier work focused on differences in social class as defined by the combination of education, occupation, and income. Consequently, differences between the lower class and the middle class were described without regard to the distinct contribution of income or poverty to the differences in parenting behavior of lower or higher income families (Hoff et al., in Vol. 2 of this *Handbook*).

The use of social-class measures such as the Hollingshead scale (1975) typifies approaches that make no attempt to untangle correlations among poverty, education, and occupational attainment (Hoff et al., in Vol. 2 of this *Handbook*). The most rigorous way to separate the impacts of income from other influences is with an experimental design that manipulates families' incomes. Such types of large-scale experiments are extremely rare. In the 1960s and 1970s four income-maintenance experiments were conducted. In each, the experimental treatment received a guaranteed minimum income (Salkind and Haskins, 1982). Unfortunately, no assessment was made of family functioning.

Given the paucity of income experiments, much of our knowledge on how poverty affects parenting has come from quasi-experimental and nonexperimental research. Quasi-experimental research capitalizes on data from "natural experiments" in which changes in a family's economic well-being are largely the result of an exogenous shock. Among the better-known developmental studies that rely on quasi-experimental variability in income is Elder's (1974) work on the effects of the Great Depression on children and parents. He relied on two sources of exogenous variability to estimate the effect of economic hardship on children. The first was the timing of the macroeconomic shock with respect to children's age. Since the timing of the Great Depression could not have been affected by when the children were born, his evidence on the differential impacts of economic hardship for children of different ages is particularly convincing. Elder also contrasted families for whom macro-economic conditions produced large income drops with families whose incomes did not fall as much. In this case, difficult-to-measure differences in families may have led to their degree of financial hardship, rendering Elder's inferences regarding the impact of economic hardship less convincing.

Most developmental studies on the impact of poverty on parenting rely on nonexperimental contrasts between parents, and consequently may suffer from serious omitted-variable bias. Income reflects (at least in part) family decisions about employment, welfare program participation, and past savings. Consequently, regression-adjusted associations between income and parenting from nonexperimental data may not be entirely causal, but may instead result from a spurious correlation between difficult-to-measure characteristics of the parents themselves and these outcomes.

Most developmental survey studies of parenting and child development devote little attention to questions on the economic characteristics of households, and income in particular, either because their designers believe that other measures of socioeconomic status (e.g., education) render them redundant or because they fear that respondents will not answer such questions truthfully. Moreover, economic questions are thought to compromise data quality by prompting some potential respondents to drop out of the survey altogether.

Duncan and Petersen (2001) show that this conventional wisdom regarding survey questions on economic characteristics is wrong. There are many examples of successful surveys that gather high-quality income and employment data without suffering unduly from high rates of item non-response. Key to these successes is asking about conceptually appropriate economic components, motivating both respondents and interviewers, probing reluctant respondents with easier-to-answer follow-on questions, and asking questions that do not overburden respondents' memories. Duncan and Petersen (2001) provide recommendations of both short and longer question sequences on income, wealth and earnings.

Methodological challenges to studying parents in poverty also arise from the uneven distribution of poverty among the United States population. As mentioned earlier in the chapter, ethnic and racial minorities are disproportionately likely to be poor and live in poor urban neighborhoods. Consequently, when studying poor parents, particularly poor urban parents, researchers must be sensitive not to confound the effects of poverty with the effects of minority status or other sources of cultural variation in parenting. Some research has found that the associations between poverty and parenting do not differ by ethnicity (Gutman and Eccles, 1999). However, researchers must continue to be sensitive to how cultural differences, ethnicity, and minority status may be confounded with poverty in their research.

Psychological Distress and Parenting

The psychological cost of economic hardship is compellingly portrayed by ethnographic work with poor families. Based on hundreds of ethnographic interviews with low-income welfare recipients and working single mothers living in three cities, Edin and Lein (Edin and Lein, 1997) described these mothers' constant struggles to provide food, housing, and other necessities as well as keep their children out of danger. Despite ongoing hardship, most of the mothers in the study adapted to their situations. They budgeted carefully and spent considerable time and energy making money in alternative ways. Despite their efforts, however, arrangements for childcare, housing, and medical care were often precarious. Any one of a number of events, such as a family or extended-family illness, could cause major disruptions in their employment and family lives. The chronic and pervasive stress that Edin and Lein documented suggests important potential links among economic stress, mental health, and parenting.

Poverty places parents at greater risk for depression and other forms of psychological distress, such as low self-worth and negative beliefs about control. Nationally representative estimates of mental health problems indicate that approximately 10% of poor and less-educated people in the United States currently experience major depressive episodes—twice the rate of others who are more advantaged (Blazer, Kessler, McGonagle, and Swartz, 1994). Using a sample of impoverished inner-city women, Hobfoll, Ritter, Lavin, Hulsizer, and Cameron (1995) found rates of clinical depression to be as high as 27.6% during pregnancy and 24.5% postpartum.

Reports of depressive symptoms among highly disadvantaged mothers suggest that an even higher percentage of mothers may be at risk for clinical depression. For example, approximately 40% of the poor women in two large samples participating in work and training programs scored at or above the cutoff for clinically significant depressive symptoms (McGroder, Zaslow, Moore, and LeMenestrel, 2000; Quint, Bos, and Polit, 1997).

Psychological distress is more prevalent among low-income populations because they experience more negative life events and have fewer resources with which to cope with adverse life experiences (Kessler and Cleary, 1980; McLeod and Kessler, 1990). In addition to elevated levels of chronic stress associated with economic strain, compared with the general population, poor women are more likely to experience threatening and uncontrollable life events such as violence and illness. Economic stress undermines marital relationships and cocaregiving relationships, and poor parents, especially single mothers, are more likely than their advantaged counterparts to be socially isolated (Brody et al., 1994; Simons et al., 1993). For some poor parents, social networks are an important part of survival strategies, but these networks may also be a source of additional stress (Belle, 1990). Finally, with limited financial resources, poor parents often depend on public or private social welfare programs for assistance with crises, but many poor women feel further dehumanized and demeaned by the social welfare system.

Psychological and affective disorders often strongly influence parents' affective interactions and responses, and consequently poor mental health is associated with harsh, inconsistent, and detached parenting (Zahn-Waxler et al., in Vol. 4 of this *Handbook*). Being nurturing, rewarding, attentive, and involved with a child requires concentration, patience, and emotional resources that may be difficult to muster under psychological distress. For example, depressed mothers often demonstrate parenting patterns that reflect the emotional symptoms of their mental state, view the role of parenting less positively and often exhibit feelings of rejection and hostility toward their children (Downey and Coyne, 1990; Field, 1995). These affective reactions are manifested in three possible patterns. Some depressed mothers withdraw from their children and respond with little affect or energy; others become hostile toward their children, usually resorting to interfering and intrusive parenting. Still others may alternate between withdrawn and intrusive behaviors. In all cases, the mothers' responses to the needs of their children tend to be less consistent, frequent, and positive (Downey and Coyne, 1990).

Research in this field has emphasized the associations among economic decline, economic strain, and parental psychological well-being, particularly depression (e.g., McLoyd, 1997). Accordingly, research on low-income families has explored whether elements of depressive parenting patterns are associated with economic hardship and children's maladjustment. It is important to note that these correlations depend on the age and gender of the child, and they do not account for all of the association between family poverty and child well-being (Watson, Kirby, Kelleher, and Bradley, 1996).

The work by Elder and colleagues on children of the Great Depression (Elder, 1974; Elder, Liker, and Cross, 1984; Elder, Nguyen, and Caspi, 1985) found strong associations among economic hardship, parental psychological well-being, and children's well-being in two-parent families. Fathers who experienced job loss and economic deprivation were more distressed psychologically and more prone to explosive, rejecting, and punitive parenting. Preschool-age children in these families, especially boys, were more likely to exhibit problem behaviors, and adolescent girls were more likely to have lower feelings of self-adequacy and to be less goal oriented. Adolescent boys fared better than either adolescent girls or younger children. Elder and colleagues (1985) speculated that the gender and age differences reflected different experiences in families during times of deprivation. During such times, adolescent boys sought economic opportunities outside of the home, which limited the time they spent with their families, perhaps also reducing the amount of negative family interactions they experienced. Younger children and adolescent girls did not have access to buffers provided by extrafamilial activities.

In a more recent application of Elder's framework, Conger and his collaborators (1992, 1993, 1994) have found similar processes operating in midwestern farm families experiencing economic decline. Parents who suffered sudden income losses experienced feelings of economic pressure, which were in turn associated with increases in depressive mood. In interactions with their children these parents were more hostile, more punishing, and less involved. Less-positive parenting was negatively related to adolescents' prosocial behavior. However, it is important to note that the adolescents' social behavior improved over the course of time. Farm families and children became more involved in social institutions, such as schools and churches, and the adolescents' resilience had much to do with their connections to these social influences (Elder and Conger, 2000).

McLoyd, Jayaratne, Ceballo, and Borquez (1994) extended the scope of Elder's and Conger's theoretical frameworks to include single-parent African American families that experience chronic economic strain, but, like Conger, she restricted her sample of children to adolescents. Among African American single mothers, mothers' unemployment was associated with heightened maternal depressive symptoms. Unemployment increased mothers' negative perceptions of their parenting role and their depressive symptoms that were in turn related to increases in punishing parenting behavior. Maternal punishment was associated with adolescents' lower self-esteem and both heightened cognitive distress (i.e., difficulty concentrating) and general anxiety.

In an extension of McLoyd's work, Gutman and Eccles (1999) compared the strength of the associations between financial strain, negative parent–adolescent relationships, and adolescents' academic achievement among African American families relative to Euro-American families, and single-parent families relative to two-parent families. The study found no differences in the pattern of associations with respect to ethnicity or family structure. In all cases, financial strain was associated with more difficulty in the parent–adolescent relationship, which in turn was associated with lower academic achievement. The authors conclude that parents and adolescents show similar responses to financial strain.

Brody and Flor (1997) proposed a model similar to that of McLoyd and colleagues, but their sample included 6- to 9-year-old children rather than adolescents. They found that among rural African-American single-parent families, reduced financial resources were associated with lower maternal self-esteem and an increase in depressive symptoms. Lower self-esteem, but not depressive symptoms, were in turn associated with deterioration in family routines and the quality of mother–child interactions. These family processes were related to the child's self-regulation and indirectly associated with children's academic achievement, as well as externalizing and internalizing problems. Likewise, the study by Harnish, Dodge, and Valente (1995) of ethnically diverse low-income children entering first grade found that the quality of mother–child interactions partially accounted for the effects of social class and maternal depressive symptoms on children's externalizing behavior.

There are important gaps in what we know about connections among income, parental mental health, parenting behaviors, and child well-being. For example, little is known about differential effects of economic hardship on parenting infants, toddlers, children, and adolescents. Although it can be argued that parental interactions with older children may be particularly vulnerable to parents' psychological well-being given the difficult issues of control and authority that are often involved (Hoff et al., in Vol. 2 of this *Handbook*), the work of Elder and colleagues (1985) suggests that children of all ages are affected, but that the nature of the effects varies for younger and older children. Moreover, older children have greater access than younger children to supportive interactions and experiences outside the home. Clearly, more attention should be given to the role of age and gender in shaping poor children's interactions within and outside their homes.

Furthermore, because different types of psychological distress tend to occur together, research should assess interactions among them (Seifer, 1995). Sameroff, Seifer, Barocas, Zax, and Greenspan (1987) argued that the number of risk factors facing children and parents might be more important than the particular types of risk factors. In addition, it is important to clarify whether particular parenting practices, such as physical discipline, are important in their own right, or because they represent more global parenting styles, negative relationships, or other experiences (Darling and Steinberg, 1993). Finally, we know little about which aspects of parenting are more or less stable as children develop and as financial circumstances change (Holden and Miller, 1999).

Poverty and the Home Environment

Pioneering work by Bradley and Caldwell (1984) delineated the important aspects of children's home environments that are associated with children's well-being. Although Bradley and Caldwell focused on multiple aspects of the home environment that, taken together, predict children's well-being, the provision of learning experiences in early childhood has been found to be a strong predictor of children's later school achievement and cognitive functioning. Actions such as providing children with a library card and learning-oriented toys or experiences, as well as reading to them and joining them in developmentally appropriate activities have been found to promote their cognitive development (Bradley and Caldwell, 1980).

Unfortunately, research has consistently found that children from poor families are less likely to have a favorable home learning environment compared with children from more affluent families (Bradley et al., 1994). Both poverty and persistent poverty are strongly associated with less optimal home environments (Garrett, Ng'andu, and Ferron, 1994). This should not be surprising, because poor parents have less money to spend on books or toys for their children. They also have less money to provide their children with enriching learning and social experiences outside of the home, such as music lessons or visits to museums. Consequently, economic resources play a strong role in parents' ability to provide their children with a stimulating learning environment.

Using data from the National Longitudinal Survey of Youth (NLSY) Child Supplement on children from 6 to 9 years old, Miller and Davis (1997) found stronger associations between a child's poverty history and the quality of the cognitive stimulation of home learning environment than between poverty and the quality of maternal emotional support. They concluded that income and poverty have a particularly direct and strong association with the provision of material and other learning resources. Similarly, Garrett, and colleagues (1994) used data from the NLSY child supplements to investigate the association of poverty experiences from birth to 4 years of age with the home environment, as measured by the short form of the HOME scale, of young children. They found, after controlling for maternal and child characteristics, that early poverty, depth of poverty, and persistence of poverty all had a significant and negative association with the quality of the home environment.

Several studies have found that the more positive home learning environments of high- versus low-income children account for as much as half of the high- versus low-income gap in test scores of preschool children, and as much as one third of the gap in the achievement scores of elementary school children. Using data from both the NLSY Child Supplements and the Infant Health and Development Program (IHDP), Smith, Brooks-Gunn, and Klebanov (1997) investigated the extent to which the home environment mediated the effect of family income on children's cognitive development. Among the 5- to 6-year-old children in the NLSY data, HOME scores from when the children were ages 3 to 4 years old reduced the effect of family income-to-need ratios on Peabody Picture Vocabulary Test (PPVT) by 42%. Also using the NLSY data, Smith et al. (1997) considered the mediating role of concurrent HOME scores and a range of other indicators of children's cognitive performance. Analyses found that the early and concurrent HOME scores reduced the effects of the income-to-needs ratio by between 18% to 42%. Using IHDP data on children at 3 and 5 years old, Smith et al. (1997) found that year three HOME scores reduced the effect of family income by 30% to 40% on indicators of cognitive development, including the PPVT and the Wechsler Preschool and Primary Scale of Intelligence.

Despite strong negative associations between poverty and the quality of the children's home learning environment, research has still not been able to establish a causal link between the two.

Economic resources that provide learning materials and parental practices are both key elements of the home learning environment, and it is virtually impossible to decompose either the relative influence of poverty on each element or the relative importance of each for children's development by relying on naturally occurring variation in study populations. Experimental interventions, which we discuss both in the following section and final section of this chapter, and quasi-experimental approaches such as sibling difference models, offer a promising approach to the task of moving from correlation to causation.

Intervention Research

Recently revived parenting-education and home-visiting programs have an extensive history in the United States (Smith, Pevou, and Lesesne, in Vol. 4 of this *Handbook*; Weiss, 1993). Many interventions to improve the life chances of low-income children have focused on parents and parenting, often targeting low-income parents or parents who face a range of social risk factors related to poverty. Parenting programs rely on strategies of educational home visits, emotional and instrumental support, and informational sessions or videos. Some have combined parent-focused strategies with childcare center-based programs. Several projects have also targeted either parental literacy or intergenerational literacy. Despite the diversity, designers of all of these programs hope to improve poor parents' interactions with their children, either by improving mental health and thus improving parent-child interactions, increasing educational and literacy activities in the home, or getting parents involved with other community resources (Seitz and Provence, 1990).

Rigorous evaluations of these programs, with random assignment of some respondents to a control comparison group, have provided both concrete information about the effectiveness of particular programs, as well as a better understanding of the ways in which poverty shapes parenting. Most evaluations of parenting programs have addressed whether the program improved child–parent interactions. Fewer attend to the ways in which the intervention may have influenced parents and parenting, including parent's mental health or parent–child interactions. Looking across these studies, however, some tentative conclusions seem warranted (Brooks-Gunn, Berlin, and Fuligni, 2000; Gomby, Cubross, and Behrman, 1999).

Surprisingly few evaluations have assessed whether parent-focused interventions have improved participating parents' mental health. Of those that have considered this question, nearly all report that the program neither helped nor harmed parents' depression, self-esteem, or other indicators of mental health (Brooks-Gunn et al., 2000). When positive impacts have been found, they are usually concentrated among mothers who are most at risk. For example, a program that targeted pregnant women with little social support found that, among particularly high-risk participants, a home-visit program with a therapeutic curriculum improved participants' reports of depressive symptoms more than a home-visiting program with an educational curriculum (Booth, Mitchell, Barnard, and Spieker, 1989).

Even in the absence of apparent effects on parental mental health, a remarkable number of intervention evaluations have documented modest improvements in parent–child interactions, including leading parents to be more sensitive, supportive, and positive, as well as less harsh. For example, an experimental evaluation of the Nurse Home Visitation Program (Olds, Henderson, Chamberlin and Tatelbaum, 1986; Olds, Henderson, Tatelbaum and Chamberlin, 1986, 1988) found that mothers who received intensive home visits from professional nurses were less restrictive and punishing with their children and showed more positive parenting skills than the control-group mothers.

Some but not all parent-centered programs have also had positive effects on the home learning environment. For example, Larson's (1980) evaluation of the Montreal Home Visitation Study found that mothers who received both prenatal and postnatal home visits until their children reached the age of 15 months provided a better home environment than control group mothers, and that effects were particularly pronounced for the provision of appropriate play materials and opportunities for variety in the daily routine. Programs have also met with mixed success in improving parents' knowledge of child development and attitudes toward childrearing (Brooks-Gunn et al., 2000).

Despite the fact that some programs have succeeded in changing parenting behavior or knowledge, programs focused solely on parents have not demonstrated a consistent ability to improve the cognitive and social well-being of poor children (Yoshikawa, 1994). The review by Olds and colleagues (1999) suggests that parent-focused interventions work best when parents perceive that they or their children need help and when parents face multiple risk factors.

To date, the various interventions undertaken to improve parental mental health have been limited in scope, with most relying on social support and instructional interventions. Despite demonstrating modest changes in parenting behavior, most interventions have not measured the outcomes necessary to determine whether the intervention has been effective at improving parental mental health. Consequently, it is difficult to know whether to attribute the lack of significant impacts on child outcomes to the fact that the parent's mental health was not improved or whether the causal associations between parental mental health, parenting, and children's outcomes are weaker than expected by program designers (Brooks-Gunn et al., 2000). If the former explanation proves to be true, it will be important to broaden the approaches that interventions take to improving parental mental health and reducing parental strain.

Neighborhood Poverty Influences on Parenting and Children

Theoretical and empirical work on how neighborhood characteristics affect families has been dominated by the question of how neighborhoods influence children rather than parents. Despite this emphasis, there are good reasons to hypothesize that neighborhood characteristics may affect parental socialization strategies. Parenting may be influenced directly by neighborhood poverty, as parents adapt to the communities in which they are rearing their children. In addition, parenting may be indirectly influenced by neighborhood characteristics because neighborhoods might affect children, and parents, in turn, may respond to their children's behavior. To date, few empirical studies have systematically investigated how neighborhood characteristics, and neighborhood poverty in particular, influence parents and families. Consequently, we discuss theories and research on how neighborhood-level poverty affects both children and parenting, and suggest that theories that have been developed to describe neighborhood influences on children may be broadened to include parenting, and therefore offer numerous hypotheses for additional research.

Wilson (1987) galvanized empirical research on community and neighborhood effects with his description and analysis of conditions in high-poverty, inner-city Chicago neighborhoods. He provided explanations of structural changes that produced these conditions as well as of how life in high-poverty urban neighborhoods affects families and children living in them. In summary, he hypothesized that massive changes in the economic structure of inner cities, when combined with residential mobility among more advantaged African Americans, have resulted in homogeneously impoverished neighborhoods that provide neither resources nor positive role models for the children and adolescents who reside within them.

Others have provided a more general summary of ways in which neighborhood and community processes may affect parenting and children's development (Coulton, 1996; Earls and Buka, 2000; Haveman and Wolfe, 1994; Jencks and Mayer, 1990), including:

(1) "Stress" theory, which emphasizes the importance of exposure to such physical toxins as lead in soil and paint, as well as to such social and psychological conditions as community violence;

(2) "Social organization" theory, based on the importance of role models and a values consensus in the neighborhood, which in turn limit and control problem behavior among young people and give parents social support in their socializing efforts;

(3) "Institutional" explanations, in which the neighborhood's institutions (e.g., schools, police protection) rather than neighbors per se make the difference;

(4) "Epidemic" theories, based primarily on the power of peer influences to spread problem behavior in children or parents.

Because adolescents typically spend a good deal of time away from their homes, explanations of neighborhood influences emanating from peer-based "epidemics," role models, schools and other neighborhood-based resources would appear to be more relevant for them than for younger children. However, interactions between preschool children and their kin, neighbors, religious communities, and childcare and health systems suggest that neighborhood influences may begin long before adolescence (Chase-Lansdale, Gordon, Brooks-Gunn, and Klebanov, 1997).

Proponents of the stress theory, such as Earls and Buka (2000), emphasize the potential importance for child development of exposure to violence. Studying a sample of patients in a Boston pediatric clinic, Taylor, Zuckerman, Harik, and Groves (1992) found that 1 in 10 children had witnessed a violent event prior to age 6. Psychiatric problems ranging from posttraumatic stress disorder and aggression to externalizing behavioral disorders are more common among children and youth who witness violence (Singer, Anglin, Song, and Lunghofer, 1995). Neighborhood violence may also have indirect effects on child development, and a direct effect on parenting if mothers in physically dangerous neighborhoods restrict their children's interactions with peers and adults (Furstenberg, 1993).

Jarrett (1997) synthesized findings from her own and others' ethnographic studies to identify the diverse strategies used by parents living in dangerous neighborhoods to limit their children's exposure to neighborhood risks. Some families will perform domestic tasks such as grocery shopping at particular times, for example in the morning, because the streets are safer before drug dealers arrive. Other families actively avoid neighbors whose lifestyles differ from their own. With regard to protecting child from neighborhood dangers, parents may isolate their children from risks by confining them to their house, selectively choosing playmates, and seeking out resources within and outside their community such as after-school enrichment programs or just safer playgrounds.

Research has documented a diverse set of parental strategies to buffer children from the risks associated with poor neighborhoods, but little work has explored determinants of these strategies. Exceptions are the work of Elder, Eccles, Ardelt, and Lord (1995) and Furstenberg, Cook, Eccles, Elder, and Sameroff (1999). Using survey data from 429 families in low-income Philadelphia neighborhoods with adolescents, Elder and colleagues found that financial stress affected parent's sense of parental efficacy, and this association was mediated by depressed affect. Parents with greater economic pressure felt less capable of making a positive difference in their children's lives. Lower parental efficacy, in turn, was strongly associated with the use of parental management strategies. Parents with greater efficacy were more likely to seek out promotive and protective activities for their children both within their household and out of the home.

Social organization in a neighborhood may well matter for families with young children. Neighborhoods in which parents frequently come into contact with one another and share values are more likely to monitor the behavior of and potential dangers to children (Sampson 1992; Sampson and Groves, 1989). Contact among parents may lead them to share ways of dealing with the inevitable problem behavior of their children, encouraging talents in their children, connecting to community health and other resources, and organizing neighborhood activities (Chase-Lansdale et al., 1997). Others argue that family management practices are key to understanding how neighborhood and community conditions may affect children's development (Furstenberg, 1993; Furstenberg et al., 1999). They point out that families formulate different strategies for rearing children in high-risk neighborhoods, ranging from extreme protection and insulation to an active role in developing community-based "social capital" networks that can help children at key points in their academic or labor market careers.

The neighborhood study of Sampson, Raudenbush, and Earls (1997) is noteworthy for its focus on the "collective efficacy" of neighborhoods. This component of a neighborhood's social organization is measured with a survey of adult residents in sampled neighborhoods rather than relying exclusively on demographic census-based measures. Collective efficacy combines social cohesion (the extent to which neighbors trust each other and share common values) with informal social control (the extent to which neighbors can count on each other to monitor and supervise youth and protect public order).

It is thus a capacity for collective action shared by neighbors. They find that collective efficacy so defined relates strongly to neighborhood levels of violence, personal victimization, and homicide in Chicago, after controlling for social composition as indicated by census variables, and for prior crime. One could imagine that lower levels of neighborhood violence and crime might change parenting practices in ways that benefit young children, although that possibility has not yet been tested with the Sampson et al. (1997) or other data.

One striking result in broad-based quantitative studies of neighborhood effects is of larger differences in parenting and children's achievement and behavior within neighborhoods than between them. Using data from the Infant Health and Development Program, Klebanov, Brooks-Gunn, and Duncan (1994) found that at most, 4% of the variation in the maternal depression, social support, and behavioral coping of mothers of preschool children could be accounted for by neighborhood conditions. With data from a diverse set of Philadelphia neighborhoods, Furstenberg et al. (1999, Table 7.1) found similar results for their measures of the psychological resources of adolescents' caregivers, and only 10% of the variance in family management practices was found across neighborhoods.

Despite explaining little of the variance in child outcomes, some neighborhood factors have proved to be consistently significant predictors of preschoolers' achievement and behavior. Notably, having high–socioeconomic status neighbors appears advantageous for school-age children (see Brooks-Gunn et al., 1997). For both preschool and older children, cognitive and achievement measures appear somewhat more sensitive to neighborhood influences than behavioral and mental health measures. Finally, correlations between neighborhood and child well-being measures were somewhat lower among African Americans than European Americans.

Although our knowledge of the importance of neighborhood and community contexts for parenting and young children's development is far from definitive, the weight of the evidence points to highly distressed neighborhoods as extremely negative environments for parents and children. Neighborhood violence, in particular, may generate a range of detrimental effects on parenting and children and should not be ignored in the design and implementation of interventions. Perceptions of violence contribute to residential mobility and thereby reduce beneficial neighborhood resources and economic integration. Crime and violence appear to reduce a neighborhood's social organization and ability to monitor its problem behavior. Harsh discipline and socially isolating parenting practices appear to develop in part as a reaction to neighborhood dangers (Furstenberg et al., 1999). And violent events themselves appear to scar the psychological development of some of the children who witness them (Osofsky, 1995). Consequently, interventions in high-stress neighborhoods that ignore these conditions are ill advised.

Neighborhood conditions outside of our nation's inner cities appear to be much less consequential for the healthy development of children. Population-based studies are consistent in showing much more variation in achievement, behavior, and parenting within than across neighborhoods. Under these conditions, family factors matter more than neighborhood factors. This certainly does not rule out the possibility of cost-effective community-based interventions outside of high-poverty urban areas. Nor does it imply that certain children aren't affected in fundamental ways by the events and conditions in their neighborhoods. Rather, the implication for children residing outside of high-poverty, urban environments is that family- or child-focused interventions should be considered first.

FUTURE DIRECTIONS FOR RESEARCH ON PARENTS IN POVERTY

Future research on parenting and poverty should take into account the crucial distinction between income-based poverty and the broader concept of socioeconomic status. To the extent that the economic dimensions of parenting and poverty matter, research designs must be able to distinguish the economic from other dimensions of socioeconomic status, and to establish causal connections between poverty and parenting. Traditional nonexperimental research designs have little power to do so. However, randomized parenting interventions as well as welfare reform and housing reform experiments offer new opportunities to further the study of poverty and parenting.

Evaluations of experimental parenting interventions offer an opportunity to investigate directly how parenting goals, values, knowledge, and behaviors can be changed. Intensive, high-quality and high-cost parenting interventions such as the Nurse Home Visitation Program (Olds, Henderson, Chamberlin, and Tatelbaum, 1986; Olds, Henderson, Tatelbaum, and Chamberlin, 1986, 1988) have been able to improve measures of parenting by low-income parents, yet many large-scale programs have failed to reproduce these effects. What accounts for differences in the effectiveness of programs, and the lack of findings in many large-scale programs? Are positive results only possible with an intensive program, or can a program of modest size produce measurable results? Are larger scale programs less effective because they offer a level of services below the threshold necessary to produce effects? Or have less intense programs suffered from poor implementation and therefore demonstrated few measurable successes? To date we have little evidence that bears on these questions, and thus conclude that additional intervention studies are needed.

A promising avenue for future research would take advantage of welfare-reform-related experimental studies involving wage and other supports that are currently underway. These studies are evaluating not only the economic well-being of families but also indicators of caregivers' mental health, parenting practices, gatekeeping activities, and home environments. Given that transitions from welfare to work may involve increases in employment and income, such studies offer a unique opportunity to understand how economic circumstances and characteristics of employment affect family life for parents and children. To date, reports from four evaluation studies have been released. Several other studies including the nonexperimental Three City Study (Johns Hopkins University, 2000) will begin to release findings in the near future.

Examples of random-assignment experiments include the National Evaluation of Welfare to Work Strategies (NEWWS, McGroder et al., 2000), which included two kinds of programs—labor force attachment and human capital development—offered to welfare recipients in Atlanta, Georgia; Grand Rapids, Michigan; and Riverside, California. The Minnesota Family Independence Program combined participation mandates, "make-work-pay" incentives, and services in what amounts to a somewhat more generous version of Minnesota's current TANF program (Knox, Miller, and Gennetian, 2000). The Canadian Self-Sufficiency Project is a pure "make-work-pay" approach offering a very generous, but temporary (3-year) earnings supplement for full-time work (at least 30 hours per week; Lui-Gurr, Vernon, and Mijanovich, 1994). Milwaukee's New Hope Project combined various "make-work-pay" strategies with some employment services (Bos et al., 1999).

Duncan and Chase-Lansdale's (2000) review of the four experiments' findings showed that the programs that offered more generous work supports had positive impacts on child outcomes. More relevant for our review are results for parenting. Changes outside the family, such as increased participation in childcare, after-school programs, and extracurricular programs, appeared to be more important than within-family changes in parent–child relationships, parental mental health, or family routines. They suggest that even supportive programs were unable to improve parental mental health, but they did enhance parents' gatekeeping ability. Ongoing synthesis efforts will yield more information about the impact of welfare-to-work transitions and low-wage employment on parenting and the home environment, and in turn on how changes in particular aspects of parenting affect children's well-being.

An opportunity to understand better how neighborhood poverty affects parents and parenting is provided by experimental public housing reforms. With funding for 10 years, the Moving to Opportunity (MTO) experiment randomly assigned housing project residents in five of the nation's largest cities in the mid-1990s to one of three groups: (1) a group receiving housing subsidies to move into low-poverty neighborhoods, (2) a comparison group receiving conventional Section 8 housing assistance but not constrained in their locations, and (3) a second comparison group receiving no special assistance. The vast majority of parents who volunteered for the program reported that escaping from gangs and drugs was their most important reason for participating in the MTO program.

Katz, Kling, and Liebman (2001) use the experimental data from the Boston MTO site to evaluate the effects of the program on maternal mental health and the health and behavior problems of children between ages 6 and 15. They found significantly more positive reports of general maternal health and suggestive evidence of less maternal depression among families offered the chance to move to low-poverty neighborhoods. They found significantly fewer injuries, accidents, and asthma attacks for children in the experimental relative to control groups. Furthermore, the behavior problems among boys in the experimental groups were significantly lower than among boys in the control groups. Additional sites are also conducting evaluations of family well-being and parenting, and will yield further information about how neighborhood-level characteristics, such as poverty, and neighborhood resources shape family life.

We suggest that experimental-design studies are one of the most promising avenues for future research, but we also identify four other areas of research that are in need of further attention. First, as pointed out previously, we know that parenting practices and styles vary considerably among poor parents, yet we still do not know enough about what circumstances or individual characteristics promote positive adaptive patterns of parenting despite the strain of poverty. A more comprehensive understanding of within-group differences among poor parents would better inform the field.

Second, recent developmental theories and research have emphasized that children's characteristics such as age, gender, or temperament may be important determinants of parenting practices. However, research on poverty and parenting has virtually ignored the variety of child traits that may influence poor parents' gatekeeping activities and their interactions with their children. We suggest that children's characteristics should be more prominently featured in models of parenting among poor families.

Third, most research on the effects of neighborhood poverty have concentrated on child outcomes rather than parenting. Greater attention should be given to how neighborhood characteristics influence parenting styles and practices. This work should also address the joint influences of both family and neighborhood poverty on parenting.

Finally, research has consistently found an association between poverty and parenting, but we know do not know how responsive parenting is to policy-relevant incremental changes in family income and economic resources. Do increases in family income have a more profound impact on parenting at the lower end of the income distribution compared with the higher end? Or is there a threshold of family income below which increases in income do not affect parenting but above which parenting practices improve with additional income? A better understanding of how parenting practices respond to incremental increases in income will refine our understanding of how poverty affects parenting.

CONCLUSIONS

Despite considerable diversity among parents in low-income families, research has documented several important differences between parenting typical in poor and nonpoor families. First, poor parents are more likely to use physical punishment and less likely to ask about and respond to their children's needs. Second, poor families are less likely to provide as rich a home-based learning environment for their children, which in turn appears to reduce their children's chances of academic success. Third, families in low-income neighborhoods adopt different and more protective gatekeeping strategies than families in more affluent neighborhoods.

The evidence further suggests that such differences result at least in part from the stresses and strains associated with low-income parents' persistent struggles to make end meet. Parental psychological distress appears key to understanding linkages between poverty and the more frequent negative interactions between poor parents and their children. Low income limits a poor parent's ability to provide an enriched home learning environment. The unsafe and violent nature of some low-income neighborhoods has been implicated in studies of parents' gatekeeping strategies.

Despite their uniformly daunting challenges, parents in poor families are far from homogeneous in terms of their parenting styles and practices. The average poor–nonpoor parenting differences cited above conceal the fact that many poor parents are as warm and responsive toward their children and provide as enriching learning environments as more affluent parents. Some of the diversity among poor parents can be accounted for by differences in the family structure, work patterns, and skills of low-income parents. However, on the whole, we are far from being able to account for this diversity with the measured characteristics of low-income parents.

We are also discouragingly far from being able to translate research knowledge about the circumstances and practices of low-income parents into effective interventions. Despite a few notable and high-cost exceptions, interventions directed at improving parenting practices have not succeeded. Interventions focused on improving the family economic and neighborhood resources of low-income parents appear to be promising routes, although much remains to be learned here as well.

In their attempts to understanding the impacts of poverty on parenting, researchers need to pay more attention to poverty's conception and measurement. Monolithic treatments of "social class" in developmental studies need to be replaced by more nuanced attention to the components of class—income, education, and occupation. More importantly, research on the impacts of these components of social class on parenting need recognize that they are not randomly assigned to different families. To the extent that difficult to measure behaviors, attitudes and even genetic dispositions affect both class and parenting, studies based on naturally occurring variation in class and parenting risk bias in their assessments of the importance of poverty or other components of class. The recent wave of random-assignment social experiments is a promising avenue for new research on parents in poverty.

ACKNOWLEDGMENT

We are grateful to Dorothy Duncan for helpful comments.

REFERENCES

Administration on Children and Families. (2000). Change in TANF Caseloads. http://www.acf.dhhs.gov/news/stats/caseload.htm

Alwin, D. F. (1984). Trends in parental socialization values: Detroit, 1958–1983. *American Journal of Sociology, 90*, 359–382.

Amato, P. R., and Gilbreth, J. G. (1999). Nonresident fathers and childrens' well-being: A meta-analysis. *Journal of Marriage and the Family, 61*, 557–573.

Bane, M. J., and Elwood, D. (1986). Slipping in and out of poverty: The dynamics of spells. *Journal of Human Resources, 21*, 1–23.

Belle, D. (1990). Poverty and women's mental health. *American Psychologist, 45*, 385–389.

Belsky, J., Hertzog, C., and Rovine, M. (1986). Causal analyses of multiple determinants of parenting: Empirical and methodological advances. In M. Lamb, A. L. Brown, and B. Rogoff (Eds.), *Advances in developmental psychology* (Vol. 4, pp. 153–202). Hillsdale, NJ: Lawrence Erlbaum Associates.

Belsky, J., and Rovine, M. J. (1988). Nonmaternal care in the first year of life and the security of infant–parent attachment. *Child Development, 59*, 157–167.

Beyer, S. (1995). Maternal employment and children's academic achievement: Parenting styles as mediating variable. *Developmental Review, 15*, 212–253.

Black, M., Dubowitz, H., and Starr, R. H. (1999). African American fathers in low-income, urban families: Development, behavior, and home environment of three-year-old children. *Child Development, 70*, 967–978.

Blazer, D. G., Kessler, R. C., McGonagle, K. A., and Swartz, M. S. (1994). The prevalence and distribution of major depression in a national community sample: The National Comorbidity Survey. *American Journal of Psychiatry, 151*, 979–986.

Booth, C. L., Mitchell, S. K., Barnard, K. E., and Spieker, S. J. (1989). Development of maternal social skills in multiproblem families: Effects on the mother–child relationship. *Developmental Psychology, 25*, 403–412.

Bos, H., Huston, A., Granger, R., Duncan, G., Brock, T., and McLoyd, V. (1999). *New hope for people with low incomes: Two-year results of a program to reduce poverty and reform welfare*, New York: Manpower Demonstration Research Corporation.

Bradley, R. H., and Caldwell, B. M. (1980). The relation of the home environment to cognitive competence and IQ among males and females. *Child Development, 51,* 1140–1148.

Bradley, R. H., and Caldwell, B. M. (1984). The HOME inventory and family demographics. *Developmental Psychology, 20,* 315–320.

Bradley, R. H., Whiteside, L., Mundform, D. J., Casey, P. H., Kelleher, K. J., and Pope, S. K. (1994). Early indications of resilience and their relation to experiences in the home environments of low birthweight, premature children living in poverty. *Child Development, 65,* 346–360.

Brody, G. H., and Flor, D. L. (1997). Maternal psychological functioning, family processes, and child adjustment in rural, single-parent, African-American families. *Developmental Psychology, 33,* 1000–1011.

Brody, G. H., and Flor, D. L. (1998). Maternal resources, parenting practices, and child competence in rural, single-parent African-American families. *Child Development, 69,* 803–816.

Brody, G. H., Flor, D. L., and Gibson, N. M. (1999). Linking maternal efficacy beliefs, developmental goals, parenting practices, and child competence in rural single-parent African American families. *Child Development, 70,* 1197–1208.

Brody, G. H., Stoneman, Z., and Flor, D. (1996). Parental religiosity, family processes, and youth competence in rural two-parent African American families. *Developmental Psychology, 32,* 696–706.

Brody, G. H., Stoneman, Z., Flor, D., McCrary, C., Hastings, L., and Conyers, O. (1994). Financial resources, parent psychological functioning, parent co-caregiving, and early adolescent competence in rural two-parent African American families. *Child Development, 65,* 590–605.

Bronfenbrenner, U. (1979). *The ecology of human development.* Cambridge, MA: Harvard University Press.

Brooks-Gunn, J., Berlin, L., and Fuligni, A. (2000). Early childhood intervention programs: What about the family? In J. P. Shonkoff and S. J. Meisels (Eds.), *Handbook of early intervention* (pp. 549–588). New York: Cambridge University Press.

Brooks-Gunn, J., and Duncan, G. (1997). The effects of poverty on children and youth. *The Future of Children, 7,* 55–71.

Brooks-Gunn, J., Duncan, G. J., and Aber, J. L. (1997). *Neighborhood poverty: Context and consequences for children* (Vols. 1 and 2). New York: Russell Sage Foundation.

Bumpass, L., and Lu, H. H. (2000). Trends in cohabitation and implications for children's family contexts in the U.S. *Population Studies, 54,* 29–41.

Chase-Lansdale, P. L., and Brooks-Gunn, J. (Eds.). (1995). *Escape from poverty: What makes a difference for children?* New York: Cambridge University Press.

Chase-Lansdale, P. L., Gordon, R. A., Brooks-Gunn, J., and Klebanov, P. K. (1997). Neighborhood and family influences on intellectual and behavioral competence of preschool and early school-age children. In J. Brooks-Gunn, G. J. Duncan, and J. L. Aber (Eds.), *Neighborhood poverty: Context and consequences for children* (Vol. 1, pp. 79–118). New York: Russell Sage Foundation.

Chase-Lansdale, P. L., and Pittman, L. (in press). Parenting and the home environment. *Future of Children, 11.*

Citro, C., and Michael, R. (Eds.) 1995. *Measuring poverty: A new approach* Washington, DC: National Academy Press.

Coley, R. L. (1998). Children's socialization experiences and functioning in single mother households: The importance of fathers and other men. *Child Development, 69,* 219–230.

Cooksey, E., and Craig, P. H. (1998). Parenting from a distance: The effects of paternal characteristics on contact between nonresidential fathers and their children. *Demography, 35,* 187–200.

Conger, R. D., Conger, K. J., Elder, G. H., Jr., Lorenz, F. O., Simons, R. L., and Whitbeck, L. B. (1992). A family process model of economic hardship and adjustment of early adolescent boys. *Child Development, 63,* 526–541.

Conger, R. D., Conger, K. J., Elder, G. H., Jr., Lorenz, F. O., Simons, R. L., and Whitbeck, L. B. (1993). Family economic stress and adjustment of early adolescent girls. *Developmental Psychology, 29,* 206–219.

Conger, R. D., Elder, G. H., Lorenz, F. O., Conger, K. J., Simons, R. L., Whitbeck, L. B., Huck, S., and Melby, J. N. (1990). Linking economic hardship to marital quality and instability. *Journal of Marriage and the Family, 52,* 643–656.

Conger, R., Ge, X., Elder, G., Lorenz, F., and Simons, R. (1994). Economic stress, coercive family process and developmental problems of adolescents. *Child Development, 65,* 541–561.

Corcoran, M. (1995). Rags to rags: Poverty and mobility in the United States. *Annual Review of Sociology, 21,* 237–267.

Corcoran, M., Danziger, S., Kalil, A., and Seefeldt, K. (2000). How welfare reform is affecting women's work. *Annual Review of Sociology, 26,* 241–269.

Coulton, C. C. (1996). Effects of neighborhoods on families and children: Implications for services. In A. J. Kahn and S. B. Kamerman (Eds.), *Children and their families in big cities.* New York: Cross-National Studies Program.

Danziger, S. K., and Radin, N. (1990). Absent does not equal uninvolved: Predictors of fathering in teen mother families. *Journal of Marriage and the Family, 52,* 636–642.

Darling, N., and Steinberg, L. (1993). Parenting style as context: An integrative model. *Psychological Bulletin, 113,* 487–496.

Desai, S., Chase-Lansdale, P. L., and Michael, R. T. (1989). Mother or market? Effects of maternal employment on intellectual ability of 4-year-old children. *Demography, 26,* 545–561.

Dix, T. (1992). Parenting on behalf of the child: Empathetic goals in the regulation of responsive parenting. In I. E. Sigel (Ed.), *Parental belief systems: The psychological consequences for children* (pp. 319–346). Hillsdale, NJ: Lawrence Erlbaum Associates.

Downey, G., and Coyne, J. C. (1990). Children of depressed parents: An integrative review. *Psychological Bulletin*, *1*, 50–76.

Duncan, G. J., Hoffman, S., Coe, R. D., Morgan, J. N., Hill, M. S., and Corcoran, M. E. (1984). *Years of poverty, years of plenty*. Ann Arbor, MI: Institute for Social Research.

Duncan, G. J., and Chase-Lansdale, P. L. (2000, September). *Welfare reform and child well-being*. Paper presented at the New World of Welfare Reform Pre-conference, Ann Arbor, MI.

Duncan, G. J., and Petersen, E. (2001). The long and short of asking questions about income, wealth and labor supply. *Social Science Research*, *30*, 248–263.

Earls, F., and Buka, S. (2000). Measurement of community characteristics. In S. Meisels and J. Shonkoff (Eds.), *Handbook of early intervention* (pp. 309–324). New York: Cambridge University Press.

Edin, K., and Lein, L. (1997). *Making ends meet*. New York: Russell Sage Foundation.

Eggebeen, D., and Lichter, D. T. (1991). Race, family structure, and changing poverty among American children. *American Sociological Review*, *56*, 801–817.

Elder, G. (1974). *Children of the Great Depression: Social change in life experience*. Chicago: University of Chicago Press.

Elder, G., and Conger, R. (2000). *Children of the land: Adversity and success*. Chicago: University of Chicago Press.

Elder, G. H., Jr., and Caspi, A. (1988). Economic stress in lives: Developmenal perspectives. *Journal of Social Issues*, *44*, 25–45.

Elder, G. H., Jr., Eccles, J. S., Ardelt, M., and Lord, S. (1995). Inner-city parents under economic pressure: Perspectives on the strategies of parenting. *Journal of Marriage and the Family*, *57*, 771–784.

Elder, G. H., Jr., Liker, J. K., and Cross, C. E. (1984). Parent–child behavior in the Great Depression: Life course and inter-generational influences. In P. B. Baltes and O. G. Brim, Jr. (Eds.), *Life-span development and behavior* (Vol. 6, pp. 109–158). New York: Academic Press.

Elder, G. H., Nguyen, T. V., and Caspi, A. (1985). Linking family hardship to children's lives. *Child Development*, *56*, 361–75.

Encyclopedia Britannica. (2001). Encyclopedia Britannica Online Dictionary SV "Poverty" http://www.eb.com/.

Field, T. (1995). Psychologically depressed parents. In M. H. Bornstein (Ed.), *Handbook of parenting* (Vol. 2, pp. 85–99). Mahwah, NJ: Lawrence Erlbaum Associates.

Furstenberg, F. F. (1993). How families manage risk and opportunity in dangerous neighborhoods. In W. J. Wilson (Ed.), *Sociology and the public agenda* (pp. 231–258). Newbury Park, CA: Sage.

Furstenberg, F. F., Cook, T., Eccles, J., Elder, G., and Sameroff, A. (1999). *Managing to make it: Urban families in high risk neighborhoods*. Chicago: University of Chicago Press.

Furstenberg, F. F., and Harris, K. M. (1993). When and why fathers matter: Impacts of father involvement on children of adolescent mothers. In R. I. Lerman and T. J. Ooms (Eds.), *Young unwed fathers: Changing roles and emerging policies* (pp. 117–138). Philadelphia: Temple University Press.

Garfinkel, I., McLanahan, S., and Hanson, T. (1998). A patchwork portrait of nonresident fathers. In I. Garfinkel, S. McLanahan, D. R. Meyer, and J. A. Seltzer (Eds.), *Fathers under fire* (pp. 31–60). New York: Russell Sage Foundation.

Garrett, P., Ng'andu, N., and Ferron, J. (1994). Poverty experiences of young children and the quality of their home environments. *Child Development*, *65*, 331–345.

Gecas, V. (1979). The influence of social class on socialization. In W. R. Burr, R. Hill, F. I. Nye, and I. L. Reiss (Eds.), *Contemporary theories about the family* (Vol. 1, pp. 365–404). New York: Free Press.

Gomby, D. S., Cubross, P. L., and Behrman, R. E. (1999). Home visiting: Recent program evaluations. *Future of Children*, *9*, 4–26.

Greene, A. D., and Moore, K. A. (2000). Nonresident father involvement and child well-being among young children in families on welfare. In E. Peters, G. W. Peterson, S. K. Steinmetz, and R. D. Day (Eds.), *Fatherhood: Research, interventions, and policies* (pp. 159–180). New York: Haworth.

Greenstein, T. N. (1995). Are the most advantaged children truly disadvantaged by early maternal employment. *Journal of Family Issues*, *16*, 149–199.

Gutman, L. M., and Eccles, J. S. (1999). Financial strain, parenting behaviors, and adolescent achievement: Testing model equivalence between African American and European American single- and two-parent families. *Child Development*, *70*, 1464–1476.

Hardy, J. B., Duggan, A. K., Masnyk, K., and Pearson, C. (1989). Fathers of children born to young urban mothers. *Family Planning Perspectives*, *21*, 159–187.

Harnish, J. D., Dodge, K. A., and Valente, E. (1995). Mother–child interaction quality as a partial mediator of the roles of maternal depressive symtomatology and socio-economic status in the development of child-behavior problems. *Child Development*, *66*, 739–753.

Harvey, E. (1999). Short-term and long-term effects of parental employment on children of the National Longitudinal Survey of Youth. *Developmental Psychology*, *35*, 445–459.

Hashima, P. Y., and Amato, P. R. (1994). Poverty, social support, and parental behavior. *Child Development*, *65*, 394–403.

Haveman, R., and Wolfe, B. (1994). *Succeeding generations: On the effect of investments in children*. New York: Russell Sage Foundation.

Hobfoll, S. E., Ritter, C., Lavin, J., Hulsizer, M. R., and Cameron, R. P. (1995). Depression prevalence and incidence among inner-city pregnant and postpartum women. *Journal of Consulting and Clinical Psychology, 63,* 445–453.

Hoffman, L. W. (1984). Maternal employment and the young child. In M. Perlmutter (Ed.), *Parent–child interactions and parent–child relationships in child development. The Minnesota symposia on child psychology* (pp. 101–127). Hillsdale, NJ: Lawrence Erlbaum Associates.

Holden, G. W., and Miller, P. (1999). Enduring and different: A meta-analysis of similarity in parents' childrearing. *Pscyhological Bulletin, 125,* 223–254.

Hollingshead, A. A. (1975). *Four-factor index of social status.* Unpublished manuscript, Yale University, New Haven, CT.

Howard, E. C. (2000). *Employment, social support, and well-being among low-income mothers: A qualitative and quantitative analysis.* Unpublished doctoral dissertation, Northwestern University, Evanston, IL.

Huston, A. C., McLoyd, V. C., and Garcìa Coll, C. (1994). Children and poverty: Issues in contemporary research. *Child Development, 65,* 275–282.

Jackson, A., Gyamfi, P., Brooks-Gunn, J., and Blake, M. (1998). Employment status, psychological well-being, social support, and physical discipline practices of single Black mothers. *Journal of Marriage and the Family, 60,* 894–902.

Jargowsky, P. (1997). *Poverty and place: Ghettos, barrios, and the American City.* New York: Russell Sage Foundation.

Jarrett, R. (1997). African American family and parenting strategies in impoverished neighborhoods. *Qualitative Sociology, 20,* 275–288.

Jencks, C., and Mayer, S. (1990). The social consequences of growing up in a poor neighborhood. In L. Lynn and M. McGeary (Eds.), *Inner-city poverty in the United States* (pp. 111–186). Washington, DC: National Academy Press.

Johns Hopkins University. (2000). Welfare, Children, and Families: A Three City Study. http://www.jhu.edu/~welfare/

Kasarda, J. (1993). Inner-city concentrated poverty and neighborhood distress: 1970–1980. *Housing Policy Debate, 4,* 253–302.

Katz, L., Kling, J., and Liebman, J. (2001). Moving to Opportunity in Boston: Early results of a randomized experiment. *Quarterly Journal of Economics, 116,* 607–654.

Kelley, M. L., Power, T. G., and Wimbush, D. D. (1992). Determinants of disciplinary practices in low-income black mothers. *Child Development, 63,* 573–582.

Kessler, R., and Cleary, P. D. (1980). Social class and psychological distress. *American Sociological Review, 45,* 463–478.

Klebanov, P., Brooks-Gunn, J., and Duncan, G. (1994). Does neighborhood and family poverty affect mothers' parenting, mental health and social support? *Journal of Marriage and the Family, 56,* 441–455.

Knox, V., Miller, C., and Gennetian, L. (2000). *Reforming welfare and rewarding work: A summary of the final report on the Minnesota Family Investment Program.* New York: Manpower Demonstration Research Corporation.

Kohn, M. L. (1963). Social class and the parent–child relationship: An interpretation. *American Journal of Sociology, 68,* 471–480.

Kohn, M. L. (1969). *Class and conformity: A study in values.* Homewood, IL: Dorsey.

Larson, C. P. (1980). Efficacy of prenatal and postpartum home visits on child health and development. *Pediatrics, 66,* 191–197.

Lichter, D. T., and Eggebeen, D. (1993). Rich kids, poor kids: Changing income inequality among american children. *Social Forces, 71,* 761–780.

Liker, J. K., and Elder, G. H. (1983). Economic hardship and marital relations in the 1930s. *American Sociological Review, 48,* 343–359.

Lui-Gurr, S., Vernon, S., and Mijanovich, T. (1994). *Making work pay better than welfare: An early look at the Self-Sufficiency Project.* New York: Manpower Research Demonstration Corporation.

Mack, J., and Lansley, S. (1985). *Poor Britain.* London: Allen and Unwin.

McGroder, S. M. (2000). Parenting among low-income, African-American single mothers with preschool-age children: Patterns, predictors, and developmental correlates. *Child Development, 71,* 752–771.

McGroder, S. M., Zaslow, M. J., Moore, K. A., and LeMenestrel, S. M. (2000). *National evaluation of welfare-to-work strategies impacts on young children and their families two years after enrollment: Findings from the child outcomes study.* Washington, DC: U.S. Department of Health and Human Services, Office of the Assistant Secretary for Planning and Evaluation Administration for Children and Families.

McLanahan, S., Garfinkel, I., Reichman N., and Teitler, J. (2001). Unwed parents or fragile families? Implications for Welfare and Child Support Reform. In L. Wu, R. Havemen, and B. Wolfe (Eds.), *Out-of-wedlock: Trends, causes and consequences of nonmarital fertility* (202–228). New York: Russell Sage Foundation.

McLeod, J. D., and Kessler, R. (1990). Socioeconomic status differences in vulnerability to undesirable life events. *Journal of Health and Social Behavior, 31,* 162–172.

McLoyd, V. (1990). The impact of economic hardship on black families and children: Psychological distress, parenting and socioeconomic development. *Child Development, 61,* 311–346.

McLoyd, V. (1997). The impact of poverty and low socioeconomic status on the socioemotional functioning of African-American children and adolescents: Mediating effects. In R. Taylor and M. Wang (Eds.), *Social and emotional adjustment and family relations in ethnic minority families* (pp. 7–34). Mahwah, NJ: Lawrence Erlbaum Associates.

McLoyd, V. C. (1998). Socioeconomic disadvantage and child development. *American Psychologist, 53*, 185–204.

McLoyd, V. C., Jayaratne, T. E., Ceballo, R., and Borquez, J. (1994). Unemployment and work interruption among African American single mothers: Effects on parenting and adolescent socioemotional functioning. *Child Development, 65*, 562–589.

McLoyd, V. C., and Wilson, L. (1992). Telling them like it is: The role of economic and environmental factors in single mothers' discussions with their children. *American Journal of Community Psychology, 20*, 419–444.

Miller, J., and Davis, D. (1997). Poverty history, marital history, and quality of children's home environments. *Journal of Marriage and the Family, 59*, 996–1007.

Moore, K. A., and Driscoll, A. K. (1997). Low-wage maternal employment and outcomes for children: A study. *Future of Children, 7*, 122–126.

Mott, F. L. (1990). When is a father really gone? Paternal–child contact in father absent homes. *Demography, 27*, 499–517.

Newman, K. (1999). *No shame in my game: The working poor in the inner-city.* New York: Russell Sage Foundation.

Ogbu, J. U. (1981). Orgins of human competence: A cultural sociological perspective. *Child Development, 52*, 413–429.

O'Higgins, M., and Jenkins, S. (1990). Poverty in the EC: Estimates for 1975, 1980, and 1985. In R. Teekens and B. van Praag (Eds.), *Analysing poverty in the European community: Policy issues, research options, and data sources* (pp. 187–212). Luxembourg: Office of Official Publications of the European Communities.

Olds, D. L., Henderson, C. R., Jr., Chamberlin, R., and Tatelbaum, R. (1986). Preventing child abuse and neglect: A randomized trial of nurse home visitation. *Pediatrics, 78*, 65–78.

Olds, D. L., Henderson, C. R., Jr., Kitzman, H., Eckenrode, J., Cole, R., and Tatelbaum, R. (1999). Prenatal and infancy home visitation by nurses: Recent findings. *Future of Children, 9*, 44–65.

Olds, D. L., Henderson, C. R., Jr., Tatelbaum, R., and Chamberlin, R. (1986). Improving the delivery of prenatal care and outcomes of pregnancy: A randomized trial of nurse home visitation. *Pediatrics, 77*, 16–28.

Olds, D. L., Henderson, C. R., Tatelbaum, R., and Chamberlin, R. (1988). Improving the life-course development of socially disadvantaged mothers: A randomized trial of nurse home visitation. *American Journal of Public Health, 78*, 1436–1445.

Osofosky, J. (1995). The effects of exposure to violence on young children. *American Psychologist, 50*, 782–788.

Parcel, T. L., and Menaghan, E. G. (1994). *Parents' jobs and children's lives.* Hawthorne, NY: De Gruyter.

Parcel, T. L., and Menaghan, E. G. (1997). Effects of low-wage employment on family well-being. *The Future of Children, 7*, 116–121.

Quint, J., Bos, J., and Polit, D. (1997). *New chance: Final report on a comprehensive program for young mothers in poverty and their children.* New York: Manpower Demonstration Research Corporation.

Raver, C. C., and Leadbeater, B. J. (1999). Mothering under pressure: Environmental, child and dyadic correlates of maternal self-efficacy among low-income women. *Journal of Family Psychology, 13*, 1–12.

Salkind, N. J., and Haskins, R. (1982). Negative income tax: The impact on children from low-income families. *Journal of Family Issues, 3*, 165–180.

Sameroff, A., and Feil, L. A. (1985). Parental concepts of development. In I. E. Sigel (Ed.), *Parental belief systems: The psychological consequences for children* (pp. 83–105). Hillsdale, NJ: Lawrence Erlbaum Associates.

Sameroff, A. J., and Fiese, B. H. (1990). Transactional regulation and early intervention, In S. Meisels and J. P. Shonkoff (Eds.), *Handbook of early childhood intervention* (pp. 119–191). New York: Cambridge University Press.

Sameroff, A. J., Seifer, R., Barocas, B., Zax, M., and Greenspan, S. (1987). IQ scores of 4-year-old children: Social environmental risk factors. *Pediatrics, 79*, 343–350.

Sampson, R. J. (1992). Family management and child development: Insights from social disorganization theory. In J. McCord (Ed.), *Advances in criminological theory* (Vol. 3, pp. 193–216). New Brunswick, NJ: Transaction Publishers.

Sampson, R. J., and Groves, W. B. (1989). Community structure and crime: Testing social disorganization theory. *American Journal of Sociology, 94*, 774–802.

Sampson, R. J., Raudenbusch, S. W., and Earls, F. (1997). Neighborhoods and violent crime: A multilevel study of collective efficacy. *Science, 277*, 918–924.

Seifer, R. (1995). Perils and pitfalls of high-risk research. *Developmental Psychology, 31*, 420–424.

Seitz, V., and Provence, S. (1990). Caregiver-focused models of early intervention. In S. J. Meisels and J. P. Shonkoff (Eds.), *Handbook of early intervention* (pp. 400–427). New York: Cambridge University Press.

Seltzer, J. A. (1991). Relationships between fathers and children who live apart: The father's role after seperation. *Journal of Marriage and the Family, 53*, 79–101.

Sigel, I. E. (1992). The belief–behavior connection: A resolvable dilemma? In I. E. Sigel, A. V. McGillicuddy-DeLisi, and J. J. Goodnow (Eds.), *Parental belief systems: The psychological consequences for children* (pp. 433–456). Hillsdale, NJ: Lawrence Erlbaum Associates.

Simons, R. L., Beaman, J. Conger, R. D., and Chao, W. (1993). Stress, support, and antisocial behavioral trait as determinants of emotional well-being and parenting practices among single mothers. *Journal of Marriage and the Family, 55*, 385–398.

Singer, M. I., Anglin, T. M., Song, L., and Lunghofer, L. (1995). Adolescents' exposure to violence and associated symptoms of psychological trauma. *Journal American Medical Association, 273*, 477–482.

Smith, J., Brooks-Gunn, J., and Klebanov, P. (1997). The consequences of living in poverty on young children's cognitive development. In G. J. Duncan and J. Brooks-Gunn (Eds.), *Consequences of growing up poor* (pp. 132–189). New York: Russell Sage Foundation.

Spencer, M. B. (1990). Development of minority children: An introduction [Special Issue: Minority Children]. *Child Development, 61*, 267–269.

Stevens, J. H. (1988). Social support, locus of control, and parenting in three low-income groups of mothers: Black teenagers, Black adults, and White adults. *Child Development, 59*, 635–642.

Taylor, L., Zuckerman, B., Harik, V., and Groves, B. (1992). Exposure to violence among inner-city parents and young children. *American Journal of the Diseases of Children, 146*, 487.

Townsend, P. (1992). *The international analysis of poverty.* Hemel Hempstead, England: Harvester-Wheatsheaf.

U.S. Bureau of the Census. (2000a). *Table 1: Weighted Average Poverty Thresholds for Families of Specified Size 1959 to 1999.* http://www.census.gov/hhes/poverty/histpov/hstpov1.html

U.S. Bureau of the Census. (2000b). *Table 3: Poverty Status of People, by Age, Race and Hispanic Origin: 1959 to 1999.* http://www.census.gov/hhes/poverty/histpov/hstpov3.html

U.S. Department of Health and Human Services. (1997). *Indicators of Welfare Dependence Annual Report to Congress.* Washington, DC: Author.

Vandell, D. L., and Ramanan, J. (1992). Effects of early and recent maternal employment on children from low-income families. *Child Development, 63*, 938–949.

Vaughn, D. (1993). Exploring the use of the public's views to set income poverty thresholds and adjust them over time. *Social Security Bulletin, 56*, 22–46.

Ventura, S. J., Bachrach, C. A., Hill, L., Kaye, K., Holcomb, P., and Koff, E. (1995). *The demography of out-of-wedlock childbearing. Report to Congress on out-of-wedlock childbearing.* Washington, DC: U.S. Department of Health and Human Services.

Wackschlag, L., Chase-Lansdale, P. L., and Brooks-Gunn, J. (1996). Not just "ghosts in the nursery." Contemporaneous intergenerational relationships and parenting in young African-American families. *Child Development, 67*, 2131–2147.

Watson, J. E., Kirby, R. S., Kelleher, K. J., and Bradley, R. H. (1996). Effects of poverty on home environment: An analysis of three-year outcome data for low birth weight premature infants. *Journal of Pediatric Psychology, 21*, 419–431.

Werthheimer, R. (1999). *Working poor families with children.* Washington, DC: Child Trends.

Weiss, H. B. (1993). Home visits: Necessary but not sufficient. *The Future of Children, 3*, 113–128.

Whitbeck, L. B., Simons, R. L., Conger, R. D., Wickrama, K. A. S., Ackley, K. A., and Elder, G. H. (1997). The effects of parents' working conditions and family economic hardship on parenting behaviors and self-efficacy. *Social Psychology Quarterly, 60*, 291–303.

Wilson, W. J. (1987). *The truly disadvantaged: The inner city, the underclass and the public policy.* Chicago: University of Chicago Press.

Wright, J. D., and Wright, S. R. (1976). Social class and parental values for children: A partial replication and extension of the Kohn thesis. *American Sociological Review, 41*, 527–537.

Yoshikawa, H. (1994). Prevention as cumulative protection: Effects of early family support and education on chronic delinquency and its risks. *Psychological Bulletin, 115*, 28–54.

6

Parenting and Social Networks

Moncrieff Cochran
Starr Niego
Cornell University

INTRODUCTION

Our purpose in this chapter is to examine the ways that parenting beliefs, attitudes, and behaviors are influenced by parents' networks of social relationships. Of primary concern are the various kinds of support and assistance provided to parents, both in meeting everyday responsibilities and in promoting the optimal development of their children. We use social networks as a framework for charting the structure and content of parents' relations as well as for tracing the lines of influence into the family from larger social systems and institutions. Guided by an ecological perspective, we consider how social relationships serve different functions and carry different meanings for families with differing life circumstances, needs, expectations, and resources. Throughout the chapter, as in the *Handbook* as a whole, "parenting" is defined broadly: grandparents, aunts and uncles, close friends, neighbors, childcare providers, and baby-sitters all have relationships with children (other than their own) that include or require some parenting activities.

We begin by presenting brief sketches of parents' networks through case studies of Cathy Conrad and Lisa and Christopher Jefferson. Drawing on these accounts, we offer a definition of the network and a strategy for its measurement. In the next part of the chapter, connections are drawn between networks and parenting, first by considering the effects of network relations on adults as parents and then on their children. Our view broadens as we examine the ways that network building opportunities are limited by parents' social position. Specifically, we review studies that illustrate the effects of culture, class, race, and family structure on the pool of potential network members available to parents. Then an overall framework is presented, and we consider some of the ways that networks may be strengthened through personal initiatives of parents as well as by policy and programmatic interventions. Finally, in the concluding section of the chapter, we suggest directions for future research.

Cathy Conrad

Cathy Conrad, age 27, is a European American, single mother with two children, Brandon (age 5) and Sally (age 2). She rents an apartment in a blue-collar neighborhood on the outskirts of a small city. During the day Cathy works as a secretary at a large insurance company. At night she attends classes at the nearby community college, where she is in training to become a nurse practitioner. The father of her children has moved to another state and pays no child support, and neither Cathy nor her children have any contact with his parents or his siblings.

Cathy's social network consists of six kinfolk and seven nonkin. She has remained close to her own mother and father, who live just four blocks away. Her sister and brother are also important to her, and her sister-in-law is sometimes helpful. She also stays in touch with a cousin of the same age, with whom she grew up.

Cathy includes three neighbors in her network. Mrs. Macomber, who lives downstairs and owns the duplex containing her apartment, is always nice to the children and hasn't hassled her when the rent check is a little late. Several times she has sat in with the children when Cathy had to run down to the store for milk or Pampers. Mrs. Jackson, who lives around the corner and down three blocks, is a family childcare provider who looks after both children while Cathy is at work. Sandy is a new friend whom Cathy met when their children were playing over at the local play park. She is also a solo parent, and her Sherri is the same age as Sally. Two other friends, Gerri and Donna, are also secretaries at the insurance company. Cathy has known them ever since she started working there four years ago. Her other two friends, Marcie and Patty, are also studying to be nurse practitioners. She met them within the last few months, when they began the training program together, but already they have become very important to her.

Cathy says that her network affects her parenting and the care of her children in a variety of ways, some helpful and others not so. Whenever she is worried about the behavior of one of the children she talks to her mother about it first. That is usually helpful, but at the same time the response is often "Then give him or her a good smack," and Cathy remembers hating it as a child when one of her parents hit her. Her sister Joan lives in another state, but calls often and is a great listener. Sandy has had some good ideas about the children when they talk over at the park, and she shares tips from the single parent support group she attends. At work Gerri and Donna give Cathy "shoulders to cry on" when she is feeling down about the struggles of parenting, but they don't have children so can't help out with advice. Marcie and Patti are so helpful with schoolwork and so much fun to talk to about other things that Cathy doesn't want to "bore" them with parenting issues.

Cathy relies quite heavily on her network for childcare support and other surrogate parenting assistance. Mrs. Jackson has the children for a total of 43 hours each week, and Cathy feels lucky to have a reasonably priced childcare provider so nearby. At the same time, Mrs. Jackson looks after three other preschool children and seems to rely pretty heavily on the TV to entertain them. On the three nights each week that Cathy has classes her mother comes over to the apartment to look after the children, but her dad has been grumbling more and more about how that disrupts his evenings, so it may not last much longer. Billy, her brother, has been great about taking the kids out to watch softball games at the local park and down to the lake front to splash in the water, but his wife Jan gets irritated easily by rambunctious little children. Cathy wants Billy to stay involved with the children because they need to know and trust good men, so she is looking for better ways to get them all together without hassling Jan.

All in all, Cathy can't imagine how she would manage to rear her children without the help of her relatives and friends.

Lisa and Christopher Jefferson

Lisa and Christopher Jefferson, both 28 years old and African American, have been married for 6 years. They live together with their 3-year-old daughter Betsy in a small Northeastern city. Two years ago, with financial assistance from Lisa's parents, the couple purchased their own home in a stable, blue-collar neighborhood where there are parks and playgrounds for Betsy to play. Close by live both sets of parents and other extended family members. Having grown up in large, tight-knit families, Lisa and Chris look forward to gatherings with their relatives throughout the year, from Christmas to summer barbecues.

Since graduating from high school, Lisa has held a number of secretarial jobs. Currently she is employed part time, 25 hours each week, at a local elementary school. Chris, who is also a high school graduate, was recently laid off from a large manufacturing company where he had worked for several years. He and his brother have formed a partnership and are planning to set up their own electrical contracting firm. Meanwhile he has enrolled in an accounting class at the local community college to sharpen his business skills.

In separate interviews each parent was asked to name the individuals "who make a difference" in their lives. The network of people Lisa nominated includes 15 relatives: her parents, in-laws, aunts, uncles, and siblings and their children. Although Lisa feels close to many of these people, it is her parents and older sister who are described as "especially important." Her mother and father offered encouragement when Lisa decided to return to work after spending 2 years at home with Betsy. Now her mother helps out by picking up Betsy from the childcare center where she spends the morning and staying with her until Lisa returns from work. Even with just part-time enrollment at the center, Lisa and Chris find themselves struggling to pay the bills; they could not afford the additional expense of a babysitter. Lisa's sister Alice is a good source of advice and comfort when Lisa feels overwhelmed with her responsibilities as a wife, mother, and worker. Alice's three children are Betsy's favorite cousins.

Apart from kin, Lisa names nine additional network members. Four of these are neighbors, including Mr. and Mrs. Mulcahy, who live next door. When the Jefferson's car breaks down, Mr. Mulcahy can often repair it. Most of all Lisa enjoys casual conversations with this older couple as they work in their garden and Betsy plays outside, sometimes helping them collect vegetables or pull weeds. Peter, Beth, and Darleen are three people Lisa has met at work. Peter, a second-grade teacher, came to the school at the same time as Lisa, and his sense of humor cheered her during the first, uncertain days on the job. Beth and Darleen are secretaries who sit beside Lisa in the main office. Darleen has worked for the district for more than 20 years and has friends in all of the schools. She has promised to look out for a full-time position that Lisa might apply for.

Finally, Lisa names two friends she has known since childhood. As working mothers, Lisa, Maggie, and Christine regularly pitch in to care for one another's children. Occasionally, though, Lisa finds herself reluctant to answer the telephone when it rings early on Saturday mornings. After a full week, she would prefer not to have extra work during her "days off." Lisa wonders when was the last time that she, Maggie, and Christine spent a day together, without their spouses or children. Having more time alone with her friends is something she looks forward to as Betsy gets a little older and enters school.

Chris Jefferson describes a smaller social network than his wife, naming a total of 13 members. Included in his network are eight relatives: his parents and in-laws, Lisa's sister Alice, his own brother Ted, Ted's wife Joan, and their 8-year-old son Charles. Apart from these kin, who are all named to Lisa's network as well, Chris mentions few additional, independent social ties. He recognizes that people would be willing to assist him but explains that he generally prefers to rely on Lisa.

Before leaving his job, Chris had enjoyed spending time with some of his coworkers at the plant. Since the layoff, though, he has lost touch. In his network he does include Mr. and Mrs. Mulcahy, both "generous and kind" neighbors. Mr. Mulcahy's help with car repairs has saved them a considerable amount of money over the past year. Three other people named are "actually Lisa's friends."

With fewer people to turn to, Chris relies on five primary relationships—his parents, parents-in-law, and brother—for nearly all of the support he receives. They provide childcare, childrearing advice, and support with practical and work-related concerns. When Chris and Lisa want to spend time together, they know they can ask his parents to watch Betsy. And he and Ted have grown particularly close as they've worked to establish their company. As partners, they complement each other. Ted talks easily and has built up contacts and potential clients throughout the city. Quieter and more organized, Chris manages the paperwork and legal documents. Chris also admires the role Ted plays as a father to Charles; their own father was pretty distant from them when they were boys. Now that he's home most afternoons, Chris has been spending more time with Betsy, reading, playing, and talking to her. Lisa appreciates some time out from childcare.

Even with his closest relations Chris chooses not to discuss financial and emotional matters. In these two areas he recognizes that Lisa's support is especially important.

WHAT IS A SOCIAL NETWORK?

The individuals who "make a difference" in Cathy Conrad's and Lisa and Chris Jefferson's lives—relatives, coworkers, neighbors, and friends—comprise the membership of each parent's social network. In this chapter we use the term *social network* to refer to specific sets of linkages between defined sets of people (Mitchell, 1969a). The linkage is operationalized through our principal question—"Who makes a difference in your life?"—and amplified by probing for the individuals whom parents "do things with" or "know and depend on." In response, parents speak about people they see with some regularity or exchange goods and services with.[1]

It is important to recognize that our sketches reveal only partial views of networks. Total networks, consisting of the web of relationships among all members of a society, are nearly impossible to map. The partial networks that we study are *personal* social networks, networks anchored to a specific individual and defined in response to specific questions and probes. Illustrated above are the personal networks of three parents. Alternatively, we might look at the network relations of Lisa and Chris' daughter Betsy, for example, or aggregate all three of their personal networks into a Jefferson family network.

Cochran and Brassard (1979, p. 601) defined personal social networks as consisting of "those people outside the household who engage in activities and exchanges of an affective and/or material nature with members of the immediate family." Two facets of this definition merit elaboration. First, applying the definition to the Jeffersons, neither Chris nor Betsy would be included in Lisa Jefferson's personal network. Family members, as long as they live together in one household, are excluded from network membership. Many investigators have found that relations with household members are qualitatively distinct from other social ties (Brassard, 1982; Crnic, Greenberg, Ragozin, Robinson, and Basham, 1983). From a conceptual standpoint, the important distinction is between the nuclear family and the personal network, a distinction well articulated by Bott (1957) in *Family and Social Network*. The study of nuclear families has a long tradition in sociology and anthropology, and the subdiscipline of family sociology has become well established during the past half century. Family historians and other social researchers conceive of the family as an emotional entity resting on sentimental ties among husband and wife and parents and children, and as a social unit with economic significance (Hareven, 1984). Thus, the nuclear family is a concept that has meaning in the real world and importance for the development of the individual, separate from the impacts of other kin, associates, and friends.

The second facet of our definition that requires elaboration is the nature of the links between the individual at the center of the network (the "anchor") and the members included within it. Cochran and Brassard (1979, p. 601) described these links as "activities and exchanges of an affective and/or material nature." Is this phrase a proxy for social support? As suggested above, there is a certain degree of affinity between the concepts of "social support" and "social network," particularly because both have been applied to assess the impact of personal relationships on human development. Yet, in constructing social networks we aim to describe relations of broader range and structural complexity than usually incorporated in studies of social support.

Most of the researchers using the social support concept refer to work of Cobb (1976), who defined such support as information that leads an individual to believe that she or he is cared for and

---

[1] Milardo (1988) notes that other methodological techniques yield alternative pictures of parents' networks.

loved, valued, and a member of a network of mutual obligation. Later Crockenberg (1988, p. 141) described social support as emotional, instrumental, or informational help that other people provide to an individual:

> With respect to families, emotional support refers to expressions of empathy and encouragement that convey to parents that they are understood and capable of working through difficulties in order to do a good job in that role. Instrumental support refers to concrete help that reduces the number of tasks or responsibilities a parent must perform, typically household and child care tasks. Informational support refers to advice or information concerning child care of parenting.

Thus, the concept of social support emphasizes the types of support provided (emotional, instrumental, informational) and the psychological state of the recipient ("cared for and loved, valued"). Those networks researchers who focus on support have tended to map the networks of their respondents with the use of probes that are explicitly oriented to support, like "Please give me the names of all the people who provide you with emotional support." Such a strategy leads to the identification of a partial network that excludes people in an individual's life not thought of primarily in terms of support.

The definition presented by Cochran and Brassard, in contrast, suggests a wider view of social relationships. The content of linkages between respondents and their network members ranges from information of various kinds (where to find work, how to rear a child, which childcare arrangement to choose) to emotional and material assistance and access to role models (Cochran and Brassard, 1979; Mitchell, 1969b). As the range of possible exchanges is broadened, naturally occurring social relationships may influence parenting in ways that extend well beyond those included within the domain of "social support." For Cathy Conrad, a working parent rearing two children on her own, having friends and relatives help with childcare is one form of assistance that is particularly important. Having her brother as a role model to her children is a second. In Cathy's network there are also friendships in which she leaves aside for a while her concerns as a parent.

At the same time, network relations, even supportive ones, may also be conflictual. Cathy and her mother sometimes express different attitudes toward childrearing, even as Cathy values and depends on her mother's assistance with childcare on the nights she attends school. Additionally, network members' expectations for reciprocal care can burden parents who feel they have little left to give. From a study of low-income mothers with young children, Belle (1982, p. 143) concluded that "one cannot receive support without also risking the costs of rejection, betrayal, burdensome dependence, and vicarious pain." Similarly, Wellman (1981, p. 173) articulated various ways in which social support may oversimplify the nature of network relations:

> Its focus on a simple "support/nonsupport" dichotomy de-emphasizes the multi-faceted, often contradictory nature of social ties. Its assumption that supportive ties form a separate system isolates them from a person's overall network of interpersonal ties. Its assumption that all of these supportive ties are connected to each other in one integrated system goes against empirical reality and creates the dubious expectation that solidary systems are invariably more desirable. Its assumption that there are no conflicts of interest between "supporters" invokes the false premise of a common good.

A final point of departure from the social support model is networks researchers' emphasis on the characteristics of the "set of linkages" between network anchors and their members. By this we refer to structural dimensions of the network, including size, diversity of role relationships, diversity of sex, age, life stage, and density, or the extent to which network members know one another. Typically, these characteristics are used to transcend individual relationships and view networks as a whole. For instance, we might be interested in comparing the extent of kin versus nonkin membership in Cathy Conrad's and Lisa Jefferson's networks. Attention to network structure stems from a concern with the limits imposed by society on personal relationships, as well as to the content of those relationships, as described above. Beginning with the earliest studies conducted by British social anthropologists in the 1950s, there has been tension between individual choice and social-structural constraints in network models. We return to this issue later in the chapter.

HOW ARE SOCIAL NETWORKS MEASURED?

A variety of techniques exists for measuring and describing network relationships. Surveys and questionnaires have been used successfully to gather information with large samples. Face-to-face interviews permit researchers to offer follow-up prompts, amplify definitions, and elicit respondents' own perspectives of their naturally occurring relations. The strategy presented below, based on a semistructured interview format, was designed for the international research project mentioned in Cochran, Larner, Riley, Gunnarsson, and Henderson (1990). The instrument was developed collaboratively, by social scientists from four Western industrialized countries. It has proved suitable for use with diverse populations, representing a range of cultural and educational backgrounds, family structures, and social environments. (Additional information regarding development and use of the instrument can be found in Cochran et al. (1990):

(1) *Name generation.* In the first part of the interview, the interviewer leads the respondent through a series of direct questions to elicit a network membership list. The interviewer begins by asking for the names of individuals outside of the immediate family "who are important to you in one way or another." The word "important" is clarified by a time frame ("people you have contact with from time to time") and by examples of the kinds of exchanges that might characterize the relationship ("I mean people whom who might turn to for general help or if you need a baby sitter. Or when you need to borrow something, or perhaps when a personal problem is on your mind.") The following role- and context-related prompts are used: neighbors, relatives, workmates, schoolmates, organizations and agencies, and other friends.

(2) *Characteristics of network members and their relationship to respondents.* The interviewer then collects and records information about the location of each relationship in time and space, including geographic proximity, frequency of contact, and duration of contact. Information concerning the age, sex, and family life stage of network members is also gathered.

(3) *Exchange content.* A checklist procedure is employed to determine which network members engage in each of 4 kinds of social exchange with the respondent: child-related support, practical support, emotional support, and social activities.

(4) *Intensity of relations.* Finally, respondents are asked to name the individuals on their membership list who are especially important to them. No limit is placed on the number of members who may be so designated.

Summarized in Table 6.1 are the questions and prompts included in the Social Networks Interview, and dimensions of the network associated with them.

THE EFFECTS OF SOCIAL NETWORKS ON ADULTS AS PARENTS

There are two main routes by which social networks affect childrearing, and thus parenting in the broadest sense. One route is through impacts on adults, who modify their parenting beliefs, attitudes, and behaviors as a result of network influences. The other route is not via the parents, but involves the direct impact of network members on children by engaging with them in face-to-face interactions affecting their development. In this section of the chapter, we are concerned with the first of these lines of influence transmission, the links between network influences and parents in their caregiving roles. Four types of network exchange content are distinguished: instrumental assistance, emotional support, childrearing advice, and other informational support. We also address the question of network stress and consider the causes and consequences of social isolation. The

TABLE 6.1
The Social Networks Interview

Questions	Network Dimensions
Name generation	
"Please give me the names of all of the people who are important to you in one way or another."	
"People in the neighborhood..."	
"Relatives of yours..."	
"People you see at work..."	Size
"People you know through school..."	Diversity of role relationships
"People who you come in contact with at agencies or organizations..."(e.g., daycare council, church)	
"Other people who don't fit into any of these categories..."	
Characteristics of network members and their relationship to respondents	
"Where does X live?"	Location in time and space (three dimensions)
"How often do you see X?"	
"How long have you known X?"	
"Please check the name of all network members who are more than 20 years older than you are."	Diversity of age, sex, and life stage
"Is X male or female?"	
"Which members have children under age ten?"	
Exchange content	
"Please check the names of people whom you turn to if you need a baby-sitter or if you want to discuss childrearing issues"	Extent of child-related support
"...people whom you turn to if you want to borrow something, if you need practical advice and information."	Extent of practical support
"...people whom who feel you can turn to if you feel down or depressed, people you can talk to about everything."	Extent of emotional support
"...people whom you do things with on your leisure time, like sports, fishing, parties, movies."	Extent of social activities
Intensity of relations	
"Please check the names of people who mean the most to you—who are especially important."	Primary network membership

section concludes with discussions of how to conceptualize the way social support affects parental behavior and child-related outcomes related to the characteristics of mothers' networks.

INSTRUMENTAL ASSISTANCE AND EMOTIONAL SUPPORT

Studies of parents' social networks conducted during the 1980s and 1990s indicate that assistance with childcare, unconditional emotional support, and advice about how to maintain authoritative control over the child's behavior proved particularly helpful to young mothers, especially when the women are single, divorced, or separated (Weinraub, Horvath, and Gringlas, in Vol. 3 of this *Handbook*). Belle (1982) studied the costs and benefits of social ties identified as important by 43 low-income mothers with young children. Although working within the broader "social support and health outcomes" tradition of Cobb (1976), with particular interest in personal mastery and depression in adults, she was also interested in the quality of interaction between the mothers and their children. Belle found that it was not network size, proximity of membership, or frequency of contact that was associated with emotional well-being, but rather the number of people reported as engaged specifically in providing childcare assistance and "someone to turn to."

Longfellow, Zelkowitz, Saunders, and Belle (1979) also considered social support in its relation to parent–child processes. Working with data from the Belle study, they found that the availability of support in the area of childcare (baby-sitting, discussions of childrearing problems) was positively related to the quality of mother–child interactions. Those women who reported access to childcare support were less dominating, emotionally warmer, and more sensitive to the needs of their children than were mothers who did not report this type of network support. The authors were careful to warn against overgeneralization, pointing out that their sample was limited to low-income mothers.

Colletta (1981) considered the significance of social supports for maternal functioning in several different studies. Working with 50 adolescent mothers, both European American and African American, she found a link between emotional support and maternal affection. Colletta (1981, p. 193) noted that "with high levels of emotional support adolescent mothers reported being less aggressive and rejecting; less likely to nag, scold, ridicule or threaten their children."

Brassard (1982) conducted a study of 20 single parents' personal social networks that included a comparison group made up of 20 married mothers, well matched with the divorced or separated women on occupation, educational level, family size, and religious background. The Brassard study also included assessment of mother–child interaction patterns gathered through direct observation. All 40 families contained preschool children, divided equally by sex in each subgroup. Brassard found that network members contributed both support and stress to the lives of the mothers she interviewed, but that support outweighed stress in this sample of employed, moderate income, European American women. The single mothers experienced more stress than did the women in two-parent homes even when differences in working hours and income were controlled for (see Weinraub et al., in Vol. 3 of this *Handbook*) Emotional support from adults in the network was especially important for these single women. This support was related to increases in activities containing egalitarian power relationships, a more neutral stance toward children of both sexes, and a more inhibiting style with sons. Brassard (1982, pp. 152–153) suggested that:

> The network supports and guides the single mother in making this role shift toward assuming primary, daily responsibility for being an authoritative leader with her child.... She needs help in sorting out a reasonable, consistent style of home discipline that maintains a workable family equilibrium. The single mother looks to her network for this guidance.

Childrearing Advice

Riley (1990) broadened the discussion of networks and parenting to include men in the parenting role by capitalizing on one of very few data sets that includes information about the networks of fathers. The question he asked was "In what ways would a father use social ties in the service of his childrearing efforts?" One important way might be to turn to network members to discuss parenting concerns and to gather childrearing advice. Whom would fathers go to for such advice? Would they prefer advice from their own parents or siblings, or from other young parents? Are there fathers who report no one with whom they talk about childrearing? To answer these questions, Riley focused on the 70 married, employed fathers from two-parent households who participated in the larger study of parental supports and stresses referred to earlier (Cochran et al., 1990). Most fathers in the sample reported that they discussed childrearing concerns with several people they knew well. The average network included about five sources of childrearing advice. But there was great variation. Eleven of the 70 fathers reported 10 or more network members willing to give advice, whereas 12 fathers reported no such people.

Riley then related aspects of the fathers' networks to the men's level of involvement in rearing their 6-year-old children. The two areas of father involvement examined were participation in routine childcare tasks and play. He found that in the two-earner families both nonkin allies and local female kin affected the childcare participation of the father. Nonkin allies are those highly elective and supportive network members who provided fathers with three or more of the following six kinds of support: practical borrowing, financial assistance, work-related support, discussion of marital issues, emotional support, and social activities. Local female kin consisted of the number of adult female relatives (including in-laws) in the father's network who lived in the same section of town. Of these two sources of network support, the nonkin allies variable was a much stronger predictor of fathers' involvement than was the number of local female kin. Riley noted that the two sources were related; fathers with fewer local kinfolk had more nonkin allies. He suggested the intriguing possibility that today some men are substituting multiply supportive nonkin bonds for the traditional extended family bonds sustained by other men.

In the case of the single earner families, in contrast, the "male network" variable exerted a powerful influence on fathers' childrearing efforts. As the percentage of men in the network increased, the father's share of parent–child play declined. The existence of local female relatives also decreased the father's play involvement. Local female kin seemed to reduce the demand for the father's assistance in childrearing, and the male peer group maintained attitudes and activities in competition with the father's role at home.

Riley concluded that fathers are often pushed into childrearing involvement, or away from it, by situational demands related to their wives' employment status. The mother's work situation (exclusively inside or also outside the family) serves to distinguish two types of American families, each apparently responding to very different network influences. The existence of a local female kin network appeared to relieve the pressure on the father to participate in childrearing (or it may have competed with him if he wanted more responsibility for his children). At the same time, there was evidence that fathers may to some extent select or construct social environments that influence them in the future, given that the male peer group and nonkin allies are amenable to active construction by the individual. Chris Jefferson's recent change in employment status, for example, offered him the opportunity to reconsider his role as a father to Betsy. Instead of nonkin allies, however, it was his brother Ted who provided guidance and modeling as Chris engaged in new activities with Betsy.

Informational Support

Cotterell (1986) was interested in the independent and joint influences on childrearing of the mother's social network, the father's workplace, and the local community. Working with a sample of 96 married mothers living in rural towns of inland Australia, he compared the personal networks and childrearing milieus provided by those women whose husbands were present on a regular basis with those whose partners' jobs routinely required periods of absence from home. Aspects of the childrearing environment were measured with the Caldwell HOME inventory (Caldwell and Bradley, 1984), and the quality of maternal expectations and beliefs was assessed with the Parent as a Teacher (PAAT) inventory (Strom, 1982). Analysis of the network data indicated that mothers with absentee husbands relied more heavily on their neighbors than those whose husbands were at home. When the "quality of childrearing" variables were analyzed by the father's presence or absence and the mother's amount of informational support from the network, the effects of support were statistically significant for six of seven childrearing measures. Cotterell concluded that network support, general character of the community, and father's work situation did not operate independently. He suggested that "the chain of influence of father's work is connected to maternal behavior via the patterns of social relationships established by the mother" (p. 371). His findings indicated that the wives of absentee husbands had smaller networks, and that these women had a more limited range of settings available for contacting network members.

Network Stress

Belle (1982), Brassard (1982), and Wellman (1981) all emphasized the importance of recognizing the stresses as well as the supports in network relationships. Cochran and Henderson (1990) were interested in how single parents' perceptions of their children might be affected not only by those network members providing the parent with child-related assistance and emotional support, but also by members whom mothers may have identified as "making life difficult for them" in one way or another. The links of interest were between those network influences and the mothers' free response to the question "Is your [3-year-old] child easy or difficult to raise?" Of the 48 European American, single-parent families in a larger study of family stresses and supports, Cochran et al. (1990), focused on a subsample of 27 in which mothers were living with no other adults (either male partners or their own parents). Their findings indicated that perception of the child varied directly with the number of kinfolk mothers included in primary networks. That is, as the number of relatives defined as "especially important" increased, mothers' views of their children became more positive. But the strength of this positive relation was affected by the educational backgrounds of the women. It was strongest for the nine mothers with less than a high school education, followed by those with a high school diploma, and then by those with more than 12 years of school. The picture that emerged was one of women with differing needs, expectations, and resources, for whom close involvement with kinfolk appeared to mean different things.

The distinction between women with more or less education was dramatized by the network variable called "difficult kin," those relatives identified as "making things more difficult" in one way or another. These were not contacts included in the network primarily because of their difficult characteristics. Rather, mothers were told not to leave someone off the list because that individual was in some sense difficult. Once the network list was completed, respondents were asked whether there was anyone included whom they found difficult in one way or another. Thus, people identified as difficult also had other characteristics, some of which may have been very supportive. Reporting more of such people was linked to more-positive perceptions by the least educated mothers, and less-positive perceptions by those with the most education. Less-educated mothers seemed willing to accept the stress associated with close kinship relations in order to benefit from the support also provided, but more educated women, perhaps with stronger and more independent personal identities, appeared to find certain kinds of relatives meddlesome and irritating. This study provided evidence that similar amounts and types of support and stress coming from network members may be perceived quite differently and translated into different perceptions of the child, depending on past educational experiences and the aspirations the mother has for her own development.

Social Isolation

Another body of research focuses not on how parents are affected by network influences, but instead on the causes and consequences of social isolation. Interest in factors causing isolation stems from evidence linking the absence of constructive social ties with child abuse and neglect. Crockenberg (1988, p. 160), in summarizing a number of findings, introduced the possibility that "characteristics of the mothers account both for their low support and their abusive parenting." One study that fits within this framework included a comparison of neglectful with nonneglectful mothers (Polansky, Gaudin, Ammons, and Davis, 1985). The researchers used a comparison group that was similar to the neglectful families not only in socioeconomic and family characteristics, but also regarding the geographic accessibility of relatives and proximity to the community where they grew up. One innovative feature of the study involved interviewing a neighbor of every neglectful and control family to determine their perceptions of the friendliness and helpfulness of neighbors, whether there were neighbors one could call on for help, and whether there were neighbors who needed help in rearing their children. The researchers found that neglectful mothers described their neighborhoods as less supportive and friendly than did parents in the control group or neighbors of the parents in either group. That is, they described a different *psychological* reality, although there was no evidence from the neighbors of *objective* differences in the supportive potential. Additional evidence suggested that neglectful parents were less helpful than control parents to others in the neighborhood, based on both their own reports and the reports of their neighbors. The researchers concluded from their data that "inadequacies of ability, and perhaps motivation, cut them off from helping networks dependent on mutuality. Related inadequacies lead to their being stigmatized and held at a distance socially" (p. 274).

Crittenden (1981, 1985a) conducted research that provides greater understanding of what the "inadequacies" referred to by Polansky et al. (1985) might consist of, as well as some indication of their origins. She proposed that adults possess internal working models of social relationships that are developed from experiences in early childhood and then modified over time based on the social relations experienced during later childhood and adolescence. Applying this conceptual orientation to network relations, Crittenden (1985b, p. 1301) suggested that "a mother may influence her relationship with her network, just as she appears to do in her relationship with her child, through the processes of generalization and repetition of ingrained patterns of behavior." This idea received support from her comparison of the networks and parent–professional relationships of adequate mothers with those of neglectful and abusive or neglectful mothers. She found that mothers in the adequate group had far more supportive and satisfying network relationships than mothers in either of the other two groups. This was true despite the fact that the adequate and maltreating mothers were often living in the same neighborhoods. The adequate mothers were also more cooperative in the parent–professional relationship, and less defensive or withdrawn. Crittenden (1985b, p. 1311) concluded that her data were "highly consistent with the notion that the mothers' approach to relationships of all kinds was reflected both in their relationships with their children and in their relationships with network members." She argued that the interaction styles of these women—cooperative, defensive, withdrawn—reflect internalized working models of relationships, and result in greater or lesser openness to and capacity for the establishment and maintenance of satisfying and supportive network relationships.

Conceptualizing How Social Support Affects Parental Behavior

Crockenberg (1988) provided a very useful review of the theories explaining how social support affects parental behavior. She identified four processes by which benefits might be conveyed. First, support can reduce the sheer number of stressful events. The instrumental assistance described earlier in this section probably operates largely in this manner. Baby-sitting, childrearing advice, and financial assistance simply provide relief from daily burdens that might otherwise accumulate to incapacitate the parent, or press her or him into inappropriate or even abusive behavior patterns.

It is possible that social support may not directly reduce the number of stressful events experienced by the parent, but instead serves as a buffer, preventing the parent from being adversely affected by a stressful event, like divorce or job loss, and enabling the parent to maintain satisfactory childrearing routines in difficult situations. This second process is probably not an alternative to sheer reduction of stressful events, but rather operates in addition to it. The effects of emotional support reported in several of the studies referenced earlier may be operating in this buffering manner.

Crockenberg identified the construction of active coping strategies as the third process by which social supports may have beneficial effects on parents. For example, a mother's self-confidence may be bolstered by praise from a supportive and more experienced network member, and her childrearing skills may improve as a result of suggestions from this person. The result of this process may be greater willingness and ability to take positive initiatives in other situations involving the child (Cochran, 1988). Riley's "nonkin allies" and Cathy Conrad's friend Sandy probably provide coping strategies of this sort.

The fourth process identified by Crockenberg also involves the emotional support that emerged from several of the studies reviewed earlier as an important predictor of more effective parenting behaviors. She ties emotional support to the idea of "working models of relationships" outlined previously in relation to maltreating parents (Crittenden, 1985b), pointing out that "ongoing emotional support or nurturance may affirm this sense [of herself or himself as a person deserving of care and capable of caring for someone else] and in doing so encourage the individual's inclination to be nurturant to others" (p. 146).

Personal Networks of Mothers and Child-Related Outcomes

Do the social resources available to parents actually have an impact on the development of their children? Three examples illustrate the link to child development. Crockenberg (1981) was interested in ways that social support might affect the nature of the emotional bond between mother and infant. She assessed infants' reactions to short periods of separation from their mothers and documented clear, consistent patterns within a middle- and working-class sample. Low social support was associated with resistant, avoidant, and anxious behavior when infants were reunited with their mothers. With irritable babies, the association was especially strong, leading Crockenberg to suggest that the "availability of social support is particularly critical when the family is under particular stress" (p. 862). The fact that the positive relationship between social support for the mother and the attachment behaviors of the child was obtained primarily in the case of irritable babies is important to note. An environmental demand, the irritable baby, appears to have created the conditions calling for mobilization of existing support.

Research by Tietjen (1985) suggested a connection between the social networks of mothers and those of their children, specifically their daughters. Her sample consisted of 72 Swedish mothers and their 8- to 9-year-old children. Mothers and children were interviewed separately. Tietjen found similarities between the networks of mothers and their daughters that were not apparent for mothers and sons. For instance, the greater the percentage of neighbors in the married mother's network, the greater the likelihood that the daughter would play with several friends together, rather than with a single friend. Among unmarried mothers in the sample, there was an association between involvement in instrumental exchange with network members and the number of friends whom daughters named, especially at school. Tietjen proposed modeling, teaching, and the provision of opportunities for interaction as the processes that might account for such commonalities.

Homel, Burns, and Goodnow (1987) interviewed the fathers, mothers, and 9- to 11-year-old children in 305 Australian families. These families were drawn from areas in Sydney defined as high, medium, and low according to the number of social risk indicators contained in each area. Information about the "family" network was gathered from one or the other parent (alternating), yielding data about the frequency, location, and dependability of relations with neighbors, friends, and relatives, as well as affiliation with community organizations. Data collected from the children included information about their happiness, negative emotions, social skills, friendship networks, and school adjustment. The authors reported that the child's happiness with the family, negative emotions, peer-related social skills, extensiveness and diversity of friendship networks, and school adjustment all related to the presence, absence, or number of dependable adult friends in the family network. Also important were local friendship networks and ties to community organizations. The family friends were nonkin, as distinguished from the kinfolk in the networks. One especially interesting detail in the larger array of findings pertained to the relation between the friendship networks of family and child, and complemented the Tietjen results previously mentioned. Where the parents reported the presence of just one dependable friend, the child was likely to report friendship with one or two children or membership in a small clique. Children whose parents reported a number of dependable friends tended themselves to describe peer contact with a number of equally liked friends.

In this section we considered the ways that social network relations influence adults in their roles as parents. Now we turn to another line of influence, this one extending from parents' adult network members directly to children.

THE EFFECTS OF SOCIAL NETWORKS ON CHILDREN

Although many parents nominate children to their networks, we focus here on adult network members and the distinct roles they may play for a developing child. The potential for such influence arises when children engage in face-to-face interaction with adults known to their parents, whether or not their parents are present at the time. Cathy Conrad presented one example in describing the outings led by her brother Jim as an opportunity to introduce her children to positive male role models. Yet despite the prevalence of such relations in daily life, only recently have researchers moved beyond the family to look at the developmental consequences for children of relationships with a broad range of people. Our discussion, then, is necessarily speculative.

It should be noted that the majority of data on which our ideas are based were gathered in studies that had as their central focus the personal networks of children. Lewis, Feiring, and Kotsonis (1984), for example, described the networks of children at two points in time, first when they were 3 years old, and again at age 6. In their analysis, these authors were able to identify important distinctions between adults and peers, and kin and nonkin contacts. But, readers may wonder, can we draw inferences from children's networks (even when reported by their mothers) about relationships with adults who are anchored to parents' social networks? Research by Tietjen (1985), as well as by Cochran and Riley (1988), sheds light on this issue. After conducting separate interviews with Swedish mothers and their 8 to 9-year-old children, Tietjen reported significant overlap of networks, especially with girls. With a sample of 225 U.S. mothers and their 6-year-old children, Cochran and Riley found that the degree of overlap varied from 46%, with nonkin adult network members in African American, two-parent families, to 85% for adult kinfolk in European American, two-parent families. From these studies we can conclude that some, and often many, of the adults included in children's networks are also named by parents to their own networks.

The Content of Adult–Child Relationships

From a developmental perspective, nonparental adults can be thought of as representing various kinds of interactive potential for the child, including parental role-related behaviors, such as child care, task-oriented activities, social outings to contexts beyond the home (e.g., parks, museums, and libraries), and formal teaching directed toward cognitive and social stimulation. In Cochran et al. (1990) mothers were asked, "What kinds of things do [child] and [adult contact] usually do when they are together?" Responses to this open-ended question were organized into five categories of activity, as shown in Table 6.2:

Few differences were found in the kinds of activities pursued with children by kin and nonkin adults.

The Impact on Children of Adult–Child Interactions

In what ways might these activities influence children's development? We hypothesize that enhanced socioemotional functioning is one possible outcome. At the most basic level, an adult who interacts with a child in any of the ways described in Table 6.2 may demonstrate through words or actions that the child is loved, cared for, and valued. Responsiveness, support, and warmth foster the child's trust in adults and, by extension, the social world that he or she is beginning to explore. We predicted that interactions that occur with some regularity, and in which both partners are actively engaged, would carry the greatest potential (Cochran and Brassard, 1979).

TABLE 6.2
The Content of Relations Between Parents' Network Members and Children

Activity	Illustration
Parent role	Paid or unpaid childcare
Task oriented	Washing the car, gardening, marketing
Outings	Trips to a park, library, nature area
Formal teaching	Paid lessons, YMCA activities
Social activities	All other adult–child activities

Time together is also likely to include the exchange of ideas and feelings that are a part of everyday conversation. With practice and encouragement, a child gains confidence and skill in expressing her or his own beliefs, as well as in listening to the views of others. Adults will encourage children to behave appropriately and follow instructions (talking quietly in museums and libraries, not wandering off in a park) to ensure that standards are met. From these social processes we identify the dimensions of "responsiveness" and "demandingness" described in Baumrind's (1980) model of authoritative parenting. In our view, the benefits of firm, warm, and flexible behavior with children transcend the biological relationship linking parent and child. Adult network members, too, through such "ordinary" activities as gardening or a visit to the park, may enhance the social and emotional well-being of children.

Evidence supporting this argument can be discerned from an investigation relating social networks to pro- and antisocial behavior among 92 16-year-old Norwegian boys (Cochran and Bφ, 1989). One key finding of the study was that boys with more educated parents and larger numbers of nonkin adults in their networks showed better school performance, less absenteeism, and more positive social behavior. Negative behaviors such as alcohol use and illegal activities, in contrast, were associated with higher neighborhood risk and less time spent by the parents with their sons. In reviewing their findings, the authors called attention to the particular benefits of adult nonkin membership for the adolescent boys in their sample. They further suggested that social processes operating to prevent antisocial behavior may differ from those that contribute to the development of constructive behavior.

In addition, older children and adolescents may take advantage of activities with adults outside the family to explore attitudes and values different from those presented at home. Teenagers seeking to define an authentic identity for themselves enjoy probing others' ideas about such varied issues as morality, personal relationships, religion, and future plans (Erikson, 1968). More practically, parents' acquaintances may provide suggestions or direct links to possible employment for part-time, internship or summer positions.

Interaction between children and adult network members can also foster gains in cognitive development. Here we draw on Cochran and his colleague's (1990) findings to suggest that task-oriented activities may offer the greatest potential. Joint participation by children and adults challenges partners to cooperate toward constructing goals and performance standards and making decisions. For adults, a primary responsibility is to provide a "scaffold" for the child, giving enough support while challenging the individual toward further mastery. In this process the child can learn metacognitive problem-solving strategies, in time acquiring the skills necessary for independent performance. In other words, joint interaction is an excellent context for social influences on cognitive development—in particular, as conceived by Vygotskian theory (Cochran and Riley, 1988).

The ecological contrasts made possible by the design of the Comparative Ecology of Human Development studies enabled us to examine whether the benefits of joint-task participation would be equal for children growing up under differing social conditions. We predicted that measures of early school success would show the greatest gains among single-parent boys. Our expectation was based on the knowledge that (1) conditions for adequate childrearing were often in jeopardy and (2) the benefits of social network resources would be greatest when the need was greatest. Analysis of the data revealed significant increases in the boys' academic achievement only when the adult accompanying the child was a relative, most often uncles or noncustodial fathers. Thus, although we previously noted that nonkin adults offered significant benefits to adolescent boys, we found that at younger ages boys appear to benefit most by interacting with their kinfolk.

It may also be possible that pre-existing differences in the children are responsible both for their school grades and their network differences. We recognize that children who are brighter, especially as demonstrated by social competence, are likely to elicit more joint activities with adults and perform better in school. Although the intellectual and social–emotional competencies of mother and child contribute strongly to their network building skills, our ecological perspective leads us to believe that the networks constructed with these skills have different effects on children living in different social contexts.

Having looked at the content within social relationships, we step back now to consider how network members represent particular, partial views of the broader social world and the possible impact of such views for the child. Who children do and do not come in contact with, and the particular roles in which adults are seen, help to shape fundamental attitudes and beliefs regarding such issues as social diversity and sex roles. For example, Cross (1990) looked at the racial homogeneity of mothers' networks and found significant differences in the images presented to European American and African American children, as well as in the content of commonplace activities and experiences. Cross found that African American children are far more likely than their European American peers to engage in bicultural experiences. We wonder about the developmental effects for European American children who have little or no early experiences with people of color, or whose impressions must be based on occasional contact with a single individual representing another race.

Additionally, we believe that the roles parents play in introducing network members to their children are related in part to parents' visions for the future of their children. Although African American mothers in two-parent families retained strong ties to kinfolk, their children were typically involved with fewer relatives than were African American children from single-parent households. This pattern recalls the earlier work of Stack (1974), who suggested that upward mobility of African American families often requires a "breaking free" from the network of social ties to the past. Through a process of anticipatory socialization, the married African American mothers in the Cross study may have been preparing their children for a future that would be different, even separate, from their own past and present. Similarly, after Lisa and Chris Jefferson moved to a predominantly European American, blue-collar neighborhood, they understood that most of the children Betsy would meet at the childcare center, and later at school, would be European American. They saw a sharp contrast between Betsy's experiences and their own, having spent much of their lives in African American communities.

Much work remains to be done in documenting the impacts on children's development of their relationships with adult network members. Nevertheless, our glimpse at some of the ways that adults outside the home "parent" children reinforces the broad definition of parenting underlying the chapter and, indeed, this *Handbook*. Importantly, we have seen how adult network members provide psychological and material resources to children at the same time as they represent partial views of the wider social world. We look further at the ways in which networks may be limited in the following section of the chapter, in which we discuss constraints to the pool of members available to parents.

CONSTRAINTS ON PARENTS' ACCESS TO NETWORK MEMBERSHIP

The implicit assumptions underlying much of the research reviewed thus far are that all parents have equal access to deep reservoirs of social ties and that if some parents are tied into more of those resources than others, it is because of the personal value they place in such relationships and the effort they exert to establish and maintain them. But as Wellman (1981, p. 195) warns us:

> There are dangers in studying interpersonal networks in isolation, as if they are the only relevant social phenomena. We must also realize that such networks are really systems that transport resources to and from individuals, and that the structure of large-scale social systems largely determines the allocation of those resources.

There is now good evidence that the network resources available to parents vary substantially depending on parents' educational experience, income, occupation, the number of parents in the household, race, and even the culture in which they live. We refer to these circumstances as *constraint factors*, because the absence of certain characteristics and conditions considered advantageous by the dominant culture constrains or limits access to some kinds of network resources. In this section we document what happens to their networks when parents are constrained by social class (as indicated by educational experiences, income, and occupational level), citizenship in societies with traditional beliefs about women's roles, single-parent status, or identification as African Americans.

Social Class

Family income, the educational level of parents, and the status and complexity of the occupations parents engage in are thought of by sociologists as defining the social class in which a family is located. Fischer (1982) was the first sociologist to provide empirical evidence for the relationships between dimensions of social class and network ties. Fischer's team interviewed a cross section of people ($n = 1,000$) in a 20-county area around San Francisco about their personal social networks. Although some were parents, others were not. The sample reflected the diversity in educational, occupational, economic, gender, and life cycle characteristics of that part of California. Of these background factors, Fischer (1982, p. 252) found that educational level had the most consistent effect on personal networks:

> Other things being equal, the more educational credentials respondents had, the more socially active they were, the larger their networks, the more companionship they reported, the more intimate their relations, and the wider the geographic range of their ties. In general, education by itself meant broader, deeper, and richer networks.

Fischer also found that household income made a sizeable difference in the networks reported, even with education held constant. People with more income included more nonkin in their networks and were more likely to report adequate amounts of companionship and practical support than were the poor.

Fischer's work also provides insight into the impacts of life cycle stage and gender on personal networks. Married people named more relatives and neighbors than did those who were unmarried, whereas single people were more involved with nonkin. Children restricted the social involvement of their parents, and especially of their mothers: "Women with children at home had fewer friends and associates, engaged in fewer social activities, had less reliable social support, and had more localized networks than did otherwise similar women without children" (Fischer, 1982, p. 253). An analysis by gender revealed that women tended to be more involved with kinfolk and to report more intimate ties than did men.

Culture and Class: Influences on Role and Identity

Cochran and Gunnarsson (1990) expanded Fischer's general approach to a comparison of parents' networks across cultures (Sweden, the United States, Wales, and West Germany), social class (blue collar versus white collar), and family structure (one- versus two-parent families). The mothers in all four countries were Caucasian, and each had a 3-year-old child when first interviewed. These researchers confirmed Fischer's finding about the effects of social class on parents' networks, and extended it across cultures. They found in all four countries that mothers in white-collar families reported larger networks than did women in blue-collar households. The magnitude of the difference proved to be about the same in every country except the United States, where the class differences were larger. When they looked beyond network size to the functions performed by network members, again differences by class were readily apparent. Mothers in the white-collar families reported involvement with a higher number of network members in every category of social support. This difference was most visible for social and recreational activities. The data suggest, as a hypothesis, that mothers in white-collar families have more leisure time at their disposal (especially in Sweden and the United States) and spend some of that "extra" time in social and recreational activities with network members.

These comparisons also uncovered consistent network size differences by culture. The pattern was illustrated most dramatically by the contrast between Germany and the United States, in which the networks of young German mothers were about half the size of those reported by the mothers of young children in the United States. A closer examination of these size data distinguished two pairs of countries; German and Welsh mothers reported smaller total networks than mothers in either Sweden or the United States. Although the most dramatic cultural contrasts were seen in the social and recreational activities mentioned earlier, even in the area of emotional support Swedish mothers reported 50%, and white-collar Americans almost 100%, more network members whom they called on for assistance (as compared to mothers in Wales and Germany).

In considering both cultural and class-bound differences in mothers' networks, Cochran and Gunnarsson suggested that the critical distinction involved both role and identity. Societies and social classes differ in terms of the roles women are permitted or encouraged to adopt (mother versus worker, for instance) and in the extent to which they can develop identities beyond those roles. From a developmental perspective, one can distinguish between development as a parent (parent role) and development as a person (personal identity). Network members can be thought of as contributing more or less to one or another of these developmental trajectories. It is reasonable to suggest, for instance, that kinfolk contribute heavily to definition and reinforcement of the parental role, whereas "other friends" are more likely to contribute to "development of self as person" or personal identity. The larger proportion of other friends engaged in social and recreational activities in the networks of white-collar women and of U.S. and Swedish mothers suggests greater involvement with personal development beyond the roles of wife and mother. This impression is reinforced by the data involving relatives and neighbors; German and Welsh mothers interacted more heavily around child-related and practical rather than social and recreational matters.

Cochran and Gunnarsson pointed out that the expectations in blue-collar families regarding the roles of men and women are somewhat more conservative than those found in white-collar families. This pattern was also reflected in their network data. Across cultures, blue-collar networks were somewhat smaller, more kin-dominated, less geographically dispersed, and more child-related and practical in content than their white-collar counterparts.

One-Parent Families

Gunnarsson and Cochran (1990) also examined whether solo parenting was associated with patterns of social relationship that differ from those maintained by parents in two-parent families. This led in the Family Matters Project to the oversampling of single-parent families by the Swedish and U.S. teams. Comparisons of these networks with those maintained by mothers in two-parent families showed that they were smaller, regardless of culture or class. A major factor accounting for the difference in total size was a smaller number of relatives in the networks of single mothers. In the U.S. sample there was an average difference of more than four relatives between single and married mothers, regardless of social class. In Sweden, where the networks of mothers in two-parent families were themselves smaller and less kin-centered than in the United States, there was still an average of two more relatives in the networks of the coupled women than in those of the single mothers.

In the "other friends" sector, single mothers in white-collar families nominated more members than mothers in blue-collar families, both in Sweden and in the United States. The average of eight nonkin friends in the networks of American white-collar single mothers outranked all the other subgroups of women by a substantial margin, and was nearly twice as large as in the case of U.S. blue-collar single mothers. Several circumstances surrounding single mothers in the United States help to explain this difference. It is important to understand that "other friends" are acquired relationships. Whereas ties to kin are ascribed by birth or marriage, individual initiative is necessary to develop and maintain friendships. Also required are access to people, interest, motivation, and the social and material resources with which to sustain the process. The white-collar single mothers in the U.S. sample were more likely to work outside the home than were the blue-collar single mothers, and thus had access to workmates. White-collar jobs are likely to provide more opportunities for socializing than is usual with blue-collar jobs. Training for white-collar jobs usually involves educational situations where opportunities to meet people are also present and social interaction and development of social skills are encouraged. Finally, financial and material resources are likely to be more available to the white-collar single mothers in the sample by virtue of the fact that their jobs pay better.

In Sweden more than 70% of the neighbors included in the networks of single mothers were themselves mothers with young children. In the United States, by contrast, the corresponding figure was only 48% to 59%. This cultural difference was especially extreme for blue-collar single parents (86% versus 48%). The difference may stem from the fact that in the United States such families are often forced by financial disadvantage to live in high-crime areas with substandard housing, where parents are suspicious of their neighbors and are afraid to allow their children to play outside. In Sweden, however, income redistribution has made it possible to ensure that all families can live in safe, relatively "child friendly" neighborhoods. Swedish single mothers tend to live in well-maintained public housing areas containing safe play areas designed specially for young children.

Differences by Race and Ethnicity

Cross (1990) examined the personal networks of African American single and married mothers and compared the size and functioning of their networks with the social ties reported by European American ethnic and nonethnic mothers from similar socioeconomic circumstances living in the same city. When he compared the networks of African American single mothers ($N = 38$) with those of their counterparts in two-parent families ($N = 27$), he found that overall the networks of the latter were more than 25% larger than those of the single women (19.1 versus 14.3 members), a pattern similar to that found by Gunnarsson and Cochran for Caucasian mothers. At the same time, the absolute number of kinfolk in these networks was virtually identical for all African American mothers regardless of family structure. Thus the larger networks of African American mothers in two-parent homes could be traced to the greater number of nonkin neighborhood and work-related contacts (workmates) included as members.

Cross then compared the networks of the 65 African American women with those of 50 ethnic and 40 nonethnic European American mothers, again distinguishing women in one-parent from those in two-parent families. He found that the networks of the ethnic European American mothers were larger than those of either nonethnic European American or African American mothers, regardless of family structure. This difference in favor of ethnic European American women was apparent both for kinfolk and for nonkin in their networks.

When he compared the networks of nonethnic European American and African American mothers, Cross found very few differences in the kin sector, and numbers of nonkin neighbors and workmates were also similar. However, the European American, nonethnic women reported many more ties with "other friends," those nonkin who lived outside the neighborhood and were not workmates (European American two-parent = 5.0; European American one-parent = 6.6; African American two-parent = 2.9; African American one-parent = 3.4).

Cross also examined the cross-race membership in the networks of these women, testing the likelihood that at least one opposite race contact would appear at the functional level of the network. The results of this analysis revealed that 21% of the African American mothers and 16% of the European American mothers in one-parent families had at least one friend of the other race. This modest disparity by race increased as family structure changed and socioeconomic level became higher; within the two-parent sample, 41% of the African American women but only 11% of the European Americans named friends of the other race. Indeed, after moving to a largely European American neighborhood and starting work at a local school, the majority of Lisa Jefferson's new friends were European American. Lisa recognized that she was the first African American friend some of these people ever had.

Cross postulated a relation between the relative lack of African Americans in the networks of European American mothers and the smaller number of "other friends" reported by the African American women. On the one hand, he suggested that the exclusion of African Americans as potential friends would not have much of an effect on the overall size of European American networks because the large numbers of European Americans in all sectors of everyday life provide numerous opportunities to meet and incorporate new European American nonkin contacts. On the other hand, he noted, this is not the case for African American people living in the same community. In the Northeastern city where this study was conducted, only about 12% of the population was African American. Thus, the pool of potential same-race network members was much smaller for African American than for European American mothers, meaning that any cross-race avoidance that might have occurred would have placed the African American women at a relative disadvantage.

In this section of the chapter we have presented evidence that structural factors operating at the levels of culture, class, education, race, ethnicity and family structure constrain the network-building opportunities of some parents more than others. Such constraints yield a relatively smaller pool of "eligibles" from which network membership will be selected. African American parents, nonethnic European American parents, parents with relatively little education, and parents living in cultures shaped by beliefs that lead to narrow definitions of the woman's role all have smaller pools of potential network membership available to them than do their more socioeconomically and socially advantaged counterparts. Constraints accumulate for single parents, who often have less access to relatives, further education, jobs paying a decent salary, and housing in neighborhoods that are supportive of neighboring activities.

PARENTING AND PERSONAL NETWORKS: A FRAMEWORK[2]

At the outset of the chapter we introduced case studies of Cathy Conrad and Lisa and Chris Jefferson to illustrate some of the ways that network members support (and sometimes interfere with) adults in their parenting roles and also engage directly with the children of these adults in parent-like roles, relationships, and activities. In subsequent sections we reviewed empirical investigations of the nature and function of network relationships, as well as of the constraints parents face in building and maintaining social ties. We proceed now to integrate all that what we have learned about parenting and social networks.

At the center of our framework we locate one or two parents and their children engaged with kin and nonkin contacts in relationships that provide more or less emotional support, instrumental assistance, and information.

Just as every network involves some combination of stress and support, so too do we find that each component relationship brings relatively greater or fewer demands. We have provided empirical evidence (where available) and informed speculation (where evidence is lacking) regarding the kinds of impacts—on parents, on parenting, and on child development—that accrue from these social processes.

But networking and parenting do not operate in a vacuum. Both processes are heavily influenced by the location of parents and network members in larger social and economic systems. We have documented the constraints imposed on the pool of potential network membership that are associated with lower levels of education, lower income, less-prestigious employment, racial characteristics deemed less desirable by American society, or even citizenship in a culture in which custom limits the roles available to women. Thus, as depicted in Figure 6.1, the pool of potential network members available to adults for assistance in their parenting roles varies quite dramatically, depending on a set of socioeconomic factors and personal characteristics, some of which are beyond their power to alter.

---

[2]The reader is referred to Cochran, Riley, Larner, Gunnarsson, and Henderson (1990, chapters 14, 15, 16) and Cochran (1991) for elaboration of this model.

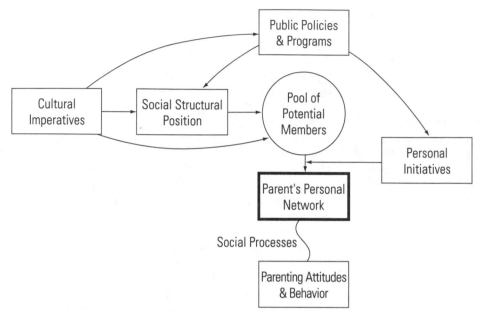

FIGURE 6.1. Parenting and personal networks: A framework.

The term *potential* connotes the possibility and need for parents to take initiative in order to realize available opportunities. Cochran (1990) included *personal initiative* in a model of parental network development, as we have in Figure 6.1, to incorporate the actions required, first, in selecting as members those people not already prescribed by kin relations, and second, to maintain relationships once established. Cochran identified nine possible factors contributing to the amount of initiative a parent might take in building and maintaining network ties: personality characteristics, human capacity, time and energy resources, stage of development, discrete life events (divorce, loss of family member, job loss), self-esteem, personal and group identity, educational experience, and social and cognitive skills. He further asserted that educational achievement beyond secondary school is so important for expanding the network because it enhances the achievement component of personal identity, raises self-esteem, and expands social and cognitive skills simultaneously. In summary, participation in higher education alters significantly the capacity and the motive of the parent to build new, highly functional social relationships and to phase out relationships that bring more stress than support to the parenting role.

It is very important to understand that the networks of parents are not static, even in those instances when parents face severe socioeconomic and culturally defined constraints. Larner (1990), for instance, documented a 22% turnover in parent network membership over just 3 years. Only 9% of kinfolk were involved in these shifts, whereas 33% of all nonkin were included. Within our framework, change is linked to factors affecting both constraint and initiative. For instance, shortly after Cathy Conrad enrolled in the local community college for training as a nurse practitioner, she added Marcie and Patty to her network. Looking toward the future, we anticipate that more networking possibilities will open up to her as she continues her education and enters the nursing profession (reduced constraint). Experiences at college give Cathy increased self-confidence, new skills in social interaction and intellectual exchange, and a new personal and professional identity as a caring person and a member of a caring profession. All of these changes make her more willing and able to approach strangers and to establish new relationships (personal initiative) even though she considers herself a rather shy person.

Network change need not be brought about only by large-scale social and economic changes in the living conditions of classes or groups, or defined simply by developmental and life cycle transitions.

There is evidence that social programs initiated by local communities can effect positive changes in parents' networks. Network changes, in turn, can facilitate healthy child development. In the next section we review studies documenting such impacts.

PROGRAMMATIC AND POLICY EFFORTS
TO ENHANCE PARENTAL NETWORKS

Is there any evidence that community-level programs can have positive effects on the natural help-ing networks of parents? One of the earliest indicators of such potential was associated with an experimental intervention carried out in Chicago by Hess, Shipman, Brophy, and Bear (1968). The focus of this project was on helping mothers in low-income families stimulate the cognitive capa-cities of their young children more effectively. The authors noted in passing that the mothers receiv-ing the intervention were more likely than those in a control group to have become involved in social activities outside the home (e.g., clubs and courses). Two implications were drawn from this find-ing: first, that a program focused on parent–child interaction might stimulate the mother to become involved with social activities outside the home, and second, that this outside social involvement might reinforce interest in parenting activities.

A more explicit emphasis on social networks was included in an intervention study carried out in a blue-collar Detroit neighborhood by Powell and his colleagues (Eisenstadt and Powell, 1987; Powell, 1979, 1987, 1988) with families containing children up to 6 months old. The Child and Family Neighborhood Program (CFNP) was designed to strengthen family supports by improving families' use of social networks and neighborhood resources for childrearing. Peer participants were identified as potential providers of informal support to parents in the program. The strategy of choice involved neighborhood group meetings, supported by home visits and health and social services.

Powell (1988, p. 130) reported that parents' social networks first came into play during the recruitment phase of the program, in several different ways:

> There were instances where mothers routinely and frequently congregated with family and friends. One individual, for example, socialized with her own mother and sisters several times a week. The program, she reported, would be duplicative of these gatherings. It also seemed that significant members of one's social network had an influence on the decision about joining. It was not uncommon to learn that a person's husband or mother did not approve of the program. There were also cases of a mothers' relatives (especially her own mother) encouraging program participation but the mother not wanting to join.

Powell also found a relation between parents' social networks and their decision to stop participating in the program. Those mothers who terminated involvement early had less extensive social networks than did mothers who remained in the program longer.

Cochran, Bronfenbrenner, and Cross designed an experimental family support initiative that had a number of features in common with Powell's Child and Family Neighborhood Program (Cochran, 1991). The Family Matters Program had five major goals, all related broadly to the parenting role: (1) to recognize parents as experts, (2) to exchange information with parents about children, the neighborhood, community services, schools, and work, (3) to reinforce and encourage parent–child activities, (4) to exchange informal resources such as babysitting, childrearing advice, and emotional support with neighbors and other friends, and (5) to facilitate concerted action by program participants on behalf of their children when parents deemed such action appropriate. The program was offered to 160 families, each containing a 3-year-old child, in 10 different urban neighborhoods. Two processes were used to involve families in activities related to their children: a home-visiting approach aimed at individual families and a cluster-building approach aimed at linking together all the Family Matters families in a given neighborhood. Families were involved with program activities for an average of

24 months. A comparison group of 128 families, living in eight other neighborhoods in the same city, was also included in the study.

The findings revealed that networks were affected positively by the program, and that networks-related changes were associated with attitudes, activities, or school performance among certain types of families.

Single Mothers

Unmarried mothers were especially responsive in network terms to program involvement. This responsivity was more evident with European American women than with their African American counterparts. By the end of the study, European American, unmarried program mothers reported more nonrelatives in their networks, both overall and at the primary level. A closer look at the content of exchanges revealed involvement with larger numbers of people for borrowing and work-related and emotional support, always with nonkin. At the primary network level, change consisted primarily of the addition of nonrelatives who were not present in the network three years earlier. Overall, these women reported contact with somewhat fewer relatives at follow-up than had been the case at baseline. In terms of outcomes, these mothers' perceptions of themselves as parents emerged as a key determinant of their children's performance in school. More positive parental self-perceptions were also associated with increases in both the primary networks and the number of activities mothers reported engaging in with their children. There is evidence that the nonkin sector of the mothers' primary networks played an especially positive role in preparing their children for entry into school.

African American unmarried mothers who participated in the program also added a significant amount of new nonkin membership to the primary portion of their networks. They were less likely, however, to report increases beyond the primary level, and the increase in new primary membership was about as likely to involve relatives as nonrelatives. This reflected a more general tendency among African American women to rely on kinship ties. In terms of outcome measures, increases in the number of relatives included in the mother's primary support network were associated with reports of more joint activity with the child. Joint activity involving household chores was linked in turn to children's higher performance in school. Expansion of nonkin membership in the primary networks of these mothers was also linked with school readiness outcomes (personal adjustment, interpersonal relationships, relationships with the teacher).

Married Mothers

Program effects were less pervasive with married women than was found with single mothers, and the effects that could be discerned were confined to relationships with kin. European American married mothers who participated in the program reported an overall decrease in network size in comparison with the appropriate controls. This decrease was found only among nonrelatives, and balanced at the primary level by an increase in kin. Closer examination showed that typically these kin had been present in the network three years earlier, but not defined as especially important at that time. Only one set of possible links to outcomes was discerned for these women, and only if they had additional schooling beyond high school. Under this condition, higher perception of self as parent, more mother–child activities, and better performance by the child in school were observed.

In the case of married African American women there was an increase at follow-up in the number of relatives reported in the primary network, many of whom were new additions. Increased involvement with kin was related to greater amounts of mother–child activity. However, neither the increases in primary kin nor the greater parent–child activity appeared to be associated with better school performance.

One of the exciting aspects of social supports as program outcomes is their potential for further development of the individual into the future. Some have used the *convoy analogy* (House, 1980;

Kahn and Antonucci, 1980; Larner, 1990). Such an analogy clearly implies that network-related changes associated with an early childhood or family support program might be as strongly linked to subsequent developments in the child as they are to more immediate ones. The findings reported earlier begin to provide outlines for the forms of transport making up such convoys. One vehicle is likely to be composed of close friends and relatives committed to the welfare of both parent and child. This is the conveyance that was the central focus the research by Powell and by Cochran and his colleagues. Another vehicle is parental self-confidence, which Cochran and his colleagues believe comes in part from the support of key network members, but is also necessary to stimulate network building or modification. A third vehicle, and perhaps the one heading the convoy, is the parent's level of formal education. Cochran (1990) suggested that schooling provides parents with both network-building skills and access to people outside the kinship circle.

Public education is itself an intervention into the childrearing process far more comprehensive than anything else undertaken by local communities. Taken as a whole, the network studies carried out by Cochran and his associates through the Family Matters Project provide compelling evidence for the argument that 40% to 50% of the support parents receive from their personal networks is strongly affected by their level of schooling. In this research the critical step appeared to involve access to postsecondary education: Those parents who had acquired such schooling were much richer in network resources than those who had not. College scholarships, student loans and programs providing incentives to adolescents and young adults for continuation of schooling through high school and beyond would seem to be an especially good investment to society from this standpoint.

Policies that stimulate job creation and continuation might also deserve high priority from a "networks in context" perspective. The workplace proved to be an important context for network building for Family Matters families and the economic returns associated with working provide some of the resources needed to sustain network relations.

The findings presented in this section have led us to conclude that public and private policies and programs must be included in our "parenting and social networks" framework because of their very real potential for altering the network resources of adults in their parenting roles. We close the chapter by identifying future directions for networks research. The results of such studies would fill in some of the major gaps in our understanding of why and how parents engage with network members around parenting issues, and just what impacts such activities have on their parenting attitudes and behaviors.

CONCLUSIONS

"It takes a whole village to rear a child," states an African proverb. Social networks represent one way of describing that village, a community defined not by geography but by relations and relationships. In this chapter we have offered a broad perspective on parenting. We showed how parents like Cathy Conrad and Lisa and Chris Jefferson turn to their network members for advice, emotional support, practical assistance, and help caring for their children. Yet, we demonstrated as well that parenting cannot be understood in isolation from the larger set of social and economic structures in which it is embedded. It is clear that poverty, unemployment, and lack of educational opportunity dramatically influence the networks of families, limiting their capacity to nurture and support parents and their children.

Although our society expects parents to accept full responsibility for rearing its future workers, citizens, and leaders, from the research reviewed in this chapter we discern the wisdom of an alternative view. In particular, the growing body of research linking social networks to parenting demonstrates that the actions of communities, states, and society as a whole are a decisive factor in determining whether parents have the resources necessary for fulfilling our expectations of them. Access to education, well-paying jobs, and secure housing enables parents like Cathy, Lisa, and Chris to build and maintain strong networks and to use those networks in support of their own development, as well as that of their children.

Strengthening parents' networks requires that we increase our knowledge of the ways in which networks develop, function, and change over time. Let us conclude, then, by identifying six key areas for future research.

To begin, we would like to see further study of the factors that encourage parents to initiate network-building activities or that inhibit them from doing so. One obvious, but as yet unexploited area of inquiry involves the possible connection between parents' personality type (extroverted/introverted, shy/outgoing) and their willingness to initiate social relationships with other parents, neighbors, or coworkers. Another approach would focus on context by investigating whether parents with sustained involvement in particular settings (the workplace, the neighborhood, elementary school) or in settings organized in one or another particular way (e.g., workplaces with hierarchical or horizontal chains of command, neighborhoods with open spaces for play, arrangement of dwellings in a housing development) engage in more or less network building.

Further inquiry is also needed on the connections between personal ideologies or belief systems and parents' propensity to engage in network-building activities. It is quite possible that some people are reared within a strong ethic of self-sufficiency, whereas others experience interdependent exchanges of assistance and support through childhood and adolescence. We expect that new parents holding such different beliefs about the appropriate functions of social relationships would respond quite differently to opportunities for parenting-related network building.

Cochran and his colleagues (1990) identified clusters of parents with similar patterns of variation along several dimensions of their networks: total size, proportion of kin versus nonkin membership, degree to which members served multiple roles, and the overlap between mothers' and fathers' membership. We are left to wonder whether there may be specific network typologies associated with particular beliefs, attitudes, and behaviors of parents toward their children. Investigating possible links between parenting and network typologies would add a strong ecological dimension to the already substantial literature on parenting styles.

In an earlier section we discussed the possible effects on children's development of interaction with adult members of parents' networks. Our broad understanding of parenting—extending well beyond biological relationships linking parents and their children—leads us to wonder about the many ways adults may promote social, emotional, and cognitive competence in children. In future studies we would like to see greater attention to the roles adults play in children's everyday lives—at childcare centers, schools, after-school programs, and in neighborhood and family gatherings. A networks perspective would enable researchers to perform fine-grained analyses in order to determine the nature and meaning of such relations, as well as the different outcomes for children associated with particular social conditions.

Changes in the nature and meaning of intrafamilial relations—between spouses and between parents and their children—have been associated with children's movement from infancy through adolescence and adulthood. As expectations and role relations are altered within the family, we would expect to find additional changes in family members' relations with individuals outside the household. Study of this issue would help us to better understand the dynamic properties of networks as well as their capacity to promote and respond to the personal identity development of family members across the life course.

Finally, our review of the literature uncovered very few evaluations of early intervention, early childhood, or family support programs that included network change as a possible outcome. From a parenting perspective, we would particularly like to see such a focus in evaluations of the family support programs now burgeoning in the United States, many of which include "parent education" as a centerpiece. Network building is possible in any program that brings parents together, or that could do so; we encourage evaluators to include measures of network-related consequences as part of their overall assessment strategy.

ACKNOWLEDGMENTS

We acknowledge with gratitude the support provided to the Cornell studies described in this chapter by the College of Human Ecology and the Africana Studies and Research Institute at Cornell University, the Department of Education at the University of Gothenburg in Gothenburg, Sweden, the Department of Educational Research at the Stockholm Institute of Education, and Rogoland College in Stavanger, Norway. This research was supported in the United States with grants from the Ford Foundation, the National Institute of Education, the William T. Grant Foundation, The Administration for Children, Youth, and families, the Carnegie Corporation, the Charles F. Kettering Foundation, the Charles Stewart Mott Foundation, the National Institute of Child Health and Human Development, the Spencer Foundation, and the Kellogg Foundation.

REFERENCES

Baumrind, D. (1980). New directions in socialization research. *American Psychologist, 35,* 639–652.

Belle, D. (1982). Social ties and social support. In D. Belle (Ed.), *Lives in stress: Women and depression.* Beverly Hills, CA: Sage.

Bott, E. (1957). *Family and social networks.* London: Havistock.

Brassard, J. (1982). *Beyond family structure: Mother–child interaction and personal social networks.* Unpublished doctoral dissertation, Cornell University, Ithaca, NY.

Caldwell, B. M., and Bradley, R. H. (1984). *Home observation for measurement of the environment.* Little Rock: University of Arkansas at Little Rock/Center for Child.

Cobb, S. (1976). Social support as a moderator of life stress. *Psychosomatic Medicine, 38,* 300–314.

Cochran, M. (1988). Parental empowerment in Family Matters: Lessons learned from a research program. In D. Powell (Ed.), *Parent education as early childhood intervention: Emerging directions in theory, research and practice* (pp. 23–52). Norwood, NJ: Ablex.

Cochran, M. (1990). Factors influencing personal social initiative. In M. Cochran, M. Larner, D. Riley, L. Gunnarsson, and C. Henderson, Jr. (Eds.), *Extending families: The social networks of parents and their children* (pp. 297–306). London/New York: Cambridge University Press.

Cochran, M. (1991). Personal social networks as a focus of support. In D. Unger and D. Powell (Eds.), *Families as nurturing systems* (pp. 45–68). New York: Haworth.

Cochran, M., and Bφ, I. (1989). The social networks, family involvement, and pro- and anti-social behavior of adolescent males in Norway. *Journal of Youth and Adolescence, 18,* 377–398.

Cochran, M., and Brassard, J. (1979). Child development and personal social networks. *Child Development, 50,* 609–615.

Cochran, M., and Gunnarsson, L. (1990). The social networks of married mothers in four cultures. In M. Cochran, M. Larner, D. Riley, L. Gunnarsson, and C. Henderson, Jr. (Eds.), *Extending families: The social networks of parents and their children* (pp. 86–104). London/New York: Cambridge University Press.

Cochran, M., Larner, M., Riley, D., Gunnarsson, L., and Henderson, C., Jr. (1990). *Extending families: The social networks of parents and their children.* London/New York: Cambridge University Press.

Cochran, M. M., and Riley, D. (1988). Mother reports of children's personal networks: Antecedents, concomitants, and consequences. In S. Salzinger, M. Hammer, and J. Antrobus (Eds.), *Social networks of children, youth and college students.* Hillsdale, NJ: Lawrence Erlbaum Associates.

Colletta, N. (1981). Social support and the risk of maternal rejection by adolescent mothers. *Journal of Psychology, 109,* 191–197.

Cotterell, J. (1986). Work and community influences on the quality of childrearing. *Child Development, 57,* 362–374.

Crittenden, P. (1981). Abusing, neglecting, problematic, and adequate dyads: Differentiating by patterns of interaction. *Merrill-Palmer Quarterly, 27,* 1–18.

Crittenden, P. (1985a). Maltreated infants: Vulnerability and resistance. *Journal of Child Psychology and Psychiatry, 26,* 85–96.

Crittenden, P. (1985b). Social networks, quality of child-rearing, and child development. *Child Development, 56,* 1299–1313.

Crockenberg, S. (1981). Infant irritability, mother responsiveness, and social support influences on the security of infant–mother attachment. *Child Development,* 857–865.

Crockenberg, S. (1988). Social support and parenting. In W. Fitzgerald, B. Lester, and M. Yogman (Eds.), *Research on support for parents and infants in the postnatal period* (pp. 67–92). New York: Ablex.

Cross, W. (1990). Race and ethnicity: Effects on social networks. In M. Cochran, M. Larner, D. Riley, L. Gunnarsson, and C. Henderson, Jr. (Eds.), *Extending families: The social networks of parents and their children* (pp. 67–85). London/New York: Cambridge University Press.

Crnic, K., Greenberg, M., Ragozin, A., Robinson, N., and Basham, R. (1983). Effects of stress and support on mothers and premature and full-term infants. *Child Development, 54*, 209–217.

Eisenstadt, J., and Powell, D. (1987). Processes of participation in mother–infant programs as modified by stress and impulse control. *Journal of Applied Developmental Psychology, 8*, 17–37.

Erikson, E. H. (1968). *Identity: Youth and crisis*. New York: Norton.

Fischer, C. (1982). *To dwell among friends: Personal networks in town and city*. Chicago: University of Chicago Press.

Gunnarsson, L., and Cochran, M. (1990). The social networks of single parents: Sweden and the United States. In M. Cochran, M. Larner, D. Riley, L. Gunnarsson, and C. Henderson, Jr. (Eds.), *Extending families: The social networks of parents and their children* (pp. 105–116). London/New York: Cambridge University Press.

Hareven, T. (1984). Themes in the historical development of the family. In R. D. Parke (Ed.), *Review of Child Development Research, 7*, 137–178. Chicago: University of Chicago Press.

Hess, R., Shipman, V., Brophy, J., and Bear, R. (1968). *The cognitive environments of urban preschool children*. Unpublished paper, University of Chicago, Graduate School of Education.

Homel, R., Burns, A., and Goodnow, J. (1987). Parental social networks and child development. *Journal of Social and Personal Relationships, 4*, 159–177.

House, J. (1980). *Work, stress, and social support*. Reading, MA: Addison-Wesley.

Kahn, R., and Antonucci, T. (1980). Convoys over the life course: Attachment, roles, and social support. In P. Baltes and O. Brim (Eds.), *Life-span Development and Behavior, 3*, 116–138. New York: Academic Press.

Larner, M. (1990). Change in network resources and relationships over time. In M. Cochran, M. Larner, D. Riley, L. Gunnarsson, and C. Henderson, Jr. (Eds.), *Extending families: The social networks of parents and their children* (pp. 181–204). London/New York: Cambridge University Press.

Lewis, M., Feiring, C., and Kotsonis, M. (1984). The social network of the young child: A developmental perspective. In M. Lewis (Ed.), *Beyond the dyad* (pp. 129–160). New York: Plenum.

Longfellow, C., Zelkowitz, P., Saunders, E., and Belle, D. (1979, March). *The role of support in moderating the effects of stress and depression*. Paper presented at the biennial meeting of the Society for Research in Child Development, San Francisco.

Milardo, R. (Ed.). (1988). *Families and social networks*. Beverly Hills, CA: Sage.

Mitchell, J. C. (1969a). The concept and use of social networks. In J. C. Mitchell (Ed.), *Social networks in urban situations*. Manchester, England: Manchester University Press.

Mitchell, J. C. (1969b). *Social networks in urban situations*. Manchester, England: Manchester University Press.

Polansky, N., Gaudin, J., Ammons, P., and Davis, K. (1985). The psychological ecology of the neglectful mother. *Child Abuse and Neglect, 9*, 265–275.

Powell, D. (1979). Family environment relations and early childrearing: The role of social networks and neighborhood. *Journal of Research and Development in Education, 13*, 1–11.

Powell, D. (1987). A neighborhood approach to family support groups. *Journal of Community Psychology, 15*, 51–62.

Powell, D. (1988). Client characteristics and the design of community-based intervention programs. In A. Pence (Ed.), *Ecological research with children and families*. New York: Teachers College Press.

Riley, D. (1990). Network influences on father involvement in childrearing. In M. Cochran, M. Larner, D. Riley, L. Gunnarsson, and C. Henderson, Jr. (Eds.), *Extending families: The social networks of parents and their children* (pp. 131–153). London/New York: Cambridge University Press.

Stack, C. (1974). *All our kin: Strategies for survival in a black community*. New York: Harper & Row.

Strom, R. D. (1982). *Parent as a teacher inventory. Manual and instructions*. Bensenville, IL: Scholastic Testing Service.

Tietjen, A. (1985). Relationships between the social networks of Swedish mothers and their children. *International Journal of Behavioral Development, 8*, 195–216.

Wellman, B. (1981). Applying network analysis to the study of support. In B. H. Gottlieb (Ed.), *Social networks and social support*. Beverly Hills, CA: Sage.

PART II

APPLIED ISSUES IN PARENTING

7

Parenting Competence

Douglas M. Teti
Margo A. Candelaria
University of Maryland

INTRODUCTION

That variations in many developmental outcomes can be at least partly accounted for by individual differences in parenting quality is a premise that has widespread empirical support. (Baumrind, 1970; Clarke-Stewart, 1973; Isabella and Belsky, 1991; Tamis-LeMonda, Bornstein, Baumwell, and Damast, 1996). Conceptualizations of competent parenting, however, will by necessity depend on the specific child outcomes of interest. Language development, for example, appears to be best fostered by caregiving environments rich in language inputs, tailored to the child's developmental level, and responsive to the child's bids to communicate (Bornstein and Tamis-LeMonda, 1997; Warren and Walker, in press). Parent-provided language mastery experiences and parental responsivity to child behavior are similarly important for promoting children's intellectual development (Bornstein and Tamis-LeMonda, 1989; Carew, 1980; Tamis-LeMonda et al., 1996), and to these we can add the adequacy with which parents structure their children's environments to be intellectually stimulating (e.g., in terms of providing appropriately stimulating play materials and variety in daily stimulation; Bradley, 1999). Attachment theorists, by contrast, would likely define competent parenting in terms of parental sensitivity, or the ability of the parent to read and respond contingently and appropriately to infant distress, bids for comfort, and cues for interaction and withdrawal (Ainsworth, Blehar, Waters, and Wall, 1978; Belsky, 1999). Conceptualizations of parenting competence would also differ in relation to age-related differences in children's developmental competencies and specific needs.

The present chapter is concerned with parenting competence in relation to socialization outcomes that are desired by parents. This particular focus is plagued by an inherent circularity. That is, parenting competence is identified by its effects, or, more specifically, competent parenting can be defined only in reference to socialization outcomes desired by a particular group. Whatever parents do that sets children on a path toward achieving these outcomes is likely to be considered "competent," and whatever parents do that derails children from this path is likely to be considered "incompetent."

Furthermore, like much of the knowledge base in the behavioral sciences, theoretical and empirical foundations underlying parenting competence are largely Western- and, in particular, U.S.-based. There does appear to be universal agreement among parents the world over that the central goal of parenting is to rear children to become productive and contributing members of society (Whiting and Edwards, 1988). What is promoted in this chapter as competent parenting, however, has a decidedly Western flavor, although evidence is accruing that at least some components of skillful parenting have cross-cultural validity.

We begin our discussion with some historical, pre–twentieth century perspectives on parenting competence, followed by brief coverage of two grand theories, psychoanalytic and learning theory, and how they guided research on parenting competence in the first half of the twentieth century. We then follow with an in-depth review of parenting quality as defined in terms of parenting style, a research tradition led by Baumrind that is still very influential today. Our focus then turns to specific parent–child behavioral and cognitive processes that underlie children's successful internalization of standards of conduct, the role of early parenting and attachment security in the first few years of life in shaping successful socialization in later childhood, and the importance of considering the child as a contextual moderator of the effects of specific socialization practices. Finally, we review some well-known and successful intervention programs, drawn from socialization theory and research covered herein, designed to promote competent parenting in families at risk.

HISTORICAL PERSPECTIVES ON PARENTING COMPETENCE

Widespread interest in what constitutes competent parenting is a relatively recent development in the Western world (French, in Vol. 4 of this *Handbook*). Indeed, the mere recognition of childhood as a separate developmental stage, that children should be prevented from being incorporated too quickly into adult society, was very slow to develop (Ariès, 1962). Children perceived as the undesired by-product of sexual relations were routinely destroyed or abandoned, with little consequence for the perpetrator (Langer, 1974). Handing infants over to wet nurses during the first two years of life was commonplace, as were other child–parent separations for purposes of entering monastic life, a nunnery, serving as a neighboring lord's page, or acquiring a trade. Typically, a child was assimilated into the work and play of adult life very early in childhood, and only a few bound manuscripts addressing "proper" infant and childcare were available to the general public during this time. Such "advice" was predicated on personal opinions, well-practiced customs of the day, and/or on religious ideologies that viewed children as creatures in need of breaking and molding to prepare them properly for the afterlife.

Pre–Twentieth Century Thoughts on Parenting Competence

Perhaps the most well-known medieval source of parental "wisdoms" was the Franciscan Bartholomew of England's *De proprietatibus rerum* (Book on the Nature of Things), an encyclopedia of ancient and modern philosophies and recommendations about proper childcare that appeared around 1230 (Goodich, 1975). Advice included keeping infants away from too much light to avoid damage to the eyes, strengthening infants' limbs with frequent baths and oil rubdowns, nursing infants with good milk, and administering medicines not to the infant but to the wet nurse so that the infant would benefit from her good health. Swaddling of the limbs with tight bandages was also recommended to prevent twisting and other deformities. Bartholomew also advocated strict upbringing with frequent corporal punishment, which he believed to be essential for successful childrearing. A second encyclopedia with specific advice for parents was Vincent of Beauvais's *Speculum majus*, appearing in the thirteenth century. In marked contrast to Bartholomew's writings and societal norms of the age, Beauvais viewed childhood as the most delicate and malleable period of life. Recommendations to parents included providing children with ample sleep and free play and to differentiate between children who could be led by gentleness and children who require firmer, more coercive discipline (Gabriel, 1962).

Such voices, however, existed on the fringes of medieval society and had little influence on parental practices and attitudes. Most of the literature at this time was written in Latin by monastic scholars and not widely circulated until much later, as the number of different translations increased. It is quite unlikely that these ideas touched the lives of the illiterate masses of the period, those of lower socioeconomic strata, whose children remained at home to work the fields and tend to domestic concerns (Ariës, 1962).

From the fourteenth through seventeenth centuries, a child's life remained quite precarious. The practice of wet nursing continued, as did sending young boys to enter the monastery or to apprentice-ships and preparing young girls for marriage (frequently pre-arranged in childhood) or the nunnery. As economic conditions improved in Europe, however, more interest was invested in children with the growth of the middle class, and a different view of children began to emerge—that they were both innocent and sweet but also weak and in need of moral "guidance" (Ariës, 1962). Ironically, although this new perspective signified a recognition that children possessed unique qualities that dis-tinguished them from adults, it also gave rise to the belief that children needed to be "strengthened" and "improved" through humiliation and physical discipline. Corporal punishment became espe-cially relevant for children, irrespective of their social class, as parents saw the need to "break" their children to ensure their moral and spiritual character. There was even a theory, developed by a Dutchman named Batty, that God formed the human buttocks in such a way that they could be beaten repeatedly without sustaining serious injury (Stone, 1975).

Moralists and pedagogues of this era preached about children's need for education, physical discipline, and segregation from adult life, and that parents were ultimately responsible for their children's moral character. The fourteenth through seventeenth centuries saw a gradual increase in institutions of learning dedicated to the education of children. Parents, in accepting the sanctity and fragility of childhood, began to feel the need to watch over their children more closely rather than send them off to live with strangers who could potentially "contaminate" them. The practice of apprenticeship slowly waned, and parents began to look to schools as the primary means of educating their young. By the seventeenth century, which witnessed the emergence of a more elaborate system of schools, parents began to push for founding schools closer to their homes (Ariës, 1962; Epstein and Sanders, in Vol. 5 of this *Handbook*).

With the increase in schools, of course, came an increase in literacy rates, and with the proliferation of printing presses and increasing investment in children, more people than ever before were probably reading childcare manuals (Greenleaf, 1978). One of the foremost philosophers and scholars of the seventeenth century, and who wrote extensively on children, was John Locke, in his 1693 publication of *Some Thoughts Concerning Education*, a compilation of letters Locke wrote from Holland to friends in England concerning the upbringing of their son. Locke's views reflected the growth in the appreciation of childhood and education that especially characterized the seventeenth century. It is also likely, however, that Locke's writings accelerated the movement that set children apart as special human beings. Locke was unique in emphasizing that education was absolutely essential to one's psychological and physical well-being. In addition, in an age in which brutality toward children was commonplace, Locke (1693/1978, para. 1) demonstrated a singular understanding of children's special nature and their treatment:

For all their innocent folly, playing, and childish acting, are to be left perfectly free and unrestrained, as far as they can consist with the respect due to those that are present; and that with the greatest allowance. If these faults of their age, rather than of the children themselves, were, as they should be, left only to time, and imitation, and riper years to cure, children would escape a great deal of misapplied and useless correction.... This gamesome humour, which is wisely adapted by nature to their age and temper, should rather be encouraged, to keep up their spirits, and improve their strength and health, than curbed or restrained: and the chief art is to make all that they have to do, sport and play too.

In advocating the use of reasoning rather than brute force in disciplining children, Locke wrote (para. 81):

> It will perhaps be wondered, that I mention reasoning with children: and yet I cannot but think that the true way of dealing with them. They understand it as early as they do language; and, if I misobserve not, they love to be treated as rational creatures sooner than is imagined. It is a pride should be cherished in them, and, as much as can be, made the greatest instrument to turn them by.

He then demonstrates remarkable insight as he goes on to say (para. 81):

> But when I talk of reasoning, I do not intend any other but such as is suited to the child's capacity and apprehension. Nobody can think a boy of three or seven years old should be argued with as a grown man. Long discourses, and philosophical reasonings, at best amaze and confound, but do not instruct, children. When I say, therefore, that they must be treated as rational creatures, I mean, that you should make them sensible, by the mildness of your carriage, and the composure, even in your correction of them, that what you do is reasonable in you, and useful and necessary for them; and that it is not out of caprice, passion, or fancy, that you command or forbid them any thing.

This passage reflects a childrearing approach that is no less modern than that which is advocated by modern scholars. Moreover, in an age where childhood was being marked out and "improved" by physical discipline, Locke (1693/1978, para. 84) expressed these views:

> . . . as I said before, beating is the worst, and there the last, means to be used in the correction of children; and that only in cases of extremity, after all gentler ways have been tried, and proved unsuccessful; which, if well observed, there will be very seldom any need of blows.

Locke's views reflected his belief in the role of the early caregiving environment in shaping children's development, and in particular in the use of reason, rather than corporal punishment, as a consequence of misbehavior. His views still fell prey to some common superstitions of the era, however, which would not be endorsed as elements of competent parenting today. For example, he advocated the use of cold baths and light clothing to build stamina and "harden" infants and cautioned parents against feeding their infants peaches, grapes, and melons because their juice was unhealthy. On balance, however, Locke was influential in focusing the attention of later generations on children in a new and different way.

Locke's influence was not so strong, unfortunately, that it led to sweeping changes in the manner in which young children were treated. The abandonment and murder of infants continued and actually may have worsened in the eighteenth and nineteenth centuries, despite deterrents such as burial alive and drowning, because it was difficult to prove that the alleged offender willfully committed murder (Langer, 1974). The practice of wet nursing remained in fashion in the eighteenth and nineteenth centuries despite the fact that nurses were responsible for scores of infant deaths by "over-laying" (smothering) the infant to death by nurses who tended to sleep with their "charges." The casual indifference regarding children's rights was exemplified by the differential severity of punishments meted out for a crime of petty larceny, which was frequently punished by death, versus putting out the eyes of children (sometimes done by beggars to arouse pity), which was punished by imprisonment for only 2 years. Furthermore, despite Locke's strong position against the use of physical punishment, the eighteenth century child continued to be brutally victimized at home and school. Parents had absolute power over their children in the eyes of the law, and parents' harsh treatment of children continued to stem from the belief that it was the parent's right and duty to curb severely children's inherently sinful passions (Ariès, 1962).

Despite this backdrop of indifference, the eighteenth and nineteenth centuries saw the systematic development of local and national welfare movements designed to save abandoned infants (e.g., the Foundling Hospital of London, established by Thomas Coram in 1739, George, 1964). In addition, with the emergence of the field of pediatrics in the eighteenth century came recommendations from physicians for the humane treatment of children. For example, the British physician William Cadogan, in "An Essay Upon Nursing and the Management of Children" (1748, George, 1964), provided advice on a host of topics, including swaddling (recommending against it) and the proper choice for a wet nurse, although Cadogan more strongly supported the nursing of infants by their own mothers. His essay also advocated frequent bathing (unusual in an era that practiced swaddling), lots of fresh air, and a balanced diet following weaning. Indeed, Cadogan emphasized a commonsense, humane approach to infant management that was unique for his era (George, 1964) and consistent with the recommendations of modern-day pediatricians (Spock and Rothenberg, 1992). Such writings indicate that the notion of parental competence was emerging in this era.

At about the same time eighteenth-century welfare movements were gaining momentum, a notable French scholar was writing books that were to have far-reaching effects on the childrearing practices and attitudes. Jean-Jacques Rousseau had already achieved notoriety in French society with his two treatises, *Sur les Sciences et les Arts* and *Sur l'Inegalite*, in which he advanced his basic philosophy that mankind's natural goodness, evidenced in childhood, was slowly corrupted by societal evils. His most influential work with regard to children was *Émile* (1911/1762) a fictitious account of a tutor who teaches the same pupil, Émile, from infancy to about the age of 20 years. *Émile* was written on the premise that childhood was a unique state of being that was important for its own sake, and Rousseau saw childhood as spanning four of his proposed five life stages: Infancy, childhood, preadolescence, adolescence, and adulthood. Unlike many other pedagogues of his era, Rousseau believed that learning begins from birth, and that infants' natural curiosity of the world should be cultivated by parents. He advised parents to be appropriate role models for their children, and to take the time to appreciate and enjoy the natural proclivities of childhood. He took special exception to the practices of swaddling and wet nursing, which he saw as devices used to maximize mothers' and nurses' comfort at the expense of the infant. Of swaddling, he wrote (Rousseau, *Émile*, Book I):

> What is the origin of this senseless and unnatural custom? Because mothers have despised their first duty and refused to nurse their own children, they have had to be entrusted to hired nurses. Finding themselves the mothers of a stranger's children, without the ties of nature, they have merely tried to save themselves trouble. A child unswaddled would need constant watching; well swaddled it is cast into a corner and its cries are unheeded... If the nurse is at all busy, the child is hung up on a nail like a bundle of clothes and is left crucified while the nurse goes leisurely about her business. Children have been found in this position purple in the face, their tightly bandaged chest forbade the circulation of the blood, and it went to the head; so the sufferer was considered very quiet because he had not the strength to cry. How long a child might survive under such conditions I do not know, but it could not be long. This, I fancy, is one of the chief advantages of swaddling clothes.

Rousseau eschewed the idea of teaching language, geography, and history to a young child, whose underdeveloped understanding of symbols precluded meaningful comprehension of such topics. More important to Rousseau was the teaching of ideas appropriate to a child's age, and that teaching be structured so that the child feels in control of what she or he is learning. This necessarily ruled out the use of corporal punishment, which he considered ineffective if not entirely debilitating.

In *Émile*, Rousseau placed much greater emphasis than did Locke on learning about children, and on discovering and enjoying children as intrinsically good creatures without the need for strict parental control. *Émile* became an instant success, owing partly to an accelerating interest in children and education (de Monvel, 1911). It became required reading in many educational settings during the French Revolution, and upper-class mothers began to stop swaddling and sending infants off to wet-nurse, although the habit of swaddling diminished much more slowly (Robertson, 1974).

The valuation of children in the Western world was enhanced further by the American experiment, whose pioneer lifestyles and evolving political structure endowed childhood with a status and power unheard of in the Old World. Indeed, the American influence, along with the humanitarian reforms taking place in Europe, ushered in at the close of the nineteenth century what has been termed the Century of the Child (Ariĕs, 1962). When the Puritans first settled Massachusetts Bay, they brought many of their customs, religious beliefs, and childrearing practices with them. Indeed, the Calvinist philosophy that children were inherently depraved and in need of parental correction was personified by the Puritans. Furthermore, infant survival rates were no different in the New World as in the Old World. The high infant mortality rate in the early colonies, however, appeared to be the result of the rigors of colonial life rather than the neglect of wet nurses. Indeed, a major difference between the colonists and the Old World was the relative absence of wet nurses and swaddling in the New World (Illick, 1974).

However, the demise of the Puritan system was well under way by the beginning of the eighteenth century, due primarily to the large infiltration of non-Puritans into Massachusetts Bay and surrounding areas, and, it has been speculated, to the Puritans' failure to look beyond their own children to propagate the Puritan spirit (Greenleaf, 1978). Hiner (1975) wrote of the Puritans' extreme investment in their children, and the strong tendency among Puritan parents to accept full responsibility for their children's salvation. The intensity of this investment was reflected by an almost negligible rate of infanticide and abandonment in Puritan society (Walzer, 1974).

As increasing numbers of settlers came to the New World, the dynamic and highly mobile society of early America gave to childhood a new optimism and importance. Children came to represent the future, the avenues through which parents' could realize the fruits of their labors. In addition, once the colonies had freed themselves from English subjugation, the spirit of democracy further enhanced the status of childhood by making each son the eventual equal of the father in the eyes of the law (Calhoun, 1918). Bremner (1970–1971) remarked that Europeans visiting the United States were struck by the freedoms of the American child, although they were uncertain as to whether the changes were for good or ill. They saw American children as less socially awkward, more independent and individualistic, more challenging of adult authority, and more assertive and opinionated than their own children. This apparent equality between American parent and child stood in marked contrast to the hierarchical, vertical family structure of Europe.

The late nineteenth and early twentieth centuries marked a period in which there was open acknowledgment of the individual rights of children and of the link between childhood experiences and later adulthood. In both Europe and America, the state took on a major role in safeguarding the welfare of children, legislating and better enforcing harsher punishments to perpetrators of cruelty to children. Childrearing advice, provided in the form of books and articles, became more commonplace. One of the most influential sources used to obtain childrearing advice during the first half of the twentieth century was Luther Emmett Holt's *The Care and Feeding of Children* (1914). Like much of the parenting literature that preceded it, Holt's recommendations were based less on empirical data and more on his conceptions of proper parenting. Some of his advice would be viewed as sound by today's standards (e.g., he preferred breast over bottle feeding), and some not (e.g., he recommended that toilet training begin at 2 months of age). Holt's work, nevertheless, served to influence the most revered pediatrician of the twentieth century, Benjamin Spock, whose volume *The Common Sense Book of Baby and Childcare* (Spock and Rothenberg, 1992) became the leading reference source for parents in the past 50 years.

Early Theories of Parenting Competence

The twentieth century witnessed a dramatic growth in efforts to develop and empirically validate early theories of child socialization (Cairns, 1983; Kessen, 1965). The two major theoretical perspectives in psychology in the early twentieth century, behaviorism and psychoanalytic theory, had much to say about parental socialization methods. However, clear-cut contributions from these perspectives to an understanding of parenting competence were dubious at best. Psychoanalytic theory saw parents as importantly influencing children's success in negotiating psychosexual stages of development (oral, anal, phallic, latency, and genital), which in turn was believed to exert a strong (and irreversible) influence on later personality (Cohler and Paul, in Vol. 3 of this *Handbook*). Competent parents were those who brought children's sexual impulses and desires under social control, resisted children's sexual impulses directed to parents, and suppressed and constructively channeled the anger and aggression that results. They understood that their children loved them, feared the loss of this love when children's parent-directed anger and sexual impulses are rejected, and resolved this conflict by identifying with the same-sexed parent. This identification, in turn, led to the emergence of a rudimentary "conscience," or primitive value system, which enabled children to monitor and suppress undesired impulses and regulate their own behavior.

Behaviorist accounts of socialization, by contrast, used the concepts of conditioned and unconditioned stimuli, reinforcement and reinforcement schedules, punishment, and extinction to explain the manner in which parents shaped behavior in children, with a focus on actual behaviors practiced by parents. Interestingly, the mission of much of the early work in socialization research was to reconcile behavioral and psychoanalytic theories by using behavioral principles to operationally define concepts (e.g., fixations and dependency needs) and test hypotheses, drawn from psychoanalytic theory, about linkages between parenting practices and children's personality (e.g., Sears, Whiting, Nowlis, and Sears, 1953). These efforts were largely unsuccessful. Sears, Rau, and Alpert (1965), for example, found few linkages between identification and socially desired traits in children, and Sears, Maccoby, and Levin (1957) reported few relations between parent-reported parenting practices and children's personality traits. Sears et al. (1957), however, did report some important findings relating parental permissiveness and punitiveness to aggression in children that contributed significantly to later conceptualizations of parenting style. Maccoby (1992) somewhat ironically noted that, had the early efforts of behaviorists chosen topics and child outcomes straightforwardly derived from behavioral theory alone (e.g., compliance to parental directives, sharing toys, and having good manners), their endeavors might have met with greater success. Indeed, that children are amenable to behavioral contingencies set up by parents and arc capable of shaping parental behavior themselves is amply supported in later literature addressing the role of behavioral contingencies in parent–child relationship (e.g., Anderson, Lytton, and Romney, 1986; Carlson, Tamm, and Hogan, 1999; Gewirtz and Pelaez-Nogueras, 1992; Patterson, 1976). These early theories of parental competence set the stage for subsequent in depth and systematic analysis of parental competence.

PARENTING STYLE

The early psychoanalytic and behavioral learning formulations about the role of parents in socializing their children, and their emphasis on parental control and parent-created emotional climate, gave rise to more focused efforts to identify specific parental modes, or styles, of behavior that shaped children in socially desirable ways. The particular dimensions that went into parenting style varied across studies, but common to this work were efforts to link particular parenting styles to particular developmental outcomes. In their sample of 379 5-year-old children and their mothers, Sears et al. (1957), for example, explored relations between parental reports of *punitiveness* (physical discipline or severe restriction of activities) and *permissiveness* (tolerance for child transgressions) in response to children's aggression. They found wide variation in parents' responses. Some reportedly responded with little tolerance of aggression and with aggression directed toward the child in kind (low permissiveness and high punitiveness). Some tolerated it with no negative consequences (high permissiveness and low punitiveness). Some tolerated it to a certain breaking point and then followed it with severe retaliation (high permissiveness and high punitiveness). Finally, some would not tolerate it but followed it with less severe, more measured consequences (low permissiveness and low punitiveness). The highest levels of child aggression were found in the high permissiveness/high punitiveness group, the lowest levels in the low permissiveness/low punitiveness group, and intermediate levels in the low permissiveness/high punitiveness and high permissiveness/low punitiveness groups. Sears et al. speculated that high levels of parental permissiveness in the face of child aggression sent a message that aggressive behavior was acceptable, and that high levels of parental punitiveness led to high levels of child frustration and in turn to aggressive behavior. Combining high punitiveness with high permissiveness thus had an additive effect on child aggression, and this particular combination appears to reflect a high degree of parental inconsistency in dealing with child aggression, which Patterson and his colleagues have identified as an important predictor of coercive, aggressive behavior in children (Chamberlain and Patterson, 1995; Patterson, 1997; Patterson and Fisher, in Vol. 5 of this *Handbook*). By contrast, low permissive/low punitive mothers sent a clear message that aggression was unacceptable but responded to it in ways that the child did not find unduly frustrating. Sears et al.'s (1957) findings were significant in that they addressed, empirically, centuries-old "wisdoms" about the use of punitive versus permissive practices in rearing children. As will become clear, the finding that high levels of parental control (i.e., parents' intolerance of child aggression) with consequences that were not harsh would prove to be key components of effective parenting in Western cultures.

At about the same time, Baldwin (1948, 1955) conducted a longitudinal study of 67 children from birth to middle childhood and identified two parental dimensions that overlapped with and extended the work of Sears et al. From factor analysis of a variety of parent-reported rating scales, Baldwin identified a parental dimension of *control* (similar, conceptually, to the permissiveness–nonpermissiveness dimension of Sears et al.) and *democracy*, which related to the degree to which parents engaged in open communication with the child and provided a rationale for discipline policies. All four combinations of high/low democracy and high/low control were found in this study. Control, with democracy held constant, was associated with child conformity, including lower levels of disobedience and quarreling but also lower levels of curiosity, assertiveness, and originality. Democracy, with control held constant, related to fearlessness, planfulness, and curiosity, but also to aggressiveness, disobedience, and cruelty. Thus, both parental control and democracy were each associated with positive and negative child attributes, and it appeared that the best child outcomes were associated with high levels of both democracy and control, which produced children who were planful, curious, engaging, and cooperative.

By far the most sweeping and influential treatment of parenting style, however, is reflected in the work of Baumrind (1966, 1967, 1970, 1980, 1989, 1991), who made great strides toward identifying components of parental competence. Her work built on and logically extended that of Sears et al. (1957) and Baldwin (1955) by first identifying a set of attributes that she believed represented child outcomes that were highly valued by middle-income parents in the United States. These included independent, social responsibility, and achievement (among others), and comprised a construct she termed *instrumental competence*. Baumrind (1970, p. 106). wrote:

> Instrumental competence refers to behavior which is socially responsible and independent. Behavior which is friendly rather than hostile to peers, cooperative rather than resistive to adults, achievement rather than non-achievement oriented, dominant rather than submissive, and purposive rather than aimless, is here defined as instrumentally competent.

Baumrind believed that instrumental competent behavior had survival value for individuals regardless of cultural context, a point that has generated its fair share of controversy to which we return later. The overall implication, from Baumrind's framework, however, was that competent parenting was whatever combination of behaviors and attitudes that served to promote instrumental competence in children.

Baumrind's conceptualization of parenting style was configurational in nature, taking into account patterns of parenting behaviors across four parenting dimensions. Two of these dimensions, *control* and *clarity of communication*, overlapped conceptually with Baldwin's (1955) dimensions of control and democracy. The remaining two were *maturity demands*, defined as parental expectations, conveyed directly to children, so that they function at a level that is commensurate with their developmental level, and *nurturance*, reflecting the degree to which parents express warmth, concern, involvement, and pleasure in parenting. Baumrind was particularly interested in the pattern of parental behavior across these four dimensions and not in the influence of any single one, and from parental interview and observations she identified three major parenting styles that were to have a profound influence on social scientists' understanding of parenting competence, at least in the United States (Baumrind, 1967, 1968). The *authoritarian parenting style* was identified by high levels of control and maturity demands, and low levels of nurturance and clarity of communication. Authoritarian parents expect absolute obedience from their children and are likely to resort to strong punitive measures whenever children deviate from that standard. Reciprocal verbal dialogue is discouraged, under the imperative that the parent's word is final. The *permissive parenting style* is characterized by high levels of nurturance and clarity of communication, and low levels of control and maturity demands. Permissive parents allow the child great freedom in choosing activities, are openly accepting and supportive of the child's behavior, and make little effort to exert control over it or set standards of conduct. Discipline involves the use of reasoning only, and the parent actively seeks out the child for input regarding household rules and regulations. The *authoritative parenting style* is described by high levels of control, nurturance, clarity of communication, and maturity demands. Authoritative parents exert firm control over their children's behavior and set clear stands of conduct for the child. At the same time, authoritative parents openly acknowledge and incorporate the child perspective in disciplinary matters, within limits that are acceptable to the parent. Discipline involves the combined use of reason and power, but not to the point of harsh physical discipline or severe restriction of the child's autonomy, with reference to established standards of conduct.

The cumulative results of Baumrind's work are well-known (Baumrind, 1967, 1973, 1989). The highest levels of instrumental competence in children were linked to authoritative parenting. Children in authoritative homes were found, on the basis of observations, standardized tests, ratings, and Q sorts, to be more friendly with peers, more independent and assertive, cooperative with parents, and achievement oriented. By contrast, children in authoritatian homes were found to be more hostile and/or shy with peers, overly dependent on parents (especially among girls), and less invested in achievement. Interestingly, children in permissive homes exhibited several of the same characteristics (e.g., nonassertiveness, dependency, and poor self-control) as those exhibited by children in authoritarian homes, prompting Baumrind's (1973) speculation that, despite the appearance of being diametrically opposite rearing styles, authoritarian and permissive parenting hold in common the propensity to minimize opportunities for children to learn to cope with stress. Authoritarian parents do this by curtailing children's pursuits of their own initiatives. Permissive parents do this by giving their children free rein and failing to establish and enforce standards of conduct. The result is a reduction in the capacity to cope with frustration and disappointment and to deal adaptively with everyday life challenges.

Research testing Baumrind's parenting typology during the past three decades has been remarkably consistent. The benefits of authoritative parenting to children's social and academic competence from early childhood through adolescence, both in the United States and abroad, are well documented. Although the findings are correlational, a number of studies have linked authoritative parenting to Dutch school children's popularity with peers (Deković and Janssens, 1992); U.S. schoolchildren's socioemotional adjustment, as rated by parents and teachers; and academic achievement (Kaufmann et al., 2000; Shumow, Vandell, and Posner, 1998); achievement motivation in Chinese pre-adolescents (Leung and Kwan, 1998); adaptive strategies for achievement in Finnish adolescents (Aunola, Stattin, and Nurmi, 2000); and achievement among U.S. adolescents (Hickman, Bartholomae, and McHenry, 2000; Steinberg, Mounts, Lamborn, and Dornbusch, 1991).

Maccoby and Martin (1983) used parenting dimensions of demandingness (control and maturity demands) and responsiveness (warmth and involvement) to extend Baumrind's typology to include a second type of permissive parenting, *permissive-neglectful*, described by low demandingness and low responsiveness. Unlike Baumrind's original permissive parent group (which Maccoby and Martin labeled *permissive-indulgent*), who were highly involved with their children, permissive-neglectful parents were emotionally and physically disengaged from their children, showing little monitoring, supervision, and support of their children's behavior. Compared to children of authoritative, authoritarian, and permissive-indulgent parents, children of permissive-neglectful parents appeared to be at highest risk for instrumental incompetence (Maccoby and Martin, 1983), a finding that was later replicated by Baumrind herself (Baumrind, 1989, 1991) and others (Lamborn, Mounts, Steinberg, and Dornbusch, 1991; Radziszewska, Richardson, Dent, and Flay, 1996). Thus, abject abdication of parental responsibilities, as reflected in permissive-neglectful homes, appears to have even worse consequences for children than in homes in which parents lack warmth, discourage dialogue, and are harsh and restrictive, as reflected in authoritarian homes. These data suggest that, generally speaking, some kind of parental involvement with children, even if it is of poor quality, is better than none at all.

The efficacy of authoritative parenting for African American children has been more controversial, stemming from Baumrind's (1972) initial study of families with preschoolers. In this study, it was more difficult, using the same observational and interview techniques as those used with European American families, to classify African American households into the authoritarian, authoritative, and permissive categories. Among the seven African American families with boys, only one could be classified, and that classification was authoritarian; among the nine African American families with girls, five were classifiable (again, all as authoritarian). Baumrind conducted comparisons between these five African American girls whose parents were classified as authoritarian and the ten European American girls whose parents were also classified as authoritarian. The African American girls were found to be more independent and domineering, and tended to be more resistive and dominant, than were the European American girls, suggesting that an authoritarian upbringing was not as maladaptive for African American girls in comparison to European American girls.

These findings must be interpreted with caution because of the very small sample size on which they are based, and because Baumrind's measurement system was derived from a sample that was predominantly European American. On the other hand, the construct validity of the authoritative parenting style for non–European American ethnicities has been questioned by Dornbusch, Ritter, Leiderman, Roberts, and Fraleigh (1987), who found authoritative parenting (as indexed from children's reports of their parents' disciplinary behaviors) to be a significant predictor of school grades among Euro-American adolescents but not among African American, Asian, or Latino adolescents (see also Steinberg, Dornbusch, and Brown, 1992). Furthermore, Baldwin, Baldwin, and Cole (1990) found higher IQs and academic achievement among high-risk minority adolescents to be associated with authoritarian, but not authoritative parenting. Such findings prompted Steinberg et al.'s (1991) speculation that authoritarian parenting may actually serve an adaptive and protective function for children living in high-stress, dangerous neighborhoods.

This matter is further complicated, however, by findings showing theoretically expected linkages between authoritative parenting, child competence, and family functioning in African American families with adolescents. Taylor, Casten, and Flickinger (1993), for example, found authoritative parenting (identified from child reports) in single-parent, African American families to correlate positively with support from adult kin and with adolescents' self-reliance, and negatively with adolescents' problem behavior. Furthermore, kinship support's relation with adolescent self-reliance and problem behavior appeared to be mediated by authoritative parenting. In a sample of 95 African American and 55 European American adolescents, Hall and Bracken (1996) found that adolescents with authoritative parents had more successful interpersonal relationships when compared to adolescents with authoritarian or permissive parents. Hill (1995) found positive associations between mothers' authoritative parenting and family cohesion, organization, achievement orientation, intellectual and cultural orientation, and moral and religious orientation. Authoritativeness in mothers was also negatively associated with family conflict. Finally, Radziszewska et al. (1996), in a study of almost 4,000 15-year-old adolescents of European American, Latino American, African American, or Asian American ethnicity, found that adolescents who described their parents as authoritative had fewer depressive symptoms and higher grades and that these linkages were not moderated by ethnicity.

Clarification of this mixed picture might come from a more careful scrutiny and accounting of additional contextual factors than describe the particular ethnic minority sample under study, such as socioeconomic status, single versus two-parent families, quality of neighborhood, and child age. It may be the case, for example, that authoritarian parenting is adaptive for children living in high-risk neighborhoods, but not so for children in safer environments, as Steinberg et al. (1991) proposed. On the other hand, we question whether parenting that is devoid of real warmth and responsivity and that relies too heavily on physical coercion (the essence of authoritarianism) can really be beneficial to any child, regardless of ethnic, socioeconomic, or neighborhood background. This view is supported by McLoyd's (1998) formulations regarding mediating factors, such as harsh, punitive parenting, that place children in poverty at risk for intellectual, academic, and socioemotional difficulties. Just as Baumrind (1972) cautioned that the African American families in her sample were assessed with a measurement system derived from a predominantly European American sample, it behooves researchers to take pains to understand how authoritative parenting might be manifested in a context that differs from European middle–socio economic status (SES) norms. For example, otherwise loving parents of children in high-risk environments may go to great lengths to restrict their children's outdoor activities in an effort to protect them from harm and may even physically punish their children who break parental rules. Questionnaire, interview, and observational measures developed from European American samples may not always be sensitive to the subtle mix of warmth and control in these contexts, leading to misperceptions of parental behavior. This concern may be especially relevant when it is not reasonable to incorporate child perceptions of parental behavior into one's assessment of parenting style, as, for example, when children are too young.

On balance, the research conducted on parenting style provides a comprehensive model of parental competence as reflected by the differential associations of parenting styles with instrumental competence in children. The parenting style model continues to be used extensive in contemporary research on parenting and its effects, and has operated as the springboard for a great deal of additional attempts to further define the essence of competent parenting.

PARENTING, INTERNALIZATION, AND THE DEVELOPMENT OF CONSCIENCE

A separate and sometimes overlapping line of research complementing the extensive work on parenting style has focused on specific parental disciplinary techniques that facilitate children's ability to internalize the parent's message underlying the discipline. That is, competent parents are those that successfully enable children to attend to the socialization process and incorporate their parents' messages as their own. Grusec and Goodnow (1994, p. 4) defined internalization as the "taking over the values and attitudes of society as one's own so that socially acceptable behavior is motivated not by anticipation of external consequences but by intrinsic or internal factors." Arguably, having children develop internalized societal standards of conduct and an appropriate understanding of right and wrong (i.e., developing a conscience) is the ultimate goal of socialization (Kochanska, 1993), and it is competent parents who achieve this goal.

Psychoanalytic accounts of internalization viewed it as arising from children's identification with the same-sexed parent in the Oedipal phase of psychosexual development (Freud, 1922/1975; Cohler and Paul, in Vol. 3 of this *Handbook*). Sears et al. (1957), however, were among the first to identify specific disciplinary practices predictive of children's internalization of values. In particular, they proposed that parents who used a combination of warmth, praise, and love withdrawal were more likely to foster internalization than were parents who used physical rewards and punishment, which included withdrawal of privileges. Among children of nurturing mothers who employed love withdrawal in response to child misdeeds, internalization of the parental message, they argued, was motivated by the child's desire to keep the mother's affection. By contrast, children of mothers who disciplined by applying or withdrawing physical rewards and punishments would be motivated to behave prosocially either for the external rewards they would receive for doing so or for the punishment that would ensue for not doing so.

Sears et al.'s work paved the way for further theorizing and empirical work on the efficacy, both singly and in combination, of three major parental disciplinary techniques: power assertion, love withdrawal, and reasoning and explanation. Power assertion refers to the threat of or actual use of force, physical punishment, or withdrawal of privileges. Love withdrawal involves ignoring the child or expressing disappointment or disapproval. Reasoning/explanation involves calling attention to the nature of the misdeed and how it infringes on the rights and feelings of others, a process that is termed *induction* or *other-oriented induction* (Damon, 1983; Grusec and Goodnow, 1994). Hoffman (1970, 1975, 1983, 1994; Hoffman and Saltzstein, 1967) has concluded that, among the three, induction has the greatest likelihood of fostering internalization. Hoffman and Saltzstein (1967), for example, examined relations between parental use of power assertion, love withdrawal, and induction and seventh graders' propensities to experience guilt, accept responsibility for wrongdoing, and make reparations to the aggrieved party. Data on internalization were obtained from the children themselves, using hypothetical vignettes (e.g., a story in which the main character contributed to another child's death through negligence); from teachers who were asked how a given child responded when caught in the act of doing something wrong; and from mothers, who were asked to rate their children in response to a question about how their child would behave if they did something wrong but the mother did not know about it yet. Sociometric ratings were also obtained on each child in response to two questions, one asking which child in the class was likely to care about the feelings of other children, and one asking which child in the class would be likely to defend a child that the class was making fun of. Children and parents separately contributed data on parental disciplinary practices, again using hypothetical situations describing a child committing a transgression (e.g., noncompliance to a parental request).

This study unequivocally supported induction as the best means of promoting internalization in children, although Hoffman and Saltzstein hastened to point out the inability to draw causal inferences from their correlational study. Among many findings in this report, parental use of induction was positively associated with children's reports of guilt in response to a transgression, their tendency to confess to wrongdoing even before the parent discovered it (from mothers' reports), their likelihood of accepting responsibility for the transgression (mothers' reports), and to be considerate of other children (from sociometric ratings). Maternal warmth, assessed from both parent and child reports, related positively to a variety of internalization indices. By contrast, power assertive disciplinary techniques almost uniformly related negatively to indices of internalization, and love withdrawal related inconsistently, and only to a few. Hoffman and Saltzstein proposed that the efficacy of inductive techniques was due to their tendency to arouse empathy, which they defined as the vicarious experience of discomfort from the knowledge that the child's act hurt someone else, either emotionally or physically, and to communicate to the child that she or he was the cause of that hurt. That knowledge, coincidental with the vicarious experience of discomfort, serves as a strong motivator to keep one's impulses under control (Hoffman, 1983, 1986, 1988).

Hoffman formalized his information processing theory of internalization (Hoffman 1983, 1994), emphasizing the point that internalization, or the lack thereof, can be understood through examination of children's cognitions and affect experiences in repeated discipline encounters across time. Power assertive and love withdrawal, though by themselves inadequate in promoting internalization, nevertheless can serve an important function if used appropriately with induction, that of elevating the child's arousal level to the point necessary to attend to the parental message. An arousal level that is too high, resulting from an overuse of power assertion, will likely direct the child's attention away from whatever message the parent may be trying to convey and toward the negative consequences that are in store for the child. Too little arousal, on the other hand, could lead the child to pay insufficient attention to the message. An appropriate level of arousal and empathy, generated by a judicious use of power assertion and/or love withdrawal, coupled with induction, is most likely to promote the child's successful processing of the parental message. Internalized standards of conduct is the hypothesized outcome of repeated discipline encounters of this type, with children's moral behavior becoming increasingly self-motivated over time.

The prerequisite that children's arousal level must be high enough to motivate their attention to parental messages is consistent with other theoretical work. Lepper (1973; Lepper and Greene, 1975, 1978; Lepper, Greene, and Nisbett, 1973), an attributions theorist, distinguished between a child's immediate compliance to a parental directive, which could occur simply because of the promise of an externally administered reward or threat of punishment, and internalization, or the incorporation of parentally set standards as one's own. Lepper (1973; Lepper et al., 1973) studied the reactions of children in the "forbidden toy" paradigm (disallowing children to play with a desired toy and systematically varying the severity of punishment (mild versus severe) if they did play with it, and of children given Magic Markers to play with followed by a salient reward or no reward for playing with them. Children in the mild threat condition showed less interest in the forbidden toy than did children in the severe threat condition, and children given no reward for playing with the markers showed much greater subsequent interest in the markers than did the children who had been rewarded for playing with them. Like Hoffman (1983), Lepper proposed that long-term behavioral change in children is best facilitated by just enough reward or coercion to change the child's behavior, but not so much that the child attends more to the incentive or threat than to the standards inherent in the parent's message. This model, which Lepper termed the *minimum sufficiency principle*, was useful in accounting for distinctions among Baumrind's authoritarian, permissive–indulgent, and authoritative parenting styles. Lepper proposed that disciplinary encounters in authoritarian homes are typified by an excessive use of power assertive and love withdrawal tactics to coerce compliance in children, leading not only to poor internalization but also to maladjustment in other relational domains. For example, harsh, coercive parenting has been linked to childhood aggression toward peers (Baumrind, 1973; Parke, Burks, Carson, Neville, and Boyum, 1994; Pettit, Clawson, Dodge, and Bates, 1996), including relational aggression (i.e., acting to subvert or sabotage another child's friendships or threatening to stop being another child's friend; Hart, Nelson, Robinson, Olson, and McNeilly-Choque, 1998). Disciplinary encounters in permissive homes, by contrast, do not provide sufficient incentives to children to attend to whatever standards the parent is trying to convey. Neither the authoritarian nor the permissive parenting style is adequate for promoting permanent behavioral change. By contrast, Lepper proposed that the minimum sufficiency principle is best applied in authoritative homes, wherein parents consistently provide just enough coercion to motivate children to attend to and process their messages, which in turn facilitates internalization and self-initiated, socially responsible behavior.

Grusec and Goodnow (1994) expanded on the work of Hoffman, Lepper, and others in proposing a working model of internalization that incorporated a variety of new, primarily cognitive, factors. This model appears to carry the potential to generate research questions about the nature of competent parenting. For example, the model takes into account Turiel's (1983) work on the nature of children's social knowledge and the fact that transgressions can be moral or social in nature. Moral transgressions involve the infliction of physical and/or emotional harm on others. Social convention violations involve acting or failing to act in a manner that conforms with social rules (e.g., showing poor table manners). Children view moral transgressions as being of higher gravity than violations of social convention, and not surprisingly believe that parents are more entitled to punish children in response to transgressions in the moral over the social domain (Tisak, 1986). The model also considers the child's developmental status and perspective-taking skills; whether the parental message focuses on the impact of the transgression on self versus other (focusing on other is hypothesized to be more effective); the relevance and specificity of the parental message (e.g., "Nice kids don't do that" should be less effective than appeals that address the specific transgression, such as, " Teasing your sister hurts her feelings and makes her sad"); the frequency and consistency of specific messages; the kind and severity of power assertion used (physical punishment versus reduction of privileges, anger displays, shaming, etc.), which may have different effects on a child's sense of autonomy and sense of security; whether reasoning and power assertion or love withdrawal should be used in a particular sequence; the child's particular temperament and mood; and specific parental attributes, such as warmth.

Grusec and Goodnow's (1994) model viewed successful internalization as a joint function of the success with which parents can package their messages so that the child can accurately perceive and accept them. Accuracy in perceiving parental messages is hypothetically influenced by such factors as their clarity, consistency, redundancy, and "fit" (i.e., their relevance and understandability) with child schemas, the ability of the child to take the parent's perspective, and whether the child perceives the parent as well meaning. Acceptance of the parent's message is hypothetically influenced by the extent to which the child views the message as appropriate (i.e., is well fitted to the kind of transgression and the child' developmental status, temperament, and mood); the message's tendency to motivate the child to attend and process it (involving empathy arousal and insecurity about the parent's love); and to facilitate, over the long haul, the child's inclination to view the message as her or his own. This "self-generational" capacity is expected to be promoted when the message is not overly punitive or restrictive and presses the child to think about the impact of the transgression on others.

Thus, whereas parenting style addresses global characteristics and the overarching tone of parenting, research on parenting and children's internalization elucidates more clearly some specific parental disciplinary behaviors (i.e., power assertion, love withdrawal, and induction, and the balance among them) that appear to be centrally relevant to the success with which children internalize parental messages and value systems. Following Grusec and Goodnow (1994), further explication of parent, child, and contextual processes that affect the quality of internalization should prove fruitful in understanding the manner in which specific parenting styles are manifested to children in day-to-day parent–child interactions.

EARLY PARENTING, ATTACHMENT SECURITY, AND "MUTUAL INTERPERSONAL ORIENTATION"

The work on parenting styles, and the process models of parenting put forth by Hoffman, Lepper, and Grusec and Goodnow, pertain most straightforwardly to parenting of children in the preschool years and older. Indeed, such constructs as clarity of communication, maturity demands, power assertion, and induction hold more meaning when parenting an organism in whom the socially constructed emotions of shame, embarrassment, guilt (i.e., the beginnings of a "moral" self), and rudimentary perspective taking and emotion understanding have already emerged (Dunn, Slomkowski, Donelan, and Herrera, 1995; Eisenberg and Valiente, in Vol. 5 of this *Handbook*; Emde, Biringen, Clyman, and Oppenheim, 1991). Of course, parenting competence is a construct that is applicable to infancy as well and may be critically important in shaping the degree to which a child orients to and accepts a parent's subsequent disciplinary messages as valid and worthy of the child's attention. In this section, we discuss attachment theory's contribution to parenting competence and, from this perspective, the role of early parenting in influencing the child's commitment to the parent as a socializing agent.

Bowlby (1969) viewed infants' propensity to attach to a caregiver as an outcome of natural selection, functioning to promote infant survival and that of the species as a whole. In addition, however, Bowlby acknowledged that the quality of infant–caregiver attachment related to the quality of the caregiving environment. It was Ainsworth, however, who transformed our understanding of infant–parent relationships by identifying three categories or classifications of attachment by the end of the first year of life that related in theoretically consistent ways to the quality of care provided to infants in the first year. She did this by using her well-known Strange Situation, a 22- to 24-minute laboratory procedure composed of eight 3-minute (or less) episodes involving infant separations from and reunions with the attachment figure and an adult (typically female). Separations from mother are designed to induce distress and activate the attachment behavioral system in the infant, and the infant's behavior toward the caregiver during reunions is used to arrive at an attachment classification. Ainsworth's conceptualization of attachment security was linked to the integrity of the infant's "secure base" behavior, or the infant's proclivity to use the attachment figure as a secure base to explore the environment (Ainsworth, 1973, 1982; Ainsworth and Bell, 1970; Ainsworth, Bell, and Stayton, 1971, 1974). Secure infants, during infant–mother reunions, seek the proximity of the caregiver, soothe quickly on pickup, and are then able to ease back into exploration with periodic checks on the caregiver's whereabouts. These infants appear able to derive sufficient security from their relationships with their caregivers and display an appropriate balance of attachment and exploratory behavior. Insecure-avoidant infants, by contrast, appear to snub or ignore the caregiver during reunions, showing an inappropriate balance of exploratory and attachment behavior that involves exploring in the caregiver's presence in an almost compulsory fashion that is devoid of any real interest in the caregiver. Ainsworth's third attachment classification was insecure-resistant (or insecure-ambivalent), characterized by infant petulance, anger, and clinginess directed toward the caregiver, and an inability to be consoled. The attachment-exploration balance in these infants is demonstrated by their overdependency on the caregiver and an inability to move back into exploration. Subsequent to Ainsworth's tripartite classification system, Main and Solomon (1986, 1990) identified a fourth attachment category, insecure-disorganized/disoriented, characterized during infant–mother reunions by expressions of fear and/or apparent confusion about how to gain access to the caregiver.

From the vantage point of attachment theory, parenting competence can be defined in terms of that which leads to the development of a secure infant–caregiver attachment, which Ainsworth viewed as most conducive to promoting an infant's physical survival and psychological well-being (Ainsworth et al., 1978; Cummings and Cummings, in Vol. 5; Demick, in Vol. 3 of this *Handbook*). Ainsworth's empirical work revealed that the single most important feature of mothering in the prediction of secure infant–mother attachment was maternal sensitivity to infant cues and signals. That is, mothers who accurately perceived and responded contingently and appropriately to basic infant needs and bids for interaction and withdrawal during feeding, play, and distress were more likely to foster secure infant–mother attachments than were mothers who were ignoring or rejecting of infant bids or who responded inconsistently (Ainsworth et al., 1978).

The central role of parental sensitivity in the development of secure attachments in infancy is well documented (Bates, Maslin, and Frankel, 1985; Crockenberg, 1981; Egeland and Farber, 1984; Erickson, Sroufe, and Egeland, 1985; Smith and Pederson, 1988; Teti, Gelfand, Messinger, and Isabella, 1995; Vondra, Shaw, and Kevenides, 1995). Insensitive parenting, by contrast, is linked to insecure attachment, although specific manifestations of insensitivity appeared to predict specific manifestations of insecurity. Controlling, overstimulating, intrusive parenting, for example, has been associated with insecure-avoidant attachments in infancy (Belsky, Rovine, and Taylor, 1984; Main and Weston, 1982), whereas unresponsive, inconsistently responsive parenting has been linked to insecure-ambivalent attachments (Cassidy and Berlin, 1994; Vondra et al., 1995). The relevance of parenting sensitivity to early attachment security has also been documented in non-U.S. samples (Grossmann, Grossmann, Spangler, Suess, and Unzner, 1985; Posada et al., 1999; Valenzuela, 1997). Parental antecedents of insecure-disorganized attachments are somewhat controversial (Lyons-Ruth and Jacobvitz, 1999), although elevated rates of these attachments have been associated with highly pathological caregiving environments, including those in which mothers were clinically depressed (De Mulder and Radke-Yarrow, 1991; Teti et al., 1995), who abused their infants (Carlson, Cicchetti, Barnett, and Braunwald, 1989; Lyons-Ruth, Connell, Grunebaum, and Botein, 1990), and who drank heavily (O'Connor, Sigman, and Brill, 1987). A largely separate literature has tied disorganized attachments to unresolved loss or trauma in the parent, which in turn may predispose the parent to behave in a frightened or frightening manner (e.g., using unusual vocal patterns, sudden looming, or "hunt-pursuit" games); (Schuengel, Bakermans-Kranenberg, van IJzendoorn, and Blom, 1999). Such parental behavior, it has been argued, creates fear and uncertainty about how to access the parent in times of stress (Lyons-Ruth and Jacobvitz, 1999; Main and Hesse, 1990; Schuengel et al., 1999).

Achieving a secure attachment in infancy is believed to bear importantly on the likelihood of success in later social relationships and in negotiating and resolving subsequent developmental tasks

(Sroufe, 1979; Thompson, 1999). A large literature documents relations between early security and later success in peer and sibling relationships (e.g., Elicker, Englund, and Sroufe, 1992; Kerns, 1994; LaFreniere and Sroufe, 1985; Teti and Ablard, 1989) and relationships with teachers (e.g., Sroufe, Fox, and Pancake, 1983) and unfamiliar adults (e.g., Easterbrooks and Lamb, 1979). Early security has also been predictive of indicators of emotional well-being, such as self-confidence, ego-resiliency, and play competence (Elicker et al., 1992; Londerville and Main, 1981; Sroufe, 1983). A full review of this literature is beyond the scope of this chapter. We do wish to focus, however, on a particular line of research that testifies to the importance of parental sensitivity and secure attachment in infancy for understanding how parenting competence may evolve over time. We refer specifically to the role that maternal sensitivity and secure infant–mother attachment plays in fostering the child's positive orientation toward and acceptance of the attachment figure as an agent of socialization. Going back to Ainsworth's seminal early work, when mothers of infants early in the first year of life were rated highly on sensitivity, acceptance, and cooperation with their infants, their infants cried and clung to their mothers less often and complied more often to mothers' requests and directives by the end of the first year than did infants whose mothers were rated poorly on these indices (Ainsworth et al., 1974; Stayton, Hogan, and Ainsworth, 1973). Thus, warm, sensitive, cooperative mothering during the first few months of life was rewarded by high levels of infant cooperation with and acceptance of the mother's bids by the end of the first year. Londerville and Main (1981) reported similarly high levels of compliance and cooperation in 21-month-old toddlers found at 12 months of age to be securely attached to their mothers, in comparison to toddlers who were insecurely attached. Furthermore, secure toddlers in this study were more cooperative with sensitive, unfamiliar adults than were insecure toddlers, suggesting that secure attachment to mothers not only fosters a positive orientation toward mothers but also toward other nurturant adults.

Kochanska (1997b; Kochanska and Thompson, 1997; Kochanska and Aksan, 1995) built on this early work in her study of parental and child contributions to the development of conscience in young children. As her work and that of others indicate, children give evidence of an emergent conscience by their emotional responses (e.g., distress, anxiety, and discomfort) to acts of wrong-doing by the second year of life (Dunn, 1988; Eisenberg, 1992; Kochanska, De Vet, Goldman, Murray, and Putnam, 1994). At this age, children become increasingly self-aware, begin to evaluate the impact of their behavior on others (Lamb, 1993; Thompson, 1998), and begin to notice and respond to violations of standards (e.g., finding trash on the floor, objects in the wrong place, or objects that are broken or have pieces missing, and transgressions by siblings; Dunn, 1988; Kagan, 1981; Kochanska, Casey, and Fukomoto, 1995). Kochanska (1997b) argued that young children's willingness to accept and incorporate standards of personal conduct depended importantly on the achievement of a secure attachment in infancy, which lays the foundation for a parent–child relationship characterized by cooperation and mutual reciprocity. This view accords with Maccoby's (1984; Maccoby and Martin, 1983) proposal that successful socialization is not a unidirectional, parent-to-child process. Rather, it is reflected by the development of a mutual interpersonal orientation, in which both the parent and the child are invested in and committed to the relationship, take into account the needs and welfare of the other before acting, and expect their own needs to be taken into account by the other. Whether or not a mutual interpersonal orientation describes a given parent–child dyad depends on the relationship history as well as the quality of current, ongoing parent–child exchanges.

That parental responsivity, warmth, and affective tone during interactions with children relate a to children's investment in the relationship with the parent was demonstrated by Kochanska and Aksan (1995) in a study of 26- to 41-month-old infants observed with their mothers in three separate control contexts. Children and mothers were observed in two "Do" tasks (one toy cleanup session at home and one in the laboratory), in which mothers were instructed to get their children to put the toys away after a period of free play, and one "Don't" task, in which mothers were asked to prohibit their children from touching some very attractive toys on a shelf in the laboratory for a period of 2 hours. Kochanska and Aksan distinguished between two qualitatively distinct forms of compliance and three forms of noncompliance. *Committed compliance* was coded when the child willfully committed to the task at hand and to the mother's agenda, with little if any prompting from the mother. *Situational compliance* was coded when the child's cooperation was dependent on maternal prompting. *Passive noncompliance* was identified when the child ignored maternal bids to comply but without overt resistance to the mother. *Refusal/negotiation* was coded when the child openly refused maternal directives but without strong oppositional behavior. Finally, *defiance* was used to describe overt noncompliance accompanied by strong opposition (e.g., temper tantrums and kicking toys) in response to maternal bids. Maternal and child affect, ranging from highly positive to highly negative, and levels of maternal control, ranging from none to gentle guidance (polite requests and suggestions) to coercive intervention, were also assessed during "Do" and "Don't" tasks. Additional observations were made to determine children's internalized conduct, involving evaluations of whether children would comply with task rules (e.g., not touching the forbidden toy) without the mother being present in the room. Finally, mothers rated the quality of their children's internalization in the home using a 20-item scale tapping maternal perceptions of their children's tendencies to adhere to family rules when alone, carrying out chores without being told, and so forth.

This study provided compelling evidence that the quality of children's compliance and degree of internalized conduct is linked significantly and, in many cases, strongly to mutually positive mother–child affect. Committed compliance and children's internalized conduct during the forbidden toy session correlated positively with mother–child mutually positive affect. Furthermore, mothers' use of negative (coercive) control correlated negatively with committed compliance, and positively with children's passive noncompliance, overt resistance, and defiance. Shared positive affect during behavioral observations was also found to relate to mothers' ratings of their children's internalization in the home. These data are purely correlational and obtained at the same point in time, and thus it is not clear if the shared positive affect between mother and child was causally related to children's quality of compliance and internalization or was in reaction to child behavior. In an earlier study, however, Parpal and Maccoby (1985) demonstrated experimentally that 3- to 4-year-old children of mothers who were trained to be responsive to their children's cues were more cooperative with their mothers during a cleanup task, which took place one week after training, than were same-aged children of mothers who did not receive training.

Kochanska (1997b) later extended this work with a longitudinal study examining relations between mother–child mutual interpersonal orientation, defined by high levels of parent–child positive affect and cooperation during behavioral observations and the quality of children's internalization at 2 to 3 and 3 to 4 years of age. Mutual interpersonal orientation related both concurrently and over time to better internalization and less maternal power assertion. Furthermore, mothers who scored highly on a measure of empathic perspective taking, considered to be an implicit component of parental sensitivity (Ainsworth et al., 1978; Pederson et al., 1990), were more likely to enter into a reciprocally positive relationship with their children than were mothers with low scores on this measure.

Attachment theory and research, along with the contributions of Maccoby, Kochanska, and others, thus stress the importance of parental sensitivity and warmth in infancy and early childhood for shaping parent–child relationships in which both partners are invested in and committed to the relationship and to each other. Indeed, achieving such a relationship appears to be one of the most important goals of early socialization, not only because it fosters an early internalization of parental values, but because it smooths the way for later socialization successes. Children who are committed to the parent should, over the long run, be easier to discipline, provided that the parent maintains her or his own high level of emotional commitment to the relationship. Darling and Steinberg (1993) addressed this point in a theoretical paper in which they conceptualized parenting style as a cluster of emotional attitudes that serve as a context within which specific parenting practices are exercised. In their model, parenting style is communicated to the child via the parent's quality of attention paid to the child, tone of voice, emotional displays, and other behaviors that convey how the parent feels about the child (e.g., love and acceptance versus indifference and/or hostility). Parenting style, they argued, is a characteristic of the parent that served to moderate the effectiveness of specific parenting practices. This moderational influence of parenting style can occur via its influence on the quality of parental behavior or its influence on the child's orientation and openness to the parent's message. For example, specific parental attempts at controlling child behavior should be more successful when they take place in a context of warmth toward and acceptance of the child than in a context of parental rejection or detachment. This view is consistent with the formulations of Maccoby (Maccoby and Martin, 1983) and Kochanska (1997b; Kochanska and Aksan, 1995; Kochanska and Thompson, 1997). Furthermore, it would appear that the influence of parenting style, when conceptualized, as Darling and Steinberg (1993) have done, as a cluster of emotional attitudes that parents convey to the child is likely felt by the child as early as infancy, as evidenced by the relation of maternal sensitivity and warmth to greater infant compliance and cooperation with maternal bids as early as 12 months of age (Ainsworth et al., 1974; Londerville and Main, 1981). That warm, caring (but not overprotective) parenting is a central feature of competent parenting throughout the lifespan is demonstrated in studies that link it to social competence in early peer relationships (Harrist, Pettit, Dodge, and Bates, 1994; Kahen, Katz, and Gottman, 1994), emotional well-being in young adults (McFarlane, Bellissimo, and Norman, 1995; Parker et al., 1999; Taris and Bok, 1996), and low levels of adolescent drug use (Clausen, 1996).

Hence, precursors of parenting style may be evident as early as the child's first year of life, although we hasten to point out that a warm, tender, sensitive parent of an infant may not necessarily remain a competent parent later in the child's life, when the child's behavioral repertoire expands and parenting becomes more challenging. Child characteristics, such as evolving temperament, the parent's own developmental history with her or his own parents, and the parent's social ecology, all may conspire to affect, positively or negatively, the quality of parenting as the child develops (see chapters by Belsky and Barends, in Vol. 3; Grych, in Vol. 4; and Cochran and Niego, in Vol. 4 of this *Handbook*). We address one important component of this equation in the following section.

THE CHILD AS CONTEXT

Despite open acknowledgment of bidirectional parent–child influences in socialization, it is only in the past decade that systematic attempts have been made to understand parenting competence in relation to variations in children's temperamental traits. Indeed, it appears that the effectiveness of specific disciplinary practices may vary depending on a child's temperamental makeup.

Conceptualizations of temperament in infancy vary, but temperament theorists generally agree that temperamental predispositions, such as activity level, proneness-to-distress, reactivity thresholds, and affective biases are constitutionally based and are somewhat stable across time and context (Goldsmith et al., 1987; Putnam, Sanson, and Rothbart, in Vol. 1 of this *Handbook*). Rothbart and Bates (1998, p. 106) defined temperament as "constitutionally-based differences in emotional, motor, attentional reactivity and self-regulation." The predictive validity of temperament assessment obtained in the first few years of life and later development is, in the main, not strong, although longitudinal linkages have been reported between early temperamental difficulty and externalizing behavior in childhood and adulthood (Bates and Bayles, 1988; Caspi, Henry, McGee, Moffitt, and Silva, 1995) and between early proneness-to-distress and shyness and internalizing symptoms in later childhood (Caspi and Silva, 1995; Kagan, Snidman, Zentner, and Peterson, 1999). Of greater interest to developmentalists has been the manner in which temperamental variations "pull" for variations in parental behavior, and in which variations in parenting might moderate longitudinal associations between early temperament and later development. Indeed, Thomas, Chess, and Birch (1970) found that parents of difficult infants, described by high amounts of negative affect, activity, reactivity, and distractibility, and poor adaptability, for the most part coped poorly in parenting their infants. Later work has demonstrated that infant temperamental traits such as high irritability and proneness-to-distress are associated with parental withdrawal, anger, and coercive discipline (Bates, Pettit, and Dodge, 1995; Lee and Bates, 1985; van den Boom, 1991).

These findings indicate that children can contribute in their own way to their own socialization and that parenting competence is in part a function of the parent's ability to understand what strategies might work, and not work, for a given child. For example, although parents may be inclined to respond to an irritable, difficult-to-soothe child with hostility and power-assertive tactics, research bears out that such reactions place the child at even greater risk for later maladjustment. Bates et al.'s (1995) work, for example, found that harsh parental reactions at 4 years of age to children found in infancy to be temperamentally difficult contributed to children's externalizing behavior in adolescence beyond the contribution of early temperamental difficulty. Paterson and Sanson (1999) similarly found difficult temperament and punitive parenting to contribute jointly to externalizing behavior problems in 5- to 6-year-old children, and Belsky, Hsieh, and Crnic (1998) found mothering characterized by negative affect and intrusiveness to predict externalizing behavior only in 3-year-old children previously judged at 1 year of age to be temperamentally difficult. Clearly, favorable child outcomes are not fostered by harsh parental reactions to temperamentally challenging children (see Campbell, 1995, for a comprehensive review).

At the same time, it is important to note that temperamental difficulty in infancy need not lead to parenting failures and child maladjustment. For example, Bates, Pettit, Dodge, and Ridge (1998) found that maternal restrictive control in the first 2 years of life (i.e., prohibitions, scolding, and restricting child behavior that was potentially harmful to the child), in the general absence of physical discipline, moderated relations between early resistance to control in the second year of life and externalizing behavior at 7 to 10 years of age. Specifically, longitudinal links between resistance to control in toddlerhood and later externalizing behavior were stronger in the absence than in the presence of maternal restrictive control. This study indicated that consistent, firm parental control, without physical coercion, was an adaptive parental response to children's temperamental difficulty. Firm, consistent parental control may have facilitated, over the long term, the child's ability to self-regulate and develop internalized standards of conduct. These findings are reminiscent of Thomas and Chess's (1977) premise that child developmental outcomes are best understood in terms of the goodness-of-fit between specific child characteristics and characteristics of the caregiving environment (Lerner, Rothbaum, Boulos, and Castellino, in Vol. 2 of this *Handbook*). They also support, broadly speaking, Wachs's (in press; Wachs and Gandour, 1983) organismic-specificity hypothesis, which posits that the effects of any particular environment on child development will depend on the particular constellation of dispositions the child brings to that setting. Both of these views explicitly acknowledge the child as a central contextual element that can influence the course of socialization and moderate the effects of specific parenting practices.

Kochanska (1993, 1994, 1995, 1998; Kochanska, Coy, Tjebkes, and Husarek, 1998; Kochanska et al., 1994; Kochanska, Murray, and Coy, 1997; Kochanska, Murray, Jacques, Koenig, and Vandegeest, 1996; Kochanska and Thompson, 1997) has studied the manner in which individual differences in child temperament influence the effectiveness of parenting and, in turn, the development of conscience. Kochanska's model incorporates two distinct components of conscience. The first is an affective discomfort component, referring to the anxiety, guilt, or remorse resulting from a transgression. The second is a behavioral control component, pertaining to the exercise of self-control and self-restraint in the face of a desired but forbidden object or activity. Each of these components is rooted in conceptualizations of temperament (Rothbart and Bates, 1998), and individual differences in each should influence the effectiveness of specific socialization techniques and subsequent internalization. Individual differences in fear/wariness in response to novel or ambiguous events, especially social events, can be observed as early as 4 months of age (Kagan et al., 1999). By contrast, individual differences in behavioral control emerges later, sometime between 12 and 18 months of age, as evidenced by toddlers' emergent ability to comply with simple requests, and its exercise is also dependent on the development of attention, language, and memory systems (Kochanska, 1993).

Kochanska (1993) proposed that temperamental variations in young children's susceptibility to anxiety arousal will relate directly to the degree of emotional discomfort experienced in response to a transgression, and children's predisposition to attend to parental input. Thus, what is considered competent parenting may vary depending on the temperamental makeup of the child. Anxiety-prone children should be more sensitive to the emotional content of parental messages regarding standards of proper conduct than should emotionally imperturbable children. High amounts of negative arousal stemming from a violation of an established rule or standard, coupled with greater sensitivity to parents' emotional reactions to the transgression, should facilitate internalization, and thus the model predicts that internalization should occur more readily in anxiety-prone children than in emotionally unreactive children. Indeed, gentle disciplinary techniques, such as induction and mild love withdrawal, should be sufficient to foster internalization among anxiety-prone children, whereas the use of high power, coercive discipline with such children would be expected to produce excessive anxiety and distorted feelings of guilt. Although emotionally unreactive children are expected to respond less well to gentle socialization pressures, Kochanska (1993) warns against the use of highly coercive discipline with emotionally unreactive children, which is expected to have uniformly detrimental effects on child development regardless of the temperamental makeup of the child. Instead, successful socialization for emotionally unreactive children may depend on the parent's ability to establish a mutually positive interpersonal orientation (discussed earlier) with the child, in which the child's emotional commitment to the parent and the relationship will be sufficient for successful internalization to take place.

With regard to behavioral control, the second component of conscience, Kochanska (1993) proposed that internalization should be more easily achieved among children with high levels of behavior control relative to children with poor behavior control, again implying that the extent to which a parent is competent is in part a function of the child's temperament. Indeed, children with poor impulse control may present special challenges to parents, who may find their children's lack of self-regulation very difficult to cope with. Such children do not respond well to gentle forms of socialization, in contrast to children with high behavioral control (Kochanska, 1993), and as a result appear to elicit harsher, more coercive parenting (Lindahl, 1998). Harsh, power-oriented parenting of children with poor behavioral control may explain the co-occurrence of attention deficit hyperactivity disorder (ADHD), a disorder defined by attentional and impulse control difficulties, and externalizing disorders such as oppositional-defiant disorder and conduct disorder (August, Realmuto, Joyce, and Hektner, 1999). However, temperamentally impulsive children may respond favorably to parental messages that are simply packaged and help the child structure his behavior and his thoughts about how it affects others (Kochanska, 1993), and as always this parenting approach should be most effective in the context of a reciprocally positive parent–child relationship.

Kochanska's model of conscience development thus emphasizes that what is considered competent parenting may depend on a given child's temperamental makeup. Support for the model is accumulating. Kochanska et al. (1997) found that inhibitory control in children appeared as a stable characteristic from toddlerhood to school age, and also found that children higher in inhibitory or effortful control evinced higher levels of committed compliance to mothers' requests and stronger internalization of conduct standards than did children lower in inhibitory control. Kochanska, Murray, and Harlan (2000) further reported that effortful control at 22 months of age predicted better regulation of anger and joy and greater ability to show restraint when tempted by attractive, "forbidden" toys at 33 months. Finally, Kochanska (1995) demonstrated that fearfulness and/or anxiety in preschool-age children was positively associated with committed compliance and indices of internalization, and anxiety-prone preschoolers responded well to maternal discipline that was "gentle" (i.e., low levels of power assertion coupled with reasoning). By contrast, gentle maternal discipline did not predict quality of compliance and internalization in fearless children, but secure attachment (i.e., an index of mutually positive parent–child orientation) did. Taken together, these findings support Kochanska's model of conscience development and stress the need to incorporate variations in children's temperaments in theories of effective socialization.

Thus, the child her- or himself presents a context through which parental competence reveals itself. Moreover, this supports the notion that the competent parent is not only one who is sensitive, responsive and successfully socializes their children with the correct balance of induction, love withdrawal and power assertion, but also is aware of who their child is and adapts their specific behavior accordingly to create a match, or mutual orientation, that ensures successful socialization.

INTERVENTIONS PROMOTING PARENTING COMPETENCE

Researchers and practitioners alike have devised a myriad of interesting interventions targeting specific populations such as conduct disordered children, infants at biological risk (e.g., preterm infants), children diagnosed with ADHD, children at risk for abuse or neglect, and other at-risk groups (Barclay and Houts, 1995; Smith, Perou, and Lesesne, in Vol. 4 of this *Handbook*). These programs have differed in form and substance, but have in common the premise that improving parental competence will lead to positive outcomes for both parents and children. Although parenting interventions have existed for over a century and in more structured forms since the early 1960s (Briesmeister and Schaefer, 1998), their evolution has not been straightforward. Programs vary in intensity, have different theoretical foundations, and target many different family types and have a wide array of expected outcomes (Cowan, Powell, and Cowan, 1998). Local churches, county officials, community professionals such as social workers and teachers, and academic professionals such as psychologists have initiated programs, each with differing intents and expectations. Furthermore, not all programs have included empirical evaluations of their effectiveness. In their review, Cowan et al. (1998) differentiated among three types of intervention approaches: child focused, aimed at helping the parent change the child's behavior; parent-focused, directly targeting parental behavior; and parent–child focused, in which the reciprocity of the parent–child relationship and the specific interactions between parent and child are the focus. More recently, interventions have become more dynamic, addressing not only the parent and child, but also directing efforts at other important relationships, such as spousal or sibling, as well as contextual supports or stressors.

Models of parenting intervention can be based on a single, overarching theory or can draw from several theoretical perspectives. Forehand's behavioral approach (Forehand and McMahan, 1981) is perhaps a good example of one that draws primarily from a single theoretical perspective, that of social learning theory. This approach, which has also been studied extensive by Patterson and his colleagues at the Oregon Social Learning Center (Patterson, Reid, and Dishion, 1992), relies on teaching the parent to reinforce positive behaviors and proper methods for disciplining noncompliance with communication and time-outs. Other programs incorporate multiple theoretical perspectives (e.g., Olds, 1997) that are assumed to work in tandem to improve parental competence and sometimes address issues that go beyond the parent and child, such as parental developmental history, social supports, and economic stress. Such an approach explicitly acknowledges the ecological or systems perspective on parenting and child development (Bronfenbrenner, 1979). Although space does not allow for an exhaustive review (see Barclay and Houts, 1995; Briesmeister and Schaefer, 1998; and Cowan et al., 1998, for comprehensive reviews), several programs are discussed below that have differing theoretical bases, target children at different points in development, and whose efficacy has been rigorously evaluated.

A well-known program targeting parental competence in infancy is the Prenatal/Early Infancy Project, designed by Olds (1997). This program focused on changing women's health related behaviors during pregnancy, shaping their parenting behavior and improving their self-sufficiency. Using a randomized clinical trial design, the program relied on a nurse-home-visiting model. Nurses visited single mothers approximately every other week, beginning prenatally and until 2 years after birth. Families were followed until the child was 15 years of age. The program was grounded in a combination of ecological (Bronfenbrenner, 1979), self-efficacy (Bandura, 1986), and attachment theory (Ainsworth et al., 1978). A major premise of the project was that a person's behavior is a result of who they are, their environment, and the processes within that environment. Home visitors focused on enhancing parents' social skills with the intention of enabling parents to seek out proper supports in their environment. They also attempted to work with friends and family members to affect the parents' contextual influences as well as identify environmental stressors. Olds and his colleagues also believed that providing opportunities for small, tangible changes in behavior would allow the mothers to feel more efficacious as parents. Nurses worked on problem solving strategies with the mothers and helped them to identify when they were successful with their children or when making other life decisions (e.g., seeking out support, making community contacts, and changing health behaviors). The object was to empower the mothers to see they could change their practices. Whereas this notion played a part in the original study, it was intensified in later studies as the researchers learned more about the parents and their needs (Olds, 1997).

In terms of shaping parenting style and behavior, the program relied on the tenets of attachment theory. That is, infants are born with a repertoire of behaviors that promote interaction with the mother (Bowlby, 1969), and that a mother's internal working model for the mother–infant relationship is largely determined by the mother's processing of her own early childhood experiences (Main, Kaplan, and Cassidy, 1985). Hence, the home visitors focused on developing trusting relationships with the mothers where they could explore their histories and guide mothers to be consistently responsive, sensitive, and engaging with their infants. This helping relationship provided a safe caregiving environment for the mothers where they could explore issues and learn from the nurses the importance of being warm, consistent, and responsive caregivers.

Results have shown improved pregnancy outcomes, increases in the quality of mother–infant interaction and greater economic self-sufficiency long-term. A strength of this program is that it has been replicated with randomized trials targeting more diverse populations. Whereas the original study included primarily poor European Americans in the Appalachian region of New York, a second study focused on an African American population in Memphis (Olds et al., 1998). The Memphis study functioned as an "effectiveness" study; that is, the researchers were intentionally less involved in program implementation, and the program operated within an existing health care system with attendant problems therein (e.g., a high level of staff turnover). Despite these limitations, the Memphis study results also indicated reduced rates of dysfunctional care for treatment mothers and fewer subsequent pregnancies. Hence, an impact on parental competence was obtained with a long-term home-visit model.

Another exemplary parent training program with a multitheoretical foundation is the Fast Track program (Conduct Problems Prevention Research Group [CPPRG], 1992, 1999). Fast Track was designed as a preventive intervention program with a mixed model of service delivery including parent training groups and home visits with family coordinators, tutoring and social skills training for school-age children, and universal school based interventions. A randomized design was employed, and the program was constructed to address culturally and geographically diverse populations with implementation taking place in four settings across the country (CPPRG, 1992, 1999). Intervention began when children identified as at risk for developing conduct problems were in kindergarten (from parent and teacher reports of externalizing behavior) and continued follow up into early high school. Components included weekly enrichment sessions with children and follow-up home visits every other week (CPPRG, 1999). During the first hour of the enrichment sessions, while children attended social-skills training groups, parents met with family coordinators (FCs) and coleaders to discuss methods of promoting their child's adjustment to school, increasing their own self control, implementing appropriate discipline strategies, improving the quality of parent–child interactions, and lessening disruptive behavior from children. Training methods included discussions, direct instruction, modeling, and role playing, and were based on the social learning models developed by Forehand and McMahon (1981) and Webster-Stratton (1989). After the parent session, children were brought in to engage with parents in semistructured activities that promoted interactions (e.g., arts and crafts and games). This allowed parents to practice techniques with staff present for support, with staff available to give suggestions and feedback about implementation of specific practices as well as the context of practices. FCs then visited families in the home to monitor the generalization of practices, offer opportunities to practice strategies discussed in group in a realistic setting, and work with families individually about their specific needs and stressors (CPPRG, 1999).

Results of the first year of intervention indicated improvements in both parental and child outcomes (CPPRG, 1999). Specifically, intervention parents evinced heightened levels of appropriate and consistent discipline, and a reduction in harsh discipline strategies. In addition, analyses revealed increased levels of parental warmth, as well as involvement with their child's school. Parents also reported positive modifications of their own behavior and conveyed feeling more effective and satisfied as parents. Hence, Fast Track yielded changes in both parental style and practices. Child outcomes included enhanced social and emotional coping skills, improved peer relationships, and progress in reading and language arts.

Irvine, Biglan, Smolkowski, Metzler, and Ary (1999) conducted an efficacy study of the Adolescent Transition Program (ATP) designed by Dishion, Andrews, Kavanagh, and Soberman (1996). The foundation of ATP rested on social learning theory, and in particular Patterson's coercion theory and his team's work at the Oregon Social Learning Center. On the premise that coercive interactions between children and parents, lack of parental monitoring, and inconsistent discipline predict substance abuse and antisocial behavior, the ATP was a behavioral approach to training parents in specific skills to modify their parenting practices (Dishion, Patterson, and Reid, 1988; Patterson, 1995, 1996). Specifically, it focused on promoting appropriate and consistent discipline methods as well as positive interactions, particularly reinforcement of positive behavior. In addition, ATP focused on communication and problem-solving techniques. Parents met for weekly sessions to discuss discipline, interaction, reinforcement, communication, and problem-solving strategies with a group leader and other parents. The group was designed to be supportive, with parents giving suggestions and feedback to each other. Parents were encouraged to go home and practice techniques and then report back to the group. Group leaders also made midweek calls to monitor families and offer support or advice, and conducted home visits as needed.

Irvine et al. (1999) examined the ATP program with middle school and junior high school children and their parents, using a randomized control trial in eight Oregon communities. A highlight of this study is that the effectiveness of ATP was demonstrated when the program was not conducted by researchers. Group leaders in this study included those with high school diplomas as well as those with advanced degrees. The goal was to have leaders reflect the likely composition of the average community center. However, the researchers admitted that their presence still permeated the program and it was not an effectiveness study in the purest sense. Results of the intervention found that treatment parents demonstrated decreased levels of parental coercive behavior. Parents also improved monitoring behaviors, positive reinforcement, limit setting, and problem-solving skills. Together, results indicated improvements in both parental affect and parental behaviors. This study demonstrates that parenting competence can be enhanced with a group training model.

Parenting interventions are still evolving, and those discussed here provide only a small sampling of parental interventions that have enjoyed success. Other notable programs include those targeting parents of children with ADHD (Anastopoulos, 1998), parents of failure to thrive children (Lachenmeyer, 1998), various programs aimed at parents of infants (e.g., Belsky, 1985; Nurcombe et al., 1984), those directed at helping parents understand direct children's behaviors (e.g., Systematic Training for Effective Parenting; Dinkmeyer and McKay, 1976), and many others (Barclay and Houts, 1995; Briesmeister and Schaefer, 1998; Cowan et al., 1998). It is encouraging that, in many of these programs, there is a dual emphasis on stylistic elements of parenting as well as specific parenting practices. Consistent with Darling and Steinberg's (1993) conceptualizations, it is common for parenting intervention programs to endorse the importance of parental warmth, sensitivity, and involvement, and to endorse specific parenting practices that should be done in the context of positive emotional climate. The success of the above projects, and others, indicates that parental quality is indeed amenable to intervention, and when interventions are theoretically sound and correctly matched with a child's developmental stage and the needs of the parent, they can be quite powerful.

CONCLUSIONS

Parenting competence is defined by its effects, and although it has been examined from a variety of perspectives, all of them converge with regard to at least three major points. The first is that warmth, acceptance, and sensitivity to children's basic needs, social cues, and to what is appropriately expected for a given child's developmental level appear to be universal components of competent parenting irrespective of the developmental stage of the child. Indeed, we would argue that the establishment of a mutually reciprocal, positive parent–child relationship as early as infancy is perhaps the first and foremost goal of early socialization because of its impact on the quality of the child's orientation to the parent and the subsequent ease with which that child can be socialized. The second is that harsh, negative, coercive parenting is universally regarded as being detrimental to children, although the degree of its debilitative impact will vary depending on the age and temperamental disposition of the child. The third is that parental involvement is probably better than no involvement at all, although involvement, by itself, is not a good index of parenting competence.

A similar point can be made about parental control, again which, by itself, does not denote competent parenting but in the context of high parental warmth and sensitivity has been found to produce more competent and well-adjusted children than does control in the absence of warmth. As the earlier work on disciplinary practices and internalization indicate, some degree of parental control in the form of either love withdrawal or power assertion may be necessary for some children to pay attention to the parent's message, but parents must take care to avoid excessive control that threatens the child's autonomy and elevates the child's arousal levels to the point where the child pays greater attention to the parent's emotion underlying the message rather than to the message itself. How much control was not addressed in this early work, and the field has taken an important step forward in explicitly incorporating information about children's temperaments in conceptualizations of competent parenting and addressing more specifically how different temperamental dispositions, either in terms of emotional reactivity or behavioral control, might facilitate our understanding of how much control might be too much for a given child. This research is only just getting under way and, in our view, holds great promise for understanding children's unique contributions to the process and success of socialization.

Despite the impressive knowledge base that now exists regarding competent parenting, there are many unresolved questions that await further research. For example, very little work has been done examining the transition from parenting in infancy, in which issues of parental control and maturity demands are not yet salient in conceptualizations of parenting competence, to parenting in the preschool years and beyond, when such issues loom larger. How likely is it, for example, that parents deemed sensitive and responsive to their children in infancy will develop an authoritative parenting style with their preschool-age children? We would argue that competent parenting in infancy, denoted by a high level of parental sensitivity, will be as likely to predict to authoritative as to permissive-indulgent parenting in the preschool years, and what might be predictive of one parental trajectory over another is unclear. Although child factors such as temperament may play some role in this, we believe it might be more fruitful to attempt to explore whether and how parents manifest some tendencies, even during infancy, to exert some level of control over the infants' physical and temporal environments and routines throughout the course of a typical day. "Authoritative" parenting in infancy might be identified by parents who are sensitive to their infants and who structure their infants' environments (with some flexibility) in such a way as to bring some structure and order to the entire family (e.g., by establishing routines for bedtime and meals, daily walks with the infant, and so forth). "Permissive" parenting in infancy, by contrast, may be manifested by sensitivity in infancy without such attempts at structure. Along similar lines, how parental insensitivity in infancy might predict to later parenting styles is, again, unclear. Parental insensitivity marked by intrusiveness and rigidity might be more likely to predict to authoritarian parenting in the preschool years, whereas insensitivity described by lack of responsiveness might be predictive of permissive-neglectful parenting. The nature of specific cross-time linkages will also likely depend on the stability of contextual features of the caregiving environment, as research on the stability of attachment has shown, as well as on the ability of the parent to be resilient in the face of change.

Another line of research awaiting further development is the extent to which the same parent disciplines similarly versus differently with different children in the same family. Much of the work on parental treatment of siblings makes use of parental and/or child reports of parent behavior in broad dimensions such as warmth, responsivity, and control, with the bulk of this work showing that differential parental treatment of siblings leads to sibling conflict and, for the disfavored sibling, maladjustment in terms of elevated rates internalizing and externalizing behaviors (see Teti, in press, for a review). This research, however, sheds little light on the reasons that underlie differential parental treatment (e.g., individual differences in children's emotional reactivity or behavioral control), nor does it make use of established observational probes (e.g., mothers' behavior in "Do" and "Don't" tasks, Kochanska, 1997a; Kochanska and Aksan, 1995) to determine more specifically how the parent (typically the mother) might use different disciplinary techniques with different children in the same family to bring about compliance. Such research would enable researchers to determine to what degree, for example, particular parenting styles and modes of discipline are characteristics of the parent versus products of temperamental differences in children. It also would enable researchers to examine differential parental discipline in relation to individual differences in children's internalization. In some families, for example, it may be the case that a parent can be "good enough" for one child but not so for another, based on differences between the two children in emotional reactivity and/or behavioral control.

Additional work is also needed in embedding parenting styles within a given socioeconomic and cultural context. Authoritative parenting, for example, may have a different face in a lower SES context, especially when parents have justifiable concerns about neighborhood quality and safety. Parents are bound to exert higher levels of control over their children's behavior and autonomy and may have little tolerance for disobedient behavior that threatens the child's safety. Such parents may look more "authoritarian" on a questionnaire measure that does not take into account such contextual features of the parent–child environment. In research involving parenting style, there is a clear need for measures that are sensitive to context and, ideally, developed specifically with that context in mind.

Along similar lines, research examining the efficacy of parental intervention programs would benefit from a stronger consideration of context. Although logic dictates that not every program will match every family, we need to demonstrate empirically that programs can have a core structure that is effective with varying cultural contexts and that details of programming simply need sensitive adaptations at the local level. Olds et al.'s (1998) program is such an example. Furthermore, given that each child her- or himself can be considered a contextual feature of the parenting environment, and in light of the exciting contributions within the past decade regarding the role of child temperament in moderating the effects of parenting practices (e.g., Kochanska, 1997a, 1997b; Kochanska et al., 2000), the field awaits the development of new parenting interventions tailored to individual differences in children's fearfulness/anxiety and behavioral control. Finally, it is important to note that parenting interventions typically target a specific age range of children, and this represents an important limitation. Whether the program is directed at children in poverty, children with behavior difficulties, or children with specific disorders, the focus is usually on strategies a parent can use within a developmental stage. What this does not provide a parent is what to expect in the future (e.g., how children's behavior changes from 2 to 5 years of age, and in turn how parents might best adapt to these developments in terms of parent–child communication and limit-setting behavior). Likely, the age ranges of programs are chosen relative to qualitative differences in developmental stages. However, parents also need help transitioning between stages and preparing for those transitions. Parenting practices can become outmoded, and research into the efficacy of interventions that incorporate an anticipatory guidance approach (e.g., Hussey-Gardner, 1999), educating parents what to expect of their children over the short and long term and how parents might best meet the challenges these new developments create, would be a welcome addition to the parenting competence literature.

REFERENCES

Ainsworth, M. (1973). The development of infant–mother attachment. In B. Caldwell and H. Riccuiti (Eds.), *Review of child development research* (Vol. 3). Chicago: University of Chicago Press.

Ainsworth, M. D. S. (1982). Attachment: Retrospect and prospect. In C. M. Parkes and J. Stevenson-Hinde (Eds.), *The place of attachment in human behavior* (pp. 3–30). New York: Basic Books.

Ainsworth, M. D. S., and Bell, S. M. (1970). Attachment, exploration, and separation: Illustrated by the behavior of one-year-olds in a strange situation. *Child Development, 41,* 49–67.

Ainsworth, M. D. S., Bell, S. M., and Stayton, D. J. (1971). Individual differences in Strange-Situation behavior of one-year-olds. In H. R. Schaffer (Ed.), *The origins of human social relations* (pp. 17–52). New York: Academic Press.

Ainsworth, M. D. S., Bell, S. M., and Stayton, D. J. (1974). Infant–mother attachment and social development: Socialization as a product of reciprocal responsiveness to signals. In M. Richards (Ed.), *The integration of the child into the social world* (pp. 99–135). Cambridge, England: Cambridge University Press.

Ainsworth, M. D. S., Blehar, M. C., Waters, E., and Wall, S. (1978). *Patterns of attachment: A psychological study of the strange situation.* Hillsdale, NJ: Lawrence Erlbaum Associates.

Anastopoulos, A. D. (1998). A training program for parents of children with attention-deficit/hyperactivity disorder. In J. M. Briesmeister and C. E. Schaefer (Eds.), *Handbook of parent training: Parents as co-theapists for children's behavior problems* (pp. 27–60). New York: Wiley.

Anderson, K. E., Lytton, H., and Romney, D. M. (1986). Mothers' interactions with normal and conduct-disordered boys: Who affects whom? *Developmental Psychology, 22,* 604–609.

Ariès, P. (1962). *Centuries of childhood: A social history of family life* (R. Baldick, Trans.). New York: Knopf.

August, G. J., Realmuto, G. M., Joyce, T., and Hektner, J. M. (1999). Persistence and desistance of oppositional defiant disorder in a community sample of children with ADHD. *Journal of the American Academy of Child and Adolescent Psychiatry, 38,* 1262–1270.

Aunola, K., Stattin, H., and Nurmi, J.-E. (2000). Parenting styles and adolescents' achievement strategies. *Journal of Adolescence, 23,* 205–222.

Baldwin, A. L. (1948). Socialization and the parent–child relationship. *Child Development, 19,* 127–136.

Baldwin, A. L. (1955). *Behavior and development in childhood.* New York: Dryden.

Baldwin, A. L., Baldwin, C., and Cole, R. E. (1990). Stress-resistant families and stress-resistant children. In J. Rolf, A. S. Masten, D. Cicchetti, K. H. Nuechterlein, and S. Weintraub (Eds.), *Risk and protective factors in the development of psychopathology* (pp. 257–280). New York: Cambridge University Press.

Bandura, A. (1986). *Social foundation of thought and action: A social-cognitive theory.* Englewood Cliffs, NJ: Prentice-Hall.

Barclay, D. R., and Houts, A. C. (1995). Parenting skills: A review and developmental analysis of training content. In W. O'Donohue and L. Krasner (Eds.), *Handbook of psychological skills training: Clinical techniques and applications* (pp. 195–228). Boston: Allyn & Bacon.

Bates, J. E., and Bayles, K. (1988). The role of attachment in the development of behavior problems. In J. Belsky and T. Nezworski (Eds.), *Clinical implications of attachment* (pp. 253–299). Hillsdale, NJ: Lawrence Erlbaum Associates.

Bates, J. E., Maslin, C. A., and Frankel, K. A. (1985). Attachment security, mother–child interaction, and temperament as predictors of behavior problem ratings at age three years. In I. Bretherton and E. Waters (Eds.), *Growing points of attachment theory and research. Monographs of the Society for Research in Child Development, 50* (Serial No. 209), 167–193.

Bates, J. E., Pettit, G. S., and Dodge, K. A. (1995). Family and child factors in stability and change in children's aggressiveness in elementary school. In J. McCord (Ed.), *Coercion and punishment in long-term perspectives* (pp. 124–138). New York: Cambridge University Press.

Bates, J. E., Pettit, G. S., Dodge, K. A., and Ridge, B. (1998). Interaction of temperamental resistance to control and restrictive parenting in the development of externalizing behavior. *Developmental Psychology, 34,* 982–995.

Baumrind, D. (1966). Effects of authoritative control on child behavior. *Child Development, 37,* 887–907.

Baumrind, D. (1967). Childcare practices anteceding three patterns of preschool behavior. *Genetic Psychology Monographs, 75,* 43–88.

Baumrind, D. (1968). Authoritarian v. authoritative parental control. *Adolescence, 3,* 255–272.

Baumrind, D. (1970). Socialization and instrumental competence in young children. *Young Children, 26,* 104–119.

Baumrind, D. (1972). An exploratory study of socialization effects on black children: Some black–white comparisons. *Child Development, 43,* 261–267.

Baumrind, D. (1973). The development of instrumental competence through socialization. *Minnesota symposium on child psychology, Vol. 7* (pp. 3–46). Minneapolis: University of Minnesota Press.

Baumrind, D. (1980). New directions in socialization research. *American Psychologist, 35,* 639–652.

Baumrind, D. (1989). Rearing competent children. In W. Damon (Ed.), *Child development today and tomorrow* (pp. 349–378). San Francisco: Jossey-Bass.

Baumrind, D. (1991). Parenting styles and adolescent development. In J. Brooks-Gunn, R. Lerner, and A. C. Petersen (Eds.), *The encyclopedia of adolescence* (pp. 746–758). New York: Garland.

Belsky, J. (1985). Experimenting with the family in the newborn period. *Child Development*, *56*, 407–414.

Belsky, J. (1999). Interactional and contextual determinants of attachment security. In J. Cassidy and P. R. Shaver (Eds.), *Handbook of attachment: Theory, research, and clinical applications* (pp. 249–264). New York: Guilford.

Belsky, J., Hsieh, K.-H., and Crnic, K. (1998). Mothering, fathering, and infant negativity as antecedents of boys' externalizing problems and inhibition at age 3 years: Differential susceptibility to rearing experience? *Development and Psychopathology*, *10*, 301–319.

Belsky, J., Rovine, M., and Taylor, D. G. (1984). The Pennsylvania Infant and Family Development Project: III. The origins of individual differences in infant–mother attachment: Maternal and infant contributions. *Child Development*, *55*, 718–728.

Bornstein, M. H., and Tamis-LeMonda, C. S. (1977). Maternal responsiveness and infant mental abilities: Specific predictive relations. *Infant Behavior and Development*, *20*, 283–296.

Bornstein, M. H., and Tamis-LeMonda, C. S. (1989). Maternal responsiveness and cognitive development in children. In M. H. Bornstein (Ed.), *Maternal responsiveness: Characteristics and consequences* (pp. 803–809). San Francisco: Jossey-Bass.

Bowlby, J. (1969). *Attachment and loss: Vol. 1. Attachment*. New York: Basic Books.

Bradley, R. H. (1999). The home environment. In S. L. Friedman and T. D. Wachs (Eds.), *Measuring environment across the life span: Emerging methods and concepts* (pp. 31–58). Washington, DC: American Psychological Association.

Briesmeister, J. M., and Schaefer, C. E. (Eds.). (1998). *Handbook of parent training: Parents as co-theapists for children's behavior problems*. New York: Wiley.

Bremner, L. (Ed.). (1970–1971). *Children and youth in America* (Vols. 1 and 2). Cambridge: Harvard University Press.

Bronfrenbrenner, U. (1979). *The ecology of human development: Experiments by nature and design*. Cambridge, MA: Harvard University Press.

Cairns, R. B. (1983). The emergence of developmental psychology. In P. Mussen (Ed.), *Handbook of child psychology: Vol. 1. History and methods* (pp. 41–102). New York: Wiley.

Calhoun, A. W. (1917–1919). *A social history of the American family* (Vols. 1, 2, and 3). New York: Barnes & Noble.

Campbell, S. (1995). Behavior problems in preschool children: A review of recent research. *Journal of Child Psychology and Psychiatry*, *36*, 113–149.

Carew, J. (1980). Experience and the development of intelligence in young children at home and in daycare. *Monographs of the Society for Research in Child Development*, *45*(6–7).

Carlson, C. L., Tamm, L., and Hogan, A. E. (1999). The child with oppositional defiant disorder and conduct disorder in the family. In H. C. Quay and A. E. Hogan (Eds.), *Handbook of disruptive behavior disorders* (pp. 337–352). New York: Kluwer Academic/Plenum.

Carlson, V., Cicchetti, D., Barnett, D., and Braunwald, K. (1989). Disorganized/disoriented attachment relationships in maltreated infants. *Developmental Psychology*, *25*, 525–531.

Caspi, A., Henry, B., McGee, R. O., Moffitt, T. E., and Silva, P. A. (1995). Temperamental origins of child and adolescent behavior problems: From age three to age fifteen. *Child Development*, *66*, 55–68.

Caspi, A., and Silva, P. A. (1995). Temperamental qualities at age three predict personality traits in young adulthood: Longitudinal evidence from a birth cohort. *Child Development*, *66*, 486–498.

Cassidy, J., and Berlin, L. J. (1994). The insecure/ambivalent pattern of attachment: Theory and research. *Child Development*, *54*, 971–991.

Chamberlain, P., and Patterson, G. (1995). Discipline and child compliance in parenting. In M. Bornstein (Ed.), *Handbook of parenting: Vol. 4. Applied and practical parenting* (pp. 205–225). Mahwah, NJ: Lawrence Erlbaum Associates.

Clarke-Stewart, K. A. (1973). Interactions between mothers and their young children: Characteristics and consequences. *Monographs of the Society for Research in Child Develoment*, *38* (6–7, Serial No. 153).

Clausen, S.-E. (1996). Parenting styles and adolescent drug use behaviours. *Childhood: A Global Journal of Child Research*, *3*, 403–414.

Conduct Problems Prevention Research Group. (1992). A developmental and clinical model for the prevention of conduct disorder: The Fast Track program. *Development and Psychopathology*, *4*, 509–527.

Conduct Problems Prevention Research Group. (1999). Initial impact of the Fast Track prevention trial for conduct problems: I. The high-risk sample. *Journal of consulting and clinical psychology*, *67*, 631–647.

Cowan, P. A., Powell, D., and Cowan, C. P. (1998). Parenting interventions: A famiy systems perspective. In W. Damon, I. Sigel, and K. A. Renninger (Eds.), *Handbook of child psychology: Child psychology in practice* (Vol. 4, pp. 3–72). New York: Wiley.

Crockenberg, S. B. (1981). Infant irritability, mother responsiveness, and social support influences on the security of infant–mother attachment. *Child Development*, *52*, 857–865.

Damon, W. (1983). *Social and personality development: Infancy through adolescence*. New York: Norton.

Darling, N., and Steinberg, L. (1993). Parenting style as context: An integrative model. *Psychological Bulletin*, *113*, 487–496.

Deković, M., and Janssens, M. A. M. (1992). Parents' child-rearing style and child's sociometric status. *Developmental Psychology*, *28*, 925–932.

De Monvel, A. B. (1911). Introduction. In J. J. Rousseau's *Émile* (B. Foxley, Trans.). London: Dent. (Original work published 1762.)

De Mulder, E. K., and Radke-Yarrow, J. (1991). Attachment with affectively ill and well mothers: Concurrent behavioral correlates. *Development and Psychopathology, 3,* 227–242.

Dinkmeyer, D., and McKay, G. (1976). *Systematic training for effective parenting (STEP): Parent's handbook.* Circle Pines, NM: American Guidance Service.

Dishion, T. J., Andrews, D. W., Kavanagh, K., and Soberman, L. H. (1996). Preventive interventions for high-risk youth: The Adolescent Transitions Program. In R. D. Peters and R. J. McMahon (Eds.), *Preventing childhood disorders, substance abuse, and delinquency* (pp. 184–214). Thousand Oaks, CA: Sage.

Dishion, T., Patterson, G., and Reid, J. (1988). Parent and peer factors associated with early adolescent drug use: Implications for treatement. In E. Rahdert and J. Grabowski (Eds.), *Adolescent drug abuse: Analyses of treatment research* (NIDA Research Monograph No. 77, pp. 69–93). Washington, DC: U.S. Government Printing Office.

Dornbusch, S. M., Ritter, P. L., Leiderman, P. H., Roberts, D. F., and Fraleigh, M. J. (1987). The relation of parenting style of adolescent school performance. *Child Development, 58,* 1244–1257.

Dunn, J. (1988). *The beginnings of social understanding.* Cambridge, MA: Harvard University Press.

Dunn, J., Slomkowski, C., Donelan, N., and Herrera, C. (1995). Conflict, understanding, and relationships: Developments and differences in the preschool years. *Early Education and Development, 6,* 303–316.

Easterbrooks, M. A., and Lamb, M. E. (1979). The relationship between quality of infant–mother attachment and infant competence in initial encounters with peers. *Child Development, 50,* 380–387.

Egeland, B., and Farber, E. A. (1984). infant–mother attachment: Factors related to its development and changes over time. *Child Development, 55,* 753–771.

Eisenberg, N. (1992). *The caring child.* Cambridge, MA: Harvard University Press.

Elicker, J., Englund, M., and Sroufe, L. A. (1992). Predicting peer competence and peer relationships in childhood from early parent–child relationships. In R. D. Parke and G. W. Ladd (Eds.), *Family–peer relationships: Modes of linkage* (pp. 77–106). Hillsdale, NJ: Lawrence Erlbaum Associates.

Emde, R. N., Biringen, Z., Clyman, R. B., and Oppenheim, D. (1991). The moral self of infancy: Affective core and procedural knowledge. *Developmental Review, 11,* 251–270.

Erickson, M. F., Sroufe, L. A., and Egeland, B. (1985). The relationships between quality of attachment and behavior problems in preschool in a high-risk sample. In I. Bretherton and E. Waters (Eds.), *Growing points of attachment theory and research. Monographs of the Society for Research in Child Development, 50* (Serial No. 209), 147–166.

Forehand, R., and McMahon, R. J. (1981). *Helping the noncompliant child: A clinican's guide to parent training.* New York: Guilford.

Freud, S. (1975). *Group psychology and the analysis of the ego* (J. Strachey, Trans. and Ed.). New York: Norton. (Original work published 1922.)

Gabriel, A. L. (1962). *The educational ideas of Vincent of Beauvais.* Notre Dame, IN: South Bend: University of Notre Dame Press.

George, M. D. (1964). *London life in the eighteenth century.* New York: Harper & Row.

Gewirtz, J. L., and Pelaez-Nogueras, M. (1992). B. F. Skinner's legacy to human infant behavior and development. *American Psychologist, 47,* 1411–1422.

Goldsmith, H. Hill, Buss, A. H., Plomin, R., Rothbart, M. K., Thomas, A., Chess, S., Hinde, R. A., and McCall, R. B. (1987). Roundtable: What is temperament? Four approaches. *Child Development, 58,* 505–529.

Goodich, M. (1975). Bartholomaeus Anglicus on child-rearing. *History of Childhood Quarterly: The Journal of Psychohistory, 3,* 75–84.

Greenleaf, B. F. (1978). *Children through the ages.* New York: McGraw-Hill.

Grossmann, K., Grossman, K. E., Spangler, G., Suess, G., and Unzner, L. (1985). Maternal sensitivity and newborns' orientation responses as related to quality of attachment in northern Germany. In I. Bretherton and E. Waters (Eds.), *Growing points of attachment theory and research. Monographs of the Society for Research in Child Development, 50* (Serial No. 209), 233–256.

Grusec, J. E., and Goodnow, J. J. (1994). Impact of parental discipline methods on the child's internalization of values: A reconceptualization of current points of view. *Developmental Psychology, 30,* 4–19.

Hall, W. N., and Bracken, B. A. (1996). Relationship between maternal parenting styles and African American and white adolescents interpersonal relationships. *School Psychology International, 17,* 253–267.

Harrist, A. W., Pettit, G. S., Dodge, K. A., and Bates, J. E. (1994). Dyadic synchrony in mother–child interaction: Relations with children's subsequent kindergarten adjustment. *Family Relations, 43,* 417–424.

Hart, C. H., Nelson, D. A., Robinson, C. C., Olsen, S. F., and McNeilly-Choque, M. K. (1998). Overt and relational aggression in Russian nursery-school-age children: Parenting style and marital linkages. *Developmental Psychology, 34,* 687–697.

Hickman, G. P., Bartholomae, S., and McHenry, P. C. (2000). Influence of parenting style on the adjustment and academic achievement of traditional college freshman. *Journal of College Student Development, 41,* 41–54.

Hill, N. E. (1995). The relationship between family environment and parenting style: A preliminary study of African American families. *Journal of Black Psychology, 21,* 408–423.

Hiner, R. (1975). Adolescence in eighteenth-century America. *History of Childhood Quarterly: The Journal of Psychohistory*, *3*, 253–280.

Hoffman, M. L. (1970). Conscience, personality, and socialization techniques. *Human Development*, *13*, 90–126.

Hoffman, M. L. (1975). Moral internalization, parental power, and the nature of parent–child interaction. *Developmental Psychology*, *11*, 228–239.

Hoffman, M. L. (1983). Affective and cognitive processes in moral internalization. In E. T. Higgins, D. Ruble, and W. Hartup (Eds.), *Social cognition and social development: A sociocultural perspective* (pp. 236–274). New York: Cambridge University Press.

Hoffman, M. L. (1986). Affect, motivation, and cognition. In R. M. Sorrentino and E. T. Higgins (Eds.), *Handbook of motivation and cognition: Foundations of social behavior* (pp. 244–280). New York: Guilford.

Hoffman, M. L. (1988). Moral development. In M. H. Bornstein and M. Lamb (Eds.), *Developmental psychology: An advanced textbook* (pp. 497–548). Hillsdale, NJ: Lawrence Erlbaum Associates.

Hoffman, M. L. (1994). Discipline and internalization. *Developmental Psychology*, *30*, 26–28.

Hoffman, M. L., and Saltzstein, H. D. (1967). Parental discipline and the child's moral development. *Journal of Personality and Social Psychology*, *5*, 45–47.

Holt, L. (1914). *The care and feeding of children*. New York: Appleton.

Hussey-Gardner, G. (1999). *Best Beginnings: Helping parents make a difference*. Palo Alto, CA: VORT Corporation.

Illick, J. E. (1974). Child-rearing in seventeenth century England and America. In L. de Mause (Ed.), *The history of childhood* (pp. 303–350). New York: Psychohistory Press.

Irvine, A. B., Biglan, A., Smolkowski, K., Metzler, C. W., and Ary, D. V. (1999). The effectiveness of a parenting skills program for parents of middle school students in small communities. *Journal of consulting and clinical psychology*, *67*, 811–825.

Isabella, R. A., and Belsky, J. (1991). Interactional synchrony and the origins of infant–mother attachment: A replication study. *Child Development*, *62*, 373–384.

Kagan, J. (1981). *The second year: The emergence of self-awareness*. Cambridge, MA: Harvard University Press.

Kagan, J., Snidman, N., Zentner, M., and Peterson, E. (1999). Infant temperament and anxious symptoms in school age children. *Development and Psychopathology*, *11*, 209–224.

Kahen, V., Katz, L. F., and Gottman, J. M. (1994). The world of parents and peers: Coercive exchanges and children's social adaptation. *Social Development*, *3*, 238–254.

Kaufmann, D., Gesten, E., Santa Lucia, R. C., Salcedo, O., Rendina-Gobioff, G., Gadd, R. (2000). The relationship between parenting style and children's adjustment: The parents' perspective. *Journal of Child and Family Studies*, *9*, 231–245.

Kerns, K. A. (1994). A longitudinal examination of links between mother–child attachment and children's friendships in early childhood. *Journal of Social and Personal Relationships*, *11*, 379–381.

Kessen, W. (1965). *The child*. New York: Wiley.

Kochanska, G. (1993). Toward a synthesis of parental socialization and child temperament in early development of conscience. *Child Development*, *64*, 325–347.

Kochanska, G. (1994). Beyond cognition: Expanding the search for the early roots of internalization and conscience. *Developmental Psychology*, *30*, 20–22.

Kochanska, G. (1995). Children's temperament, mothers' discipline, and security of attachment: Multiple pathways to emerging internalization. *Child Development*, *66*, 597–615.

Kochanska, G. (1997a). Multiple pathways to conscience for children with different temperaments: From toddlerhood to age 5. *Developmental Psychology*, *33*, 228–240.

Kochanska, G. (1997b). Mutually responsive orientation between mothers and their young children: Implications for early socialization. *Child Development*, *68*, 94–112.

Kochanska, G. (1998). Mother–child relationship, child fearfulness, and emerging attachment: A short-term longitudinal study. *Developmental Psychology*, *34*, 480–490.

Kochanska, G., and Aksan, N. (1995). Mother–child mutually positive affect, the quality of child compliance to requests and prohibitions, and maternal control as correlates of early internalization. *Child Development*, *66*, 236–254.

Kochanska, G., Casey, R. J., and Fukumoto, A. (1995). Toddlers' sensitivity to standard violations. *Child Development*, *66*, 643–656.

Kochanska, G., Coy, K. C., Tjebkes, T., and Husarek, S. J. (1998). Individual differences in emotionality in infancy. *Child Development*, *64*, 375–390.

Kochanska, G., De Vet, K., Goldman, M., Murray, K., and Putnam, S. P. (1994). Maternal reports of conscience development and temperament in young children. *Child Development*, *65*, 852–868.

Kochanska, G., Murray, K., and Coy, K. C. (1997). Inhibitory control as a contributor to conscience in childhood: From toddler to early school age. *Child Development*, *68*, 263–277.

Kochanska, G., Murray, K. T., and Harlan, E. T. (2000). Effortful control in early childhood: Continuity and change, antecedents, and implications for social development. *Developmental Psychology*, *36*, 220–232.

Kochanska, G., Murray, K., Jacques, T. Y., Koenig, A. L., and Vandeceest, K. (1996). Inhibitory control in young children and its role in emerging internalization. *Child Development*, *67*, 490–507.

Kochanska, G., and Thompson, R. A. (1997). The emergence and development of conscience in toddlerhood and early childhood. In J. E. Grusec and L. Kuczynski (Eds.), *Parenting and children's internalization of values: A handbook of contemporary theory* (pp. 53–77). New York: Wiley.

Lachenmeyer, J. R. (1998). Parent training for failure to thrive. In J. M. Briesmeister and C. E. Schaefer (Eds.), *Handbook of parent training: Parents as co-theapists for children's behavior problems* (pp. 261–280). New York: Wiley.

LaFreniere, P. J., and Sroufe, L. A. (1985). Profiles of peer competence in the preschool: Interrelations between measures, influence of social ecology, and relation to attachment history. *Developmental Psychology, 21,* 56–69.

Lamb, S. (1993). First moral sense: An examination of the appearance of morally related behaviors in the second year of life. *Journal of Moral Education, 22,* 97–109.

Lamborn, S., Mounts, N., Steinberg, L., and Dornbusch, S. M. (1991). Patterns of competence and adjustment from authoritative, authoritarian, indulgent, and neglectful families. *Child Development, 62,* 1049–1065.

Langer, W. L. (1974). Checks on population growth: 1750–1850. *Scientific American, 226,* 92–99.

Lee, C. L., and Bates, J. E. (1985). Mother–child interaction at age two years and perceived difficult temperament. *Child Development, 56,* 1314–1325.

Lepper, M. R. (1973). Dissonance, self-perception, and honesty in children. *Journal of Personality and Social Psychology, 25,* 65–74.

Lepper, M. R., and Greene, D. (1975). Turning play into work: Effects of adult surveillance and extrinsic rewards on children's intrinsic motivation. *Journal of Personality and social Psychology, 31,* 479–486.

Lepper, M. R., and Greene, D. (Eds.). (1978). *The hidden costs of reward: New perspectives on the psychology of human motivation.* Potomac, MD: Lawrence Erlbaum Associates.

Lepper, M. R., Greene, D., and Nisbett, R. E. (1973). Undermining children's intrinsic interest with extrinsic rewards: A test of the over-justification hypothesis. *Journal of Personality and social Psychology, 28,* 129–137.

Leung, P. W. L., and Kwan, K. S. F. (1998). Parenting styles, motivational orientations, and self-perceived academic competence: A mediational model. *Merrill-Palmer Quarterly, 44,* 1–19.

Lindahl, K. M. (1998). Family process variables and children's disruptive behavior problems. *Journal of Family Psychology, 12,* 420–436.

Locke, J. (1964). *Some thoughts concerning education.* New York: Bureau of Publications. (Original work published 1693.)

Londerville, S., and Main, M. (1981). Security of attachment, compliance, and maternal training methods in the second year of life. *Developmental Psychology, 17,* 289–299.

Lyons-Ruth, K., Connell, D., Grunebaum, H., and Botein, S. (1990). Infants at social risk: Maternal depressive and family support services as mediators of infant development and security of attachment. *Child Development, 61,* 85–98.

Lyons-Ruth, K., and Jacobvitz, D. (1999). Attachment disorganization: Unresolved loss, relational violence, and lapses in behavioral and attentional strategies. In J. Cassidy and P. R. Shaver (Eds.), *Handbook of attachment: Theory, research, and clinical applications* (pp. 520–554). New York: Guilford.

Maccoby, E. E. (1984). Socialization and developmental change. *Child Development, 55,* 317–328.

Maccoby, E. E. (1992). The role of parents in the socialization of children: An historical overview. *Developmental Psychology, 28,* 1006–1007.

Maccoby, E. E., and Martin, J. (1983). Socialization in the context of the family: Parent–child interaction. In E. M. Hetherington (Ed.) and P. H. Mussen (Series Ed.), *Handbook of child psychology: Vol. 4. Socialization, personality, and social development* (pp. 1–101). New York: Wiley.

Main, M., and Hesse, E. (1990). Parents' unresolved traumatic experiences are related to infant disorganized attachment status: Is frightening and/or frightened parental behavior the linking mechanism? In M. T. Greenberg, D. Cicchetti, and E. M. Cummings (Eds.), *Attachment in the preschool years* (pp. 121–160). Chicago: University of Chicago Press.

Main, M., Kaplan, N., and Cassidy, J. (1985). Security in infancy, childhood, and adulthood: A move to the level of representation. In I. Bretherton and E. Waters (Eds.), *Growing points of attachment theory and research. Monographs of the society for research in child development, 50,* 66–104.

Main, M., and Solomon, J. (1986). Discovery of an insecure-disorganized/disoriented attachment pattern. In T. B. Brazelton and M. W. Yogman (Eds.), *Affective development in infancy* (pp. 95–124). Norwood, NJ: Ablex.

Main, M., and Solomon, J. (1990). Procedures for identifying disorganized/disoriented infants in the Ainsworth Strange Situation. In M. T. Greenberg, D. Cicchetti, and E. M. Cummings (Eds.), *Attachment in the preschool years: Theory, research, and intervention* (pp. 121–160). Chicago: University of Chicago Press.

Main, M., and Weston, D. R. (1982). Avoidance of the attachment figure in infancy: Descriptions and interpretations. In C. Parkes and J. Stevenson-Hinde (Eds.), *The place of attachment in human behavior* (pp. 31–59). New York: Basic Books.

McFarlane, A. H., Bellissimo, A., and Norman, G. R. (1995). Family structure, family functioning, and adolescent well-being: The transcendent influence of parental style. *Journal of Child Psychology and Psychiatry and Allied Disciplines, 36,* 847–864.

McLoyd, V. C. (1998). Socioeconomic disadvantage and child development. *American Psychologist, 53,* 185–204.

Nurcombe, B., Howell, D. C., Rauh, V. A., Teti, D. M., Ruoff, R., and Brennan, J. (1984). An intervention program for mothers of low-birthweight infants: preliminary results. *Journal of American Academy of Child Psychiatry, 23,* 319–325.

O'Connor, M. J., Sigman, M., and Brill, N. (1987). Disorganization of attachment in relation to maternal alcohol consumption. *Journal of Consulting and Clinical Psychology, 55,* 831–836.

Olds, D. (1997). The Prenatal/Early Infancy Project: Fifteen years later. In G. W. Albee and T. P. Gullotta (Eds.), *Primary prevention works: Vol. 6. Issues in children's and families' lives* (pp. 41–67). Thousand Oaks, CA: Sage.

Olds, D., Henderson, C., Jr., Kitzman, H., Eckenrode, J., Cole, R., and Tatelbaum, R. (1998). The promise of home visitation: Results of two randomized trials. *Journal of community psychology, 26,* 5–21.

Parke, R. D., Burks, V. M., Carson, J. L., Neville, B., and Boyum, L. A. (1994). Family–peer relationships: A tripartite model. In R. D. Parke and S. Kellan (Eds.), *Exploring family relationships with other social contexts* (pp. 115–145). Hillsdale, NJ: Lawrence Erlbaum Associates.

Parker, G., Roy, K., Wilhelm, K., Mitchell, P., Austin, M.-P., and Hadzi-Pavlovic, D. (1999). An exploration of links between early parenting experiences and personality disorder type and personality functioning. *Journal of Personality Disorder, 13,* 361–374.

Parpal, M., and Maccoby, E. E. (1985). Maternal responsiveness and subsequent child compliance. *Child Development, 56,* 1326–1334.

Paterson, G., and Sanson, A. (1999). The association of behavioural adjustment to temperament, parenting and family characteristics among 5-year-old children. *Social Development, 8,* 293–309.

Patterson, G. R. (1976). The aggressive child: Victim and architect of a coercive system. In E. J. Mash, L. A. Hamerlynck, and L. C. Handy (Eds.), *Behavior modification and families* (pp. 267–316). New York: Brunner/Mazel.

Patterson, G. R. (1995). Coercion as a basis for early age of onset for arrest. In J. McCord (Ed.), *Coercion and punishment in long-term perspective* (pp. 81–105). New York: Cambridge University Press.

Patterson, G. R. (1996). Some characteristics of a developmental theory for early-onset delinquency. In M. F. Lenzenweger and J. J. Haugaard (Eds.), *Frontiers of developmental psychopathology* (pp. 81–124). New York: Oxford University Press.

Patterson, G. R. (1997). Performance models for parenting: A social interactional perspective. In J. E. Grusec and L. Kuczynski (Eds.), *Parenting and children's internalization of values: A handbook of contemporary theory* (pp. 193–226). New York: Wiley.

Patterson, G. R., Reid, J. B., and Dishion, T. J. (1992). *Antisocial boys: A social interactional approach* (Vol. 4). Eugene, OR: Castalia.

Pederson, D., Moran, G., Sitko, C., Campbell, K., Ghesqure, K., and Acton, H. (1990). Maternal sensitivity and the security of infant–mother attachment. *Child Development, 67,* 915–927.

Pettit, G. S., Clawson, M. A., Dodge, K. A., and Bates, J. E. (1996). Stability and change in peer-rejected status: The role of child behavior, parenting, and family ecology. *Merrill-Palmer Quarterly, 42,* 267–294.

Posada, G., Jacobs, A., Carbonell, O. A., Alzate, G., Bustamante, M. R., and Arenas, A. (1999). Maternal care and attachment security in ordinary and emergency contexts. *Developmental Psychology, 35,* 1379–1388.

Radziszewska, B., Richardson, J. L., Dent, C. W., and Flay, B. R. (1996). Parenting style and adolescent depressive symptoms, smoking, and academic achievement: Ethnic, gender, and SES differences. *Journal of Behavioral Mediine, 19,* 289–305.

Robertson, P. (1974). Home as a nest: Middle-class childhood in nineteenth-century Europe. In L. de Mause (Ed.), *The history of childhood* (pp. 407–431). New York: Psychohistory Press.

Rothbart, M. K., and Bates, J. E. (1998). Temperament. In W. Damon (Ed.) and N. Eisenberg (Vol. Ed.), *Handbook of child psychology: Vol. 3: Social, emotional, and personality development* (5th ed., pp. 105–176). New York: Wiley.

Rousseau, J. J. (1911). Émile (B. Foxley, Trans.). London: Dent. (Original work published 1762.)

Schuengel, C., Bakermans-Kranenberg, M., van IJzendoorn, M. H., and Blom, M. (1999). Unresolved loss and infant disorganization: Links to frightening maternal behavior. In J. Solomon and C. George (Eds.), *Attachment disorganization* (pp. 71–94). New York: Guilford.

Sears, R. R., Maccoby, E., and Levin, H. (1957). *Patterns of childrearing.* Evanston, IL: Row, Peterson.

Sears, R. R., Rau, L., and Alpert, R. (1965). *Identification and childrearing.* Stanford, CA: Stanford University Press.

Sears, R. R., Whiting, J. W. M., Nowlis, V., and Sears, P. S. (1953). Some child-rearing antecedents of aggression and dependency in young children. *Genetic Psychology Monographs, 47,* 135–234.

Shumow, L., Vandell, D. L., and Posner, J. K. (1998). Harsh, firm, and permissive parenting in low-income families: Relations to children's academic achievement and behavioral adjustment. *Journal of Family Issues, 19,* 483–507.

Smith, P. B., and Pederson, D. R. (1988). Maternal sensitivity and patterns of infant–mother attachment. *Child Development, 59,* 1097–1101.

Spock, B., and Rothenberg, M. B. (1992). *Dr. Spock's baby and childcare* (6th ed.). New York: Pocket.

Sroufe, L. A. (1979). The coherence of individual development. *American Psychologist, 34,* 834–841.

Sroufe, L. A. (1983). infant–caregiver attachment and patterns of adaptation in preschool: The roots of maladaptation and competence. In M. Perlmutter (Ed.), *Minnesota Symposia on Child Psychology: Vol. 16. Development and policy concerning children with special needs* (pp. 41–83). Hillsdale, NJ: Lawrence Erlbaum Associates.

Sroufe, L. A., Fox, N. E., and Pancake, V. R. (1983). Attachment and dependency in developmental perspective. *Child Development, 54,* 1615–1627.

Stayton, D., Hogan, R., and Ainsworth, M. D. S. (1973). Infant obedience and maternal behavior: The origins of socialization reconsidered. *Child Development, 42,* 1057–1070.

Steinberg, L., Dornbusch, S., and Brown, B. (1992). Ethnic differences in adolescent achievement: An ecological perspective. *American Psychologist, 47,* 723–729.

Steinberg, L., Mounts, N. S., Lamborn, S. D., and Dornbusch, S. M. (1991). Authoritative parenting and adolescent adjustment across varied ecological niches. *Journal of Research on Adolescence, 1,* 19–36.

Stone, L. (1975). The rise of the nuclear family in the early modern England: The patriarchal stage. In C. E. Rosenberg (Ed.), *The family in history* (pp. 13–57). Philadelphia: University of Pennsylvania Press.

Tamis-LeMonda, C. S., Bornstein, M. H., Baumwell, L., and Damast, A. M. (1996). Responsive parenting in the second year: Specific influences on children's language and play. *Early Development and Parenting, 5,* 173–183.

Taris, T. W., and Bok, I. A. (1996). Effects of parenting style upon psychological well-being of young adults: Exploring the relations among parental care, locus of control and depression. *Early Child Development and Care, 132,* 93–104.

Taylor, R. D., Casten, R., and Flickinger, S. M. (1993). Influence of kinship social support on the parenting experiences and psychosocial adjustment of African-American adolescents. *Developmental Psychology, 29,* 382–399.

Teti, D. M. (in press). Sibling relationships. In J. McHalg and W. Grolnick (Eds.). *Interiors: Retrospect and prospect in the psychological story of families.* Hillsdale, NJ: Erlbaum.

Teti, D. M., and Ablard, K. E. (1989). Infant-sibling relationships and child–parent attachment: A laboratory study. *Child Development, 60,* 1519–1528.

Teti, D. M., Gelfand, D. M., Messinger, D., and Isabella, R. (1995). Maternal depression and the quality of early attachment: An examination of infants, preschoolers, and their mothers. *Developmental Psychology, 31,* 364–376.

Thomas, A., and Chess, S. (1977). *Temperament and development.* New York: Brunner/Mazel.

Thomas, A., Chess, S., and Birch, H. G. (1970). The origin of personality. *Scientific American, 223,* 102–109.

Thompson, R. A. (1998). Early sociopersonality development. In W. Damon (Ed.) and N. Eisenberg (Vol. Ed.), *Handbook of child psychology: Vol. 3. Social, emotional, and personality development* (5th ed., pp. 25–104). New York: Wiley.

Thompson, R. A. (1999). Early attachment and later development. In J. Cassidy and P. R. Shaver (Eds.), *Handbook of attachment: Theory, research, and clinical applications* (pp. 265–286). New York: Guilford.

Tisak, M. (1986). Children's conceptions of parental authority. *Child Development, 57,* 166–176.

Turiel, E. (1983). *The development of social knowledge: Morality and convention.* New York: Cambridge University Press.

Valenzuela, M. (1997). Maternal sensitivity in a developing society: The context of urban poverty and infant chronic under-nutrition. *Developmental Psychology, 33,* 845–855.

Van den Boom, D. C. (1991). The influence of infant irritability on the development of the mother–infant relationship in the first six months of life. In J. K. Nugent, B. M. Lester, and T. B. Brazelton (Eds.), *The cultural context of infancy* (Vol. 2, pp. 63–89). Norwood, NJ: Ablex.

Vondra, J. I., Shaw, D. S., and Kevenides, M. C. (1995). Predicting infant attachment classification from multiple contemporaneous measures of maternal care. *Infant Behavior and Development, 18,* 415–425.

Wachs, T. D. (in press). Person–environment "fit" and individual development. In D. M. Teti (Ed.), *Handbook of research methods in developmental psychology.* London: Blackwell.

Wachs, T. D., and Gandour, M. J. (1983). Temperament, environment, and six-month cognitive-intellectual development: A test of the organismic specificity hypothesis. *International Journal of Behavioral Development, 6,* 135–152.

Walzer, J. F. (1974). A period of ambivalent: Eighteenth-century American childhood. In L. de Mause (Ed.), *The history of childhood* (pp. 351–382). New York: Psychohistory Press.

Warren, S. F., and Walker, D. (in press). Fostering early communication and language development. In D. M. Teti (Ed.), *Handbook of research methods in developmental psychology.* London: Blackwell.

Webster-Stratton, C. (1989). *The parents and children series.* Eugene, OR: Castalia.

Whiting, B., and Edwards, C. P. (1988). *Children of different worlds: The formation of social behavior.* New Haven, CT: Yale University Press.

8

Maternal Deprivation

Michael Rutter
University of London

INTRODUCTION

The concept of maternal deprivation was first firmly established by Bowlby's World Health Organization (WHO) monograph, *Maternal Care and Mental Health* (1951), which sought to assess the mental health consequences for children who were being reared in group care residential institutions. Bowlby (1951, p. 46) concluded that "the prolonged deprivation of the young child of maternal care may have grave and far-reaching effects on his character and so on the whole of his future life." Indirectly, although importantly, this work constituted the roots of attachment theory (Bowlby, 1969, 1973, 1980), which continues as a dominant force today in thinking about normal and abnormal development (Rutter, 1995a; Rutter and O'Connor, 1999; Rutter and Sroufe, 2000; Thompson, 1998). The historical development of the concepts and the controversies to which it gave rise were reviewed in the first edition of this *Handbook* (Rutter, 1995b), and these will not be repeated, except insofar as they are relevant to current issues and disputes. Much of the controversy concerned unwarranted extrapolations from residential group care to different forms of daycare and from severely stressful separations to separations of all kinds. Those topics will not be considered here, but the relevant concepts and findings are reviewed in other chapters (see Clarke-Stewart and Allhusen, in Vol. 3 of this *Handbook*, on nonparental caregiving; Haugaard and Hazan, in Vol. 1, on foster parenting; Hetherington and Stanley-Hagan, in Vol. 3, on divorce and remarriage; Weinraub, Horvath, and Gringlas, in Vol. 3, on single parenthood; and Zahn-Waxler, Duggal, and Gruber, in Vol. 4, on parental mental illness). Although the issue of selective attachments remains central to considerations of residential group care, the broader issues of attachment are not dealt with in this chapter, but are discussed in Cummings and Cummings (in Vol. 5 of this *Handbook*). Rather, this chapter considers maternal deprivation in relation to six main issues, some of which derive from earlier concerns and some of which are new: (1) whether deprivation of individualized parental caregiving has substantial adverse effects that are environmentally mediated, (2) whether the effects of institutional rearing are behaviorally specific, (3) whether there are age-related sensitive periods for such effects, (4) to what extent there is heterogeneity in outcome after comparable adverse experiences, (5) to what extent adverse effects persist, even after high quality parental care is restored, and (6) what are the mechanisms by which adverse effects are carried forward in development, the implication being the need to understand the processes involved in environmental effects on the organism, together with queries about the concept of developmental programming. Finally, the chapter concludes with a few words on heterogeneity in the concept of maternal deprivation.

TESTING FOR ENVIRONMENTAL MEDIATION

During the last decade there has been a string of vigorous attacks on the very idea that variations in the qualities of parenting make any substantial difference to children's psychological development (Harris, 1998; Rowe, 1994; Scarr, 1992, 1997). The main basis of these critiques has been the evidence of gene-environment correlations that raise the possibility that some of the effects of adverse environments are actually mediated genetically rather than environmentally. In fact, as several reviews have brought out, there are good research methods by which environmental mediation can be tested (Rutter, Pickles, Murray and Eaves, 2001-a) and the empirical evidence is clear cut in showing the importance of environmental effects for a range of parenting features (Collins, Maccoby, Steinberg, Hetherington, and Bornstein, 2000; Rutter, 2000a; Wachs, 1992). However, because the issue is so fundamental to the whole concept of maternal deprivation, the concepts and findings need to be considered in some detail.

The main genetic basis for the dismissal of substantial parenting effects was summarized in the influential papers by Plomin and Daniels (1987) and by Plomin and Bergeman (1991). The first concluded that nonshared environmental effects were vastly more important than shared ones, and that shared environmental effects were of negligible importance for many psychological traits. In other words, the implication from quantitative genetic analyses was that, insofar as environmental effects were important, they tended to make children within the same family different rather than similar. The findings were useful in serving as a reminder that family-wide influences as observed (such as neglect or discord) frequently impinged in differing ways and to differing degrees on different children in the same family. To an important extent, that comes about because children's own characteristics serve to influence the interactions they have with their parents. Also, children actively appraise and process their experiences, both cognitively and affectively. As a consequence, what looks like the same experience may be felt quite differently by different children.

The implication was that psychosocial researchers needed to examine environmental effects of risks as experienced at the individual level, rather than the family level. Nevertheless, the assumption that these findings meant that family-wide influences such as discord or neglect were unimportant was quite mistaken, for four main reasons. First, whether or not an environmental effect is shared or nonshared has everything to do with whether the effects serve to make children similar or different, and nothing to do with whether the risk experience is or is not family wide (Rutter, 2000a; Rutter, Silberg, O'Connor, and Simonoff, 1999a; Rutter et al., 2001-a). Second, there are some psychological features, most especially antisocial behavior, where it is usual for several children in the same family to be affected. Third, the empirical findings on the supposed importance of nonshared environmental effects are much less secure than usually supposed (Reiss, Niederhiser, Hetherington, and Plomin, 2000; Rutter et al., 1999a; Rutter et al., 2001-a). That is because most of the findings in the 1987 review derived from univariate analyses of cross-sectional data, and these will have been artificially inflated by measurement error. Bivariate analyses, focusing on variance that excludes measurement error, have produced much lower estimates of nonshared environmental effects (Rutter et al., 1999a), as have analyses of traits as shown longitudinally over time (Reiss et al., 2000). There is also concern that some studies that have shown shared effects to be greater than nonshared effects presented their data in ways that obscured that fact (see, e.g., Pike, McGuire, Hetherington, Reiss, and Plomin, 1996). Fourth, both twin and adoptee studies have been consistent in showing that nongenetic effects usually account for something approaching half of the population variance, and often more than that (Rutter, Silberg, O'Connor, and Simonoff, 1999b).

The second paper (Plomin and Bergeman, 1991), together with a broader range of quantitative genetic evidence that has accumulated since (Plomin 1994; Plomin, de Fries, McClearn, and Rutter, 1997), reviewed evidence on gene–environment correlations (rGE) and concluded that there was an important genetic component in almost all environmental measures. This led some critics to dismiss psychosocial research because so much of it had failed to take into account the possibility of genetic mediation (Harris 1998; Rowe, 1994; Scarr, 1992). Once more, the challenge was both real and important, and it had to be accepted that much psychosocial research had assumed environmental mediation without taking the necessary steps to test the alternative possibility of genetic mediation. Nevertheless, the rejection of psychosocial influences was unwarranted for several reasons. Most importantly, there is a substantial body of rigorous research that has tested for genetic mediation, or has used designs that obviate the possibility, and has produced findings that demonstrate clear environmental effects (see Collins et al., 2000; Rutter, 2000a; Shonkoff and Phillips, 2000). Second, although indeed there is good evidence showing the role of genetic factors in individual differences in the liability to various aspects of parenting (Kendler, 1996; Wade and Kendler, 2000) and to divorce (Jockin, McGue, and Lykken 1996), to mention but two examples, it is also apparent that genetic factors rarely account for more than a minority of the population variance in liability (typically of the order of 20% to 40%). That still leaves substantial scope for environmentally mediated risks from the variables showing some genetic influence. Third, the genetic analyses have implicitly assumed that the origins of a risk factor and its mode of risk mediation are synonymous. Obviously, that does not follow logically, as the effects of smoking clearly illustrate (Rutter, Silberg, and Simonoff, 1993). People smoke for a whole range of reasons deriving from personality features, cultural attitudes, and access to cigarettes, but the risk processes linking smoking with cardiovascular disease, lung cancer, osteoporosis, and other somatic conditions have nothing to do with those risk factors for smoking. Rather, they concern physical influences such as nicotinic effects on blood vessels, carbon monoxide, and carcinogenic tars. The origin of a risk factor is an important datum to have but, on its own, it is uninformative about the process of risk mediation. As a result, the usual practice, as followed in most behavior genetic analyses, of attributing the whole of rGE correlations to a genetic effect is seriously misleading. Causal effects involving rGE derive, not from nature or nurture on their own, but rather from their coming together.

Third Variable Effects

Although the main focus of behavior genetic critiques has been on the possibility that supposed environmental effects have been genetically mediated, it is important to appreciate that this constitutes but one example of the broader scientific concern to consider possible third variable effects before concluding that the impact of the risk factor being considered is truly responsible for the effect on the psychological outcome being examined. So far as children placed in residential group care when they are young are concerned, the possibility of genetic mediation risks is real enough because of the extensive evidence of the raised rates of psychopathology in parents who fail to parent successfully, whose children are taken away from them because of abuse and neglect, or who give up their children to residential care for other reasons (see, e.g., Quinton and Rutter, 1988). Parents with chronic or recurrent mental disorders, particularly if they involve personality disorder, show much increased rates of family discord and hostility focused on their children (Rutter and Quinton, 1984). The need to be concerned with possible genetic mediation is obvious. Do risks for psychopathology in the children derive mainly from the atmosphere of discord, conflict, and hostility in which they are reared, or, rather, from their genetic predisposition? Parents both pass on genes and shape and select the rearing environments for their children.

It is important, however, to realize that genetic mediation is simply one example of a possible third variable effect, and there are others that need to be considered in relation to the possible environmentally mediated risks associated with maternal deprivation. For example, the rate of heavy drinking and frank alcohol abuse is raised in the parents who give up their children into residential care. Do the risks to the children derive from alcohol damage during the early months of the pregnancy or from rearing patterns after birth? Longitudinal studies have shown that there are important sequelae associated with alcohol exposure in early pregnancy—sequelae that perhaps particularly involve cognitive impairment and patterns of hyperactivity and inattention (Spohr and Steinhausen, 1996; Stratton, Howe, and Battaglia, 1996). Similarly, serious social disadvantage is associated with an increased likelihood of poor quality prenatal care and with an increased risk of low birthweight and premature gestation. Could it be that prenatal complications play a part in the psychopathological risk? Serious parental neglect may also be associated with malnutrition after birth. Could this predispose a child to psychopathology?

Person Effects on the Environment

The second major challenge to the inference that maternal deprivation causes psychopathology through environmentally mediated processes comes from the possibility that the causal arrow runs in the opposite direction. In other words, it is children's behavior that is eliciting particular negative reactions from their parents, rather than that poor parenting leads to adverse consequences for children's psychological development. In a seminal paper written over three decades ago, Bell (1968) was the first to provide a systematic challenge to socialization explanations. Since that time, an increasing number of studies have provided good evidence that children do, indeed, have effects on the behavior of those people with whom they interact (see Bell and Chapman, 1986; Engfer, Walper, and Rutter, 1994; Lytton, 1990). Most of the evidence, however, concerns rather short-term effects, and much less is known about enduring effects. It is also the case that the research findings are consistent in showing bidirectional influences, so that the question is not whether parents influence children or children influence parents but, rather, how to sort out the relative importance of each in particular circumstances for particular outcomes.

As part of this overall concern with possible child effects, there has been an appreciation that the child qualities that elicit responses from other people are likely to be genetically influenced in part. This has led, among other things, to adoption designs in which the focus is on the effects of genetic risk in the biological parents (who did not rear the children), on the behavior of the adoptive parents who did rear the children (but who do not share their genes). Significant effects with respect to parental negativity and children's disruptive behavior have been found (Ge et al., 1996; O'Connor, Deater-Deckard, Fulker, Rutter, and Plomin, 1998), with the mediating variable being the negative behavior of the child. The O'Connor et al. (1998) study is informative in going on to consider the extent to which genetic influences are crucial in this effect. Interestingly, they found that genetic effects constituted only a small part of the picture. In other words, there were associations between negative parenting by the adoptive parents and disruptive behavior in the children, even in those children who did not have a mother with a genetic risk as indexed by antisocial behavior or drug problems. The implication is that, as Lehrman (1965) pointed out many years ago, we need to think about organisms influencing their environments and not genes doing so. Genes have a crucial role to play, but they do so through their effects on organisms rather than independently of them. Nevertheless, research designs are needed to take account of the possibility that causal effects run from the child to the parent, rather than the other way round.

Tests of Environmentally Mediated Effects of Maternal Deprivation

Behavior geneticists often write and talk as if the only way to deal with these issues is through twin and adoptee designs (or molecular genetic designs as and when specific susceptibility genes are identified). Such designs do have an important place in the research strategies that need to be used, but there is a range of other designs of equal importance, of which carefully planned "natural experiments" are crucial (Rutter et al., 2001-a). Several examples serve to illustrate both the rationale of the "natural experiment" strategy and some of the key substantive findings.

The first example is provided by the follow-up study of children from severely depriving Romanian orphanages who were adopted into U.K. families (O'Connor, Rutter, Beckett, Keaveney, and Kreppner, 2000b; Rutter and the ERA Research Team, 1998b; Rutter et al., 2000). Because the children were placed in institutions within the first few weeks of life in almost all instances, this effectively rules out the possibility of any substantial person effect on the environment, particularly as the environmental conditions being investigated involved gross and pervasive neglect that applied to all children in the institutions. The experiment involved several different components. The first test was whether the children's psychological functioning changed after their removal from the institution and placement in a U.K. adoptive family providing good quality rearing experiences. The findings were dramatic in indicating huge developmental gains across the board. At the time of leaving the institutions, over half the children were functioning in the severely retarded range, their behavior was strikingly abnormal, and about half were severely malnourished. By the age of 4 years, there had been a rise in developmental level that was equivalent to approximately 40 IQ points, with the great majority of the children functioning within the normal range. The further follow-up, at age 6, showed a comparable pattern.

The second test was provided by determination of whether or not the degree of developmental catch-up showed a systematic linear dose-response relation with the duration of severe institutional deprivation. Again, the findings were clear cut. The average general cognitive index score, at age 6 years, was some 24 points lower in those over the age of 2 at the time of leaving the institution, as compared with both those who left at under the age of 6 months and, also, the comparison group of nondeprived within U.K. children adopted within infancy. Because the children usually moved more or less directly from the Romanian institution to the adoptive home, there was, inevitably, a complete confound between the duration of institutional deprivation and the time the children had spent in the adoptive home. However, this confound could be removed by considering longitudinal data provided by the assessments at both 4 years and 6 years. The findings showed that, after a period of some two and a half years in the adoptive home, the same very large effect of duration of institutional deprivation remained.

The third test required consideration of whether or not the developmental catch-up and/or the continuing sequelae were a function of the malnutrition that was present in some, but not all, children. The findings showed that the children's weight at the time of leaving the institution had a modest, but statistically significant, effect on psychological outcome, but an effect that was much weaker than the overall duration of institutional care. Moreover, the pattern of catch-up and of deficit was much the same in the subgroup of late adopted children who did *not* show malnutrition as indexed by a weight below the fifth percentile (Rutter and O'Connor, submitted). It may be concluded that malnutrition may well have played a contributory role, but the psychosocial deprivation of a prolonged kind was probably more important. The limited findings on the effects of variations in the quality of care among institutions in Romania pointed in the same direction (Castle et al., 1999).

The fourth test was provided by a quite different study that was concerned with interventions within Romanian institutions. Ramey and Ramey (2000) showed that steps taken to improve the quality of care within institutions had a worthwhile, measurable effect, although they did not lead to complete cognitive catch-up.

The findings of these studies have been given in some detail because they illustrate how steps can be taken to use natural experiments to test environmental mediation hypotheses but the results of somewhat comparable studies of adoptees in Canada from Romanian orphanages provide much the same picture (Ames, 1997; Chisholm, 1998; Chisolm, Carter, Ames, and Morrison, 1995; Fisher, Ames, Chisholm, and Savoie, 1997; Marcovitch et al., 1997). Of course, the findings concern quite gross deprivation of all forms of individualized parental care, and it could be argued that it is scarcely surprising that such extreme conditions had such serious effects. The question is whether lesser degrees of poor care have effects that are at all comparable.

To answer that question, we need to turn to other samples and other designs. Roy, Rutter, and Pickles (2000) focused on the variations in patterns of alternative care provided in the United Kingdom for children whose parents had been unable to continue childcare, or whose children had been removed because of neglect. The key comparison was between those reared in residential nurseries where care was provided on a group basis and those placed in individual foster families. Blind analysis of case records showed that both groups came from homes characterized by severe parental psychopathology, but they did not differ in that connection. In order to avoid the possible problems of children's effects on the environment, and in order to avoid confounding due to major experiences before the children were taken into the care of the local authority, the samples were confined to children taken into care in the first year of life (the mean age in both was about 3 months). Both groups were compared with classroom controls as well as with each other. The findings showed that the institution-reared children had raised rates of inattention/overactivity, as measured both by direct observation and by questionnaire ratings, whereas this was not so for the family-fostered children other than to a minor, statistically nonsignificant, extent. The institution-reared group also showed more difficulties in selective attachments and social relationships, these difficulties overlapping to a significant extent with the inattention/overactivity (Roy, Rutter, and Pickles, submitted; Rutter, Roy, and Kreppner, in press).

The design of the study enabled the inference to be made that something about the experience of residential group care had led to this behavioral difference. There needs to be caution with respect to that inference because of the inevitably small sample size, but the findings are important in relation to the study of Romanian adoptees in that this group of children in British residential nurseries was not malnourished and was not generally deprived. They did experience a lack of individualized caregiving with substantial turnover of caregivers, but there was a good range of experiences, with ample play and conversational activities. The implication is that the key variable does not derive from global sensory or experiential deprivation, or from malnutrition, but rather from the particular pattern of relationships experienced in residential caregiving provided on a group basis. Systematic comparisons between family foster home and residential care would be informative, but there are major limitations in most of the studies undertaken to date (Rushton and Minnis, 2001).

An earlier study by Hodges and Tizard (1989a, 1989b) similarly focused on the possible effects of residential group care but employed a somewhat different design. Their starting point was a group of children, all of whom had been admitted in very early life to residential nurseries. As in the Roy study, the overall quality of care in the nurseries was high, but there was the same feature of a high rate of turnover of caregivers. The main comparison in the Hodges and Tizard study concerned the children who were returned to their biological parents (and, usually, to a discordant, disadvantageous family environment), those who were adopted (usually into reasonably well-functioning families), and a small group who remained in institutions. Classroom controls were used for comparison.

Not surprisingly, many features of the children's behavior at 16 (when they were followed up) were related to their living conditions at that time. What was less expected at the time was that all the groups who had experienced residential group care when young tended to show impairments in selective, committed, relationships with peers, irrespective of their family circumstances at 16. Although the children in the adoptive families had generally seemed to develop selective attachments to their parents, it nevertheless appeared that there were important remaining differences in their peer relationships. The implication was that these may have been a consequence of the relative lack of opportunities for forming selective social attachments with caregivers when they were young. More recently, the groups have been followed up by Jewett (1998) when they were in their early 30s. She found surprisingly few differences between the ex-institutional and comparison groups on a range of self-report questionnaires. Most were generally well functioning, but the ex-institutional individuals tended to have more difficulties in relationships with their families and more had been in trouble with the police since age 16. There was more individual variability in outcome in the ex-institutional group, and adult functioning in that group showed greater continuity with functioning in childhood/adolescence than was the case in the comparison group. The implication is that there were some enduring effects from early institutional rearing in a minority subgroup.

Four other studies have focused, not on residential group care but, rather, on the effects of poor parenting in the early years. Schiff and Lewontin (1986) compared children within the same family who had been reared by their biological mother in generally disadvantageous circumstances and children born to the same mothers but who had been adopted into well-functioning families. They found that the latter group had a mean IQ some dozen points higher than the former group, with the implication that the cognitive deficit was a function of the poorer quality parenting in the biological family. The inference is a plausible one, but it is weakened by uncertainties as to what it was that led one child to remain and another child to be adopted, by the fact that most of the children had different fathers, and by the fact that the inference relied on a between-group difference rather than changes within individuals as a result of changed living circumstances. Capron and Duyme (1989, 1991) improved on the design by seeking out a sample of adopted children whose biological families and adoptive families represented both the upper and lower ends of the socio-economic/educational distribution. The two-by-two table thereby enabled the children's IQ (the outcome variable being examined) to be examined in relation to biological parentage controlling for family of rearing, and vice versa. The findings were closely comparable to those of Schiff and Lewontin in showing that the family of rearing accounted for a mean IQ difference of about a dozen points, the effects of the biological parentage having a similar sized effect. The implication was that the qualities of the family of rearing made an important difference with respect to intellectual outcome, even after having taken account of the effects of genetic background. There was, however, the same limitation of reliance on between-group differences rather than within-individual change.

Somewhat similarly, Maughan, Collishaw, and Pickles (1998) compared the educational outcome of illegitimate children (studied during an era when illegitimacy was atypical and subject to community condemnation) who remained with their biological mothers and those who were adopted. They found that the adopted children fared much better. Again, the inference is that the qualities of the rearing environment made an important difference, but there is the same limitation that the main leverage had to be obtained from between-group comparisons rather than within-individual change.

In a later study, Duyme, Dumaret, and Tomkiewicz (1999) went on, to examine the matter further, using an improved design that did focus on within-individual change over time. They scoured France to sort out a sample of children who had been removed from their parents because of abuse or neglect, who had been adopted between the ages of 4 and $6\frac{1}{2}$ years, and for whom there was a preadoption IQ. The group was followed up into adolescence. In addition to the focus on within-individual change, the other crucial innovation concerned the study of the extent to which changes over time were a function of the qualities of the adoptive family. The findings were striking in three main respects. First, the group as a whole showed a substantial rise in IQ from pre-adoption to adolescence. The implication was that the change in family of rearing, from a disadvantageous one to a higher quality one, was followed by important IQ gains. Second, the extent of these gains was related in a systematic way to the socioeconomic/educational qualities of the adoptive parents. This finding is particularly important because it was the first to provide direct evidence of the impact of variations in family qualities within the normal range, using a genetically sensitive design. The effects were substantial, the mean rise in the upper group of adoptive families being 20 points, and that in the lower group being 8 points. The third point was different but equally important. That is, the correlation between the preadoption IQ and the IQ in adolescence was substantial and did not differ among the three groups that varied in qualities of the adoptive family. The implication is that it is possible for a change in environment to have a substantial impact on the overall levels of a trait without it making much difference to individual variation. This last study is clearly the most rigorous, but the results of all four point in the same direction, indicating a substantial effect of the family rearing environment on cognitive development.

There is an extensive literature showing statistical associations between early parental loss (through family breakup or death) and many different forms of psychopathology in both childhood and adult life (Rodgers and Pryor, 1998; Tennant, 1988). Initially, the element of loss or separation was seen as the key risk feature, but it soon became clear that this was unlikely to be the case because the risks were so much lower with parental death than with family breakup (Rutter, 1971); because comparisons between the relative effects of separation and of discord/conflict indicated that the main risks were associated with the latter (Fergusson, Horwood and Lynskey, 1992); and because it was found (with respect to the risks for adult depression) that the risk was primarily mediated by poor parenting (Brown and Harris, 1986). Poor parenting provided a risk in the absence of parental loss, but parental loss did not constitute a substantial risk when it was not followed by poor parenting. However, all of these earlier studies suffered from the important limitation that the possibility of at least partial genetic mediation could not be taken into account. Kendler et al. (1996) used the extended twin-family design in order to control for genetic effects with respect to the environmental risks following early parental loss for the development of later alcoholism. In this design, the genetic component is taken into account through the correlations between psychopathology in parent and child at the same age period by use of the MZ-DZ comparison, and by making use of the correlation between parental psychopathology and the postulated environmental risk factor (in this case, parental loss). A significant causal effect of environmentally mediated risk stemming from parental loss was found. Meyer et al. (2000) used the same research design to examine the effects of family maladaptation as a risk factor for antisocial behavior in the children, and, again, an environmentally mediated risk was found.

A broader spectrum of research strategies has been used to examine a range of different aspects of children's early psychosocial experiences. These include examination of the effects on psychopathology of differences in experiences within monozygotic pairs (where the effects must be environmentally mediated because the twins share all their genes); the use of twin designs in which experiences are treated as an individual phenotype, thereby allowing the association between the experience and the psychological trait of interest to be partitioned into the various genetic and environmental components; migration strategies (in which the effects of a massive change in living conditions can be examined by comparisons between the population of origin and the population who moved); and a range of other natural experiments, all focusing unusual circumstances that pull apart variables that ordinarily go together (Rutter et al., 2001-a). Taken together, the findings provide compelling evidence that rearing experiences do have a substantial effect. When the evidence is put together, the inference is that there are substantial risks associated with a lack of ongoing, harmonious, selective, committed relationships (Rutter, 2000a). These risks arise when there is a lack of such relationships (as may be the case in most forms of institutional rearing), when the relationships are profoundly negative (as with rejection, scapegoating, and neglect), and when relationships are of a kind that engender uncertainty and insecurity.

Earlier animal studies, looking at the effects of severe social isolation on the behavior of infant monkeys, by Harlow and Harlow (1969) and Suomi, Harlow, and Novak (1974), together with studies of mother–infant separation in monkeys by Hinde and McGinnis (1977), were important in demonstrating experimentally the effects of various forms of maternal deprivation (see Rutter, 1981, 1995b, for summarizing reviews). More recent research, both in nonhuman primates and in rodents, has been succinctly reviewed by Collins et al. (2000) and Shonkoff and Phillips (2000). Although the findings do not, for the most part, directly address the issues with respect to human maternal deprivation, they do clearly indicate the behavioral effects of variations in qualities of parenting.

SPECIFICITY OF BEHAVIORAL CONSEQUENCES OF MATERNAL DEPRIVATION

One of the main reasons for a degree of skepticism about possible centrality of the role of maternal deprivation (or other forms of psychosocial adversity) in the causal processes leading to psychopathology has been an apparent lack of specificity of effects. It is entirely possible for a single risk factor to have very diverse consequences. Nevertheless, the causal inference is much strengthened, other things being equal, by the demonstration of specific effects (Bradford Hill, 1977). One of the problems, however, with the detection of specificity has been that a single major experience may lead to quite a varied range of consequent risk experiences. Each of these may have specific effects, but they will be concealed by the fact that the same general risk factor actually incorporates many different risk mechanisms. The effects of smoking in leading to outcomes as heterogeneous as osteoporosis, lung cancer, cardiovascular disease, chronic bronchitis, and skin wrinkling, provide a well-known example (see Rutter, 1997). In this case, it is not that a single-risk process has very diverse effects but, rather, that smoking includes quite varied effects that are mediated by carcinogenic tars, carbon monoxide in the smoke, nicotine effects on blood vessels, and so forth. There is specificity in these effects, and they represent quite different causal mechanisms. One of the issues, then, is whether the same applies to the risks associated with maternal deprivation. Quite obviously, the experiences that tend to get included under that general heading are actually very varied.

The studies of residential group care noted above illustrated the issues and provided some substantive findings. Thus, within the British study of Romanian adoptees (O'Connor et al., 2000b; Rutter et al., 1998b), not only was cognitive impairment substantially more frequent in the children who had experienced severe institutional privation in Romania and in the nondeprived within-U.K. comparison group, but the degree of cognitive deficit showed a strong dose-response relation with the duration of institutional privation. That finding, together with the very substantial cognitive catch-up following adoption, provided strong support for the causal inference that the institutional privation had caused cognitive impairment. However, the other studies of group residential care in the United Kingdom, which did not involve the severe deprivation evident in Romanian institutions, have been consistent in failing to show any significant cognitive impairment (Hodges and Tizard, 1989a; Roy et al., 2000), the findings being in keeping with the earlier literature that had considered a range of institutions (see Rutter, 1981). It is clear that group style residential care is not, in itself, a substantial risk factor for cognitive impairment. Rather, the evidence both from the studies of institutions, and from studies of variations within ranges of more normal environments (see Rutter, 2000a), indicates that the key mediating variables are likely to lie in the qualities of conversational interchange, the availability of play materials, and the provision of a range of active experiences that tap children's curiosity and which allow them to explore and learn from their environment.

The findings with respect to patterns of quasi-autistic behavior (Rutter et al., 1999) provide a parallel. Within the sample of British adoptees from severely depriving Romanian institutions, there was a strong association between this pattern of behavior and the duration of institutional care, and the pattern was not seen in the nondeprived within-U.K. adoptees. Somewhat similar quasi-autistic features have been observed in other studies of Romanian adoptees. By contrast, these features have not been reported in any of the studies of children in residential group care that did not involve social isolation or other more widespread forms of severe deprivation. Together with the evidence that broadly comparable patterns of autistic-like behavior have been found in congenitally blind children (Brown, Hobson, Lee, and Stevenson, 1997; Hobson, Brown, Minter, and Lee, 1997), it may be concluded that it is not residential care as such that constitutes the risk factor but some aspect of accompanying social isolation. On the evidence available to date, however, it is not clear why such isolation should sometimes lead to uncomplicated cognitive impairment, whereas in other cases it leads to quasi-autistic patterns.

The two other behavioral patterns showing a strong association with institutional deprivation and a strong dose–response relation with the duration of such deprivation in the Romanian adoptees were patterns of inattention/overactivity and impairments in selective, committed, social relationships (Chisholm et al., 1995; Chisolm, 1998; Kreppner, O'Connor, and Rutter, and the ERA Study Team in press; Rutter, Kreppner and O'Connor, and the ERA Research Team, 2001-b). Unlike the findings with autistic features and with cognitive deficits, both these behavioral patterns have been reported in studies of children in nondepriving residential care (Hodges and Tizard, 1989a, 1989b; Roy et al., 2000; Rutter et al., 2001-b). Moreover, the evidence has shown that there is a substantial overlap between the patterns of inattention/overactivity and the impairments in selective social relationships.

The suggestion (but it is no more than a suggestion at this point) is that the inattention/overactivity may have a somewhat different meaning from more "ordinary" varieties of attention deficit disorder with hyperactivity (Rutter et al., in press).

The question also arises as to the meaning of the relationship features found. Sometimes these have been described in terms of "indiscriminate friendliness" (Chisholm, 1998; Chisholm et al., 1995). Also, there has been concern to consider the features as part of the concept of attachment disorder (O'Connor, Rutter, and the ERA Study Team, 2000a). The concept of attachment disorder remains somewhat ill-defined (Zeanah, 2000; Zeanah, Boris, and Larrieu, 1997), but the usual concept has been to consider attachment disorders in terms of varieties of insecurity of attachment, in line with the usual classification approaches to the Ainsworth's "Strange Situation" procedure (Ainsworth, Blehar, Waters, and Wall, 1978). Findings using the strange situation, or modifications of it, with the Romanian adoptees (Goldberg, 1997; O'Connor et al., submitted) suggest that neither the notion of "indiscriminate friendliness" nor "attachment insecurity" provides the most appropriate conceptualization of the relationship features observed. The children do not appear either anxious or insecure; indeed, it is the lack of both of those features that is most striking in the separation–reunion procedures. It would be going too far to describe the children's social approaches as indiscriminate, because they do vary their interaction styles with different people. Also, it does not appear that they are unusually friendly, at least as that term might ordinarily be understood. Rather, there seems to be a relative failure to pick up social cues and to appreciate social boundaries, together with an apparent lack of emotional intensity in their closest social relationships. In short, the limited evidence available suggests that the features are perhaps best considered in terms of limitations in quality of selective social attachments, together with limitations in appreciation of social cues and other people's social responses. The implication is that it may be that this is the relatively specific consequence of the severe limitations in opportunities for selective social attachments with caregivers that is a feature of most forms of group style residential care.

It is necessary to go on to ask whether something comparable could result from poor parenting or parental neglect in children reared in family settings of various kinds. Possibly it could, but most studies of children exposed to seriously adverse rearing conditions within a family context show either marked patterns of attachment insecurity or disorganized patterns of attachment or some combination of the two (Rutter, 1995a). The evidence is much too fragmentary to justify strong conclusions, but the tentative inference would seem to be that a serious lack of opportunities to form selective social attachments in the first 2 or 3 years of life may result in an impaired ability to develop such relationships (with both family members and with peers) at a later age. This seems to be different from the various forms of attachment insecurity that result from family situations that provide the opportunity for attachments but where they are damaged as a result of negative features that may include neglect, hostility, scapegoating, abuse, or the various forms of impaired interaction associated with severe parental depression.

We are left with the many findings that parental loss and poor parenting not only predispose to these rather more specific behavioral features but also increase the risk for a much broader range of psychopathology in childhood and adult life. The associations seem reasonably robust and well replicated, but the mechanisms remain poorly understood. Their elucidation remains an important research challenge for the future.

SENSITIVE PERIOD EFFECTS?

For obvious reasons, human studies provide few clear-cut comparisons of possible sensitive period or age-specific effects. The findings discussed above all concern experiences in the first few years of life. Insofar as there have been studies of residential group care at later ages (e.g., Wolkind, 1974), the findings do not suggest the same patterns. Animal studies, too, suggest that the findings are relatively specific to maternal deprivation in the early (rather than later childhood) years, but the data are very limited (Rutter, 1981). What is clear is that the patterns found with respect to early maternal deprivation are not a feature of the reports of later experiences of either residential group care or seriously poor parenting. It cannot possibly be claimed that there has been a rigorous test of the sensitive period hypothesis, but such evidence as there is points to the likelihood of the sequelae being a consequence of maternal deprivation in the early years, rather than in the later periods of childhood and adolescence.

HETEROGENEITY IN OUTCOME

The findings have been discussed so far in terms of group trends that are reasonably consistent, both within and across studies. It is important to emphasize, however, that all studies have shown very marked heterogeneity in outcome. It might be supposed, for example, that the very extreme conditions in Romanian institutions would have led to a relatively uniform outcome for the children exposed to the severe, pervasive, and persistent deprivation. However, that is not what has been found. Thus, for example, in the subgroup of children adopted after the age of 2 years, the spread of IQ in the British study extended from a few individuals with severe retardation to one with an IQ in the highly superior range (above 130), with the rest distributed widely between the two extremes. It could be argued that that is simply a consequence of the fact that there are many features, both genetic and environmental, that influence cognitive development, and that the varied outcome is simply the expected result of multifactorial causation. Doubtless, to some extent, that is the case. On the other hand, it is not so obvious that such a coming together of multiple influences that operate within the normal range applies to the pattern of severe limitation in selective social relationships evident in this sort of sample. That is not a pattern that one ordinarily sees in children reared outside of extreme institutional conditions. Nevertheless, although this form of attachment disorder was a common feature of the late-adopted children, over half the children did not show the pattern. Moreover, even when extremely stringent rules were set to define normality of functioning across a wide range of areas of functioning, one fifth of the late-adopted children showed no abnormalities on any of the areas of functioning considered (Rutter et al., 2001-b). The inescapable conclusion is that, although very serious maternal deprivation has serious effects that are both common and persistent, they are not inevitable. The topic of resilience in the face of serious adversity has received increasing attention in recent years (Luthar, Cicchetti, and Becker, 2000; Rutter, 2000b), but the mechanisms involved remain poorly understood.

One question that needs to be asked is whether the consequences described above are a "pure" effect of maternal deprivation or, rather, whether they apply only to children who are unusually vulnerable by virtue of their genetic predisposition or prior experiences. The evidence on this point is decidedly limited, but it is noteworthy that, in their study of children in Romanian orphanages, Vorria, Rutter, Pickles, Wolkind, and Hobsbaum (1998a, 1998b) found that there were few differences from the classroom comparison group for children admitted to institutions largely as a result of family poverty and who did not have adverse experiences in the family before admission. Whether or not their relative protection against the adverse effects of institutional experiences stemmed from a lack of genetic risk factors or a lack of predisposing family adversities remains unknown. It should be added, also, that the relative resilience did not apply so strikingly to the qualities of the peer group relationships associated with an institutional upbringing. Other research has produced evidence of gene–environment interactions with respect to family adversity/poor parenting in relation to the risk for antisocial behaviour (Cadoret, Cain, and Crowe, 1983; Cadoret, Yates, Troughton, and Stewart, 1995; Crowe, 1974) and to stressful life events in relation to the liability for depressive disorders (Kendler et al., 1995; Silberg, Rutter, Neale, and Eaves, 2001). Although there is good reason, from a much broader range of evidence in biology and medicine more generally, to suppose that genetic factors will be important in an individual's differences in susceptibility to environmental hazards (Rutter, 2000a; Rutter et al., 1997), it is likely that they constitute but one of many influences on resilience and vulnerability (Rutter, 1999; Rutter, 2000b).

PERSISTENCE OF EFFECTS OF EARLY MATERNAL DEPRIVATION

Although there is abundant evidence that psychosocial experiences throughout life have major effects on behavior (Rutter, 1996; Rutter, 2000a), and although the long-term effects of adverse experiences in infancy tend to fade markedly provided that later experiences are good (Clarke and Clarke, 1976, 2000), the studies of severe maternal deprivation seem to provide a partial exception to this trend. With respect to cognitive impairment, inattention/overactivity, and impairments in selective social relationships, the sequelae in the studies of Romanian adoptees have been surprisingly persistent over a period of several years after the children left the depriving institutions and after adoption into well-functioning families (Rutter et al., 2000). There was relatively little change between the ages of 4 and 6 years; there was high stability in individual differences over this period, and the effects of duration of institutional privation were as marked at age 6 as they had been at age 4. Although, obviously, the good qualities of the adoptive families had been tremendously important in the remarkable developmental catch-up and behavioral improvement that took place, variations in the qualities of the adoptive home (which were mostly within a range of good qualities) were not systematically related to the children's progress between 4 and 6 years. Findings from the Canadian studies of Romanian adoptees (Ames, 1997) tell the same story. The follow-up of the Hodges and Tizard sample of children in group residential care in the United Kingdom (where there was no general deprivation apart from the marked turnover of caregivers) also showed a degree of persistence into adult life of the variations in qualities of social relationships found at age 16. Accordingly, it is evident that the adverse effects are by no means fixed and immutable, but they have proved much more enduring than the earlier literature would have one suppose. What remains unknown, however, is whether the persistence is more a function of the effects of the adverse early experiences on the organism or of a lack of appropriate remedial experiences postadoption. Very little is known about the types of interventions that are likely to make a difference to the sequelae (Rushton and Minnis, 2001; Rutter et al., 2000). That remains a considerable research and clinical challenge to be met in the future.

Effects on the Organism: Developmental Programming?

The findings on persistence raise important questions about the effects of early experiences on the organism and on the processes by which effects are carried forward in time. Several rather different sorts of mechanisms need to be considered (Rutter, 1989). The simplest, and most straightforward, possibility is that the children have learned particular styles or habits of behavior as a result of their experiences. Inevitably, there will be a neural substrate for such learning, but the implication would be that there are no particular constraints with respect to new learning or unlearning if experiences change. That does not necessarily mean that children's behavior will automatically change if their experiences alter. Thus, for example, one of the effects of a severely frightening experience may be that the person thereafter seeks to avoid the feared object. The mechanisms involved in the persistence and remission of phobias are by no means fully understood, but it certainly is clear that avoidance of the feared object tends to predispose to persistence of the phobia. In other words, the new learning needs to involve encounters with the feared objects—encounters that provide the opportunity for effective coping and for different outcomes that alter the experience and thereby alter the learning that takes place.

In the same sort of way, it could be that children in depriving institutions, or in families character-ized by poor parenting or neglect, learn styles of interpersonal interaction that may be adaptive in the adverse environment but maladaptive in more ordinary circumstances. Processes of this kind may account, at least in part, for the well-replicated finding that antisocial children have a much increased rate of later adverse experiences such as falling out with friends, multiple marital breakdowns, lack of social support, and very frequent changes of jobs (Champion, Goodall, and Rutter, 1995; Robins, 1966). The learned patterns of negative interpersonal interactions serve to bring about further adverse social experiences. Something comparable could apply in the case of children suffering severe institutional deprivation. On the other hand, at least with respect to the Romanian adoptees, it does not seem that this mechanism fits the findings at all well. The main characteristic of the institutional environment was not so much negative interpersonal experiences (although that played a part) but rather an overall lack of conversation, play, learning experiences, and social interaction. Moreover, the behavioral patterns seen following adoption did not, for the most part, constitute continuations of behavior that was apparent in the institution, but rather the development of new patterns. Furthermore, it is not at all clear why the radical change in social environment was not accompanied by a greater normalization of social behavior.

An alternative model is provided by the mechanisms involved in children's cognitive and affective processing of their experiences. The old-style notion that experiences impinge on a passive organism has long since been abandoned. Even quite young children think about what happens to them, conceptualize and add meaning to their experiences, and develop mental sets both about themselves and about their relationships with other people, as well as what they may expect from the world about them. Whereas this active processing of the environment is present in infancy onward, children's abilities to conceptualize increase greatly over the early childhood years (Flavell and Miller, 1998; Mandler, 1998; Rutter and Rutter, 1993). Although it is clear that implicit learning in early childhood persists into later life (for example, that is obviously the case with respect to language), most children's memories of specific experiences and specific events in the first 2 to 3 years of life are extremely limited—the so-called phenomenon of infantile amnesia (Rutter, Maughan, Pickles, and Simonoff, 1998a). So far as can be judged, it is not so much that experiences are not registered, but rather that children's abilities to retrieve memories from the early years are quite limited. It is because of this that Kagan (1980) argued that this accounted for the finding that there were so few enduring effects from experiences in the first few years of life. That is, experiences have their effects through children's thought processes about such experiences and, if their thought processes are quite limited at the time, it follows that the effects of such experiences are likely to be comparably evanescent. What is not known, however, is whether children's tendency to forget specific events and experiences in early life is paralleled by a comparable loss of the self-concepts or internal working models to which such experiences gave rise. Attachment theorists have seen the role of such internal working models as the key mechanism by which early experiences have effects on later social relationships. Nevertheless, findings from use of the "Strange Situation" procedure show that the main characteristic is not anxious insecurity, but rather a lack of social boundaries. In other words, the main feature is not deviant qualities in social relationships, but rather a relative lack of selectivity and emotional intensity, together with a limited apparent level of commitment in close social relationships. Clearly, the findings run completely counter to Kagan's (1980) expectation that there would not be persistent effects from early experiences, and there are no strong reasons for supposing that aberrant cognitive processing constitutes the key mediating mechanism. Nevertheless, in the absence of a proper understanding of the developmental course of cognitive processing in the early years, it is not possible to draw any firm conclusions on the role of such processing in the persistence of the effects of severe institutional deprivation.

The key proposition of attachment theory has always been that children's early selective attachments with caregivers constitute the basis for all later social relationships (Bowlby, 1969, 1973, 1980; Cassidy and Shaver, 1999). Certainly, the findings with respect to the effects of early institutional privation are in keeping with this proposition. What is not at all apparent, however, is what mechanism is supposed to mediate these links across relationships. The implication seems to be that it is necessary, in some way, to have developed selective attachment relationships during the first few years if there is to be fully normal later development of peer relationships, love relationships, and the ability to provide optimal parenting for the person's own children. Presumably, if this proposition is correct, there is likely to be some underlying neural process that is involved.

Neuroendocrine effects constitute another possibility for mediation. It has long been known, from systematic animal studies, that early stressful experiences have enduring effects on the development, structure, and function of the neuroendocrine system (Hennessey and Levine, 1979; Levine, 1982). On the whole, however, the animal evidence suggests that these effects tend to be somewhat protective against later stresses rather than giving rise to an increased vulnerability. Human studies are much more limited but, if anything, suggest the reverse (Sandberg and Rutter, in press). That is, early stresses tend to sensitize, rather than steel, the organism with respect to responses to later stresses and adversities. There has been some research into the neuroendocrine functioning of children from Romanian orphanages, and patterns that differ from normal have been found (Carlson and Earls, 1997). It is not apparent, however, what behavioral implications there are from these, fairly subtle, neuroendocrine changes. It does not seem likely that they constitute the key mediating mechanism for the enduring effects of early institutional privation, if only because the consequences do not seem to be mainly manifest in either an increased or decreased autonomic or neuroendocrine sensitivity to stress. It may be that the neuroendocrine changes play some role, but it is doubtful whether they are at all central.

Finally, it is necessary to consider the possibility of some form of developmental programming. The reality of such a biological effect is well established, but the precise biological processes remain poorly understood, and it is not at all clear how heterogeneous are the mechanisms implicated. It is known, for example, that early experiences play a key role in development of immune responses (Bock and Whelan, 1991). Barker (1997, 1999) postulated a comparable programming effect to account for the well-demonstrated association between a poor early nutrition and growth and an increased vulnerability in adult life to hypertension, cardiovascular disease, and diabetes. The notion is that the organism is programmed to deal adaptively with subnutrition, and that this then creates a maladaption when, in later life, the organism has to deal with overnutrition.

The best demonstrated example of developmental programming with respect to brain functioning (albeit of a kind different from that postulated by Barker) constitutes the effect of visual input from the development of the visual cortex, as first demonstrated by Hubel and Wiesel (1970) in their Nobel prize–winning research, subsequently confirmed and extended by many other investigators (Blakemore, 1991). The well-known human consequence of this effect is the fact that, if children's squints are not corrected within the first few years of life, it is highly likely that normal binocular vision will not be possible later. Greenough, Black, and Wallace (1987) and Greenough and Black (1992) have discussed the phenomenon using the concept of experience-dependent development. That is, the genetically programmed brain development requires certain forms of experience (which are universally available in all ordinary circumstances) for it to proceed normally. Furthermore, there is a sensitive period during which these experiences have to occur. The concept of a critical period was first established in relation to the phenomenon of imprinting, and there was an expectation of a biologically fixed critical period with firm time limits and no flexibility thereafter. Research soon showed that this rather rigid concept was misleading (Bateson, 1966; Bornstein, 1987) but, nevertheless, there is ample evidence of sensitive periods in development. For example, it has been shown that some phonological discriminations are retained and others lost in early language learning (Kuhl, 1994; Kuhl et al., 1997). Older children or adults have no particular difficulty in learning the vocabulary of second, third, or even more languages later in life. On the other hand, second language learning later in life is much less likely to include basic phonological discriminations that are not present in the first language acquired, and there are also some difficulties in the ease with which certain grammatical constructions are learned when they are markedly different from those in the first language (de Groot and Kroll, 1997). The phenomenon seems roughly comparable to that seen in visual development.

In recent years, psychosocial researchers, and more particularly advocates of early intervention, have sought to use neuroscience findings to argue for the critical role of early experiences (see Bruer, 1999, for a critique of both the findings and the inference). Reliance has been placed on two main sorts of evidence. First, there are the well-demonstrated findings on early brain development. It is well established that brain growth is particularly rapid and particularly radical during the first two or three years of life. That is, when neuronal migration takes place, when there is a massive proliferation of synapses, and when there is myelination of nerve fibers. This is followed by a period of pruning which seems to provide a fine-tuning function that is guided in part by experiential input. This has led to claims that brain development is sculpted by experiences, and that it is those experiences that shape later brain functioning (Eliot, 2000). The second basis of the claims comes from animal studies showing that enriched environments bring about enhanced brain growth that is accompanied by improved function (Greenough and Black, 1992). Again, the implication is that environmental input determines brain growth and functioning.

There are several major problems with this overall line of argument. To begin with, it is not the case that brain development more or less comes to an end after the first three years of life, and that there is no plasticity after that point. To the contrary, brain development continues right through adolescence and into early adult life; and recent research has shown that there is much more plasticity later in development than was once supposed. Even the growth of new neurons has been shown to be possible for at least some parts of the brain, in some circumstances (Eriksson et al., 1998; Gould, Reeves, Graziano, and Gross, 1999; Nelson and Bloom, 1997). Second, experience-dependent effects on brain development have mainly been evident in relation to quite gross forms of sensory input of a kind that occurs in all ordinary environments. The extrapolations from such forms of gross sensory restriction to variations in the quality of experiences within the normal range are not supported by the evidence available so far. It is doubtful whether the environmental enrichment research with laboratory rats provides an appropriate model. The findings are sound, and the research was high quality, but the findings probably say more about the extreme artificial restriction of environments in laboratory caged rats (as compared with the natural, wild environment) than anything to do with enrichment as applied to the human situation. There is no evidence so far that, for example, brain growth is enhanced by better quality conversational interchange between parents and children. Naturally, there will be neural consequences of such variations in experiences, but that is not at all the same thing as developmental programming as ordinarily understood. There must be a good deal of skepticism about the extravagant claims that experiences must occur during the first 3 years of life if they are going to have important effects on later psychological development.

Nevertheless, even accepting such cautions, the fact remains that, for whatever reason, surprisingly enduring effects have been found following institutional deprivation. A distinction must be drawn, however, between studies of grossly depriving institutions such as those seen in Romania and studies of residential group care in the much better circumstances of children's homes in most Western countries. So far as the former is concerned, the degree of social and sensory restriction undoubtedly exceeded anything that could reasonably be included in the average, expectable environment. It would not be unreasonable to suppose that this did have a lasting effect on those aspects of brain development that subserve later cognitive functioning. It is noteworthy that, although there was a complete catch-up in children's weight, the catch-up in head size was incomplete. It might be supposed that that was a consequence of malnutrition rather than psychosocial deprivation, but the head sizes of the Romanian adoptees whose weight at the time of leaving the institution was in the normal range were also below population norms at age 6 (Rutter and O'Connor, submitted). Intellectual impairment, as already noted, was not a feature of the studies of children in nondepriving children's homes in the United Kingdom.

The real query concerns the persistent effects on social relationships and on inattention/overactivity. Biological functioning ordinarily provides for normal development to take place under an extremely wide range of environmental conditions. Thus, human societies over time and across a widely divergent range of cultures have included a wide diversity of patterns of childcare (Werner, 1984). Children can cope well with caregiving by several adults, and there is no reason to suppose that the conventional nuclear family is needed, or is even necessarily optimal. Also, it has been found that children develop selective attachments even when there are gross physical handicaps such as blindness, deafness, or missing limbs (Rutter, 1981). Such disabilities may impede the development of social relationships, but they do not prevent it. The question, then, is whether a pattern of institutional care in which caregiving is provided by a very large number of ever changing adults falls outside the limits of what is needed for the development of whatever brain systems underpin the development of relationships (in the Tizard study, the average was some 50 different caregivers during the preschool years, Hodges and Tizard, 1989b). In other words, is this form of deprivation of a sufficient severity and of the necessary quality to interfere with the programming of brain development? There is, at the moment, no satisfactory answer to that question, but the possibility certainly seems to be present. In that connection, it should be added that the programming effects of early subnutrition (see O'Brien, Wheeler, and Barker, 1999) seem to involve variations in experiences within the normal range, unlike the programming effects on brain development (see previous discussion). The processes involved may be quite different.

Animal studies are potentially very informative, but so far they have not provided resolution. Studies with rodents have shown the effects of severe deprivation on brain structure and function (Robbins, Jones, and Wilkinson, 1996), and it is noteworthy that the effects seem to be somewhat different from those seen with stressful experiences (Matthews, Wilkinson, and Robbins, 1996). The evidence to date is too fragmentary for any firm conclusions, but animal studies will be needed in order to provide a better understanding of the effects of maternal deprivation on the organization of brain development.

IS MATERNAL DEPRIVATION A USEFUL CONCEPT?

There is clear continuity between the findings on early institutional rearing discussed here and the work that gave rise to the initial concept of maternal deprivation, as exemplified in Bowlby's WHO monograph. Nevertheless, as earlier reviews (Rutter, 1972, 1981, 1995b) have made clear, the term comprises rather heterogeneous phenomena. Also, the adjective *maternal* might seem to imply (wrongly) that the deprivation is solely concerned with maternal care. To the contrary, the studies reviewed in this chapter all concern deficits in parental care, not just that provided by the mother (or, even, that provided by the main caregiver). Unquestionably, the concept has been important in highlighting the consequences of variations in the quality and nature of early childcare. On the other hand, it is crucial to "unpack" the overall concept into different forms of suboptimal parenting. It is highly likely that both the effects, and the underlying mechanisms associated with them, will vary according to the nature of what is being deprived. At the very least, the evidence to date suggests that distinctions need to be drawn among, first, the effects associated with global social and sensory isolation (which predisposes to general cognitive impairment); second, caregiving that is dispersed among a large number of ever changing individuals and accompanied by a lack of social interchange and communicative interaction (which seems to predispose to difficulties in later intimate relationships and also patterns of inattention/overactivity); and, third, other forms of parental neglect, rejection, and abuse (which give rise to a broader range of somewhat different forms of psychopathology). Across all of these circumstances, however, substantial heterogeneity in outcome has always been found. Conclusions that this outcome or that outcome is inevitable are wrong. What accounts for heterogeneity in outcome is not at all well understood. That remains one of the most important challenges for the future because, if the mechanisms could be delineated, it is likely that they would have implications for both prevention and intervention.

CONCLUSIONS

In this chapter, there has been a preponderant focus on six main questions. First, does deprivation of individualized caregiving have substantial adverse effects that are environmentally mediated? A range of different rigorous research designs have provided clear evidence that there are such environmentally mediated effects. Second, are the negative effects of institutional rearing behaviorally specific? Although, as with all risk experiences, there may be a variety of sequelae, there appear to be several psychological patterns that are relatively specific. These comprise a form of "disinhibited" attachment problems and a variety of attention deficit difficulties sometimes accompanied by overactivity. In addition, if the institutional care has been characterized by severe general deprivation, but not otherwise, an unusual quasi-autistic pattern and also cognitive impairment may be evident. Third, are there age-related sensitive periods for such effects? The evidence on this issue is meager, but possibly the effects are a function of depriving experiences in the early years of life rather than in later childhood or adolescence. Fourth, to what extent is there heterogeneity in outcome after comparable adverse experience? It is abundantly clear that heterogeneity is marked, but relatively little is known on the mechanisms that mediate it. Fifth, to what extent do adverse effects persist even after high quality parental care is restored? The findings from the very few studies of severe institutional deprivation are striking in showing an interesting mix of a remarkable degree of restoration of normal psychological functioning in most instances but also quite marked, and clinically important, sequelae in a substantial minority of those suffering deprivation for at least a year or two. Sixth, what are the mechanisms by which these adverse effects are carried forward in development despite a massive improvement in rearing conditions? So far, there has been little research directed at this crucially important question but it seems that some form of developmental programming by which early experiences influence brain structure and functioning needs to be considered as a possibility. Finally, it is concluded that, although the concept of maternal deprivation comprises a rather heterogeneous range of risk experiences that probably operate in different ways, it has been useful in drawing attention to a most important phenomenon and in focusing research attention on key issues in parenting.

REFERENCES

Ainsworth, M. D. S., Blehar, M. C., Waters, E., and Wall, S. (1978). *Patterns of attachment: A psychological study of the strange situation*. Hillsdale, NJ: Lawrence Erlbaum Associates.

Ames, E. W. (1997). The development of Romanian orphanage children adopted to Canada. (*Final Report to Human Resources Development, Canada*). Available upon request from the Adoptive Families Association of British Columbia, Ste #205, 15463 104th Avenue Surrey BC V3R INO Canada.

Barker, D. J. P. (1997). Fetal nutrition and cardiovascular disease in later life. *British Medical Bulletin, 53,* 96–108.

Barker, D. J. P. (1999). Fetal programming and public health. In P. M. S. O'Brien, T. Wheeler, and D. J. P. Barker (Eds.), *Fetal programming: Influences on development and disease in later life* (pp. 3–11). London: RCOG.

Bateson, P. P. (1966). The characteristics and context of imprinting. *Biological Review, 41,* 177–211.

Bell, R. Q. (1968). A reinterpretation of the direction of effects in studies of socialization. *Psychological Review, 75,* 81–95.

Bell, R. Q., and Chapman, M. (1986). Child effects in studies using experimental or brief longitudinal approaches to socialization. *Developmental Psychology, 22,* 595–603.

Blakemore, C. (1991). Sensitive and vulnerable periods in the development of the visual system. In G. Bock and J. Whelan (Eds.), *The childhood environment and adult disease: CIBA Foundation Symposium* (pp. 129–154). Chichester, England: Wiley.

Bock, G. R., and Whelan, J. (Eds.). (1991). *The childhood environment and adult disease.* Chichester, England: Wiley.

Bornstein, M. (1987). *Sensitive periods and development.* Hillsdale, NJ: Lawrence Erlbaum Associates.

Bowlby, J. (1951). *Maternal care and mental health.* Geneva, Switzerland: World Health Organization.

Bowlby, J. (1969). *Attachment and loss: Vol. 1. Attachment.* London: Hogarth.

Bowlby, J. (1973). *Attachment and loss: Vol. 2. Separation, anxiety and anger.* London: Hogarth.

Bowlby, J. (1980). *Attachment and loss: Vol. 3. Loss, sadness and depression.* London: Hogarth.

Bradford Hill, A. (1977). *A short textbook of medical statistics,* London: Hodder and Stoughton.

Brown, G. W., and Harris, T. O. (1986). Establishing causal links: The Bedford College studies of depression. In H. Katschnig (Ed.), *Life events and psychiatric disorders: Controversial issues* (pp. 107–187). London: Cambridge University Press.

Brown, R., Hobson, R. P., Lee, A., and Stevenson, J. (1997). Are there autistic-like features in congenitally blind children? *Journal of Child Psychology and Psychiatry, 38,* 693–704.

Bruer, J. T. (1999). *The myth of the first three years.* New York: Free Press.

Cadoret, R. J., Cain, C. A., and Crowe, R. R. (1983). Evidence for gene–environment interaction in the development of adolescent antisocial behavior. *Behavior Genetics, 13,* 301–310.

Cadoret, R. J., Yates, W. R., Troughton, G. W., and Stewart, M. A. (1995). Genetic–environmental interaction in the genesis of aggressivity and conduct disorders. *Archives of General Psychiatry, 52,* 916–924.

Capron, C., and Duyme, M. (1989). Assessment of the effects of socioeconomic status on IQ in a full cross-fostering study. *Nature, 340,* 552–554.

Capron, C., and Duyme, M. (1991). Children's IQ and SES of biological and adoptive parents in a balanced cross-fostering study. *European Bulletin of Cognitive Psychology, 11,* 323–348.

Carlson, M., and Earls, F. (1997). Psychological and neuroendocrinological sequelae of early social deprivation in institutionalized children in Romania. *Annals of the New York Academy of Sciences, 807,* 419–428.

Cassidy, J., and Shaver, P. R. (Eds.). (1999). *Handbook of attachment: Theory, research, and clinical applications.* New York: Guilford.

Castle, J., Groothues, C., Bredenkamp, D., Beckett, C., O'Connor, T., Rutter, M., and the English and Romanian Adoptees (ERA) Study Team (1999). Effects of qualities of early institutional care on cognitive attainment. *American Journal of Orthopsychiatry, 69,* 424–437.

Champion, L. A., Goodall, G. M., and Rutter, M. (1995). Behavioural problems in childhood and stressors in early adult life: A 20-year follow-up of London school children. *Psychological Medicine, 25,* 231–246.

Chisholm, K. (1998). A three-year follow-up of attachment and indiscriminate friendliness in children adopted from Romanian orphanages. *Child Development, 69,* 1092–1106.

Chisholm, K., Carter, M. C., Ames, E. W., and Morison, S. J. (1995). Attachment security and indiscriminately friendly behavior in children adopted from Romanian orphanages. *Development and Psychopathology, 7,* 283–294.

Clarke, A. M., and Clarke, A. D. B. (1976). *Early experience: Myth and evidence.* London: Open Books.

Clarke, A. M., and Clarke, A. D. B. (2000). *Early experience and the life path.* London: Jessica Kingsley.

Collins, W. A., Maccoby, E. E., Steinberg, L., Hetherington, E. M., and Bornstein, M. H. (2000). Contemporary research on parenting: The case for nature and nurture. *American Psychologist, 55,* 218–232.

Crowe, R. R. (1974). An adoption study of antisocial personality. *Archives of General Psychiatry, 31,* 785–791.

De Groot, A. M. B., and Kroll, J. F. (1997). *Tutorials in bilingualism: Psycholinguistic perspectives.* Mahwah, NJ: Lawrence Erlbaum Associates.

Duyme, M., Dumaret, A.-C., and Tomkiewicz, S. (1999). How can we boost IQs of "dull children"? A late adoption study. *Proceedings of the National Academy of Sciences, 96,* 8790–8794.

Eliot, L. (2000). *What's going on in there? How the brain and mind develop in the first five years of life.* London: Allen Lane, Penguin Press.

Engfer, A., Walper, S., and Rutter, M. (1994). Individual characteristics as a force in development. In M. Rutter and D. F. Hay (Eds.), *Development through life: A handbook for clinicians* (pp. 79–111). Oxford: Blackwell Scientific.

Eriksson, P. S., Perfilieva, E., Bjork-Eriksson, T., Alborn, A. M., Nordborg, C., Peterson, D. A., and Gage, F. H. (1998). Neurogenesis in the adult human hippocampus. *Nature Medicine, 4,* 1313–1317.

Fergusson, D. M., Horwood, L. J., and Lynskey, M. T. (1992). Family change, parental discord and early offending. *Journal of Child Psychology and Psychiatry, 33,* 1059–1075.

Fisher, L., Ames, E. W., Chisholm, K., and Savoie, L. (1997). Problems reported by parents of Romanian orphans adopted to British Columbia. *International Journal of Behavioural Development, 20,* 67–82.

Flavell, J. H., and Miller, P. H. (1998). Social cognition. In: W. Damon, D. Kuhn, and R. S. Siegler (Eds.), *Handbook of child psychology: Vol. 2. Cognition, perception, and language* (5th ed., pp. 851–898). Wiley.

Ge, X., Conger, R. D., Cadoret, R. J., Neiderhiser, J. M., Yates, W., Troughton, E., and Stewart, M. A. (1996). The developmental interface between nature and nurture: A mutual influence model of child antisocial behavior and parenting. *Developmental Psychology, 32,* 574–589.

Goldberg, S. (1997). Attachment and childhood behavior problems in normal, at risk, and clinical samples. In L. Atkinson and K. J. Zucker (Eds.), *Attachment and Psychopathology.* New York: Guilford.

Gould, E., Reeves, A. J., Graziano, M. S., and Gross, C. G. (1999). Neurogenesis in the neocortex of adult primates. *Science, 286,* 548–552.

Greenough, W. T., and Black, J. E. (1992). Induction of brain structure by experience: Substrates for cognitive development. In M. R. Gunnar and C. M. Nelson (Eds.), *Developmental behavior neuroscience* (Vol. 24, pp. 155–200). Hillsdale, NJ: Lawrence Erlbaum Associates.

Greenough, W. T., Black, J. E., and Wallace, C. S. (1987). Experience and brain development. *Child Development, 58,* 539–559.

Harlow, H. F., and Harlow, M. K. (1969). Effects of various mother–infant relationships on rhesus monkey behaviours. In B. M. Foss (Ed.), *Determinants of infant behaviour* (pp. 15–36). London: Methuen.

Harris, J. R. (1998). *The Nurture Assumption: Why children turn out the way they do.* London: Bloomsbury.

Hennessey, J. W., and Levine, S. (1979). Stress, arousal, and the pituitary–adrenal system: A psychoendocrine hypothesis. In J. M. Sprague and A. N. Epstein (Eds.), *Progress in psychobiology and physiological psychology* (pp. 79–111). New York: Academic Press.

Hinde, R. A., and McGinnis, L. (1977). Some factors influencing the effect of temporary mother–infant separation: Some experiments with rhesus monkeys. *Psychological Medicine, 7,* 197–212.

Hobson, R. P., Brown, R., Minter, M. E., and Lee, A. (1997). "Autism" revisited: The case of congenital blindness. In V. Lewis, and G. M. Collis (Eds.), *Blindness and psychological development in young children* (pp. 99–115). Leicester, England: British Psychological Society.

Hodges, J., and Tizard, B. (1989a). IQ and behavioural adjustment of ex-institutional adolescents. *Journal of Child Psychology and Psychiatry, 30,* 53–75.

Hodges, J., and Tizard, B. (1989b). Social and family relationships of ex-institutional adolescents. *Journal of Child Psychology and Psychiatry, 30,* 77–97.

Hubel, D. H., and Wiesel, T. N. (1970). The period of susceptibility to the physiological effects of unilateral eye closure in kittens. *Journal of Physiology, 206,* 419–436.

Jewett, J. (1998). *The long-term outcomes of early institutional care.* Unpublished doctoral thesis, University of London.

Jockin, V., McGue, M., and Lykken, D. T. (1996). Personality and divorce: A genetic analysis. *Journal of Personality and Social Psychology, 71,* 288–299.

Kagan, J. (1980). Perspectives on continuity. In O. G. Brim and J. Kagan (Eds.), *Constancy and change in human development* (pp. 26–74). Cambridge, MA: Harvard University Press.

Kendler, K. S. (1996). Parenting: A genetic-epidemiologic perspective. *American Journal of Psychiatry, 153,* 11–20.

Kendler, K. S., Kessler, R. C., Walters, E. E., MacLean, C., Neale, M. C., Heath, A. C., and Eaves, L. J. (1995). Stressful life events, genetic liability, and onset of an episode of major depression in women. *American Journal of Psychiatry, 152,* 833–842.

Kendler, K. S., Neale, M. C., Prescott, C. A., Kessler, R. C., Heath, A. C., Corey, L. A., and Eaves, L. J. (1996). Childhood parental loss and alcoholism in women: A causal analysis using a twin-family design. *Psychological Medicine, 26,* 79–95.

Kreppner, J., O'Connor, T., Rutter, M., and the ERA Study Team. (in press). *Can inattention/overactivity be an institutional deprivation disorder?* Journal of Abnormal Child Psychology.

Kuhl, P. K. (1994). Learning and representation in speech and language. *Current Biology, 4,* 812–822.

Kuhl, P. K., Andruski, J. E., Chistovich, I. A., Chistovich, L. A., Kozhevnikova, E. V., Ryskina, V. L., Stolyarova, E. I., Sundberg, U., and Lacerda, F. (1997). Cross-language analysis of phonetic units in language addressed to infants. *Science, 277,* 684–686.

Lehrman, D. S. (1965). Interaction between internal and external environments in the regulation of the reproductive cycle of the ring dove. In F. A. Beach (Ed.), *Sex and behavior* (pp. 355–380). New York: Wiley.

Levine, S. (1982). Comparative and psychobiological perspectives on development. In W. A. Collins (Ed.), *Minnesota Symposia on Child Psychology: Vol. 15. The concept of development* (pp. 29–53). Hillsdale, NJ: Lawrence Erlbaum Associates.

Luthar, S. S., Cicchetti, D., and Becker, B. (2000). The construct of resilience: A critical evaluation and guidelines for future work. *Child Development, 71,* 543–562.

Lytton, H. (1990). Child and parent effects in boys' conduct disorder: A reinterpretation. *Developmental Psychology, 26,* 683–697.

Mandler, J. M. (1998). Representation. In W. Damon, D. Kuhn, and R. S. Siegler (Eds.), *Handbook of child psychology: Vol. 2. Cognition, perception, and language* (5th ed., pp. 255–308). New York: Wiley.

Marcovitch, S., Goldberg, S., Gold, A., Washington, L., Wasson, C., Krekewich, K., and Handley-Derry, M. (1997). Determinants of behavioural problems in Romanian children adopted in Ontario. *International Journal of Behavioural Development, 20,* 17–32.

Matthews, K., Wilkinson, L. S., and Robbins, T. W. (1996). Repeated maternal separation of preweanling rats attenuates behavioral responses to primary and conditioned incentives in adulthood. *Physiology and Behavior, 59,* 99–107.

Maughan, B., Collishaw, S., and Pickles, A. (1998). School achievement and adult qualifications among adoptees: A longitudinal study. *Journal of Child Psychology and Psychiatry, 39,* 669–685.

Meyer, J. M., Rutter, M., Silberg, J. L., Maes, H. H., Simonoff, E., Shillady, L. L., Pickles, A., Hewitt, J. K., and Eaves, L. J. (2000). Familial aggregation for conduct disorder symptomatology: The role of genes, marital discord and family adaptability. *Psychological Medicine, 30,* 759–774.

Nelson, C. A., and Bloom, F. E. (1997). Child development and neuroscience. *Child Development, 68*, 970–987.

O'Brien, P. M. S., Wheeler, T., and Barker, D. J. P. (Eds.). (1999). *Fetal programming: Influences on development and disease in later life* (pp. 3–11). London: RCOG.

O'Connor, T. G., Deater-Deckard, K., Fulker, D., Rutter, M., and Plomin, R. (1998). Genotype–environment correlations in late childhood and early adolescence: Antisocial behavioral problems and coercive parenting. *Developmental Psychology, 34*, 970–981.

O'Connor, T. G., Marvin, R. S., Rutter, M., Olrick, J., Britner, P. A., and the (ERA) Study Team. (submitted). *Child–parent attachment following early institutional deprivation.*

O'Connor, T. G., Rutter, M., and the ERA Study Team. (2000a). Attachment disorder behavior following early severe deprivation: Extension and longitudinal follow-up. *Journal of the American Academy of Child and Adolescent Psychiatry, 39*, 703–712.

O'Connor, T., Rutter, M., Beckett, C., Keaveney, L. Kreppner, J. M., and the ERA Study Team. (2000b). The effects of global severe privation on cognitive competence: Extension and longitudinal follow-up. *Child Development, 71*, 376–390.

Pike, A., McGuire, S., Hetherington, E. M., Reiss, D., and Plomin, R. (1996). Family environment and adolescent depressive symptoms and antisocial behavior: A multivariate genetic analysis. *Developmental Psychology, 32*, 590–603.

Plomin, R. (1994). *Genetics and experience: The interplay between nature and nurture.* Thousand Oaks, CA: Sage.

Plomin, R., and Bergeman, C. S. (1991). The nature of nurture: Genetic influence on "environmental" measures. *Behavioral and Brain Sciences, 14*, 373–427.

Plomin, R., and Daniels, D. (1987). Why are children in the same family so different from one another? *Behavioral and Brain Sciences, 10*, 1–15.

Plomin, R., DeFries, J. C., McClearn, G. E., and Rutter, M. (1997). *Behavioral Genetics* (3rd ed.). New York: Freeman.

Quinton, D., and Rutter, M. (1988). *Parenting breakdown: The making and breaking of inter-generational links.* Aldershot, England: Avebury.

Ramey, S. L., and Ramey, C. T. (2000). Early childhood experiences and developmental competence. In S. Danziger and J. Waldfogel (Eds.), *Securing the future: Investing in children from birth to college* (pp. 122–150). New York: Russell Sage Foundation.

Reiss, D., Neiderhiser, J. M., Hetherington, E. M., and Plomin, R. (2000). *The relationship code: Deciphering genetic and social influences on adolescent development.* Cambridge, MA: Harvard University Press.

Robbins, T. W., Jones, G. H., and Wilkinson, L. S. (1996). Behavioural and neurochemical effects of early social deprivation in the rat. *Journal of Psychopharmacology, 10*, 39–47.

Robins, L. (1966). *Deviant children grown up: A sociological and psychiatric study of sociopathic personality.* Baltimore: Williams and Wilkins.

Rodgers, B., and Pryor, J. (1998). *Divorce and separation: The outcomes for children.* York, England: Joseph Rowntree Foundation.

Rowe, D. C. (1994). *The limits of family influence: Genes, experience, and behavior.* New York: Guilford.

Roy, P., Rutter, M., and Pickles, A. (2000). Institutional care: Risk from family background or pattern of rearing? *Journal of Child Psychology and Psychiatry, 41*, 139–149.

Roy, P., Rutter, M., and Pickles, A. (submitted). *Institutional care: Associations between overactivity and a lack of selectivity in attachment relationships.*

Rushton, A., and Minnis, H. (in press). Residential and foster family care. In M. Rutter and E. Taylor (Eds.), *Child and adolescent psychiatry* (4th ed.). Oxford, England: Blackwell Scientific.

Rutter, M. (1971). Parent–child separation: Psychological effects on the children. *Journal of Child Psychology and Psychiatry, 12*, 233–260.

Rutter, M. (1972). *Maternal deprivation reassessed.* Harmondsworth, England: Penguin.

Rutter, M. (1981). *Maternal deprivation reassessed* (2nd ed.). Harmondsworth, England: Penguin.

Rutter, M. (1989). Pathways from childhood to adult life. *Journal of Child Psychology and Psychiatry, 30*, 23–51.

Rutter, M. (1995a). Clinical implications of attachment concepts: retrospect and prospect. *Journal of Child Psychology and Psychiatry, 36*, 549–571.

Rutter, M. (1995b). Maternal deprivation. In M. H. Bornstein (Ed.), *Handbook of parenting: Vol. 4. Applied and practical parenting* (pp. 3–31). Mahwah NJ: Lawrence Erlbaum Associates.

Rutter, M. (1996). Transitions and turning points in developmental psychopathology: As applied to the age span between childhood and mid-adulthood. *International Journal of Behavioral Development, 19*, 603–626.

Rutter, M. (1997). Comorbidity: Concepts, claims and choices. *Criminal Behaviour and Mental Health, 7*, 265–285.

Rutter, M. (1999). Resilience concepts and findings: Implications for family therapy. *Journal of Family Therapy, 21*, 119–144.

Rutter, M. (2000a). Psychosocial influences: Critiques, findings, and research needs. *Development and Psychopathology, 12*, 375–405.

Rutter, M. (2000b). Resilience reconsidered: Conceptual considerations, empirical findings, and policy implications. In J. P. Shonkoff and S. J. Meisels (Eds.), *Handbook of early childhood intervention* (2nd ed., pp. 651–682). New York: Cambridge University Press.

Rutter, M., Andersen-Wood, L., Beckett, C., Bredenkamp, D., Castle, J., Groothues, C., Kreppner, J., Keaveney, L., Lord, C., O'Connor, T. G., and the ERA Study Team. (1999). Quasi-autistic patterns following severe early global privation. *Journal of Child Psychology and Psychiatry, 40*, 537–549.

Rutter, M., Dunn, J., Plomin, R., Simonoff, E., Pickles, A., Maughan, B., Ormel, J., Meyer, J., and Eaves, L. (1997). Integrating nature and nurture: Implications of person–environment correlations and interactions for developmental psychology. *Development and Psychopathology, 9*, 335–364.

Rutter, M., Kreppner, J. K., O'Connor, T. G. , and the ERA Research Team. (2001-b). Specificity and heterogeneity in children's responses to profound privation. *British Journal of Psychiatry, 179*, 97–103.

Rutter, M., Maughan, B., Pickles, A., and Simonoff, E. (1998a). Retrospective recall recalled. In R. B. Cairns, L. R. Bergman, and J. Kagan (Eds.), *Methods and models for studying the individual. Essays in honor of Marian Radke-Yarrow* (pp. 219–242). Thousand Oaks, CA: Sage.

Rutter, M., and O'Connor, T. (submitted). *Are there biological programming effects for psychological development?*

Rutter, M., O'Connor, T., Beckett, C., Castle, J., Croft, C., Groothues, C., Kreppner, J., and the ERA Study Team. (2000). Recovery and deficit following profound early deprivation. In P. Selman (Ed.), *Intercountry adoption: Developments, trends and perspectives* (pp. 89–107). London: British Agencies for Adoption and Fostering.

Rutter, M., Pickles, A., Murray, R., and Eaves, L. (2001-a). Testing hypotheses on specific environmental causal effects on behavior. *Psychological Bulletin, 127*, 291–324.

Rutter, M., and Quinton, D. (1984). Parental psychiatric disorder: Effects on children. *Psychological Medicine, 14*, 853–880.

Rutter, M., Roy, P., and Kreppner, J. (in press). Institutional care as a risk factor for inattention/overactivity. In S. Sandberg (Ed.), *Hyperactivity disorder* (2nd ed.).

Rutter, M., and Rutter, M. (1993). *Developing minds: Challenge and continuity across the lifespan.* Harmondsworth, England: Penguin Books; New York: Basic Books.

Rutter, M., Silberg, J., O'Connor, T., and Simonoff, E. (1999a). Genetics and child psychiatry: I. Advances in quantitative and molecular genetics. *Journal of Child Psychology and Psychiatry, 40*, 3–18.

Rutter, M., Silberg, J., O'Connor, T., and Simonoff, E. (1999b). Gentics and child psychiatry: II. Empirical research findings. *Journal of Child Psychology and Psychiatry, 40*, 19–55.

Rutter, M., Silberg, J., and Simonoff, E. (1993). Whither behavioral genetics? A developmental psychopathological perspective. In R. Plomin and G. E. McClearn (Eds.), *Nature, nurture, and psychology* (pp. 433–456). Washington, DC: American Psychological Association.

Rutter, M., and Sroufe, L. A. (2000). Developmental psychopathology: Concepts and challenges. *Development and Psychopathology, 12*, 265–296.

Rutter, M., and the ERA Research Team. (1998b). Developmental catch-up, and deficit, following adoption after severe global early privation. *Journal of Child Psychology and Psychiatry, 39*, 465–476.

Sandberg, S., and Rutter, M. (in press). The role of acute life stresses. In M. Rutter and E. Taylor (Eds.), *Child and adolescent psychiatry* (4th ed.). Oxford, England: Blackwell Scientific.

Scarr, S. (1992). Developmental theories for the 1990s: Development and individual differences. *Child Development, 63*, 1–19.

Scarr, S. (1997). Behavior-genetic and socialization theories of intelligence: Truth and reconciliation. In R. J. Sternberg and E. L. Grigorenko (Eds.), *Intelligence, heredity, and environment* (pp. 3–41). Cambridge, England: Cambridge University Press.

Schiff, M., and Lewontin, R. (1986). *Education and class: The irrelevance of IQ genetic studies.* Oxford, England: Clarendon.

Silberg, J., Rutter, M. Neale, M., and Eaves, L. (2001). Genetic moderation of environmental risk for depression and anxiety in adolescent girls. *British Journal of Psychiatry, 179*, 116–121.

Shonkoff, J. P., and Phillips, D. A. (2000). *From neurons to neighborhoods: The science of early childhood development.* Washington, DC: National Academy Press.

Spohr, L., and Steinhausen, C. (Eds.). (1996). *Alcohol, pregnancy and the developing child.* Cambridge, England: Cambridge University Press.

Stratton, K., Howe, C., and Battaglia, F. (1996). *Fetal alcohol syndrome: Diagnosis, epidemiology, prevention, and treatment.* Washington, DC: National Academy Press.

Suomi, S. J., Harlow, H. F., and Novak, M. A. (1974). Reversal of social deficits produced by isolation rearing in monkeys. *Journal of Human Evolution, 3*, 527–534.

Tennant, C. (1988). Parental loss in childhood. *Archives of General Psychiatry, 45*, 1045–1050.

Thompson, R. A. (1998). Early sociopersonality development. In W. Damon and N. Eisenberg (Eds.), *Handbook of child psychology: Vol. 3. Social, emotional and personality development* (5th ed.). New York and Chichester, England: Wiley.

Vorria, P., Rutter, M., Pickles, A., Wolkind, S., and Hobsbaum, A. (1998a). A comparative study of Greek children in long-term residential group care and in two-parent families: (I) Social, emotional and behavioural differences. *Journal of Child Psychology and Psychiatry, 39*, 225–236.

Vorria, P., Rutter, M., Pickles, A., Wolkind, S., and Hobsbaum, A. (1998b). A comparative study of Greek children in long-term residential group care and in two-parent families: (II) Possible mediating mechanisms. *Journal of Child Psychology and Psychiatry, 39*, 234–245.

Wachs, T. D. (1992). *The nature of nurture.* Newbury Park, CA: Sage.

Wade, T. D., and Kendler, K. S. (2000). The genetic epidemiology of parental discipline. *Psychological Medicine, 30,* 1303–1313.

Werner, E. E. (1984). *Child care: Kith, kin and hired hands.* Baltimore: University Park.

Wolkind, S. N. (1974). The components of "affectionless psychopathology" in institutionalized children. *Journal of Child Psychology and Psychiatry, 15,* 215–220.

Zeanah, C. H. (2000). Disturbances of attachment in young children adopted from institutions. *Developmental and Behavioral Pediatrics, 21,* 230–236.

Zeanah, C. H., Boris, N. W., and Larrieu, J. A. (1997). Infant development and developmental risk: A review of the past 10 years. *Journal of the American Academy of Child and Adolescent Psychiatry, 36,* 165–178.

9

Marital Relationships and Parenting

John H. Grych
Marquette University

INTRODUCTION

Jim and Jean were a couple in their mid 30s who sought help at a university mental health clinic because their 8-year-old son, Peter, was becoming increasingly defiant and aggressive. The therapists concluded that differences in Jim and Jean's parenting styles were contributing to their son's behavior problems: Jean, who took primarily responsibility for disciplining Peter, tended to be permissive, whereas Jim was quite strict. Jean thought that Jim was too hard on Peter and would often soften the consequences that Jim had levied. The therapists began meeting regularly with the couple to improve their ability to work together in parenting Peter. However, after several sessions little change in their behavior had occurred. It became apparent that tension in their marriage made it difficult for them to parent effectively together. Their relationship lacked emotional closeness, and attempts to address their differences often resulted in angry fights. The focus of therapy changed to their marriage, and Jean and Jim worked for months to address feelings of hurt and disappointment that they had experienced in their relationship and to change destructive patterns of relating to each other. Over time, they began to communicate more effectively and to support each other emotionally, and only then did they begin to exhibit the parenting skills and strategies that had been discussed early in therapy.

Stories like Jim and Jean's are common in clinical practice. Systems-oriented family therapists have long argued that marital and parent–child relationships are interdependent (e.g., Haley, 1976; Minuchin, 1974), but prior to the 1980s there were few attempts to examine this hypothesis empirically. Since that time, increasing attention has focused on understanding how marriage and parenting are related (for a review, see Erel and Burman, 1995), and this research has supported the general proposition that the quality of the marital relationship is associated with the quality of parent–child relationships. However, both marital quality and parenting are multifaceted constructs, and we know relatively little about which dimensions of marital functioning are related to which aspects of parenting. Moreover, documenting the existence of this association is only a first step toward understanding how marital relationships and parenting affect each other. Although a number of mechanisms have been proposed to explain how marital functioning influences parenting, few studies have directly tested those mechanisms. Describing the processes by which marriage affects parenting has important conceptual and applied significance because identifying the factors that guide effective parenting is essential for developing programs to enhance parenting quality (see Smith, Pevere, and Lesesne, in Vol. 4 of this *Handbook*) and for helping couples who are struggling with marital and parenting difficulties.

This chapter examines the theoretical and empirical underpinnings of research on the relation between marriage and parenting. Although parenting experiences undoubtedly affect marital functioning as well, the chapter focuses on understanding how marital relationships may support or undermine parenting. After a brief overview of the development of research in this area, the conceptual perspectives that have informed this work are described and the body of empirical findings linking marital quality with different aspects of parenting, including behavior, affect, cognition, and coparenting processes, are reviewed. The chapter closes by considering critical issues that need to be investigated if we are to more fully understand the links between marriage and parenting.

THE ASSOCIATION BETWEEN MARITAL QUALITY AND PARENTING

Research on the links between marriage and parenting began in earnest in the early 1980s. In 1981, Belsky highlighted the lack of attention paid in psychological research to the way that relationships within the family influence each other. Noting that the study of marriage historically had been the province of sociologists whereas psychologists focused on the relationship between mother and child (also see Aldous, 1977), Belsky (1981) argued that understanding child development required understanding the broader family system and called for psychologists to study how marriage affects parenting, how parenting affects marriage, and how children affect both parenting and marriage.

The initial empirical studies in this area examined links between marriage and parenting during the transition to parenthood, arguing that marital functioning may be particularly important when spouses first take on the parenting role. Cross-sectional studies documented an association between marital satisfaction and parents' behaviors and attitudes, fathers' involvement in caregiving, and the quality of parent–infant attachment (e.g., Goldberg and Easterbrooks, 1984; Pederson, Anderson, and Cain, 1980), and several longitudinal studies were launched that supported a causal link between marital quality and these parenting dimensions (e.g., Belsky Youngblade, Rovine, and Volling, 1991; Cowan and Cowan, 1992; Cox, Owen, Lewis, and Henderson, 1989). Researchers interested in associations between marriage and parenting then broadened the scope of investigation to involve older children and adolescents and other aspects of parenting, including affect, disciplinary practices, and teaching (Brody, Pillegrini, and Sigel, 1986; Deal, Halverson, and Wampler, 1989; Stoneman, Brody, and Burke, 1989).

Relations between marriage and parenting also have been explored in work on marital discord and on coparenting. One pathway by which interparental conflict is proposed to affect children is by undermining the quality of parent–child relationships or the consistency of parental discipline practices (e.g., Cox, Paley, and Harter, 2001; Fincham, Grych, and Osborne, 1994). Several studies have shown that parenting partially mediates the association between interparental conflict and child adjustment, although it does not wholly account for this association (e.g., Fauber, Forehand, Thomas, and Wierson, 1990; Harold and Conger, 1997; Harold, Fincham, Osborne, and Conger, 1997; Osborne and Fincham, 1996). Coparenting refers to the process by which spouses support each other in the parenting role and share the responsibilities and tasks of childrearing (e.g., McHale, 1995; McHale, Khazan, Rotman, DeCourcey and McConnell, in Vol. 3 of this *Handbook*; Minuchin, 1974), and thus sits squarely at the interface of marriage and parenting. Investigations of coparenting have generated data concerning ways that the marital relationship may impact parents' interactions with their children and have expanded the focus of analysis from dyadic to triadic interactions involving children and both parents.

The empirical research on links between marriage and parenting was reviewed by Erel and Burman (1995), who conducted a meta-analysis of 68 studies examining associations between marital quality and parenting, nearly all published between 1979 and 1992. Marital quality was assessed in a variety of ways across studies, including both self-reported and observed measures of marital satisfaction, overt conflict, and the strength of the marital alliance. Parenting similarly was assessed with diverse measures, including global measures of quality, consistency between parents, satisfaction with parenting, covert control of children (e.g., protectiveness, use of child for emotional support), harshness of discipline, and within-parent consistency. The average effect size for the association between measures of marriage and parenting was 0.46, a medium-size effect according to Cohen's (1977) criteria, but ranged from −0.52 to 2.30 across studies (Erel and Burman, 1995). Thus, most studies supported a spillover effect in which positive (or negative) affect and behavior flows from one relationship to the other. However, a number of studies reported a negative association between the constructs, supporting a compensatory model in which parents invest more in their relationship with their children when there are problems in the marriage or, conversely, are less focused on their children when marital satisfaction is high.

In an effort to understand the variability in effect sizes across studies, Erel and Burman (1995) attempted to identify conditions under which the nature of the association between marriage and parenting differed. They tested 13 factors, including methodological, demographic, and conceptual variables, as potential moderators of the relation between marriage and parenting. A moderator changes the magnitude or direction of the association between two other variables (Baron and Kenny, 1986); in the context of the meta-analysis, moderation would be demonstrated if different categories of a proposed moderator (e.g., boys vs. girls) produced homogenous effect sizes that differed significantly from each other (Erel and Burman, 1995). For example, children's age would act as a moderator if studies demonstrated a consistent positive relation between marital quality and parenting in families with school-age children, but no association between these constructs in families of adolescents. One factor of particular interest in Erel and Burman's analysis was gender, because several studies have reported stronger associations between marriage and parenting for men than women (e.g., Belsky et al., 1991; Cowan and Cowan, 1992; Goldberg and Easterbrooks, 1984), with some suggesting that the father–daughter relationship is particularly vulnerable to the effects of marital discord (e.g., Belsky et al., 1991; Stoneman et al., 1989).

Although differences in effect sizes were found for several factors, including parent and child gender, none of the proposed moderators produced different *and* homogeneous effects. For example, across the 68 studies, the average effect size for the association between marital quality and parenting was 0.51 for fathers and 0.37 for mothers; however, the sizes of the effects varied significantly across studies for both mothers and fathers, and so it cannot be concluded that fathers exhibited a reliably stronger association than mothers. The failure to identify significant moderators means that the factors that influence the strength and direction of the association between marriage and parenting are not well understood. It should be noted that the potential moderators identified by Erel and Burman (1995) were examined singly, and so their analysis cannot address whether combinations of these factors may produce significantly different effect sizes. In addition, the number of studies representing some of these variables was relatively small, limiting the power to detect moderating effects.

Thus, although there is ample evidence that marriage and parenting are related, precisely how they affect each other is a question that remains unanswered. A number of hypotheses have been proposed to explain this association, and the next section of the chapter reviews the theoretical perspectives that have been most influential in guiding thinking and research in this area.

RESEARCH ON MARRIAGE AND PARENTING:
CONCEPTUAL FOUNDATION

Understanding the process by which marital functioning influences parenting depends on the development of conceptual models that describe pathways linking particular aspects of marital functioning with particular aspects of parenting. Most models propose that there is a positive association, or spillover, between the two constructs, but differ in the processes believed to account for this effect and the degree to which the hypothesized processes are based on broader theoretical paradigms.

Family Systems Theory

Family systems theory is the primary theoretical perspective underlying much of the research on links between marriage and parenting. Family systems theory became prominent in psychology in the 1960s and 1970s, primarily through the work of family therapists who were attempting to understand the origins of child and family dysfunction and formulate new models for clinical intervention. This theoretical approach was based on ideas drawn from general systems theory (e.g., von Bertallanfy, 1950) and cybernetics (e.g., Weiner, 1950), both of which describe how the relations between elements of a system define and maintain the system. Although different variations of family systems theory have been developed, they share certain core principles (Cox and Paley, 1997; Minuchin, 1985). First, the family is viewed as an organized whole comprised of interdependent elements or subsystems (individuals and relationships between individuals). As such, it has properties that are not reducible to its constituent parts. Most notably, the family system has a hierarchy denoting the power relations among the members and boundaries that demarcate and define the "rules" for interactions between subsystems. Second, causal relations among the elements of the system are circular rather than linear; each element both affects and is affected by the other elements. Third, stability, or homeostasis, is maintained through negative feedback, which serves to "correct" deviations from families' usual way of functioning. Finally, families are open systems that are influenced by events occurring in their environment. Families continually change as they adapt to these outside forces, as well as to internal forces such as the development of their individual members.

These basic principles, particularly the idea of circular causality, began to influence the empirical study of the family in the early 1980s. Since that time, the systemic perspective has become widespread in family and child research, although many studies adopting this approach use the theory more as a philosophical backdrop than a source of specific hypotheses. In fact, all but one of the hypotheses described in this section are consistent with the systemic principle that family relationships are interdependent; however, only those discussed in the next paragraph explicitly reflect hypotheses derived specifically from family systems theory.

One legacy of translating systems theory through family therapy is that pathological rather than adaptive family processes have been emphasized. Processes such as triangulation, detouring, scapegoating, formation of cross-generational coalitions, and boundary violations have been proposed to explain how tension or difficulties in the marriage can undermine the parent–child relationship. The term *triangulation* has been used somewhat differently by different theorists (see Buchanan and Waizenhofer, 2001; Westerman, 1987), but essentially refers to a process whereby conflict between parents is diverted or avoided by involving the child (Minuchin, 1974; Westerman, 1987). This may take a number of different forms. Detouring, or scapegoating, occurs when couples avoid confronting marital difficulties by focusing on problems exhibited by the child, such as misbehavior or illness. As a result, parents may become hostile toward or overinvolved with the child. Alternatively, a cross-generational coalition may be formed in which a parent and a child become allied against the other parent. This process disrupts the boundary between the parent and child subsystems and may create tension between the child and the parent who is excluded from the coalition, and overinvolvement or enmeshment between the allied parent and child.

Margolin, Oliver, and Medina (2001) argued that boundary dissolution is at the root of all of these processes, stating that "marital conflict is a risk factor for children because marital power struggles are accompanied by an intensification of either intimacy, rejection, or both, in the parent–child relationship" (p. 11). When difficulties in the marriage undermine the marital subsystem, the boundaries that define the marriage and separate it from other relationships become weakened, and conflict spreads from the marriage to parent–child relationships. What is common to these processes is that parents' inability to resolve tension in the marriage changes the nature of parent–child relationships (Wilson and Gottman, in Vol. 4 of this *Handbook*). Even if children's involvement helps to resolve a parental disagreement, it is likely to be maladaptive because it prevents parents from resolving their differences and may lead parents to direct hostility or aggression toward the child (Emery, 1989).

Although systems theory provides a clear conceptual basis for understanding how marriage affects parenting, relatively few studies have directly tested these hypotheses. One of the first such studies was conducted by Christensen and Margolin (1988), who examined boundary violations in a small sample of families, half reporting both marital distress and child behavior problems. The families participated in two structured interactions and reported daily on the occurrence of conflict in the family over a 2-week period. Christensen and Margolin (1988) found that distressed families were more likely to exhibit cross-generational coalitions and a tendency for conflict in the marriage to spread to other family relationships.

Kerig (1995) assessed systemic processes with a creative self-report measure of family structure that asked family members to use a set of circles to portray visually the nature of the relationships in the family. These family configurations were classified as cohesive, detouring, triangulated, or disengaged. She found that triangulated families, who were characterized by cross-generational coalitions between parents and children, reported more marital conflict and lower marital satisfaction. In contrast, detouring families did not differ in marital satisfaction from families describing themselves as cohesive, supporting the family systems hypothesis that detouring is functional for the marriage because it detracts attention from marital difficulties by focusing on the child. The maladaptive nature of this pattern was illustrated by the findings that children in detouring families had higher levels of internalizing problems and felt more responsibility for their parents' quarrels than did children in cohesive and triangulated families.

Finally, Lindahl and her colleagues (Lindahl, Clements, and Markman, 1997) examined systemic processes in a study assessing family interaction prior to and 5 years after the birth of a child. Mothers and fathers reporting higher levels of current marital conflict were more likely to triangulate children and involve them in cross-generational coalitions during a conflict resolution task. In addition, fathers exhibiting more negative escalation during marital conflict 5 years earlier were more likely to triangulate their child in the family discussion task. In contrast, greater cohesion was seen in families reporting greater marital satisfaction at both time points.

Systems theory also suggests two reasons why marital and parenting quality may be inversely related. First, experiencing a lack of affection or intimacy in the marital relationship may lead parents to meet their emotional needs by seeking a closer relationship with their child. Alternatively, a problematic relationship between a child and one parent may lead the other parent to become more involved with the child in an effort to compensate for the troubled relationship. Studies reporting a negative association between marriage and parenting provide support for each of these possibilities. For example, Engfer (1988) found that mothers with conflictual marriages reported greater emotional involvement with their infants at 4 months and were more protective of their infants at 4 and 18 months. However, the qualities captured by the measures of these constructs are not necessarily indicative of good parenting. High scores on the measure of emotional involvement reflected inappropriate expectations about receiving love, comfort, and affection from the child, and high scores on protectiveness reflected excessive anxiety about the health and well-being of their child. Moreover, overinvolved mothers were viewed as less sensitive toward their newborns by observers, suggesting that this type of involvement reflected mothers' emotional needs rather than their children's.

In contrast, other studies suggest that maternal overinvolvement may occur in response to difficulties in the father–child relationship rather than mothers' own unmet emotional needs. Belsky and his colleagues (1991) followed 100 families from the third trimester of pregnancy until their children were 36 months of age. Different associations between marriage and parenting were found for fathers and mothers. Fathers whose marital satisfaction remained stable or improved over the 3 years of the study exhibited more positive, faciliative behavior with children, whereas fathers experiencing a decrease in marital satisfaction were more intrusive during an interaction with their child. In contrast, for mothers, declines in marital satisfaction were related to more positive and faciliative behavior with their child. Moreover, in almost all of the families in which fathers were highly intrusive and mothers highly positive toward their child, one or both spouses showed a decline in marital satisfaction over tune (Belsky et al., 1991). Although it is possible that mothers' involvement with their child fuels marital dissatisfaction and stimulates intrusive fathering, these data suggest that mothers' involvement reflects an attempt to compensate for a problematic father–child relationship.

Stress and Coping Perspective

A second conceptual approach to understanding the association between marriage and parenting focuses on the marital relationship as a source of stress or support for the parenting role (e.g., Belsky, 1984; Rutter, 1988). Discord in the marriage can be a source of subjective distress that saps parental resources, energy, and attention, and thus interferes with parents' capacity to be attuned to and responsive toward their children (Belsky, 1984). For example, parents preoccupied with worries about the future of their marriage may be less able to focus on their children's needs and desires. Stress also elicits negative emotions, which may lead to impaired, harsh, or even abusive parenting (see Dix, 1991). The role of the marital relationship as a source of support was highlighted in Belsky's (1984) model of the determinants of effective parenting. In that model, parenting quality is conceptualized as the product of three kinds of forces: individual parent characteristics (e.g., personality), child factors (e.g., temperament), and contextual sources of stress and support, which include the marital relationship.

The marital relationship can support parenting in several ways (Belsky, 1984). Spouses provide emotional support (e.g., love and acceptance), instrumental support (e.g., help with parenting tasks and advice), and social expectations about appropriate parental behavior. For example, a spouse may learn more effective discipline strategies from a partner, and experiencing warmth and caring in the marital relationship may facilitate the expression of similar qualities with their children. Easterbrooks and Emde (1988) suggest that the role of marriage as a support may be more salient at certain challenging times, such as the transition to parenthood, the first few months of toddlerhood, and adolescence.

This approach also suggests that marital relationships may have indirect or buffering effects on parenting in addition to direct effects. An indirect effect occurs when interactions between spouses affect some aspect of individual functioning, which then influences parenting. For example, feeling valued by their spouse may increase parents' sense of self-worth and well-being, which in turn may help them to be empathic and warm toward their children (Belsky, 1984). Alternatively, stress in the marriage could undermine parents' psychological health, which in turn may compromise parenting. Buffering entails a process in which support in the marriage reduces the impact of other sources of stress on parenting (e.g., Crockenberg and McCluskey, 1986; Simons et al., 1992). For example, Crockenberg and McCluskey (1986) found that the adverse impact of having a child with a difficult temperament was decreased when parents reported higher levels of spousal support. Similarly, Cowan and Cowan (1992) reported that parenting difficulties exhibited by mothers with insecure models of parent–child attachment did not occur when these women were married to secure men.

The stress and coping approach, particularly Belsky's model, has been influential in raising awareness of the range of factors that impinge on parenting, but very few studies have explicitly tested hypotheses examining how support in the marriage affects parenting. Most studies in this area employ fairly global measures of marital satisfaction or conflict that provide little information about the quality or quantity of support experienced in the marriage. Even though ratings of marital satisfaction can be considered an index of the degree of warmth and acceptance experienced in the relationship, they are not specific enough to test hypotheses about either the quality or quantity of support experienced in the marriage. Only a handful of studies provides data that assess support more directly, and these focus on emotional support.

Cox and her colleagues (1989) studied 38 married couples in the third trimester and again when their children were 3 months of age. Their measure of marital quality, which was based on interviews with the couples and observations of their interactions, tapped the extent to which spouses shared ideas and activities, expressed affection and appreciation for each other, and confided in each other. For fathers, greater marital closeness and support predicted more positive attitudes toward their infant and the parenting role but was not related to parenting behavior. For mothers, greater marital closeness was related to greater warmth and sensitivity in parenting and more positive attitudes in mothers with girls but not boys. Cox and her colleagues concluded that supportive marital relationships allow parents to meet their emotional needs, which in turn enables them to be more sensitive and responsive toward their children (also see Engfer, 1988; Pederson, 1982). Stress in the parenting role was directly assessed by Grych and Clark (1999), who examined fathers' report of stress in three aspects of parenting: balancing parenting with other roles and responsibilities, feeling competent as a parent, and experiencing reinforcement from their infant. Marital quality was assessed with a questionnaire that tapped both rewards experienced in the marriage (e.g., good communication and effective conflict resolution) and costs such as fighting and being criticized. When infants were 4 months of age, higher marital quality was associated with less stress resulting from role strain, and at 12 months, fathers reporting greater marital satisfaction experienced less stress on all three parenting dimensions. The associations between marital quality and parenting stress were significantly stronger at 12 than 4 months. Thus, the limited data suggest that, at least for fathers, a positive and supportive marital relationship appears to help parents cope with the stress associated with the transition to parenthood.

Affective Spillover

As noted above, the term *spillover* has been used in a broad sense to refer to the idea that the positivity or negativity of the marriage leads to a similar quality in parent–child relationships. This definition does not distinguish between theoretically distinct mechanisms predicting positive associations between marriage and parenting, and so spillover will refer more narrowly here to a process in which the affect expressed in the marriage influences expression of affect in the parent–child relationship (see also Margolin et al., 2001). Easterbrooks and Emde (1988) argued that parents are better able to tune into their children's needs when they are emotionally open and available, and emotional availability, in turn, is fostered by warmth and caring in the marriage. Similarly, experiencing anger and frustration in the marriage may make a parent hostile or punitive when they interact with their child (Fincham, Grych, and Osborne, 1994; Margolin et al., 2001).

To test this hypothesis, affective experience or expression must be assessed in both relationships, and although a number of studies have assessed parents' warmth or hostility toward their children, most rely on global measures of martial satisfaction rather than more specific indices of affective experiences. An exception is Easterbrooks and Emde's (1988) study of marriage and parenting during the transition to parenthood. They assessed self-reported emotional experiences in both marital and parent–child relationships and observed parents' affective expression in marital and parent–child interactions in the laboratory. They found that observed marital harmony was associated with positive affect sharing, physical affection, and expressions of approval while interacting with their children. Parents who reported greater marital satisfaction also reported experiencing less negative affect in their relationships with their children. However, self-reported satisfaction was not related to mothers' or fathers' emotional expression in the lab, suggesting that measures of subjective experience and observed affect may be tapping different constructs. These findings also raise the possibility that method variance may have inflated the associations between similar types of measures. This is a particular concern for self-report methods because response biases (e.g., social desirability and yay- or nay-saying) tend to increase correlations among questionnaire measures.

In sum, although the affective spillover hypothesis is an intuitively appealing explanation for a positive association between marriage and parenting, it has not received the kinds of empirical tests needed to confirm or disconfirm it. Studies employing more precise measures of emotional expression and experience in both marital and parent–child relationships are needed to investigate this hypothesis; such research will be facilitated by the development of conceptual models proposing specific processes by which emotion in one relationship may affect emotion in the other relationship. Moreover, in the absence of research that examines causal paths between emotion in marital and parental relationships, the possibility that associations between these constructs reflect a third variable, such as negative affectivity, cannot be discounted (see Common Factor Hypothesis, discussed later).

Withdrawal

Another hypothesis proposed to account for the spillover effect is that unhappily married parents may withdraw from their children. They may be too preoccupied with or exhausted by marital problems to be fully engaged with their children, and, consequently, parenting might become lax or overly permissive, or their children may feel rejected (e.g., Osborne and Fincham, 1996). This pattern may be particularly characteristic of men, who are more likely to withdraw from their spouse when marital conflict is high (Christensen and Heavey, 1990). Furthermore, because the parenting role is less well defined for men than for women, there may be fewer barriers to men disengaging from parental responsibilities (see Parke, in Vol. 3 of this *Handbook*). Interestingly, however, studies examining this hypothesis have found that men's withdrawal from their wives is not associated with withdrawal from their children. Rather, withdrawal in the parent–child relationship has been related to greater interparental hostility (Lindahl and Malik, 1999; Lindahl et al., 1997), and spouses' withdrawal during marital conflict has been associated with greater hostility and intrusiveness with their children (e.g., Katz and Gottman, 1996; Lindahl and Malik, 1999). In fact, one study (Lindahl et al., 1997) found that fathers who were more withdrawn from their wives showed *greater* involvement with their children. Thus, although disengagement from children may be associated with marital problems, it does not appear to reflect a general style of withdrawing from family interactions.

Common Factor Hypothesis

A final hypothesis for the link between marriage and parenting is that this association does not reflect a causal relation between these constructs but rather a shared association with a third variable, such as personality or stable relational styles, that explains adults' behavior in both contexts (Belsky and Pensky, 1988; Caspi and Elder, 1988; Engfer, 1988; Rutter, 1988). Belsky's (1984; Belsky and Barends, in Vol. 3 of this *Handbook*) model places particular emphasis on parents' personality as a determinant of parenting because it affects their marital relationship, social networks, and work experiences in addition to directly influencing their parenting. Heinicke (1984; in Vol. 3 of this *Handbook*) identified three personality characteristics that may be particularly important for influencing the quality of an individual's parenting: adaptation-competence, capacity for positive sustained relationships, and self-development. The capacity for developing positive relationships, defined as empathy and positive mutuality expressed by the parent in ongoing relationships (Heinicke, 1995), would seem to be especially important for maintaining a positive marital relationship. Caspi and Elder (1988) argued that learned interactional styles, rather than personality traits, may account for consistencies in marital and parent–child relations. They proposed that adults with "aversive personalities," marked by quarrelsome, difficult, and negativistic behaviors, are likely to have conflictual relationships with both spouses and children. These individuals often select partners with similar characteristics and elicit problematic interactions with others, and through exposure to discordant marital and parent–child relationships their children are likely to develop similar interactional styles that maintain the pattern in successive generations.

Empirical findings support the importance of personal characteristics as a determinant of both marital and parent–child relationships. Caspi and Elder's (1988) analysis of the Berkeley growth study found evidence for a multigenerational pattern in which negativistic interpersonal behaviors are transmitted from parents to children. Women with aversive personalities had more discordant marriages and were more likely to lose control of their feelings and actions as adults in parental situations. Within a given generation, the data suggested that spouses' personality "drives" the quality of marital and parent–child interactions, but a different picture emerged for understanding the associations among these constructs across generations. Examining personality and patterns of interaction across four generations, Caspi and Elder (1988, p. 229) concluded that "from generation to generation, unstable personalities are reproduced through a socialization environment characterized by marital tension and nonoptimal parenting. Unstable adults are significantly more likely to establish a conflicted relational context in which parenting difficulties are likely to result in children's problem behaviors."

Engfer (1988) also found support for personality as a predictor of marital and parent–child relationships. Maternal personality characteristics were only weakly related to marital conflict, communication, and affection 4 months after delivery, but predicted marital functioning consistently at 43 months. In particular, neuroticism, "depressiveness," and composure showed correlations with the marriage indices ranging from 0.31 to 0.59. This is consistent with research showing that neuroticism is a reliable of predictor of diminishing marital satisfaction and divorce (Karney and Bradbury, 1995).

The common factor hypothesis also points to the potential role of biological or genetic factors in understanding links between marriage and parenting. Many of the characteristics associated with problems in close relationships (e.g., neuroticism and antisocial tendencies) are heritable to some degree and may interact with life experiences to increase or decrease the likelihood of developing difficulties in both marital and parent–child relationships. There has been little theoretical or empirical work investigating this issue, which may provide another lens for understanding the continuity of relationship difficulties over time (for an exception, see Rutter, 1994).

The mechanisms summarized above describe a variety of pathways by which marital relations can influence the quality of parenting. Some support has been provided for each, but relatively few studies have included measures of marriage and parenting that are specific enough to explicitly test these proposed processes (Katz and Gottman, 1996). Most investigations offer descriptive data concerning links between diverse aspects of marital and parental functioning that may be consistent with more than one of these hypotheses. In the next section, the literature describing the nature of associations between marital relationships and parenting is reviewed.

RESEARCH ON MARRIAGE AND PARENTING:
EMPIRICAL FOUNDATION

Both marriage and parenting are multifaceted constructs, and there is wide variation across studies in which aspects of marital functioning are examined in relation to which aspects of parenting, and in how each of these constructs is measured. Consequently, relatively few studies provide data on associations between the same indices of marriage and parenting. To organize this literature and place it in a meaningful conceptual context, the dimensions of parenting considered to be most important for fostering healthy child adjustment are identified, and then research investigating relations between marital functioning and these dimensions is reviewed.

The "Ingredients" of Effective Parenting

Despite changes in the demands placed on parents as children develop, there is considerable consensus among theorists regarding the key "ingredients" of competent or effective parenting in childhood and adolescence. For example, Belsky, Robins, and Gamble (1984, p. 254) wrote:

> Across childhood, it is parenting that is *sensitively* attuned to children's capabilities and to the developmental tasks they face that promotes the kinds of developmental outcomes thought important: emotional security, behavioral independence, social competence, and intellectual achievement. In infancy, this sensitivity translates into being able to read babies' often subtle cues and to respond appropriately to their needs within relatively brief periods of time.... In childhood, sensitivity means continuing the warmth and affection provided in the early years, but increasing the demands for age-appropriate behavior. Parents must be willing and able to direct their children's behavior and activities without squelching their developing independence and industry.

Dix (1991, p. 11) touched on similar themes: "Parents of socially competent children tend to be responsive, to express warmth and affection, to reason and communicate openly, to make appropriate demands for mature behavior, to establish and enforce consistent rules, and to avoid arbitrary, restrictive, or punitive control."

Competent parenting thus involves certain classes of behavior: sensitivity and responsivity to children's needs; expression of affection and acceptance; and exertion of appropriate control or discipline, which involves encouraging increasingly mature and autonomous behavior in addition to setting limits, providing consequences for behavior, and monitoring (see Bornstein, in Vol. 1 of this *Handbook*; Teti, in Vol. 4 of this *Handbook*). Parental behavior, in turn, is guided by affective and cognitive processes. Parenting is an emotional experience, at turns joyous and frustrating, and how parents regulate and express their affect is critical for their capacity to care for their children (see Dix, 1991). Similarly, cognition plays a central role in parenting: to be responsive to their children, parents must accurately perceive their needs and know how to respond to them, and reasonable discipline requires parents to understand children's capacities, have appropriate developmental expectations, and make appropriate attributions for their behavior (Crouter and Head, in Vol. 3 of this *Handbook*). However, there have been few attempts to develop conceptual models that link parents' behavior, affect, and cognition.

Dix (1991) developed one such model. He argued that affect plays a central role in organizing parenting behavior, and that cognition is essential for the experience and regulation of affect. Dix described three sets of affective processes that shape parenting. First, *activation processes* determine what emotion will occur and when. Cognition is a fundamental part of this process because the emotion a person experiences in a situation depends on their appraisal of the likely outcomes, obstacles, and supports present in the situation (Dix, 1991). Once affect is elicited, *engagement processes* guide individuals' responses to events; they "prepare people to perceive and evaluate particular features of events (cognition), activate motives to seek particular outcomes (motivation), communicate to others the person's affective stance (expressive behavior) and prepare response tendencies likely to be needed" (p. 5). Finally, *regulation processes* help individuals to control and cope with emotions that threaten to disrupt or undermine their functioning. There is not space here to describe Dix's model in more detail; what is most notable for the present chapter is that the model underscores the idea that competent parenting arises from the integration of emotional and cognitive processes.

The next section reviews research on links between marital functioning and the quality of parenting, focusing on representative studies of the aspects of parenting most closely associated with healthy child development: sensitivity and responsivity, warmth and acceptance, and appropriate control or discipline. Although the expression of warmth may often be a sign of sensitive, responsive parenting, in this review sensitivity and responsivity will be defined as parents' ability to accurately perceive and appropriately react to their children's signals, and warmth and acceptance will refer to the expression of positive affect and positive regard toward children. In addition, even though few studies have directly examined the cognitive processes that underlie parenting, given their importance for understanding parents' emotions and behavior research on links between marital relationships and parental cognition also will be reviewed. Finally, studies expanding the focus from the individual parent to the coparenting relationship will be examined. When there are two parents in a household, they must coordinate their parenting goals and methods to provide a sense of stability and consistency for their children. Coparenting processes are a relatively recent topic of investigation, but have the potential to shed light on ways that spouses may support or undermine each other in the parenting role (McHale, Khazan, Rotman, DeCourcey, and McConnell, in Vol. 3 of this *Handbook*).

The review will emphasize studies employing independent measures of marriage and parenting to reduce the impact of method variance on the strength of the association between these constructs. However, independence of methods is difficult to achieve in studies of cognition because virtually all such studies use self-report measures to assess constructs such as beliefs and attributions. This section also considers the extent to which associations between marriage and parenting are consistent for men and women. Even though parent gender was not found to be a significant moderator of the association between marriage and parenting in Erel and Burman's (1995) meta-analysis, narrative reviews (e.g., Parke, 1995) consistently document differences in findings for mothers and fathers, and consequently the effects of gender are still in question.

Parental Sensitivity and Responsivity

Bowlby (1980) argued that parents' capacity to tune into their children's signals and provide for their needs were fundamental for the development of secure parent–child attachment. As noted above, parenting theorists similarly emphasize the importance of these behaviors for promoting healthy adaptation throughout childhood, and several studies examining the links between marriage and parenting have investigated these dimensions of parenting.

For example, Cox and her colleagues (1989) studied 38, middle-income married couples in the third trimester of pregnancy and again when their child was 3 months old. They interviewed the couples and observed them interacting, and videotaped each parent interacting with their infant in the home. The measure of marital quality employed in the study tapped two dimensions, closeness and intimacy of communication, which were combined to form a single scale. Parenting was assessed with a measure that combined attitudes about the infant and the level of warmth, sensitivity, and responsiveness exhibited by each parent during the interaction. Cox and her colleagues (1989) found that after accounting for parents' mental health, marital closeness predicted fathers' attitudes toward parenting but not their parenting behavior. Greater marital closeness and intimacy predicted warm, sensitive responding by mothers, especially those with daughters.

Other studies have supported an association between these parenting dimensions and indices of marital functioning. Engfer (1988) found that maternal sensitivity was associated with measures of marital communication, mutual disclosure, and lower levels of conflict shortly after birth and at 8 months, and Heineke (1995) reported that husbands' and wives' marital adjustment prior to the birth of their child predicted parent responsiveness to infant needs at 1 and 48 months, even after accounting for parents' psychological functioning. In contrast, the extent to which parents stimulated their infant cognitively and verbally was not predicted by marital quality (Heineke, 1995), suggesting that marital functioning does not affect all aspects of parenting similarly.

Two studies also examined parents' intrusiveness in their interactions with their infants, which reflects a lack of sensitivity to the child's cues. Belsky and his colleagues (1991) found that fathers who reported a decline in love for their spouse and growing ambivalence about the marriage from the third trimester to 3 years of age were more negative and intrusive during free play with their children but not during a teaching task, and their children were more negative toward them in both situations. No associations were found for mothers, suggesting that they may be better able to maintain boundaries between their spousal and parental roles. Similarly, Katz and Gottman (1996) observed both marital and triadic interactions in 56 families with 4- to 5-year-old children and found that greater marital hostility was associated with higher levels of fathers' intrusiveness and lower levels of positive involvement with the child during the triadic interaction. Fathers' withdrawal during the marital interaction was correlated with mothers' being more intrusive and critical and less involved with their children.

Most studies examining relations between marital quality and parents' sensitivity or responsiveness have involved couples with infants or toddlers. An exception is Brody, Pillegrini and Sigel's (1986) examination of families with $5^{1}/_{2}$- to $7^{1}/_{2}$-year-old children. As noted earlier, these parenting qualities continue to be important as children develop, although their expression may change. In the study, parents and children were videotaped in two contexts: reading a book together and engaged in a teaching task in which parents helped their children to do origami. Marital quality was assessed with a questionnaire inquiring about the frequency of disagreement about a variety of topics. A compensatory effect was found for mothers: Those in more conflictual marriages were more engaged with their children during the teaching task, asked more questions, provided more information and positive feedback, were less intrusive than more maritally satisfied mothers, and were more engaged and less intrusive than maritally dissatisfied fathers.

There also have been several studies investigating links between marital relationships and parent–child attachment (also see Cummings and Cummings, in Vol. 5 of this *Handbook*). Because attachment quality is presumed to reflect the degree of sensitivity and responsiveness exhibited by parents, these studies also provide insights into the influence of marriage on parenting. Goldberg and Easterbrooks (1984) examined 75 families with a toddler and assessed marital quality with self-report and observational measures, parenting attitudes and behavior, and attachment with the Strange Situation paradigm. Couples were classified into three groups based on their scores on the Dyadic Adjustment Scale (Spanier, 1976). The low-satisfaction group had more children with insecure attachments and fewer with secure attachments than expected by chance, and the couples reporting the highest level of marital quality included more children with secure and fewer insecure attachments than expected by chance. Observed parental sensitivity was correlated, albeit fairly weakly, with self-reports of marital quality for mothers, but not fathers, whereas observed marital harmony was correlated, again fairly weakly, with fathers' but not mothers' observed sensitivity. Similarly, Howes and Markman (1989) found that parents reporting higher levels of marital satisfaction and communication quality and lower levels of interparental conflict were more likely to have children with secure attachments. However, in contrast to studies showing stronger relations between marriage and parenting for fathers, Isabella and Belsky (1985) reported that decreasing marital satisfaction was related to insecure attachment between infants and their mothers, but not their fathers.

In sum, most studies have found that parents in satisfied, low-conflict marriages are more sensitive and responsive to their children and more likely to have children with secure parent–child attachments. The majority of these studies were conducted with very young children, however, and so it is not clear whether marital relationships predict these dimensions in older children and adolescents. In fact, the one study including older children found support for a compensatory effect, at least for mothers (Brody et al., 1986). There is little consistency across studies in documenting the presence or nature of parent gender effects. Some studies report links between marriage and parenting sensitivity and attachment in mothers and fathers (Goldberg and Easterbrooks, 1984; Heinecke, 1995; Howes and Markman, 1989; Owen and Cox, 1997), others find significant results only for fathers (Belsky et al., 1991; Volling and Belsky, 1991), and yet others report this association only for mothers (Cox et al., 1989; Engfer, 1988; Isabella and Belsky, 1985).

Parental Warmth and Acceptance

A second quality considered to be central to competent parenting is the expression of warmth and acceptance. One of the earliest and most influential descriptions of parenting included warmth as one of two primary dimensions that define parenting style (Baumrind, 1971). Accordingly, there have been numerous studies assessing parental warmth and acceptance (e.g., Cowan and Cowan,

1992; Engfer, 1988; Vandewater and Lansford, 1998) as well as studies examining their opposites, rejection and hostility (e.g., Fauber et al., 1990; Harold and Conger, 1997; Lindahl and Malik, 1999). However, very few studies have gone beyond measuring these qualities to investigate other aspects of emotional experience, such as parents' ability to manage frustration and negative affect.

As with sensitivity and responsivity, most of the studies of parental warmth focus on parents of young children. For example, Cowan and Cowan (1992) followed 96 couples from the third trimester of pregnancy until their children were $3\frac{1}{2}$ years old. They reported that a decline in marital satisfaction from pregnancy to 18 months was related to more angry, competitive, and cold marital interactions when the child was $3\frac{1}{2}$; this conflictual style of marital interaction in turn was related to both mothers' and fathers' expressing less warmth toward their child, and distressed fathers exhibiting greater irritability and anger toward their children, especially their daughters.

Easterbrooks and Emde (1988) assessed both affect as expressed by parents during a family interaction and parents' self-report of their experiences of affect in the parenting role. Parents reporting higher levels of marital satisfaction also reported that they experienced less negative affect in parent–child interactions, an association that was stronger at 18 months than at 6 months. Correlations between marital adjustment and positive emotions were nonsignificant at 6 months and marginally significant at 18 months. However, self-reported marital satisfaction was not related to mothers' or fathers' observed hedonic tone during parent–child interaction in the laboratory. Observed marital harmony was marginally associated with parents exhibiting more approval and physical affection and more positive affect sharing (mutual gaze and smiling displayed by parent and child).

Other studies have looked at the other side of warmth and acceptance, examining rejection or hostility in parent–child relationships. For example, Lindahl and Malik (1999) observed 113 Latin American, European American, and biethnic families with a 7- to 11-year-old son during couple and family interaction tasks. Couples were classified into one of three conflict styles based on their behavior during a problem-solving interaction: harmonious, destructive, and disengaged. Fathers from couples exhibiting destructive conflict were more coercive, rejecting, withdrawn, and less supportive when interacting with their sons than fathers from harmonious or disengaged families. These associations were moderated by marital distress: distressed fathers showed stronger associations between conflict styles and their behavior with their children than did nondistressed fathers. Fewer differences were found for mothers: European American mothers from marriages exhibiting destructive conflict were more withdrawn with their sons, an association not found in Latino mothers. Contrary to the hypothesis that withdrawal in the marriage would be associated with withdrawal in parent–child relationships, Lindahl and Malik (1999) found that disengaged parents did not show higher levels of withdrawal when interacting with their children (see also Lindahl et al., 1997).

Lindahl and Malik (1999) also classified couples according to the distribution of power in the marriage: traditional (male dominated), balanced, and power struggle. They found that mothers from male dominated homes were more emotionally supportive of their sons than mothers from marriages characterized by power struggles, but only when these mothers were not distressed. This may reflect a role division in traditional households in which mothers take primary responsibility for providing emotional nurturance for the family and fathers are responsible for instrumental and financial support in the family. Fathers from male-dominated marriages were more coercive toward their sons, but only if they were distressed.

Relations between marriage and rejection in parents' relationships with adolescents also have been examined. Harold and Conger (1997) conducted a 1-year prospective study with 451 rural families who had a child in seventh grade at the time of the first assessment. Reports of marital conflict and parent–child relationships were obtained from the adolescents and their parents, and observers rated hostility exhibited during couple and parent–child interactions. The measure of hostility combined behavior (e.g., criticized, shouted or yelled at, or argued) and affect (e.g., got angry at him or her). Harold and Conger (1997) found that observer and parent reports of marital conflict reliably predicted parental hostility toward the adolescent 1 year later. Moreover, adolescents' perceptions of parental hostility mediated the association between conflict and internalizing symptoms for boys and externalizing symptoms for boys and girls. That is, their data supported the hypothesis that inter-parental conflict leads adolescents to view their parents as hostile, which in turn leads to adjustment problems. Harold and colleagues (1997) replicated these findings and, in addition, showed that adolescents' perceptions of marital conflict were related to increased hostility in their relationships with both their mothers and their fathers. Similarly, Fauber and his colleagues (1990) found that higher levels of interparental conflict were associated with increased parental rejection, an association that was stronger in divorced than intact families. It may be that divorced parents embroiled in conflict are particularly likely to withdraw from or perhaps express anger at their children (see Hetherington and Stanley-Hagan, in Vol. 3 of this *Handbook*).

These studies of parental warmth or rejection consistently show that greater satisfaction and intimacy in the marriage is associated with greater warmth expressed toward children, whereas higher levels of marital conflict predict greater hostility or rejection in parent–child relationships. There also is evidence that observational and self-report measures of parental harmony and warmth yield different findings, with each type of measure correlating more highly with like measures and often failing to correlate with different measures of the same constructs. Thus, it is not clear to what extent findings regarding marital quality and parental warmth may be inflated by method variance. This is less of a problem for the studies linking interparental conflict and parental hostility, which have tended to combine different methods of assessing the constructs. Although it would appear that these findings provide strong support for the affective spillover hypothesis, firm conclusions about the reasons why marital quality is related to parental warmth and rejection cannot be drawn because these studies did not assess possible third variables, such as interpersonal style.

Parental Control and Discipline

Exercising appropriate control over children's activities is another fundamental aspect of effective parenting and represents the second of Baumrind's (1971) two-dimensional scheme for defining parenting styles. Control involves setting limits and using rewards and punishment judiciously, but also providing structure for children when it is needed and fostering autonomy. There has been relatively little research examining whether marital quality predicts this aspect of parenting, however. This section focuses on parenting or discipline styles, including the occurrence of aggression or abuse in parent–child relationships.

Fauber and his colleagues (1990) examined the association between interparental conflict, parenting styles, and adjustment in a sample of 97 adolescents, half from intact and half from divorced families. Three dimensions of parenting were assessed through adolescents' self-report and a video-taped interaction between adolescents and their mothers: acceptance and rejection, which reflected the degree of closeness and warmth in the relationship; psychological control, which reflected the induction of guilt, shame, and anxiety as a method of discipline; and lax control, which reflected the degree to which parents monitored and regulated their adolescents' conduct. The results of a path analysis with the intact families indicated that higher levels of interparental conflict were related to higher levels of rejection and use of psychological control, but did not predict lax control. In the divorced sample, conflict was related to all three dimensions of parenting, with the strongest associations found for rejection.

Cowan and Cowan (1992) assessed parenting style in terms of Baumrind's (1971) categories of authoritative (high warmth, high control), authoritarian (low warmth, high control), permissive (high warmth, low control), and disengaged (low warmth, low control). They found that maritally dissatisfied mothers and fathers were more authoritarian and less authoritative with children, especially when their daughters asserted themselves. They also provided evidence for the importance of parents' well being for shaping both marital and parent–child relationships. Parents reporting depressive symptoms were more likely to engage in marital conflict, and conflict, in turn, was associated with less authoritative parenting. However, Cowan and Cowan (1992) also reported that a warm and supportive marital relationship could reduce the negative effects of depression on parenting, supporting the hypothesis drawn from the stress and coping perspective that marital support can serve as a buffer when parents' well-being is undermined.

Stoneman and her colleagues (Stoneman et al., 1989) examined several dimensions of discipline, including parents' beliefs about the acceptability of different discipline strategies, within-parent consistency in enforcing limits, and similarity between parents in attitudes about discipline. Their sample included 47 parents of 4½- to 6½-year-old children, all from middle- to upper middle–income families. Parents reporting higher levels of marital satisfaction and lower levels of conflict tended to express more similar ideas about appropriate disciplinary strategies. Fathers who were in happier, less conflicted marriages also were more consistent in their enforcement of limits and use of consequences, especially with their daughters. In contrast, mothers did not exhibit significant relations between marital quality and consistency. Finally, attitudes about particular discipline strategies were related less reliably to the measures of marital satisfaction. Parents of boys were more likely to endorse authoritarian methods of discipline when they were happier in their marriage, and happily married fathers of girls were more likely to support rational approaches to discipline. Fathers who reported more conflict in their marriage were less likely to report using authoritarian methods, rational control, and nonpunitive discipline with their sons, and mothers in more conflictual marriages were less likely to endorse authoritarian methods of discipline with their daughters. The meaning of these apparently discrepant findings is not clear, but the small sample sizes that resulted when the families were divided according to both child and parent gender may have undermined the reliability of the results.

Finally, there is a significant body of research that examines the relations between spousal abuse and child maltreatment (see Azar, in Vol. 4 of this *Handbook*). Appel and Holden (1998) reviewed this literature and found that the strength of the association between these types of abuse varied across studies, from 0.28 to 0.56. They concluded that the cooccurrence of spousal and child abuse is greater when levels of violence in either relationship are higher: Samples drawn from battered women's shelters or documented cases of child maltreatment find that, on average, nearly half of the families reporting one type of violence also report the other, whereas studies surveying families in the community suggest that 5.6% to 11% of couples reporting physical aggression in the marriage also acknowledge physical aggression in their relationships with their children.

Cognitions About Parenting

Work on the role of parental cognition in understanding the association between marital and parenting relationships lags behind research on behavior and affect, both conceptually and empirically. Although the study of cognition in marriage is well developed, it has proceeded relatively independently of research on cognition in parenthood (Brody, Arias, and Fincham, 1996). Investigations of the relations between marriage and parental cognitions reflect two different traditions in studying cognition. One set of studies has focused on assessing parental attitudes toward their children or childrearing in general, under the assumption that attitudes guide behavior. Empirical support for this assumption, as Holden and Buck (in Vol. 3 of this *Handbook*) point out, is inconsistent at best.

Several studies of the transition to parenthood assessed new parents' attitudes toward and perceptions of their children and the parenting role. Generally, these studies have found that happily married couples tend to perceive their children and parenthood in a more positive light (Cox et al., 1989) and view their children as temperamentally easier, less aggravating, and less of an interference (Easterbrooks and Emde, 1988; Goldberg and Easterbrooks, 1984). Some gender differences also have been reported (e.g., Easterbrooks and Emde, 1988), but these findings are not consistent. In contrast, Kurdek (1996, 1998) found that satisfaction with parenting was not strongly related to satisfaction with the marriage. He followed a sample of newlyweds over the first 8 years of their marriage, and those who became parents during that time completed measures of both types of satisfaction on a yearly basis. Concurrent correlations between marital and parenting satisfaction were only significant in half of the analyses and change in marital satisfaction over time was not related to change in parenting satisfaction. Kurdek (1996) concluded that the links between these constructs are weak because many of the factors that influence marital quality and parenting satisfaction are independent. For example, whether spouses are happy with their marriage depends a great deal on their partner and relatively little on their child, whereas their partner may have a minimal effect on parents' satisfaction with their child. However, this explanation does not account for the possibility of indirect effects; that is, marital (or parenting) satisfaction may increase adults' sense of well-being, which in turn may affect their satisfaction with other aspects of their lives.

The second approach to studying cognition focuses on cognitive structures and processes involved in the construction of meaning about parenting and child behavior. These types of studies have focused primarily on parental beliefs and attributions for children's behavior (see Bugental and Happaney, in Vol. 3 of this *Handbook*). The rationale for investigating parental beliefs was articulated by McGillicuddy-DeLisi and Sigel (1995, p. 349):

> Beliefs enable adults to organize their world in a psychologically consistent manner, make predictions, perceive similarities, and relate new experiences to past ones. . . . In addition, beliefs provide parents with a means for setting parental priorities, evaluating success in parenting as well as a means of preserving self-efficacy. . . . Beliefs can serve as a source of parental teaching and management behaviors, influencing the child's intellectual and personal-social development.

Individuals' beliefs about parenting arise from a variety of interactions over the life course, but may be shaped most prominently by their experiences of being parented in childhood. Interactions with a spouse or partner also can influence parental beliefs, and consequently studying relations with marital functioning is particularly relevant. Similarly, attributions for children's behavior may be extremely important for guiding parents' emotional and behavioral responses to child misbehavior (e.g., Bugental, 1992; Dix and Grusec, 1985; Dix et al., 1986), and may be influenced by the quality of the marital relationship. For example, Bugental (1992) proposed that abusive parents have "threat-oriented schemas" that make them prone to attribute high levels of control to their children and low levels of control to themselves when problems arise in interactions with their children. If parents perceive themselves as unable to exert control in caregiving situations they are unlikely to be effective, and viewing their children as blameworthy in these situations is likely to lead to punitive behavior (also see Daggett, O'Brien, Zanolli, and Petyon, 2000). Marital support may increase parents' sense of competence and worth, and thus may influence the way they perceive themselves in the parenting role (Belsky, 1984). Rubin and Mills (1992) note that attributions for child behavior are a product, in part, of parents' knowledge of child development, and parents can serve as an important source of information about appropriate expectations for child behavior.

This approach to parental cognition is represented by a study conducted by Brody and colleagues (1996), who examined the idea that parents' attributions for marital interaction also may affect their behavior with their children. Earlier, Fincham and Grych (1991) had found that distressed couples made similar attributions for spousal and child behavior, but did not examine whether these attributions were related to parents' behavior toward their child. Brody and his colleagues used structural equation modeling to examine associations between husbands' and wives' attributions and parent–child interaction in a sample of 170 families with a 10- to 12-year-old child. Significant direct paths were found between attributions made for marital interactions and harsh parenting for mothers and fathers, and for involved parenting by mothers. The direct effects of attributions on parent–child relationships were stronger for fathers than for mothers, leading Brody et al. (1996) to conclude that wives may be better able to separate their views of the marriage and child than are fathers, who may be characterized by a more general attributional style that is applied to all family interactions.

The relation between marriage and parenting cognitions has not been explored in detail, but existing data largely support the hypothesis that happily married parents hold more positive attitudes and perceptions of their children. Much work needs to be done to explore the mechanisms by which marital interaction may influence cognitions, and to expand understanding of the kinds of cognitive structures and processes that are most relevant for guiding parenting.

Coparenting

Most of the research on marriage and parenting has examined each parent independently, an approach which neglects the fact that many parents have partners. Successful childrearing requires parents to mesh their goals, styles, and strategies to provide consistent and coherent expectations and consequences for their children. Spouses' abilities to communicate, collaborate, and resolve disagreements play an important role in their ability to coparent effectively, and thus marital and coparenting relationships are tightly interwoven. They are not entirely synonymous, however, because the coparenting subsystem involves a third member, the child, who also affects the nature of the interactions that occur.

Although not framed as studies of coparenting per se, studies assessing parental agreement about childrearing issues tap an important aspect of coparenting. These studies generally have found that greater marital satisfaction is related to higher levels of accord on childrearing issues. For example, Deal and his colleagues (1989) found that the level of positivity and avoidance observed during a marital interaction was related to parental agreement about childrearing. However, self-reported marital satisfaction was not related to parental agreement.

McHale (1995) studied the association between marital quality and parents' mutual support and mutual involvement in parenting in a sample of 47 married couples with an $8\frac{1}{2}$- or 11-month-old child. Marital quality and six dimensions of coparenting (intimacy of communication, leadership/power, autonomy, warmth, problem solving, and conflict) were coded from an interview with the parents, but factor analyses showed that the coparenting dimensions all loaded on a single factor. Triadic interactions involving the parents and child also were coded and yielded three dimensions: hostility and competitiveness, family harmony, and discrepancy in parents' involvement and warmth with the child. McHale (1995) reported that self-reports of marital quality were weakly associated with observed coparenting in the triadic interaction; only one of the three correlations was significant for mothers, and none was significant for fathers. In contrast, higher levels of observed marital distress were associated with more hostility and competitiveness between parents of boys even after accounting for level of marital distress, and with greater discrepancies in parents' involvement with girls. McHale (1995) also examined power balance in the marriage and found that nonegalitarian power predicted parenting discrepancy after controlling for marital distress. Similarly, Katz and Gottman (1996) reported that parents in more conflictual marriages reported less cooperation and more disagreement and competitiveness in the coparenting relationship.

Floyd, Gilliom, and Costigan (1998) proposed that marital quality would affect parenting through the coparenting relationship, and tested this hypothesis in a longitudinal study with 79 families that had a child with mental retardation. They found that they could distinguish marital quality and coparenting empirically, and that the parenting alliance (coparenting) mediated the effects of marital quality on parenting experiences. That is, the data supported the idea that marital functioning has an influence on parenting through the coparenting relationship. In addition, negative child behavior directed at fathers increased more over time when fathers reported both marital dissatisfaction and a poor parenting alliance. Finally, Floyd and his colleagues tested reciprocal effects of parenting on the marriage but found little evidence that difficulties in parent–child interaction led to decreased marital quality or weakened the coparenting alliance.

Research on coparenting is promising because it affords an opportunity to provide more fine-tuned analysis of the aspects of the marital relationship most pertinent to the parenting role and because it focuses attention on triadic interaction. However, it is important to be clear about how coparenting is similar to and different from other dimensions of marital functioning so that studies do not merely replace "old" constructs, such as marital conflict, with new ones. For example, demonstrating that parental conflict about childrearing predicts parenting difficulties may simply reflect the well-documented finding that marital conflict is related to diminished parenting unless the coparenting measure predicts parenting above and beyond a more general measure of marital discord.

Limitations of Research on Marriage and Parenting

The empirical literature investigating links between marital relationships and parenting has thoroughly documented that these constructs are related. However, this research has a number of characteristics that limit its ability to illuminate *how* marriage may affect parenting. First, the majority of these studies have used global measures that provide little information about which aspects of marital functioning are associated with which aspects of parenting. This is particularly problematic in the assessment of the marital relationship: Of the 68 studies reviewed by Erel and Burman (1995), 57 used a global measure of marital satisfaction. Second, most studies have tested fairly simple, direct pathways between these constructs, examining, for example, whether marital satisfaction is correlated with harsh parenting. Although many of these studies acknowledge the reciprocal nature of marital and parent–child relationships, little attention has been paid to the effects of marriage on parenting, and rarely has the interplay between multiple subsystems been evaluated. In part, this state of affairs reflects the fact that testing hypotheses involving circular causation or the interactions among more than two individuals is quite complex methodologically. It has only been in the last decade or so that the sophisticated statistical techniques needed to test systemic hypotheses and have become widely available (Osborne and Fincham, 1996). Similarly, methods for assessing triadic interactions have become more well developed in recent years (see Kerig and Lindahl, 2000). Moreover, few studies have tested multivariate models. Because parenting is influenced by a number of factors, many of which may also affect the marital relationship (e.g., stress and parental personality), it is important to examine the relation between marriage and parenting when other variables are considered. Finally, although theoretical rationales have been offered for expecting both spillover and compensatory effects, there is no clear basis for predicting when each type of effect may occur. Most studies show that there is a positive association between marriage and parenting, but the handful of investigations documenting a compensatory effect cannot be ignored. How to account for both processes will be an important challenge for future research. Other key questions that remain to be addressed if we are to more fully understand the links between marriage and parenting are discussed in the final section of the chapter.

FUTURE DIRECTIONS IN THE STUDY OF MARRIAGE AND PARENTING

A number of issues that require further study have been identified in prior sections, and this section highlights seven themes that are particularly important for advancing research in this area.

Gender of Parents and Children

It remains unclear whether associations between marriage and parenting are similar for fathers and mothers and for sons and daughters. There is considerable support for the notion that marital quality affects fathers' parenting more than mothers, but enough studies have failed to find gender differences or report gender differences in the opposite direction that Erel and Burman's (1995) meta-analysis showed no reliable effects of gender. To better understand how gender may affect links between marital and parent–child relationships, studies must test for both parent and child gender effects and, if sample size permits, the interaction of parent and child gender. However, sorting out what are likely to be inconsistent findings ultimately will require the development of a more sophisticated theoretical understanding of how the gender of both parents and children affects marriage and parenting.

Diversity in Family Life

Virtually all of the studies reviewed in this chapter were conducted with European American, middle-income samples. Consequently, the generalizability of this work to families from different ethnic and socioeconomic backgrounds is open to question. Given that two-parent families with children constitute a decreasing proportion of family life in the United States, it also is important to examine whether the findings reported here apply to families in which couples are in remarriages or are not married. There is a small but growing body of research on stepfamilies (see Hetherington and Stanley-Hagan, in Vol. 3 of this *Handbook*), which suggests that links between family relationships may be different in remarried families. For example, Fine and Kurdek (1995) found that the relation between marital quality and the stepparent–stepchild relationship was stronger than that between marital quality and the relationship between the biological parent and child. In contrast, little attention has been paid to cohabiting couples and gay and lesbian parents, and consequently we simply do not know whether these family forms show similar or different patterns of relations between the intimate partner and parent roles.

The Role of Development

It has been suggested that marriage may be a more important influence on parenting at different points in childhood (e.g., Easterbrooks and Emde, 1988), but few studies have directly tested developmental hypotheses. The majority of studies in this area have included families with very young children, and consequently it is difficult to draw conclusions across studies about the relative influence of marriage on different parenting processes at different times. Testing the idea that "a transition point for any family member is a challenge for the entire system" (Minuchin, 1985, p. 294) could be an important starting point for building a literature that is developmentally informed. Longitudinal designs in particular are needed to provide sensitive tests of developmental changes.

Examining "Child Effects"

The emphasis on children's development also highlights the need to consider what children contribute to the process of parenting. For example, parental sensitivity and responsivity are likely to be influenced by children's temperament (see Putnam, Sanson, and Rothbart, in Vol. 1 of this *Handbook*). A handful of studies has assessed children's behavior in addition to parents' (e.g., Floyd et al., 1998; Kerig, Cowan, and Cowan, 1993) and thus provides insight into the transactional nature of parent–child relationships. Understanding more about the role that children play in eliciting parental behavior, affect, and cognition will help to complete the picture of family interaction. Examining child effects is especially important for testing hypotheses drawn from systems theory, which posits that children are active participants in family interaction patterns rather than simply recipients of parenting. Similarly, we know little about how children affect marriage beyond the simple statement that, in general, they appear to be hard on marital satisfaction. Testing hypotheses regarding reciprocal effects requires longitudinal research designs in order to untangle the direction of causal relations.

Parent Characteristics

The emphasis on systems theory has led researchers to neglect the role that parental personality and interpersonal style may play in explaining links between marriage and parenting (see Belsky and Barends, in Vol. 3 of this *Handbook*). Examining the role of more or less stable intrapersonal characteristics may shed light on genetic factors that may influence both marriage and parenting, and also could illuminate the contribution of social learning and attachment theories to understanding family interaction. Transactional models that posit processes by which individual characteristics transform and are transformed by relationships are needed to integrate intrapersonal and systemic perspectives.

Increasing Sophistication in Research Design

Now that the existence of a relationship between marriage and parenting has been thoroughly documented, it is essential to examine how these constructs are related and what other factors may affect this relationship. In particular, investigating the processes (affective, cognitive, and behavioral) that link marriage and parenting is critical. Moving from testing fairly simple direct associations to developing models that include indirect, moderating, or mediating pathways will provide a more complete and ecologically valid understanding of the ways in which individual, dyadic, and family factors influence each other. Testing more sophisticated hypotheses depends on increasing the precision of measurement of the central concepts. The broad conclusions that can be drawn from much of the existing research could be oversimplified to the single statement that "good things go together"; to go beyond such unhelpful conclusions requires researchers to propose and test specific hypotheses. Clear strides are being made in that direction (e.g., Lindahl and Malik, 1999) and bode well for the potential for research in this area to enhance our understanding of the ways in which marriage can support, or undermine, parenting.

CONCLUSIONS

As psychological research on the family has broadened from focusing primarily on parent–child interaction to investigating how individuals and relationships within the family influence each other (Gable, Belsky, and Crnic, 1992), the effect of marital quality on parenting has become an increasingly important topic of study. This literature generally supports the family systems hypothesis that marital and parent–child relationships are interdependent, but the specific nature of this association is yet to be fully articulated. The most consistent findings indicate that happily married parents are more sensitive, responsive, warm, and affectionate toward their children; links between marital quality and parental discipline and cognition are less consistent. A number of processes have been proposed to explain how marital functioning may influence parenting, including several drawn from family systems and stress and coping perspectives, mechanisms based on the transfer of affect from one relationship to the other, and the hypothesis that the association is due a common factor affecting both types of relationships, such as personality characteristics. However, at present, findings from empirical research in this area do not clearly support one type of process over another, with one exception: It does not appear that individuals who tend to withdraw from their partner in the face of marital distress also withdraw from their children. Although much still needs to be done to fully understand the processes by which marriage affects parenting, the existing research has some important implications for professionals who work with couples and families.

First, the research supports the proposition that promoting marital satisfaction promotes good parenting. As Belsky (1981) proposed, the marital relationship appears to serve as a primary source of support for parenting. When parents report greater intimacy and better communication in their marriage, they tend to be more attuned to and affectionate toward their children. One important, if unintended, benefit of marriage enhancement programs therefore may be the improvement of parenting, and, consequently, healthier child development. The data also suggest that programs and courses focused on enhancing parenting skills would be well served by including attention to participants' marriages. As in the case of Jim and Jean that opened this chapter, having skills and knowledge is not sufficient for competent parenting if marital tensions and conflict undermine the coparenting alliance. Providing support and improving communication in the marriage is instrumental for developing a foundation for effective parenting.

Second, this work has implications for clinical practice. Family therapists (e.g., Haley, 1976; Minuchin, 1974) have argued that examining a particular problem in isolation, whether it involves a child, the parents, or their marriage, is bound to present an incomplete and inaccurate picture. Research on marriage and parenting makes a clear case for considering the context in which family problems occur. Child problems may be affected by parenting difficulties, but parenting difficulties in turn may be strongly influenced by marital difficulties. Clinicians who work primarily with couples thus should be attuned to the effects that marital difficulties may have on parenting, and clinicians who work with children and parents should learn to assess for marital problems. Putting the "pieces" of the family together will result in a more accurate and more useful picture of family functioning.

REFERENCES

Aldous, J. (1977). Family interaction patterns. *Annual Review of Sociology, 3*, 105–135.

Appel, A. E., and Holden, G. W. (1998). The co-occurrence of spouse and physical child abuse: A review and appraisal. *Journal of Family Psychology, 12*, 578–599.

Baron, R. M., and Kenny, D. A. (1986). The moderator-mediator variable distinction in social psychological research: Conceptual, strategic, and statistical considerations. *Journal of Personality and Social Psychology, 51*, 1173–1182.

Baumrind, D. (1971). Current patterns of parental authority. *Developmental Psychology Mongraphs, 4*(1, Pt. 2).

Belsky, J. (1981). Early human experience: A family perspective. *Developmental Psychology, 17*, 3–23.

Belsky, J. (1984). The determinants of parenting: A process model. *Child Development, 55*, 83–96.

Belsky, J., and Pensky, E. (1988). Marital change across the transition to parenthood: Pregacy to three years pospartum. *Journal of Marriage and Family, 52*, 5–19.

Belsky, J., Robins, E., and Gamble, W. (1984). The determinants of parental competence: Toward a contextual theory. In M. Lewis (Ed.), *Beyond the dyad* (pp. 251–280). New York: Plenum.

Belsky, J., and Volling, B. L. (1987). Mothering, fathering, and marital interaction in the family triad: Exploring family systems processes. In P. Berman and F. Pederson (Eds.), *Men's transitions to parenthood: Longitudinal studies of early family experience* (pp. 37–63). Hillsdale, NJ: Lawrence Erlbaum Associates.

Belsky, J.,Youngblade, L., Rovine, M., and Volling, B. (1991). Patterns of marital change and parent–child interaction. *Journal of Marriage and Family, 53*, 487–498.

Bowlby, J. (1980). *Attachment and loss: Vol. 1. Attachment* (2nd ed.). New York: Basic Books.

Brody, G. H., Arias, I., and Fincham, F. D. (1996). Linking marital and child attributions to family processes and parent–child relationships. *Journal of Family Psychology, 10*, 408–421.

Brody, G. H., Pillegrini, A. D., and Sigel, I. E. (1986). Marital quality and mother–child and father–child interactions with school-aged children. *Developmental Psychology, 22*, 291–296.

Buchanan, C. M., and Waizenhofer, R. (2001). The impact of interparental conflict on adolescent children. In A. Booth, A. Crouter, and M. Clements (Eds.), *Couples in conflict* (pp. 149–160). Mahwah, NJ: Lawrence Erlbaum Associates.

Bugental, D. B. (1992). Affective and cognitive processes with: Threat-oriented family systems. In I. E. Sigel, A . McGillicuddy-DeLisi and J. Goodnow (Eds.), *Parental belief Systems: The psychological consequences for children* (pp. 219–248). Hillsdale, NJ: Lawrence Erlbaum Associates.

Caspi, A., and Elder, G. H. (1988). Emergent family patterns: the intergenerational construction of problem behavior and relationships. In R. Hinde and J. Stevenson-Hinde (Eds.), *Relationships within families* (pp. 218–240). Oxford, England: Oxford University Press.

Christensen, A., and Heavey, C. L. (1990). Gender and social structure in the deman/withdraw pattern of marital interaction. *Journal of Personality and Social Psychology, 59*, 73–81.

Christensen, A., and Margolin, G. (1988). Conflict and alliance in distressed and nondistressed families. In R. Hinde and J. Stevenson-Hinde (Eds.), *Relationships within families* (pp. 263–282). Oxford, England: Oxford University Press.

Cohen, J. (1977). *Statistical power analysis for the behavioral sciences*. New York: Academic Press.

Cowan, C. P., and Cowan, P. A. (1992). *When partners become parents: The big life change for couples*. New York: Basic Books.

Cox, M. J., Owen, M T., Lewis, J. M., and Henderson, V. K. (1989). Marriage, adult adjustment, and early parenting. *Child Development, 60*, 1015–1024.

Cox, M. J., and Paley, B. (1997). Families as systems. *Annual Review of Psychology, 48*, 243–267.

Cox, M. J., Paley, B., and Harter, K. (2001). Interparental conflict and parent–child relationships. In J. Grych and F. Fincham (Eds.), *Interparental conflict and child development: Theory, research, and applications* (pp. 249–272). Cambridge, England: Cambridge University Press.

Crockenberg, S., and McCluskey, K. (1986). Change in maternal behavior during the baby's first year of life. *Child Development, 57*, 746–753.

Daggett, J., O'Brien, M., Zanolli, K., and Petyon, V. (2000). Parents' attitudes about children: Associations with parental life histories and childrearing quality. *Journal of Family Psychology, 14*, 187–199.

Deal, J. E., Halverson, C. F., and Wampler, K. S. (1989). Parental agreement on child-rearing orientation: Relations to parental, marital, family, and child characteristics. *Child Development, 60*, 1025–1034.

Dix, T. H. (1991). The affective organization of parenting: Adaptive and maladaptive processes. *Psychological Bulletin, 110*, 3–25.

Dix, T. H., and Grusec, J. E. (1985). Parent attribution processes in the socialization of children. In I. Sigel (Ed.), *Parental belief systems* (pp. 201–233). Mahwah, NJ: Lawrence Erlbaum Associates.

Dix, T., Ruble, D. N., Grusec, J. E., and Nixon, S. (1986). Social cognition in parents: Inferential and affective reactions to children of three age levels. *Child Development, 57*, 879–894.

Easterbrooks, M. A., and Emde, R. N. (1988). Marital and parent–child relationships: The role of affect in the family system. In R. Hinde and J. Stevenson-Hinde (Eds.), *Relationships within families.* (pp. 83–103). Oxford, England: Oxford University Press.

Emery, R. E. (1989). Family violence. *American Psychologist, 44*, 321–328.

Engfer, A. (1988). The interrelatedness of marriage and the mother–child relationship. In R. Hinde and J. Stevenson-Hinde (Eds.), *Relationships within families* (pp. 104–118). Oxford, England: Oxford University Press.

Erel, O., and Burman, B. (1995). Interrelatedness of marital relations and parent–child relations: A meta-analytic review. *Psychological Bulletin, 118*, 108–132.

Fauber, R., Forehand, R., Thomas, A. M., and Wierson, M. (1990). A mediational model of the impact of marital conflict on adolescent adjustment in intact and divorced families: The role of disrupted parenting. *Child Development, 61*, 1112–1123.

Fincham, F. D., and Grych, J. H. (1991). Explaining family events in distressed and nondistressed couples: Is one type of explanation used consistently? *Journal of Family Psychology, 4*, 341–353.

Fincham, F. D., Grych, J. H., and Osborne, L. N. (1994). Does marital conflict cause child maladjustment? Directions and challenges for longitudinal research. *Journal of Family Psychology, 8*, 128–140.

Fine, M. A., and Kurdek, L. A. (1995). Relation between marital quality and (step)parent–child relationship quality for parents and stepparents in stepfamilies. *Journal of Family Psychology, 9*, 216–223.

Floyd, F. J., Gilliom, L. A., and Costigan, C. L. (1998). Marriage and the parenting alliance: Longitudinal prediction of change in parenting perceptions and behaviors. *Child Development, 69*, 1461–1479.

Gable, S., Belsky, J., and Crinic, K. (1992). Marriage, parenting, and child development: Progress and prospects. *Journal of Family Psychology, 5*, 276–294.

Goldberg, W. A., and Easterbrooks, M. A. (1984). Role of marital quality in toddler development. *Developmental Psychology, 20*, 504–514.

Grych, J. H., and Clark, R. (1999). Maternal employment and development of the father–infant relationship in the first year. *Developmental Psychology, 35*, 893–903.

Haley, J. (1976). *Problem-solving therapy*. San Francisco: Jossey-Bass.

Harold, G. T., and Conger, R. D. (1997). Marital conflict and adolescent distress: The role of adolescent awareness. *Child Development, 68*, 333–350.

Harold, G. T., Fincham, F. D., Osborne, L. N., and Conger, R. D. (1997). Mom and dad are at it again: Adolescent perceptions of marital conflict and adolescent psychological distress. *Developmental Psychology, 33*, 333–350.

Heinicke, C. M. (1984). Impact of pre-birth parent personality and marital functioning on family development: A framework and suggestions for further study. *Developmental Psychology, 20*, 1044–1053.

Heinicke, C. M. (1995). Determinants of the transition to parenting. In M. Bornstein (Ed.), *Handbook of parenting* (Vol. 3, pp. 277–304). Mahwah, NJ: Lawrence Erlbaum Associates.

Holden, G. W. (1995). Parental attitudes toward childrearing. In M. Bornstein (Ed.), Handbook of parenting (Vol. 3, pp. 359–392). Mahwah, NJ: Lawrence Erlbaum Associates.

Howes, P., and Markman, H. J. (1989). Marital quality and child functioning: A longitudinal investigation. *Child Development, 60*, 1044–1051.

Isabella, R., and Belsky, J. (1985). Marital change during the transition to parenthood and security of infant–parent attachment. *Journal of Family Issues, 6*, 505–522.

Karney, B. R., and Bradbury, T. N. (1995). The longitudinal course of marital quality and stability: A review of theory, method, and research. *Psychological Bulletin, 188*, 3–34.

Katz, L. F., and Gottman, J. M. (1996). Spillover effects of marital conflict: In search of parenting and coparenting mechanisms. In J. McHale and P. Cowan (Eds.), *Understanding how family-level dynamics affect children's development Studies of two-parent families*. San Francisco: Jossey-Bass.

Kerig, P. K. (1995). Triangles in the family circle: Effects of family structure on marriage, parenting, and child adjustment. *Journal of Family Psychology, 9*, 28–43.

Kerig, P. K., Cowan, P. A., and Cowan, C. P. (1993). Marital quality and gender differences in parent–child interaction. *Developmental Psychology, 29*, 931–939.

Kerig, P. K., and Lindahl, K. M. (2000). *Family observational coding systems: Resources for systematic research*. Mahwah, NJ: Lawrence Erlbaum Associates.

Kurdek, L. A. (1996). Parenting satisfaction and marital satisfaction in mothers and fathers with young children. *Journal of Family Psychology, 10*, 331–342.

Kurdek, L. A. (1998). Prospective predictors of parenting satisfaction for fathers and mothers with young children. *Journal of Family Psychology, 12*, 56–65.

Lindahl, K. M., Clements, M., and Markman, H. (1997). Predicting marital and parent functioning in dyads and triads: A longitudinal investigation of marital processes. *Journal of Family Psychology, 11*, 139–151.

Lindahl, K. M., and Malik, N. M. (1999). Observations of marital conflict and power: Relations with parenting in the triad. *Journal of Marriage and the Family, 61*, 320–330.

Margolin, G. (1981). The reciprocal relationship between marital and child problems. In J. Vincent (Ed.), *Advances in family intrevention, assessment, and theory* (Vol. 2, pp. 131–182). Greenwich, CT: JAI.

Margolin, G., Oliver, P. H., and Medina, A. M. (2001). Conceptual issues in understanding the relation between interparental conflict and child adjustment. In J. Grych and F. Fincham (Eds.), *Interparental conflict and child development: Theory, research, and applications* (pp. 9–38). Cambridge, England: Cambridge University Press.

McGillicuddy-DeLisi, A. V., and Sigel, I. E. (1995). Parental beliefs. In M. Bornstein (Ed.), *Handbook of parenting* (Vol. 3, pp. 333–358). Mahwah, NJ: Lawrence Erlbaum Associates.

McHale, J. P. (1995). Coparenting and triadic interactions during infancy: The roles of marital distress and child gender. *Developmental Psychology, 31*, 985–996.

Minuchin, P. (1985). Families and individual development: Provocations from the field of family therapy. *Child Development, 56*, 289–302.

Minuchin, S. (1974). *Families and family therapy*. Cambridge, MA: Harvard University Press.

Osborne, L. N., and Fincham, F. D. (1996). Marital conflict, parent–child relationships, and child adjustment: Does gender matter? *Merrill-Palmer Quarterly, 42*, 48–75.

Owen, M. T., and Cox, M. J. (1997). Marital conflict and the development of infant–parent attachment relationships. *Journal of Family Psychology, 11*, 152–164.

Parke, R. D. (1995). Fathers and families. In M. H. Bornstein (Ed.), *Handbook of Parenting* (Vol. 3, pp. 27–63). Hillsdale, NJ: Lawrence Erlbaum Associates.

Pederson, F. (1982). Mother, father, and infant as an interactive system. In J. Belsky (Ed.), *In the beginning: Readings on infancy*. New York: Colombia University Press.

Pederson, F. A., Anderson, B. J., and Cain, R. L. J. (1980). Parent–infant and husband–wife interactions observed at age five months. In F. A. Pederson (Ed.), *The father–infant relationship* (pp. 71–96). New York: Praeger.

Rutter, M. (1988). Functions and consequences of relationships: Some psychopathological considerations. In R. Hinde and J. Stevenson-Hinde (Eds.), *Relationships within families* (pp. 332–353). Oxford, England: Oxford University Press.

Rutter, M. (1994). Family discord and conduct disorder: Cause, consequence, or correlate? *Journal of Family Psychology, 8*, 170–186.

Simons, R. L., Lorenz, F. O., Conger, R. D., Wu, C. (1992). Support from spouse as mediator and moderator of the disruptive influence of economic strain on parenting. *Child Development, 63*, 1282–1301.

Spanier, G. B. (1976). Measuring dyadic adjustment: New scales for assessing the quality of marriage and similar dyads. *Journal of Marriage and the Family, 38*, 15–28.

Stoneman, Z., Brody, G. H., and Burke, M. (1989). Marital quality, depression, and inconsistent parenting: Relationship with observed mother–child conflict. *American Journal of Orthopsychiatry, 59*, 105–117.

Vandewater, E. A., and Lansford, J. E. (1998). Influences of family structure and parental conflict on children's well-being. *Family Relations, 47*, 323–330.

Von Bertallanfy, L. (1950). An outline of general systems theory. *British Journal of the Philosophy of Science, 1*, 134–165.

Volling, B. L., and Belsky, J. (1991). Multiple determinants of father involvement during infancy in dual-earner and single-earner families. *Journal of Marriage and the Family, 53*, 46–474.

Weiner, N. (1950). *Cybernetics, or control and communication in the animal and machine*. New York: Wiley.

Westerman, M. A. (1987). "Triangulation," marital discord, and child behavior problems. *Journal of Social and Personal Relationships, 4*, 87–106.

10

Marital Conflict, Repair, and Parenting

Beverly J. Wilson
Seattle Pacific University
John M. Gottman
University of Washington

Anna starts the "Hands Game" with enthusiasm and energy. She bounces up and down in her seat in an animated manner and leans in close to her father as she tries to capture his large hands with her own. Anna laughs loudly when she finally catches him and shouts, "Ha, I got ya!" Anna's father appears more tentative than Anna, smiling only slightly when she catches him. He makes few comments when she succeeds in her attempts but continues to watch her intently, as if trying to gauge her every response. The game continues for several more turns with Anna playing the "catcher" and her father the "catchee." When her father suggests that they switch roles, Anna agrees reluctantly. Her father quickly reassures her that she can catch him again after a couple turns. She manages to elude her father's attempts to catch her hands for several turns but eventually he is able to capture her. As her father shouts, "I got ya back," she quickly pulls her hands back and up to her chest as if she has been hurt. She looks shocked and says, "Ya...that's not...don't," and averts her gaze. Her father fails to see her response at first and continues to talk to her, stating that she will be able to get him again soon. When he finally notices her displeasure, he tries unsuccessfully to coax her to continue the game. She whines and turns her body away from him, drawing her leg up she kicks at him. He asks, "What's wrong, are you tired?" She looks angry and pulls both legs up toward her chest and sits in her chair with her arms wrapped around her legs. She refuses to talk or look at him except for occasional glares. Her father asks, "Are ya hungry? I'll bet you're hungry. Come on, we can play any game that you want. You tell me what game you want to play and we'll play it. Whatever you want." Although her father clearly understands that something is wrong, he asks about Anna's physical state but fails to inquire or address Anna's emotional distress.

INTRODUCTION

Anna and her parents are participating in a study investigating the role of family interaction patterns in children's conduct and social problems (see Wilson, 2001, for more information). Anna's parents report that they are concerned about her temper, she seems to get angry easily and has few friends at school or in her neighborhood. They feel frustrated about how to help her. Anna's father states that he does not understand her behavior and that he only wants her to be happier. Questionnaires completed by Anna's mother indicate that she is unhappily married to Anna's father and feels very little support from her husband in parenting Anna. When interacting in triadic family sessions, Anna's mother and father have difficulty coordinating their efforts to help her complete a homework assignment or build a world in a sandbox with toy people, animals, and buildings. There is little mutual fun or enjoyment in their interactions; negativity and competition dominate.

Relationships within the family may be the most intimate and influential forces in the lives of individuals. Theories of individual differences have failed to predict which child will be kind and which will be aggressive, which child will enjoy learning and which will be unable to learn, which will be happy and which will be anxious or depressed. On the other hand, family factors do predict many of these things in the longitudinal course of a child's life.

Over the past 25 years numerous studies have linked processes within the family to children's prosocial behavior (Heinicke, Guthrie, and Ruth, 1997; Hetherington, Cox, and Cox, 1985; Janssens and Dekovic, 1997; Putallaz, 1987), social and cognitive competence (Brody and Flor, 1998; Long, Forehand, Fauber, and Brody, 1987; Long, Slater, Forehand, and Fauber, 1988; O'Connor, Caspi, DeFries, and Plomin, 2000; Strassberg, Dodge, Bates, and Pettit, 1992), aggression (Borkhuis and Patalano, 1997; Hetherington et al., 1985; Johnston, Gonzalez, and Campbell, 1987; Patterson, 1971, 1982; Short, 1998), conduct problems/disorders (Anderson, Greene, Hetherington, and Clingempeel, 1999; Johnson and O'Leary, 1987; Jouriles, Murphy, and O'Leary, 1989; Pagani, Boulerice, Tremblay, and Vitaro, 1997; Jouriles, Pfiffner, and O'Leary, 1988; Simons, Lin, Gordon, Conger, and Lorenz, 1999), delinquency/antisocial behavior (Emery and O'Leary, 1982; Patterson and Stouthamer-Loeber, 1984; Peterson and Zill, 1986; Short, 1998), depression (McCabe, 1997), and anxiety/withdrawal (Johnston et al., 1987; Long et al., 1987; Patterson, 1993; Sheets, Sandler, and West, 1996).

Recent research has found especially good predictability from the quality of couples' marriages to children's development. It is even the case that we can predict from what the marriage is like before children arrive to what the children will be like when they are in preschool (Cowan and Cowan, 1992). The mechanisms that account for these predictions, however, are not well understood at this point. In the following pages we attempt to link processes in marriage to child development. In doing this we wish to explore three major themes. First, although parental conflict has typically been associated with negative outcomes for children, we believe that it is not conflict per se that leads to deleterious effects but a deficit or failure in the repair of negative interactions. We will describe a theoretical model of dynamic homeostasis, set point, feedback, and repair that will be helpful for organizing the research we will review about families. We suggest that conflict and miscoordinations in relationships are a normal and healthy part of family life. It is their resolution and the ultimate proportion of positive to negative interactions that are critical.

Second, we suggest that families serve as what we will call "emotion cultures." It is within families that individuals learn when and how to feel and how to think about these feelings, and hence develop a meta-emotional life. Families report a wide diversity of feelings and cognitive structures about emotions. For example, some families think that anger in themselves and in their children is harmful and should not be expressed, especially by children. Others think that anger is natural but ought to be ignored. Others believe anger should be expressed and explored with the child. We have also found that these meta-emotional cultures are emotion and gender specific. Fathers often have different attitudes toward sadness expressed by sons versus daughters, for example. These emotion cultures within families lead to different experiences for children. These experiences, in turn, have important consequences for individuals and relationships. When two individuals come together to form a new family, they bring these distinct attitudes, beliefs, and biases with them.

Third, we want to make two types of recommendations: One type of recommendation is for families who must deal with a number of normative and nonnormative transitions, and a second type of recommendation concerns public policy related to families. For this second type of recommendation we will propose a cumulative stress model. We will review research that shows that cumulative stress in children's lives is associated with numerous child deficits. Social policy can be developed to assist families during transitions and restructuring.

The following sections summarize research related to the linkage between marriages and child development. We start by discussing research on potential mechanisms for this relationship and discuss the influence of marital interaction, quality, and processes related to repair of negativity. This information is used to build a model for the regulation of negativity in families. A typology of marriages and families based on this model is presented with a discussion of potential risks and benefits to children in the different types of marriages. We also discuss a number of buffers and risk factors that may mediate the effects of marital interaction on children.

THE SEARCH FOR MECHANISMS THAT LINK MARITAL INTERACTION AND CHILD OUTCOMES

The challenge that must be met in the area of research dealing with the transfer of marital interaction to children is the development of theory that provides operational and testable mechanisms capable of accounting for observed relationships. This is now quite feasible, and we suggest that the field develop an aesthetic preference for precise theories over those that are vague and more metaphor than mechanism. The following section summarizes research on three potential mechanisms: modeling, cumulative stress, and parenting practices.

Modeling

Marital conflict may affect child development in a number of ways. Modeling or imitating the aggressive behavior of others is one possible direct mechanism (Bandura, 1973; Bandura, Ross, and Ross, 1963). Parents provide especially potent models for children because of their role as attachment and authority figures. The salience of same-sex parents as models (Bandura, 1973; Isley, O'Neil, Clatfelter, and Parke, 1999) may also help to explain findings that boys are more likely to evidence externalizing behavior and girls internalizing behavior (Block, Block, and Morrison, 1981; Emery, 1982). Research suggests that children do not need to observe actual physical aggression to evidence an increase in these behaviors. Cummings, Iannotti, and Zahn-Waxler (1985) found that children were more aggressive with familiar peers after observing a staged angry argument between adults.

Parents who engage in marital aggression are also more likely to use aversive methods, such as physical punishment, in dealing with their children (Jouriles, Barling, and O'Leary, 1987). Recent evidence also suggests that children in these families are more likely to be victims of physical abuse (Jouriles and Norwood, 1995; Ross, 1996). Thus, many children are given multiple opportunities to observe aggressive behaviors and possibly experience them firsthand. Children exposed to interparent aggression may learn that this is an acceptable strategy for dealing with disagreements. In families where parents are disengaged, inattentive, or insensitive to typical communicative signals, children's aversive or aggressive behavior may prove quite reinforcing, in that the parent's attention is redirected to the child (Patterson, 1971).

Unfortunately, in everyday (nonexperimental) settings it has proved impossible to operationalize "modeling" or even to reliably measure when one person is imitating another (G. R. Patterson, personal communication, 1993). Consequently, other mechanisms, those involving processes that can be operationalized and measured, must be explored. One such mechanism is the child's experience of stress during parental conflict.

Stress

Interparental conflict may also affect children because they experience it as very stressful. Children as young as 1 year of age show signs of distress when witnessing angry interactions between family members (Cummings, Zahn-Waxler, and Radke-Yarrow, 1981). A history of observing conflict in the home is related to greater emotional and behavioral reactivity in response to marital conflict such as increased fear, distress, hypervigilance, and covert hostility (Davies and Cummings, 1994). For example, children are more distressed at witnessing interadult anger when they have observed repeated incidences of interadult anger or had a history of exposure to interparent physical aggression (Cummings et al., 1985; Cummings, Pellegrini, Notarius, and Cummings, 1989; Cummings, Vogel, Cummings, and El-Sheikh, 1989; El-Sheikh and Reiter, 1995). Not surprisingly, children who have been exposed to marital aggression are also more anxious and engage in more distracting behaviors, such as being silly, when their parents are hostile toward them (Gordis, Margolin, and John, 1997).

It may be that children coping with frequent marital conflict become hypersensitive to or over-whelmed by conflict (Davies and Cummings, 1994). The effect of marital stress on children may be mediated through the child's physiology (i.e., measures of internal stress), such as heart rate and levels of stress-related hormones in the child's urine (El-Sheikh, Cummings, and Goetsch, 1989; Gottman and Katz, 1989). Gottman and Katz (1989) found that children from homes in which parents are unhappily married have higher levels of stress-related urinary hormones (catecholamines) and engage in more parallel and less joint play with peers, probably in the service of avoiding interper-sonal conflict. Wilson, Staley, Gottman, and Katz (2001) found that these same children have more difficulty recovering from the physiological arousal associated with making angry facial expressions. Children from conflict-ridden homes may also have lower levels of psychological coping resources or less-effective coping styles. In times of high stress, individuals tend to use coping strategies that are well learned. Derensky and Tarabulsy (1991) found that children from divorced homes had a tendency to select and use a single coping style with little consideration for the situation or its effectiveness.

Parenting Practices

Parenting factors also mediate between marital conflict and child dysfunction. Several processes may help to account for this association.

Inconsistent parenting. It has been proposed that the association between marital conflict, parenting, and child behavior problems can often be explained by disruptions in parenting practices (Fauber, Forehand, Thomas, and Wierson, 1990; Hess and Camara, 1979). Patterson (1982) suggested that parental conflict is associated with increases in child aversive behavior because parents become absorbed by their own conflict and are less consistent or effective in their discipline practices. Incon-sistent discipline is associated with both marital conflict and child behavior problems (Block, Block, and Morrison, 1981; Stoneman, Brody, and Burke, 1989). For example, poor maternal monitoring of child behavior is the best predictor of delinquent behavior in a nonclinic sample of boys (Patterson and Stouthamer-Loeber, 1984). There is also support for the negative reinforcement model, which suggests that a child's aggression is reinforced by the subsequent reduction of negativity by others (Patterson, 1982; Snyder, Schrepferman, and St. Peter, 1997).

Marital dissolution, ineffective parenting, and marital conflict. Marital dissolution has also been associated with child behavior problems and ineffective parenting practices (Hetherington and Stanley-Hagan, in Vol. 3 of this *Handbook*). Hetherington (1979) reported that divorced parents are more likely than nondivorced parents to be inconsistent, use poor communication, make fewer maturity demands, and be less affectionate with their children. These changes in parenting were greatest one year after the divorce. Because processes leading to marital dissolution typically evolve some time before the actual dissolution (Gottman and Levinson, 1992), changes in parenting and child behavior should also be evident much earlier. Several researchers have investigated this hypothesis and found that child behavior problems could be identified up to 12 years before parents divorced (Amato and Booth, 1996; Block, Block, and Gjerde, 1986). Signs of interparental tensions and unsupportive parenting patterns also differentiated between those parents who eventually divorced and those who did not (Block, Block, and Gjerde, 1988). Years before the dissolution of their marriages, fathers reported being more angry, disengaged, conflicted, and less warm and intimate with their sons. Mothers also reported being more strict, tense, and conflicted with their sons. Katz and Gottman (1993), in a longitudinal study, found that marital interaction patterns that predicted later divorce (mostly mutual contempt) were also predictive of later antisocial behavior in the children (as rated by teacher); however, actual divorce or separation did not correlate with antisocial behavior in the children.

There is also evidence that marital conflict plays a prominent role in the association between children's behavior problems and parental divorce. Hetherington (1999) compared the adjustment of children from divorcing families (i.e., parents who later divorce) with children from high- and low-conflict nondivorcing families. Children in high-conflict nondivorcing families had more externalizing and internalizing problems and were lower in cognitive agency, self-esteem, social responsibility, and social competence than other groups. The adjustment of children from divorcing homes fell in between these two groups but was not significantly different from either. It is important to note that these findings do not indicate that divorce does not have a negative influence on children's development. Hetherington also compared the long-term adjustment of children in high- and low-conflict divorced and high- and low-conflict nondivorced families. In the first 2 years after the divorce, girls of divorced parents, regardless of the level of parental conflict, had poorer adjustment (i.e., a higher percentage of these girls were above the clinical cutoff on the Child Behavior Checklist) than girls of nondivorced parents. In contrast, boys in the high-conflict divorced families were more likely to be above the clinical cutoff, whereas, boys in low-conflict nondivorced families were less likely to be in this range. Beyond 2 years after the divorce, the level of continuing conflict in divorced and nondivorced families began to differentiate between the outcomes of both boys and girls from these families. Although children from high-conflict divorced families had the poorest adjustment, children from high-conflict nondivorcing families had the second poorest outcome. Hetherington concluded that if parental conflict is going to continue after the divorce, "it is better for children to remain in an acrimonious two-parent household than to divorce" (p. 101). On the other hand, if the relationship between parents becomes more harmonious after the divorce, it is beneficial to both boys and girls if their parents divorce. The relations between marital discord, parenting, and child outcomes have also been investigated by examining normative transitions in families such as the transition to parenthood (Heinicke, in Vol. 3 of this *Handbook*).

Stressful life transitions: First-time parenthood. Families encounter numerous periods of stress and adjustment throughout the course of their development. Transitions, such as first-time parenthood, generate many new joys and pleasures but also require major reorganization of routines, roles, and relationships (Bornstein, in Vol. 1 of this *Handbook*). These are stressful events and are frequently associated with increases in marital conflict. For example, conflicts and disagreements between couples increase with the birth of a baby (Cowan et al., 1985), and marital satisfaction decreases from pregnancy to early childhood (Belsky and Kelly, 1994; Belsky, Lang, and Rovine, 1985; Cowan et al., 1985, Grossman, Eichler, and Winickoff, 1980).

Cowan and Cowan (1992) found that parents' attitudes about their marriages during this transition influenced the quality of their interactions with their children and their children's development. Mothers who were unhappily married were more authoritarian and less authoritative with their sons and daughters during play interactions, especially when their daughters asserted themselves. This pattern of results also extended to the father–daughter relationship. Fathers who were unhappily married responded more negatively (i.e., they were more cold and critical, set more limits, and were less encouraging of independence) with their daughters regardless of their daughters' behavior. Fathers' interaction with their sons, on the other hand, was unaffected by their relationship with their wives. Cowan and Cowan suggest that fathers' relationship with their sons may be more dependent on how fathers feel about themselves and life while becoming a parent than how they feel about their marriage. This means that daughters whose parents are unhappily married are less likely than sons to have at least one parent who is warm, responsive, and encourages age-appropriate independence.

Preexisting factors within the marriage also appear to mediate some of the changes in marital satisfaction with first-time parenthood. Shapiro, Gottman, and Carrere (2000) found that how couples viewed their marriage predicted how their marital satisfaction changed after the baby arrived. They interviewed couples about their relationship history and philosophy. They found that mothers were more likely to show stability or increases in marital satisfaction after the birth of the baby if fathers expressed fondness toward their wives and each member of the couple was aware of details about their spouses' lives and their relationship history. Mothers' marital satisfaction was most likely to decrease when (1) husbands expressed high levels of negativity during the interview (i.e., they were critical of their wives, vague about what attracted them to their wives, or displayed negative affect toward their wives), (2) husbands verbalized disappointment in the marriage, or (3) when either partner described their marriage as chaotic.

Coparenting and the parenting alliance.   Another factor that predicts changes in marital satisfaction in new parents is the degree to which they engage in unsupportive coparenting. Belsky and Hsieh (1998) investigated the role of personality variables, the division of labor, and coparenting in couples' marital satisfaction. They looked at the role of these factors in differentiating between couples who initially had high marital satisfaction at 10-month postpartum and those who showed a decline versus no decline in satisfaction (i.e., stays good and good-gets-worse marriages, respectively). The percentage of unsupportive coparenting behaviors differentiated between these groups. An example of unsupportive coparenting might be when one parent picks up a child and holds her after the other parent has instructed the child to stay in her chair. Personality variables and division of labor did not differentiate between stays-good and good-gets-worse marriages, although these variables did differentiate between groups of parents who initially had low marital satisfaction and either remained stable or showed declines in satisfaction. Block, Block, and Morrison (1981) found that parental disagreement about childrearing practices related to both subsequent marital dissolution and externalizing behavior in boys and internalizing behavior in girls.

Frequent conflict between spouses may be related to more negative parenting and child outcomes because it reduces the availability of an important source of support in childrearing, one's partner. The observation of triadic interactions among mothers, fathers, and their infants provides invaluable information about how this system of support functions. Spouses with higher levels of marital satisfaction are more positive and less negative in their marital interactions and more harmonious when interacting with their infants (Frosch, Mangelsdorf, and McHale, 1998). Belsky and Volling (1987) looked at triadic interaction patterns in the home among mothers, fathers, and infants during the first year of life. High levels of positive behaviors between parents such as sharing pleasure, showing affection, and complimenting each other were associated with positive and responsive parenting behaviors. This "spillover effect," or continuity between the affective tone of the marital dyad and parent–child triad, has also been reported by Kitzmann (2000): She found that negativity in the martial dyad was related to less democratic coparenting and more negativity and less warmth, engagement, and support in triadic interactions between parents and children. Marital distress has also been linked to greater hostility and competitive coparenting with boys in triadic settings (McHale, 1995).

The more affective or evaluative aspects of supporting ones partner's parenting have also been referred to as the parenting alliance (Weissman and Cohen, 1985; Floyd and Zmich, 1991). Weissman and Cohen define the parenting alliance as the degree to which parents acknowledge, respect, and value the parenting and judgement of their partner. Parenting alliance has been shown to influence the parenting behavior of parents of at-risk children (Floyd and Zmich, 1991) and the involvement of fathers' in childrearing activities (McBride and Rane, 1998). McBride and Rane found that fathers were more involved with their children when (1) they perceived their wives as having confidence in their own parenting (2) their wives made positive emotional appraisals of their partner's parenting, and (3) mothers perceived a shared philosophy of parenting with the father. Supporting the parenting of one's partner may also be observed in the behavior patterns of couples. E. Fivaz (personal communication, June 1993) observed subtle ways that parents support each other and how these behaviors may be disrupted by marital discord. She described how the interaction of one well-functioning triad gives the impression of quiet harmony, smooth synchrony, with the three partners alternating their expressive exchanges. When one parent actively engages the infant, the other parent's body and gaze remain oriented toward the pair as he or she waits. Fivaz refers to this spatial arrangement as "framing" the interaction and believes it suggests supportive engagement in the partner's parenting role. A second more conflicted couple exhibits patterns that are disordered and without synchrony. These parents attempt different strategies to attract the baby's attention without success. Turn taking is often indistinct as they compete for the infant's attention. When one parent does interact with the baby, the other withdraws instead of remaining oriented toward the pair. The effect of the couple's disharmony is immediately evident: The baby remains disengaged during much of the session and ultimately begins to cry.

Cross-generational alliances and coalitions. Family systems theory suggests that marital conflict may also influence child outcomes because some parents engage in intergenerational alliances within the family (Minuchin, 1974). In these instances children are drawn into their parents' conflict by one or both parents. For example, a parent lacking emotional closeness with a spouse may form a close alliance with a child to meet these needs. Intergenerational alliances often result in a coalition between the child and parent dyad against the other parent (Minuchin, 1974). Minuchin suggested that triangulations involving parent–child alliances may provide parents with some immediate relief from their marital stress but hinder the long-term resolution of their differences and compromise the well-being of their children. Although support for the role of compensatory processes, such as triangulation, in linking marital conflict to child outcomes is limited (see Erel and Burman, 1995, for a meta-analyses), recent studies have highlighted the prevalence and detrimental effects associated with these patterns. For example, parents and children in triangulated families report more parental conflict, negative affect, and lower marital satisfaction (Kerig, 1995). Alliances between fathers and daughters during childhood have also been associated with higher levels of depression, anxiety, and lower self-esteem in young adult women (Jacobvitz and Bush, 1996). Although triangulated relationships appear to provide some benefit to the child by providing them with a close relationship with one parent, their relationship with the second parent becomes more conflictual and the ultimate outcome is greater negativity within the family. Erel and Burman conclude that maintaining a positive parent–child relationship in the midst of marital distress is difficult at best.

Parenting factors and children's peer relationships. Factors related to parenting may also help to explain the negative relation between marital conflict and children's ability to form positive peer relationships. Long et al. (1987) found that school-age children whose parents were unhappily married showed low levels of sociability in school. Rejection by peers has also been shown to be more common among children whose parents have recently separated or divorced than children who have not had these experiences (Patterson, Vaden, and Kupersmidt, 1991). Several factors may help to explain these findings. First, parents may influence their child's social competence through the quality of the parent–child relationship (Harrist and Ainslie, 1998). Substantial research indicates that marital conflict is related to more negative and less positive parent–child interactions. The quality of parent–child interactions has also been linked to the quality of children's peer relationships. Stocker and Youngblade (1999) found that fathers' hostility toward their children mediated the association between conflict in the marriage and children's peer relationship difficulties. In general, children are more likely to be low in peer acceptance if parents are demanding, directive, and express high levels of negative affect (Barth and Parke, 1993; MacDonald and Parke, 1984; Parke, Cassidy, Burks,

Carson, and Boyum, 1992; Putallaz, 1987). Harrist and Ainslie (1998) found that marital conflict predicted lower quality interactions between parents and children and that these interactions predicted greater aggressiveness in children. The association between marital conflict and child aggression is especially problematic because aggression is associated with rejection by peers (Pope, Bierman, and Mumma, 1991).

Opportunities for positive peer contact may also be reduced for children whose parents are unhappily married. Children whose parents are dissatisfied with their marriages, especially those in active conflict, may be less likely to invite other children to their homes. An unpredictable and affectively negative environment would not encourage this practice. Marital conflict may also steal emotional energy from the parent–child relationship. As parents focus more on their own issues, they may become less effective providers and facilitators of social opportunities for their children (Bhavnagri and Parke, 1991; Ladd and Golter, 1988; O'Neal and Parke, 2000).

Children whose parents are in conflict may also modify their interactions with peers to avoid confrontation and conflict. Recall that Gottman and Katz (1989) identified disruptions in the play behavior of children from maritally distressed homes. Children whose parents reported lower levels of marital satisfaction played at lower levels with their best friends than children from more satisfied marriages. Higher levels of play are thought to require greater emotion regulation and interpersonal coordination on the part of children (Gottman, 1983).

Emotion regulation and social and emotional outcomes. The regulation of negative affect appears to be particularly critical for effective peer interactions. Sroufe, Schork, Motti, Lawaroski, and LaFreniere (1984) found a negative relation between the expression of negative affect and peer sociometric ratings. Children who expressed more negative affect were seen as less desirable playmates by other children. The expression of negative affect also predicts the quality of children's peer relationships over time. Isley, O'Neil, Clatfelter, and Parke (1996) found that children's expression of negative affect in kindergarten predicted their social competence with peers in first grade.

A recent review of studies investigating the link between parenting behavior and children's peer competence found substantial support for the mediational role of emotion regulation (Mize, Pettit, and Meece, 2000). Emotion regulation, defined as emotional reactivity and internal representations of parent's marital relationship, partially mediated between marital distress and children's externalizing and internalizing problems (Davies and Cummings, 1998). More specifically related to peer competence, emotion regulation, defined as mother's report of the child needing to "down regulate," partially mediated between parental awareness and coaching regarding the child's emotional experience and the child's peer relationships (Gottman, Katz, and Hooven, 1996). These findings suggest that emotion regulation abilities and the coordination of interactions may be skills that children from maritally distressed homes have difficulty learning.

To understand the processes that link the marital and parent–child systems, we first need to understand marital conflict. Children are born into existing familial systems that have developed their own ways of dealing with stress and conflict. This preexisting system has a tremendous effect on the developing child, as does the child on the existing system.

MARITAL INTERACTION, MARITAL SATISFACTION, AND REGULATION

In this section we discuss research that indicates negative affect reciprocity is the most consistent behavioral discriminator between happily and unhappily married couples. A theory is also suggested for this observation, namely, that the greater negative affect reciprocity of unhappily married couples is due to a failure of regulation in which repair processes are inoperative. This theory is then used as a base for proposing how two particular behavioral systems in families are regulated and repaired, the *irritability system* and the *affectional system*.

Patterns That Discriminate Between Maritally Satisfied and Dissatisfied Couples

Statistical techniques such as sequential analyses have enabled researchers to identify a number of patterns in marital interactions that discriminate between satisfied and dissatisfied couples. The basic idea of these analyses is to predict some future behavior from a current behavior. For example, dissatisfied couples are more likely than satisfied couples to engage in cycles of negative reciprocity (Gottman, 1998; Margolin and Wampold, 1981). Margolin and Wampold hypothesized that there is a suppression of positivity following a negative event in distressed couples but found no evidence for this suppression for nondistressed couples.

Revenstorf, Vogel, Wegener, Hahlweg, and Schindler (1980) found a number of sequences that differentiated between distressed and nondistressed couples. Nondistressed couples engaged in more positive interchanges such as *validation sequences* (problem description followed by positivity) and *positive reciprocity sequences* (positive followed by positive). On the other hand, distressed couples engaged in more negative interchanges than nondistressed couples. These included "devaluation" sequences (negative follows positive), *negative continuance sequences* (which they called "fighting on" or "fighting back" in three-chain sequences), and *negative startup sequences* (which they called "yes-butting," meaning that somewhere in a four-chain sequence, negative follows positive).

It appears that distressed couples become caught up in cycles of negativity. Revenstorf et al. called these cycles "distancing" and suggested that they measure the extent to which negativity becomes an absorbing state (a state that is difficult to exit once entered). Positive reciprocity was called "attraction" and may indicate the extent to which positivity becomes an absorbing state. For most sequences (e.g., for positive reciprocity) the differences between the groups are not very great. However, the evidence is very clear that negative cycles represent an absorbing state for distressed couples but not for nondistressed couples. By the second turn, nondistressed couples begin to escape from the negativity, but distressed couples cannot escape.

What is consistent across these two studies and numerous others is that dissatisfied or distressed couples engage in long chains of reciprocated negativity (Fitzpatrick, 1988; Gottman, 1979; Raush, Barry, Hertel, and Swain, 1974; Revenstorf et al., 1980; Revenstorf, Hahlweg, Schindler, and Vogel, 1984; Ting-Toomey, 1983). Furthermore, it appears that once dissatisfied couples enter into cycles of negativity they find it very difficult to escape from this pattern. To better understand how dissatisfied couples become trapped in cycles of reciprocal negativity it is necessary to examine the different phases of marital conflict.

The Three Phases of Marital Conflict

Gottman (1979) divided the conflicts of couples he has studied into three phases, an agenda-building phase, an arguing phase, and a negotiation phase. The task of the agenda-building phase is to air issues. The tasks of the arguing phase are to find areas of common ground, to persuade one another, and to argue for one's own point of view. This arguing phase is usually quite hot emotionally, and it is here that one sees codes and sequences designed to repair the interaction, such as *metacommunication* and *feeling probe messages*. Gottman (1998) found that repair attempts are frequent events in these interactions, happening at a rate of about one to three times a minute even in unhappy marriages. Finally, the goal of the negotiation phase is to come to a mutually satisfying resolution of the issue. Within each phase, specific sequences discriminate between satisfied and dissatisfied couples.

The agenda-building phase. In general, during the agenda-building phase of the conflict discussion, satisfied couples engage in more validation of each other's comments and ideas than dissatisfied couples. They follow descriptions of an issue with verbal or nonverbal signals that communicate that they are listening (e.g., "Mmmhmmm," "Oh," "I see," gazing toward the speaker, or head nodding) and suggest agreement with the feelings being expressed. This is not to say that the partners agree with their spouse's point of view, but rather that it makes sense to feel that way. Dissatisfied couples, on the other hand, tend to respond to an expression of feelings about a problem with disagreement or a cross complaint. The interspersed agreement is far less likely to be there.

The disagreement phase.   In the disagreement phase two repair processes among satisfied couples are important: One is the *feeling probe*, and the other is *metacommunication*. Couples do not tend to discuss or ask about feelings directly. Instead, they use "mindreading," an attribution of feelings, motives, or past behaviors to the partner. An example of this is that, instead of asking her husband about how he feels about going to dinner at her mother's house, a wife might say, "You always get tense at my mother's." Stems of "you always" or "you never" are common in mindreading. The feeling probe is a sequence of neutral affect mindreading followed by agreement and elaboration by the partner. For example:

> Wife: You always get tense at my mother's (neutral affect).
> Husband: Yeah I do, and I think it's because she criticizes the way I discipline Jason.

If the mindreading was delivered with negative affect, the sequence most common in dissatisfied couples, the response would be disagreement and elaboration. For example:

> Wife: You always get tense at my mother's (negative affect).
> Husband: "I don't always get tense at your mother's, but when I do I think it's because she criticizes the way I discipline Jason, and you never stand up for me."

The latter response is far more self-protective and defensive than the first.

Metacommunication was identified in the classic double-bind paper of Bateson, Jackson, Haley, and Weakland (1956). It is a communication about communication, and as such it may qualify or change communication itself. A simple example is the statement "You're interrupting me." Gottman found that metacommunication is equally likely for both satisfied and dissatisfied couples. However, satisfied couples use it often, with neutral affect, in short chains that end with agreement. For example:

> Husband: You're interrupting me.
> Wife: Sorry. What were you saying?

In dissatisfied couples the metacommunication is delivered with negative affect, and the chains are longer and lead to counter-metacommunication. For example:

> Husband: You're interrupting me.
> Wife: Maybe I wouldn't have to if I could get a word in edgewise.
> Husband: Oh, now I talk too much.
> Wife: You don't give me a chance to tell you how I feel.

The metacommunication cannot function as a repair mechanism because the negative affect from the interaction transferred to what was supposed to be a repair mechanism. It may be in this sense that negative affect reciprocity works in constricting the social processes available to a couple in the course of trying to resolve an area of disagreement. That is the meaning of the negative affective absorbing state.

The negotiation phase.   A similar differentiation involving agreement is found in the negotiation stages of the discussion. Satisfied couples are more likely to enter into negotiation sequences, whereas counterproposals are more characteristic of the interaction of dissatisfied couples.

Theoretical Formulation of Greater Negative Reciprocity Among Dissatisfied Couples

The finding that negative reciprocity becomes an absorbing state for dissatisfied couples has profound implications for the discussion of interaction process and the functioning of families. Couples typically express the most negative affect during the middle arguing phase of conflict resolution, and their major attempts at repair of the interaction are usually delivered in this phase as well. Attempts at interaction repair are often delivered with negative affect. For example, statements like "Stop interrupting me!" or "We're getting off the subject" may be accompanied by irritation, tension, sadness, or some other form of distress. Thus, repair attempts usually have two components, a negative affective nonverbal component and a metacommunication content component attempting to repair the interaction.

The implication of negativity as an absorbing state for dissatisfied couples is that they may attend primarily to the negative affect component of repair attempts, whereas satisfied couples attend primarily to the repair component. Thus, repair processes may not work very well in dissatisfied marriages. Instead, what will predominate in dissatisfied couples' attempts to use these social processes is the negative affect. The usual social processes that are present during conflict that repair the interaction (such as metacommunication) do not work in unhappy marriages. These processes are the mechanisms used by satisfied couples for exiting a negative state (Gottman, 1979). They include metacommunication, feeling probes that explore feelings, information exchange, social comparison, humor, distraction, gossip, finding areas of common ground, and appeals to basic philosophy and expectations in the marriage.

To summarize, there is greater negative affect reciprocity in the interactions of dissatisfied compared to satisfied couples. There is also evidence of negative affect turning the normal social processes available to satisfied couples into a negative-affect absorbing state for dissatisfied couples. That is, the normal repair processes that enable couples to regulate their interactions and return to a more positive state after negativity are inoperative for dissatisfied couples. Social processes have less chance of working because what people attend to, and respond to, is the negativity. This results in a less-flexible system for unhappy couples, a system that leaves fewer options open to them. It is as if they have no way of escaping a negative state once it is entered. All roads lead to this particular Rome.

A MODEL FOR THE REGULATION OF NEGATIVITY IN FAMILIES

In the following section, we attempt to build a model of the regulation of negativity in families. To build this model we must draw on research concerning the mechanisms that link marriages, families, and children's development. In particular, we focus on research on repair processes in social interaction. Before we introduce elements of this model, we must present a number of key concepts related to regulatory processes.

The Theoretical Language of Regulation

The theoretical language of regulation can assist in building a theory of family functioning. What do we mean by "regulation"? If we want to demonstrate that a system is regulated, we actually need to show that several things are true. First, we need to identify the quantity that is regulated. Second, we have to show that this quantity has a *set point* and that this set point has validity, that is, that it matters what the set point is in terms of something external to the regulated system. Third, it is necessary to show that the *error signal*, the difference between the set point and the actual behavior of the system, has some feedback implications for the operation of the system; that is, there has to be a deviation threshold. This shows that it matters that the system is far away from

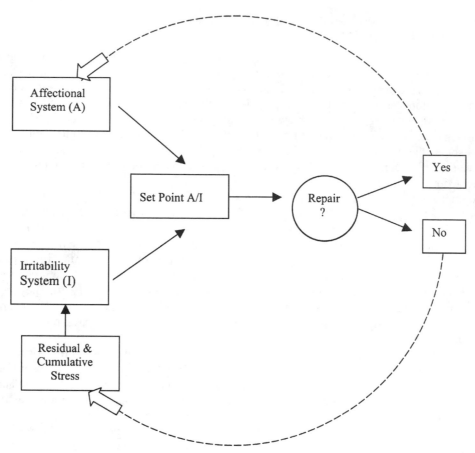

FIGURE 10.1. A model for the regulation of negativity in families.

the set point; once the threshold is exceeded, there has to be some action, or some consequences of inaction.

Hence, demonstrating that a system is regulated is no easy matter. An example may be helpful. One system that is regulated is body weight. The media recently reported the case of a 500-pound man who died; his body defended his weight (it was very hard for him to diet) even though his health was clearly compromised by his weight. This example illustrates the importance of the set point variable to systems, and some set points are functional, whereas others are dysfunctional. The latter point may be particularly applicable to our discussion of couples in unhappy marriages and interaction patterns present in their families. Figure 10.1 presents a model for the regulation of negativity in families. In our formulation, the set point for regulating interactions in families is determined by the relative influences of the Irritability (I) and Affectional (A) systems. These systems and other parameters in our model are presented in the following sections.

The Irritability System

The Irritability System involves processes that result in greater negativity (e.g., hostility, criticism, depression, and disengagement) within the family system. These processes may originate within the family system, such as in the case of parental psychopathology or chronic illness, or outside the family, such as in the work environment. Each of these events increases the level of stress experienced by families.

Residual and cumulative stress.   Residual stress may be conceptualized as stress that exceeds available resources. For example, recent research has underscored the deleterious effects of economic stress on family functioning (Bolger, Patterson, Thompson, and Kupersmidt, 1995; Conger, Elder, Lorenz, Simons, and Whitbeck, 1992; Conger et al., 1993; Magnuson and Duncan, in Vol. 4 of this *Handbook*; Hoff, Laursen, and Tardif, in Vol. 2 of this *Handbook*). Conger et al. found that economic pressure was associated with father and mother depression and resulted in greater marital conflict and disruption of several positive aspects of parenting. Changes in parenting were related to developmental outcome for both adolescent girls and boys.

Multiple unresolved stressors or residual stress may also have a cumulative effect on the well-being of marriages, families, and children's development. One particularly disturbing finding is that children's ability to form effective peer relationships may be compromised by certain familial events and stressors (Patterson, Vaden, and Kupersmidt, 1991). Peers play important functions in the socialization and development of children, and the long-term outcome for children who are rejected by peers in childhood is quite poor (Parker and Asher, 1987). These children are at risk for dropping out of school and criminality. Family background variables, such as absence of mother or father from the home, economic difficulties, and lack of educational stimulation have a cumulative effect on children's rejection by peers, the presence of each additional variable significantly raising the probability of peer rejection (Patterson et al., 1991). Peer rejection is also influenced by two life events, being transferred to a new school and parental separation or divorce.

Corrosive patterns in marital conflict.   Although a number of forms of negativity contribute to the Irritability System, recent work suggests that some are more corrosive than others. Katz and Gottman (1993) identified two patterns of marital conflict that predicted child behavior problems. The first, the *Mutually Hostile pattern*, involves behaviors such as husband and wife contempt and belligerence and wife anger. The presence of this pattern in marital interactions when children were 4 to 5 years old predicted teacher report of child externalizing behavior 3 years later. A second pattern, "Husband Angry and Withdrawn," involves husband anger and stonewalling behavior and predicted teacher report of child internalizing behavior 3 years later. Subsequent research by Katz and Kahen (1993) identified several parenting behaviors that appear to mediate these associations. Children whose parents exhibited a Mutually Hostile pattern during marital interactions had fathers who were more intrusive with their children during a triadic teaching situation. Their children also displayed more anger during the parent–child session. Father intrusiveness was associated with subsequent teacher report of externalizing behavior in the child. Father Anger and Withdrawal during marital conflict was associated with mother criticism and intrusiveness during the parent–child task. Mother criticism and intrusiveness was related to the child being unresponsive during the parent–child session and to teacher's report of internalizing behaviors 3 years later. In contrast, the Husband Angry and Withdrawn pattern was not related to marital satisfaction or dissolution. The Mutually Hostile pattern, on the other hand, was related to marital dissatisfaction and predictive of dissolution of the marriage. Thus, reciprocal exchanges of negative affect and behavior, which is the most consistent pattern associated with marital dissatisfaction, is also associated with child externalizing behaviors.

Negative affect.   Several studies indicate positive associations between parents' expression of negative affect in the parent–child setting and children's externalizing and social problems (Cowan, Cowan, Schulz, and Heming, 1994; Isley, O'Neil, and Parke, 1996). Cowan et al. (1994) found that parental warmth during parent–child interactions was predictive of children's externalizing problems, whereas parenting style was not. Isley et al. examined parents' affect and parenting behaviors, such as control and directiveness, as they interacted in a physical game with their children. The expression of negative affect by parents was the strongest predictor of children's social acceptance by peers, especially within same-sex dyads. The contribution of parental control and directiveness were less substantial than those of parents' negative affect.

Parental psychopathology.   We have primarily been discussing the hostile or aggressive part of the irritability system in families. Parental psychopathology is another process that may introduce negativity into a system, especially depression (Davies and Windle, 1997; Jacob and Johnson, 1997; Zahn-Waxler, Duggal, and Gruber, in Vol. 4 of this *Handbook*; Zahn-Waxler, Kochanska, Krupnick, and McKnew, 1990). Maternal depression is associated with increased negativity in parent–child interactions (Jacob and Johnson, 1997). It is also associated with children's responses to conflict and stress. Zahn-Waxler et al. (1990) reported that 5- to 6-year-old children of depressed mothers exhibited atypical patterns of overarousal in hypothetical situations concerning interpersonal conflict and distress. These children showed significantly more responsibility/involvement in the conflict and distress of others than children of nondepressed mothers. The themes of their responses were more likely to include expressions of remorse, self-punishment, reparation, blame-worthiness, combined with attempts to comfort or help others. Because depression is associated with self-attributions of responsibility for negative events, Zahn-Waxler et al. suggested that depressed mothers may recruit their children into sharing their affective burdens and guilt. The immature cognitive skills of young children make them less able to assign responsibility for the distress and conflict experienced by others. Children of depressed caregivers may find that sharing responsibility results in some positive effects such as adult attention and relief from aversive events.

Although most previous work has focused on the role of maternal psychopathology in parent–child interactions and child outcomes, other work indicates that paternal psychopathology also plays a role. Arnold, O'Leary, and Edwards (1997) found paternal symptoms of attention deficit hyperactivity disorder (ADHD) moderated the relation between father involvement and negative parenting patterns. Greater father involvement was associated with greater self-report of overreactivity in parenting when fathers had many ADHD symptoms. It is interesting to note that the positive association between paternal ADHD and overreactivity occurred only when the level of father involvement was high. The authors suggest that ADHD symptoms may interfere with fathers' ability to be patient and to employ more effective parenting practices when fathers are involved in many of the day to day childcare tasks required of parents. When paternal ADHD symptoms were not present, fathers' involvement in daily childrearing was related with more effective parenting behaviors. In the latter example, frequent involvement in childcare activities may create more opportunities for positive interactions between fathers and their children.

The Affectional System

The affectional system includes all factors that result in a more positive influence in families (e.g., positive attention and engagement, positive emotions such as joy, showing physical affection, reciprocal humor, validation, and affect sharing as well as positive play). Many of these are important processes in the repair of interactions. Unfortunately, there is a great deficit in the research literature about the role of positivity in families, particularly with respect to child developmental outcomes. One exception is face-to-face play between parents and their young infants. This research will be reviewed in the context of Tronick's (1980, 1989; Cohn and Tronick, 1983, 1989) theory of mutual regulation and repair.

The face-to face play of infants and parents: Miscoordination and repair.   Early interactions between infants and their parents provide an excellent example of how social interactions involve periods of negativity or miscoordination that require repair. Face-to-face play provides infants with their first opportunity to learn important lessons about interactions and repair. Coordinated states between parents and infants involve mutual regulation of affect and behavior in which one person follows the lead of the other. Infants signal their intent to communicate or disengage through gaze and affect, such as looking away when they are overstimulated.

Gianino and Tronick (1988) conceptualized miscoordinated states as interactive errors and the transition from miscoordinated states to coordinated ones as interactive repair. Interactive errors are frequent events. Infants and parents spend approximately 70% of the time in miscoordinated states. Consequently, all dyads experience states of miscoordination, the difference between well-functioning and more poorly functioning pairs is in the proportion of repairs. When caregivers are sensitive to infant signals, high proportions of repairs and positive interactions result. Infants learn that miscoordinated states are reparable and that they can create changes in these states. We think a high proportion of interactive repairs adds positivity to the family system.

When caregivers and infants are chronically miscoordinated, such as depressed mothers and their infants, infants experience prolonged periods of interactive failure, negative affect, and low rates of interactive repair (Tronick, 1989). Parents embroiled in marital conflict may have difficulty attending to the sometimes subtle signals used by infants to communicate their needs. For example, Owen and Cox (1997) found that parents involved in chronic marital conflict were less sensitive and involved in their parenting of their infants. Infants in these homes may learn that caregivers are unreliable sources of information or assistance in stressful situations. Owen and Cox found that marital conflict predicted infant's attachment status. Dickstein and Parke (1988) found that 11-month-old infants were less likely to socially reference their maritally dissatisfied fathers than infants of more satisfied fathers.

Physical play.   A second way that researchers have attempted to study the role of positivity in families is by examining the physical play of parents and their children. Young children acquire important skills about playing with others and the repair of negative affect in parent–child settings, especially in situations that elicit strong affect. The acquisition of these skills has powerful implications for children's peer relationships. MacDonald (1987) compared the dyadic play interactions of parents and their sons classified as popular or rejected by peer sociometric ratings. Popular boys and their parents were able to maintain longer bouts of physical play and showed more positive affect than rejected boys and their parents. The play of popular dyads appears to flow smoothly between participants. Exchanges are filled with reciprocal positive affect involving laughter, smiles, teasing, and playful affection. Physical play is an especially useful setting for examining regulation processes because of the potential for overstimulation and the need for mutual regulation. Children typically express their displeasure when their optimal level for stimulation is exceeded. MacDonald found that the frequency of overstimulation was much higher in rejected dyads than the popular dyads, especially for boys and their fathers. Parents of rejected children were less able to keep stimulation within levels appropriate for their child. Children in these dyads were more likely to try to avoid and to make negative responses to parental stimulation.

Carson (1993) studied the physical play interactions of 4- and 5-year-old children and their parents. He found that parents of rejected children displayed more neutral and angry cues, whereas parents of popular children gave more instructions about affect and more apologetic cues. Popular children also laughed and showed more positive affect than rejected children, who gave more neutral cues to their parents. Sequential analyses indicated that rejected boys and their fathers were more likely than popular boys and their fathers to engage in reciprocal negative affect. These chains of negativity were just as likely to start with fathers as with sons. In contrast, popular boys and their fathers were more likely to respond to negative affect by the other with neutral affect. This sequence is reminiscent of the interactions of maritally satisfied couples. Popular boys and their fathers and satisfied couples have developed ways to diffuse or regulate the negative affect in their interactions. The higher frequency of positive affect expressed in these pairs may help to explain this. Gottman (1993a) noted that stable marriages have a much higher ratio of positive to negative behaviors in their marital interactions than unstable marriages. Patterson (1982) also noted in passing that the homes of aggressive children do not contain very much love, fun, or affection. This observation raises the possibility that the child's aggression is a response to this lack of fun, affection, and intimacy in the family.

In summary, children learn important lessons about repairing interactions with others in the parent–child system. During the early months of life, face-to-face interactions provide opportunities for learning that interactions are reparable and that one can play a role in this process. Response tendencies that predispose some individuals to continue interactions despite temporary disruptions versus disengaging may have their genesis in these early experiences (Kopp, 1989). Play interactions with parents during early childhood provide an important context for learning about sharing fun and regulating positive and negative affect with others. In ineffective parent–child settings, expectations for mutual repair are repeatedly violated. Subsequent miscoordinations and overstimulation may trigger negative affect and withdrawal instead of attempts at repair. Thus, the ability to learn about repair mechanisms and apply them in different settings may be hampered.

Set Points: Uninfluenced and Influenced Set Points

The ratio of the total number of acts in the Affectional System (all positivity) to the total number of acts in the Irritability System is the set point variable. The start value of this ratio at the beginning of an interaction can be considered the initial state, or the "uninfluenced set point" of this system. As the family continues to interact, members affect one another, and we can compute a new or "influenced set point" for the family. This set point is regulated in family systems in the sense that an error signal is generated when deviations from the setpoint occur. The family system typically responds to this error signal by adjusting its interaction patterns in a way that maintains this set point (e.g., increasing negativity or positivity). Longitudinal work on marital stability, separation, and divorce suggests a set point of 5.0 (i.e., 5 positive events to one negative event) is characteristic of stable marriages, whereas a set point of 0.8 (1 positive to every 0.8 negative event) is characteristic of unstable marriages on the course to dissolution (Gottman, 1994).

The set point variable is important because it influences the probability of repair within the system. Families with a high ratio of positive to negative events are less likely to enter and become trapped in cycles of negativity, much like the stable marriage types described by Gottman (1993). For unstable marriages and ineffective family systems, negativity tends to become an "absorbing state." Individuals in these systems are unable to utilize repair processes used by individuals in more positively balanced systems for exiting negative cycles. What is particularly interesting about the set point idea in marriages and families is that a set point will be defended by a given system regardless of how functional it is for the long-term health of that system. Thus, families may continue to engage in cycles of coercion, such as those described by Patterson (1982), even though marital and child behavior problems increase.

The Emotion Bank Account: Positive and Negative Sentiment Override

The set point variable represents the emotional history of the couple or family. In our earlier discussion of repair processes in satisfied and dissatisfied couples, we noted that dissatisfied couples are more likely to combine repair attempts with negative affect and that this was associated with greater negative reciprocity. It is important to note that dissatisfied couples are also more likely than satisfied couples to respond to neutral affect expressed by their spouse with negative affect. Weiss (1980) proposed that couples' interactions were influenced by *positive and negative sentiment overrides*. That is, their reactions are determined not only by the immediate situation but by a global dimension of affection or disaffection in the relationship. Notarius, Benson, and Sloane (1989) investigated this hypothesis by examining the sequential patterns of behavior and cognitions in distressed and nondistressed couples' interactions. Distressed wives were more likely to perceive their partners' neutral and negative messages as negative than nondistressed wives. These findings support the idea that a negative sentiment override is in effect for distressed couples. Positive sentiment override, on the other hand, enables couples to recover more quickly from negative events during their interactions. Gottman (1998) called this idea the *Emotional Bank Account* model of marriage. Positive sentiment override is determined by how much *emotional money*, or positive sentiment, the couple has deposited in their account. Although a couple's account balance may be influenced by conflict and negativity, a more powerful determinant may actually be how they interact during more typical or mundane periods. For example, during daily interactions spouses vary on their contingent responsiveness to each other's neutral interest or excitement, what Gottman calls "turning toward each or turning away from each other." Consequently, a couple's history of overall affection and involvement influences how well they are able to repair negativity. We believe a similar process is at work within families.

"Inertia," or the Characteristic Flexibility of a System

"Inertia" refers to how flexible a system is, or how much it stays in a particular state once the state is entered. Dissatisfied marriages are prone to a state of inertia. Once these couples enter a cycle of negativity, it is very difficult for them to leave it. One reason repair processes fail is a constriction in social processes. Whereas satisfied couples are able to use repair processes to break away from the cycle of negativity, dissatisfied couples are unable to use these processes; they are more likely to focus on the negative affect component of the repair attempt or negative sentiment override takes over. For many dissatisfied couples, repair attempts actually add to the cycle of negativity rather than break it. Cycles of negativity described by Patterson (1982) and Hetherington (1989; Hetherington and Stanley-Hagan, in Vol. 3 of this *Handbook*) suggest that similar processes function in the parent–child setting. For example, Hetherington described "spontaneous startups" of negative cycles between divorced mothers and adolescent sons that occur when the mother or son responds negatively to a neutral or even positive statement made by the other.

TYPES OF MARRIAGES AND FAMILIES: RISKS AND BENEFITS TO CHILDREN

A Typology of Marriages

It is important at this point to distinguish among different types of marriages because they have different implications and risks for children. Gottman (1993a) reported two unstable and three stable types of marriages.

Unstable types of marriage include Hostile and Hostile/Detached marriages. The interactions of these couples are characterized by direct engagement in conflicts, high levels of negativity, and reciprocal attacks and defensiveness. The Hostile/Detached marriage type is more detached and less emotionally involved with one another than the Hostile type, but these couples still engage in episodes of reciprocated attack and defensiveness. Several behavior patterns discriminate between the two unstable types. Husbands from Hostile marriages are more likely than husbands from Hostile/Detached marriages to show interest in their wives, smile, and show affection and less likely to express disgust or contempt toward their wives. Wives in Hostile marriages show more interest, smile more, show less sadness, and express less disgust or contempt than wives in Hostile/Detached marriages. During a general discussion about the events of the day, wives in Hostile marriages are also more likely than wives in Hostile/Detached marriages to interject humor into the conversation, an important repair mechanism.

Although the balance between positive and negative interactions in the two unstable types is quite similar, both are more negative than the stable marriage types, which appears to be true across situations and time. Individuals in unstable types have lower marital satisfaction and are more likely to consider marital dissolution and separation. It may be that the two unstable types are really the same type at different stages of marital dissolution, with Hostile/Detached marriages closer to dissolution. However, at this point there is no evidence to support this speculation.

Stable types of marriages include Volatile, Conflict Avoiders, and Validators. Stable types of marriage have developed a balance or adaptation that enables them to handle (or avoid) conflict and remain together. Although the balance between positive and negative interactions within these marriages is roughly equivalent, approximately 5:1, the absolute level of negativity expressed is quite different. Volatile couples express high levels of negativity but balance this with much positivity, such as humor, positive affect, and passion. These couples tend not to inhibit feelings and may have long chains of reciprocated negativity as well as positivity. Validating couples express more moderate levels of negative and positive emotions. They carefully pick and choose when to disagree and confront conflict, and then convey some measure of support when their partner expresses negative feelings about an issue. This does not mean that the partner agrees with the other's view, but that it makes sense to feel a certain way given the other's perspective. Validating couples are typically good at resolving important conflicts and have lots of repair mechanisms. Conflict Avoiders eschew disagreement at any cost. If a potential conflict comes up in an interaction, these couples will suppress or minimize the importance of the difficulty. Conflict avoiding couples do not have specific strategies for resolving conflict and often refer to the passing of time alone as solving problems or the need for each spouse to work things out individually.

Characteristic Patterns of Influence in Marriages and Families

Marriage partners and members of families develop characteristic patterns for influencing each other. This pattern or "influence function" is an index of the possibility of repair within the family. In marriage, Cook, Tyson, White, Rushe, Gottman, and Murray (1995) found that Hostile, Hostile/Detached, and Volatile couples influenced one another only with negativity. Of these three, only Volatile couples balanced these negative behaviors with large amounts of positivity. On the other hand, Avoiders influenced each other only through positivity. Expressed negativity was typically ignored or quickly minimized by the other spouse in these marriages. Cook et al. (1995) found that Validating couples were able to influence their spouses with both positive and negative behaviors. Overall negative behavior had a negative influence, whereas positive behavior had a positive influence in this type of marriage.

The existing marital system and its characteristic influence function also affect interactions within families and children's development. We know that the only way some families create change in other family members is by continual escalation of negativity. Patterson (1982) described a cycle of coercion in which one member of a family uses aversive behaviors to gain compliance from another member. For example, a parent may scream or use physical aggression to gain compliance from a defiant child. Initially this tactic may be one-sided, but as the child learns aversive methods are effective in eliciting change from others, the pattern becomes reciprocal. More and more aversive events become necessary as the coercive cycle continues. Negative reinforcement (escaping pain) maintains this type of system. Members are reinforced when the aversive behavior of the other is stopped. Zahn-Waxler et al. (1990) suggested another type of cycle of negativity in the self-blame and guilt patterns of young children and their depressed mothers. Once patterns of negative reciprocity have been established, individuals may enter the cycle at many different points. As we described earlier, spontaneous startups of negative cycles between divorced mothers and adolescent sons can begin with neutral or even positive behavior on the part of one partner (Hetherington, 1989; Hetherington and Stanley-Hagan, in Vol. 3 of this *Handbook*). It appears to be difficult to break away from this cycle of negativity; just as in the marital relationship, negativity in families can become an absorbing state. We believe this is also due to the failure of repair processes.

Speculations About Risks and Benefits to Children
in Different Types of Families

Gottman (1993a) reported that unstable marriage types have a low set point of positive to negative interactions and frequent cycles of negative reciprocity and withdrawal, and are not likely to use repair mechanisms effectively. We see many dangers for children in these settings. It may be that the interaction patterns these couples use to influence each other become ingrained in parent–child interactions. Because these couples rarely inhibit feelings or behaviors, there is also the potential for violence in these homes. Couples in unstable marriages are also more likely to engage in the Mutually Hostile and Husband Anger and Withdrawal patterns that appear to be particularly corrosive to children's development (Katz and Gottman, 1993). The open, bitter, and unresolved conflicts within these homes also provide a poor atmosphere for children to observe and acquire appropriate skills necessary for interpersonal coordination and repair.

The two unstable types of marriage may pose somewhat different risks for children. Because Hostile/Detached marriages are closer to dissolution, they may be particularly toxic. There is some evidence of greater negativity, particularly contempt and disgust, as well as greater detachment of both husbands and wives in the Hostile/Detached compared to the Hostile group.

The stable marital types described by Gottman (1993a) also have a number of potential risks and benefits associated with them. Volatile marriages are similar to the unstable marriage types described above, except that they balance negativity with high levels of positivity. Parents in these homes are not afraid of intense feelings; both positive and negative emotions are expressed openly. Consequently, their children may also learn to recognize and express their own feelings and observe successful examples of repair processes. Children in these homes may also experience a great deal of warmth, fun, and closeness. On the other hand, the high level of negativity expressed in these marriages is concerning. Gottman (1993b) suggests that these marriages are at risk for violence because of their tendency to express feelings without inhibition. Cummings and his colleagues (Cummings, Ballard, El-Sheikh, and Lake, 1991; Cummings et al., 1989) have demonstrated that children as young as 5 years of age were less negative in response to angry parental interactions that are resolved than by those that are unresolved. Given their immature cognitive skills and relative lack of social experience and resources, toddlers and early preschool children may be particularly vulnerable to negativity in families. Even if marriages achieve a stable balance with a 5:1 ratio of positive to negative events and conflicts being resolved, young children may need a much higher level of positivity for proper emotional and social development. Alternately, it may be that their relative immaturity provides some protective function for younger children. It may also be that a high proportion of repairs in relation to expressed negativity provides a buffering effect for all children. At this point, we know of no research that has attempted to address this question.

Avoiders attempt to maintain a high level of positivity within their homes and avoid negativity as much as possible. Although at first glance the absence of all conflict appears beneficial to children, this may also be a high-risk strategy. Gottman and Krokoff (1989) found that although negative statements such as complaints are disruptive to marriages in the short term, they can be adaptive over the long term. Occasional misunderstandings and disagreements are inevitable in close relationships. Couples who avoid dealing with problems and issues in their marriage by ignoring and reprioritizing them as unimportant may experience immediate relief from the negative affect but fail to successfully resolve problems. The continued use of this pattern over the long-term course of marriage may lead to feelings of separateness, interpersonal distance, and low levels of companionship and sharing. Gottman (1994) also speculates that these couples lack basic skills for conflict resolution. When problems surface that cannot be ignored, they may be ill prepared to handle them. Although children from these marriages may not be exposed to frequent arguing or the negative affect present in more discordant homes, they miss opportunities to see disagreements openly discussed and resolved. Lacking examples of successful repair, children from these homes may also come to see conflict and negativity as overwhelming states.

Validating marriages expose children to more moderate levels of negative affect and high levels of positivity and repair. During the agenda building phase of marital conflict, children in these families are more likely to see differing views presented and validated. Although negative affect is still expressed in these marriages, it is less likely to escalate into cycles of reciprocal negativity. Thus, children in these homes are able to observe examples of effective repair mechanisms. These children may also come to see that conflict and negative emotions are not overwhelming states but aspects of human interaction that are both inevitable and reparable.

Changing System Parameters

Are there ways to change existing family patterns? Several "system parameters" can be manipulated to alter the functioning of an existing system. Several of these parameters are also interrelated. To change the set point of a particular system one can increase the number of positive interactions and/or decrease the number of negative interactions. According to our model, relatively large changes in positivity are needed to create change in a system's set point. In contrast, a small change in negativity can have a powerful effect on a system.

What about inertia within the system, or the degree to which the family is able to exit an affective state once it is entered? One possibility for manipulating this parameter is through families' expectations and beliefs regarding stressful events and concomitant emotions.

The Power of Violated Expectations During the Transition to First-Time Parenthood

Violated expectations play a powerful role in the quality of couples' marriages and their children's development during the transition to first-time parenthood. Cowan and Cowan (1992) reported that greater discrepancy between couples' expectations about the division of labor and roles before the baby's birth and their actual behavior and roles after the birth were predictive of declines in marital satisfaction. Children's academic and peer relationship problems were also predicted by the degree to which parents' expectations were violated. Greater discrepancy was related to more child aggression, shyness, a decreased ability to concentrate in school, and lower reading and math scores.

Transitions and conflicts are inevitable factors in family life. Dealing constructively with these stressful events is critical for the long-term health of marriages and children. The Cowans' work points to the importance of preparation and realistic expectations in negotiating first-time parenthood. Expectations, beliefs, and biases filter life experiences. Couples may attribute the cause of a current stress to flaws in their relationship or to elements of the current situation. A 6-month intervention program developed by Cowan and Cowan (1992, 1995) provided expectant couples with opportunities for discussing expectations, adjustments, and feelings related to the birth of their child. Couples in intervention groups maintained higher levels of marital satisfaction and were less likely to separate or divorce up to 3 years after the intervention than couples in nonintervention groups. The intervention couples still experienced the adjustments and conflicts typical for this period, but the stress and strain did not transfer to their marital relationship or children. According to Cowan and Cowan, these couples were better able to come back together after arguing over some problem or issue and to continue functioning as a team rather than as opponents.

Families as Emotion Cultures

In discussions of how families deal with stressful events we must also examine families' beliefs about these events and the emotions associated with them. For example, some individuals believe that strong negative emotions in themselves and their children should be controlled and not expressed. Other families believe that these experiences are healthy and seek out intense emotional interchanges.

Families develop specific belief systems about emotions, especially about particular emotions (e.g., anger and sadness). The nature of this belief system may be related to whether parents choose to notice and accept their children's emotions and whether they assist when their children are experiencing a particular strong emotion. This is important because the emotional world of the child and the child's ability to regulate his or her own emotions are related to the development of peer-related social competence (Gottman, 1983; Gottman et al., 1996; Sroufe et al., 1984; Wilson and Gottman, 1996).

The Meta-Emotion Interview (Gottman and Katz, 1986) assesses parents' meta-emotion philosophy, or how they think and feel about emotional experiences in themselves and their children. There is a parent meta-emotion philosophy we call emotion coaching, in which parents notice low-intensity emotions in their children and see these emotion moments as opportunities for teaching and building intimacy with their child. These parents are accepting of their child's emotions but also set limits on behaviors associated with emotions. They also participate in problem solving with their child about these emotional experiences. A second type of philosophy is the emotion-dismissing meta-emotion philosophy. Parents with this type of philosophy feel that sadness and anger are dangerous emotions and parents should help their child get over these feelings as quickly as possible. Some emotion-dismissing parents talk about teaching their children that these emotions aren't important, that they don't last long, and that their child needs to learn to "ride out" these affective states.

Longitudinal data on the effects of meta-emotion processes indicate that children of emotion-coaching parents experience numerous positive outcomes not associated with children of emotion-dismissing parents. They are better able to regulate their emotions, stay organized when experiencing negative emotions, and focus their attention (Gottman et al., 1996). They also have less negative interactions with friends and peers at school, fewer behavior problems, and are rated more positively by their teachers. At age 8, children with emotion-coaching parents had higher reading and mathematics scores in school, even when controlling for their general intelligence at age 5. Thus, the type of emotion culture experienced by children has implications for their social and academic development.

The relation between meta-emotion variables and many child outcomes appears to be mediated by children's regulatory physiology (i.e., their vagal tone). The vagus nerve is the tenth cranial nerve and the major nerve associated with the parasympathetic nervous system. It also innervates the thymus gland, which is involved in the production of T cells. Children with emotion-coaching parents tend to have higher vagal tone and are also more resistant to illness (Gottman et al., 1996). Children with emotion-coaching parents also have lower heart rates and recover more quickly from the physiological arousal associated with negative emotions than children with emotion-dismissing parents.

We might ask why talking about emotional experiences would have such a profound influence on children's development. Vygotsky (1962) described how language could play a mediational role in children's processing of emotional experiences and their subsequent behavior. Pine (1985, p. 139) also suggested that "Words provide a moment of recognition and delay in which discomfort over feelings might have a chance to be handled in ways other than denial or immediate discharge through action." Gottman (1998) described a mechanism for this process. He believes that when parents coach their children regarding emotions, the emotion is processed in a different area of the child's brain. Emotional experiences that would usually be processed in the right hemisphere become a left-frontal or bilateral process. Negative emotions that are related to withdrawal from stimulation (e.g., sadness, fear, and disgust) are usually processed in the right frontal lobe. Joy, interest, curiosity, amusement, and even anger are emotions related to greater engagement in the world and tend to be processed in the left frontal lobe. Language centers are also located in the left hemisphere and are engaged when parents talk to their children about emotions. Gottman believes that right frontal lobe activation during withdrawal emotions leads to increases in physiological arousal (e.g., increases in heart rate) because the right frontal lobe has direct connections with the limbic system and the brain stem, and finally to autonomic centers. Emotion-coaching increases left frontal lobe activity and subsequently the processing of emotional experience. This shift in the processing of emotional experience enables children to soothe the physiological arousal associated with negative withdrawal emotions.

Research (Gottman et al., 1996; Katz and Gottman, 1997) has also found evidence that parents' meta-emotion philosophy influences children's regulatory physiology, such as their baseline vagal tone and suppression of vagal tone. This is important because children's regulatory physiology serves as a buffer, protecting children from many of the negative effects associated with marital hostility, conflict, and dissolution. Before discussing the results of these studies, a brief description of the vagal tone indices used in this research is needed. During periods when environmental challenges are minimal, vagal influences act as a brake on the heart, slowing its intrinsic rhythm. According to

Porges, Doussard, Portales, and Greenspan (1996) this assists in the maintenance of physiological homeostasis, promoting growth and restoration. During periods of environmental challenge, withdrawal of these inhibitory influences (suppression of vagal tone) results in rapid changes in cardiac functioning. Porges et al. suggest that the appropriate withdrawal of vagal tone enables individuals to more effectively engage and disengage with their environments.

Katz and Gottman (1995) found a strong relation between martial hostility and child externalizing behavior when children had low-baseline vagal tone, but this association was not found when children had high vagal tone. Subsequent research (Katz and Gottman, 1997) investigated whether baseline vagal tone and suppression of vagal tone buffered children from the negative effects associated with martial conflict and marital dissolution. They found that both vagal indices served as buffers against emotion regulation difficulties in children whose parents were experiencing marital conflict and dissolution.

We believe that similar processes may also influence how children deal with unresolved marital conflict. Cummings and Wilson (1999) found that, even when marital conflicts were not resolved, explanations such as "It is okay to disagree" improved 6- to 21-year-olds' representations of their parents' relations. For some children (10 to 12 and 14 to 16 years old), explanations involving potential negative consequences of nonresolution such as parental divorce were more helpful than no explanation at all. We suggest that the more parents notice, discuss, and assist children with their emotional reactions to parents' unresolved conflicts, the more helpful their explanations will be. As Cummings and Wilson's research suggests, it appears that any discussion of unresolved martial conflict is more helpful than no discussion at all, especially for older children.

Education about stressful life transitions and emotion-coaching philosophies are two important processes that can help to alleviate the detrimental effects of stressful life events such as marital conflict. The following section presents research on other factors that may serve to buffer children from negative effects or may place children at additional risk for negative outcomes associated with marital conflict.

RISK AND PROTECTIVE FACTORS IN THE TRANSFER
OF MARITAL CONFLICT TO CHILDREN

Individual Differences

A number of child characteristics influence the relation between marital conflict and child development. Positive personality characteristics provide a protective function against stress for children (Garmezy, 1983). A more difficult temperament, on the other hand, may place children at risk for more negative outcomes (Sanson, Putnam, and Rothbart, in Vol. 1 of this *Handbook*). For example, Easterbrooks, Cummings, and Emde (1994) found that young children (ages 12 to 36 months) with difficult temperaments were more reactive during marital disputes. The temperamentally difficult child is also more likely to elicit and be the target of aversive interchanges with parents (Rutter, 1987; Putnam et al., in Vol. 1 of this *Handbook*). This is especially true when difficult temperament is combined with deficits in the parent's support or personal resources (Belsky, 1984). For example, Hetherington (1989) found that difficult temperament was related to aversive maternal responses only when it was combined with high levels of stress or maternal personality problems.

It is likely that the relation between child temperament/characteristics and marital conflict is bidirectional in nature. Marital conflict may create a stressful environment for children, and a difficult child may prove to be a stressor on the marital relationship. On the other hand, the effects of these factors are probably not uniform. O'Leary (1984) found that the conditional probability of the occurrence of marital conflict given child problems was smaller than the conditional probability of child behavior problems given marital conflict.

Physiological Functioning

As described in the section on meta-emotion philosophy, aspects of children's physiological functioning may affect their ability to cope adaptively with stress and challenges. Environmental stressors
are physiologically costly to individuals; a quick expenditure of physiological resources is needed
to meet a challenge and then return to some previous homeostatic state. Environmental challenges
may be as simple as sustaining attention toward a partner during a conversation or as demanding
as coping with an angry and potentially violent parent. Thus, flexibility in physiological responses
and recovery are important aspects of adaptability. A substantial amount of research (Fox, 1989;
Fox and Field, 1989; Katz and Gottman, 1995, 1997; Stanley [Wilson] and Katz (1991) suggests
that vagal tone is associated with better emotion regulation abilities in young children. Fox found
that 5-month-old infants with high vagal tone were more likely than infants with low vagal tone to
use emotion regulation strategies such as looking at mother or self in a mirror when they were distressed. At 14 months, infants with high vagal tone were less reticent to approach an unfamiliar adult
(with mother present) and a novel toy. Fox suggested that early successful experiences with emotion
regulation strategies enable infants with high vagal tone to encounter potentially stressful situations
(such as novelty) with less apprehension and stress. Perceptions of self-efficacy may also increase
in these individuals as they encounter stressful situations and are able to successfully regulate their
physiological responses.

Physiological correlates of play have also been investigated. The ability to coordinate play with
others is a particularly complex task that necessitates managing conflict, attending to the affective
signals of others, and regulating one's emotions (Gottman, 1983; Wilson and Gottman, 1996). Fox
and Field (1989) examined the relation between vagal tone and preschoolers' adaptation to a new
classroom environment. They found that children with high vagal tone, high activity levels, and
low distractibility were more likely to move from solitary to group play over the 6 weeks of their
observations. Stanley [Wilson] and Katz (1991) found that 4- to 6-year-old children with high vagal
tone were better able than children with low vagal tone to maintain a joint play activity with their
best friend, a task that often involves negotiating roles and ownership of preferred objects.

Variables related to physiological reactivity and recovery may also influence an individual's tendency to engage in or avoid potentially stressful situations. If an individual reacts to challenging situations with high levels of arousal or is unable to return to a state of physiological homeostasis quickly
after stressful events, this person may learn to avoid potentially stressful situations in the future.

Gender

Rutter (1979) observed that males are generally more vulnerable to stress including psychosocial
stressors. Recent work suggests that it may be more accurate to talk about gender differences in
response patterns than greater vulnerability. In general, boys are more likely to develop externalizing
problems, whereas girls are more likely to develop internalizing problems in response to marital
conflict or violence (Davies, Myers, and Cummings, 1996; Emery and O'Leary 1982; Jouriles and
Norwood, 1995). It is also the case that distress or internalizing responses may not be readily
apparent to observers, but aggression is likely to draw the attention of parents, schools, and health
care professionals. Gender differences in children's response to stress and interparental conflict may
be related to these child outcomes.

Boys typically respond to stress by becoming more aggressive, whereas girls are more likely to
withdraw or become anxious (Block et al., 1981, 1986; Cohn, 1991). Cummings and colleagues
(Cummings et al., 1985; Cummings et al., 1989) reported that boys were more likely than girls to
respond to interadult anger with increased anger and aggression, whereas girls were more likely than
boys to respond with distress.

Gender differences in children's perception of and involvement in interparental anger also exist.
Crockenberg and Forgays (1996) found that girls perceived their fathers as more angry than boys

or objective observers did. This may be related to the tendency of girls to withdraw from parental conflicts. Boys, on the other hand, appear more aware of marital conflict than girls (Cummings, Davies, and Simpson, 1994) and are more likely to become engaged in their parents' conflicts (e.g., trying to help parents resolve the issue; Davies et al., 1996). Greater involvement in parents' marital conflict is related to poorer outcomes in children (O'Brien, Margolin, and John, 1995). Greater involvement may also be related to the finding that boys whose parents are in violent marriages are more likely than girls to become the target of aggression by their parents (Jouriles and Norwood, 1995).

There are also gender differences in the way maritally distressed parents interact with their children (see Snyder, 1998, for a recent review). There are some indications that girls are more likely than boys to encounter inconsistent discipline and parental involvement when their parents are in marital conflict. Recall that Cowen and Cowen (1992) found that fathers were more likely to engage in authoritarian parenting toward daughters when they were unhappily married. This was not true for fathers with sons. Mothers who were unhappily married, on the other hand, were more authoritarian with both their sons and daughters during play interactions. McHale (1995) found that fathers in distressed marriages showed lower levels of engagement with their infant daughters during triadic play than mothers. Snyder suggests that these differences may be related to the higher incidence of internalizing problems among girls. She reasoned that discrepancies in parenting would result in greater parental conflict over childrearing issues. Conflict over childrearing issues is more likely than other conflict situations to result in self-blame and shame in children (Grych and Fincham, 1993; McHale, Fritag, Crouter, and Bartko, 1991). A positive association between girls' internalizing problems and self-blame related to parents' conflict has also been identified (Cummings et al., 1994).

Age

Work by Cummings and his colleagues (Cummings et al., 1981) suggests that children as young as 1 year of age are distressed by interadult conflict. Young children are more likely than older children to respond to conflictual adult interactions with increased aggression (Cummings et al., 1985). Positive associations between externalizing problems in preschool children and parental disagreement about childrearing and toddler conduct problems and marital discord have been identified (Block et al., 1981; Jouriles, Pfiffner, and O'Leary, 1988; Mahoney, Jouriles, and Scavone, 1997). Parental divorce has also been shown to relate to increases in aggression and irritability in preschoolers (Wallerstein and Kelly, 1980). Because of their less developed cognitive skills, preschool children may need help understanding the source of interparental conflicts. Preschool children are less able than adolescents to infer the resolution of parental conflict based only on how the conflict ended (Davies et al., 1996). Young preschool children tend to feel responsible for their parents' conflicts and often benefit from simple explanations that absolve them of blame. These children may also benefit from seeing overt positive resolutions to parental conflict, such as physical displays of affection (Davies and Cummings, 1994).

As children move from toddlerhood and preschool to the early elementary school years, they are less likely to show overt distress responses to interadult conflict but are more likely to attempt to intervene (Cummings et al., 1989; Cummings, Zahn-Waxler, and Radke-Yarrow, 1984). This may occur because older children are better able to determine the cause of their distress and become more active in attempts to relieve it (Kopp, 1989). Interventions may involve pleading with parents to stop fighting or comforting a crying parent. However, the intensity of interparental conflict will influence children's coping responses. Johnston, Campbell, and Mayes (1985) reported the responses of latency age children to witnessing intense parental hostility after divorce. Parents reported that 79% of the young latency children (6 to 8 years) displayed a submissive distress response such as becoming highly anxious, staring helplessly or freezing, crying as well as somatic complaints after witnessing interparent hostility. These responses decreased with age, by 9 to 12 years only 32% showed this type of distress. In addition, over 25% of 9- to 12-year-old children showed distress responses involving aggression. Cummings et al. (1984) found very few older children responded with distress or anger to interadult conflicts, but the conflicts children viewed in Cummings's studies were less aversive and possibly less personally threatening.

Although preschoolers are not bothered by logical inconsistencies or mixed emotions in interparental conflict, early latency children in the Johnston et al. study (1985) were highly confused about these issues. They struggled to understand who was right and who was wrong in parental conflicts. According to Piaget (Piaget and Inhelder, 1969), children in this age range are able to think more logically about their world and to weigh different solutions to problems. Research also suggests that older children are able to infer the resolution of interadult conflicts that have occurred behind closed doors from a number of channels such as changes in parent's affect, voice, and interaction (Cummings, Simpson, Pennington, and Wilson, 1993). Children's ability to understand conflict contexts that are relatively complex also increases with age (e.g., when resolutions involve mixed messages such as an angry apology; Simpson and Cummings, 1996). Although these children can infer resolution, they may still benefit from seeing some conflicts worked out. For example, children of this age can appreciate discussions of resolutions based on rules and the principles of justice and fairness.

Adolescence presents many new challenges for parents. Whereas abstract reasoning skills allow adolescents a wider variety of strategies for responding to stress, their strivings to resolve issues regarding their own identity and place in the world present significant challenges. The family system during this time must provide continued structure and support, while encouraging movement toward greater responsibility and age-appropriate independence. Chronic conflict between parents often makes families less adaptable to change and may, consequently, complicate this process. This is especially true when adolescents feel caught between their parents. Buchanan, Maccoby, and Dornbusch (1991) found adolescents whose parents continued to engage in high levels of conflict and hostility after their divorce were more likely than other adolescents to feel caught in the middle of their parents' conflicts. When adolescents felt caught in the middle they were more likely to feel depressed and anxious. When parents can work effectively on resolving their disputes, adolescents benefit from seeing these negotiated and resolved. They are better able than younger children to understand underlying motives and themes in interpersonal conflicts and benefit from resolutions based on understanding of one's self, a psychological resolution.

Cummings and Wilson (1999) found age differences in children's ability to discriminate between different explanations for unresolved conflicts. They found that 6- to 12-year-old children differentiated between explanations about nonresolution that suggested positive versus negative future consequences. These children showed a preference for explanations associated with positive consequences regardless of the constructiveness of the explanations (i.e., how realistic versus vague parents' explanations were about the plan for resolution). Adolescents and young adults (14 to 21 years old), on the other hand, differentiated between explanations based on how realistic versus unrealistic the plans were for resolution.

CONCLUSIONS

Social-affective processes within families are linked to child outcome: There is now evidence of good predictability from the quality of marriages to child outcomes. However, the mechanisms mediating these effects are not well understood. We reviewed research suggesting that parenting behaviors mediate between marital distress and many child outcomes. We contend that it may not be conflict per se (i.e., nonphysical conflict) that leads to negative child outcomes, but a failure of repair mechanisms. To explain this notion of the failure of repair mechanisms, we reviewed research on marital quality, showing that the most consistent discriminator across studies between happy and unhappy marriages is negative affect reciprocity, and that this is probably the case because of the failure of repair mechanisms such as metacommunication.

It is fruitful to extend the concept of repair to the entire family system. Processes, such as negative affect reciprocity, that are detrimental to marriages, are also corrosive to child development. We also extend the idea of the set point variable (i.e., the ratio of positive to negative events) from research on marriage to the family system. A high ratio of positive to negative events, or what we might think of as a positive balance in families' emotional bank account (Gottman, 1998), is needed to utilize repair processes effectively. Thus, the failure of repair processes can be seen as the major deficit in both unstable marriages and ineffective family systems.

When couples are unable to use repair mechanisms effectively to resolve conflict and repair negativity, their marriages and children suffer. Specifically, unresolved and chronic conflict and negativity in marriages steal emotional energy from important parental roles, such as being providers and facilitators of children's social opportunities. It undermines the ability of parents to support each other's parenting and spills over into the parent–child setting, particularly corroding positive affect and increasing irritability. Chronic conflict and negativity between parents may also interfere with children's acquisition of effective strategies for repair of negativity through modeling and direct experiences with repair failure in the parent–child setting. When children are unable to observe and participate in successful repair in the familial setting, they are less likely to acquire their own strategies for repair and may also come to experience conflict and negative affect as overwhelming or "absorbing states."

We also suggested that families are emotion cultures and that their "meta-emotion systems," or their feelings about feelings, determine the management of the Affectional and Irritability systems. In particular, a family's ratio of positivity to negativity is the regulated quantity of interest in predicting child outcome. Furthermore, there are characteristics of children that provide buffers against the negative effects of marital discord. It is also necessary to consider the cumulative effects of stress on families and children, which has implications for social policy.

Social policy needs to be developed to assist families during difficult normative and nonnormative transitions. Cowan's and Cowan's (1992, 1995) work with expectant parents suggests that marital dissatisfaction, dissolution, and a number of negative child outcomes can be reduced when families have a safe place to learn and to share their expectations, struggles, and feelings concerning first-time parenthood. Programs preparing families for stressful transitions should be implemented in all local hospitals and community centers. Many new mothers and fathers would also benefit from programs that continue until the end of the first postpartum year. Many role adjustments are required during this time, and it is important that new parents develop effective coparenting skills (Belsky and Hsieh, 1998; Matthey and Barnett, 1999; McHale, Khazan, Rotman, DeCourcey, and McConnell, in Vol. 3 of this *Handbook*). Other important forms of support needed by families are reliable and affordable daycare and family leave policies (Clark-Stewart and Allhusen, in Vol. 3 of this *Handbook*). These preventive forms of assistance could have immediate and long-term effects on the health and stability of marriages and the development of children. The need for social and economic support during crisis situations is also evident. Counseling and supportive services are needed for families struggling with marital conflict and dissolution. These services are also needed for families facing the challenges of educating and caring for children with special needs such as disabilities or developmental delays. In addition, many families face major life stressors such as a loss of income, terminal illness, or the death of a loved one. Providing services for families encountering these events should be a top priority for any health care system.

ACKNOWLEDGMENTS

We acknowledge support to the second author by the National Institute of Mental Health, including grant MH47083 and Research Scientist Award MHK00257, held since 1979. We are grateful to C. K. Craig and J. Cunningham for their helpful editing and comments on an earlier version of this chapter. We also wish to thank T. Osborn for assistance in the gathering research articles for this chapter.

REFERENCES

Amato, P. R., and Booth, A. (1996). A prospective study of divorce and parent–child relationships. *Journal of Marriage and the Family, 58,* 356–365.

Anderson, E. R., Greene, S. M., Hetherington, E. M., and Clingempeel, W. G. (1999). The dynamics of parental remarriage: Adolescent, parent, and sibling influences. In E. M. Hetherington (Ed.), *Coping with divorce, single parenting, and remarriage: A risk and resiliency perspective* (pp. 295–319). Mahwah, NJ: Lawrence Erlbaum Associates.

Arnold, E. H., O'Leary, S. G., and Edwards, G. Y. (1997). Father involvement and self-reported parenting of children with attention deficit-hyperactivity disorder. *Journal of Consulting and Clinical Psychology, 65,* 337–342.

Bandura, A. (1973). *Aggression: A social learning analysis.* Englewood Cliffs, NJ: Prentice-Hall.

Bandura, A., Ross, D., and Ross, S. A. (1963). Imitation of film-mediated aggressive models. *Journal of Abnormal and Social Psychology, 66,* 3–11.

Barth, J. M., and Parke, R. (1993). Parent–child relationship influences on children's transition to school. *Merrill Palmer Quarterly, 39,* 173–195.

Bateson, G., Jackson, D. D., Haley, J., and Weakland, J. (1956). Toward a theory of schizophrenia. *Behavioral Science, 1,* 251–264.

Belsky, J. (1984). The determinants of parenting: A process model. *Child Development, 55,* 83–96.

Belsky, J., and Hsieh, K. (1998). Patterns of marital change during the early childhood years: Parent personality, coparenting, and division-of-labor correlates. *Developmental Psychology, 12,* 511–528.

Belsky, J., and Kelly, J. (1994). *The transition to parenthood: How a first child changes a marriage. Why some couples grow closer and others apart.* New York: Dell.

Belsky, J., Lang, M. E., and Rovine, M. (1985). Stability and change in marriage across the transition to parenthood: A second study. *Journal of Marriage and the Family, 47,* 855–865.

Belsky, J., and Volling, B. L. (1987). Mothering, fathering, and marital interaction in the family triad during infancy: Exploring family system processes. In P. W. Berman and F. A. Pederson (Eds.), *Men's transitions to parenthood: Longitudinal studies and early family experiences* (pp. 37–63). Hillsdale, NJ: Lawrence Erlbaum Associates.

Bhavnagrei, N. P., and Parke, R. D. (1991). Parents as direct facilitators of children's peer relationships: Effects of age of child and sex of parent. *Journal of Social and Personal Relationships, 8,* 423–440.

Block, J. H., Block, J., and Gjerde, P. F. (1986). The personality of children prior to divorce: A prospective study. *Child Development, 57,* 827–840.

Block, J., Block, J. H., and Gjerde, P. F. (1988). Parental functioning and home environments in families of divorce: Prospective and concurrent analyses. *The American Academy of Child and Adolescent Psychiatry, 27,* 207–213.

Block, J. H., Block, J., and Morrison, A. (1981). Parental agreement–disagreement on child-rearing orientations and gender-related personality correlates in children. *Child Development, 52,* 965–974.

Bolger, K. E., Patterson, C. J., Thompson, W. W., and Kupersmidt, J. B. (1995). Psychosocial adjustment among children experiencing persistent and intermittent family economic hardship. *Child Development, 66,* 1107–1129.

Brody, G. H., and Flor, D. L. (1998). Maternal resources, parenting practices, and child competence in rural, single-parent African American families. *Child Development, 69,* 803–816.

Buchanan, C. M., Maccoby, E. E., and Dornbusch, S. M. (1991). Caught between parents: Adolescents' experience in divorced homes. *Child Development, 62,* 1008–1029.

Carson, J. L. (1993, March). *Sociometric status differences in affect sequences in preschool children's play with parents.* Paper presented at the biennial meeting of the Society for Research in Child Development, New Orleans, LA.

Cohn, J. F. (1991). Sex differences in the course of personality development: A meta-analysis. *Psychological Bulletin, 109,* 252–266.

Cohn, J. F., and Tronick, E. Z. (1983). Three-month-old infants' reaction to simulated maternal depression. *Child Development, 54,* 185–193.

Cohn, J. F., and Tronick, E. Z. (1989). Specificity of infants' response to mothers' affective behavior. *Journal of the American Academy of Child and Adolescent Psychiatry, 28,* 242–248.

Conger, R. D., Conger, K. J., Elder, G. H., Lorenz, R. O., Simons, R. L., and Whitbeck, L. B. (1993). Family economic stress and adjustment of early adolescent girls. *Developmental Psychology, 29,* 206–219.

Conger, R. D., Elder, G. H., Jr., Lorenz, F. O., Simons, R. L., and Whitbeck, L. B. (1992). A family process model of economic hardship and influences on adjustment of early adolescent boys. *Child Development, 60,* 1015–1024.

Cook, J., Tyson, R., White, J., Rushe, R., Gottman, J., and Murray, J. (1995). The mathematics of marital conflict: Qualitative dynamics and mathematical modeling of marital interaction. *Journal of Family Psychology, 9,* 110–130.

Cowan, P. P., and Cowan, P. A. (1992). *When partners become parents.* New York: Basic Books.

Cowan, C. P., and Cowan, P. A. (1995). Interventions to ease the transition to parenthood: Why they are needed and what they can do. *Family Relations, 44,* 412–423.

Cowan, C. P., Cowan, P. A., Heming, G., Garrett, E., Coysh, W. S., Curtis-Boles, H., and Boles, A. J. (1985). Transitions to parenthood: His, hers, and theirs. *Journal of Family Issues, 6,* 451–481.

Cowan, P. A., Cowan, C. P., Schulz, M. S., and Heming, G. (1994). Prebirth to preschool family factors in children's adaptation to kindergarten. In R. D. Parke and S. G. Kellam (Eds.), *Exploring family relationships with other social contexts* (pp. 75–114). Hillsdale, NJ: Lawrence Erlbaum Associates.

Crockenberg, S., and Forgays, D. K. (1996). The role of emotion in children's understanding and emotional reactions to marital conflict. *Merrill-Palmer Quarterly, 42,* 22–47.

Cummings, E. M., Ballard, M., El-Sheikh, M., and Lake, M. (1991). Resolution and children's responses to interadult anger. *Developmental Psychology, 27,* 462–470.

Cummings, E. M., Davies, P. T., and Simpson, K. S. (1994). Marital conflict, gender, and children's appraisals and coping efficacy as mediators of child adjustment. *Journal of Family Psychology, 8,* 141–149.

Cummings, E. M., Iannotti, R. J., and Zahn-Waxler, C. (1985). Influence of conflict between adults on the emotions and aggression of young children. *Developmental Psychology, 21,* 495–507.

Cummings, J. S., Pellegrini, D. S., Notarius, C. I., and Cummings, E. M. (1989). Children's responses to angry adult behavior as a function of marital distress and history of interparent hostility. *Child Development, 60,* 1035–1043.

Cummings, E. M., Simpson, K., Pennington, L., and Wilson, A. (1993, March). *Fighting constructively: Children's reactions to everyday contexts of interpersonal conflict resolution.* Paper presented at the biennial meeting of the Society for Research in Child Development, New Orleans, LA.

Cummings, E. M., Vogel, D., Cummings, J. S., and El-Sheikh, M. (1989). Children's responses to different forms expression of anger between adults. *Child Development, 60,* 1392–1404.

Cummings, E. M., and Wilson, A. (1999). Contexts of marital conflict and children emotional security: Exploring the distinction between constructive and destructive conflict from the children's perspective. In M. J. Cox and J. Brooks-Gunn, *Conflict and cohesion in families: Causes and consequences* (pp. 105–129). Mahwah, NJ: Lawrence Erlbaum Associates.

Cummings, E. M., Zahn-Waxler, C., and Radke-Yarrow, M. (1981). Young children's responses to expressions of anger and affection by others in the family. *Child Development, 52,* 1274–1282.

Cummings, E. M., Zahn-Waxler, C., and Radke-Yarrow, M. (1984). Developmental changes in children's reactions to anger in the home. *Journal of Child Psychology and Psychiatry, 25,* 63–74.

Davies, P. T., and Cummings, E. M. (1994). Martial conflict and child adjustment: An emotional security hypothesis. *Psychological Bulletin, 116,* 387–411.

Davies, P. T., and Cummings, E. M. (1998). Exploring children's emotional security as a mediator of the link between marital relations and child adjustment. *Child Development, 69,* 124–139.

Davies, P. T., Myers, R. L., and Cummings, E. M. (1996). Responses of children and adolescents to interadult anger: A functionalist perspective. *Developmental Psychology, 31,* 677–684.

Davies, P. T., and Windle, M. (1997). Gender-specific pathways between maternal depressive symptoms, family discord, and adolescent adjustment. *Developmental Psychology, 33,* 657–668.

Derensky, J. L., and Tarabulsy, G. (1991, April). *An empirical examination of the applications of stress-coping theory for children from divorced homes.* Paper presented at the biennial meeting of the Society for Research in Child Development, Seattle, WA.

Dickstein, S., and Parke, R. D. (1988). Social referencing in infancy: A glance at fathers and marriage. *Child Development, 59,* 506–511.

Easterbrooks, M. A., Cummings, E. M., and Emde, R. N. (1994). Young children's responses to constructive marital disputes. *Journal of Family Psychology, 8,* 160–169.

El-Sheikh, M., Cummings, E. M., and Goetsch, V. L. (1989). Coping with adults' angry behavior: Behavioral, physiological, and verbal responses in preschoolers. *Developmental Psychology, 25,* 490–498.

El-Sheikh, M., and Reiter, S. L. (1995, March). *Inter-adult anger: A comparison of mothers' and children's responses to videotaped interactions.* Poster session presented at the biennial meeting of the Society for Research in Child Development, Indianapolis, IN.

Emery, R. E. (1982). Interparent conflict and the children of discord and divorce. *Psychological Bulletin, 92,* 310–330.

Emery, R. E., and O'Leary, K. D. (1982). Children's perceptions of marital discord and behavior problems of boys and girls. *Journal of Abnormal Child Psychology, 10,* 11–24.

Erel, O., and Burman, B. (1995). Interrelatedness of martial relations and parent–child relations: A meta-analytic review. *Psychological Bulletin, 118,* 108–132.

Fauber, R., Forehand, R., Thomas, A. M., and Wierson, M. (1990). A mediational model of the impact of marital conflict on adolescent adjustment in intact and divorced families: The role of disrupted parenting. *Child Development, 61,* 1112–1123.

Fitzpatrick, M. A. (1988). *Between husbands and wives: Communication in marriage.* Beverly Hills, CA: Sage.

Floyd, F. J., and Zmich, D. E. (1991). Marriage and the parenting partnership: Perceptions and interactions of parents with mentally retarded and typically developing children. *Child Development, 62,* 1434–1448.

Fox, N. A. (1989). Psychophysiological correlates of emotional reactivity during the first year of life. *Developmental Psychology, 25,* 364–372.

Fox, N. A., and Field, T. M. (1989). Individual differences in preschool entry behavior. *Journal of Applied Developmental Psychology, 10,* 527–540.

Frosch, C. A., Mangelsdorf, S. C., and McHale, J. L. (1998). Correlates of marital behavior at 6 months postpartum. *Developmental Psychology, 34*, 1438–1449.

Garmezy, N. (1983). Stressors of childhood. In N. Garmezy and M. Rutter (Eds.), *Stress, coping, and development of children.* New York: McGraw-Hill.

Gianino, A., and Tronick, E. Z. (1988). The mutual regulation model: The infant's self and interactive regulation, coping, and defense. In T. Field, P. McCabe, and N. Schneiderman (Eds.), *Stress and coping* (pp. 47–68). Hillsdale, NJ: Lawrence Erlbaum Associates.

Gordis, E. B., Margolin, G., and John, R. S. (1997). Marital aggression, observed parental hostility, and child behavior during triadic family interaction. *Journal of Family Psychology, 11*, 76–89.

Gottman, J. M. (1979). *Marital interaction: Experimental investigations.* San Diego, CA: Academic Press.

Gottman, J. M. (1983). How children become friends. *Monographs of the Society for Research in Child Development, 48* (Serial No. 201).

Gottman, J. M. (1993a). The roles of conflict engagement, escalation, and avoidance in marital interaction: A longitudinal view of five types of couples. *Journal of Consulting and Clinical Psychology, 61*, 6–15.

Gottman, J. M. (1993b). *What predicts divorce?* Hillsdale, NJ: Lawrence Erlbaum Associates.

Gottman, J. M. (1994). An agenda for marital therapy. In S. M. Johnson and L. S. Greenberg (Eds.), *The heart of the matter: Perspectives on emotion in marital therapy* (pp. 256–293). New York: Brunner/Mazel.

Gottman, J. M. (1998). Toward a process model of mean in marriages and families. In A. Booth and A. C. Crouter (Eds.), *Men in families: When do they get involved? What difference does it make?* (pp. 149–192). Mahwah, NJ: Lawrence Erlbaum Associates.

Gottman, J. M., and Fainsilber, L. (1986). *The meta-emotion interview.* Unpublished manuscript, University of Illinois, Champaign.

Gottman, J. M., and Katz, L. F. (1989). Effect of marital discord on young children's peer interaction and health. *Developmental Psychology, 25*, 373–381.

Gottman, J. M., and Katz, L. F. (1993). Patterns of marital conflict predict children's internalizing and externalizing behaviors. *Developmental Psychology, 29*, 940–950.

Gottman, J. M., Katz, L. F., and Hooven, C. (1996). Parental meta-emotion philosophy and the emotional life of families: Theoretical models and preliminary data. *Journal of Family Psychology, 10*, 243–268.

Gottman, J. M., and Krokoff, L. J. (1989). The relationship between marital interaction and marital satisfaction: A longitudinal view. *Journal of Consulting and Clinical Psychology, 57*, 47–52.

Gottman, J. M., and Levinson, R. W. (1992). Toward a typology of marriage-based affective behavior: Preliminary differences in behavior, physiology, health, and risk for dissolution. *Journal of Personality and Social Psychology, 63*, 221–233.

Grossman, F., Eichler, L., and Winickoff, S. (1980). *Pregnancy, birth, and parenthood.* San Francisco, CA: Jossey-Bass.

Grych, J. H., and Fincham, F. D. (1993). Children's appraisals of martial conflict: Initial investigations of the cognitive-contextual framework. *Child Development, 64*, 215–230.

Harrist, A. W., and Ainslie, R. C. (1998). Marital discord and child behavior problems: Parent–child relationship quality and child interpersonal awareness as mediators. *Journal of Family Issues, 19*, 140–163.

Heinicke, C. M., Guthrie, D., and Ruth, G. (1997). Marital adaptation, divorce, and parent–infant development: A prospective study. *Infant Mental Health Journal, 18*, 282–299.

Hess, R. D., and Camara, D. A. (1979). Post-divorce relationship as mediating factors in the consequences of divorce for children. *Journal of Social Issues, 35*, 79–96.

Hetherington, E. M. (1979). *Toward a life-course conception of divorce and its effects on children.* National Institute of Education.

Hetherington, E. M. (1989). Coping with family transition: Winners, losers, and survivors. *Child Development, 60*, 1–14.

Hetherington, E. M. (1999). Should we stay together for the sake of the children? In M. E. Hetherington (Ed.), *Coping with divorce, single parenting, and remarriage: A risk and resiliency perspective* (pp. 93–116). Mahwah, NJ: Lawrence Erlbaum Associates.

Hetherington, E. M., Cox, M., and Cox, R. (1985). Long-term effects of divorce and remarriage on the adjustment of children. *Journal of American Academy of Psychiatry, 24*, 518–530.

Isley, S., O'Neil, R., Clatfelter, D., and Parke, R. D. (1999). Parent- and child-expressed affect and children's social acceptance and competence: Modeling direct and indirect pathways. *Developmental Psychology, 35*, 547–560.

Isley, S., O'Neil, R., and Parke, R. D. (1996). The relation of parental affect and control behaviors to children's classroom acceptance: A concurrent and predictive analysis. *Early Education & Development, 7*, 7–23.

Jacob, T., and Johnson, S. L. (1997). Parent–child interaction among depressed fathers and mothers: Impact on child functioning. *Journal of Family Psychology, 11*, 391–409.

Jacobvitz, D. B., and Bush, N. F. (1996). Reconstructions of family relationships: Parent–child alliances, personal distress, and self-esteem. *Developmental Psychology, 32*, 732–743.

Janssens, J. M. A. M., and Dekovic, M. (1997). Child rearing, prosocial moral reasoning, and prosocial behavior. *International Journal of Behavioral Development, 20*, 509–527.

Johnson, P. L., and O'Leary, K. D. (1987). Parental behavior patterns and conduct disorders in girls. *Journal of Abnormal Child Psychology, 15*, 573–581.

Johnston, J. R., Campbell, L. E., and Mayes, S. S. (1985). Latency children in post-separation and divorce disputes. *Journal of American Academy of Child Psychiatry, 24*, 563–574.

Johnston, J. R., Gonzalez, R., and Campbell, L. E. (1987). Ongoing post divorce conflict and child disturbance. *Journal of Abnormal Child Psychology, 15*, 493–509.

Jouriles, E. N., Barling, J., and O'Leary, S. G. (1987). Predicting child behavior problems in maritally violent families. *Journal of Abnormal Child Psychology, 15*, 165–173.

Jouriles, E. N., Murphy, C. M., and O'Leary, K. D. (1989). Interspousal aggression, marital discord, and child problems. *Journal of Abnormal Child Psychology, 16*, 197–206.

Jouriles, E. N., and Norwood, W. D. (1995). Physical aggression toward boys and girls in families characterized by the battering of women. *Journal of Family Psychology, 9*, 69–78.

Jouriles, E. N., Pfiffner, L. J., and O'Leary, S. G. (1988). Marital conflict, parenting, and toddler conduct problems. *Journal of Abnormal Psychology, 16*, 197–206.

Katz, L. F., and Gottman, J. M. (1991). Marital discord and child outcomes: A social psychophysiological approach. In J. Garber and K. A. Dodge (Eds.), *The development of emotion regulation and dysregulation* (pp. 129–155). New York, NY: Cambridge University Press.

Katz, L. F., and Gottman, J. M. (1993). Patterns of marital conflict predict children's internalizing and externalizing behaviors. *Developmental Psychology, 29*, 940–950.

Katz, L. F., and Gottman, J. M. (1995). Vagal tone protects children from marital conflict. *Development & Psychopathology, 7*, 83–92.

Katz, L. F., and Gottman, J. M. (1997). Buffering children from marital conflict and dissolution. *Journal of Clinical Child Psychology, 26*, 157–171.

Katz, L. F., and Kahen, V. (1993, March). *Marital interaction patterns and children's externalizing and internalizing behaviors: The search for mechanism.* Paper presented at the biennial meeting of the Society for Research in Child Development, New Orleans, LA.

Kerig, P. K. (1995). Triangles in the family circle: Effects of family structure on marriage, parenting, and child outcomes. *Journal of Family Psychology, 9*, 28–43.

Kitzmann, K. M. (2000). Effects of marital conflict on subsequent triadic family interactions and parenting. *Developmental Psychology, 36*, 3–13.

Kopp, C. B. (1989). Regulation of distress and negative emotions: A developmental view. *Developmental Psychology, 25*, 343–354.

Ladd, G. W., and Golter, B. S. (1988). Parents' management of preschoolers' peer relations: Is it related to children's social competence? *Developmental Psychology, 24*, 109–117.

Long, N., Forehand, R., Fauber, R., and Brody, G. (1987). Self-perceived and independently observed competence of young adolescents as a function of parental marital conflict and recent divorce. *Journal of Abnormal Child Psychology, 15*, 15–27.

Long, N., Slater, E., Forehand, R., and Fauber, R. (1988). Continued high or reduced interparental conflict following divorce: Relation to young adolescent adjustment. *Journal of Consulting and Clinical Psychology, 56*, 467–469.

MacDonald, D., and Parke, R. D. (1984). Bridging the gap: Parent–child play interactions and peer interactive competence. *Child Development, 55*, 1265–1277.

MacDonald, K. (1987). Parent–child physical play with rejected, neglected, and popular boys. *Development Psychology, 23*, 705–711.

Mahoney, A., Jouriles, E. N., and Scavone, J. (1997). Marital adjustment, marital discord over childrearing, and child behavior problems: Moderating effects of child's age. *Journal of Clinical Child Psychology, 4*, 415–423.

Margolin, G., and Wampold, B. F. (1981). A sequential analysis of conflict and accord in distressed and nondistressed marital partners. *Journal of Consulting and Clinical Psychology, 49*, 554–567.

Matthey, S., and Barnett, B. (1999). Parent–child classes in the early postpartum period: Need and participation by fathers and mothers. *Infant Mental Health Journal, 20*, 278–290.

McBride, B. A., and Rane, T. R. (1998). Parenting alliance as a predictor of father involvement: An exploratory study. *Family Relations, 47*, 229–236.

McCabe, K. M. (1997). Sex difference in the long-term effect of divorce on children: Depression and heterosexual relationship difficulties in young adult years. *Journal of Divorce and Remarriage, 27*, 123–135.

McHale, J. P. (1995). Coparenting and triadic interactions during infancy: The roles of martial distress and child gender. *Developmental Psychology, 31*, 985–996.

McHale, J. P., Freitag, M. K., Crouter, A. C., and Bartko, W. T. (1991). Connections between dimensions of marital quality and school age children's adjustment. *Journal of Applied Developmental Psychology, 12*, 1–17.

Minuchin, S. (1974). *Families and family therapy.* Cambridge, MA: Harvard University Press.

Mize, J., Pettit, G. S., and Meece, D. (2000). Explaining the link between parenting behavior and children's peer competence: A critical examination of the "Mediating Process" Hypothesis. In K. A. Kerns, J. M. Contreras, and A. M. Neal-Barnett (Eds.), *Families and peers: Linking two social worlds* (pp. 137–168). Westport, CT: Praeger.

Nortarius, C. I., Benson, P. R., and Slone, D. (1989). Exploring the interfaces between perception and behavior: An analysis of martial interaction in distressed and nondistressed couples. *Behavioral Assessment, 11*, 39–64.

O'Brien, M., Margolin, G., and John, R. S. (1995). Relation among marital conflict, child coping, and child adjustment. *Journal of Clinical Child Psychology, 24*, 346–361.

O'Connor, T. G., Caspi, A., DeFries, J. C., and Plomin, R. (2000). Are associations between parental divorce and children's adjustment genetically mediated? An adoption study. *Developmental Psychology, 36*, 429–237.

O'Leary, K. D. (1984). Marital discord and children: Problems, strategies, methodologies and results. In A. B. Doyle, D. Gold, and D. S. Modkowitz (Eds.), *Children in families under stress* (pp. 35–46). San Francisco, CA: Jossey-Bass.

O'Neal, R., and Parke, R. D. (2000). Family–peer relationships: The role of emotion regulation, cognitive understanding, and attentional processes as mediating processes. In K. A. Kerns, J. M. Contreras, and A. M. Neal-Barnett (Eds.), *Family and peers: Linking two social worlds* (pp. 195–226). Westport, CT: Praeger.

Owen, M. T., and Cox, M. J. (1997). Marital conflict and the development of infant–parent attachment relationships. *Journal of Family Psychology, 11*, 152–164.

Pagani, L., Boulerice, B., Tremblay, R. E., and Vitaro, F. (1997). Behavioral developmental in children of divorce and remarriage. *Journal of Child Psychology and Psychiatry and Allied Disciplines, 38*, 769–781.

Parke, R. D., Cassidy, J., Burks, V. M., Carson, J. L., and Boyum, L. (1992). Familial contribution to peer competence among young children: The role of interactive and affective processes. In R. D. Ross and G. W. Ladd (Eds.), *Family–peer relationships: Modes of connection* (pp. 107–134). Hillsdale, NJ: Lawrence Erlbaum Associates.

Parker, J. G., and Asher, S. R. (1987). Peer relations and later personal adjustment: Are low-accepted children at risk? *Psychological Bulletin, 102*, 357–389.

Patterson, C. J., Vaden, N. A., and Kupersmidt, J. B. (1991). Family background, recent life events and peer rejection during childhood. *Journal of Social and Personal Relationships, 8*, 347–361.

Patterson, G. R. (1971). *Families: Applications of social learning to family life*. Champaign, IL: Research Press.

Patterson, G. R. (1982). *Coercive family process*. Eugene, OR: Castalia.

Patterson, G. R. (1993). Orderly change in a stable world: The antisocial trait as a chimera. *Journal of Consulting and Clinical Psychology, 61*, 911–919.

Patterson, G. R., and Stouthamer-Loeber, M. (1984). The correlation of family management practices and delinquency. *Children Development, 55*, 1299–1307.

Peterson, J. L., and Zill, N. (1986). Marital disruption, parent–child relationships, and behavior problems in children. *Journal of Marriage & the Family, 48*, 295–307.

Piaget, J., and Inhelder, B. (1969). *The psychology of the child*. New York: Basic Books.

Pine, F. (1985). *Developmental theory and clinical process*. New Haven, CT: Yale University Press.

Pope, A. W., Bierman, K. L., and Mumma, G. H. (1991). Aggression, hyperactivity, and inattention-immaturity: Behavior dimensions associated with peer rejection in elementary school boys. *Developmental Psychology, 27*, 663–671.

Porges, S. W., Doussard-Roosevelt, J. A., Portales, A. L., and Greenspan, S. I. (1996). Infant regulation of the vagal "brake" predicts child behavior problems: A psychobiological model of social behavior. *Developmental Psychobiology, 29*, 697–712.

Putallaz, M. (1987). Maternal behavior and children's sociometric status. *Child Development, 58*, 324–340.

Raush, H. L., Barry, W. A., Hertel, R. K., and Swain, M. A. (1974). *Communication, conflict, and marriage*. San Francisco, CA: Jossey-Bass.

Revenstorf, D., Hahlweg, K., Schindler, L., and Vogel, L. (1984). Interaction analysis of marital conflict. In K. Halhweg and S. Jacobson (Eds.), *In marital interaction: Analysis and modification* (pp. 159–181). New York: Guilford.

Revenstorf, D., Vogel, B., Wegener, C., Hahlweg, K., and Schindler, L. (1980). Escalation phenomena in interaction sequences: An empirical comparison of distressed and nondistressed couples. *Behavioral Analysis and Modification, 4*, 97–115.

Ross, S. M. (1996). Risk of physical abuse to children of spouse abusing parents. *Child Abuse and Neglect, 20*, 589–598.

Rutter, M. (1979). Protective factors in children's responses to stress and disadvantage. In M. W. Dent and J. E. Rolf (Eds.), *Primary prevention of psychopathology: Vol 3. Social competence in children*. Hanover, NH: University Press of New England.

Rutter, M. (1987). Psychosocial resilience and protective mechanisms. *American Journal of Orthopsychiatry, 57*, 316–331.

Shapiro, A. F., Gottman, J. M., and Carrere, S. (2000). The baby and the marriage: Identifying factors that buffer against decline of marital satisfaction after the first baby arrives. *Journal of Family Psychology, 14*, 59–70.

Sheets, V., Sandler, I., and West, S. G. (1996). Appraisals of negative events by preadolescent children of divorce. *Child Development, 67*, 2166–2182.

Short, J. L. (1998). Evaluation of a substance abuse prevention and mental health promotion program for children of divorce. *Journal of Divorce and Remarriage, 28*, 139–155.

Simons, R. L., Lin, K., Gordon, L. C., Conger, R. D., and Lorenz, F. O. (1999). Explaining the higher incidence of adjustment problems among children of divorce compared with those in two-parent families. *Journal of Marriage and the Family*, *61*, 1020–1033.

Simpson, K. S., and Cummings, E. M. (1996). Mixed message resolution and children's responses to interadult conflict. *Child Development*, *67*, 437–448.

Snyder, J. R. (1998). Marital conflict and child adjustment: What about gender? *Developmental Review*, *18*, 390–420.

Snyder, J. R., Schrepferman, L., and St. Peter, C. (1997). Origins of antisocial behavior: Negative reinforcement and affect dysregulation. *Behavior Modification*, *21*, 187–215.

Sroufe, L. A., Schork, E., Motti, F., Lawaroski, N., and LaFreniere, P. (1984). The role of affect in social competence. In C. E. Izard, J. Kagan, and R. B. Zajonc (Eds.), *Emotions, cognition, and behavior*. New York: Cambridge University Press.

Stanley (Wilson), B. J., and Katz, L. F. (1991, April). *Vagal tone, gender, and the peer interactions of preschool children*. Paper presented at the biennial meeting of the Society for Research in Child Development, Seattle, WA.

Stocker, C. M., and Youngblade, L. (1999). Marital conflict and parental hostility: Links with children sibling and peer relationships. *Journal of Family Psychology*, *13*, 598–609.

Stoneman, Z., Brody, G. H., and Burke, M. (1989). Marital quality, depression, and inconsistent parenting: Relationship with observed mother–child conflict. *American Journal of Orthopsychiatry*, *59*, 105–117.

Strassberg, Z., Dodge, K. A., Battes, J. E., and Pettit, G. S. (1992). The longitudinal relation between parental conflict strategies and children's sociometric standing in kindergarten. *Merrill-Palmer Quarterly*, *38*, 477–494.

Ting-Toomey, S. (1983). An analysis of communication patterns in high and low marital adjustment groups. *Human Communication Research*, *9*, 306–319.

Tronick, E. Z. (1980). On the primacy of social skills. In D. B. Sawin, L. O. Walder, and J. H. Penticuff (Eds.), *The exceptional infant: Psychosocial risks in infant environment transactions* (pp. 144–158). New York: Brunner/Mazel.

Tronick, E. Z. (1989). Emotions and emotional communication in infants. *American Psychologist*, *44*, 112–119.

Vygotsky, L. S. (1962). *Thought and language*. Cambridge, MA: MIT Press.

Wahler, R. G., and Dumas, J. E. (1986). "A chip off the old block": Some interpersonal characteristics of coercive children across generations. In P. Strain and M. Guralnick (Eds.), *Social development problems in children* (pp. 49–91). New York: Academic Press.

Wallerstein, J. S., and Kelly, J. B. (1980). Effects of divorce on the visiting father–child relationship. *American Journal of Psychiatry*, *137*, 1534–1539.

Weiss, R. L. (1980). Strategic behavioral martial therapy: Toward a model for assessment and intervention. In J. P. Vincent (Ed.), *Advances in family intervention, assessment, and theory* (Vol. 1, pp. 229–271). Greenwich, CT: JAI.

Weissman, S. H., and Cohen, R. S. (1985). The parenting alliance and Adolescence. *Adolescent Psychiatry*, *12*, 24–45.

Wilson, B. J. (2001). *The role of attentional processes in children's conduct and social problems: Focusing and shifting attention*. Manuscript submitted for publication.

Wilson, B. J., and Gottman, G. M. (1996). Attention-the shuttle between cognition and emotion: Risk, resiliency, and physiological bases. In M. Hetherington and E. A. Blechman (pp. 189–228). *Stress, coping and resiliency in children*. Hillsdale, NJ; US: Lawrence Erlbaum Associates.

Wilson, B. J., Staley, J. Gottman, J. M., and Katz, L. F. (2001, August). *Children's physiological recovery from angry facial expressions:* Marital, stress, and parenting contributions. Poster session presented at the annual meeting of the American psychological Association, San Francisco, CA.

Zahn-Waxler, C., Kochanska, G., Krupnick, J., and McKnew, D. (1990). Patterns of guilt in children of depressed and well mothers. *Developmental Psychology*, *26*, 51–59.

11

Parenting With a Sensory or Physical Disability

Kathryn P. Meadow-Orlans
Gallaudet University

INTRODUCTION

This chapter provides a review of the special functional and social circumstances of parenting by those who are deaf, blind, or physically disabled,[1] the devices or strategies utilized to cope with these conditions, and the effects on children reared in such families. Primary attention is given to persons whose disabilities are severe or profound rather than mild or moderate and who became disabled before their children were born. A context for the research review is provided through summaries of the demographics of disability, the historical treatment of these groups as reflected in social attitudes and legal rights, and shared socialization experiences that may influence future parenting. This contextual frame is followed by a review of relevant social and psychological theories and of research on parenting, information on educational programs and assistive devices available to parents with disabilities, and issues of research design and methodology. Finally, suggestions are made for future research that might contribute to understanding parenting in these populations.

---

[1]Increased sensitivity to the importance of language used to describe subgroups in society has led to rapidly changing linguistic conventions to reference racial, ethnic, religious, and disability groupings. In this chapter, I have attempted to employ language that is currently accepted as appropriate by professional journals that deal with deafness, blindness, or physical disability, and by individuals who are members of these groups. Deafness is a complex case because many adults who are deaf view themselves as members of an ethnic or cultural subgroup rather than a disability group, and prefer the term "Deaf adults" who are members of a "Deaf community."

A CONTEXT FOR UNDERSTANDING PARENTING WITH DISABILITIES: DEMOGRAPHY, HISTORY, AND CHILDHOOD SOCIALIZATION

The Demographic Context

The research literature on parenting by adults with disabilities is limited. One reason is the low incidence of any severe or profound disability, which means that sample selection and participant recruitment are difficult and that data collection and analysis may be demanding and expensive. Even demographic data are scarce for adults whose disabilities were acquired in childhood. Added to the research problems associated with low incidence are those related to heterogeneity within each disability group. Variations in etiology contribute to functional and social diversity, and age at onset or degree of impairment are associated with cognitive functioning and educational achievement.

Incidence and prevalence of sensory and physical disability. Data reported by educational systems may provide the most accurate picture of prevalence because population counts of adults usually include those with late onset as well as those whose conditions were acquired in childhood. For example, hearing impairment is one of the most common disabilities, with an estimated overall prevalence rate in the United States of 86 per 1,000 persons. However, deafness (defined broadly as the inability to hear speech unaided) is relatively rare, with a rate of about 6 per 1,000, and prelingual deafness (occurring before the age of 3 years) has an estimated rate of 0.8 per 1,000 (Schein, 1996). The changing picture at increasing ages is similar for visual impairment: Data from a 1977 Health Interview Survey collected by the National Center for Health Statistics show the prevalence of visual disability (the inability to see well enough to read ordinary newspaper print, even with glasses) as 1 per 1,000 persons under the age of 45, 6 per 1,000 at ages 45 to 64, and 44.5 per 1,000 at ages 65 or older (Kirchner and Peterson, 1988).

The prevalence of disabilities in the school-age population, estimated by the U.S. Department of Education, remained quite stable from the 1950s through the 1980s. Of 40 million school children in 1986, about 11% were enrolled in special education classes: 0.17% were hard of hearing and deaf; 0.14% orthopedically impaired; 0.14% other health impaired; and 0.07% visually handicapped (Hallahan and Kauffman, 1988). There are numerous problems in interpreting these estimates. Federal regulations require that a child be counted only once, even if he or she has two or more impairments requiring special services. A special survey of children ages 0 to 21 of children enrolled in special education classes resulted in an estimate of 93,600, 65% of whom had a disability in addition to the visual impairment (Kirchner and Diament, 1999). Of about 50,000 deaf children receiving special education, one third had additional impairments (Holden-Pitt and Diaz, 1998). With a prevalence rate of approximately 1.5 per thousand live births, cerebral palsy accounts for about half of all orthopedically disabled school children. In 1986 it was estimated that there were 1.7 million people homebound with permanent disabilities, and as many as 13.5 million who were temporarily disabled (Fox, 2000). About 1.5 million adults (1% of the population) use a wheelchair (Olkin, 1999).

Within-group heterogeneity. Heterogeneity within disability groups may stem from etiological or biological factors associated with severity of impairment and multiple disabling conditions, from socioeconomic status affecting accessibility of medical treatment (Williams, 1990) and early diagnosis leading to prompt intervention, and from family characteristics such as the hearing, visual, or mobility status of parents and siblings. Most disability studies show higher prevalence rates for males and lower rates for upper socioeconomic and highly educated groups (Altman, Cooper, and Cunningham, 1999; Gliedman and Roth, 1980; Schein, 1996). In fact, there is a strong relation between disability and social stratification (Alexander, 1976). Three fifths of all adults with disabilities live at the poverty level; more than half are outside the labor force (Bowe, 1980). There is a higher concentration of disabilities among African Americans and Native Americans, compared to whites and Hispanics (Thompson-Hoffman and Storck, 1991).

Age at onset of the disabling condition can be a powerful determinant of both functional and psychological adjustment. Several researchers have concluded that those losing their vision early in life were more likely to be employed in competitive, home-based, or community rehabilitation programs, whereas those losing vision later were more likely to be unpaid family workers or unemployed. However, no differences were found between those with congenital and adventitious vision loss employed by National Industries for the Blind (Crudden and Hanye, 1999; Leonard, D'Allura, and Horowitz, 1999).

Further examples of within-group heterogeneity are found in data from school-age children with disabilities. (It must be emphasized that this population, grown to adulthood, is the primary focus of this chapter.) About 33% of deaf children enrolled in special education classes have additional handicapping conditions with educational significance (Schildroth and Hotto, 1996). At least 50% of congenital deafness is genetic (Arnos, 1999; Israel, Cunningham, Thumann, and Arnos, 1992), but more than 90% of deaf persons have hearing parents. Those who are deaf from an early age are likely to marry deaf partners at the estimated ratio of 9:1. Nine of 10 children born to two deaf parents have normal hearing (Schein, 1996). With the completion of the human genome project, the identification of deafness-related genes is expected to accelerate (Willems, 2000) and genetic counseling will become more important (Arnos, 1999). Some Deaf people view this work as part of a "conspiracy" to eliminate deafness (Mowl, 1996).

It is expected that the prevalence of blindness among adults will increase in the future, as the number of children with visual impairments has, with the rate of severely limiting blindness rising from 0.9% to 2% in a 20-year period (Kirchner, 1990). (However, this apparent increase may be due to improved reporting.) A study of all children in British Columbia who were born blind between 1944 and 1973 ($N = 454$) gives an indication of the characteristics of adults with visual limitations today: 35% had no visual acuity or light perception only; 84% were blind from birth; and heredity accounted for about 40% of cases. Almost 70% had one or more additional handicaps (Jan, Freeman, and Scott, 1977). A more recent analysis of characteristics of children seen over a 10-year period in one low-vision clinic showed that only 10% had either no visual acuity or light perception only (Wilkinson and Stewart, 1993).

A large proportion of persons with cerebral palsy have additional disabling conditions. The range of mental abilities is the same as that in the general population, but proportionately more are mentally retarded. Other conditions associated with limited physical mobility include spina bifida, muscular dystrophy, arthritis, and congenital malformations of the limbs (Hallahan and Kauffman, 1988). There are many types of cerebral palsy and many different etiologies; half result from prenatal brain damage and one third from perinatal factors (Harris, 1987).

A secondary analysis of U.S. Census Bureau data from the 1993 Survey of Income and Program Participation showed that 56% of adults with either physical or sensory disabilities were married. However, 27% with physical disabilities and 39% with sensory disabilities had children. Among adults with cognitive disabilities, 22% are married and 16% have children (Barker and Maralani, 1997).

Reports of the incidence and prevalence of disabilities can be misleading. Advocates for those with disabilities may use the broadest possible definitions in order to establish a rationale for increased public funding. Low estimates may result from the reluctance of caregivers to include children in a census because of their fear of stigma resulting from a disability label (Hobbs, 1975). Discrepancies in various databases can be sizeable. For example, a carefully monitored 1986 pilot study in the state of Virginia (selected because of the care with which data were collected) showed that the number of blind children included in official statistics was 35% fewer than the number actually enrolled in special education classes (Kirchner, 1990).

The Historical Context

From ancient Greece and Rome to biblical and medieval periods, attitudes of fear, scorn, and pity have helped to create the context for the lives of individuals with disabilities (Lane, 1984; Rée,

1999; Winzer, 1997). During many historical periods, they were not allowed to marry or to bear children. These attitudes continue to influence the lives of disabled persons, although dramatic changes have occurred in their legal status, as reflected in a number of recent legal cases and judicial decisions.

Social views of sensory and physical disability. The instrumental or functional adaptations to parenting made necessary by deafness, blindness, and physical disabilities are quite different. However, these groups share the stigmatization of disability because historically they have been viewed negatively. These attitudes were often based on a low tolerance for people whose economic contributions were limited: those who could not plow fields and harvest crops, hunt for game, or travel easily to new grazing areas. One modern analysis echoes that linkage of human value with economic productivity: "It is unpardonable in an individualist society to fail to be 'self-sufficient'" (Connors, 1985, p. 97).

Throughout history, people with disabilities had less chance of growing to adulthood than did their siblings. In ancient Greece and Rome, babies with recognizable handicaps were often abandoned at birth (French, in Vol. 2 of this *Handbook*). (Those who were deaf, however, probably escaped that fate since their condition was invisible.) As early as 530 A.D., the Justinian legal code provided that individuals deaf from birth were without any legal rights, including the right to form a family. Those who became deaf after birth were allowed to conduct their own affairs, to marry, and to have children, provided they could read and write (Bender, 1970; Winzer, 1997).

Religious feelings and beliefs helped to improve the treatment of disabled groups. For example, the education of deaf persons in the sixteenth century was motivated by the desire to add converts to Christianity by teaching them to read scripture (Levine, 1969). However, religious teaching was also responsible for the Augustinian view that a child's handicap served to punish a father's sins, a belief that exists in some religious and ethnic communities even today (Steinberg, Davila, Collazo, Loew, and Fischgrund, 1997).

Stigma continues to be attached either to visible or invisible conditions distinguishing an individual from some idealized norm (Barker, with Wright, Meyerson, and Gonick, 1953; Gliedman and Roth, 1980; Goffman, 1963; Monbeck, 1973; Safilios-Rothschild, 1970). Disability creates special barriers to women's parenting rights and opportunities (Asrael, 1982; Deegan and Brooks, 1985; Hanna and Rogovsky, 1991). There is impressive evidence to support the position that "disability is a more severely handicapping condition for women than for men" (Fine and Asch, 1985, p. 6). Economic data suggest that at least 65% of all women with disabilities are unemployed and are more likely than comparable men to live at the poverty level. They are less likely to marry than are men with disabilities. Often they are advised not to have children and find it difficult to receive professional advice about conception and childbearing: "Disabled women, in self-perceptions and as perceived by others, are viewed more negatively than are disabled men" (Fine and Asch, 1985, p. 8). "Fears that disabled women would produce children with similar conditions . . . have mingled with convictions that they would harm, deprive, or burden children they attempted to rear" (Asch and Fine, 1988, p. 21). Women with disabilities, whether they are deaf, blind, or physically limited, tend to accept negative stereotypes about themselves and are alienated from the mainstream of the women's movement, the disability movement, and party politics (Danek, 1992; Lloyd, 1992). However, motherhood can link a woman with a disability to other women, demonstrating that her imperfect body can perform a vital function (Baskin and Riggs, 1988).

Legal status of those with disabilities. Important to the more recent history of the status of people with disabilities are their legal struggles to gain or maintain the right to conceive and bear (or adopt) and rear children. These rights, taken for granted by most people, have been won only through continuing court procedures by those with a disability.

An important chapter in this history was the 1942 Supreme Court ruling that procreation is a basic right, thus outlawing mandatory sterilization (*Skinner v. Oklahoma*, 1942). Today, the right of a person with a disability to become a parent has strong judicial protection, although judges may still remove a child from a home solely on the basis of a parent's disability. However, most states require evidence of repeated abuse or neglect before terminating parental rights (Gilhool and Gran, 1985; Pagliocca, Melton, Lyons, and Weisz, in Vol. 5 of this *Handbook*).

Section 504 of the Civil Rights Act of 1964, enacted in 1973, and the Comprehensive Services for Independent Living provisions of the Rehabilitation Act of 1978 authorized resources for independent living for those with disabilities (Bowe, 1980). This legislation informed the decision of a 1979 case in which a judge awarded custody of two sons to their father who had recently become a quadriplegic, noting "legislation designed to enhance the participation of handicapped persons in the everyday life of the community" (*Marriage of Carney*, 1979). The judge proposed that "Handicap can strengthen family unity; can help children become more responsible; and can enhance the ethical, emotional and intellectual environment for the child" (Gilhool and Gran, 1985, pp. 20–21).

In a 1985 Michigan case, the lower court awarded custody for the hearing children of a deaf mother to grandparents on grounds that the children needed daily exposure to oral language. The Court of Appeals ordered a new trial on the basis of psychologists' testimony that the mother could provide necessary language stimulation. The mother's custody was restored (*Bednarski v. Bednarski*, 1985; Geer, 1985). In California, a judge ruled that a deaf couple should not be permitted to adopt a child, and his judgment turned solely on the basis of the parents' disability. On appeal this decision was reversed, and the judge was rebuked: his "irrebuttable presumption of the parents' incapacity to raise a child violated [their] right to due process and equal protection of the law" (*Adoption of Richardson*, 1967; Gilhool and Gran, 1985, p. 17).

In another custody battle, the court decided in favor of the father on the assumption that a normal life was impossible for a child with mother who used a wheelchair. A different view was expressed by another judge: the state "can supplement the parent–child relationship with housekeeping, nutritional, and child development services. It cannot produce a substitute for something for which no substitute exists: the love of a parent for its child, and of a child for its parent" (*People v. C.A.K.*, 1982).

Court decisions and contemporary legislation have greatly expanded the rights and opportunities of those with disabilities. The Americans with Disabilities Act (1990), adopted in July, extended civil rights protection to this population, with guarantees for access to employment and public accommodations (DeJong and Batavia, 1990). The direct and indirect effects on parenting are wide ranging. A Michigan couple, both with severely limiting cerebral palsy, used the ADA as the basis for demanding a full-time attendant to help care for their infant (Mathews, 1992). Increased government support for such individuals in independent living units and group homes provides them with expanded opportunities for romantic attachments, marriage, and family formation. Issues of adequate parenting and family life are certain to become more visibly public in the future. Some observers believe that sociopolitical realities "mandate that human services professionals and organizations provide the necessary resources and support to parents with disabilities to facilitate and enhance their parenting roles and responsibilities" (Kelley, Sikka, and Venkatesan, 1997, p. 106).

Social responsibility versus individual rights.   Questions about the requisites of adequate parenting have been raised most often for those with mental retardation. Legally, minimal qualities have included the provision of love and affection, performance of household tasks, adequate attention to physical needs, the provision of cognitive stimulation, and the ability to plan for the "lifelong needs" of the child (Tymchuk, Yokota, and Rahbar, 1990, p. 97). Social responsibility for children's physical comfort, emotional well-being, safety, and health must be balanced against adults' rights to become parents and to care for their children. Legal and ethical issues intersect with social, psychological, and developmental knowledge that can contribute to evolving policy (Baumrind and Thompson, in Vol. 6 of this *Handbook*; Pagliocca, Melton, Lyons, and Weisz, in Vol. 5 of this *Handbook*). However, the judicial decisions summarized above make clear that a physical or sensory disability no longer restricts an individual's legal right to parent a child.

The Context of Childhood Socialization

Persons with disabilities must learn to cope with general attitudes and behaviors that separate them from others, and with the functional behavioral modifications required for coping with visual, auditory, or physical limitations. Six decades of research on infants and children at biological risk demonstrate that the resilience of the human organism and creative familial response to potentially disabling conditions can overcome many effects of perinatal stress. "Human development is, in fact, remarkably resistant to a wide range of biological insults" (Kopp and Krakow, 1983, p. 1102). These children share some experiential commonalities with potential for influencing future parenting patterns. If these patterns are to be understood, they must be viewed within a context of parenting which is different from birth onward for those with a disability.

Most of those with disabilities were viewed by their own parents as "different." From the time the family of procreation receives the diagnosis of a disability, parents' views of potential and future capabilities shift. This family process begins at birth or the time of diagnosis (Featherstone, 1980) and continues through childhood and adolescence. Experiences at each stage help shape the desire to become a parent and the emotional readiness to cope with parenthood.

Infancy and early childhood. The diagnosis of a disability in an infant or young child is almost always a shock experienced by parents as a tragedy. From that point onward, parental reactions vary enormously, but grief, depression, and guilt are common (Barsch, 1968; Fraiberg, 1977; Gregory, 1995; Hewett, 1970; Richardson, 1969; Schlesinger, 1987; Shonkoff, Hauser-Cram, Krauss, and Upshur, 1992). An immediate parental response of grief and shock may be replaced by continuing depression and chronic sorrow (Moses, 1985) that can interfere with effective parenting (Cohn, Matias, Tronick, Connell, and Lyons-Ruth, 1986; Zahn-Waxler, Duggal, and Gruber, in Vol. 4 of this *Handbook*).

However, parents' resilience and social support systems can overcome these negative parenting responses (Meadow-Orlans, 1994; Meadow-Orlans and Steinberg, 1993; Prendergast, 1992), and infants begin early to develop positive coping skills. Those who are deaf gaze earnestly at their mothers' faces and receive more visual and tactile stimulation than do other infants (Koester, 1995; Meadow-Orlans and Spencer, 1996). Young children exposed to visual language acquire sign communication as rapidly as hearing infants acquire speech (Bonvillian, Orlansky, and Folven, 1994; Schlesinger and Meadow, 1972). Infants who are blind become unusually attentive to sound (Preisler, 1991), although they lag in acquisition of fine-motor and locomotor skills (Preisler, 1997; Troster and Brambring, 1993). Blind children are delayed in some areas of language (Erin, 1990), even though syntax is acquired "roughly on time and develops normally" (Landau, 1997, p. 13). Infants born without arms use their feet to manipulate objects (Roskies, 1972).

Attachment patterns of infants with disabilities appear to be within the normal range: Those who are deaf become securely attached to their mothers, either deaf or hearing (Greenberg and Marvin, 1979; Lederberg and Mobley, 1990; Meadow, Greenberg, and Erting, 1985) as did a group of limb-deficient thalidomide infants (Roskies, 1972). Fraiberg (1977), in a study of 10 infants who were blind, found that nine were emotionally attached to their mothers and were either creeping or toddling around the house at 18 months. (The mother of the tenth infant was unable to relate to him and had relegated most of his early care to others.)

A child's disability often encourages or exacerbates maternal directiveness and overprotectiveness. Hearing mothers whose children are deaf have repeatedly been described as more directive or intrusive than mothers in comparison groups (Musselman and Churchill, 1992; Nienhuys, Horsborough, and Cross, 1985; Schlesinger and Meadow, 1972; Wedell-Monnig and Lumley, 1980; White and White, 1984). Similar reports are found for mothers whose children are blind (Conti-Ramsden and Perez-Pereira, 1999; Kekelis and Andersen, 1984) and for those whose children have physical disabilities (Kogan and Tyler, 1973). Blind children who were the most passive had mothers who were the most dominant (Rogow, 1999).

Overprotectiveness is prevalent in families with children who are deaf (Gregory, 1995), blind (Scott, 1969b), or have physical disabilities (Barsch, 1968; Davis, 1963; Roskies, 1972). However, behaviors interpreted as "overprotective" may result from a realistic assessment of a child's vulnerability to environmental risk. The difficulty of distinguishing between appropriate limitation and developmental facilitation creates additional dilemmas for parents.

In these families, the mother frequently becomes the primary caregiver, and the father sometimes excludes himself or is excluded by others (Barsch, 1968; Gregory, 1995; Gregory, Bishop, and Sheldon, 1995). Marital conflict may be exaggerated or focused on the special needs of the child with a disability (Bristol, Gallagher, and Schopler, 1988). An alternative pattern, however, is the strengthening of family ties as members work together to overcome the consequences of disability (Gallagher, Beckman, and Cross, 1983; Koester and Meadow-Orlans, 1990).

Later childhood.   As children grow older and more aware of their "differences," negative self-concepts often develop in those who are blind (Leung and Hollins, 1989; Tuttle, 1984) or physically disabled (Molnar, 1989; Olkin, 1999; Richardson, 1969). Children who are deaf and have hearing parents have lower levels of self-esteem compared to those whose parents are deaf, possibly because of their participation in a Deaf community and their sign language proficiency (Marschark, 1993; Meadow, 1980).

Particular educational settings can influence the development of older children. Historically, residential school placements were common for children with a profound sensory impairment, although the trend for many years has been toward a decreasing proportion of residential placements compared to those in day schools or regular classrooms (Moores, 1992; Moores, 1996; Moores and Kluwin, 1986). The passage of Public Law 94–142, the Equal Education for All Handicapped Children Act (1976), accelerated the shift to mainstreaming for children with disabilities and fostered wide-ranging changes in residential practices as well. In residential schools for children with visual impairments, major changes included service to increasingly complex populations, the provision of services delivered in other settings, and the expansion of support services (Erin, 1993; Head, Maddock, Healey, and Griffing, 1993). Despite many changes, outmoded ideas about residential schools persist—one of these is that children placed in these schools are isolated and overprotected—even though enlightened administrators work to combat these tendencies (Bina, 1993). Residential placement may serve to reduce social isolation by providing opportunities for interaction with similar peers even though separation from parents and siblings limits the experience of family life.

Socialization for intimacy and parenthood.   "Socialization for both marriage and parenthood begins in the parental family. In this setting more is 'caught' than is formally taught . . . " (Hill and Aldous, 1969, p. 888). Children who are either deaf or blind have fewer opportunities to "catch" untaught lessons that socialize other children to the nuances of intimacy: those who are deaf and have hearing parents because they often have minimal communication skills, those who are blind because they are excluded from the nonverbal gestures, facial expressions, and body language that convey much interpersonal meaning. As Scott (1969b, p. 1034) noted, "the blind child is limited . . . in his opportunity to observe how fathers and mothers relate to their children. . . . Because he misses many facets of other paternal and maternal interactions, his experience with the role of father or mother is limited to one person in each case until a much later date in his life." These observations are most pertinent to those who are profoundly deaf or totally blind. Partial disability increases opportunities for absorbing some of this nonverbal communication, but also increases the likelihood of processing incomplete or distorted information.

Children with disabilities who live at home may be isolated from peers, have few opportunities to interact outside the family, and therefore may not develop the social skills important for intimate relationships. Children in residential placements have abundant opportunities for peer socializing, but limited exposure to family life and parenting role models (Coker, 1979; Gregory et al., 1995).

Although residential institutions have changed a great deal in the past three decades, even the most enlightened cannot provide socialization experiences precisely like those that take place within a family setting. Living with many same-age peers rather than a few siblings and having infrequent contact with parents may reduce experiences that give other children role models and socialization for future parenting and family life.

One study of court records showed that children with disabilities were "2.2 times more likely to be victims of sexual abuse than nondisabled children" (Sullivan, Brookhouser, and Scanlan, 2000, p. 155). Periodically, scandals involving sexual abuse erupt in residential schools, where the subject has traditionally been handled by a "conspiracy of silence" (Mertens, 1996). Those who experience this abuse clearly receive negative socialization for sexual intimacy.

The healthy expression of sexuality is an important part of parenting, but adults often find the expression of sexuality by adolescents difficult to accept. These views can be exacerbated when adolescents have disabilities and contribute to deficiencies in sex education in these populations. In the past, most residential schools permitted boy–girl activities only in groups (Evans, 1987; Schlesinger and Meadow, 1972). Thus, it is not surprising that more than half of a group of deaf adults interviewed in the early 1960s reported having no dates while in school (Rainer, Altshuler, and Kallmann, 1969). Many signs related to sexual acts or body functions are graphic and iconic, and may be banned by school authorities (Fitz-Gerald and Fitz-Gerald, 1978).

Children with visual impairments may be unaware of physical sex differences, as this awareness depends initially on sight. "In the absence of sight there are no socially approved means for understanding what these differences are" (Scott, 1969b, p. 1042). Taboos against tactile body exploration of the other sex can lead to difficulties in sexual relationships and the family relationships that contribute to successful parenting (Warren, 1977).

Early onset physical disabilities can affect sexual development (and therefore the preparation for parenting) in a variety of ways: "Many children with disabilities experience far more 'handling' than tender loving caresses. Similarly, having a disability that requires medical attention presents the possibility of more public nudity than that experienced by a typical child" (Cole and Cole, 1993, p. 193). There is some evidence that girls with congenital physical disabilities have a significantly earlier mean age for the onset of the menarche compared to girls without physical disabilities (Dalton and Dalton, 1978, cited in Craft and Craft, 1979), suggesting that sex education should begin earlier for this group, although actually it begins later or is considered unnecessary altogether.

The needs or "tasks" of those who become disabled in late adolescence differ, of course, from those of the population discussed in this section. However, like other adolescents, their "family tasks" include changing the nature of relationships with parents, developing a capacity for intimacy, establishing a firm identity, and finding a place for themselves in society (Erikson, 1959, 1963; Ireys and Burr, 1984).

Summary

Some important differences among those with various disabilities have been reviewed, including issues of incidence, prevalence, variations in etiology, and severity of conditions that influence adult functioning and parenting capability. In addition to these differences for individuals in each of three main disability groupings, other important demographic factors include race and socioeconomic status. The problems of controlling many separate characteristics multiply the difficulties of research on parenting by adults with disabilities.

The potential conflict between the rights of adults with disabilities and the cost to society of providing the assistance that enables them to exercise their rights to conceive, bear, and rear children is at the heart of many court cases. Establishing the principle that disability alone does not make a person unable to parent was a landmark in the history of disability rights.

The children with disabilities who will become parents of their own children have developmental trajectories different from those of individuals without a disability. Their parents probably struggled to overcome grief and, perhaps, the chronic sorrow associated with bearing a child different from themselves and from the anticipated "perfect baby." They may have been sheltered and protected during their middle years, perhaps isolated from age-mates during adolescence, with experiences that contribute to negative images of themselves as competent and sexually attractive adults. Although these experiences can create strengths as well as weaknesses, parental adequacy as well as inadequacy, parenting by individuals who are deaf, blind, or physically disabled must be viewed within the context of those childhood experiences in order to be understood.

SOCIAL AND PSYCHOLOGICAL THEORY
RELEVANT TO PARENTING AND DISABILITY

Consideration of parenting by adults with disabilities leads to a new appreciation of the theoretical importance of the lifespan/lifecycle approach to human development. The preceding section focused on the family of orientation. As children with disabilities become adults and form their own families, the role of the disability status of grandparents becomes a factor in the circumstances of the next generation. As Bronfenbrenner (1979) emphasized, it is a mistake to focus on the role of the mother alone, the father alone, or the parents alone in understanding family dynamics. Many factors create the ecology of an individual's life: family, friends, educational and religious institutions, legal statutes, social attitudes as expressed in written and visual media. The failure to view children with disabilities in the context of the lifespan may help to explain the paucity of research on families formed by persons with disabilities. Most of the research on these adults is focused on vocational or work adjustment rather than on family issues. (An exception to the usual separation of children from adults in the literature on disabilities is a review of behavioral research with mentally retarded children; Berkson, 1993.) Much of the available research with both children and adults with disabilities is driven by applied or clinical concerns rather than by theory, and is informed by a "deficit" rather than a "coping" framework, ignoring the natural adjustments made by the human organism to biological risk and disability. Summarized below are some social and psychological theories with special relevance for parenting and disability.

Impact of a Disabling Condition on Personality

A question that has intrigued social scientists as well as the general public is whether there are specific personality types or behavioral patterns associated with sensory and physical disabilities. Myth and popular lore have suggested positive talents as well as negative characteristics that may accompany a disabling condition. If there were clusters of traits or personality patterns associated with deafness, blindness, and physical disability, they would influence parenting styles and capabilities.

The psychology of disability.   The linkage of personality types or descriptions to disability is outmoded (Shontz, 1975). The notion of a "psychology of deafness" or a "psychology of blindness" has been discarded, because there is as much variation within each disability grouping as between it and the groupings of hearing, sighted, and able-bodied persons. Deafness provides an interesting example of changing approaches to this issue. Work published before 1970 (Altshuler, 1964; Levine, 1956, 1969; Myklebust, 1960) argued that deafness invariably elicits certain personality traits. Deaf people were described as "primitive" and incapable of abstract thought, conditions linked to auditory deprivation rather than to social-psychological experiences or impoverished educational and communicative opportunities. These formulations by psychologists and psychiatrists were common before American Sign Language (ASL) was recognized as a sophisticated form of communication, a language with the properties of other languages, through which abstract and symbolic ideas could be expressed. Stokoe (1960; Stokoe, Casterline, and Croneberg, 1965) opened the door to this understanding, changing the assumptions of social and psychological as well as linguistic research with deaf people. Deaf children's early communication ranges from almost none, for those with hearing parents, to a language-rich environment for those with deaf, educated, signing parents. With these perspectives, behavioral scientists moved from a monolithic view of "the" deaf experience to analyses of subgroups with diagnostic or experiential differences (Pollard, 1992b).

Similar debates about blindness are found. Some authors minimize the effects of absence of vision and insist that it is only a nuisance; others declare that "blindness changes and utterly reorganizes the entire mental life of the individual" (Lowenfeld, 1981, pp. 223–224). A moderate view is that, although there is no personality of the blind, lack of vision affects those behaviors that result from visual feedback, such as eye contact and facial expression of emotion (Foulke, 1972). Others agree that there is no unique psychology of blindness, asserting that the self-concepts of blind and sighted people develop in similar ways (Leung and Hollins, 1989; Tuttle, 1984).

Children who are deaf and those who are blind have frequently been characterized as egocentric, impulsive, or lacking in empathy (Greenberg, 2000; Marschark, 1993; McAndrew, 1948; Meadow, 1980; Meadow-Orlans, 1984; Scott, 1969b). They also are at greater risk for emotional disturbance compared to children without disabilities (Chess, Korn, and Fernandez, 1971; Hindley, 2000; Jan et al., 1977; Schlesinger and Meadow, 1972). Some of these conditions are associated with traumatic or genetic conditions responsible for the sensory deficit: "Up to one-half of the causes of blindness and at least a third of the causes of deafness arise through genetic anomalies which may also be responsible for mental disabilities" (Bond, 2000, p. 127).

Among physically disabled persons especially, the onset of disability in childhood or adulthood has very different consequences, necessitating a change in body image or self-concept. Depression and denial followed by gradual acceptance is a common form of adaptation; age at onset, the severity of impairment, and the nature of functional limitations influence response to later onset (Berrol, 1989; Safilios-Rothschild, 1970; Trieschmann, 1989). In those with early onset, the transition to adulthood can be difficult. A group of young adults with cerebral palsy was described as "unhappy, worried, isolated from peers and lacking self-esteem" (Clark and Hirst, 1989, p. 271). These characteristics might be appropriate reactions rather than "personality" traits. Personality is too complex to be accounted for by one characteristic, even one with the global implications of deafness, blindness, or physical limitation (Belsky and Barends, in Vol. 3 of this *Handbook*).

Psychological effects of sensory deprivation: Generalized deficiency and compensatory mechanisms. Either implicit or explicit in much of the speculation and research on personality traits of persons with sensory deficits are the effect of that deficit on perceptual ability and the resulting effects on behavior. Research attention has concentrated on two major hypotheses. The generalized-perceptual-deficiency hypothesis examines the idea that the absence of one major perceptual modality has a negative effect on "the neurological development and organization of other perceptual systems and, therefore, the total reactivity of an organism" (Hoemann, 1978, p. 44). Almost the mirror image of this hypothesis is that of sensory compensation, which suggests that, because it is necessary to rely on other modalities, persons who are deaf or blind will depend on them more and develop heightened capabilities in those senses that are available. Support for these hypotheses has been ambiguous at best. Myklebust's and Brutten's (1953) early research concluding that deaf people suffered generalized deficiencies was not replicated and has been criticized on the basis of research design (Reynolds, 1978). A related hypothesis proposes that experiential deficiencies contribute to differences in the cognitive and language development of deaf persons, leading to poor performance compared to hearing controls (Furth, 1966, 1971). One reviewer stated that the construct of experiential deficiency was neither defined nor assessed clearly, and "thus has limited predictive power ... " (Parasnis, 1983, p. 149).

Warren (1978, p. 84) concluded that "the vast majority of studies that have isolated sensory discrimination abilities have failed to find differences between blind and sighted groups or among various blind groups." He stressed the complexity of the issue of compensation in persons who are blind, proposing that it is necessary to separate the ability to discriminate on the basis of auditory and tactile cues from practice and training in effective attention to or functional use of information. A study of blind and sighted children showed no differences between the two groups in short-term memory, memory strategies, or metamemory (Wyler and Markham, 1998). Another researcher found that people who were blind early in life performed better than sighted people on a task designed to measure ability to localize sound but only when one ear was blocked (Lessard, Pare, Lepore, and Lassonde, 1998). One commentator believes that "These experimental findings raise as many problems as they solve" (Morgan, 1999, p. R54).

Reynolds's (1993) research on the ability of deaf persons to utilize peripheral vision illustrates the complexity of compensation for auditory deprivation. Utilizing a complicated design varying the interfering stimuli and presentation in the visual field (right vs. left), he concluded that hearing persons made better use of peripheral vision under some conditions whereas those who are deaf were superior under other conditions. Likewise, researchers who controlled for age, gender, language mode, and etiology, concluded that, under some conditions deaf people do compensate for auditory loss through vision, but that superior performance is limited to attention-dependent tasks and does not develop until adulthood (Rettenbach, Diller, and Sireteanu, 1999).

Developmental-Stage Theories

Because the primary concern in this chapter is with parenting by persons disabled from birth or early childhood, a lifespan perspective becomes imperative. In order to understand both the possible advantages and the possible weaknesses or challenges of parenting with a disability, it is necessary to understand the experiences of those parents from infancy through adolescence, and to appreciate the parenting challenges that may differ at varying stages of the children.

At least two research groups concerned with disabilities (Schlesinger and Meadow, 1972; Sutkin, 1984) have utilized Erikson's (1959, 1963) developmental framework in discussions of the impact of disability on the individual. Despite legitimate criticisms of this perspective (e.g., development rarely follows the smooth trajectory implied by the construct; "tasks" earmarked for a single stage overlap and remain issues at later stages), the perspective encourages a consideration of the life course often absent in research on families with disabled members (Freeman, Goetz, Richards, and Groenveld, 1991; Ireys and Burr, 1984).

According to Erikson's theory, the central task of adolescence is the development of "identity." This concept is often summarized as self-image or self-concept and is frequently the focus or organizing principle of research on the consequences of disability (e.g., Super and Block, 1992), and more specifically, on parents with disabilities. Self-image is often assumed to develop, in part, from the "reflected appraisals of others" (Mead, 1934) and referred to as "the looking glass self" (Cooley, 1902). Stigmatizing attitudes about disability, thus, are theorized as being communicated by significant others, incorporated into the self-concept and internalized as a negative self-image (Goffman, 1963).

Intuitive Parenting

The Papoušeks proposed that parents intuitively monitor and modulate their young infants' exposure to environmental stimuli and that infants' responses reinforce these caregiving behaviors (Koester, Papoušek, and Papoušek, 1987; Papoušek and Papoušek, in Vol. 2 of this *Handbook*). They investigated reciprocal behaviors, such as eye gaze, vocalizations, and tactile, rhythmic, and temporal communications that help infants to maintain, regain, or regulate optimal states. This theory is particularly relevant for parents with a sensory disability. If parents' intuitive or unconscious interactive patterns are inappropriate for their infants because of a mismatch in communicative abilities, it may be necessary for the parent to make conscious adjustments. The extent to which parents are able to shift their "preprogrammed" interactive styles has both practical and theoretical significance (Koester, 1992). Investigations of substitutions of one modality for another, and the maintenance of reciprocity when one modality (sound, vision, or mobility) is absent, would provide tests or extensions of the theory. For example, it would be instructive to compare the parenting styles of mothers who are deaf and have same-status parents to those with hearing parents. Differences in their use of visual and tactile cues with their own infants could help to explain the basis of intuitive parenting.

The Social Model of Disability

The case for the "social construction" of disability is presented clearly by Scott (1969a, p. 119): "The behavior of blind men comes to correspond with the assumptions and beliefs that blindness workers hold about blindness." Thus, "Blind men are not born they are made" (p. 121). Much of the current literature representing this position is written by advocates who hold that treatment by society creates the social and psychological handicaps of people with disabilities (Bowe, 1980; Davis, 1997; Hughes and Paterson, 1997). A frequent starting point is a critique of the "medical model" or of "pathologizing constructions." A radical extension of this position is found in Lane's (1992) charge that hearing professionals and parents ("audists") mistakenly try to force deaf people into a hearing mold, depriving them of their natural language (ASL) and their Deaf culture by forcing them to speak and to lipread. Hiding behind a "mask of benevolence," the professional (teacher, audiologist, researcher, or sign language interpreter) deliberately exploits those who are deaf for economic gain. Lane reserves especially harsh criticism for surgeons who perform cochlear implants to restore hearing. A more moderate position is taken by Deshen and Deshen (1989), who concluded that blindness is neither an all-encompassing fact of life (the stigmatizing position) nor is it a trivial condition (the position of some advocates for people with disabilities). Like deafness and physical disability, blindness can be understood only "within a broad human context."

Summary

Several theoretical frameworks emphasize the importance of a cross-generational perspective for understanding parenting by those with disabilities. Intuitive parenting assumes the unconscious repetition of caregiving received by the parent in his or her own childhood. An emphasis on the importance of a parent's positive self-concept in providing appropriate caregiving to a child assumes the roots of that self-image are in childhood. Evaluation of the development of the child whose parents are disabled must take place within the entire context of that child's life. In addition to the parents, important influences include grandparents, neighbors, teachers, peers, and representatives of community institutions.

RESEARCH ON PARENTS WITH DISABILITIES AND THEIR CHILDREN

Research on children with disabilities and their families has increased at an exponential rate since 1920, with thousands of reports added to the literature (Berkson, 1993). Despite this increased attention to children, there is little research on their subsequent family lives as adults. One reason is that whereas federal and private funding sources support educational research on children with disabilities and rehabilitation or work adjustment research on adults with disabilities, these sources provide little or no support for research on the family lives of those with disabilities. Another reason for the continuing neglect of research on disability, family processes, and childrearing is that research with this population is expensive and time-consuming, partly because of heterogeneity of target groups, as previously discussed. Contributing to this heterogeneity is the potential diversity of family composition, which can have a profound effect on parenting practices and family power constellations. Parenting in families where both husband and wife are deaf may be quite different from that where the husband is deaf, the wife hearing, and both may be different from the family where the husband is hearing and the wife deaf. Further complications may be added to research that includes spouses with differing physical, sensory, mental, or emotional disabilities (Craft and Craft, 1979). Family communication, spousal dominance, and discipline may all be related to disability status. Any of the possible spousal combinations may produce children with or without a disability, yielding additional implications and consequences for caregiving and childrearing problems and opportunities. Another important research consideration is a description of modifications in caregiving and communication made necessary by the functional parenting accommodations required by deafness, blindness, and physical disability. Parents who are deaf and do not speak will use sign language and must modify their response to infant cries and toddler behavior outside the range of sight. Those who are blind need to modify the customary approach to safeguarding toddler exploration; those who use wheelchairs or have missing limbs or limited strength must find unconventional ways of managing the physical care of their children.

Paths to Parenthood

Generativity is one of the adult "tasks" in Erikson's epigenetic theory of development. The desire to have children of one's own is strong and widespread. Morelli and Tronick (1991, p. 91) proposed that parental caregiving strategies across cultures include "all mechanisms by which parents attempt to insure the survival of their offspring, and consequently *the perpetuation of their genes in future generations*" (italics added). When those genes appear to be responsible for the survival of an undesired trait, the urge for generativity may be threatened. For example, the father of an autistic boy says: " ... I thought by marrying outside of my race that bad genes [diabetes and mental illness] could be eliminated. Instead, I have further scattered bad genes" (Greenfeld, 1979, cited in Meyer, 1986, p. 46).

Many deaf adults have positive feelings about giving birth to a deaf child, like the brother of this woman interviewed by Preston (1994, p. 107):

> My [deaf] brother married a deaf girl and they had a baby boy. The baby is profoundly deaf. And my brother wrote me a letter saying, "I was so happy to find out he was deaf because he will always be one of us."

The hope that one's child will be like oneself would generally be seen as a reflection of positive self-image. It is less likely that it would have been felt, or at least expressed by previous generations of deaf adults. Several of Preston's informants commented on what appeared to be a growing number of younger deaf parents who wanted deaf children. "The stigma of having a 'defective' child was increasingly displaced by wanting to have a child who was like themselves" (Preston, 1994, p. 192). The self-confidence reflected by this attitude may result from the sense of positive identity that comes from an increasingly proud and cohesive Deaf community (Padden and Humphries, 1988). A study conducted with readers of the *British Deaf News* showed that 2% to 3% of each group of deaf, hard-of-hearing, and hearing respondents said they would have prenatal diagnosis to terminate a fetus who was deaf, whereas 2 of 482 deaf respondents would have this procedure to terminate a fetus who was hearing (Middleton, Hewison, and Mueller, 1998, cited in Arnos, 1999).

Anecdotal accounts suggest that parents who are blind may fear the genetic transmission of blindness to their children (Fries, 1980). A woman who was blind like both her parents was shocked to learn that her mother had known of the possible transmission of blindness. The daughter admitted that she was, indeed, enjoying her life without sight. Nevertheless, she planned to be childless (Hocken, 1978).

Conception and childbirth are no more physically problematic for individuals with sensory disabilities than for the general population. Nevertheless, women who are either deaf or blind may lack access to information about pregnancy and childbirth. A nursing teacher and practitioner was surprised at the lack of anatomical information demonstrated by blind women in a childbirth preparation class. "Some students did not even know the meaning of 'uterus' or 'cervix' " (Bobek, 1984, p. 350). Physically disabled women also may lack information about pregnancy and childbirth, knowledge about reproductive health care and contraception, and meet social resistance to their reproduction and mothering (Kallianes and Rubenfeld, 1997).

Physical disabilities may make becoming a parent difficult. However, a team of medical rehabilitation specialists reported an increase in the number of women paraplegics who have married and have borne children (Turk, Turk, and Assejev, 1983). They reported on 10 of their patients who had no difficulty with the conception, pregnancy, and delivery of their children. Another study of the pregnancy and birth experiences of 10 mothers with physical disabilities (spinal cord injury, multiple sclerosis, postpolio, and spina bifida) reported that one had a preterm infant, two delivered by C-section, and the remaining seven had uncomplicated vaginal deliveries (Shaul, Dowling, and Laden, 1985). Interviews with 36 disabled women who had experienced pregnancy suggested that it is the severity of the disability, rather than the type, that helps to predict how difficult a pregnancy will be. They also suggested that, unlike most women, they are under pressure not to have children, and therefore are exposed to public disapproval when their pregnancy becomes apparent (Rogers, 1993).

Caregiving by Parents With Disabilities

Parents who are deaf.   An investigation of the family situations of literate people with profound deafness in New York state showed that 86.1% of the women aged 45 and older were or had been married, compared to 89.4% of the general population; 69.7% of the married women were mothers, compared to 79% in the general population. About 5% of women born deaf (and 8.7% of those deafened adventitiously) were married to hearing men. Thirty percent of families where both spouses were deaf had at least one deaf child (Rainer, Altshuler, and Kallmann, 1969).

The chief handicap of early profound deafness is the inability to learn language and speech through audition or to learn to lipread others. If visual communication is not initiated early, the communication handicap associated with deafness may extend to educational underachievement, especially in the area of reading, which then becomes a secondary handicap for many adults who are deaf. However, most have become proficient in sign language long before they become parents. Those whose parents are deaf learn sign language early: from birth onward. Indeed, sign language is more than a means of communication, it is an important part of Deaf culture (Meadow-Orlans and Erting, 2000). Deaf persons with hearing parents may learn to sign from peers at school. As adults, they are likely to marry a partner who also is deaf; their children, deaf or hearing, will communicate with them by means of ASL or signed English. Their main functional handicaps lie in monitoring their children's safety or behavior by means of the auditory channel and in their inability to teach and monitor spoken language.

The first studies from which inferences can be drawn about the effect of deafness on parenting were conducted in the 1960s and early 1970s, spurred by questions about the socioeducational effects of the early use of sign language by children who were deaf. Because the oral approach was used exclusively in schools, children whose home language was signed (that is, those whose parents were deaf) were the only possible participants. The findings of several different research studies with this population showed the academic achievement of children who were deaf like their parents equaled or exceeded the academic achievement of children who were deaf but whose parents were hearing. When social adjustment or self-image was included in the research design, results were similar (Brasel and Quigley, 1977; Meadow, 1968; Stuckless and Birch, 1966; Vernon and Koh, 1970). This research promoted the educational use of sign language; by inference, it also supported the parenting efficacy of deaf adults.

However, some child psychiatrists challenged this inference. At a mental health clinic serving a school for children who were deaf, they observed four children of deaf parents, ages 7 to 31 months, for varying periods. The mothers introduced self-bottle feeding by 3 months and discouraged self-feeding of solids. During their second year, the children exhibited severe separation anxiety and sleep disturbances, which the researchers concluded were the result of disturbed mother–infant relationships exacerbated by the mothers' "characterology," contributing to infants' unstable sense of self (Galenson, Miller, Kaplan, and Rothstein, 1979). A later study reported differing results: Neither the attachment patterns (Meadow, Greenberg, Erting, and Carmichael, 1981) nor social behaviors (Meadow et al., 1985) of preschool children who were deaf and had deaf parents differed from children who were hearing like their parents. The second set of authors suggested that parents participating in the earlier study represented a different population: They had enrolled their children in a school where sign language was neither used nor accepted, despite the fact that it was their home language. Parents in the second study were more highly educated, had the support of an active Deaf community, and had placed their children in a school where sign language was accepted and used. More recently, studies of very early interaction have demonstrated that mothers who are deaf are highly responsive to their infants, also deaf (Meadow-Orlans, 1997; Spencer, Bodner-Johnson, and Gutfreund, 1992), and modify their signed communication to maximize infants' visual input (Erting, Prezioso, and Hynes, 1994; Erting, Thumann-Prezioso, and Benedict, 2000; Mohay, 2000; Swisher, 2000). Mothers who are deaf have also been observed to use more tactile contact with their infants compared to other mothers (Mohay, Milton, Hindmarsh, and Ganley, 1998; Rea, Bonvillian, and Richards, 1988).

Family life when both parents and children are deaf has been portrayed in a positive way. However, the picture in families where parents are deaf and children hearing is more problematic. Free-play interactions of mothers who are deaf with babies who are hearing were rated somewhat less positively (e.g., less sensitive mothers, less attentive infants) than those of deaf deaf and hearing hearing dyads, although somewhat more positively than hearing-mother/deaf-infant dyads (Meadow-Orlans, 1997; Meadow-Orlans and Spencer, 1996).

Speech therapists have found that hearing children whose parents are deaf experience speech and language delays (Schiff and Ventry, 1976), but there is no evidence that these delays create long-term difficulties (Mayberry, 1976). The personal accounts of children of deaf adults usually report positive family experiences (Preston, 1994): They did not as children, nor do they as adults, consider their parents "handicapped" (Hoffmeister, 1985). They recount the burdens of interpreting for their parents (Mallory, Schein, and Zingle, 1992; Preston, 1996), the need to protect parents from cruel strangers or insensitive family members (including hearing grandparents), but also express strong affection and close emotional ties (Davis, 2000; Sidransky, 1990; Walker, 1986). In her autobiography, Walker (1986) reported that both she and her sister sometimes imagined that their parents could "really" hear and were only pretending to be deaf, a fantasy also reported by some children whose parents are blind.

Results of one study suggest that hearing children (ages 7 to 13 years) of deaf parents had more influence on family decisions than the hearing children of hearing parents, and that fathers who were deaf had less influence than their counterparts with normal hearing (Rienzi, 1990). Interviews with firstborn 9- to 15-year-old hearing children whose parents were deaf revealed that negative feelings were often related to interpreting for their parents. Younger children were proud of that responsibility, but older children believed their siblings to be unfairly relieved of interpreting chores (Buchino, 1993).

Parents who are blind.   Jan et al. (1977) contacted almost the complete British Columbia population of children who were blind ($N = 92$) from 1973 to 1974. Based on their psychological adjustment and educational achievement levels, the researchers concluded that the prospects for these people's future work and family adjustments were not good. However, a 1987 to 1988 follow-up, during which 69 of the original participants were interviewed, revealed that these young adults greatly exceeded earlier expectations (Freeman et al., 1991). Of the 16- to 34-year-olds responding to family-related queries, 11 of 24 women (46%) and 18 of 33 men (55%) reported having had a romantic relationship. Seventeen percent of the women and 23% of the men were partnered, all to sighted persons. Three of the men but none of the women had one or more children. An analysis of autobiographies written by persons blind before adulthood showed that two of the eight women had married, compared to all seven of the men. All spouses were sighted (Asch and Sacks, 1983).

Like other parents or parents-to-be with disabilities, those who are blind often do not have easy access to self-help groups or parenting classes. Some of their practical childcare problems and solutions include: (birth to age 5) strapping a young baby for diaper changes, use of harnesses and shoe bells for safety, and marking medicine bottles in braille; (ages 6–12 years) dealing with school entry, handwriting, homework, embarrassment, and sneaking; (ages 13–19 years) monitoring appearance, driving a car, and reading mail for parents (Arsnow, Dichiera, Mould, Sauerbrauer, and Peaco, 1985). Interviews with 42 blind and low-vision mothers showed that one of the leading concerns of these mothers was the extra time, effort, and expense that parenting required, compared to that demanded of sighted peers. They also emphasized the importance of contact with other parents with visual impairments (Conley-Jung, 1996).

An ethnographic study of eight Israeli families (mostly immigrants from developing countries) consisting of parents who were blind and their sighted children is an excellent introduction to parenting problems and children's adjustments, ranging from pride to shame, social contributions to social pathology, and helpfulness to avoidance. The parents needed to learn the nature of sighted childhood; the children, the nature of blindness. Between the ages of 7 and 11, children were observed "testing" their parents' blindness, sometimes in a hostile or aggressive manner. Some expressed anxiety about a parent's inability to return home if a mishap were to interfere with their sense of place. As hearing children often interpret for parents who are deaf, sighted children often serve as guides for parents who are blind (Deshen and Deshen, 1989).

A case study describes the interactions of a sighted infant with a mother, congenitally blind, and a father, adventitiously blinded (Adamson, Als, Tronick, and Brazelton, 1977). During the first year, the infant was observed to avert her gaze from the mother's face, to look occasionally at the father (who was more likely than the mother to direct his own gaze to others), and to gaze avidly at the researchers' faces during their visits. The mother used auditory and tactile behaviors to monitor the infant and played games utilizing vocal rather than visual imitation. This mother was a successful primary caregiver, as were the 10 similar mothers participating in another study, taking complete responsibility for the daily needs of their infants and toddlers (Ware and Schwab, 1971). Mothers in the second study lived in rural nonfarm or urban areas of eastern Nebraska and were legally blind at the birth of at least one child. Most had childcare help from a sighted person during the first month of the infant's life. (Although information about the status of husbands was not included, it is implied that all were sighted.) Several mothers had help from their husbands in cleansing the child after removal of a soiled diaper, and help from a sighted person was called on if it was suspected that the child had a fever. Their most difficult tasks were toilet training and the introduction of solid foods. Because the mothers were unable to determine the location of the child's mouth, some delayed giving nonliquids, others put cereal into a bottle, enlarging the hole in the nipple.

One study reports interviews with 10 families consisting of one parent with a visual impairment, a spouse with normal sight, a sighted child, and a control group of 10 families in which all members had normal vision. Children whose parents were visually impaired exerted more influence on purchases of goods and services. This difference was related to the withdrawal of the parent, rather than to increased domination by the child (Gill-Williamson, 1991).

A social worker conducted nonstructured interviews with 18 mothers who were blind in an effort to determine whether their children were "deprived." In seven families, both parents were totally blind; in one, the wife was blind, the husband partially sighted; in two, wives were blind and husbands sighted; eight wives were partially blind and had sighted husbands. Conclusions were impressionistic: "a number of children (were) suffering in some way from a lack or lacks in their home life due to their parent's blindness" (Shepherdson, 1967, p. 284). Perhaps the most striking impression from the descriptions of individual cases is the wide variation in living conditions: Housekeeping habits and home environments varied from pleasant to slum-like; most children were allowed freedom to explore, but one was confined to his cot during toddlerhood because of the mother's fear for his safety; some parents demanded their children devote a great deal of time to serving as their guides; others never required this service. In 15 of the 18 families, some problems existed; 9 children from 7 families exhibited school difficulties. Nine families included 12 children with behavior problems. Four mothers were inadequate housekeepers. Families most likely to have problems were those where blindness was complicated by another disability.

These studies, all with a limited number of subjects, illustrate the wide variation in parenting practices among parents who are blind. They also illustrate the concept that some of the problems encountered by parents with disabilities can be related to system failures rather than to individual difficulties. If community services were provided at a reasonable level, parents would not need to turn to their children for assistance (Olkin, 1999).

Parents with physical limitations. Since 1990, numbers of parents with disabilities have increased rapidly. This seems to be due to the independent living movement, the civil rights movement for those with disabilities, and increasing participation of adults with disabilities in all aspects of life. About half of all parents who are disabled have physical disabilities, and about 6 million children under 18 live with at least one parent who has a physical disability (Tuleja, Rogers, Vensand, and DeMoss, 1998).

Results of a national survey of 1,200 parents with disabilities showed that one fourth of respondents live with a partner who also has a disability. Half became disabled before the age of 18. One fourth have one or more children with a disability (Barker and Maralani, 1997).

Individuals with cerebral palsy comprise about half of those with physical disabilities, with this condition occurring in 1 to 2 per 1,000 live births. Life expectancy is normal and the estimated living American population is 400,000 (Alexander and Bauer, 1988). About 60% are mentally retarded. As adults, only 10% are entirely self-supporting; 15% are quite dependent, some living in institutions (Batshaw and Perret, 1992). Results from a study of adults with cerebral palsy suggest that the mental health of those who become parents is above average and that they are enthusiastic in their commitment to this role (Greer, 1985).

A 10-year follow-up of 89 English adolescents with cerebral palsy was conducted in 1988 when individuals were 25 to 27 years old (Clark and Hirst, 1989). Questionnaire data on their current work and family arrangements were collected from the 44 who could be located. Fifty-nine percent were living with their parents and satisfied with that arrangement; 11% were looking for different housing; 23% were living in their own households; 14% were in residential care (seen by them as a step toward independent living). Three men and three women were partnered (two of the men had children); two were engaged; four hoped for a future marriage. Thus, only a quarter of the respondents even hoped to establish a family.

Adoption is one option of those physically unable to conceive children (Brodzinsky and Pinderhughes, in Vol. 1 of this *Handbook*). However, adults with disabilities are sometimes denied this alternative because they are seen as unable to provide suitable childcare (Kallianes and Rubenfeld, 1997). An anecdotal account describes the experience of a woman, a polio quadriplegic married to a nondisabled spouse (Sandness, 1981). The couple adopted a "hard to place" G.I. baby from Korea, then a child with mild cerebral palsy, another paralyzed from polio, and 11 others. This mother advises women like herself to adopt younger children who will be comfortable riding on a mother's lap in a wheelchair and being "nuzzled" affectionately. She gives such parents advice on disciplining (e.g., "Don't threaten punishments you can't enforce" and "Use a lot of humor") and for handling a child's embarrassment at having a parent who is different (e.g., "Ask your child's teacher to let you explain your wheelchair or crutches to the class").

Anecdotal accounts from parents with physical limitations can flesh out research studies. One mother with chronic illness interviewed others and reported their reactions to various aspects of their lives, including their parenting experiences. A major concern was frequent fatigue that interfered with parenting chores, but a child's ability to cope with these limitations is impressive (Register, 1987). A woman with cerebral palsy described how her adopted infant managed the mother's disability: "Whenever he'd bump into something, he'd crawl over to me and pull himself on my wheelchair up to a standing position so that I could lift him into my lap to comfort him. He started doing that at 6 months" (Jacobson, 1993, p. 51).

Fatigue and uncertain physical health are primary parenting concerns for women with multiple sclerosis (McNary, 1999; Monroe, 1989). Women participating in one study reported that disability-related problems were most likely to occur when children are younger than age 5 and that more challenges came from architectural and attitudinal barriers than from the mothers' abilities to parent their children (Cohen, 1998).

Ten mothers whose physical limitations resulted from a variety of causes reported that they found few commercial devices to help them care for an infant or young child. With a limited supply of physical energy, caregiving often left them exhausted. They believed that their children benefited from the independence required of them and showed increased sensitivity to individuals with disabilities (Shaul et al., 1985). Similarly positive evaluations of parenting by a group of 10 paraplegic mothers have also been reported. The pediatrician member of a Yugoslavian rehabilitation medicine team visited the homes on a regular basis. Her observations included these comments (Turk et al., 1983, p. 190):

> There are no signs of negligent nursing, upbringing or negative development. These children are great favorites of their mothers and families, without communication problems in mixing with other children of their own age. They make their mothers happy, and clearly demonstrate the . . . progress . . . by paraplegic women.

A study of 124 children (ages 7 to 11) with one parent with multiple sclerosis, the other one healthy, compared the children's body images to those of a control group of children with two healthy parents. Girls whose mothers were disabled had greater "body image distortion" than did those whose fathers were disabled, whereas the two groups of boys did not differ (Olgas, 1974). Another study compared two groups of adults: one whose fathers had spinal cord injuries ($N = 45$), the other whose fathers did not ($N = 36$). Half the fathers with disabilities were war veterans; 82% were paraplegic, 18%, quadriplegic. Children whose fathers were disabled "were well-adjusted, emotionally stable persons who had attained normal sex role identities. Health patterns, body image, recreational interests, interpersonal relationships, and family relations were not . . . associated with the disability status of the father" (Buck and Hohmann, 1981, p. 432). The authors concluded that parents with disabilities may provide children with heightened coping skills, illustrated by this quotation from a woman who grew up in a similar home (Buck, 1980, cited in Buck and Hohmann, 1983, p. 234):

> I feel I am more capable of facing anything that may come up than my friends. I have benefited greatly from watching and participating in the survival of a family where life depended on strength and courage. I have learned how to take care of myself and others. I know many secrets to the art of living as well as surviving in the face of many tragedies and disappointments. I have learned the tricks to success (not just survival) through my father . . .

A previous review of parenting by disabled adults noted that research in this area often confounds early and later onset disability, and may include both acute and chronic physical and mental illness without differentiating among these groups (Buck and Hohmann, 1983). When a parent becomes disabled after the birth of one or more children, the family may undergo almost unbearable stress. Stress level is not necessarily related to the severity of the disability and is more likely with cognitive and mental than physical disability (Peterson, 1979). Divorce after disability is more frequent for women than men, among young and poor couples and those with fewer than three children (Nagi and Clark, 1964; Olkin, 1999). A study of women with spinal cord injuries found that the relationships of 15 of the 29 dissolved after their injuries. Five lost custody of their children; eight gave up plans to have children (Bonwich, 1985). The Minnesota Spinal Cord Injury Study emphasizes the differences in early and late onset disability. Marital satisfaction and general life satisfaction was found to favor those who married postdisability (Crewe, 1993).

One difficulty in making sense of the sparse information about parents with mobility limitation is the wide variety of conditions included under this rubric. Each condition may require somewhat different modifications in the usual or expected parenting and caregiving arrangements. Too often these differences are not taken into account, and those with different challenges are lumped together. Another frequent problem is the inclusion of persons who are mentally retarded and the combining of participants with early and late onset of disability. Each of these differences can skew research results and necessitate the construction of different research questions. A common thread that seems to run through accounts of parenting with a physical disability is the increased time required for parenting tasks and the greater fatigue experienced by these parents compared to able-bodied adults.

Summary

Adults with sensory and physical limitations usually express the same desire to give birth to children and to participate in family life as do similar adults without disabilities. The ability to conceive and to deliver children is not affected by deafness or blindness, but conception may be more difficult and delivery may create additional health risks for mothers with physical disabilities. Most studies of mothers who are deaf show them capable of high levels of caregiving; indeed, recent research with these mothers has been used to learn more effective ways for hearing mothers to communicate with their children who are deaf. Mothers who are deaf have more problems with children who are hearing than with those who are deaf. As adults, these children express positive feelings about their early experiences, although some also report parental dependence on children and embarrassment at having parents who are "different." Likewise, adults with visual and physical limitations have developed special ways of coping with children from infancy onward. Those who are blind often need more help with caregiving tasks, compared to parents who are deaf. Depending on level of impairment, parents with physical disabilities may need still more help with everyday childrearing tasks. The theme of most research and narrative reports, however, is the high level of coping and the development of substitute skills that enable these parents to provide high levels of care for their children.

PRACTICAL INFORMATION

Parenting Information and Support

Parents with disabilities increasingly are forming their own support and educational groups. Parents who are blind, who are deaf, and who have limited mobility all have e-mail lists and Web sites for the purpose of exchanging information and experiences.[2] Kids of Deaf Adults is an organization that promotes family awareness and individual growth in hearing children of deaf parents. Children of Deaf Adults is an international organization for the (adult) hearing children of deaf parents (Bull, 1988, 1998). The cohesive Deaf community in large metropolitan areas can offer strong support to parents who are deaf. Those who are relatively isolated in rural areas or small towns may need more help from other sources.

Through the Looking Glass (TLG) is an organization in Berkeley, California, that serves as a clearinghouse for information and advocacy for parents with disabilities. With support from the U.S. Department of Education's National Institute on Disability and Rehabilitation Research, TLG established a National Task Force on Parents with Disabilities in 1997. The mission of this task force is "to promote social changes which will improve the lives of parents with disabilities and keep our families together" (Preston and Jakobson, 1997, p. 1).

Parents with disabilities encounter everyday barriers when dealing with established facilities for their children. Teachers and mental health professionals with no special training lack understanding about coping strategies and may unwittingly penalize children of parents with disabilities. Increasingly, journals carry articles advising nonspecialists in appropriate helping services for these families (Kirshbaum, 1994). For working with deaf-parented families, advice to professionals emphasizes the importance of familiarity with Deaf culture and appropriate use of interpreters (Filer and Filer, 2000; Singleton and Tittle, 2000).

---

[2]Some pertinent Web addresses include: blind-parents@egroups.com; http://www.disabledparents.net; http://www.koda.org; http://www.coda-international.org; and http://www.lookingglass.org.

DeafPride, a community-based organization working for the human rights of those who are deaf, has contracted with the Washington, DC, Commission of Public Health to provide health advocacy classes for clients. Participating mothers, all with hearing children, are mostly single African Americans who live in the inner city. Some have themselves experienced neglect and abuse. The program is designed to help the mothers meet their own broadly defined health needs as well as those of their children. A second purpose is that of encouraging the mothers to become advocates for themselves and others.

Several parent education programs, designed for the general population (Smith and Drew, in Vol. 3 of this *Handbook*), have been adapted for parents of children with disabilities (Farran, 1990; Fine, 1980; Preston and Lou, 1998) and other "atypical" families such as single-parent, adoptive, and reconstituted (Marr and Kennedy, 1980). However, little attention has been given to parents with disabilities, even though these programs would be appropriate with only slight modifications. A sign language interpreter and captioning for film or video materials would be needed by parents who are deaf, and tactile aids might be helpful for those who are blind.

Because many with disabilities come from impoverished backgrounds or have experiential deficits, parenting programs developed for economically deprived families might be useful to them (Bryant and Ramey, 1987). Examples include the Carolina Abecedarian Project (Campbell, Helms, Sparling, and Ramey, 1998), AVANCE for Mexican-American families, and MIHOW for Appalachian families (Halpern, 1990). Programs developed for those with mental disabilities could serve as models for this disadvantaged population (Whitman and Accardo, 1990; see also Parks, 1984), because they provide basic information about a child's physical, health, and nutritional needs, time management, and the organization of basic household chores. The St. Louis project developed curriculum modules focusing on child development (appropriate behaviors expected of children at various ages), children's basic needs (for affection, play, independence, safety), and parent–child interaction (sharing and use of toys), personal and child hygiene, daily routines, time concepts, and medical care (Whitman and Accardo, 1990). Goals included improving mothers' self-esteem and providing positive mother–child experiences.

Through the Looking Glass has developed a model and materials for parents with mobility disabilities that was adapted for parents who are deaf. As they are careful to note, many deaf families have raised their children successfully, but some need special help because of risk factors exacerbated by exclusion from resources more widely available to able-bodied and hearing, sighted parents (Preston and Lou, 1998).

The whole concept of parent education has been questioned and largely replaced with programs broadly characterized as "parent–professional partnerships" or "family centered" (Harbin and McNulty, 1990; Mahoney et al., 1999).

Assistive Devices and Technology

Technical devices providing visual assistance for persons who are deaf are related to telephone communication, broadcast media, face-to-face communication, and environmental awareness (Harkins, 1991; Marschark, 1997). Telecommunication Devices for the Deaf (TDD) make communication by telephone possible, if both caller and receiver possess a TDD. Telephone relay services allow calls to be placed through a third party who serves as interpreter. Captioning of television programs and videotapes has made much popular culture and public information programming newly available to those who are deaf. In 1984, the Food and Drug Administration approved a cochlear implant system, the Nucleus 22 channel, for use in the postlinguistically deafened adult population (Nevins and Chute, 1996). In 1990, the device was approved for use with children. By 1999, according to the manufacturer, Nucleus 22 systems had been implanted in 25,000 deaf people throughout the world (Cochlear Corporation, 1999). Implants have been the subject of bitter opposition in the Deaf community. Some deaf people believe that the implant's development, like research on the genetics of deafness, reflects a plot to eradicate their culture (Mowl, 1996): "Of all the controversies surrounding [deafness] . . . none seem to touch the raw nerves that the issue of cochlear implants does" (Moores, 1992, p. 109).

These advances, and others on the horizon related to fax, computer, and video and telephone technology, serve to decrease the isolation created by deafness and increase the independence of this population (Boothroyd, 1998; Levitt, 1998; Stinson and Stuckless, 1998). Assistive technology with direct relevance for parenting include environmental awareness devices: flashing lights or vibration signals for telephones and doorbells, child monitors (Baby Cry), alarm clocks, and visual fire and security alarms (Harkins, 1991). Each of these devices can decrease reliance on children for contacts with the hearing community.

As the number of sign language interpreters increases and federally funded institutions (including hospitals) are required to make their services accessible to people with disabilities, prenatal, childbirth, and parenting classes have become more available to this population. A Washington, DC, sign language service assigns an interpreter to accompany an expectant couple to the delivery room when the wife goes into labor. However, many physicians resist providing interpreters for procedures such as ultrasound testing and pediatric visits. If parents must pay interpreters themselves, access is obviously related to economic privilege.

Cost and lack of information about assistive technology are named as the two major barriers to access by those who are blind. Three basic types of electronic devices exist for accessing computers and print documents: those that magnify screen images, those that provide synthetic speech to translate print, and tactile output devices such as braille printers. These devices may cost anywhere from $1,000 to $20,000 (Uslan, 1992). After many years of research, a team of German scientists has developed an artificial human eye that should give blind people "moderate sight." It will be tested on a volunteer in 2002 (Brookman, 2000).

"Parenting without Vision in 1,000 Easy Lessons" (Cranston, 1982), a publication that summarizes assistive devices for parents who are blind, provides hints and resources on feeding, safety, setting limits, toilet training, and the importance of "talking a lot" to the child. The author, blind from birth and the mother of 2-year-old twins, interviewed 11 other mothers in preparing the booklet. The "lessons" yield insights into their everyday lives:

> The dilemma of taking a baby's temperature "is real and frustrating." There is a talking thermometer available. (p. 5)
>
> "Always remember to face the baby when nursing. That way she can see you clearly. . . . Be aware of your facial expression. Try to smile at the baby a lot . . . " (p. 11)
>
> Baby bottle nipples sometimes collapse or clog: "When milk is flowing through smoothly, there is a small whistling or bubbling sound." (p. 14)
>
> For crawlers and toddlers: "Many parents said that they experienced great fear that they would lose track of the child. . . . Some tried to keep the child contained in a playpen or harness. Several put bells on their child's shoes. One mother, with four little children at home, bought four bells with different tones . . . " (p. 25)

Parents with physical disabilities have found few devices designed to help them in childcare. In response to this lack, a grant was awarded to the National Rehabilitation Research and Training Center on Families of Adults with Disabilities to develop parenting equipment. The focus was on the design or adaptation of baby care equipment for these activities: Feeding, diapering, bathing, dressing, bedtime, transferring, carrying and moving, holding, and playing. Also evaluated were adaptive parenting techniques for burping, transferring, diapering, and undressing (Tuleja et al., 1998).

Computer-Mediated Communication has been defined as a medium that "equalizes status cues," enabling interactions that are "not mediated by the disability-related stigma." The World Wide Web opens many new possibilities for information gathering that can be especially beneficial for parents with disabilities (Fox, 2000, p. 333). For example, an Internet search—"blindness and parents," yielded 54 sites for "assistive technology" and a host of e-mail lists, including one for blind parents: "... for parents who *themselves* are blind, and who wish to discuss topics related to parenthood. The sharing of resources and solutions to problems is the focus of discussion on *Blind-Parents*" (BLIST, 2000).

Summary

Very little attention has been paid to printed information for parents with disabilities, even though minor adaptations could make existing materials accessible to these special populations. Assistive technology includes a number of telecommunication and electronic devices. Few special devices have been developed for those with physical limitations, but this may change as a result of legislation designed to promote independent living for adults with disabilities.

FUTURE RESEARCH DIRECTIONS

Research mirrors "the political, social, and scientific events of the times" (Kopp and Krakow, 1983, p. 1100). Traditional reasons for conducting research about disability and family life remain cogent: providing data for policy makers, service providers, clinicians, and parents about child development, family processes, the assumption of gender roles, childrearing practices, parental competence, role modeling, family adjustment and coping strategies in the face of biological risk or violation (Thurman, Whaley, and Weinraub, 1985). Like other research on special populations, parenting research contrasting the special challenges faced and solutions found by parents with disabilities can contribute to general knowledge and to theories of human development.

Lessons From the Past

Wars provide a powerful incentive for disability research: World War I led to the mass production of collapsible, lightweight wheelchairs (Olkin, 1999); veterans injured in World War II inspired extensive research on disability and rehabilitation (Hollis, 1989); the Vietnam war focused attention on spinal cord injuries (Knight, 1989). Polio and rubella epidemics and the thalidomide tragedy inspired other important research with broad implications for persons with disabilities. The contemporary women's movement sparked a call from women with disabilities for broad-based, cross-disciplinary, longitudinal research. Useful data would include prevalence, age, race, marital status, education, employment, number of children, particular disability and age at onset; family characteristics, including sex experiences, courting, marriage, birth control, and pregnancy, childbearing; marital roles and decision making; contributions of teachers, counselors, social workers and therapists; family stresses, including deteriorating physical conditions, illness, unemployment, childcare and availability of aides; the role of friends, church, support networks, and government assistance (Baskin and Riggs, 1988).

In their review of research on the adjustment of children reared by parents with disabilities, Buck and Hohmann (1983) detailed recurring methodological problems: extensive use of self-report questionnaires; failure to control for sex of children; absence of control or standardization in research designs; no concern for the need to explore variables associated with parental disability, or to "use multiple and appropriate comparison groups to assess alternative hypotheses, and employ diverse, objective behavioral measures" (p. 230). A more recent review of this area notes the continuing paucity of research and the need for studies that examine the interaction of many variables: "disability from a developmental perspective, support and the socioecological context, family life cycle and functioning, financial resources, communication patterns. ... [L]ongitudinal studies ... are also needed to aid in identifying points for intervention over the life course" (Kelley et al., 1997, p. 118).

Because of the relative absence of research, ethnographic studies would be particularly useful. The report by Deshen and Deshen (1989) illustrates their potential value. Based on 800 pages of field notes collected from intensive observations of parents who are blind, they provide an in-depth account of family problems and solutions.

Discussions of qualifications necessary for conducting research on disability issues began to appear in disability publications in the mid-1990s (Oliver, 1996). Those with disabilities often took the position that able-bodied people were incapable of truly understanding the conditions and situations of those with disabilities and should therefore remove themselves from the disability research arena. One author asked able-bodied researchers, "What are you doing here?" (Branfield, 1998). Another entitled his book *Nothing About Us Without Us* (Charlton, 1998). Others countered with proposals for including the disabled perspective by designing "participatory" or "emancipatory" research (Darling, 2000; Foster, 1996; Mertens, 1998). Another sensitive observer noted that "the focus of much social-psychological research on disability has been to determine the impact of contact with disability on people without impairments. Such a question, *particularly when framed by a researcher outside the disability experience*, makes the person with the disability the object, not the subject, of study and distances the research from the disabled person's life experience (Fine and Asch, 1995, p. 553, emphasis added). "It is phenomenal how undeterred we are from pursuing 'outsider' research by the able-bodied about disability. For no other out-group is the pervasive exclusion of voices from within so stifled and stilled" (Olkin, 1999, pp. 319–320).

Research Design

Research with these groups is particularly challenging, and methodological compromises may sometimes be necessary. Lewis and Collis (1997) emphasized the importance of case studies, because group designs force the comparison of participants whose within-group characteristics may be more extreme than those between groups. Coates and colleagues (1985) emphasized the interplay of theory and method and the importance of age at onset of parental disability. They proposed two paradigms for contrasting research designs. In Paradigm A, child variables are hypothesized outcomes in families where parents are disabled before the birth of children; Paradigm B hypothesizes that family processes as well as child outcomes may be affected when parental disability is adventitious.

Participant selection.   A recurring theme of this review is the low incidence of early onset sensory and physical disability, making definition and recruitment of appropriate research participants more difficult. If the definition is too broad participants will be so heterogeneous—in age at onset, severity of condition, etiology, stage of family cycle, birth order, age, disability status of spouse—that the conclusions are meaningless. If the definition is too narrow, inability to generalize becomes a danger, and participant recruitment becomes even more difficult, time-consuming, and expensive. Once the sample is defined, located, and recruited, it becomes a "precious commodity," another reason for considering a longitudinal design (Coates et al., 1985).

Careful thought must be given to the definition and recruitment of a control group and whether more than one control group is needed for particular research questions. For example, if the researcher is testing the effect of parental deafness on parent–child communication, it may be important to recruit, in addition to comparable hearing families, parents who are deaf with children who are either deaf or hearing. Depending on the research question, it may be important to recruit families where the disability status of mothers and fathers, or gender and birth order of children, differ.

Hoemann (1978, p. 47) noted that hearing participants have frequently been used as controls in research on deafness "even though they have not been appropriately matched on such important variables as educational background, socioeconomic status, or linguistic competence in English." A review of research on blindness points to similar difficulties. The author questioned whether it is ever appropriate to use a blindfolded, sighted sample as a control group for comparison with blind subjects (Warren, 1978).

Selection of instruments. Frequently used instruments for measuring psychological status, family interaction, or parental beliefs may not have been translated for or standardized appropriately with people who are disabled. Moreover, the language of some test items may be inappropriate. For example, "Do you hear voices?" has a very different meaning for participants with differing hearing status. Equivalent sign language forms are difficult to develop; a questionnaire may be translated into braille or read to participants who are blind, but care must be taken to use equivalent procedures with control groups.

Data collection and analysis. Freeman and his colleagues (1991) made a persuasive argument for using interviews rather than questionnaires when studying people who are blind. Their Canadian interview follow-up of adolescents had an impressive participation rate of 85%, compared to a 44% rate for a questionnaire follow-up of English adolescents with cerebral palsy (Clark and Hirst, 1989). Participants clearly responded in a positive manner to the Canadian interviews, conducted by two experienced clinicians.

Selecting interviewers for studies with deaf participants poses several unique problems. Interpreters are expensive and may reduce rapport with the researcher. A skilled signer, trained in interviewing, is a valuable member of a research team. Interviews should be conducted in the form of sign language (ASL, Signed English, or Contact Sign) preferred by participants. Note-taking or audio recording interviews with deaf respondents presents special problems and may not be feasible. Video recording is an option, but transcriptions are difficult and expensive.

Bias is a persistent problem particularly with observational methods. It is practically impossible for coders to remain naive to the identity of "experimental groups" when, for example, they are coding live or videotaped interactions. Coders should be unaware of the research hypotheses (Coates et al., 1985). However, the general nature of hypotheses may be clear to all but naive or ignorant coders, who may also be less able to make reliable and valid judgments. It is necessary to weigh the disadvantages and benefits of experience and naiveté.

Ethical concerns. Distinctive ethical concerns arise in research with special populations (Baumrind and Thompson, Vol. 5 of in this *Handbook*). In low-incidence groups, the same participants may be overtaxed, their privacy endangered, and they may lose the innocence often assumed by researchers. Informed consent is a special concern, especially in research where participants "have impairments that would limit understanding and/or communication" (American Psychological Association, 1982, p. 3). Psychologists should "identify situations in which particular . . . assessment techniques or norms may not be applicable or may require adjustment in administration or interpretation because of factors such as individuals' gender, age, race, ethnicity, national origin, religion, sexual orientation, disability, language, or socioeconomic status" (American Psychological Association, 1992, Standard 2.04c). Pollard (1992a) proposed that research in the Deaf community use ethical guidelines developed for cross-cultural research, being sure to include community members in the research team and advisory board.

Confidentiality assumes additional importance in small communities or subcultures. Descriptors for individual cases should be modified or eliminated to assure anonymity. In her research with mothers of thalidomide children, Roskies (1972, p. ix) found it "both more important and harder than usual to keep the pledge of confidentiality." In populations where participants are difficult to find or to enlist, the inadvertent disclosure of identities can cost the trust of and future access to an entire community.

Videotaped data collection increases the need to guard confidentiality carefully, because there is no simple way to mask people's identity. Most institutional review boards for the protection of human subjects require special consent forms for videotaping and an additional clause of consent to the future use of videotapes for training or dissemination purposes. Even with this consent, an ethical issue arises in showing tapes as "negative examples." (There may also be a legal issue of guarding participants' reputations; Department of Health and Human Services, 1991.) Revised federal regulations for the protection of human subjects contain new provisions related to obtaining a child's assent. "In determining whether children are capable of assenting, the IRB shall take into account the ages, maturity, and psychological state of the children involved" (Department of Health and Human Services, 1991, p. 16). As in research with children (Thompson, 1990), it may be especially important to develop clear explanations of research procedures and sensitive debriefings for populations of adults with limited experience or sophistication.

Summary

Much of the existing research on adults with disabilities resulted from particular concerns related to historical events. Current social issues, like the contemporary women's movement, that helps to fuel advocacy for mothers with disabilities will undoubtedly influence future research in this area. Difficulties of recruiting research participants in groups with low prevalence rates, the lack of measurement instruments appropriate for and standardized with these special groups, and the high cost of data collection and analysis have all contributed to the absence of a large body of research literature. In addition, special care must be taken to protect the rights of these participants who may be at greater risk for loss of privacy. Each of these areas must be addressed by future researchers if meaningful data are to be collected about the effects of deafness, blindness, and physical disability on parenting effectiveness.

CONCLUSIONS

Although conditions for people with disabilities have improved greatly with marked legislative and judicial advances in the past decade, stigmatizing attitudes remain, especially regarding the parenting skills of those with sensory or physical disabilities. These parents share a number of childhood and adolescent experiences that could contribute both strengths and problems in family relationships and adult parenting. Some negative socialization experiences include the chronic sorrow of their own parents, family protectiveness that promotes dependency, lack of information about and experience with sexual intimacy, and isolation from peers. Positive experiences include a host of opportunities to practice coping skills and meet the exigencies of daily life with humor and ingenuity. Even the most disadvantaged members of disability groups may "defy the negative predictions" (Freeman et al., 1991, p. 365) of their adult adjustment, illustrating again the resilience of individuals and their ability to overcome adverse life events.

Compared to those who are congenitally blind or physically disabled, people who are deaf face fewer disability-related obstacles to family life in adulthood. They marry and form families as often as adults in the general population. Blindness and physical disability lead to fewer opportunities for marriage and parenthood, especially for women. Parenting presents functional challenges to adults with limited sight, hearing, and mobility. However, technical devices or coping strategies enable them to meet these challenges. Obstacles to optimal family processes include: (1) the temptation to overly burden children with requests to perform tasks for the parents, (2) role reversal, with children taking the responsible adult's role, (3) shame or embarrassment about a parent who is different, and (4) distorted power relationships between parents with and without disabilities, leading to accelerated marital strife. Many families headed by parents with disabilities demonstrate their abilities to surmount potential obstacles, and their children express appreciation for the affection and strength exhibited by those parents. Although the research is sparse, there is little evidence of negative effects of growing up with parents who are blind or deaf or physically limited. Because these populations have been neglected, there are many opportunities for contributions from future researchers.

ACKNOWLEDGMENTS

For library assistance I thank staff members at the National Library of Medicine and Gallaudet University, especially Susan Davis, and Donna Harrison, Mary Jane McGoey, Catherine Metz, Sybil Smith-Gray; also Kathleen Arnos, Marc H. Bornstein, Marita M. Danek, Corinne Kirchner, Lynne Sanford Koester, Harold Orlans, Randall Parker, H.N. Reynolds, Patricia E. Spencer, and Edna Syzmanski for substantive and editorial suggestions.

REFERENCES

Adamson, L., Als, H., Tronick, E., and Brazelton, T. B. (1977). The development of social reciprocity between a sighted infant and her blind parents. *Journal of the American Academy of Child Psychiatry, 16*, 194–207.

Adoption of Richardson, 251C.A, 2d 222 (1967).

Alexander, K. L. (1976). Disability and stratification processes. In G. L. Albrecht (Ed.), *The sociology of physical disability and rehabilitation* (pp. 169–200). Pittsburgh: University of Pittsburgh Press.

Alexander, M. A., and Bauer, R. E. (1988). Cerebral palsy. In V. B. Van Hasselt, P. S. Strain, and M. Hersen (Eds.), *Handbook of developmental and physical disabilities* (pp. 227–246). New York: Pergamon.

Altman, B. M., Cooper, P. F., and Cunningham, P. J. (1999). The case of disability in the family: Impact on health care utilization and expenditures for nondisabled members. *The Milbank Quarterly, 77*, 39–75.

Altshuler, K. Z. (1964). Personality traits and depressive symptoms in the deaf. In J. Wortis (Ed.), *Recent advances in biological psychiatry* (Vol. 6, pp. 63–73). New York: Plenum.

American Psychological Association. (1982). *Ethical principles in the conduct of research with human participants.* Washington, DC: Author.

American Psychological Association. (1992). *Ethical principles of psychologists and code of conduct* [Online]. Available: http://apa.org/ethics

Americans with Disabilities Act of 1990, 42 U.S.C.A. § 12101–12213 (1990).

Arnos, K. S. (1999). Genetic counseling for hearing loss. In S. Epstein (Ed.), *Medical aspects of hearing loss for the consumer and the professional* [Monograph]. *The Volta Review, 99*, 85–96.

Arsnow, G. F., Dichiera, J., Mould, L., Sauerbrauer, D., and Peaco, F. (1985). Blind parents rearing sighted children. *Journal of Visual Impairment and Blindness, 79*, 193–198.

Asch, A., and Fine, M. (1988). Introduction: Beyond pedestals. In M. Fine and A. Asch (Eds.), *Women with disabilities: Essays in psychology, culture, and politics* (pp. 1–37). Philadelphia: Temple University Press.

Asch, A., and Sacks, L. H. (1983). Lives within, lives without: Autobiographies of blind women and men. *Journal of Visual Impairment and Blindness, 77*, 242–247.

Asrael, W. (1982). An approach to motherhood for disabled women. *Rehabilitation Literature, 43*, 214–218.

Barker, L. T., and Maralani, V. (1997). *Challenges and strategies of disabled parents: Findings from a national survey of parents with disabilities.* Berkeley, CA: Through the Looking Glass.

Barker, R. G., in collaboration with Wright, A., Meyerson, L., and Gonick, R. (1953). *Adjustment to physical handicap and illness: A survey of the social psychology of physique and disability* (Bulletin 55, Rev.). New York: Social Science Research Council.

Barsch, R. H. (1968). *The parent of the handicapped child: Study of child rearing practices.* Springfield, IL: Thomas.

Baskin, B. H., and Riggs, E. P. (1988). Mothers who are disabled. In B. Birns and D. F. Hay (Eds.), *The different faces of motherhood* (pp. 239–257). New York: Plenum.

Batshaw, M. L., and Perret, Y. M. (1992). *Children with handicaps, A medical primer* (3rd ed.). Baltimore: Brookes.

Bednarski v. Bednarski, Docket No. 74532 (Mich. Ct. of App. 1985).

Bender, R. E. (1970). *The conquest of deafness: A history of the long struggle to make possible normal living to those handicapped by lack of normal hearing* (Rev. ed.). Cleveland, OH: Press of Western Reserve University.

Berkson, G. (1993). *Children with handicaps: A review of behavioral research.* Hillsdale, NJ: Lawrence Erlbaum Associates.

Berrol, S. (1989). Psychosocial implications and treatment of persons with multiple sclerosis. In B. W. Heller, L. M. Flohr, and L. S. Zegans (Eds.), *Psychosocial interventions with physically disabled persons* (pp. 137–146). New Brunswick, NJ: Rutgers University Press.

Bina, M. J. (1993). Do myths associated with schools for students who are blind negatively affect placement decisions? *Journal of Visual Impairment and Blindness, 87*, 213–215.

BLIST. (2000). *BLIST: The comprehensive index of blindness-related emailing lists* [Online]. Available: http://www.hicom.net/~oedipus/blist.html

Bobek, B. (1984). Use the common senses: Childbirth education for blind and visually impaired persons. *Journal of Visual Impairment and Blindness, 78*, 350–351.

Bond, D. E. (2000). Mental health in children who are deaf and have multiple disabilities. In P. Hindley and N. Kitson (Eds.), *Mental health and deafness* (pp. 127–148). London: Whurr.

Bonvillian, J. D., Orlansky, M. D., and Folven, R. J. (1994). Early sign language acquisition: Implications for theories of language acquisition. In V. Volterra and C. J. Erting (Eds.), *From gesture to language in hearing and deaf children* (pp. 219–232). Washington, DC: Gallaudet University Press.

Bonwich, E. (1985). Sex role attitudes and role reorganization in spinal cord injured women. In M. J. Deegan and N. Brooks (Eds.), *Women and disability: The double handicap* (pp. 56–67). New Brunswick, NJ: Transaction.

Boothroyd, A. (1998). The perception of speech by children with hearing loss. In A. Weisel (Ed.), *Issues unresolved: New perspectives on language and deaf education* (pp. 103–116). Washington, DC: Gallaudet University Press.

Bowe, F. (1980). *Rehabilitating America: Toward independence for disabled and elderly people.* New York: Harper & Row.

Branfield, F. (1998). What are you doing here? "Non-disabled" people and the disability movement: A response to Robert F. Drake. *Disability and Society, 13*, 143–144.

Brasel, K. E., and Quigley, S. P. (1977). Influence of certain language and communication environments in early childhood on the development of language in deaf individuals. *Journal of Speech and Hearing Research, 20*, 81–94.

Bristol, M. M., Gallagher, J. J., and Schopler, E. (1988). Mothers and fathers of young developmentally disabled and nondisabled boys: Adaptation and spousal support. *Developmental Psychology, 24*, 441–451.

Bronfenbrenner, U. (1979). *The ecology of human development.* Cambridge, MA: Harvard University Press.

Brookman, J. (2000, July 21). Teamwork brings gift of sight. *The Times Higher Education Supplement* (London), p. 30.

Bryant, D. M., and Ramey, C. T. (1987). An analysis of the effectiveness of early intervention programs for environmentally at-risk children. In M. J. Guralnick and F. C. Bennett (Eds.), *The effectiveness of early intervention for at-risk and handicapped children* (pp. 33–78). Orlando, FL: Academic Press.

Buchino, M. A. (1993). Hearing children of deaf parents: Perspectives on the parent–child relationship. *American Annals of the Deaf, 138*, 40–45.

Buck, F. M. (1980). *The influence of parental disability on children: An exploratory investigation of the adult children of spinal cord injured fathers.* Unpublished doctoral dissertation, University of Arizona, Tucson.

Buck, F. M., and Hohmann, G. W. (1981). Personality, behavior, values, and family relations of children of fathers with spinal cord injury. *Archives of Physical and Medical Rehabilitation, 62*, 432–437.

Buck, F. M., and Hohmann, G. W. (1983). Parental disability and children's adjustment. In E. L. Pan, T. E. Backer, and C. L. Vash (Eds.), *Annual review of rehabilitation* (Vol. 3, pp. 203–241). New York: Springer.

Bull, T. H. (Ed.). (1988). *Reflections: CODAs and cultures.* Proceedings of the Second National CODA Conference, Santa Barbara, CA: C.O.D.A.

Bull, T. (1998). *On the edge of deaf culture: Hearing children/deaf parents.* Alexandria, VA: Deaf Family Research Press.

Campbell, F. A., Helms, R., Sparling, J. J., and Ramey, C. T. (1998). Early-childhood programs and success in school: The Abecedarian study. In W. S. Barnett and S. S. Boocock (Eds.), *Early care and education for children in poverty: Promises, programs, and long-term results* (pp. 145–166). Albany: State University of New York Press.

Charlton, J. I. (1998). *Nothing about us without us: Disability, oppression and empowerment.* Berkeley CA: University of California Press.

Chess, S., Korn, S. J., and Fernandez, P. B. (1971). *Psychiatric disorders of children with congenital rubella.* New York: Brunner/Mazel.

Clark, A., and Hirst, M. (1989). Disability in adulthood: Ten-year follow-up of young people with disabilities. *Disability, Handicap and Society, 4*, 271–283.

Coates, D. L., Vietze, P. M., and Gray D. B. (1985). Methodological issues in studying children of disabled parents. In S. K. Thurman (Ed.), *Children of handicapped parents: Research and clinical perspectives* (pp. 155–180). Orlando, FL: Academic Press.

Cochlear Corporation. (1999). *Annual report* [Online]. Available: http://cochlear.com

Cohen, L. J. (1998). *Mothers' perceptions of the influence of their physical disabilities on the developmental tasks of children.* Unpublished doctoral dissertation, California School of Professional Psychology, Berkeley/Alameda (UMI Proquest Digital Dissertations Abstracts).

Cohn, J. F., Matias, R., Tronick, E. Z., Connell, D., and Lyons-Ruth, K. (1986). Face-to-face interactions of depressed mothers and their infants. In E. Z. Tronick and T. Field (Eds.), *Maternal depression and infant disturbance* (pp. 31–46). San Francisco: Jossey-Bass.

Coker, G. (1979). A comparison of self-concepts and academic achievement of visually handicapped children enrolled in a regular school and in a residential school. *Education of the Visually Handicapped, 11*, 68–74.

Cole, S. S., and Cole, T. M. (1993). *Sexuality, disability, and reproductive issues through the lifespan. Sexuality and Disability, 11*, 189–205.

Conley-Jung, C. (1996). *The early parenting experiences of mothers with visual impairments and blindness.* Unpublished doctoral dissertation, California School of Professional Psychology, Berkeley/Alameda (UMI ProQuest Digital Dissertation Abstracts).

Connors, D. (1985). Disability, sexism and the social order. In S. E. Browne, D. Connors, and N. Stern (Eds.), *With the power of each breath: A disabled women's anthology* (pp. 92–107). Pittsburgh: Cleis.

Conti-Ramsden, G., and Perez-Pereira, M. (1999). Conversational interactions between mothers and their infants who are congenitally blind, have low vision, or are sighted. *Journal of Visual Impairment and Blindness, 92,* 691–703.

Cooley, C. H. (1902). *Human nature and the social order.* New York: Scribners.

Craft, A., and Craft, M. (1979). *Handicapped married couples.* London: Routledge and Kegan Paul.

Cranston, R. (1982). *Parenting without vision in 1000 easy lessons.* Oakland, CA: Child Care Information and Referral Service.

Crewe, N. M. (1993). Spousal relationships and disability. In F. P. Haseltine, S. S. Cole, and D. B. Gray (Eds.), *Reproductive issues for persons with physical disabilities* (pp. 141–152). Baltimore: Brookes.

Crudden, A., and Hanye, R. (1999). Employment differences among persons with congenital and adventitious vision loss. *Journal of Vocational Rehabilitation, 12,* 19–23.

Dalton, M. E., and Dalton, K. (1978). Menarcheal age in the disabled. *British Medical Journal, 2,* 475.

Danek, M. M. (1992). The status of women with disabilities revisited. *Journal of Applied Rehabilitation Counseling, 23,* 7–13.

Darling, R. B. (2000). Only for individuals with disabilities? *Footnotes* (Newsletter of the American Sociological Association), *28,* 6.

Davis, F. (1963). *Passage through crisis: Polio victims and their families.* Indianapolis, IN: Bobbs-Merrill.

Davis, L. J. (1997). Constructing normalcy: The bell curve, the novel, and the invention of the disabled body in the nineteenth century. In L. J. Davis (Ed.), *The disability studies reader* (pp. 9–28). New York: Routledge.

Davis, L. J. (2000). *My sense of silence: Memoirs of a childhood with deafness.* Urbana: University of Illinois Press.

Deegan, M. J., and Brooks, N. (Eds.). (1985). *Women and disability: The double handicap.* New Brunswick, NJ: Transaction.

DeJong, G., and Batavia, A. I. (1990). The Americans with Disabilities Act and the current state of U.S. disability policy. *Journal of Disability Policy Studies, 1,* 65–75.

Department of Health and Human Services. (1991). *Protection of Human Subjects* (Title 45, Code of Federal Regulations, Part 46. Rev. June 18, 1991). Washington, DC: U.S. Government Printing Office.

Deshen, S., and Deshen, H. (1989). Managing at home: Relationships between blind parents and sighted children. *Human Organization, 48,* 262–267.

Equal Education for All Handicapped Children Act, (1976). 20 U.S.C. § 1401–1420, 45 C.F.R. § 1219.1 (1977).

Erikson, E. H. (1959). *Identity and the life cycle.* New York: International Universities Press.

Erikson, E. H. (1963). *Childhood and society.* New York: Norton.

Erin, J. N. (1990). Language samples from visually impaired four- and five-year olds. *Journal of Childhood Communication Disorders, 13,* 181–191.

Erin, J. N. (1993). The road less traveled: New directions for schools for students with visual impairments. *Journal of Visual Impairment and Blindness, 87,* 219–223.

Erting, C. J., Prezioso, C., and Hynes, M. O. (1994). The interactional context of deaf mother–infant communication. In V. Volterra and C. J. Erting (Eds.), *From gesture to language in hearing and deaf children* (pp. 97–106). Washington, DC: Gallaudet University Press.

Erting, C. J., Thumann-Prezioso, C., and Benedict, B. S. (2000). Bilingualism in a deaf family: Fingerspelling in early childhood. In P. E. Spencer, C. J. Erting, and M. Marschark (Eds.), *The deaf child in the family and at school: Essays in honor of Kathryn P. Meadow-Orlans* (pp. 41–54). Mahwah, NJ: Lawrence Erlbaum Associates.

Evans, A. D. (1987). Institutionally developed identities: an ethnographic account of reality construction in a residential school for the deaf. *Sociological Studies of Childhood, 2,* 161–184.

Farran, D. C. (1990). Effects of intervention with disadvantaged and disabled children: A decade review. In S. J. Meisels and J. P. Shonkoff (Eds.), *Handbook of early childhood intervention* (pp. 501–539). New York: Cambridge University Press.

Featherstone, H. (1980). *A difference in the family: Life with a disabled child.* New York: Basic Books.

Filer, R. D., and Filer, P. A. (2000). Practical considerations for counselors working with hearing children of deaf parents. *Journal of Counseling and Development, 78,* 38–43.

Fine, M., and Asch, A. (1985). Disabled women: Sexism without the pedestal. In M. J. Deegan and N. Brooks (Eds.), *Women and disability: The double handicap* (pp. 6–22). New Brunswick, NJ: Transaction.

Fine, M., and Asch, A. (1995). Disability beyond stigma: Social interaction, discrimination, and activism. In N. R. Goldberger and J. B. Veroff (Eds.), *The culture and psychology reader* (pp. 536–558). New York: New York University Press.

Fine, M. J. (1980). The parent education movement: An introduction. In M. J. Fine (Ed.), *Handbook on parent education* (pp. 3–26). New York: Academic Press.

Fitz-Gerald, D., and Fitz-Gerald, M. (1978). Sexual implications of deafness. *Sexuality and Disability, 1,* 57–69.

Foster, S. (1996). Doing research in deafness: Some considerations and strategies. In P. C. Higgins and J. E. Nash (Eds.), *Understanding deafness socially, Continuities in research and theory* (2nd ed., pp. 3–20). Springfield, IL: Thomas.

Foulke, E. (1972). The personality of the blind: A non-valid concept. *New Outlook for the Blind, 66*, 33–37, 42.

Fox, S. A. (2000). The uses and abuses of computer-mediated communication for people with disabilities. In D. O. Braithwaite and T. L. Thompson (Eds.), *Handbook of communication and people with disabilities* (pp. 319–336). Mahwah, NJ: Lawrence Erlbaum Associates.

Fraiberg, S. (1977). *Insights from the blind.* Ann Arbor: University of Michigan Press.

Freeman, R. D., Goetz, E., Richards, D. P., and Groenveld, M. (1991). Defiers of negative prediction: A 14-year follow-up study of legally blind children. *Journal of Visual Impairment and Blindness, 85*, 365–370.

Fries, E. B. (1980). *But you can feel it.* Portland, OR: Binford and Mort.

Furth, H. G. (1966). *Thinking without language: Psychological implications of deafness.* New York: Free Press.

Furth, H. G. (1971). Linguistic deficiency and thinking. Research with deaf subjects, 1964–1969. *Psychological Bulletin, 76*, 58–72.

Galenson, E., Miller, R., Kaplan, E., and Rothstein, A. (1979). Assessment of development in the deaf child. *Journal of the American Academy of Child Psychiatry, 18*, 128–142.

Gallagher, J. J., Beckman, P., and Cross, A. H. (1983). Families of handicapped children: Sources of stress and its amelioration. *Exceptional Children, 50*, 10–19.

Geer, S. (1985). Family law: Issues raised by deafness. *Gallaudet Today, 15*, 11.

Gilhool, T. K., and Gran, J. A. (1985). Legal rights of disabled parents. In S. K. Thurman (Ed.), *Children of handicapped parents: Research and clinical perspectives* (pp. 11–34). Orlando, FL: Academic Press.

Gill-Williamson, L. M. (1991). The impact of a visually impaired parent on a family's decision making. *Journal of Visual Impairment and Blindness, 85*, 246–248.

Gliedman, J., and Roth, W. (1980). *The unexpected minority: Handicapped children in America.* New York: Harcourt Brace Jovanovich.

Goffman, E. (1963). *Stigma: Notes on the management of spoiled identity.* Englewood Cliffs, NJ: Prentice-Hall.

Greenberg, M. T. (2000). Educational interventions: Prevention and promotion of competence. In P. Hindley and N. Kitson (Eds.), *Mental health and deafness* (pp. 311–336). London: Whurr.

Greenberg, M., and Marvin, R. (1979). Attachment patterns in profoundly deaf preschool children. *Merrill-Palmer Quarterly, 25*, 265–279.

Greenfeld, J. (1979). *A child called Noah.* New York: Pocket.

Greer, B. C. (1985). Children of physically disabled parents: Some thoughts, facts, and hypotheses. In S. K. Thurman (Ed.), *Children of handicapped parents, research and clinical perspectives* (pp. 131–143). Orlando, FL: Academic Press.

Gregory, S. (1995). *Deaf children and their families.* Cambridge, England: Cambridge University Press.

Gregory, S., Bishop, J., and Sheldon, L. (1995). *Deaf young people and their families.* Cambridge, England: Cambridge University Press.

Hallahan, D. P., and Kauffman, J. M. (1988). *Exceptional children, Introduction to special education* (4th ed.). Englewood Cliffs, NJ: Prentice-Hall.

Halpern, R. (1990). Community-based early intervention. In S. J. Meisels and J. P. Shonkoff (Eds.), *Handbook of early childhood intervention* (pp. 469–498). New York: Cambridge University Press.

Hanna, W. J., and Rogovsky, B. (1991). Women with disabilities: Two handicaps plus. *Disability, Handicap and Society, 6*, 49–63.

Harbin, G. L., and McNulty, B. A. (1990). Policy implementation: Perspectives on service coordination and interagency cooperation. In S. J. Meisels and J. P. Shonkoff (Eds.), *Handbook of early childhood intervention* (pp. 700–722). New York: Cambridge University Press.

Harkins, J. E. (1991). *Visual devices for deaf and hard of hearing people: State-of-the-art* (GRI Monograph Series A, No. 3). Washington, DC: Gallaudet University.

Harris, S. R. (1987). Early intervention for children with motor handicaps. In M. J. Guralnick and F. C. Bennett (Eds.), *The effectiveness of early intervention for at-risk and handicapped children* (pp. 175–212). Orlando, FL: Academic Press.

Head, D. N., Maddock, J., Healey, W. C., and Griffing, B. L. (1993). A comparative study of residential schools for children with visual impairments. *Journal of Visual Impairment and Blindness, 87*, 216–218.

Hewett, S. (1970). *The family and the handicapped child: A study of cerebral palsied children in their homes.* Chicago: Aldine.

Hill, R., and Aldous, J. (1969). Socialization for marriage and parenthood. In D. A. Goslin (Ed.), *Handbook of socialization theory and research* (pp. 885–950). Chicago: Rand McNally.

Hindley, P. (2000). Child and adolescent psychiatry. In P. Hindley and N. Kitson (Eds.), *Mental health and deafness* (pp. 42–74). London: Whurr.

Hobbs, N. (Ed.). (1975). *Issues in the classification of children* (Vol. 1). San Francisco: Jossey-Bass.

Hocken, S. (1978). *Emma and I.* New York: Dutton.

Hoemann, H. W. (1978). Perception by the deaf. In E. C. Carterette and M. P. Friedman (Eds.), *Handbook of perception, Perceptual ecology* (Vol. 10, pp. 43–64). New York: Academic Press.

Hoffmeister, R. J. (1985). Families with deaf parents: A functional perspective. In S. K. Thurman (Ed.), *Children of handicapped parents, Research and clinical perspectives* (pp. 111–130). Orlando, FL: Academic Press.

Holden-Pitt, L., and Diaz, J. A. (1998). Thirty years of the annual survey of deaf and hard-of-hearing children and youth: A glance over the decades. *American Annals of the Deaf, 142*, 72–76.

Hollis, M. (1989). *Understanding blindness: An integrative approach.* Hillsdale, NJ: Lawrence Erlbaum Associates.

Hughes, B., and Paterson, K. (1997). The social model of disability and the disappearing body: Towards a sociology of impairment. *Disability and Society, 12*, 323–340.

Ireys, H. T., and Burr, C. K. (1984). Apart and a part: Family issues for young adults with chronic illness and disability. In M. G. Eisenberg, L. C. Sutkin, and M. A. Jansen (Eds.), *Chronic illness and disability through the life span* (pp. 184–206). New York: Springer.

Israel, J., Cunningham, M., Thumann, H., and Arnos, K. S. (1992). Genetic counseling for deaf adults: Communication/language and cultural considerations. *Journal of Genetic Counseling, 1*, 135–153.

Jacobson, D. S. (1993). Rethinking expectations. In F. P. Haseltine, S. S. Cole, and D. B. Gray (Eds.), *Reproductive issues for persons with physical disabilities* (pp. 49–52). Baltimore: Brookes.

Jan, J. E., Freeman, R. D., and Scott, E. P. (1977). *Visual impairment in children and adolescents.* New York: Grune and Stratton.

Kallianes, V., and Rubenfeld, P. (1997). Disabled women and reproductive rights. *Disability and Society, 12*, 203–221.

Kekelis, L. S., and Andersen, E. S. (1984). Family communication styles and language development. *Journal of Visual Impairment and Blindness, 78*, 54–65.

Kelley, S. D. M., Sikka, A., and Venkatesan, S. (1997). A review of research on parental disability: Implications for research and counseling practice. *Rehabilitation Counseling Bulletin, 41*, 105–121.

Kirchner, C. (1990). Trends in the prevalence rates and numbers of blind and visually impaired schoolchildren. *Journal of Visual Impairment and Blindness, 84*, 478–479.

Kirchner, C., and Diament, S. (1999). Estimates of the number of visually impaired students, their teachers, and orientation and mobility specialists: Part 1. *Journal of Visual Impairment and Blindness, 93*, 600–606.

Kirchner, C., and Peterson, R. (1988). Data on visual disability from NCHS, 1977. In C. Kirchner (Ed.), *Data on blindness and visual impairment in the U.S.* (2nd ed., pp. 19–24). New York: American Foundation for the Blind.

Kirshbaum, M. (1994). Family context and disability culture re-framing: Through the looking glass. *Family Psychologist, 10*, 8–12.

Knight, S. E. (1989). Sexual concerns of the physically disabled. In B. W. Heller, L. M. Flohr, and L. S. Zegans (Eds.), *Psychosocial interventions with physically disabled persons* (pp. 183–199). New Brunswick, NJ: Rutgers University Press.

Koester, L. S. (1992). Intuitive parenting as a model for understanding parent–infant interactions when one partner is deaf. *American Annals of the Deaf, 137*, 362–369.

Koester, L. S. (1995). Face-to-face interactions between hearing mothers and their deaf infants. *Infant Behavior and Development, 18*, 145–153.

Koester, L. S., and Meadow-Orlans, K. P. (1990). Parenting a deaf child: Stress, strength, and support. In D. F. Moores and K. P. Meadow-Orlans (Eds.), *Educational and developmental aspects of deafness* (pp. 299–320). Washington, DC: Gallaudet University Press.

Koester, L. S., Papoušek, H., and Papoušek, M. (1987). Psychobiological models of infant development: Influences on the concept of intuitive parenting. In H. Rauh and H. C. Steinhausen (Eds.), *Psychobiology and early development, Advances in psychology series* (Vol. 45, pp. 275–287). North Holland, the Netherlands: Elsevier.

Kogan, K. L., and Tyler, N. (1973). Mother–child interaction in young physically handicapped children. *American Journal of Mental Deficiency, 77*, 492–497.

Kopp, C. B., and Krakow, J. B. (1983). The developmentalist and the study of biological risk: A view of the past with an eye toward the future. *Child Development, 54*, 1086–1108.

Landau, B. (1997). Language and experience in blind children: Retrospective and prospective. In V. Lewis and B. M. Collis (Eds.), *Blindness and psychological development in blind children* (pp. 9–28). Leicester, England: British Psychological Society.

Lane, H. (1984). *When the mind hears: A history of the deaf.* New York: Random House.

Lane, H. (1992). *The mask of benevolence.* New York: Knopf.

Lederberg, A. R., and Mobley, C. E. (1990). The effect of hearing impairment on the quality of attachment and mother–toddler interaction. *Child Development, 61*, 1596–1604.

Leonard, R., D'Allura, T., and Horowitz, A. (1999). Factors associated with employment among persons who have a vision impairment: A follow-up of vocational placement referrals. *Journal of Vocational Rehabilitation, 12*, 33–43.

Lessard, N., Pare, M., Lepore, F., and Lassonde, M. (1998). Early-blind human subjects localize sound sources better than sighted subjects. *Nature, 395*, 278–280.

Leung, E. H. L., and Hollins, M. (1989). The blind child. In M. Hollins (Ed.), *Understanding blindness: An integrative approach*. Hillsdale, NJ: Lawrence Erlbaum Associates.

Levine, E. (1956). *Youth in a soundless world: A search for personality*, New York: New York University Press.

Levine, E. (1969). Historical review of special education and mental health services. In J. D. Rainer, K. Z. Altshuler, and F. Kallmann (Eds.), *Family and mental health problems in a deaf population* (2nd ed., pp. xvii–xxvi). Springfield, IL: Thomas.

Levitt, H. (1998). Automatic speech recognition and its applications. In A. Weisel (Ed.), *Issues unresolved: New perspectives on language and deaf education* (pp. 133–140). Washington, DC: Gallaudet University Press.

Lewis, V., and Collis, G. M. (1997). Methodological and theoretical issues associated with the study of children with visual impairment. In V. Lewis and B. M. Collis (Eds.), *Blindness and psychological development in blind children* (pp. 1–8). Leicester, England: British Psychological Society.

Lloyd, M. (1992). Does she boil eggs? Towards a feminist model of disability. *Disability, Handicap and Society, 7*, 207–221.

Lowenfeld, B. (1981). *Berthold Lowenfeld on blindness and blind people: Selected papers*. New York: American Foundation for the Blind.

Mahoney, G., Kaiser, A., Girolametto, L., MacDonald, J., Robinson, C., Safford, P., and Spiker, D. (1999). Parent education in early intervention: A call for renewed focus. *Topics in Early Childhood Special Education, 19*, 131–140.

Mallory, B. L., Schein, J. D., and Zingle, H. W. (1992). Hearing offspring as visual language mediators in deaf-parented families. *Sign Language Studies, 76*, 193–213.

Marr, P. C., and Kennedy, C. E. (1980). Parenting atypical families. In M. J. Fine (Ed.), *Handbook on parent education* (pp. 181–200). New York: Academic Press.

Marriage of Carney. (1979). 24 Cal.3d 725, 157 Cal. Rptr. 383, 598 P. 2d 36.

Marschark, M. (1993). *Psychological development of deaf children*. New York: Oxford University Press.

Marschark, M. (1997). *Raising and educating a deaf child*. New York: Oxford University Press.

Mathews, J. (1992, August 18). Custody battle. The disabled fight to raise their children. *Washington Post Health, 8*,10–13.

Mayberry, R. (1976). An assessment of some oral and manual language skills of hearing children of deaf parents. *American Annals of the Deaf, 121*, 507–512.

McAndrew, H. (1948). Rigidity and isolation: A study of the deaf and the blind. *Journal of Abnormal and Social Psychology, 43*, 476–494.

McNary, M. E. (1999). Themes arising in the motherhood decision for women with multiple sclerosis: An exploratory study. *Journal of Vocational Rehabilitation, 12*, 93–102

Mead, G. H. (1934). *Mind, self and society*. Chicago: University of Chicago Press.

Meadow, K. P. (1968). Early manual communication in relation to the deaf child's intellectual, social, and communicative skills. *American Annals of the Deaf, 113*, 29–41.

Meadow, K. P. (1980). *Deafness and child development*. Berkeley: University of California Press.

Meadow, K. P., Greenberg, M. T., and Erting, C. (1985). Attachment behavior of deaf children with deaf parents. In S. Chess and A. Thomas (Eds.), *Annual progress in child psychiatry and child development, 1984* (pp. 176–187). New York: Brunner/Mazel.

Meadow, K. P., Greenberg, M. T., Erting, C., and Carmichael, H. (1981). Interactions of deaf mothers and deaf preschool children: Comparisons with three other groups of deaf and hearing dyads. *American Annals of the Deaf, 126*, 454–468.

Meadow-Orlans, K. P. (1984). Social adjustment of preschool children: Deaf and hearing, with and without other handicaps. *Topics in Early Childhood Special Education, 3*, 27–40.

Meadow-Orlans, K. P. (1994). Stress, support, and deafness: Perceptions of infants' mothers and fathers. *Journal of Early Intervention, 18*, 91–102.

Meadow-Orlans, K. P. (1997). Effects of mother and infant hearing status on interactions at twelve and eighteen months. *Journal of Deaf Studies and Deaf Education, 2*, 26–36.

Meadow-Orlans, K., and Erting, C. (2000). Deaf people in society. In P. Hindley and N. Kitson (Eds.), *Mental health and deafness* (pp. 3–24). London: Whurr.

Meadow-Orlans, K. P., and Spencer, P. E. (1996). Maternal sensitivity and the visual attentiveness of children who are deaf. *Early Development and Parenting, 5*, 213–223.

Meadow-Orlans, K. P., and Steinberg, A. G. (1993). Effects of infant hearing loss and maternal support on mother–infant interactions at eighteen months. *Journal of Applied Developmental Psychology, 14*, 407–426.

Mertens, D. M. (1996). Breaking the silence about sexual abuse of deaf youth. *American Annals of the Deaf, 141*, 352–358.

Mertens, D. M. (1998). *Research methods in education and psychology, Integrating diversity with quantitative and qualitative approaches*. Thousand Oaks, CA: Sage.

Meyer, D. J. (1986). Fathers of handicapped children. In R. R. Fewell and P. F. Vadasy (Eds.), *Families of handicapped children* (pp. 35–73). Austin, TX: Pro-Ed.

Middleton, A., Hewison, J., and Mueller, R. F. (1998). *Attitudes of deaf, hard of hearing and hearing adults towards genetic testing for deafness*. Proceedings of the National Society of Genetic Counselors Seventeenth Annual Education Conference, Denver, CO.

Mohay, H. (2000). Language in sight: Mothers' strategies for making language visually accessible to deaf children. In P. E. Spencer, C. J. Erting, and M. Marschark (Eds.), *The deaf child in the family and at school: Essays in honor of Kathryn P. Meadow-Orlans* (pp. 151–166). Mahwah, NJ: Lawrence Erlbaum Associates.

Mohay, H., Milton, L., Hindmarsh, G., and Ganley, K. (1998). Deaf mothers as communication models for hearing families with deaf children. In A. Weisel (Ed.), *Issues unresolved, New perspectives on language and deaf education* (pp. 76–87). Washington, DC: Gallaudet University Press.

Molnar, G. E. (1989). The influence of psychosocial factors on personality development and emotional health in children with cerebral palsy and spina bifida. In B. W. Heller, L. M. Flohr, and L. S. Zegans (Eds.), *Psychosocial interventions with physically disabled persons* (pp. 87–107). New Brunswick, NJ: Rutgers University Press.

Monbeck, M. E. (1973). *The meaning of blindness, Attitudes toward blindness and blind people*. Bloomington: Indiana University Press.

Monroe, G. N. (1989). *Mothers with multiple sclerosis: their perceptions of the effects of physical disability on parenting.* Unpublished doctoral dissertation, University of San Francisco (UMI Digital Dissertations Abstract).

Moores, D. F. (1992). An historical perspective on school placement. In T. N. Kluwin, D. F. Moores, and M. G. Gaustad (Eds.), *Towards effective public school programs for deaf students, Context, process, and outcomes* (pp. 7–29). New York: Teachers College Press.

Moores, D. F. (1996). *Educating the deaf, Psychology, principles, and practices* (4th ed.). Boston: Houghton Mifflin.

Moores, D. F., and Kluwin, T. N. (1986). Issues in school placement. In A. N. Schildroth and M. A. Karchmer (Eds.), *Deaf children in America* (pp. 105–124). San Diego, CA: College-Hill.

Morelli, G. A., and Tronick, E. Z. (1991). Parenting and child development in the Efe foragers and Lese farmers of Zaire. In M. H. Bornstein (Ed.), *Cultural approaches to parenting* (pp. 91–113). Hillsdale, NJ: Lawrence Erlbaum Associates.

Morgan, M. (1999). Sensory perception: Supernormal hearing in the blind? *Current Biology 9*, R53–R54.

Moses, K. L. (1985). Infant deafness and parental grief: Psychosocial early intervention. In F. Powell, T. Finitzo-Hieber, S. Friel-Patti, and D. Henderson (Eds.), *Education of the hearing impaired child* (pp. 86–102). San Diego, CA: College-Hill.

Mowl, G. E. (1996). Raising deaf children in hearing society: Struggles and challenges for deaf native ASL signers. In I. Parasnis (Ed.), *Cultural and language diversity and the deaf experience* (pp. 232–245). New York: Cambridge University Press.

Musselman, C., and Churchill, A. (1992). The effects of maternal conversational control on the language and social development of deaf children. *Journal of Childhood Communication Disorders, 14*, 99–117.

Myklebust, H. (1960). *The psychology of deafness, sensory deprivation, learning and adjustment*. New York: Grune and Stratton.

Myklebust, H., and Brutten, M. (1953). A study of the visual perception of deaf children. *Acta Otolaryngological Supplement*, 105.

Nagi, S. Z., and Clark, D. L. (1964). Factors in marital adjustment after disability. *Journal of Marriage and the Family, 26*, 215–216.

Nevins, M. E., and Chute, P. M. (1996). *Children with cochlear implants in educational settings*. San Diego, CA: Singular.

Nienhuys, T. G., Horsborough, K. M., and Cross, T. G. (1985). Interaction between mothers of deaf or hearing children. *Applied Psycholinguistics, 6*, 121–139.

Olgas, M. (1974). The relationship between parents' health status and body image of their children. *Nursing Research, 23*, 319–324.

Olkin, R. (1999). *What psychotherapists should know about disability*. New York: Guilford.

Oliver, M. (1996). *Understanding disability, From theory to practice*. New York: St. Martin's.

Padden, C., and Humphries, T. (1988). *Deaf in America: Voices from a culture*. Cambridge, MA: Harvard University Press.

Parasnis, I. (1983). Visual perceptual skills and deafness: A research review. *Journal of the Academy of Rehabilitative Audiology, 16*, 148–160.

Parks, S. (Ed.). (1984). *HELP: When the parent is handicapped*. Palo Alto, CA: VORT.

People v. C.A.K., 638 p.2d 136 (Colo. Ct. App. 1981), rev'd, 652P.2d 603 (Colo. 1982).

Peterson, Y. (1979). The impact of physical disability on marital adjustment: A literature review. *The Family Coordinator, 28*, 47–51.

Pollard, R. Q. (1992a). Cross-cultural ethics in the conduct of deafness research. *Rehabilitation Psychology, 37*, 87–101.

Pollard, R. Q. (1992b, August). *One hundred years in psychology and deafness: A centennial retrospective*. Division 26 invited address, annual meetings of the American Psychological Association, Washington, DC.

Preisler, G. M. (1991). Early patterns of interaction between blind infants and their sighted mothers. *Child: Care, Health and Development, 17*, 65–90.

Preisler, G. (1997). Social and emotional development of blind children: A longitudinal study. In V. Lewis and B. M. Collis (Eds.), *Blindness and psychological development in blind children* (pp. 69–85). Leicester, England: British Psychological Society.

Prendergast, S. G. (1992, October). *Maternal manual communication and deaf toddler gaze in play: A comparison of dyads with deaf and hearing mothers*. Proceedings of the Seventh Annual Conference on Issues in Language and Deafness, Omaha, NE: Boys Town Research Hospital.

Preston, P. (1994). *Mother father deaf: Living between sound and silence*. Cambridge, MA: Harvard University Press.

Preston, P. (1996). Chameleon voices: Interpreting for deaf parents. *Social Science and Medicine, 42*, 1681–1690.

Preston, P., and Jakobson, M. (1997). *Keeping our families together: A report of the national task force on parents with disabilities and their families* (Final Rep.). Berkeley, CA: Through the Looking Glass.

Preston, P., and Lou, M. (1998). *Adapting through the Looking Glass' intervention model for deaf parents and their children* (Final Rep.). Berkeley, CA: Through the Looking Glass.

Rainer, J. D., Altshuler, K. Z., and Kallmann, F. (Eds.). (1969). *Family and mental health problems in a deaf population* (2nd ed.). Springfield, IL: Thomas.

Rea, C. A., Bonvillian, J. D., and Richards, H. C. (1988). Mother–infant interactive behaviors: Impact of maternal deafness. *American Annals of the Deaf, 133*, 317–324.

Rée, J. (1999). *I see a voice: Deafness, language and the senses—A philosophical history*. New York: Holt.

Register, C. (1987). *Living with chronic illness: Days of patience and passion*. New York: Free Press.

Rehabilitation Act, 29, U.S.C. § 794 (1978).

Rettenbach, R., Diller, G., and Sireteanu, R. (1999). Do deaf people see better? Texture segmentation and visual search compensate in adult but not in juvenile subjects. *Journal of Cognitive Neuroscience, 11*, 560–583.

Reynolds, H. N. (1978). Perceptual effects of deafness. In R. D. Walk and H. L. Pick, Jr. (Eds.), *Perception and experience* (pp. 241–259). New York: Plenum.

Reynolds, H. N. (1993). The effects of foveal stimulation on peripheral visual processing and laterality in deaf and hearing subjects. *American Journal of Psychology, 106*, 23–40.

Richardson, S. A. (1969). The effect of physical disability on the socialization of a child. In D. A. Goslin (Ed.), *Handbook of socialization theory and research* (pp. 1047–1064). Chicago: Rand McNally.

Rienzi, B. M. (1990). Influence and adaptability in families with deaf parents and hearing children. *American Annals of the Deaf, 135*, 402–408.

Rogers, J. G. (1993). A guide to pregnancy, labor, and delivery for women with disabilities. In F. P. Haseltine, S. S. Cole, and D. B. Gray (Eds.), *Reproductive issues for persons with physical disabilities* (pp. 83–96). Baltimore: Brookes.

Rogow, S. M. (1999). The impact of visual impairment on psychosocial development. In V. L. Schwean and D. H. Saklofske (Eds.), *Handbook of psychosocial characteristics of exceptional children* (pp. 523–539). New York: Kluwer Academic/Plenum.

Roskies, E. (1972). *Abnormality and normality: The mothering of thalidomide children*. Ithaca, NY: Cornell University Press.

Safilios-Rothschild, C. (1970). *The sociology and social psychology of disability and rehabilitation*. New York: Random House.

Sandness, G. (1981). Adoption by parents with disabilities. *Rehabilitation Gazette, 24*, 23–25.

Schein, J. D. (1996). The demography of deafness. In P. C. Higgins and J. E. Nash (Eds.), *Understanding deafness socially, Continuities in research and theory* (2nd ed., pp. 21–43). Springfield, IL: Thomas.

Schiff, N. B., and Ventry, I. M. (1976). Communication problems in hearing children of deaf parents. *Journal of Speech and Hearing Disorders, 41*, 348–358.

Schildroth, A. N., and Hotto, S. A. (1996). Changes in student and program characteristics, 1984–85 and 1994–95. *American Annals of the Deaf, 141*, 68–71.

Schlesinger, H. S. (1987). Effects of powerlessness on dialogue and development: Disability, poverty, and the human condition. In B. W. Heller, L. S. Flohr, and L. S. Zegans (Eds.), *Psychosocial interventions with sensorially disabled persons* (pp. 1–27). Orlando, FL: Grune and Stratton.

Schlesinger, H. S., and Meadow, K. P. (1972). *Sound and sign: Childhood deafness and mental health*. Berkeley: University of California Press.

Scott, R. A. (1969a). *The making of blind men*. New York: Russell Sage Foundation.

Scott, R. A. (1969b). The socialization of blind children. In D. A. Goslin (Ed.), *Handbook of socialization theory and research* (pp. 1025–1045). Chicago: Rand McNally.

Shaul, S., Dowling, P. J., and Laden, B. F. (1985). Like other women: Perspectives of mothers with physical disabilities. In M. J. Deegan and N. Brooks (Eds.), *Women and disability: The double handicap* (pp. 133–142). New Brunswick, NJ: Transaction.

Shepherdson, K. L. (1967). Deprivation: A study of sighted children of blind parents. *The New Beacon: The Journal of Blind Welfare, 51*, 282–288.

Shonkoff, J. P., Hauser-Cram, P., Krauss, M. W., and Upshur, C. C. (1992). Development of infants with disabilities and their families. *Monographs of the Society for Research in Child Development, 57*, (Serial No. 232).

Shontz, F. C. (1975). *The psychological aspects of physical illness and disability*. New York: Macmillan.

Sidransky, R. (1990). *In silence: Growing up in a deaf world*. New York: St. Martin's.

Singleton, J. L., and Tittle, M. D. (2000). Deaf parents and their hearing children. *Journal of Deaf Studies and Deaf Education*, *5*, 221–236.

Skinner v. Oklahoma, 316 U.S. 535 (1942).

Spencer, P. E., Bodner-Johnson, B. A., and Gutfreund, M. K. (1992). Interacting with infants with a hearing loss: What can we learn from mothers who are deaf? *Journal of Early Intervention*, *16*, 64–78.

Steinberg, A. G., Davila, J. R., Collazo, J., Loew, R., and Fischgrund, J. E. (1997). "A little sign and a lot of love...": Attitudes, perceptions, and beliefs of Hispanic families. *Qualitative Health Research*, *7*, 202–222.

Stinson, M. S., and Stuckless, E. R. (1998). Recent developments in speech-to-print transcriptions systems for deaf students. In A. Weisel (Ed.), *Issues unresolved, New perspectives on language and deaf education* (pp. 126–132). Washington, DC: Gallaudet University Press.

Stokoe, W. C. (1960). Sign language structure: An outline of the visual communication of the American deaf. *Studies in Linguistics. Occasional Papers*, *8*. Buffalo, NY: University of Buffalo Press.

Stokoe, W. C., Casterline, D. C., and Croneberg, C. G. (Eds.). (1965). *A dictionary of American Sign Language on linguistic principles*. Washington, DC: Gallaudet College Press.

Stuckless, E. R., and Birch, J. W. (1966). The influence of early manual communication on the linguistic development of deaf children. *American Annals of the Deaf*, *111*, 452–460; 499–504.

Sullivan, P., Brookhouser, P., and Scanlan, J. (2000). Maltreatment of deaf and hard of hearing children. In P. Hindley and N. Kitson (Eds.), *Mental health and deafness* (pp. 149–185). London: Whurr.

Super, J. T., and Block, J. R. (1992). Self-concept and need for achievement of men with physical disabilities. *Journal of General Psychology*, *119*, 73–80.

Sutkin, L. C. (1984). Introduction. In M. G. Eisenberg, L. C. Sutkin, and M. A. Jansen (Eds.), *Chronic illness and disability through the life span: Effects on self and family* (pp. 1–19). New York: Springer.

Swisher, M. V. (2000). Learning to converse: How deaf mothers support the development of attention and conversational skills in their young deaf children. In P. E. Spencer, C. J. Erting, and M. Marschark (Eds.), *The deaf child in the family and at school: Essays in honor of Kathryn P. Meadow-Orlans* (pp. 21–40). Mahwah, NJ: Lawrence Erlbaum Associates.

Thompson, R. A. (1990). Vulnerability in research: A developmental perspective on research risk. *Child Development*, *61*, 1–16.

Thompson-Hoffman, S., and Storck, I. F. (1991). *Disability in the United States: A portrait from national data*. New York: Springer.

Thurman, S. K., Whaley, A., and Weinraub, M. A. (1985). Studying families with handicapped parents: A rationale. In S. K. Thurman (Ed.), *Children of handicapped parents, research and clinical perspectives* (pp. 1–9). Orlando, FL: Academic Press.

Trieschmann, R. B. (1989). Psychosocial adjustment to spinal cord injury. In B. W. Heller, L. M. Flohr, and L. S. Zegans (Eds.), *Psychosocial interventions with physically disabled persons* (pp. 117–136). New Brunswick, NJ: Rutgers University Press.

Troster, H., and Brambring, M. (1993). Early motor development in blind infants. *Journal of Applied Developmental Psychology*, *14*, 83–106.

Tuleja, C., Rogers, J., Vensand, K., and DeMoss, A. (1998). *Continuation of adaptive parenting equipment development* (Final Rep.). Berkeley, CA: Through the Looking Glass.

Turk, R., Turk, M., and Assejev, V. (1983). The female paraplegic and mother–child relations. *Paraplegia*, *21*, 186–191.

Tuttle, D. W. (1984). *Self-esteem and adjusting with blindness, the process of responding to life's demands*. Springfield, IL: Thomas.

Tymchuk, A. J., Yokota, A., and Rahbar, B. (1990). Decision-making abilities of mothers with mental retardation. *Research in Developmental Disabilities*, *11*, 97–109.

Uslan, M. M. (1992). Barriers to acquiring assistive technology: Cost and lack of information. *Journal of Visual Impairment and Blindness*, *86*, 402–407.

Vernon, M., and Koh, S. D. (1970). Early manual communication and deaf children's achievement. *American Annals of the Deaf*, *115*, 527–536.

Walker, L. A. (1986). *A loss for words: The story of deafness in a family*. New York: Harper & Row.

Ware, M. A., and Schwab, L. O. (1971). The blind mother providing care for an infant. *The New Outlook for the Blind*, *65*, 169–174.

Warren, D. H. (1977). *Blindness and early childhood development*. New York: American Foundation for the Blind.

Warren, D. H. (1978). Perception by the blind. In E. C. Carterette and M. P. Friedman (Eds.), *Handbook of perception, Perceptual ecology* (Vol. 10, pp. 65–90). New York: Academic Press.

Wedell-Monnig, J., and Lumley, J. (1980). Child deafness and mother–child interaction. *Child Development*, *51*, 766–774.

White, S. J., and White, R. E. C. (1984). The deaf imperative: Characteristics of maternal input to hearing-impaired children. *Topics in Language Disorders*, *4*, 38–49.

Whitman, B. Y., and Accardo, P. J. (Eds.). (1990). *When a parent is mentally retarded*. Baltimore: Brookes.

Wilkinson, M. E., and Stewart, I. (1993). Characteristics of students evaluated at a residential school's low vision clinics, 1981–1991. *Journal of Visual Impairment and Blindness*, *87*, 180–182.

Willems, P. J. (2000). Genetic causes of hearing loss. *New England Journal of Medicine*, *342*, 1101–1109.

Williams, D. R. (1990). Socioeconomic differentials in health: A review and redirection. *Social Psychology Quarterly*, *53*, 81–99.

Winzer, M. A. (1997). Disability and society before the eighteenth century, Dread and despair. In L. J. Davis (Ed.), *The disability studies reader* (pp. 75–109). New York: Routledge.

Wyler, S. R., and Markham, R. (1998). Do children with visual impairments demonstrate superior short-term memory, memory strategies, and metamemory? *Journal of Visual Impairments and Blindness*, *91*, 799–811.

12

Parental Psychopathology

Carolyn Zahn-Waxler
Sunita Duggal
Reut Gruber
National Institute of Mental Health

There was one important way in which Maria Alexandrova did not die. Her tormented soul lives on in us, but we reveal what she concealed. Her rebellion, her madness, her longing have grown in us to the level of a scream.

—Pierpont (2000)

INTRODUCTION

Poets, novelists and biographers often describe with special clarity and eloquence their own experiences with mental illness or growing up with an emotionally disturbed parent. Their gifts of language and insight provide others with a glimpse into a realm of despair and turmoil that would otherwise be rendered impenetrable. In the quotation above, the Russian poet, Marna Tsvetaeva, encapsulates a childhood lived with a deeply unhappy mother who was required by her own father to forsake love and career, resigning herself to a dignified but deadening life with a man she didn't love and children she didn't want. Tsvetaeva (who herself later committed suicide) thus describes the legacy of suffering left by her mother who died from tuberculosis when the poet was on the verge of adolescence (Pierpont, 2000). The mother's final words according to the poet were "I shall miss only the music and the sun." Both fiction and nonfiction are replete with variations on this theme of the anguish wrought by mental illness and the adverse impact on individuals, their partners, and (if they become parents) their children. Art is one important means by which these experiences have been expressed. While powerfully rendered and capable of reaching many, biography and autobiography are select (in terms of who provides the information) and selective (in terms what that individual chooses, or can remember, to tell). Representative accounts also require the role of science.

Scientific interest in the role of parental psychopathology on the quality of caregiving and influence on offspring is relatively recent. Modern research on this topic originated, in part, from psychodynamic explanations of childhood origins of adult mental illness first advanced over half a century ago. Patients' descriptions of childhood experiences during psychoanalysis often focused on negative characteristics of their parents. This led to theories about how parents, particularly mothers, "caused" their children to become depressed or delusional over time. Most of these conceptions were overly simplistic and did little to advance knowledge about the developmental origins of later emotional and behavioral problems.

Some of the early clinical observations, however, provided insights that helped to stimulate what is now a vigorous and productive research enterprise. Initial ideas focused mainly on aspects of parenting processes per se, deemed to be psychologically healthy or unhealthy (e.g., sensitive and affirming versus punitive and rejecting). As psychodynamic theories evolved, however, maladaptive parenting also came to be viewed within the broader context of parental mental illness. That is, parents who were viewed as rejecting, indifferent, or overprotective were not just "bad" parents. They might be individuals who suffered serious affective, behavioral, and cognitive impairments that limited their capacity to foster healthy psychological development. Soon thereafter, investigators began to study parents with what were then termed psychotic and neurotic conditions.

As these issues came under scientific scrutiny, there was a shift in the primary questions of interest, from early causes of later mental illness to how adult mental illness can affect offspring (Grunebaum, Weiss, Cohler, Hartman, and Gallant, 1975). These issues, however, are never fully disconnected. Mental disorders studied in offspring research typically show familial aggregation of psychiatric and psychological problems. A large body of research suggests that symptoms of mental illness in parents become reflected in family and parent–child interactions, affecting the nature and quality of caregiving and, in turn, both short- and long-term child outcomes. There is reason to believe that these parenting processes are part of a larger set of factors that contribute to patterns of intergenerational transmission of problems. What is less clear is how socialization experiences interact with the other factors to explain why only some children are affected and why different children are affected in different ways.

Contemporary interest in parents with psychopathology, in addition to its clinical origins, is strongly grounded in concepts and research in developmental science. Beginning in the 1950s and 1960s, behavioral scientists began to study processes such as parental modeling, teaching, discipline, and other childrearing practices thought to influence children's functioning. The socialization constructs developed to study and explain normal individual differences are of clear relevance to abnormal development as well, and have been applied to research on the childrearing practices of parents with psychopathology. Research in this area has benefited from the adoption of a developmental psychopathology perspective, a theoretical and research approach that has achieved prominence over the past 2 decades. This framework merges developmental and clinical issues in a manner that facilitates the simultaneous study of adaptive and maladaptive development (Cicchetti, Ganiban, and Barnett, 1991; Sroufe and Rutter, 1984).

Early models of parenting had focused primarily on parent-centered or child-centered models: The former emphasized the influence of parental personality and behaviors on their children (e.g., the classic literature on the schizophrenogenic mother). The latter emphasized children's behaviors and characteristics, and the responses that they evoke from parents (e.g., the temperamentally difficult or hyperactive child). Developmental psychopathology models emphasize interactive processes for understanding individual differences in parenting and children's development. Within a developmental psychopathology framework, transactional models focus on mutual influences of parents and children, and diathesis-stress models posit biologically based vulnerability to external stressors (see review by Cummings, Davies, and Campbell, 2000). The two are not mutually exclusive.

Whereas interactive models are necessary for understanding how parental psychopathology is manifest in childrearing practices and child outcomes, relatively few studies are designed to permit optimal testing of transactional and diathesis stress models. Multivariate research is more common now than in the past, increasing the probability that a broad array of influences on parenting and development can be assessed.[1] However, it is difficult to establish equally reliable and valid measures for each of the constructs examined during the course of hypothesis testing. One aspect of parenting may show a stronger influence than another because it is easier to assess and not always because it is, in fact, more important or relevant. Hence, generalizations from data often must be tempered. Moreover, despite the call for researchers to relinquish the more simplistic either-nature-or-nurture stances, there is a natural tendency (reinforced by difficulties in funding large-scale investigations) to focus on a relatively small number of constructs.

Longitudinal studies in which mentally ill parents and their offspring are followed over extended periods of time are optimal to studying the role of psychopathology in parenting and child outcomes. These designs also make it possible to learn more about why only some offspring are adversely affected and also about factors that protect children and promote resilience. Nondevelopmental studies, too, provide important descriptive information. Much of the existing research literature, in fact, is based on comparisons of mentally ill versus well parents and their offspring at a particular point in time.

We consider both kinds of research here, focusing first on schizophrenia and depression in parents. These forms of parental psychopathology have received major attention in theories and empirical research. We next consider other highly relevant but less studied psychiatric disorders expected to affect the care for offspring, in particular anxiety, eating, and personality disorders (e.g., antisocial behavior, borderline personalities, and narcissism). This is followed by a discussion of the relevance of these cumulative bodies of information for clinical and applied issues pertaining to parenting and child development. Finally, we consider next steps for the field, including topics that merit further inquiry, for example, fathers with psychopathology, cultural factors that influence symptom expression, and the complex relations between mental illness and criminality. Before turning to the specific disorders, we discuss aspects of theory and research design that have both enabled and impeded our understanding of the parenting of caregivers with serious emotional and behavioral disturbances. In so doing, we describe several central issues in this field that are relevant to understanding parental psychopathology regardless of the particular disorder. These include (1) the characterization of psychopathology (categorical versus dimensional), (2) factors that influence individual differences in child outcomes, (3) reliability and validity of assessments of psychopathology, (4) the disproportionate focus on maternal psychopathology, (5) specific dimensions and analysis of parenting processes, and (6) the role of socioeconomic status or family disadvantage in parental mental health problems.

PARENTAL PSYCHOPATHOLOGY: CENTRAL THEMES

A variety of genetic/biological and environmental factors, singly and in combination, have been hypothesized to explain the role of parental psychopathology in children's development. Some of these factors may be common across disorders, whereas others may have greater relevance to a particular disorder. Research designs that include more than one diagnostic group as well as a normal comparative sample maximize the opportunity to examine what is general and what is specific. Most investigations of parental psychopathology, however, have not included more than one psychiatric

---

[1] Multivariate, multirespondent, developmental (ideally longitudinal), designs make it possible to examine complex effects of independent variables, in combination with intervening variables, on dependent variables. The goal is to better capture the array of naturally occurring processes in the real world, which contribute to parental problems and, ultimately, to child outcomes. These designs, in combination with more sophisticated statistical analytic approaches, are used to test different causal models and to distinguish different kinds of direct and indirect effects on outcomes. In this chapter we use language based on these approaches to describe particular patterns of influence (Baron and Kenny, 1986; Holmbeck, 1997). The term *mediator* is used to specify how a given effect occurs. A mediating variable represents the mechanism through which the independent variable influences the dependent variable. The term *moderator* is used to characterize the relations between two variables. A moderator variable interacts with the independent variable in such a way as to impact the level of the dependent variable.

298   Zahn-Waxler, Duggal, and Gruber

disorder. Another layer of complexity for understanding the impact of psychopathology on parenting processes and child outcomes is created by the fact that comorbidity of certain key psychiatric disorders is quite high. This highlights the somewhat arbitrary nature of focusing on a particular disorder to the exclusion of other coexisting problems. Before turning to the extant literature, we highlight some of the central themes in parental psychopathology.

Characterizations of Parental Psychopathology

Thus far, we have referred to parental psychopathology solely in terms of psychiatric disorders, which is how research in this area began. Children with a schizophrenic parent were compared with those of normal and clinically depressed parents (Goodman and Brumley, 1990; Grunbaum, Cohler, Kauffman, and Gallant, 1978; Sameroff, Seifer, Zax, and Barocas, 1987; Watt, Anthony, Wynne, and Rolf, 1984). Diagnoses of psychiatric disorders are based on categorical classification systems. A clinical disorder is a qualitatively distinct entity; it is construed as a disease that is either present or absent depending on whether specific diagnostic criteria are met (American Psychiatric Association, 1994). Within psychology, dimensional classification systems typically have been used to describe emotional and behavioral disturbances; that is, symptoms exist on a continuum. This approach does not yield psychiatric diagnoses, although scores are typically normed to distinguish normal, subclinical, and clinical problems. In this chapter we review research based both on dimensional and categorical measures. This permits access to a wider array of relevant information but makes cross-study comparisons more difficult. The difficulties reflect both the problems inherent in trying to integrate knowledge across disciplines and the fact that this is a relatively new area of research.

Factors That Influence Individual Differences in Child Outcomes

In evaluating the impact of parent clinical problems, one issue concerns the relative roles of diagnostic status and severity of problems. Are children more affected by the nature of the disorder or by or the overall level of impairment in parental functioning regardless of the form of psychopathology? Related issues concern (1) the impact of chronic versus acute but short episodes of mental illness and (2) the extent to which impairments in parenting behaviors continue to be present between episodes of illness. Irrespective of disorder, more severe disturbance may create greater difficulty, both cognitively and affectively, in accurately perceiving and responding to children's needs and communications (Rogosch, Mowbray, and Bogat, 1992). In terms of general effects of parental psychopathology across disorders, efforts of the ill parent to meet her or his own magnified needs would be expected to interfere with the ability to meet the child's needs with warmth and sensitivity. The child's needs are likely to be experienced as burdensome, given the parent's diminished internal resources. Negative transactional effects would also ensue, where the child's unmet needs lead to behavior that is difficult for the parent to manage.

Effects of Symptoms on Reliability and Validity of Parental Reports

Assessments of psychopathology, childrearing practices, and child outcomes are based on a variety of sources that differ across studies. Psychopathology, as noted, is assessed through structured diagnostic interviews and questionnaires. Although clinical observations may play a role, this is not commonly a part of the research enterprise. In assessment of children's and adolescents' problems, multiple perspectives are sometimes obtained that may include reports by parents (typically mothers), teachers, and also the children when they are old enough to effectively provide information on symptoms. The assessment of parental psychopathology typically is based solely on interview or questionnaire data from only the parent. It is not uncommon in research for parents also to provide some data on their childrearing practices and the psychological functioning of their children.

The shared method variance that results from these assessment limitations can create biased information. It becomes a particularly serious problem in studies based solely on data from the parent. The problem is hardly unique to research on parents with mental illness, but it may become compounded or exaggerated by the increased likelihood that distortions, biases, and memory impairments could compromise objectivity of their reports. Some investigators conclude that current mental health impairment appears to have a substantial effect on the reporting of child behavior problems, raising questions about the validity of reports by mothers who are currently emotionally distressed (Najman, Andersen, Bor, O'Callaghan, and Williams, 2000). Richters (1992) noted though that what may sometimes appear as bias (e.g., "overreporting" of emotional and behavioral problems in offspring by depressed mothers) may actually reflect accurate perceptions on their part.

Relative Impact of Maternal and Paternal Psychopathology

For most of the disorders studied the focus has been primarily on the mother. With regard to schizophrenia, relatively few men marry, have children, and become part of a stable family unit. For this reason alone, their parenting is an unlikely object of scientific inquiry. Assortative mating is a common characteristic of many psychiatric disorders and may affect offspring for both biological and psychosocial reasons. Mating between a schizophrenic mother and a father who suffered from schizophrenia spectrum disorder has been shown to increase the offspring's risk of developing a schizophrenia spectrum disorder (Parnas, 1985).

A higher proportion of depressed men than schizophrenic men are likely to marry, have children, and be part of an ongoing family unit. Hence they would be more likely to have an impact on their children by virtue of their socialization practices as well as for more biologically based reasons. Assortative mating occurs frequently with regard to depression. However, the literature on parental depression is based almost exclusively on mothers. Their caregiving relationships with young children are typically seen as more central and proximal than those of fathers, and they are more willing research participants. For many reasons then, what we know is mainly about the parenting of mothers with mental health problems.

Dimensions of Parenting

Research in this area requires careful analysis of how different domains of parenting (e.g., discipline, instruction, modeling, and affect expression and regulation) may be affected by different symptoms that, in turn, could have an impact on different domains of children's functioning (e.g., cognitive, social, emotional) to compromise the mental health of offspring. Variations exist within domains for a particular disorder, across domains for a given disorder, and across both domains and disorders. Specific examples are discussed in subsequent sections. Comprehensive, conceptually guided assessments of these domains facilitate analysis of the mediating and moderating roles of different aspects of parenting when relations between maternal psychopathology (unless otherwise noted) and child outcomes are found.

The timing, severity, and duration of maternal symptoms may have different implications depending on the child's age and the stage-salient developmental issues for a particular time period (Goodman and Gotlib, 1999; Weissman and Paykel, 1974; Weissman, Paykel, and Klerman, 1972). Qualities of parenting in a number of different domains have been associated with more (or less) optimal functioning in children. Early in development, provision of sensitive care and warmth is central to the promotion of secure attachments and good parent–child relationships. Also critical are the abilities to facilitate development of emotion regulation, allow for individuation, and constructively set limits. Scaffolding in cognitive development and provision of opportunities for peer interaction become increasingly salient as the child grows older, as does the judicious support of autonomy seeking by adolescents. All parenting domains of course are important at all stages of children's development. But mental illness may have an impact on aspects of parenting that are especially central to a particular point in development.

Socioeconomic Status and Parental Psychopathology

One of the most consistent findings in psychiatric epidemiology has been the inverse relations between socioeconomic status and prevalence of a variety of types of disorders (Dohrenwend, 1990; Garmezy, 1987; Sameroff and Seifer, 1990). Social causation theory and social selection theory have been used to explain why low socioeconomic status (SES) is associated with risk for psychiatric disorders (Johnson, Cohen, Dohrenwend, Link, and Brook, 1999). These theories were tested using data from a community-based longitudinal study (Johnson et al., 1999). Low family SES was associated with offspring anxiety, depressive, disruptive, and personality disorders even after offspring IQ and parental psychopathology were controlled. Different processes associated with the two theories varied in importance, depending on the particular psychiatric disorder. Eating disorders are associated with economic affluence (American Psychiatric Association, 1994), a rare example of psychopathology that might disproportionately affect the parenting of more financially secure individuals.

The studies reviewed here, and others as well (see review by Gotlib and Avison, 1995), indicate complex and powerful links between SES and parental mental illness. However, in recent years research interest in the role of economic adversity in psychiatric disorders has been declining (Dohrenwend, 1990). Given the likely negative effect on the parenting of already compromised caregivers, this is an unfortunate turn of events. While research on economic disadvantage and poverty in relation to parenting and child development has increased, the possible mediating or moderating roles of parental psychopathology have not been emphasized.

PARENTS WITH SCHIZOPHRENIA

Schizophrenia is a psychiatric condition characterized by both positive and negative signs (American Psychiatric Association, 1994). Positive symptoms reflect an excess or distortion of normal functions. They include distortions of thoughts (delusions), perceptions (hallucinations), language and communication (disorganized speech), and behavioral monitoring (grossly disorganized or catatonic behavior). Negative symptoms include restrictions in the range and intensity of emotional expression (flat affect), fluency of thought and speech, and goal-directed behavior. There are subtypes and also a spectrum of disturbance, with schizophreniform disorder as a less severe condition. In schizoaffective disorder, mood symptoms are prominent.

The role of hereditary factors in risk for schizophrenia has been demonstrated in twin, adoption, and cross-fostering studies (e.g., Fowles, 1992). However, the moderate rates of concordance (40%–60%) for schizophrenia in monozygotic twins have led researchers to endorse environmental as well as genetic etiologic factors (Gottesman and Shields, 1982; Stabenau and Pollin, 1993). Interactive etiologic models have been examined (Gabbard and Goodwin, 1996; Rosenthal, 1970; Tsuang, 2000; Zubin and Spring, 1977), with suggestive evidence in support of the diathesis-stress model (i.e., stressful environments will tend to produce schizophrenia in genetically predisposed individuals). The assumption is that schizophrenics and people with schizotypal personality disorder are comparably predisposed to schizophrenia and that environmental factors determine whether the full schizophrenic syndrome will develop (Burman, Mednick, Machon, Parnas, and Schulsinger, 1987; Hans and Marcus, 1988; Parnas, Teasdale, and Schulsinger, 1985; Walker and Diforio, 1997; Walker, Diforio, and Baum, 1999).

Associations between parental major mental illness and subsequent disturbances in the child are well documented (Laucht, Esser, and Schmidt, 1994; Rutter, 1996; Rutter and Quinton, 1984). Exposure to a schizophrenic parent is positively related to later maladjustment (e.g., Skagerlind,

Perris, and Eismann, 1996; Walker, Hoppes, Mednick, Emory, and Schulsinger, 1981). The timing and severity of disorder are also important. In a longitudinal study of offspring of schizophrenic mothers, psychopathology in offspring was predicted by the mother's age at first hospitalization and by institutionalization of the mother during the first 5 years of the child's life (Parnas et al., 1985).

Several studies of children of schizophrenic mothers have found that those reared by their mothers show a slightly lower incidence of psychopathology (including schizophrenia spectrum disorders) compared to those separated early in life and reared apart (e.g., Higgins et al., 1997). A similar pattern was found in a matched control study on kibbutzim in Israel (Breznitz, 1985). Schizophrenic parents who continued to perform parental tasks when their children lived with them full time were better able to protect their children from psychological difficulties. Children of schizophrenic parents who lived in kibbutzim and saw their parents for short and emotionally intense periods developed more psychological difficulties, which were evident at 15 years. This may reflect a greater genetic predisposition of the reared-apart children. The fact that by a young age the primary rearing of these children was carried out by metaplot may indicate more severe illness in the mother.

Investigations of specific aspects of parenting have revealed differences between normal and schizophrenic mothers. During the first year of the infant's life, women diagnosed with schizophrenia, when compared to women with no mental illness, tend to show more negative and less positive affect, and to be less responsive and less involved (e.g., Goodman and Brumley, 1990). Schizophrenic mothers were found to provide less environmental stability and nurturance when compared to normal control mothers (e.g., Ragins, Schacter, and Elmer, 1975; Seeman, 1996). Similar patterns were observed in mother–infant interactions, with schizophrenic mothers showing less spontaneity and expressiveness and providing little sensory and motor stimulation (e.g., Hipwell and Kumar, 1996; McNeil, Naslund, Persson-Blennow, and Kaij, 1985; Riordan, Appleby, and Faragher, 1999; Snellen, Mack, and Trauer, 1999; Sobel, 1961).

Relations between specific symptoms and deficits in parenting have received relatively little attention in the literature. Several studies have documented risks associated with psychotic symptoms (e.g., infant neglect, abuse and infanticide, in Brockington, 1996; terrorizing attacks on children that occurred as a consequence of the psychosis, in Anthony, 1986). Snellen et al. (1999) examined the relation between the mental state of women with a postpartum schizophrenic illness and the quality of mother–infant interactions both at admission and discharge from hospital. Severity of maternal illness correlated with the quality of mother–infant interactions. On admission, mothers with more positive symptoms had worse interactions with their infants. They were unresponsive, understimulating, and showed little positive affect, but more hostility and disorganized parenting. At discharge, however, the mothers with more negative symptoms had worse interactions with their infants (as above), with the exception of hostility. Hostility was associated with persistent positive symptoms.

Researchers and clinicians have reported that the inability of schizophrenic mothers to fulfill the daily parental roles can have a serious impact on the daily life of their children. Often these children must provide their own physical care and assume adult-like responsibility in the family household (e.g., Mander, Norton, and Hoare, 1987; Webster, 1992). These processes are elaborated in a first-person account by the daughter of a schizophrenic mother (Lanquetot, 1984). The daughter eloquently describes the chaos, disorganization, and progressive deterioration of a parent over time, the parentification that occurs, the conflicting emotions, and the legacy left by parental major mental illness. With schizophrenia (as with other major mental disorders), the quality of social supports and alternative/adjunct childrearing arrangements would be expected to matter greatly for how the child develops, copes, and functions in a difficult milieu.

Some investigators have reported few differences between schizophrenic and depressed mothers (e.g., Goodman and Brumley, 1990), with the quality of parenting found to be more important than the mother's diagnostic status in determining children's intellectual and social functioning. However, greater parenting dysfunction was found in mothers with schizophrenia. Sameroff et al. (1987) found that both schizophrenic and neurotic depressed mothers were less spontaneous and proximal with their 40-month-old infants than were mothers without psychiatric disturbances. The severity and chronicity of the mother's illness, across diagnostic groups, were negatively related to indices of quality of maternal care. Others, too, have reported that parental depression and parental schizophrenia carry similar psychiatric risks for children (e.g., Rutter and Quinton, 1984; Sameroff, Seifer, and Zax, 1982; Watt et al., 1984). Although parental mental illness increased risk for psychiatric problems in children, in most cases the main risk did not stem from the illness itself (Rutter and Quinton, 1984). Rather, it derived from the associated, continuing psychosocial disturbances in the family. Even if phenotypic similarities exist, the mechanisms still may differ according to the type of parental mental disorder. In other words, although depression and schizophrenia seem to carry similar risks for children, it could be for different reasons. Research methods may not yet be sufficient to detect diagnostic group differences in parenting that matter in important ways for children's development.

Some recent studies found greater deficits in women with schizophrenia in interactions with their infants than in women with other mental disorders. For example, Riordan et al. (1999) found that schizophrenic mothers were more remote, insensitive, intrusive, and self-absorbed than mothers with an affective disorder. Their infants were more avoidant, and the overall quality of mother–infant interaction was poor. In another study, the interactions of schizophrenic mothers with their children were more impaired than those of mothers with unipolar depression during admission to the hospital (Hipwell and Kumar, 1996). Impaired interaction was judged in terms of the appropriateness of the mothers' observed caregiving behaviors on several dimensions, including maintaining contact with the baby, sensitivity and responsiveness, and the ability to maintain routine care. In a longitudinal study by Goodman (1987), although both schizophrenic and depressed mothers were rated as less affectively involved and less responsive than well mothers, schizophrenic mothers provided the poorest overall environment based on assessments of global functioning, role performance, and social competence.

The deficits in parenting of schizophrenic caregivers would be expected to have an adverse impact on different aspects of children's development. There is a substantial body of literature demonstrating a range of disturbance in social, emotional, cognitive, physical, physiological, anatomical, and neurological domains—as well as psychiatric disorders and psychological symptoms. A selective review is provided below. Numerous deficits are documented, but the specific contributing factors are often not clear. It is also important to note that some studies have not found deficits in the functioning of offspring of schizophrenic parents (e.g., Hanson, Gottesman, and Heston, 1976; Rieder and Nichols, 1979; Sameroff et al., 1987).

Compared with controls, processes of separation–individuation were found to be less developed in the children of schizophrenic parents (Vartiovaara, Maekelae, and Pykaelaeinen, 1990). Infants of schizophrenic mothers exhibited more anxious attachment (D'Angelo, 1986; Naslund, Persson-Blennow, McNail, Kaij, and Malmquist-Larsson, 1984b). Infants of mothers with schizophreniform and depressive psychoses showed a lack of positive interaction with and approach toward their mothers on reunion after separation (Gamer, Gallant, and Grunebaum, 1976). In addition, offspring of mothers with schizophrenia were particularly likely to show a total absence of fear of strangers in the first year (Naslund et al., 1984a). At older ages their interpersonal relationships were negatively affected, and they experienced adverse emotional illness (e.g., Webster, 1992). Increased prevalence of antisocial behavior in offspring of mothers with schizophrenia (Silverton, 1988), and other impairments in social development (Goodman, 1987; Goodman and Brumley, 1990) also have been documented.

A number of cognitive problems in offspring have been identified (e.g., Goodman, 1987; Goodman and Brumley, 1990; Sameroff et al., 1987; Vartiovaara et al., 1990; Yoshida, Marks, Craggs, Smith, and Kumar, 1999). Marcus et al. (1987), for example, found that 63% of children with a schizophrenic parent, and who showed early neurobehavioral deficits, also received poor parenting compared with 15% of the offspring who did not show early behavioral deficits. Offspring of women with schizophrenia have shown reduced physiological arousal compared to offspring of affective, schizoaffective, and well mothers (Schubert, Blennow, and McNeil, 1996). Brain abnormalities in the offspring of schizophrenic mothers have been reported: Offspring of schizophrenic parents who developed schizotypal personality disorder had greater cortical sulcal enlargment than did those with nonspectrum outcomes (Cannon et al., 1994), as well as increased cortical and ventricular cerebrospinal fluid–brain ratio as a function of level of genetic risk for schizophrenia (Cannon et al., 1993). Some of these problems are more likely to have genetic/biological origins, but environmental factors might also play a role. For example, mothers who provide little cognitive stimulation or enrichment are unable to provide an environment that will nourish intellectual growth.

In summary, children of schizophrenic mothers are a high-risk group. This likely results from a combination of the child's increased genetic vulnerability and environmental strains that stem both directly and indirectly from the mother's illness. Many questions remain unanswered. The lack of specificity of the impact of parental schizophrenia compared to other psychiatric disorders, when it occurs, warrant further examination. It will be important to know more about the circumstances under which quality of parenting may matter more for child outcomes than either the nature or severity of psychiatric diagnoses. Even within the broad category of schizophrenia, there is enormous variation in how the disorder is manifest and, hence, how it is displayed and then how it is likely to be experienced by the children. Examples of such variations include whether or not the parent is appropriately medicated; whether the symptoms are mainly positive, mainly negative, or both; the extent to which negative symptoms are characterized by psychosis, disorganization, or both; the levels of social dysfunction, emotion dysregulation, and self-care; and the extent to which the child is represented in paranoia and other delusions as the cause of problems. One viable approach would be to focus on clusters of symptoms and to categorize schizophrenic parents based on symptoms rather than disorder per se. The same is true of other disorders as will become evident in subsequent sections.

DEPRESSION IN PARENTS

Depression is an affective disorder with different subtypes. The central defining feature involves mood dysregulation in the form of prolonged sadness and/or an inability to experience pleasure, but there are several other diagnostic indicators. In order to diagnose depression, at least four symptoms must be present for a minimum of two weeks, though specific symptoms may vary. There are vegetative disturbances (e.g., sleeping or eating too much or too little, fatigue, loss of energy, or restlessness); cognitive impairments (e.g., loss of concentration and memory, distorted perceptions); and psychological and affective symptoms (e.g., guilt, low self-esteem, suicidal ideation, irritability, loss of interest, and social withdrawal).

Psychotic symptoms are not confined to schizophrenia but can be manifest in severe cases of mood disorders as well. Psychotic symptoms typically involve delusions and/or auditory hallucinations congruent with mood-related themes (American Psychiatric Association, 1994). In a depressive episode, an individual may experience delusions such as delusional guilt (believing, for example, that she or he caused a relative to get sick or die) or auditory hallucinations involving a voice berating the person (saying they are worthless, etc.). In a manic episode, a person may experience delusions relating to grandiosity (e.g., believing that one is a great historical figure) or auditory hallucinations (e.g., a voice saying the person has special powers or that no one is up to their standards). The number of psychotically depressed mothers in research is thought to be relatively low. However, studies do not necessarily probe for or report psychotic features of depression. Severe postpartum depression is probably the form of maternal depression most likely to contain psychotic features, but even here it is relatively rare.

There is now a large body of literature documenting adverse effects of parental depression on offspring (see reviews by Cummings and Davies, 1994; Cummings et al., 2000; Downey and Coyne, 1990; Gelfand and Teti, 1990; Goodman and Gotlib, 1999; Zuckerman and Beardslee, 1987). This work began several decades ago when depressed parents and their children were studied as a psychiatric comparison group in studies of schizophrenic parents and their offspring. Research on children of depressed parents quickly came into its own as the scope and severity of problems in parenting and child outcomes became evident. From infancy through adolescence, these children are at risk for a number of different kinds of problems. At the same time, many children of depressed parents do not develop psychopathology, and family relations can be supportive and positive. Findings summarized below are based on a large body of literature, referenced extensively in the reviews just cited. Detailed case studies of parenting of depressed mothers can be found in Radke-Yarrow (1998).

Infants of depressed mothers more often have difficult temperament, dysregulated emotion, atypical frontal lobe activity, lower motor and mental development, and less secure attachments than infants of well mothers. Note here and below, the similarity of problems to those of young offspring of schizophrenic mothers. Toddlers and preschool-age children show cognitive and emotional problems parallel to those of infants of depressed mothers. They also begin to show additional disturbances in the development of functional autonomy. They react more negatively to stress, have less effective self-regulation strategies, and show fewer interpersonal skills in interactions with playmates compared with children of well mothers. Their lack of social competence can be seen in aggressive, withdrawn, and inappropriate behaviors toward peers. By middle childhood, problems with peers are more entrenched, and cognitive problems are now reflected in poor school performance. Clinical problems including anxiety, mood, and disruptive behavior disorders are increasingly evident. Difficulties continue through adolescence, another time period important for both adaptive and maladaptive development. Maternal depression may even affect hormonal functioning (Ellis and Garber, 2000). Early puberty in daughters has been associated with a history of maternal mood disorder and also with the entry of an unrelated father figure into their lives.

Depression is one of the most prevalent psychiatric disorders. The lifetime risk of depression for children with a depressed parent has been estimated at 45% (Hammen, Burge, Burney, and Adrian, 1990). Childbearing and childrearing are associated with increased risk of depression among women. Hence there is a relatively high likelihood that children will be exposed to maternal depression at some point in their life. Offspring research thus provides a unique opportunity to study intergenerational transmission of affective and behavioral disorders, including the development of sex differences in depression. While disruptive behavior problems are more frequent in males than females beginning in early childhood, mood disorders are two to three times more common in females than males, beginning in adolescence (American Psychiatric Association, 1994; Zahn-Waxler, 2000). Factors that contribute to gender differences in developmental trajectories are particularly amenable to study in offspring of depressed parents because they show high rates of both internalizing and externalizing problems.

As with schizophrenia, the symptoms required to diagnose depression can vary from one individual to the next. Therefore, different configurations of symptoms may have different meanings and experiences for children. For example, depression may be reflected in anger, distraction, and restless behavior. Or it may manifest itself in withdrawal, pervasive sadness, and rumination. Parents who show one or the other patterns will be quite different social partners for their spouses and children. Again, this highlights the need for more differentiated and symptom-based profiles of clinical problems in order to understand what children experience. Depression is commonly comorbid with other psychiatric disorders, particularly anxiety disorders. Having a parent who is both anxious and depressed has additional ramifications, as it involves exposure to a potentially wider range of symptomatology.

Depression often co-occurs with other disorders including personality problems. Underlying comorbid personality disorder increases the probability of both parenting difficulties and depression. Personality disorders or pervasive patterns particularly relevant to depression include (1) schizoid, i.e., detachment from social relationships and a restricted range of social expression; (2) paranoid, i.e., mistrust and suspiciousness of others such that their motives characteristically are viewed as malevolent; (3) avoidant, i.e., social inhibition, feelings of inadequacy, and hypersensitivity to negative evaluation; (4) dependent, i.e., excessive need to be taken care of that leads to submissive and clingy behavior and fears of separation; and (5) borderline, i.e., instability in interpersonal relationships, self-image and affects, and marked impulsivity (American Psychiatric Association, 1994). The latter two disorders are diagnosed predominantly in females.

Personality disorder symptoms in depressed individuals have been associated with greater severity of affective illness (DeMulder, Tarullo, Klimes-Dougan, Free, and Radke-Yarrow, 1995). Moreover, the nature of affectively ill mothers' interactions with their young children could be predicted from personality symptoms. For example, mothers with dependent and borderline symptoms show extremely high levels of engagement, a possible sign of overinvolvement. In contrast, depressed mothers with paranoid or schizoid symptoms show lack of involvement. Maternal personality disorder symptoms also have been associated with a diagnosis of depression in children in this sample of depressed and well mothers (Radke-Yarrow, 1998). Avoidant, dependent, and borderline personality symptoms were most common among depressed mothers. Avoidant and dependent personality symptoms were associated with disruptive behavior in the child. One might expect avoidant patterns to translate into unavailable or uninvolved mothering, with dependency linked to overinvolvement.

Impairments associated with depression do not necessarily disappear between episodes (Radke-Yarrow, 1998). Thus, parenting of depressed individuals may be continuously problematic to some degree despite the episodic nature of depression. Andrews, Brown, and Creasy (1990) found that disorder in daughters of mothers with psychiatric disorders was associated with a disorder in the mother only when it had been chronic or recurrent during the daughter's lifetime. In another study (Thomas, Forehand, and Neighbors, 1995), increases in maternal depressed mood over time predicted more internalizing and externalizing problems and lower social competence in adolescents than could be predicted just from initial levels of maternal depressed mood.

The heterogeneity in types, severity, comorbidity and timing of depression, in conjunction with how it is conveyed in parent–child interaction illustrates why it is difficult to determine how offspring are affected. Based on almost 3 decades of research on children and adolescents of depressed mothers, a number of group differences in offspring of depressed and well caregivers have been identified. Substantially less is known about why the differences occur, what they mean, and why some children more than others are affected.

Goodman and Gotlib (1999) have discussed these issues in a recent integrative review. They note that little attention has been paid to the mechanisms explaining the intergenerational transmission of risk, emphasizing the need for developmentally sensitive, transactional models. Four major mechanisms for transmission of problems and psychopathology are discussed. One is genetic (i.e., depression is inherited via DNA that differs in important ways for children of depressed and well mothers). As with schizophrenia, evidence from adoption, twin, and family study designs suggests some degree of inheritance in the etiology of depression. It is not clear, however, whether the disorder is inherited directly, or indirectly due to other associated factors.

A second explanation for how problems are transmitted across generations, also more biologically based, is that children of depressed mothers are born with dysfunctional neuroregulatory mechanisms. This makes it difficult to regulate arousal and affect, and hence may create vulnerability to depression. Depressed mothers, for example, are more likely than well mothers to have abnormal neuroendocrine functioning during pregnancy. Consequently, the fetus experiences the mother's higher cortisol levels and reduced blood flow. This may restrict growth and movement, alter the infants' physiological arousal, and hence contribute to the development of regulatory problems.

A third transmission mechanism focuses on disturbed interpersonal processes or socialization experiences that result from children's exposure to their mothers' negative cognitions, emotions, and behaviors associated with their depression. Often the quality of the parent–child attachment relationship becomes compromised quite early in development. This has been shown in a number of observational studies documenting disproportionately high numbers of insecure attachments (e.g., Murray, 1992; Radke-Yarrow, Cummings, Kuczynski, and Chapman, 1985). Radke-Yarrow et al. (1985) also found that expressed emotion (more negative and less positive) predicted insecure attachments independent of diagnosis. One of the most consistent findings from research on depressed caregivers is the adverse consequences for offspring of mothers' displays of negative emotions, including sadness, flat affect, and irritability. Children may learn parental depressive attributional styles through imitation of parental styles modeled and through direct internalization of parental criticism.

A number of observed impairments in childrearing and discipline processes of depressed caregivers have been reported (Goodman and Brumley, 1990; Zahn-Waxler, 2000). Depressed caregivers are more likely than well caregivers to manifest qualities of parenting known to be associated with problems in children's cognitive, social, and emotional development (Maccoby and Martin, 1983). Compromised functioning has been seen in deficient modeling of social skills and constructive coping; relational disturbances; low nurturance and sensitivity; angry, negative, and retaliatory behavior; intrusiveness; and ineffective conflict resolution (e.g., Cohn, Campbell, Matias, and Hopkins, 1990; Field, Healy, Goldstein, and Guthertz, 1990; Goodman, Adamson, Riniti, and Cole, 1994; Hammen, 1991a). Depressed mothers are more likely than well mothers to use negative discipline and control practices reflected in harsh, hostile, and coercive parenting styles (e.g., Kochanska, Kuczynski, Radke-Yarrow, and Welsh, 1987), sometimes alternating with lax undercontrol (Dumas, Gibson, and Albin, 1989) and anxiety and guilt-induction (Davenport, Zahn-Waxler, Adland, and Mayfield, 1984). These disturbances reflect an array of cognitive, social, emotional, and relational problems that stem from the demands of parenting. A more complete summary of research on the parenting of depressed caregivers can be found in the comprehensive review by Goodman and Gotlib (1999).

Through a variety of socialization processes, symptoms of depression, particularly the negative affect and self-critical features of the disorder may transfer to the child over the course of time. Depressed mothers have more negative social cognitions than nondepressed mothers. They make more negative attributions about their children, as well as other critical, unsupportive statements to the child, including feeling disappointed by the child. There is some evidence that negative attributions of child behavior mediate relations between maternal depressed mood and child psychological problems by fostering "harsh parenting practices" (Geller and Johnson, 1995). White and Barrowclough (1998) found that depressed mothers attributed problem behaviors of their preschool children to stable, controllable, causes personal to the child (rather than universal to children of that age) to a greater extent than did nondepressed mothers. Attributing negative events to internal, stable, and global causes ("It's my fault; I am responsible for all bad things that happen; It will always be that way") is a central, defining feature of a depressive orientation. Mothers with such attributional styles have children with similar styles, suggesting that the cognitions maintaining depression can transfer to offspring.

The fourth mechanism summarized by Goodman and Gotlib focuses on stressors that affect the quality of family relationships and create risk for the development of psychopathology. Children of depressed mothers are exposed to a greater number of stressors than children of well mothers (e.g., financial burdens, job problems, and social or interpersonal stresses, in the marital relationship in particular). Hammen (1991b, p. 64) has suggested, based on findings of a link between child outcomes and maternal mood state at the time of assessment and chronic stress, that "any condition that renders the mothers depressed, even nonclinically, and demoralized and stressed by ongoing problems in relationships, finances, health, or work, poses a risk to children's adjustment to the extent that such conditions are severe or persistent."

Marital discord is a stressor whose effects are likely to be experienced in an immediate, direct manner. Maternal depression and marital discord are very highly correlated. The children (boys in particular) in high-distress, high-conflict families are likely to be undercontrolled, aggressive, and develop disruptive behavior disorders. The link between maternal depression and marital conflict is a complex one. Marital conflict often precedes the onset of depressive episodes, and it is associated with the course of depression (Gotlib and Hooley, 1988).

Marital conflict not only may play a causal role in the onset and maintenance of depression but may also hinder its response to treatment and promote relapse (Downey and Coyne, 1990). It is therefore quite possible that direct effects of maternal depression on parenting may be indirectly caused by marital conflict, which creates and maintains some cases of maternal depression. There is also evidence for bidirectional influences between parental depression and marital conflict (Whisman, 2000). If stressors like marital discord mediate effects of maternal depression but are not directly examined, adverse effects of depression on child outcomes may be overestimated.

Depression in a parent not only helps to create a social and emotional milieu in which the whole family operates, it is itself affected by the social and emotional context of the family. Hops et al. (1987) found evidence of functional relations between dysphoric affect and aggressive displays in families with depressed mothers. In a study directly measuring family behavior in the home, the mother's dysphoric affect served to suppress the family's aggressive affect immediately after the dysphoric display; similarly, the family's aggressive affect served to suppress the mother's dysphoric affect immediately after the behavior. Families with a depressed parent may develop interactional patterns characterized by attempts to control aversive affect of various family members.

Longitudinal research with the same sample has focused on observed differences between the responses of adolescent daughters and sons to depressive parental behavior (Davis, Sheeber, Hops, and Tildesley, 2000). Daughters, but not sons, who provided comfort and suppressed their own aggression showed an increase in depressive symptoms over time. These findings are consistent with those of Klimes-Dougan and Bolger (1998), who reported that adolescent daughters (but not sons) cope with maternal depression by becoming overinvolved. They provide mothers with active support, become withdrawn, and express feelings of guilt, sadness, and responsibility for the depression. These patterns actually begin much earlier in development, manifest initially as anxiety, indicative of an emerging depressive orientation in some girls of depressed mothers (Zahn-Waxler, 2000). There is accumulating longitudinal data to support links between early anxiety and later depression (Zahn-Waxler, Klimes-Dougan, and Slattery, 2000). In cross-sectional research, Breslau, Davis, and Prabucki (1987) found that major depressive disorder in mothers was associated with increased risk for overanxious disorder in younger children and major depressive disorder in older children, suggesting that anxiety in children may be a developmental precursor of other disorders like depression.

In summary, there is an extensive body of literature documenting the adverse effects of maternal depression on children's well-being in several domains of functioning. Much of the information is descriptive, documenting overall differences between groups of depressed and well mothers and their offspring. Process-oriented questions and causal pathways have been more difficult to address and unravel using the necessary multivariate, multirespondent longitudinal research designs. Hammen, Burge, and Stansbury (1990) pointed out that causality cannot be reduced to a one-way effect of maternal depression on the adjustment of the child. Using structural equation modeling, they found bidirectional influences between maternal depression and child characteristics, including negativity and age, and direct effects of both on child adjustment. Hammen, Burge, and Adrian (1991) also found that diagnoses of depression in children occurred in proximity to maternal episodes of depression, either preceding or following the episodes. Both maternal and child depression might be related to external stressors, with symptoms in mother or child serving as an additional stressor for the other.

PARENTAL ANXIETY

Anxiety disorders are one of the most prevalent forms of adult mental illness and would be expected to have a major impact on parenting and the functioning of children. These disorders take a variety of forms including panic disorder, agoraphobia, specific phobia, social phobia, obsessive-compulsive disorder, generalized anxiety disorder, and posttraumatic stress disorder (American Psychiatric Association, 1994). As with depression, anxiety disorders occur much more frequently in females than males (American Psychiatric Association, 1994), and mother–child transmission patterns have received major emphasis. In contrast to depression, there is relatively little research on maternal anxiety. What does exist focuses mainly on general anxiety, assessed either as disorder or on a continuum of distress. To complicate matters further, anxiety and depression are highly comorbid disorders. In studies of depressed mothers, significant anxiety is present more often than not, just as depression is common in studies of anxious mothers. Yet, typically, the secondary symptoms are not assessed, and one is left with the impression that the focus is solely on parents who are either anxious or depressed.

Offspring of parents with anxiety disorders are at risk for anxiety disorders (Bernstein and Borchardt, 1991; Turner, Beidel, and Costello, 1987). Children of parents with anxiety disorders were found to be seven times more likely to have an anxiety disorder than children of parents without psychiatric diagnoses, and twice more likely to have an anxiety disorder than children of parents with dysthymic disorder (Turner et al., 1987). The risk of anxiety disorders among offspring of parents with anxiety disorders compared to controls averages 3.5 (range 1.3–13.3) within broad subtypes of anxiety disorders, suggesting some specificity of parent–child concordance. But there is lack of specificity with regard to parents with depressive disorder, whose offspring also have increased rates of anxiety disorders.

Only one study of parents with anxiety disorders has been based on observations of parenting interactions (Whaley, Pinto, and Sigman, 1999). They found that anxious mothers catastrophize and criticize more than controls, and show less granting of autonomy, warmth, and positivity. These behaviors were more strongly associated with child anxiety than were maternal diagnostic status or ongoing strain, and hence may mediate linkages between maternal and child anxiety symptoms. There was some evidence of interactive processes; low maternal warmth and positivity was most strongly associated with maternal anxiety, but maternal granting of autonomy was most strongly associated with child anxiety. Another study suggests that quality of parenting does not differ for anxiety-disordered mothers and nonpsychiatric controls (Merikangas, Avenevoli, Dierker, and Grillon, 1999). Rather, intergenerational group differences are thought to be a product of genetic transmission. However, the measure of parenting was based solely on adolescents' perceptions in response to a limited set of questions.

A high rate of insecure attachment (80%) was found among offspring (aged 18 to 59 months) of mothers with anxiety disorders (Manassis, Bradley, Goldberg, Hood, and Swinson, 1995). Insecure attachment at 1 year has been predicted from prebirth maternal anxiety and 3-month maternal management of infant distress (Del Carmen, Pedersen, Huffman, and Bryan, 1993). In another study, mothers with agoraphobia reported more separation anxiety than mothers with no history of psychiatric disorder. Moreover, a higher level of maternal separation anxiety was associated with a lower level of perceived control in the 11-year-old children. Modeling was suggested to be involved in the intergenerational transmission of anxiety (Capps, Sigman, Sena, Henker, and Whalen, 1996). In this study, the majority of children (68%) of agoraphobic mothers met diagnostic criteria, particularly for internalizing disorders like anxiety and depression. These children also reported more fear and anxiety and less control over various risks than did comparison children. Maternal history of anxiety disorder also has been associated with less monitoring of children aged 8 to 11 (Chilcoat, Breslau, and Anthony, 1996).

Associations between trait anxiety (enduring anxiety that may not reach clinical levels) and maternal unresponsiveness, maternal intrusiveness, and restricted infant exploratory play have been identified (Biringen, 1990; Nover, Shore, Timberlake, and Greenspan, 1984). Decreases in maternal trait anxiety from 3 to 9 months predicted an increase in mother sensitivity (Feldman, Greenbaum, Mayes, and Erlich, 1997). Maternal anxiety was associated with perceptual distortions of and less responsive, more interfering behavior with their 9-month-old infants (Nover et al., 1984). Mothers who reported low anxiety prenatally were more likely to have securely attached infants at 12 months than mothers who reported more anxiety. Independent of infant temperament, maternal prenatal anxiety also appeared relevant in determining the quality of attachment (Del Carmen et al., 1993).

Primiparous mothers with high anxiety report more distress, less confidence in themselves, and less adequate social supports than mothers with low anxiety at 1 and 5 years postpartum. Maternal anxiety at both times also predicted more social, emotional, and behavioral problems in firstborns as reported by mothers, and fathers also reported more social problems (Barnett, Schaafsma, Gusman, and Parker, 1991). Parents of children with anxiety disorders have been observed to allow less psychological autonomy than parents of children without internalizing problems (Siqueland, Kendall, and Steinberg, 1996). Children of mothers with panic disorder view their families as less cohesive, more conflictual, less independent, and more controlling than control children (Silverman, Cerny, and Nelles, 1988).

In general, issues pertaining to loss and controllability figure prominently in the small body of literature on parental anxiety. According to Capps et al. (1996), children of anxious parents describe themselves as more fearful and anxious, endorsing less control over various risks than did comparison children. Evidence from a variety of sources suggests that early experience with diminished control may foster a cognitive style characterized by the increased probability of interpreting or processing subsequent events as out of one's control, representing a psychological vulnerability for anxiety (Chorpita and Barlow, 1998). Lack of controllability over one's environment has also been hypothesized as a precursor of depression, again suggesting early developmental links between anxiety and depression. These issues are illustrated in Appendix A, in a hypothetical composite case of maternal anxiety and overprotection, and the adverse impact on the child in a particular situation.

PARENTS WITH EATING DISORDERS

Anorexia nervosa and bulimia, the two main eating problems characterized as psychiatric disorders, are on the rise, and the population most affected is young women. These disorders are typically accompanied by depression and anxiety. Little is known about the effects on children, and this topic is ripe for research. Extreme body dissatisfaction is part of a larger set of self-related problems expected to have an adverse impact on parenting processes. Infants of mothers with eating disorders have been found to weigh less on average than comparison infants (Stein et al., 1994). Mother–infant conflict, particularly during mealtime, was the strongest predictor of infant weight (Stein, Woolley, Cooper, and Fairburn, 1994). There is no evidence to suggest that the eating-disordered mothers were deliberately limiting the food intake of their infants (Stein, Murray, Cooper, and Fairburn, 1996). Stein, Woolley, and McPherson (1999) found that mothers with eating-disorder psychopathology had difficulty reading infant cues and setting aside their own concerns during mealtimes. For example, they had a tendency to put their own need for cleanliness above the 12- to 14-month-old infant's need for feeding autonomy. People with eating disorders are typically preoccupied with food and body weight and shape, and have extreme attitudes concerning these issues. Woolley and colleagues argued that these preoccupations and attitudes interfere with mother–infant interactions such that they miss infant cues, find infant self-feeding stressful, and are overly concerned about messiness associated with eating.

PERSONALITY DISORDERS IN PARENTS

Given the apparent relevance of chronicity of psychological problems to parenting, it is surprising that there have been so few investigations of the parenting of individuals with personality disorders. Personality disorders are, by definition, enduring maladaptive patterns of perceiving, relating to, and thinking about the environment and oneself exhibited in a wide range of contexts (*DSM-IV*, 1994). At their core, these patterns are stable and inflexible.

There is considerable overlap between criteria for particular personality disorders and symptoms of clinical/mental disorders. The DSM system is based on multiaxial assessment. There are five axes, two of which are most relevant to this chapter. Each axis refers to a different domain of information that the clinician can use to plan treatment and predict outcome. Axis 1 refers to clinical disorders (schizophrenia, anxiety, and mood), whereas Axis II refers to personality disorders. Axis II cluster

A personality disorders that include the paranoid, schizoid, and schizotypal features may be related to Axis 1 psychotic disorders. Schizotypal personality disorder is a pattern of acute discomfort in close relationships, cognitive or perceptual distortions, and eccentricities of behavior. Cluster C personality disorders, including avoidant, dependent, and obsessive-compulsive behavior patterns may manifest in ways that are similar to Axis 1 anxiety or mood disorders. While personality disorders are rarely diagnosed before early adulthood, it is difficult to imagine that they are not anchored in traits that have an earlier developmental course. One of the Cluster B personality disorders, antisocial personality disorder, not only is related to, but must also be preceded by, conduct disorder. Behavioral patterns associated with other Cluster B personality disorders, for example, borderline, histrionic, and narcissistic symptoms, may be more distinct from criteria for Axis 1 disorders but still closely related in terms of patterns of comorbidity, as noted earlier. The dramatic, emotional, or erratic behaviors that characterize these individuals are likely to have pronounced effects on parenting.

Parental Antisocial Personality Disorder (APD) and Conduct Disorder (CD)

Several characteristics of antisocial disorder are incompatible with responsive parenting. People with APD often present inappropriate expressions of anger or violence and have core difficulties relating to other individuals. They may also present a preoccupation with self, lack of empathy, instability in personal relationships, and a wide range of impulsive emotional reactions. Thus, they may have substantial difficulties to meet the basic requirements for good parenting (e.g., patience, tolerance for frustration, and an ability to empathize with the child). In the literature, the major issues studied pertaining to the parenting of individuals with APD include (1) cross-generational transmission of APD and (2) parental discipline as a possible mediator of CD in children of individuals with APD. In addition, indirect aspects of the functioning and characteristics of individuals with APD may also have impact on the quality of their parenting. Examples include high hostility, social disadvantage, and substance and alcohol use.

Cross-generational transmission of APD. The general findings support the idea of a cross-generation linkage risk for antisocial behavior. Parents who are antisocial are at significant risk of producing boys who are antisocial. A substantial amount of research has shown that parental externalizing spectrum of psychopathology, that is, antisocial personality disorder, aggression, imprisonment, and substance abuse is associated with CD in the children, as well as with ADHD/CD in the children (e.g., Biederman, Munir, and Knee, 1987; Lahey, Hartdagen et al., 1998; Lahey, Piacentini et al., 1988; Lahey, Russo, Walker, and Piacentini, 1989; Morrison and Stewart, 1971). The direct relation between parental antisocial personality disorder and child conduct disorder is especially prominent for fathers (Frick et al., 1992; Lahey et al., 1995; Walker, Cudek, Mednick, and Schulsinger, 1981).

Paternal CD/APD is also associated with alcoholism and/or substance abuse (Clark et al., 1997; Kuperman, Schlosser, Lidral, and Reich, 1999). It has been shown that CD children who exhibited the greatest amount of physically aggressive and other serious lawbreaking behavior had fathers who were markedly more likely to exhibit the same kind of antisocial behavior. There is also some evidence supporting the association between maternal externalizing disorders and CD in offspring (Cassidy, Zoccolillo, and Hughes, 1996; Patterson and Capaldi, 1991). Additionally, mothers of children with conduct disorder had higher scores on MMPI scales associated with antisocial behavior, histrionic behavior, and disturbed adjustment than mothers of children with attention deficit disorder with hyperactivity (*DSM-III*, 1980) and mothers of children without either of these disorders (Lahey, Russo, Walker, and Piacentini, 1989). However, in some studies the associations were not significant (e.g., Pfiffner et al., 1999), possibly because of small sample size or an imprecise measurement of externalizing problems in female participants. And in other studies, yet different patterns prevail. For example, higher rates of child (male) overt antisocial behaviors observed in a naturalistic summer program were associated more with maternal than paternal characteristics (neither of which involved parental externalizing behaviors); in particular, child antisocial behaviors were associated primarily with maternal presence of major depression, absence of generalized anxiety disorder, higher neuroticism, and lower conscientiousness (Nigg and Hinshaw, 1998).

The observed stability of antisocial behavior has been explained as indicating a predisposition toward antisocial behavior (Kendrick and Funder, 1988; Lytton, 1990), which could be acquired genetically, through behavioral learning within the family or a combination of mechanisms (Patterson and Dishion, 1988). Adoption designs have been used to demonstrate mutual influence between heritable child antisocial characteristics (e.g., based on antisocial personality disorder in the biological parent) and family environment (e.g., indexed by negative parenting practices of adoptive parents; Ge et al., 1996).

As a predictor of adult antisocial personality, having an antisocial parent places the child at risk for antisocial behavior; having two antisocial parents puts the child at even higher risk (Robins and Earls, 1986). Concordance across three generations has been documented (Elder, Caspi, and Downy, 1983; Huesmann, Eron, Lefkowitz, and Walder, 1984; Robins, West, and Herjanic, 1975). Highly specific associations of the same type of disorder across generations are consistent with genetic risk models. However, they also fit with psychological explanations that emphasize the role of the parents' behaviors and attitudes in the cross-generational transmission of the disorder. This may include modeling of parental dysfunction, parental demonstration of abnormal cognitive-emotional reactions, or parental unintentional reinforcement of emergent child symptoms. The relative contributions of parenting and child traits to antisocial behavior continue to be an important issue because of the implications for treatment. It has been shown that changes in parenting can reduce antisocial behavior (e.g., Kazdin, 1987).

Parenting skills of individuals with APD.   Antisocial parents are likely to engage in ineffective discipline practices. Families of antisocial children are characterized by harsh and inconsistent discipline, little positive parental involvement with the child, and poor monitoring and supervision of the child's activities (Loeber and Dishion, 1983; McCord, McCord, and Howard, 1963). Ineffective discipline is significantly related to risk of having an antisocial child. There is increasing evidence that parental discipline practices may be an important mediating mechanism in the transmission of antisocial behaviors from parents to children. Patterson and Dishion (1988) found a significant correlation between retrospective reports of grandparental explosive reactions in the home and parental antisocial traits. Furthermore, effects of the parents' antisocial traits on their children's antisocial behaviors were mediated by parental discipline practices. Huesmann et al. (1984) were among the first to show that discipline practices may be the mediating link between antisocial traits in one generation and antisocial traits several generations later. In a longitudinal study spanning 22 years, they collected data on the aggressiveness of three generations in the same families and found significant correlations between grandparental discipline practices and antisocial behavior in the grandsons.

In more recent work (Bosquet and Egeland, 2000) the relation between scores on the Antisocial Practices content scale of the MMPI-2 and parenting behaviors was examined in a sample of low-income women. Antisocial mothers were observed to be less understanding and more hostile and harsh in their parenting styles than mothers in the other groups of clinical and nonclinical controls. Another study (Cassidy et al., 1996) examined the relation between adolescent maternal psychopathology and the quality of mother–infant interactions. Severity of maternal antisocial history correlated positively with maternal unresponsiveness and infant passivity. It would be interesting to know the extent to which antisocial mothers also experienced significant depression. These externalizing and internalizing problems often are comorbid, particularly in females. The findings described here are reminiscent of those discussed earlier with respect to maternal depression. With respect to adolescent fathers, several researchers have found that boys who become adolescent fathers are more likely than their peers to have a history of antisocial behavior problems (Elster, Lamb, and Tavare, 1987; Kessler et al., 1997; Ketterlinus, Lamb, and Nitz, 1994; Lerman, 1993).

Finally, in a sample of 177 clinic-referred children age 7 to 13, an association was found between parental adjustment, including paternal antisocial personality disorder, and several aspects of family functioning and children's outcome (Frick et al., 1992). Mothers of children with CD were significantly more likely than mothers of control children to be poor at supervising their child's behavior and inconsistent in applying discipline. When both paternal APD and deviant maternal parenting were entered into prediction analyses, only parental APD was significantly associated with CD.

Borderline and Narcissistic Personality Disorders

Borderline and narcissistic personality disorders have not received research attention in relation to parenting. They are described here, however, because of their obvious relevance to disturbances in parenting and with the goal of stimulating research in this area. The chaotic interpersonal world of individuals with borderline personality disorder would be expected to have direct effects on children. Any exposure to its more dramatic behaviors, including recurrent suicidal behavior, gestures, threats, self-mutilating behavior, or impulsivity (which may include reckless driving or substance abuse that could put the child at risk) could be frightening and traumatic. Additionally, as with other serious disorders hospitalization may entail disruptions in caregiving as well as questions and fears about why the parent (usually the mother) is gone. In contrast to antisocial personality disorders more common in men, borderline and narcissistic personality problems are more frequently diagnosed in women.

The exaggerated focus in BPD on not being abandoned, which frequently underlies self-harming behaviors, may have a variety of effects on parenting. Although a focus on parent needs rather than child needs (and the concomitant emotional unavailability) may be common to other disorders, it is likely to be extreme in BPD. There may be general deficits in affection, sensitivity, and warmth with respect to the child in addition to neglect of particular emotional needs of the child. Feldman and Guttmann (1984) observed that children with a borderline personality disordered parent tend to become a target of that parent's projections and distortions of reality. The child may be viewed as a stress on a fragile intimate relationship and treated with covert, if not overt, hostility. Or the child may be perceived as a stable source of care for the parent. Similar to what has been observed in some children of depressed mothers, there may be an erosion of parent–child boundaries, as the child becomes overburdened with adult concerns, and begins to feel responsible for the parent's well-being. The parent might have particular difficulty with developmental periods in which the child is working toward greater autonomy, such as in the toddler years and in adolescence.

In addition to possible instability in how the child is viewed, the child is likely to be exposed to instability in other relationships of the parent with BPD. Moreover, the child may be exposed to parent figures with little investment in the child's welfare. (A parent with BPD may, for example, remain with a substance abusing and abusive partner rather than risk a sense of abandonment.) Finally, the marked reactivity of mood, often related to real or perceived interpersonal crises, may be unpredictable, confusing, and frightening. Difficulty controlling intense anger may increase the risk of emotional and/or physical abuse. Additionally, transient paranoid ideation or severe dissociative symptoms may result in neglect if not actual mistreatment of the child. More generally, the parent's inability to model and guide emotion regulation for the child may result in the child believing that emotions can themselves be frightening and overwhelming. Similarly, the child may not develop skills relevant to resolving interpersonal conflict or misunderstandings. Appendix B provides a description based on a composite of cases, of a child's experience with a borderline-personality-disordered parent.

With regard to narcissistic personality disorder, here, too, there has been some theoretical consideration of parenting processes but no systematic research. Theories do not suggest that having a narcissistic parent would put the child at risk for developing narcissism. Imbesi (1999, p. 43) suggested that "at the most basic level the parental fault consists in the failure to provide optimal, gradual frustrating experiences early in the child's life, including the setting of appropriate generational boundaries" (p. 42). Although having a narcissistic parent may not be a risk factor for narcissism per se, the grandiosity and self-centeredness suggests many additional ways in which both parenting and child functioning would be compromised.

Research on the offspring of parents with personality disorders is clearly warranted. It is an important topic in its own right. Moreover, because there is substantial comorbidity of Axis 1 and Axis 2 disorders, it provides one means of parsing the heterogeneity of ways in which a parent with a given clinical disorder might be perceived and experienced by the child. For example, the depressed mother with borderline symptoms would differ from another mother whose mood disorder is accompanied by an avoidant pattern. Caution is also in order. Reliability and validity of assessment of psychiatric disorders is an ongoing concern. It becomes a particularly critical issue with regard to personality; judgments of what is problematic may be quite subjective and the values of different cultures and subcultures are likely to come into play. The intersection of clinical disorder or deviance, and behaviors that are idiosyncratic, eccentric, unusual, or atypical in certain cultural contexts (but not necessarily pathological) is often blurred.

APPLIED AND CLINICAL IMPLICATIONS OF PARENTAL PSYCHOPATHOLOGY

The current zeitgeist is far more supportive of research on genetic/biologic factors than on environmental influences on the etiology of mental health problems. There are many reasons why the pendulum has swung toward a strong biological deterministic position where problems are viewed as clinical disorders that reside within individuals. Included are rapidly advancing technologies and sophisticated instrumentation (e.g., brain imaging and mapping the genome), economic factors including health costs and reimbursement plans, and certain political, social, and public policies. The strong biological focus also reflects a reaction against early environmental explanations of mental illness that were at once simplistic, naive, and judgmental, attributing major responsibility to horrific parenting and ascribing greater volition than was warranted. And although this judgmental quality is less prevalent now, the fact that research systematically identifies negative aspects of parenting in caregivers with psychopathology continues to make these parents "look bad." The generalizations often are strong and portray strikingly negative parental behaviors. In identifying parenting problems we run the risk of creating other communication problems that interfere with fostering adaptive development for troubled parents and their offspring.

The history of neglect of biological factors was most apparent in research on the origins of schizophrenia. As noted earlier, this thought disorder was considered a result of maternal behavior lacking in warmth and sensitivity. As the genetic component of schizophrenia and other disorders became evident, there was a reaction against the idea that problematic parenting could play a role in the development of mental health problems. This backlash was uninfluenced by the finding that even schizophrenia, a disorder with an increasingly clear biological component, could not be fully explained by genes. Similarly, perceptions of biological scientists and the public have changed little even as evidence for the diathesis-stress hypothesis, emphasizing the interaction between genetic vulnerability and environmental stress, has emerged.

There is a compelling need for advocacy, to educate the public about mental disorders so that these problems are not viewed as problems of lesser stature and importance for treatment. The biases and stigma associated with admitting to difficulties, seeking treatment, and concerns about negative attributions continue, despite major strides and efforts on the part of mental health professionals. There is a need for greater emphasis on psychiatric illness as clinical disorders that deserve treatment as much as other illness, that is, similar to addressing home and child needs of a parent with cancer or dementia. Society is much less blaming of the individual in these cases.

An important challenge for the future involves how to change perceptions that research on parental psychopathology is an inherently judgmental process, resulting in a sense of "blame." The distinction between understanding, explaining, and intervening on the one hand, and judging and blaming on the other, is a subtle but crucial one. This distinction should be emphasized both in scientific writings and media communications, with careful attention paid to the language used. Greater consideration of resources and support (or lack thereof) available to parents, in addition to developmental challenges faced by the parents themselves, is needed. Parents with clinical problems often experience stressors that are implicated not only in their psychopathology, but also directly in their parenting difficulties. It is important to make it clear that less than optimal parenting does not imply a lack of effort and may, in fact, describe the parenting of individuals who are doing the best they can. Frequent, explicit acknowledgment of the considerable challenges involved in parenting is essential, with parenting discussed as a multifaceted endeavor involving a wide range of skills and continually changing demands.

Many families, especially those with caregivers who have more severe disorders (e.g., schizophrenia or bipolar disorder) have the added struggle of low socioeconomic status, difficulty receiving appropriate care (both due to insurance bias and lack of resources of where to go) and limited social support in general. In addition, current treatments leave much to be desired. While very effective in controlling (not curing) psychosis, most of the antipsychotic medications (and many mood stabilizers and "older" antidepressants that are still used partly because they are less expensive) have side effects of sedation and blunting. This makes the patient appear "out of it" and emotionally unavailable, which would definitely contribute adversely to parenting quality. This is often a major issue for patients who dislike the side effects and become noncompliant in order to "feel real" at the risk of exacerbation of their illness (M. Slattery, personal communication, 2001).

A more balanced perspective on the parenting of individuals with psychopathology would place greater emphasis on the parental contribution to resilience in children. Children of parents with psychopathology who do not develop psychological difficulties themselves may be inherently stronger in certain respects. But they also may have parents who promote more adaptive functioning. Despite impairment from psychopathology (or other related stresses), these parents may be directing considerable internal and external resources toward their parental roles. Some studies have begun to identify positive aspects of parenting in risk populations that predict adaptive functioning in children. Childrearing practices of depressed mothers of toddlers that contributed to positive outcomes for children 3 years later have been identified (Zahn-Waxler, Iannotti, Cummings, and Denham, 1990). Depressed mothers who engaged in more positive and fewer negative practices with their toddlers had children whose behavioral problems decreased over time. These mothers more often used proactive childrearing approaches. They anticipated the child's needs and perspectives, exerted modulated but firm control, and provided positive structure during children's peer play. Further work in this area will be critical not only for advancing scientific knowledge, but also for establishing effective interventions.

These findings were replicated in a similar risk study, where risk was defined by young children's disruptive behaviors. Here, fathers as well as mothers were observed interacting with their children, and when they engaged in proactive parenting, their children showed less aggression over time (Denham et al., 2000). Fathers' contributions were evident in addition to those of mothers. These results underscore the role of fathers in influencing children's development and speak to the potential of including them in intervention efforts.

Whereas continued research is necessary and important for understanding the effects of psychopathology on parenting, there is sufficient basis to conclude that intervention is warranted. The evidence is most clear with respect to the parenting of depressed mothers only because the preponderance of research has focused on this group of mothers. Given evidence for nonspecific effects of psychopathology on parenting, it would be reasonable at this point in time to develop some broadly based interventions applicable to parenting across disorders. Common to all forms of psychopathology is a heightened need for parents to develop some awareness of their own needs, to recognize and manage the child's needs, and to resolve conflicts between parent and child needs in a manner that promotes adaptive social, emotional, cognitive, and behavioral qualities in the child.

Existing interventions focus largely on changing parental *behavior* in order to obtain child compliance. An increased emphasis on ways in which *emotions* are implicated in parenting (Dix, 1991) may be especially relevant to the development of interventions for parents with psychopathology. As parents become more attuned to their own emotional functioning, learn how their emotions affect parenting, and learn strategies to help them regulate emotions, they will be better equipped for the challenging task of parenting. They will then be in a better position to benefit from information regarding appropriate expectations and from cognitive-behavioral strategies.

Even with respect to parental depression, where much is known about the impact on parenting processes, there is no mention of parenting problems in the associated features section of the *DSM-IV* (1994). A reference to decreased role functioning is the only suggestion of such problems. This is particularly unfortunate, because the *DSM-IV* often serves as a starting point for clinicians considering areas of impairment. With some emphasis on parenting problems, clinicians would be reminded to assess and address these problems even if not initially presented by the client. The clinician may also be reminded to consider the possibility of emergent problems in the children, whose difficulties could affect the parent, rather than treating the individual in isolation.

Parents rarely present for therapy focused on parenting or child adjustment prior to the emergence of clear child problems. There is a need for systematic efforts to identify parents with psychopathology who could benefit from parent training in addition to individual treatment. A variety of institutions could serve as entry points for on-site or off-site parenting work, including, for example, hospitals (where a parent is receiving psychiatric care) and prisons (where a parent with antisocial and/or substance abuse and dependency problems is incarcerated).

Additionally, pediatricians' offices could be instrumental in identifying potential cases of postpartum depression in mothers. Psychoeducational materials and referrals could be provided, not just for individual treatment of the depression but for parenting support and training. Other institutions that assist parents at-risk of developing psychopathology (such as welfare agencies) could also be utilized. Mental health professionals treating adults need also to be reminded to routinely assess parenting problems, and to reassess over time, because parenting involves different qualities and skills as the child enters into successive developmental stages. Once cases are identified, intervention should include an individual component to treat the parental psychopathology, a general parenting skills component, and a component tailored to particular issues associated with the parent's presentation and with particular challenges presented by the child and/or the child's emerging difficulties.

FUTURE DIRECTIONS IN PARENTING AND PSYCHOPATHOLOGY

The literature reviewed indicates that children of mentally ill parents, on average, face more formidable hurdles and challenges in their life journeys than those whose parents are more psychologically healthy. This in itself does not come as any great surprise. What is new is the increased recognition that disordered thoughts, behaviors, and emotions are features of clinical syndromes that manifest themselves in parent–child relationships; moreover, this can profoundly affect how parents and children view themselves and others and how they approach the different worlds they live in. It is important that this knowledge begin to transcend the boundaries of the scientific communities that have generated this information. This will require stronger working alliances between researchers and individuals who work more directly with parents, children, and families.

Clearly there is need for more and better research that helps to address the many issues raised in this chapter. It will be important to continue to wrestle with basic issues of what constitutes a mental disorder; how disorders differ from one another, whether and how they overlap, the circumstances under which problems of both parents and children become significant clinical entities, how problems are passed forward across generations, and, in particular, the contributory role of parenting in the transmission of psychopathology. The ultimate value of such work, however, will rest on its potential for application to the lives of people in emotional turmoil. One point of intersection for basic and applied issues involves the development, implementation, and effective application of interventions to alter maladaptive parenting patterns. In closing, we elaborate on several topics within parental psychopathology that will be important to pursue in future initiatives.

Assessment of Mental Illness

Research would benefit from use of both categorical and continuous measures of psychopathology within the same research designs. This would make it possible to learn more about the points at which and the ways in which quantitative increases in clinical symptoms begin to reflect qualitative changes, not only in psychopathology per se but how it is manifest in the parent–child relationship. More studies are needed that involve direct observations of parent–child interactions, other family interactions, and children's relationships with significant others outside the family. Similarly, experimental paradigms that pose specific challenges to both caregivers and offspring would provide valuable information. But such studies will be useful only to the extent to which more differentiated assessment and coding systems can be developed that will better capture subtle but potentially profound variations in how parents engage in the many tasks, responsibilities, problems and pleasures of caring for children.

Paternal Influence

The absence of systematic research on the role of the father remains a significant concern. There is good reason to believe that fathers as well as mothers have important direct influences on their children's emotional well-being. We need to better understand paternal influences within a systems perspective in terms of their capacity to (1) provide emotional support to mentally ill mothers if mothers are the primary caregivers, (2) meet the child's needs (emotional and otherwise) that the mother is less able to provide, and (3) serve to buffer the child against direct effects of maternal psychopathology.

About a decade ago, a comprehensive examination of research on paternal psychopathology was conducted (Phares and Compas, 1992). It was noted then that fathers were dramatically under-represented in developmental research on psychopathology. Based on the existing studies, partic-ularly studies of children of clinically referred fathers and of nonreferred samples of children and their fathers, an impact of paternal psychopathology could be ascertained. Findings from studies of fathers of clinically referred children were stronger for fathers' effects on children's externalizing than internalizing problems. Most often the degree of risk associated with paternal psychopathology was comparable to that of maternal psychopathology. It was concluded that the presence of paternal psychopathology was a sufficient but not necessary condition for child or adolescent psychopathol-ogy. Phares (1992) also provided a comprehensive discussion of the multiple reasons why research on fathers with psychopathology is underrepresented in the developmental and clinical literature and made a number of recommendations for future research. An additional review of this literature can in found in Phares (1997). Despite these efforts to stimulate more interest in this important topic, research continues to lag. In addition to there being many fewer studies of fathers, the research that does exist focuses mainly on more distal aspects of parenting. For example, psychopathology or personality of the father is considered, but the study of actual interactions with the child are still quite rare. The research continues to mirror the more distant role many fathers play in the lives of their children and adolescents.

Culture and Psychopathology

An issue that has received relatively little attention pertains to the relations between culture, ethnicity, and psychopathology. Most of the research conducted is based on Western samples and perspec-tives. Some psychiatric disorders such as schizophrenia are thought to occur at similar rates across different cultures. However, symptoms may manifest themselves differently in different cultures and even in different ethnic and racial groups within a given culture. For example, differences in the nature of the hallucinations, delusions, dysphoric affect, and personality patterns of Black and White schizophrenics have been described (Chu, Sallach, Zakeria, and Klein, 1985). It is reasonable to infer (and important to study) potential differences in how parenting processes are impacted as well.

Earlier we noted that depression is two to three times more common in women than men, again based on studies of Western samples. While adult depressive disorders and syndromes are more prevalent in females than males in all cultures, the ratios differ markedly (Kleinman and Cohen, 1997). Depression in women in Santiago, Chile, for example, occurs at five times the rate as for men and may be linked to high levels of abuse and maltreatment experienced by these women. In China, the gender ratio is even more disproportionate. Moreover, women in China are at high risk for neurotic disorders, including neurasthenia, which has symptoms in common with both depressive and anxiety disorders. Somatic complaints are central to the experience of depression in several other cultures as well. Individuals who complain of headaches, weakness, or other aches and pains, rather than sadness or guilt, may not be diagnosed and treated for depression, particularly if seen by professionals from other cultures. There is increased recognition of these possibilities; for example, the *DSM-IV* (1994) provides a glossary of culture-bound syndromes that includes symptoms, sometimes observed in a particular cultural context, which have local names. However, this recognition has not yet been translated into the research process that would provide examination of the ways in which culturally based expressions of psychiatric symptoms become manifest in parenting processes.

Access to treatment and the existence of community support and resources for parenting also differs cross-culturally. Additionally, culture influences the extent to which extended family members are involved in childrearing. This is a very important variable to consider in cross-cultural work. Diffusion of childcare responsibilities (with substantial involvement of grandparents for example) could decrease the effect of parental psychopathology on parenting.

In contrast to Western cultures, females in China are more likely to commit suicide than males, with suicide described as a "normative" response for poverty-stricken rural females who have no accepted role in the social structure. Moreover, the relatively high rate of suicide in females in China not restricted to rural areas. In her novels and narratives, Tan (2001) has provided compelling accounts of cultural processes that may contribute to this form of self-destruction. Tan described her own first suicide attempt at age 6, her mother's constant suicidal threats, and the actual suicides of four female family members, including her grandmother, her mother having witnessed this event when she was 9 years old. The influence of ghosts plays a prominent role in Tan's explanation and understanding of intergenerational patterns of transmission of depression and suicidality in Chinese culture. The belief in her family and many others was that if you killed yourself, your ghost could come back and wreak havoc on those who had wronged you, including other family members. Suicidal threats, too, were linked to purported wrongs perpetrated by the children. Self-anger and guilt became part of an enduring depressive experience that would haunt one's existence. The ghosts were perceived as other wispy-edged relatives, frowning and shaking their heads.

The theme of being haunted by ghosts and their role in emotional suffering is deeply rooted in Chinese legends and mythology and has been articulated in the writings of other Chinese authors (e.g., Kingston, 1976). What might be viewed as a delusion or hallucination, indicative of psychosis within one cultural framework, may not be so in another. This illustrates one way in which the phenomenology of (the etiology of) depression may differ in different cultural contexts. Kingston described her mother as a champion talker who educated her children with "talk stories," which included myth, legend, family history, and ghost tales. These talking stories were double edged, enriching imagination but sowing seeds of depression as well. They also illustrate another potential transmission mechanism that is not culture specific, but may help to explain why females are at greater risk for depression than males.

Autobiographical memory, the internalization of scripts regarding early life experiences develop, in part, through parental verbal communications with children beginning in the first years of life

(Nelson, 1993). This is a little studied aspect of socialization that may have a bearing on the etiology and intergenerational transmission of depression. Ruminative coping (Nolen-Hoeksema, 1987) involves perseveration or dwelling on past negative events and views of the self. It is more characteristic of females than males, involves passive rather than active coping with distress, and is known to predict subsequent depressive episodes. The reasons why females are more likely than males to become sad and worried, and to develop an internalized focus on negative feelings and interpersonal problems are overdetermined and not explained by any single factor.

However, there is now a large body of literature on mother–child communications about emotions and emotional issues (e.g., Fivush, 1989, 1991; Reese and Fivush, 1993; Zahn-Waxler, Ridgeway, Denham, Usher, and Cole, 1993), that suggest ways in which young girls more than boys are drawn into a process of communication that is depressogenic in nature. Mothers talk more about emotions, providing greater detail and more elaboration with daughters than sons. Both depressed and well mothers talk more about negative emotions (e.g., sadness and distress) with their preschool daughters than sons (Zahn-Waxler et al., 1993), and depressed mothers talk more about negative emotions than well mothers. Thus, there would be more frequent occasions to internalize negative scripts, providing ready access to emotionally charged material. The nature and extent of such discussions would influence retrieveability, as those elements of events, reactivated or rehearsed through discussion become strengthened in memory (see Zahn-Waxler, 2000, for further details). The narratives of distressed caregivers may have profound implications beyond the transmission of information per se—they may shape some children's early inclinations to dwell on the more negative and painful aspects of life.

Mental Illness, Criminality, and Parenting

Another important issue concerns the intersect of mental illness and the justice system. When is a particular emotional or behavioral problem a mental health problem? When is it an illegal act or set of criminal behaviors punishable by law? When is it both and how does one deal with this interface? What are the diverse motives that come into play when harm is inflicted on others? How is this relevant to parenting? These are questions and dilemmas that have existed for all human societies at all points in time. They remain unresolved and probably unresolvable. But it is necessary to continue to address them in an effort to better understand the complex ways in adult behaviors are deviant, deviate from the norm, and affect offspring both in the short term and across generations. Overt and covert criminal behaviors, violent and nonviolent, are externalizing problems that "fit" the psychiatric diagnostic category of antisocial personality disorder. Child maltreatment, of course, represents a form of antisocial behavior. But research on the parenting of maltreating caregivers does not tend to incorporate a psychiatric/clinical perspective in efforts to understand the implications for socialization practices and children's development.

We have considered some of the ways in which antisocial personality disorder and behavior problems may affect parenting processes and compromise development of offspring. However, relatively little is known about the caregiving patterns of mothers at the extremes, in particular, women who are sociopathic and violent. What is known comes mainly in the form of case report, sometimes provided retrospectively by the offspring (who have survived) or biographical histories based on criminal records. Antisocial personality disorder is much more common in males than females. (American Psychiatric Association, 1994). Although few women engage in serious antisocial behavior, violent crimes in particular, a small minority do, and their children will be influenced by these activities.

Schone and Walker (2001) have provided an in-depth autobiographical account of a sociopathic mother, Sante Kimes, currently on trial with her son for the murder of a Manhatten philanthropist and having spent an entire life participating in criminal behavior and conning others. Of particular interest are the descriptions of her efforts to engage her two sons as accomplices in shoplifting, car thefts, and other illegal activities from an early age. Often she put them in harms way, for example, having set up an explosive device in their home in an arson attempt as part of an insurance scam, she sent one son back in to retrieve a folder. He barely escaped with his life. At the same time, she was fiercely protective and loved by her offspring, albeit in an ambivalent and deeply painful manner. In writing the memoir, Walker hoped it would help him cope with his past. It didn't, however, and he described growing up with the Kimeses as like walking through glue that you can never get off.

Another compelling account of sociopathic mothering can be found in the book '*Small Sacrifices*' (Rule, 1987). Diane Downs was characterizied as histrionic as well as antisocial, and had attempted to kill all three of her children in order to be with her boyfriend, who did not want her with the children. She engaged in other illegal activities as well. She was sufficiently charming and attractive that prior to the attempted killings (two of the three children survived) she was accepted into a program as a surrogate mother. She received national coverage as an early pioneer in surrogate mothering and impressed the reporters as especially emotionally mature—a testimony to the glibness and ease with which sociopathic individuals are able to charm others into false impressions. She, too, engaged in arson as a means to obtain money and participated in other small crimes and illegal activities as well.

Women with other psychiatric conditions kill their children, most notably mothers with severe postpartum depression, often with psychotic features. These "decisions" are not based on calculated, remorseless acts like those of Diane Downs, but rather appear to reflect a mental state of unmitigated despair and disordered thought. However, what one defines as mental illness, where one deemed not guilty of a criminal act by reason of insanity, another views as calculated and premeditated. There are no clear guidelines. We make these points, to emphasize the extreme ways in which parental psychopathology can affect parenting and the arbitrary ways in which it is parsed. It is also worth noting that infanticide is not necessarily linked to mental illness. Though less common than in the past, offspring in some cultures (particularly females) may be killed if they are a severe financial burden or if they interfere with the ability to have a male child (e.g., in China, with its one child per family rule). This process may begin even prior to birth. Selective (female) abortion also is practiced in some cultures where males are highly valued (Bumiller, 1990).

Most mothers with postpartum depression do not murder their children. Eighty percent of all new mothers experience the baby blues; 1 in 10 mothers are said to develop from this a full-blown clinical depression; and 1 in 1,000 develops psychosis, which is 16 times more common during the postpartum period than at any other point (Najman et al., 2000; O'Hara, 1987). Andrea Yates, who told the police officer who came to the home that she had drowned her five young children in the bathtub, was described as suffering from postpartum depression (Duggan, 2001). It had begun 2 years earlier after the birth of the fourth child and was eventually treated successfully with medication. Following the birth of her fifth child she relapsed into a severe depression. Although she did not respond as well to antidepressant drugs this time, she was not seen as a threat to the children. This mother could not differ more from Diane Downs, yet the mental instability of both had similar grave consequences for their children. The motives and consequences of major mental illness are incomprehensible to most people, who remain unaware of the symptoms of severe major depression, including psychotic depression and severe personality disorders that represent a breakdown of functioning.

There has been an increased scientific interest in postpartum depression in recent years (Murray and Cooper, 1997; Murray, Sinclair, Cooper, Ducournau, and Turner, 1999). To date, however, there have been few studies of prevention of depression in women, and there are no randomized controlled trials focusing on depression during pregnancy and the postpartum period. Longitudinal studies are needed to address many crucial questions about the course and effects of maternal depression, which in turn can inform approaches to preventive interventions with pregnant and postpartum women (NIMH Maternal Depression Roundtable, 2001). The issues of course are not unique to maternal depression, but are relevant to other psychiatric disorders or other aspects of maternal (parental) impairment that may or may not be couched explicitly within a psychopathology framework. This is also an important arena within which to consider cross-cultural issues, illustrated for example in research done in a South African settlement (Cooper et al., 1999). The rate of postpartum depression in Khayelitsha was around three times that found in British postpartum samples.

In conclusion, we are at the edge of a new era with enhanced potentials for reducing psychological suffering across generations. Promotion of healthy development will require major investment in helping parents to deal with problems that interfere with their capacity to optimize the quality of their interactions with their children. Although this is a universal issue that transcends class and culture, as we have seen here, it is particularly pertinent to parents plagued with mental health problems. Despite many scientific advances, much remains to be discovered, and advances will need to occur simultaneously on several societal, conceptual, and institutional fronts if the goals of helping to alleviate suffering and enhance the quality of life of caregivers and their offspring are to be more fully realized.

ACKNOWLEDGMENTS

We wish to thank Ann Brand and Marcia Slattery for their thoughtful and incisive comments on an early version of this chapter, Marc Bornstein for his encouragement and constructive feedback, and Eleanor Race for her assistance in the preparation of the manuscript.

REFERENCES

American Psychiatric Association. (1994). *Diagnostic and statistical manual of mental disorders* (4th ed.). Washington, DC: Author.

Andrews, B., Brown, G. W., and Creasy, L. (1990). Intergenerational links between psychiatric disorder in mothers and daughters: The role of parenting experiences. *Journal of Child Psychology and Psychiatry, 31*, 1115–1129.

Anthony, E. J. (1986). Terrorizing attacks on children by psychotic parents. *Journal of the American Academy of Child Psychiatry, 25*, 326–335.

Barnett, B., Schaafsma, M. F., Gusman, A. M., and Parker, G. B. (1991). Maternal anxiety: A 5-year review of an intervention study. *Journal of Child Psychology and Psychiatry and Allied Disciplines, 32*, 423–438.

Baron, R. M., and Kenny, D. A. (1986). The moderator–mediator variable distinction in social psychological research: Conceptual, strategic, and statistical considerations. *Journal of Personality and Social Psychology, 51*, 1173–1182.

Bernstein, G. A., and Borchardt, C. M. (1991). Anxiety disorders of childhood and adolescence: A critical review. *Journal of the American Academy of Child and Adolescent Psychiatry, 30*, 519–532.

Biederman, J., Munir, K., and Knee, D. (1987). Conduct and oppositional disorder in clinically referred children with attention deficit disorder: A controlled family study. *Journal of the American Academy of Child and Adolescent Psychiatry, 26*, 724–727.

Biringen, Z. C. (1990). Direct observation of maternal sensitivity and dyadic interactions in the home: Relations to maternal thinking. *Developmental Psychology, 26*, 278–284.

Bosquet, M., and Egeland, B. (2000). Predicting parenting behaviors from antisocial practices content scale scores of the MMPI-2 administered during pregnancy. *Journal of Personality Assessment, 74*, 146–162.

Brockington, I. (1996). *Motherhood and mental health* (p. 612). Oxford, England: Oxford University Press.

Breslau, N., Davis, G. C., and Prabucki, K. (1987). Searching for evidence on the validity of generalized anxiety disorder: Psychopathology in children of anxious mothers. *Psychiatry Research, 20*, 285–297.

Breznitz, S. (1985). Chores as a buffer against risk in interaction. *Schizophrenia Bulletin, 11*, 257–360.

Bumiller, E. (1990). *May you be the mothers of a hundred sons: A journey among the women of India.* New York: Ballentine.

Burman, B., Mednick, S., Machon, R., Parnas, J., and Schulsinger, F. (1987). Children at high risk for schizophrenia: Parent and offspring perceptions of family relationships. *Journal of Abnormal Psychology, 96*, 364–366.

Cannon, T. D., Mednick, S. A., Parnas, J., Schulsinger, F., Praestholm, J., and Verstergaard, A. (1993). Developmental brain abnormalities in the offspring of schizophrenic mothers: I. Contributions of genetic and perinatal factors. *Archives of General Psychiatry, 50*, 551–564.

Cannon, T. D., Mednick, S. A., Parnas, J., Schulsinger, F., Praestholm, J., and Verstergaard, A. (1994). Developmental brain abnormalities in the offspring of schizophrenic mothers: II. Structural brain characteristics of schizophrenia and schizotypal personality disorder. *Archives of General Psychiatry, 51*, 955–962.

Capps, L., Sigman, M., Sena, R., Henker, B., and Whalen, C. (1996). Fear, anxiety and perceived control in children of agoraphobic parents. *Journal of Child Psychology and Psychiatry and Allied Disciplines, 37*, 445–452.

Cassidy, B., Zoccolillo, M., and Hughes, S. (1996). Psychopathology in adolescent mothers and its effects on mother–infant interactions: A pilot study. *Canadian Journal of Psychiatry, 41*, 379–384.

Chilcoat, H., Breslau, N., and Anthony, J. C. (1996). Potential barriers to parent monitoring: Social disadvantage, marital status, and maternal psychiatric disorder. *Journal of the American Academy of Child and Adolescent Psychiatry, 35*, 1573–1682.

Chorpita, B. F., and Barlow, D. H. (1998). The development of anxiety: The role of control in the early environment. *Psychological Bulletin, 124*, 3–21.

Chu, C., Sallach, H. S., Zakeria, S. A., and Klein, H. E. (1985). Differences in psychopathology between Black and White schizophrenics. *International Journal of Social Psychiatry, 31*, 252–257.

Cicchetti, D., Ganiban, J., and Barnett, D. (1991). Contributions from the study of high-risk populations to understanding the development of emotion regulation. In J. Garber and K. Dodge (Eds.), *The development of emotion regulation and dysregulation. Cambridge studies in social and emotional development* (pp. 15–48). New York: Cambridge University Press.

Clark, D. B., Moss, H. B., Kirisci, L., Mezzich, A. C., Miles, R., and Ott, P. (1997). Psychopathology in preadolescent sons of fathers with substance use disorders. *Journal of the American Academy of Child and Adolescent Psychiatry, 36*, 495–502.

Cohn, J., Campbell, S. B., Matias, R., and Hopkins, J. (1990). Face-to-face interactions of postpartum depressed and nondepressed mother–infant pairs at 2 months. *Developmental Psychology, 26*, 15–23.

Cooper, P. J., Tomlinson, M., Swartz, L., Woolgar, M., Murray, L., and Molteno, C. (1999). Postpartum depression and the mother–infant relationship in a South African peri-urban settlement. *British Journal of Psychiatry, 175*, 554–558.

Cummings, E. M., and Davies, P. T. (1994). Maternal depression and child development. *Journal of Child Psychology and Psychiatry, 35*, 73–112.

Cummings, E. M., Davies, P. T., and Campbell, S. B. (2000). Applications of developmental psychopathology: Parental depression, families, and children's development. In *Developmental psychopathology and family process: Theory, research, and clinical implications* (pp. 299–340). New York: Guilford.

Davenport, Y., Zahn-Waxler, C., Adland, M., and Mayfield, A. (1984). Early rearing practices in bipolar families. *American Journal of Psychiatry, 141*, 230–235.

D'Angelo, E. J. (1986). Security of attachment in infants with schizophrenic, depressed, and unaffected mothers. *The Journal of Genetic Psychology, 147*, 421–422.

Davis, B., Sheeber, L., Hops, H., and Tildesley, E. (2000). Adolescent responses to depressive parental behaviors in problem-solving interactions: Implications for depressive symptoms. *Journal of Abnormal Child Psychology, 5*, 451–465.

Del Carmen, R., Pedersen, F. A., Huffman, L. C., and Bryan, Y. E. (1993). Dyadic distress management predicts subsequent security of attachment. *Infant Behavior and Development, 16*(2), 131–147.

DeMulder, E. K., Tarullo, L. B., Klimes-Dougan, B., Free, K., and Radke-Yarrow, M. (1995). Personality disorders of affectively ill mothers: Links to maternal behavior. *Journal of Personality Disorders, 9*, 199–212.

Denham, S., Workman, E., Cole, P. M., Weissbrod, C., Kendziora, K., and Zahn-Waxler, C. (2000). Prediction of externalizing behavior problems from early to middle childhood: The role of parental socialization and emotion expression. *Development and Psychopathology, 12*, 23–45.

Dix, T. (1991). The affective organization of parenting: Adaptive and maladaptive processes. *Psychological Bulletin, 110*, 3–25.

Dohrenwend, B. P. (1990). Socioeconomic status (SES) and psychiatric disorders: Are the issues still compelling? *Social Psychiatry and Psychiatric Epidemiology, 25*, 41–47.

Downey, G., and Coyne, J. C. (1990). Children of depressed parents: An integrative review. *Psychological Bulletin, 10*, 50–76.

Duggan, P. (2001, June 2). "She wasn't in the right frame of mind." *The Washington Post*, p. 2.

Dumas, J. E., Gibson, J. A., and Albin, J. B. (1989). Behavioral correlates of maternal depressive symptomatology in conduct-disorder children. *Journal of Consulting and Clinical Psychology, 57*, 516–521.

Elder, G. H., Caspi, A., and Downey, G. (1983). Problem behavior in family relationships: A multigenerational analysis. In A. Sorenson, F. Weinert, and L. Sherrod (Eds.), *Human development: Interdisciplinary perspective* (pp. 93–118). Hillsdale, NJ: Lawrence Erlbaum Associates.

Ellis, B. J., and Garber, J. (2000). Psychosocial antecedents of variation in girls' pubertal timing: Maternal depression, stepfather presence, and marital and family stress. *Child Development, 71*, 485–501.

Elster, A. B., Lamb, M. E., and Tavare, J. (1987). Association between behavioral and school problems and fatherhood in a national sample of adolescent youths. *Journal of Pediatrics, 111*, 932–936.

Feldman, R., Greenbaum, C. W., Mayes, L. C., and Erlich, S. H. (1997). Change in mother-infant interactive behavior: Relations to change in the mother, the infant, and the social context. *Infant Behavior and Development, 20*, 151–163.

Feldman, R., and Guttman, H. A. (1984). Families of borderline patients: Literal-minded parents, borderline parents, and parental protectiveness. *American Journal of Psychiatry, 141*, 1392–1396.

Field, T., Healy, B., Goldstein, S., and Guthertz, M. (1990). Behavior state matching and synchrony in mother–infant interactions of nondepressed versus depressed dyads. *Developmental Psychology, 31*, 358–363.

Fivush, R. (1989). Exploring sex differences in the emotional content of mother–child conversations about the past. *Sex Roles, 20*, 675–691.

Fivush, R. (1991). Gender and emotion in mother–child conversations about the past. *Journal of Narrative and Life History, 1*, 325–341.

Fowles, D. C. (1992). Schizophrenia: Diathesis-stress revisited. *Annual Review of Psychology, 43*, 303–336.

Frick, P. J., Lahey, B. B., Loeber, R., Stouthamer-Loeber, M., Christ, M. G., and Hanson, K. (1992). Familial risk factors to oppositional defiant disorder and conduct disorder: Parental psychopathology and maternal parenting. *Journal of Consulting and Clinical Psychology, 60*, 49–55.

Gabbard, G., and Goodwin, F. (1996). Integrating biological and psychosocial perspectives. *American Psychiatric Press Review of Psychiatry, 15*, 527–548.

Gamer, E., Gallant, D., and Grunebaum, H. (1976). Children of psychotic mothers: An evaluation of 1-year-olds on a test of object permanence. *Archives of General Psychiatry, 33*, 311–317.

Garmezy, N. (1987). Stress, competence, and development: Continuities in the study of schizophrenic adults, children vulnerable to psychopathology, and the search for stress-resistant children. *American Journal of Orthopsychiatry, 57*, 159–174.

Ge, X., Conger, R. D., Cadoret, R. J., Neiderhiser, J. M., Yates, W., Troughton, E., and Stewart, M. A. (1996). The developmental interface between nature and nurture: A mutual influence model of child antisocial behavior and parent behaviors. *Developmental Psychology, 32*, 574–589.

Gelfand, D., and Teti, D. (1990). The effects of maternal depression on children. *Clinical Psychology Review, 10*, 329–353.

Geller, J., and Johnson, C. (1995). Depressed mood and child conduct problems: Relationships to mothers' attributions for their own and their children's experiences. *Child and Family Behavior Therapy, 17*, 19–34.

Goodman, S. H. (1987). Emory University project on children of disturbed parents. *Schizophrenia Bulletin, 13*, 411–423.

Goodman, S. H., Adamson, L. B., Riniti, J., and Cole, S. (1994). Mothers' expressed attitudes: Associations with maternal depression and children's self-esteem and psychopathology. *Journal of the American Academy of Child and Adolescent Psychiatry, 33*, 1265–1274.

Goodman, S. H., and Brumley, H. E. (1990). Schizophrenic and depressed mothers: Relational deficits in parenting. *Developmental Psychology, 26*, 31–39.

Goodman, S. H., and Gotlib, I. H. (1999). Risk for psychopathology in the children of depressed mothers: A developmental model for understanding mechanisms of transition. *Psychological Review, 106*, 458–490.

Gotlib, I. H., and Avison, W. R. (1995). Children at risk for psychopathology. In C. G. Costello (Ed.), *Basic issues in psychopathology* (pp. 271–319). New York: Guilford.

Gotlib, I. H., and Hooley, J. M. (1988). Depression and marital distress: Current status and future directions. In S. Duck, D. F. Hay, S. E. Hobfoll, W. Ickes, and B. M. Montgomery (Eds.), *Handbook of personal relationships: Theory, research, and interventions* (pp. 543–570). Chichester, England: Wiley.

Gottesman, I., and Shields, J. (1982). *Schizophrenia the epigenetic puzzle*. Cambridge, England: Cambridge University Press.

Grunebaum, H., Cohler, B. J., Kauffman, C., and Gallant, D. (1978). Children of depressed and schizophrenic mothers. *Child Psychiatry and Human Development, 8*, 219–228.

Grunebaum, H., Weiss, J. L., Cohler, B. J., Hartman, C. R., and Gallant, D. H. (1975). *Mentally ill mothers and their children*. Chicago: University of Chicago Press.

Hammen, C. (1991a). *Depression runs in families: The social context of risk and resilience in children of depressed mothers*. New York: Springer-Verlag.

Hammen, C. (1991b). Generation of stress in the course of unipolar depression. *Journal of Abnormal Psychology, 100*, 555–561.

Hammen, C., Burge, D., and Adrian, C. (1991). Timing of mother and child depression in a longitudinal study of children at risk. *Journal of Consulting and Clinical Psychology, 59*, 341–345.

Hammen, C., Burge, D., Burney, E., and Adrian, C. (1990). Longitudinal study of diagnoses in children of women with unipolar and bipolar affective disorder. *Archives of General Psychiatry, 47*, 1112–1117.

Hammen, C., Burge, D., and Stansbury, K. (1990). Relationship of mother and child variables to child outcomes in a high-risk sample: A causal modeling analysis. *Developmental Psychology, 26*, 24–30.

Hans, S. L., and Marcus, J. (1988). A process model for the development of schizophrenia. *Psychiatry, 50*, 631–370.

Hanson, D. R., Gottesman, I. I., and Heston, L. L. (1976). Some possible childhood indicators of adult schizophrenia inferred from children of schizophrenics. *British Journal of Psychiatry, 129*, 142–154.

Higgins, J., Gore, R., Gutkind, D., Mednick, S. A., Parnas, J., and Schulsinger, F. (1997). Effects of child-rearing by schizophrenic mothers: A 25-year follow-up. *Acta Psychiatrica Scandinavica, 96*, 402–404.

Hipwell, A. E., and Kumar, R. (1996). Maternal psychopathology and prediction of outcome based on mother–infant interaction ratings (BMIS). *British Journal of Psychiatry, 169*, 655–661.

Holmbeck, G. N. (1997). Toward terminological, conceptual and statistical clarity in the study of mediators and moderators: Examples from the child-clinical and pediatric psychology literatures. *Journal of Consulting and Clinical Psychology, 4*, 599–610.

Hops, H., Biglan, A., Sherman, L., Arthur, J., Friedman, L., and Osteen, V. (1987). Home observations of family interactions of depressed women. *Journal of Consulting and Clinical Psychology, 55*, 341–346.

Huesmann, L. R., Eron, L. D., Lefkowitz, M. M., and Walder, L. O. (1984). Stability of aggression over time and generations. *Developmental Psychology, 20*, 1120–1134.

Imbesi, L. (1999). The making of a narcissist. *Clinical Social Work Journal, 27*, 41–54.

Johnson, J. G., Cohen, P., Dohrenwend, B. P., Link, B. G., and Brook, J. (1999). A longitudinal investigation of social causation and social selection processes involved in the association between socioeconomic status and psychiatric disorders. *Journal of Abnormal Psychology, 108*, 490–499.

Kazdin, A. E. (1987). Treatment of antisocial behavior in children: Current status and future directions. *Psychological Bulletin, 102*, 187–203.

Kendrick, D. T., and Funder, D. C. (1988). Profiting from controversy: Lessons from the person-situation debate. *American Psychologist, 43*, 23–35.

Kessler, R. C., Berglund, P. A., Foster, C. L., Saunders, W. B., Stang, P. E., and Walters, E. E. (1997). Social consequences of psychiatric disorders: II. Teenage parenthood. *American Journal of Psychiatry, 154*, 1405–1411.

Ketterlinus, R., Lamb, M. E., and Nitz, K. A. (1994). Adolescent nonsexual and sex-related problem behaviors: Their prevalence, consequences, and co-occurrence. In R. D. Ketterlinus and M. E. Lamb (Eds.), *Adolescent problem behaviors: Issues and research* (pp. 17–39). Hillsdale, NJ: Lawrence Erlbaum Associates.

Kingston, M. H. (1976). *The woman warrior: Memoirs of a girlhood among ghosts.* New York: Knopf.

Klimes-Dougan, B., and Bolger, A. (1998). Coping with maternal depressed affect and depression: Adolescent children of depressed and well mothers. *Journal of Youth and Adolescence, 27*, 1–15.

Kleinman, A., and Cohen, A. (1997, March). Psychiatry's global challenge. *Scientific American*, 86–89.

Kochanska, G., Kuczynski, L., Radke-Yarrow, M., and Welsh, J. (1987). Resolutions of control episodes between well and affectively ill mothers and their young children. *Journal of Abnormal Child Psychology, 15*, 441–456.

Kuperman, S., Schlosser, S. S., Lidral, J., and Reich, W. (1999). Relationship of child psychopathology to parental alcoholism and antisocial personality disorder. *Journal of the American Academy of Child and Adolescent Psychiatry, 38*, 686–692.

Lahey, B. B., Hartdagen, S. E., Frick, P. J., McBurnett, K., Connor, R., and Hynd, G. W. (1988). Conduct disorder: Parsing the confounded relation to parental divorce and antisocial personality. *Journal of Abnormal Psychology, 97*, 334–337.

Lahey, B. B., Loeber, R., Hart, E. L., Frick, P. J., Applegate, B., Zhang, Q., Green, S. M., and Russo, M. F. (1995). Four-year longitudinal study of conduct disorder in boys: Patterns and predictors of persistence. *Journal of Abnormal Psychology, 104*, 83–93.

Lahey, B. B., Piacentini, J. C., McBurnett, K., Stone, P., Hartdagen, S., and Hynd, G. (1988). Psychopathology in the parents of children with conduct disorder and hyperactivity. *Journal of the American Academy of Child and Adolescent Psychiatry, 27*, 163–170.

Lahey, B. B., Russo, M. F., Walker, J. L., and Piacentini, J. C. (1989). Personality characteristics of the mothers of children with disruptive behavior disorders. *Journal of Consulting and Clinical Psychology, 57*, 512–515.

Lanquetot, R. (1984). First person account: Confessions of the daughter of a schizophrenic. *Schizophrenia Bulletin, 10*, 467–471.

Laucht, M., Esser, G., and Schmidt, M. H. (1994). Parental mental disorder and early child development. *European Child and Adolescent Psychiatry, 3*, 125–137.

Lerman, R. (1993). A national profile of young unwed fathers. In R. Lerman and T. Ooms (Eds.), *Young unwed fathers: Changing roles and emerging policies* (pp. 27–51). Philadelphia: Temple University Press.

Loeber, R., and Dishion, T. (1983). Early predictors of male delinquency: A review. *Psychological Bulletin, 94*, 68–99.

Lytton, H. (1990). Child and parent effects in boys' conduct disorder: A reinterpretation. *Developmental Psychology, 26*, 683–697.

Maccoby, E. E., and Martin, J. A. (1983). Socialization in the context of the family: Parent–child interaction. In P. H. Mussen (Ed.), *Handbook of child psychology: Socialization, personality and social development* (pp. 1–102). New York: Wiley.

Manassis, K., Bradley, S., Goldberg, S., Hood, J., and Swinson, R. P. (1995). Behavioural inhibition, attachment and anxiety in children of mothers with anxiety disorders. *Canadian Journal of Psychiatry, 40*, 87–92.

Mander, A. J., Norton, B., and Hoare, P. (1987). The effect of maternal psychotic illness on a child. *British Journal of Psychiatry, 151*, 848–850.

Marcus, J., Hans, S. L., Nagler, S., Auerbach, J. G., Mirsky, A. F., and Aubrey, A. (1987). Review of the NIMH Israeli Kibbutz-city study and the Jerusalem infant development study. *Schizophrenia Bulletin, 13*, 425–438.

McCord, W., McCord, J., and Howard, A. (1963). Familial correlates of aggression in nondelinquent male children. *Journal of Abnormal and Social Psychology, 62*, 79–93.

McNeil, T. F., Naslund, B., Persson-Blennow, I., and Kaij, L. (1985). Offspring of women with nonorganic psychosis: Mother-infant interaction at three-and-a-half and six months of age. *Acta Psychiatrica Scandinavica, 71*, 551–558.

Merikangas, K. R., Avenevoli, S., Dierker, L., and Grillon, C. (1999). Vulnerability factors among children at risk for anxiety disorders. *Biological Psychiatry, 46*, 1523–1535.

Morrison, J. R., and Stewart, M. A. (1971). A family study of the hyperactive syndrome. *Biological Psychiatry, 3*, 189–195.

Murray, L. (1992). The impact of postnatal depression on infant development. *Journal of Child Psychology and Psychiatry, 33*, 543–561.

Murray, L., and Cooper, P. J. (1997). *Postpartum depression and child development.* New York: Guilford.

Murray, L., Sinclair, D., Cooper, P., Ducournau, P., and Turner, P. (1999). The socioemotional development of children of postnatally depressed mothers. *Journal of Child Psychology and Psychiatry and Allied Disciplines, 40*, 1259–1271.

Najman, J. M., Andersen, M. J., Bor, W., O'Callaghan, M. J., and Williams, G. M. (2000). Postnatal depression—myth and reality: Maternal depression before and after the birth of a child. *Social Psychiatry and Psychiatric Epidemiology, 35,* 19–27.

Naslund, B., Persson-Blennow, I., McNeil, T., Kaij, L., and Malmquist-Larsson, A. (1984a). Offspring of women with nonorganic psychosis: Fear of strangers during the first year of life. *Acta Psychiatrica Scandinavica, 69,* 435–444.

Naslund, B., Persson-Blennow, I., McNeil, T., Kaij, L., and Malmquist-Larsson, A. (1984b). Offspring of women with nonorganic psychosis: Infant attachment to the mother at one year of age. *Acta Psychiatrica Scandinavica, 69,* 231–241.

Nelson, K. (1993). The psychological and social origins of autobiographical memory. *Psychological Science, 4,* 7–14.

Nigg, J. T., and Hinshaw, S. P. (1998). Parent personality traits and psychopathology associated with antisocial behaviors in childhood attention-deficit hyperactivity disorder. *Journal of Child Psychology and Psychiatry and Allied Disciplines, 39,* 145–159.

NIMH Maternal Depression Roundtable. (2001). *Prevention and treatment of depression in pregnancy and the postpartum period.* http://www.nimh.nih.gov/wmhc/mat_depsum.cfm

Nolen-Hoeksema, S. (1987). Sex differences in unipolar depression: Evidence and theory. *Psychological Bulletin, 101,* 257–282.

Nover, A., Shore, M. F., Timberlake, E. M., and Greenspan, S. I. (1984). The relationship of maternal perception and maternal behavior: A study of normal mothers and their infants. *American Journal of Orthopsychiatry, 54,* 210–223.

O'Hara, M. W. (1987). Post-partum "blues", depression, and psychosis: A review. *Journal of Psychosomatic Obstetrics and Gynecology, 7*(3), 205–227.

Parnas, J. (1985). Mates of schizophrenic mothers: A study of assortative mating from the American-Danish high risk project. *British Journal of Psychiatry, 146,* 490–497.

Parnas, J., Teasdale, T. W., and Schulsinger, H. (1985). Institutional rearing and diagnostic outcome in children of schizophrenic mothers. *Archives of General Psychiatry, 42,* 762–769.

Patterson, G. R., and Capaldi, D. M. (1991). Antisocial parents: Unskilled and vulnerable. In P. A. Cowan and E. M. Hetherington (Eds.), *Family transitions. Advances in family research series* (pp. 195–218). Hillsdale, NJ: Lawrence Erlbaum Associates.

Patterson, G. R., and Dishion, T. J. (1988). Multilevel family process: Traits, interactions and relationships. In R. A. Hinde and J. Stevenson-Hinde (Eds.), *Relationships within families: Mutual influences* (pp. 283–310). Oxford, England: Clarendon.

Pfiffner, L., McBurnett, K., Lahey, B. B., Loeber, R., Green, S., and Frick, P. J. (1999). Association of parental psychopathology to the comorbid disorders of boys with attention deficit–hyperactivity disorder. *Journal of Consulting and Clinical Psychology, 67,* 881–893.

Phares, V. (1992). Where's poppa? The relative lack of attention to the role of fathers in child and adolescent psychopathology. *American Psychologist, 47,* 656–664.

Phares, V. (1997). Psychological adjustment, maladjustment, and father–child relationships. In M. E. Lamb (Ed.), *The role of the father in child development* (3rd ed., pp. 261–283). New York: Wiley.

Phares, V., and Compas, B. E. (1992). The role of fathers in child and adolescent psychopathology: Make room for daddy. *Psychological Bulletin, 111,* 387–412.

Pierpont, C. R. (2000). *Passionate minds.* New York: Knopf Vintage.

Radke-Yarrow, M. (1998). *Children of depressed mothers.* Cambridge, England: Cambridge University Press.

Radke-Yarrow, M., Cummings, E. M., Kuczynski, L., and Chapman, M. (1985). Patterns of attachment in two- and three-year-olds in normal families and families with parental depression. *Child Development, 56,* 884–893.

Ragins, N., Schachter, J., and Elmer, E. (1975). Infants and children at risk for schizophrenia: Environmental and developmental observations. *Journal of the American Academy of Child Psychiatry, 14,* 150–177.

Reese, E., and Fivush, R. (1993). Parental styles of talking about the past. *Developmental Psychology, 29,* 596–606.

Richters, J. E. (1992). Depressed mothers as informants about their children: A critical review of the evidence for distortion. *Psychological Bulletin, 112,* 485–499.

Rieder, R., and Nichols, P. (1979). Offspring of schizophrenics III: Hyperactivity and neurological soft signs. *Archives of General Psychiatry, 36,* 665–674.

Riordan, D., Appleby, L., and Faragher, B. (1999). Mother–infant interaction in post-partum women with schizophrenia and affective disorders. *Psychological Medicine, 29,* 991–995.

Robins, L. N., and Earls, F. (1986). A program for preventing antisocial behavior for high risk infants and preschoolers: A research perspective. In R. Hough, P. Gongola, V. Brown, and S. Goldston (Eds.), *Psychiatric epidemiology and prevention: The possibilities* (pp. 73–83). Los Angeles: Neuropsychiatric Institute.

Robins, L. N., West, P. A., and Herjanic, B. L. (1975). Arrests and delinquency in two generations: A study of black urban families and their children. *Journal of Child Psychology and Psychiatry, 16,* 125–140.

Rogosch, F. A., Mowbray, C. T., and Bogat, G. A. (1992). Determinants of parenting attitudes in mothers with severe psychopathology. *Development and Psychopathology, 4,* 469–487.

Rosenthal, D. (1970). *Genetic theory and abnormal behavior.* New York: McGraw-Hill.

Rule, A. (1987). *Small sacrifices.* New York: Penguin.

Rutter, M. (1996). Connections between child and adult psychopathology. *European Child and Adolescent Psychiatry, 5*, 4–7.

Rutter, M., and Quinton, D. (1984). Parental psychiatric disorder: Effects on children. *Psychological Medicine, 14*, 853–880.

Sameroff, A., and Seifer, R. (1990). Early contributors to developmental risk. In J. E. Rolf and A. S. Masten (Eds.), *Risk and protective factors in the development of psychopathology* (pp. 52–66). New York: Cambridge University Press.

Sameroff, A., Seifer, R., and Zax, M. (1982). Early development of children at risk for emotional disorder. *Monographs of the Society for Research in Child Development, 47*, 1–82.

Sameroff, A., Seifer, R., Zax, M., and Barocas, R. (1987). Early indicators of developmental risk: Rochester longitudinal study. *Schizophrenia Bulletin, 13*, 383–394.

Schone, M., and Walker, K. (2001). *Son of a grifter: The twisted tale of Sante and Kenny Kimes, the most notorious con artists in America: A memoir by the other son.* New York: Morrow/Avon.

Schubert, E. W., Blennow, G., and McNeil, T. (1996). Wakefulness and arousal in neonates born to women with schizophrenia: Diminished arousal and its association with neurological deviations. *Schizophrenia Research, 22*, 49–59.

Seeman, M. V. (1996). The mother with schizophrenia. In M. Geopfert, J. Webster, and M. V. Seeman (Eds.), *Parental psychiatric disorder: Distressed parents and their families* (pp. 190–200). New York: Cambridge University Press.

Silverman, W. K., Cerny, J. A., and Nelles, W. B. (1988). The familial influence in anxiety disorders: Studies on the offspring of patients with anxiety disorders. In B. B. Lahey and A. E. Kazdin (Eds.), *Advances in clinical child psychology* (Vol. 11, pp. 223–248). New York: Plenum.

Silverton, L. (1988). Crime and the schizophrenia spectrum: A diathesis-stress model. *Acta Psyhiatrica Scandinavica, 78*, 72–81.

Siqueland, L., Kendall, P. C., and Steinberg, L. (1996). Anxiety in children: Perceived family environments and observed family interaction. *Journal of Clinical Child Psychology, 25*, 225–237.

Skagerlind, L., Perris, C., and Eisemann, M. (1996). Perceived parental rearing behaviour in patients with a schizophrenic disorder and its relationship to aspects of the course of the illness. *Acta Psychiatrica Scandinavica, 93*, 403–406.

Snellen, M., Mack, K., and Trauer, T. (1999). Schizophrenia, mental state, and mother–infant interaction: Examining the relationship. *Australian and New Zealand Journal of Psychiatry, 33*, 902–911.

Sobel, D. E. (1961). Infant mortality and malformations in children of schizophrenic women. *Psychiatric Quarterly, 32*, 60–65.

Sroufe, A., and Rutter, M. (1984). The domain of developmental psychopathology. *Child Development, 55*, 17–29.

Stabenau, J. R., and Pollin, W. (1993). Heredity and environment in schizophrenia, revisited: The contribution of twin and high-risk studies. *Journal of Nervous and Mental Disease, 181*, 290–297.

Stein, A., Murray, L., Cooper, P., and Fairburn, C. G. (1996). Infant growth in the context of maternal eating disorders and maternal depression: A comparative study. *Psychological Medicine, 26*, 569–574.

Stein, A., Wooley, H., Cooper, S. D., and Fairburn, C. G. (1994). An observational study of mothers with eating disorders and their infants. *Journal of Child Psychology and Psychiatry and Allied Disciplines, 35*, 733–748.

Stein, A., Woolley, H., and McPherson, K. (1999). Conflict between mothers with eating disorders and their infants during mealtimes. *British Journal of Psychiatry, 175*, 455–461.

Tan, A. (2001). *Writers on writing: Family ghosts hoard secrets that bewitch the living.* The New York Times, on the Web: http://www.nytimes.com, February 26, 2001.

Thomas, A., Forehand, R., and Neighbors, B. (1995). Change in maternal depressive mood: Unique contributions to adolescent functioning over time. *Adolescence, 30*, 43–52.

Tsuang, M. (2000). Schizophrenia: Genes and environment. *Biological Psychiatry, 47*, 210–220.

Turner, S. M., Beidel, D. C., and Costello, A. (1987). Psychopathology in the offspring of anxiety disorders patients. *Journal of Consulting and Clinical Psychology, 55*, 229–235.

Vartiovaara, A., Maekelae, S., and Pykaelaeinen, R. (1990). Effects of parental schizophrenia on children's mental health. *Psychiatria Fennica, 21*, 87–103.

Walker, E. F., Cudeck, R., Mednick, A., and Schulsinger, F. (1981). Effects of parental absence and institutionalization on the development of clinical symptoms in high-risk children. *Acta Psychiatrica Scandinavica, 63*, 95–109.

Walker, E. F., and Diforio, D. (1997). Schizophrenia: A neural diathesis-stress model. *Psychological Review, 104*, 667–685.

Walker, E. F., Diforio, D., and Baum, K. (1999). Developmental neuropathology and the precursors of schizophrenia. *Acta Psychiatrica Scandinavica, 99*, 12–19.

Walker, E., Hoppes, E., Mednick, S., Emory, E., and Schulsinger, F. (1981). Environmental factors related to schizophrenia in psychophysiologically labile high-risk males. *Journal of Abnormal Psychology, 49*, 313–320.

Watt, N., Anthony, J. A., Wynne, L. C., and Rolf, J. E. (Eds.). (1984). *Children at risk for schizophrenia: A longitudinal perspective.* Cambridge, England: Cambridge University Press.

Webster, J. (1992). Split in two: Experiences of the children of schizophrenic mothers. *British Journal of Social Work, 22*, 309–329.

Weissman, M. M., and Paykel, E. S. (1974). *The depressed woman.* Chicago: University of Chicago Press.

Weissman, M. M., Paykel, E. S., and Klerman, G. L. (1972). The depressed woman as a mother. *Social Psychiatry, 7*, 98–108.

Whaley, S. E., Pinto, A., and Sigman, M. (1999). Characterizing interactions between anxious mothers and their children. *Journal of Consulting and Clinical Psychology, 67*, 826–836.

Whisman, M. A. (2000). Marital distress and depression: Findings from community and clinical studies. In S. R. H. Beach (Ed.), *Marital and family processes in depression: A scientific foundation for clinical practice* (pp. 3–24). Washington, DC: American Psychological Association.

White, C., and Barrowclough, C. (1998). Depressed and non-depressed mothers with problematic preschoolers: Attributions for child behaviours. *British Journal of Clinical Psychology*, 37, 385–398.

Yoshida, K., Marks, M. N., Craggs, M., Smith, B., and Kumar, R. (1999). Sensorimotor and cognitive development of infants of mothers with schizophrenia. *British Journal of Psychiatry*, 175, 380–387.

Zahn-Waxler, C. (2000). The development of empathy, guilt and internalization of distress: Implications for gender differences in internalizing and externalizing problems. In R. Davidson (Ed.), *Anxiety, depression, and emotion: Wisconsin symposium on emotion* (pp. 222–265). New York/Oxford, England: Oxford University Press.

Zahn-Waxler, C., Iannotti, R. J., Cummings, E. M., and Denham, S. (1990). Antecedents of problem behaviors in children of depressed mothers. *Development and Psychopathology*, 2, 271–291.

Zahn-Waxler, C., Klimes-Dougan, B., and Slattery, M. J. (2000). Internalizing problems of childhood and adolescence: Prospects, pitfalls and progress in understanding the development of anxiety and depression. *Development and Psychopathology*, 12, 443–466.

Zahn-Waxler, C., Ridgeway, D., Denham, S., Usher, B., and Cole, P. (1993). Pictures of infants' emotions: A task for assessing mothers' and young children's verbal communications about affect. In R. Emde, J. Osofsky, and P. Butterfield (Eds.), The IFEEL pictures: A new instrument for interpreting emotions. *Clinical Infant Report Series of the Zero to Three/National Center for Clinical Infant Programs* (pp. 217–236). Madison, CT: International Universities Press, Inc.

Zubin, J., and Spring, B. (1977). Vulnerability—a new view of schizophrenia. *Journal of Abnormal Psychology*, 86, 103–126.

Zuckerman, B. S., and Beardslee, W. R. (1987). Maternal depression: A concern for pediatricians. *Pediatrics*, 79, 110–117.

APPENDIX A

Ms. Karen Scaird brings her 5-year-old girl, Lilly, to her first morning of kindergarten. The teacher smiles and says hello to Lilly. Lilly takes a small step back toward her mother. Ms. Scaird's brow is furrowed and she speaks in a hushed, concerned tone: "I think she's scared—first day and all. I mean, she was fine in preschool but it took a long time for her to feel okay there. Do you have my home number handy? I'm going to sit by the phone today just in case you need me. Oh no—I have to go to the bank. Well, so I'll be out for a few minutes but I'll head straight back home after that. Just be sure that she drinks from the water fountain. She sometimes forgets to and becomes dehydrated." The teacher assures Ms. Scaird that Lilly is in good hands, telling her not to worry about a thing. Ms. Scaird turns to Lilly to say good-bye. Lilly is serious and quiet but does sneak a glance at some children building a tower with brightly colored blocks. Mrs. Scaird says, "Good-bye sweetie, Mommy will see you in just a few hours. And if you need me, ask the teacher." She gives Lilly a hug and a kiss, then watches as the teacher leads Lilly toward the other children. Lilly looks back and Ms. Scaird asks her if she needs another hug. Lilly returns to her mother and says she does not want her to leave.

  This mother appears to be struggling with her own anxiety about Lilly being in a new place and her behavior is largely driven by her own worries and needs rather than those of her daughter. She interprets Lilly's behavior in terms of anxiety rather than novelty, expectable inhibition, or reserve. And she does this in front of Lilly. She also communicates that Lilly might not be able to get through the morning without her. She extends her good-bye, suggesting to Lilly that leaving her mother at this point is sad, frightening, and/or weighty rather than routine or positive. Cumulatively, such experiences might be expected to lead to feeling fearful, ineffectual, and despondent in a more pervasive sense.

APPENDIX B

Ms. Delores Mesh has a long history of hospitalizations for suicide attempts and self-cutting. Ms. Mesh was impregnated during a one-night stand with a man who insisted that his sexual pleasure was diminished by the use of condoms. In an effort to please him and perhaps initiate a relationship with him, Ms. Mesh complied, resulting in her daughter Brandy. Brandy is an 11-year-old girl who is starting to get more focused on her appearance and boys. Since her birth, Ms. Mesh has been involved with 11 men, 4 of whom have lived in the home for brief periods. Her current boyfriend, Joe, is living in the home at present. Joe is working part-time but spends most of his time watching television and drinking. He shows a great deal of irritability toward Ms. Mesh, often resulting in emotional turmoil for her. On one recent occasion she cut her wrist after an argument with Joe, resulting in a 3-day hospitalization. Ms. Mesh believes that she loves him and could not live without him. Ms. Mesh spends a great deal of time with Brandy and is proud of their girlfriend-like relationship. Although money is tight, they shop frequently and get manicures together every month. The mother freely discusses her relationship with Joe with Brandy, even discussing details of their intimate relations. Ms. Mesh recently confided the true reasons for her many hospitalizations to Brandy (who had stayed with an aunt during these periods). Brandy is now terrified that her mother may commit suicide. She believes that she plays an important role as her mother's confidante in keeping her mother safe. She regularly turns down social invitations because she fears that her mother might become overwhelmed if she and Joe get into a fight and Brandy is not there.

Although another child with a different temperament might react differently, and although child gender might play a role in the nature of the mother–child relationship (with a boy becoming less enmeshed), negative outcomes would be anticipated in most cases.

13

Substance Abuse and Parenting

Linda C. Mayes
Sean D. Truman
Yale Child Study Center

INTRODUCTION

Like other descriptors such as socioeconomic status or parental depression that are used to denote a potential high-risk condition for impairments in parenting, the term *substance abuse* encompasses a large number of factors that may either independently or interactively contribute to parenting abilities. To a great extent, studies of substance abuse and parenting have adopted definitions that are categorical, and as such do not readily permit consideration of interactions among the multiple factors contributing both to the adult's substance abuse and difficulties with parenting. This issue is further complicated by the fact that all substances of abuse are not equally impairing, and as such different drugs affect parenting idiosyncratically, depending on the type, amount, and rates of use.

Parenting among substance-abusing adults is often presumed to be fragile and impaired in its execution and damaging and defeating in its influence (e.g., Burns, 1986; Wellisch and Steinberg, 1980). Historically, the assumptions made about the effects of substance abuse on parenting have been broad but rest on a relatively weak empirical foundation. Individuals with substance abuse problems are frequently assumed to be incapable of adequately fulfilling a variety of social roles, including the role of parent. This issue is complicated by the fact that drug abuse is frequently considered a problem of the under class, and the connotations of "substance abuse" reverberate beyond the diagnostic categorization.

The quality of parenting among substance abusing adults, and the effects of that parenting on children are potentially affected by drug use through several interactive pathways. First, during the course of pregnancy most abused drugs readily cross the placenta and expose the fetus during pregnancy. As we will discuss below, the effects of drug exposure on fetal development vary, but a range of illicit and licit substances has been shown to compromise fetal neural development (as well as other processes of organogenesis) and has been implicated in poor long-term developmental and behavioral outcomes in children (Hans, 1992; Mayes, Bornstein, Chawarska, Haynes, and

Granger, 1996; Streissguth et al., 1991; Streissguth, Barr, Bookstein, Sampson, and Olson, 1999). These effects may in turn compromise how infants respond to their parents' caregiving activities. Second, the effects of parental drug use are not limited to exposure during pregnancy. After birth, the infant is passively exposed to drugs whose route of ingestion is through smoking and inhalation (e.g., marijuana, tobacco, or crack) and, hence, exposure occurs during another phase of active neurogenesis. Third, after children are born, substance abuse has the potential to disrupt parenting behavior, as many abused drugs impede awareness of and sensitivity to environmental cues, interfere with emotion regulation, judgment, and aspects of executive functioning, and impair motor skills (Lief, 1985; Miller, Smyth, and Mudar, 1999; Seagull et al., 1996; Tucker, 1979). All of these capacities are central to providing timely, responsive, and stable parenting for a child. Fourth, in addition to the direct effects of substance abuse on parenting behaviors, many parenting problems among substance abusing adults are also a function of specific psychological and environmental factors that co-occur with the substance abuse (Bernstein and Hans, 1994; Hans, Bernstein, and Henson, 1999; Lester, Boukydis, Zachariah, and Twomey, 2000). Understanding the role of substance abuse in parenting is also essential if we are to develop effective treatment modalities, legislative initiatives, and public health policy. If our assumptions about how substance abuse affects parenting are inaccurate, then it follows that many of approaches designed to address this issue may be misguided, inefficient, or ineffective.

In order to facilitate understanding of this complex topic, we begin with a historical and social context for our discussion of how substance abuse may affect parenting and developmental outcomes in children. The literature is presented in a number of conceptually distinct sections. As we will discuss below, substance abuse is frequently a multigenerational problem. Literature that addresses how the families of origin of parents who are substance abusers differ from other "normal" families (even before they become parents themselves) is reviewed in terms of the environmental conditions of the family and the psychological profiles of substance abusing parents in general. Although substance abuse may affect global family function in the family of origin of substance abusing parents, the effects of substance abuse can affect children in other contexts as well. Many commonly abused substances taken during pregnancy result in problems with fetal development; these teratologic and developmental effects of exposure to both licit and illicit drugs are described in some detail. Finally, the ways in which substance abuse affects a parent's conceptualization of, and attitudes and behavior toward, their children is presented. We conclude the chapter by suggesting an approach to developing models for the effects of substance abuse on parenting and children.

HISTORICAL TRENDS IN SUBSTANCE ABUSE

The urgency of the recent upsurge in cocaine use has prompted not only the labels of a new epidemic but also belied the impression that these are new problems visited on an especially vulnerable group—women and their children. Moreover, the prevailing myth has been that women have traditionally been less involved in substance abuse (Heath, 1991) and that addiction was predominantly a male problem. However, for centuries, women have been involved in alcohol, opiate, and, more recently, cocaine abuse, and concern about the effects of such substances on a pregnancy are long-standing. In the Old Testament, Samson's mother on learning of her pregnancy was advised, "Thou shall conceive and bear a son. Now therefore beware, I pray thee, and drink not wine nor any strong drink" (Judg. 13:7, cited in Heath, 1991). Recognition that opium use during pregnancy compromised the pregnancy is found in Hippocrates association of "uterine suffocation" with maternal opiate use (Hans, 1992; Zagon and McLaughlin, 1984).

At certain periods in the United States, women were more likely than men to be opiate abusers. In the mid-eighteenth century, opium (and alcohol) were widely available in patent medicines and were frequently prescribed by physicians for nervous disorders. Indeed, the typical opiate addict of the late eighteenth century was a middle-age, middle-class woman whose addiction began with the medical prescription of opium for nervousness and stress (Courtwright, 1982). Not until the mid-1940s did that profile change to the urban poor male as the typical heroin abuser. Furthermore, opium ingested through smoking was particularly common among women prostitutes in the late nineteenth century and was a common currency exchanged for sex (Courtwright, 1982).

Cocaine became more prevalent between 1895 and 1900, again among the underclass and prostitutes. In the late 1800s, the Committee on the Acquirement of the Drug Habit surveyed physicians along the East Coast through a questionnaire. Less than half responded, but among those who did, the consensus of their report was that "The use of cocaine by unfortunate women generally . . . in certain parts of the country is simply appalling. . . . The police officers of these questionable districts tell us that the [addicts] are made wild by cocaine, which they have no difficulty at all in buying, sometimes peddled around from door to door . . ." (Musto, 1973, p. 17). The use of alcohol was not included on the questionnaire, but it was estimated on the basis of the survey that there were 200,000 addicts in the country, with a large proportion of these being women. How many children were involved was not recorded, nor has there been a systematic historical study of how children were a part of these early patterns of opiate, alcohol, and cocaine use. That women addicts regardless of social class had children and that these children were involved in various ways in their parents' addictions is certain, though not documented, except in individual stories and anecdotal accounts (see, for example, Courtwright, 1982, p. 89, for descriptions of addictions among early adolescents).

LIMITATIONS OF THE LITERATURE ON SUBSTANCE ABUSE

A remarkably small number of studies directly addresses the role of substance abuse on parenting. Given this fact, we have drawn from the more general adult substance abuse literature, but that literature is primarily focused on variables outside (although pertinent to) parenting. There are findings that suggest that many of the individuals who participate in substance abuse studies may not be representative of the population of substance abusers as a whole. This is a significant problem in the substance abuse literature in general, but it is particularly important in contextualizing findings as these relate to parenting.

A number of recent findings (reported below) demonstrates that substance abusers are at higher risk for comorbid psychopathology and other conditions than are nonusers in the population. Many of the studies in the substance abuse (and the effects of substance abuse on parenting) literature do not provide adequate measures of baseline conditions known to be prevalent in the substance abusing population. This issue is highly problematic in any attempt to assess the contribution of substance abuse to parenting separate from other comorbidity, such as personality disorders, anxiety, and depression, which are known to affect parenting independent of substance abuse.

Finally, in the literature that does directly address substance abuse and parenting, studies have used relatively restricted measures of parenting, and limited numbers and kinds of outcome variables in children have been measured. This fact makes it difficult to link systematically particular parental behaviors, attitudes, or styles to specific developmental outcomes in children. If we are to understand the role that substance abuse (or any other variable for that matter) has on parenting, careful and well-operationalized parenting variables must be linked to discrete outcomes in children.

Sample Bias and Methodological Problems in Substance-Abuse Research

Fried (1992) found that studies of substance-abusing populations are frequently biased in terms of a number of selection factors and do not always, if ever, adequately represent the overall population of alcohol, cocaine, or heroin abusers. This issue is a problem for research in substance exposed children as well, as many studies are poorly controlled and have problems with participant recruitment and attrition that may affect research findings (Olson and Toth, 1999). There may be a socioeconomic and ethnic bias in the samples most often referred for treatment or reported to police or child-protective agencies (Chasnoff, Landress, and Barrett, 1990). Study samples often consist of adults who have reported their addiction or have been present at a health care facility for a sufficient number of visits to have a positive urine drug screen. Other samples consist of those adults who have accepted and are actively involved in treatment for their addiction or have in some way or another indicated their desire to stop their substance abuse. In either case, both samples, particularly those consisting of adults who actively participate in treatment programs, may be biased either toward those most overwhelmed by the substance abuse, and thus who are at greatest risk for dysfunction in a number of areas including parenting, or those who are more motivated and have greater psychic resources to seek help. Rarely is it possible to compare those adults who participate in any program with those who do not, except on the most general measures such as age and ethnicity. This is a significant problem in the literature, as there are data that suggest that refusal to participate in treatment and/or involvement in treatment may be important predictors of long-term follow up in adults (Stout, Brown, Longabaugh, and Noel, 1996). Participants who were active during the treatment phase of the study were far less likely to "disappear" to follow up. Thus, the authors point out the necessity of carefully following all participants over time, including intention-to-treat controls, so that biased follow-up does not distort findings regarding the effectiveness of treatment.

Given the nature of the study samples and of referral and detection biases, nearly every reported sample of substance-abusing adults is marked by the multiple, already cited, confounding, and interactive factors that both contribute to substance abuse and may affect any area of functioning being assessed. These include the effects of chronic substance abuse on physical health, unemployment, and homelessness, and potentially on basic neuropsychological functions involved in memory and learning. The more chronic the adult's substance abuse history and the more that individual is involved with more than one drug, the more likely they are to have chronic medical problems related to substance abuse (e.g., HIV infection) and to be homeless, unemployed, and involved in a more violent and unpredictable lifestyle.

Study samples such as the ones described above may be representative of individuals most seriously affected by substance abuse, but they provide limited insight into deficits of parenting that may occur in individuals with substance abuse problems who have fewer comorbid problems. Thus, studies of populations with a less chronic substance abuse history from less socially disadvantaged circumstances are alternative samples for certain questions about substance abuse and parenting and represent a less often investigated group. Comparison groups from different socioeconomic conditions may highlight areas of impaired functioning that are not related to substance abuse per se but rather to the cumulative effects of poverty, poor health, chronic violence, and environmental chaos and stress.

Substance Abuse and Psychiatric Comorbidity

Within the last 15 years it has become apparent that many substance abusing individuals suffer from a variety of comorbid psychiatric impairments, such as depression, anxiety, and personality disorders (Kessler et al., 1997; Rounsaville et al., 1991; Verheul et al., 2000), many of which go unidentified and untreated (Kessler et al., 1996). Some have argued that the use of substances such as cocaine and alcohol represents an attempt to treat the symptoms of these disorders. Moreover, for the majority of addicted women, the onset of their psychopathology typically predates their first pregnancy (Beckwith, Howard, Espinosa, and Tyler, 1999; Howard, Beckwith, Espinosa, and Tyler, 1995; Luthar, Cushing, Merikangas, and Rounsaville, 1998) and the onset of substance abuse (Hans et al., 1999). The nature and type of the psychiatric impairments comorbid with substance abuse may have profound effects on both the individual's choice of drug and on their ability to stop the substance abuse and to lead a more adaptive life (Glantz, 1992; Ziedonis, 1992). Recognizing the underlying psychiatric and psychological contributions to substance abuse may also clarify potential genetic factors that will be influential for the substance-abusing adult's children. For example, a certain proportion of adults using cocaine may do so because stimulant effects ameliorate their problems with attention that are characteristic of attention deficit disorder (Clure et al., 1999; Khantzian, 1983; Khantzian et al., 1984). Similar problems with attention in their children may be due to a potential genetic loading for attention deficit disorder and may not be related either to the effects of a cocaine using parenting environment or the teratogenic effects of cocaine on the child's brain.

Comorbid maternal psychopathology may contribute to greater impairments in parenting interactions among substance-abusing adults compared to nonsubstance abusers and to those substance abusers with no coexisting psychiatric disturbance. Hans and colleagues (Hans, Bernstein, and Henson, 1990, reported in Griffith and Freier, 1992) reported that mothers using methadone who were also diagnosed as having antisocial personality disorders were significantly less responsive in their interactions with their 24-month-old infants than were methadone-maintained mothers either having no significant psychopathology or affective disorders alone. Moreover, the latter group did not differ in their interactions from drug-free mothers with similar psychopathology. Another study of cocaine and opiate using mothers and their children found that many of the women had comorbid psychiatric disturbance, and these impairments were significantly related to their children's lower levels of social function and higher levels of disruptive behavior (Luthar et al., 1998). In another study using a sample of inner-city opioid-addicted mothers, over half of the women met criteria for a personality disorder, and over one third of the sample met criteria for either current or past history of major depression. These diagnoses were linked to insensitive, unresponsive, and punitive parenting styles. Perhaps most importantly, the children of mothers with comorbid psychopathology, (and particularly antisocial personality disorder) rated their mothers as being highly rejecting of them (Hans et al., 1999). Findings such as these point to the importance of not considering drug use alone as the single determining variable for observed differences in maternal interactive behaviors, but rather as a marker for several predictor variables that are more often associated with substance abuse.

Restricted Parenting Variables and Developmental Outcomes

One of the central limitations of the parenting and substance abuse literature is the paucity of studies that provide clearly operationalized child variables that are empirically linked to well-defined and carefully measured parenting styles or behaviors. This methodological problem consistently limits the types of conclusions that we are able to draw from the literature of substance-abusing parents and their children. Below, we provide a review of some of the more specific methodological problems in the literature.

A rather restricted range of child outcomes has been used as dependent variables in the substance-abuse parenting literature, and what constitutes the impairments in parenting has not usually been adequately specified or operationalized. Rather, impairments have been presumed either because of the presence or absence of substance abuse, or assessments are based on indirect measures such as the occurrence of child abuse or neglect (Azar, in Vol. 4 of this *Handbook*). As a result of these problems, it is difficult to make claims about the ways in which specific parenting styles or deficits affect specific outcomes in children.

The child outcomes most studied are the incidence of problem behaviors or psychiatric disorders, such as conduct or oppositional disorders, antisocial behavior or personality, teenage pregnancy, alcoholism or other substance abuse, criminal involvement, or early incarceration (Johnson and Pandina, 1991; Lohr, Gillmore, Gilchrist, and Butler, 1992; Mutzell, 1993). Rarely have studies of children living in substance-abusing homes focused on adaptation or resiliency (Johnson, Glassman, Fiks, and Rosen, 1990; Luthar and Zigler, 1991). Moreover, with the exception of the increasing literature on the children of alcoholic parents (Ackerman and Michaels, 1990; Mutzell, 1993), fewer studies have assessed more individualized outcomes such as personality characteristics dealing with affective and impulse regulation, modulation of anxiety and self-esteem, or the capacity for sustained relationships, all of which are central to adult function (Belsky and Barends, in Vol. 3 of this *Handbook*).

A more comprehensive evaluation of the effect of maternal drug (opiate and cocaine) use on children has been made by Luthar and colleagues (Luthar et al., 1998). The authors used a multimodal and multirater approach to evaluate maternal psychopathology, cognitive ability, and sensation seeking. Child outcomes included diagnoses of psychopathology, cognitive ability, and social adjustment. A number of both risk and protective factors emerged from their study. Children who had mothers who scored high on sensation seeking were at higher risk for developing conduct and oppositional/defiant disorders. This risk increased if high-sensation-seeking women were psychiatrically impaired. Maternal cognitive ability was inversely related to psychosocial outcomes in children; that is, children were more likely to be diagnosed with disruptive behavior and rated as less socially competent if their mothers had higher levels of cognitive function. This finding was stronger in African American families than in European American families. Higher levels of cognitive ability in children were related to higher levels of adaptive social behavior. This study represents a departure from the usual, less-sophisticated evaluation of children with substance abusing parents, in that specific risk and protective factors and interaction effects among variables are identified.

As noted above, study designs linking child outcomes to parental substance-abuse are rare. Most of the literature on the subject relies on single case reports, has retrospectively assessed exposure to substance abuse in an identified population with specific impairments, or has compared the incidence of a given outcome between children from substance-abusing and non-substance-abusing families (Frick et al., 1992; Mutzell, 1993). It is also important to note that to date very few studies have examined information-processing performance or use of language which have been shown to be predictive of later childhood cognitive outcomes (Bornstein, 1989; Bornstein, Mayes, and Park, 1998; McCall and Carriger, 1993).

Although the accumulated evidence from multiple studies such as these (particularly for children of alcoholics—see also Pihl, Peterson, and Finn, 1990; Tesson, 1990) suggests that substance abuse in one or both parents constitutes a significant risk for poor later adjustment, poor impulse control, and problems with conduct, many of the studies do not allow for investigation of interactive effects between parenting functions and child characteristics. Nor do such studies allow for a clear understanding of potential mechanisms of effect. Certain child characteristics, such as poor impulse control, may be related to the effects of prenatal drug exposure, and the later expression of these characteristics may be less related to the effects of growing up in the care of a substance abuser and more to the sequelae of the prenatal exposure. Similarly, as will be reviewed later, many substance-abusing adults have preexisting psychiatric and neuropsychological disorders that both predispose them to substance abuse and carry genetic risks for their offspring. Again, problems such as depressive or anxiety disorders in the children of a substance abuser may reflect these genetic contributions independently or in combination with sequelae of dysfunctional parenting.

CHARACTERISTICS OF FAMILIES OF ORIGIN
AND MULTIGENERATIONAL SUBSTANCE ABUSE

Although there are significant limitations to the literature of substance abuse and parenting, a number of studies have examined the role of drug and alcohol abuse on family function and have noted that substance abuse may be highly disruptive to families. Parental death or desertion, marital discord, divorce, substance abuse, and high rates of physical and sexual abuse have been repeatedly identified as characteristics of the families of origin of substance abusers (Chambers, Hinesby, and Moldestad, 1970; Raynes, Clement, Patch, and Ervin, 1974). Brookoff, O'Brien, Cook, Thompson, and Williams (1997) evaluated the characteristics of families involved in domestic violence by going to the scene of over 60 consecutive domestic assaults that resulted in calls to the police. The vast majority of perpetrators of assaults (86%) had used alcohol the day of the assault, and over half of the assailants who submitted urine toxicology were positive for cocaine. In their sample, children were witnesses to violent incidents in 85% of the cases and were themselves victims of violence in approximately 15% of the cases. Nearly half of the women in the sample reported had been previously assaulted by the perpetrator during a pregnancy.

In a prospective study of children, Windom and White (1997) found that children who were abused or neglected before the age of 11 were at higher risk for developing substance-abuse problems and were more likely to be arrested for nonviolent crimes. Rohsenow, Corbett, and Devine (1988) found that 77% of female drug users in treatment reported childhood sexual abuse. Rounsaville and colleagues (1982) reported that disruptive events such as family violence, hospitalizations, or unexpected separations were very common historical incidents in the early experiences of substance abusers. Wolock and Magura (1996) found that when child protective services were involved with families, substance abuse predicted reopening of closed cases within a 2-year follow-up period. A considerable amount of research with alcoholic adults has demonstrated the increased frequency of unstable family environments and poor family cohesion (McCord and McCord, 1960; Robins, 1966). However, as with many other aspects of studies of parenting in substance abusers, these relations are not singular but multivariate.

A central empirical dilemma, then, is whether or not substance-abusing parents have impaired relationships with their children. Do patterns of parent–child relatedness with substance abuse differ from the impairments found in other dysfunctional or disadvantaged families not affected by substance abuse? Stated another way, does substance abuse impair function as a parent, and does that impairment in turn translate into different developmental courses in children when compared to non-substance-abusing parents?

A number of studies have examined how substance-abusing adults describe their own parents. A frequently quoted and replicated finding is the description by narcotic abusers of their mothers as overprotective and fathers as ineffective or weak (Ben-Yehuda and Schindell, 1981). In a study of 110 adults referred for detoxification from alcohol or narcotics compared to 127 controls (Bernardi, Jones, and Tennant, 1989), substance-abusing adults were more likely to describe both their mothers and their fathers as overprotective on the Parental Bonding Instrument (Parker, Tupling, and Brown, 1978). However, for both groups, ratings for caring were lower and for overprotectiveness higher if there was also a family history of alcoholism. Thus, the perception of parenting often reported by substance-abusing adults (and, at times, acted on in their relations with their own children) may be in part a reflection of the effects of substance abuse on their own families of origin. In other words, it is not just the parental behaviors that are necessarily etiologic for the substance abuser's addiction but also the effects of substance abuse on the parent that contributes to her or his own parenting and to a pattern of multigenerational continuity of substance abuse.

In a large epidemiological survey, 8,865 secondary school students were asked about their own and their parents use of drugs and alcohol (Smart and Fejer, 1972). A total of 12 drugs (including alcohol) were studied, and for all 12 there was a high agreement between students' and parents' use of drugs, and the specific drug was often concordant. The strongest relation in parent–child use was between maternal and children's use of tranquilizers. Annis (1974) studied 539 adolescents and their families and found a significant relation between parents' and adolescents' use of alcohol with similar patterns of use grouping within mother–daughter or father–son pairs. In a study using child and separate mother and father interviews (Fawzy, Coombs, and Gerber, 1983), teenagers were significantly more likely to use drugs or alcohol if their parents were users or if the teenager perceived the parent to be a user. For example, of the parents reported by the teenager to be marijuana users, 78% of mothers and 81% of fathers had substance-abusing adolescents. Similarly, if parents reported themselves to have at least one drink of beer or wine per day, 77% of mothers and 72% of fathers were likely to have a substance-abusing teenager.

Each of these studies raises the question of how drug use is transmitted across generations and what are the genetic as well as environmental contributions to the notable concordance in parental and child (and sibling) drug and alcohol use (Deren, 1986; Prescott and Kendler, 1999;

Schuckit, 1999; Yates, Cadoret, Troughton, and Stewart, 1996). The multigenerational transmission patterns of substance abuse may be mediated by gender. Among families of addicts, higher rates of alcoholism have been found in fathers, and conversely higher rates of affective disorders are found in mothers (Mirin, Weiss, Griffin, and Michael, 1991). Similarly, in a sample of adolescents in treatment, the extent of drug or alcohol use by the child was related to the extent of alcohol use by the father. However, the extent of the child's drug use was more strongly related to the mother's use of drugs rather than alcohol (Friedman, Pomerance, Sanders, Santo, and Utada, 1980).

Few studies have moved beyond the correlational design to examine other factors, such as socioeconomic status and parental psychological and psychiatric characteristics, that may contribute both to the parental substance abuse and compound the genetic risk for the children. For example, among substance abusers' parents and siblings, there is a high rate of psychiatric disorders such as depression and antisocial personality disorder, which are also comorbid with substance abuse (Mirin et al., 1991; Rounsaville et al., 1991). In a study of 492 parents and 673 siblings of cocaine abusers and 400 parents and 476 siblings of opiate abusers (Luthar, Merikangas, and Rounsaville, 1993), several variables including gender and psychiatric status of the parent, ethnicity, and type of drug abused seemed to mediate the relation between parental and child drug use. Maternal depression was associated with both depression and drug use in the adult offspring. Similarly, paternal alcoholism was significantly associated with alcoholism or drug abuse in adult offspring, but only for African American and not European American families. Studies such as these inform a more complex model of interactive effects among psychiatric disorders, substance abuse, and intrafamilial transmission of similar impairments that may have profound effects on parenting.

ENVIRONMENTAL CONDITIONS OF SUBSTANCE-ABUSING FAMILIES

Many of the samples for studies of substance abusing parents and families are drawn disproportionately from poor, urban households with low levels of education and high levels of unemployment. Although the following findings are important for setting the context in which many children of substance-abusing families grow up, it must always be borne in mind that substance abuse affects a broad socioeconomic and ethnic range. Adults participating in substance-abuse treatment programs, seeking individual treatment for their addiction, or who are involved in chronic substance abuse without ever seeking treatment come from a wide range of environmental conditions, each of which contributes to the adult's ability to parent children.

The factors most studied and most reported on are the confluence of conditions relating to extreme poverty, homelessness, prostitution, and violence, which may not be representative of the larger population of substance abusers. Multiple studies from substance abuse treatment programs document the high incidence of unemployment and less than a high school education among participating substance-abusing women (Hawley and Disney, 1992). In this population, the rate of unemployment has been shown as high as 96% (Suffet and Brotman, 1976). Many report few to no friendships or contacts with supportive persons who are not also substance abusers, and substance-abusing adults often describe long-standing social detachment (Tucker, 1979). The level of violence in substance-abusing families, particularly between women and their spouses or male friends, is markedly high and exposes children to a considerable amount of witnessed violence (Brookoff et al., 1997; Regan, Leifer, and Finnegan, 1982). Notably, there are few data about how often children in substance-abusing families are being reared by a single mother, although the quoted percentages usually exceed 70% (Boyd and Mieczkowski, 1990), or how often and in what ways fathers are involved. The reluctance of many substance-abusing adults to reveal details about their households contributes in part to this lack of knowledge, but it also reflects in part the broader lack of adequate data about the family structure in substance-abusing households—how many adults usually care for a child, how many households may a child move among, how often are substance-abusing mothers and their children virtually homeless.

PSYCHOLOGICAL PROFILES OF SUBSTANCE ABUSING PARENTS

Substance-abusing parents have been characterized as egocentric and narcissistically oriented (Burns and Burns, 1988; Coppolillo, 1975; Escalmilla-Mondanaro, 1977; Lawson and Wilson, 1979) and punitive toward their children (Miller, Smyth, and Mudar, 1999). Those running ongoing treatment programs for substance-abusing adults and their children report that participating women have great difficulty understanding their infants' and children's communications as expressions of needs and not as demanding and inappropriate (Burns and Burns, 1988). Often deprived and neglected themselves, many substance-abusing mothers have unrealistic expectations of what infants or children can do for themselves (Fiks, Johnson, and Rosen, 1985; Lawson and Wilson, 1979). The infant may be seen as a gift or as an extension of the mother's own needs. Those women who deny that their drug use has any effect on their infant or child have been reported to be at much greater risk for impaired parenting manifest, for example, by neglect (Mondanaro, 1977).

On psychological testing, substance-abusing women often score high on externalizing traits, a finding reflecting a commonly reported belief that their lives and fates are controlled by forces and persons outside of themselves and their control (Aron, 1975; Davis, 1990). Feelings of worthlessness, poor self-esteem, anxiety, and depression are commonly reported (Black and Mayer, 1980; Lawson and Wilson, 1979; Mondanaro, 1977), although these feelings may also be exacerbated by chronic substance abuse. A sample of polydrug-using mothers who were participating in a substance abuse treatment program completed the Minnesota Multiphasic Personality Inventory (Burns and Burns, 1988). In this select and small sample, ratings were consistently highest on subscales characterizing difficulties sustaining relationships and in anticipating consequences of behavior. Much more work is required in far larger samples of substance-abusing women to characterize the most common personality and psychiatric profiles. The highly selective and at times subjective nature of currently available studies limits the conclusions that can be drawn from the available data except to say that there is a marked increase in severe depression and personality disorders particularly among substance-abusing mothers (Hans et al., 1999; Rounsaville et al., 1985; Zuckerman et al., 1989), which have been linked to a variety of poorly responsive parenting behaviors (Dawson, Klinger, Panagiotides, and Spieker, 1992; Zahn-Waxler, Duggal, and Gruber, in Vol. 4 of this *Handbook*).

Relevant to this point is also the comorbidity of substance abuse with other psychiatric disorders among the families of substance-abusing adults. An addict's family of origin may also show increased incidences of depression, antisocial personality disorders, and alcoholism and other substance abuse (Mirin et al., 1991; Rounsaville, Kosten et al., 1991). Additionally, the comorbidity appears not to be an aggregation of specific disorders, that is, a concordance for depression or antisocial personality, but rather a general conveyance of risk and an elevation in the incidence of several disorders (Luthar, Anton, Merikangas, and Rounsaville, 1992; Merikangas, Rounsaville, and Prusoff, 1992), which also will have implications for the transmission of similar disorders in the third-generation offspring of these families.

To this point we have presented data that describe the ways in which parents who are substance abusers differ from "normal" parents in the population. We now turn to address the ways in which parental substance abuse affects developmental outcomes in children. These domains of influence include the teratologic effects of substances on prenatal development (in particular fetal brain development). In addition, the literature on substance abusing parents' "style" of parenting will be examined; specific attitudinal sets and deficits of parenting appear to be related to particular substances of abuse. Finally, literature directly assessing linkages between particular agents and discrete measures of parenting behavior and attitudes will be presented.

TERATOLOGIC AND DEVELOPMENTAL EFFECTS
OF PRENATAL DRUG EXPOSURE

More information is available about short- and long-term outcomes of prenatal alcohol and heroin exposure than for cocaine, but it is important to note that abuse of each of these agents is often associated with other factors that contribute to poor fetal health and infant outcome apart from the specific teratologic effects of any one agent. Women who are chronic alcoholics, heroin, or cocaine abusers often fail to seek prenatal care and are themselves in sufficiently poor health to compromise the growth and well-being of the fetus. Thus, among pregnant women who are substance abusers, associated complications include preterm deliveries and infants who are intrauterine growth retarded or small-for-gestational age (SGA). The difficulties of caring for preterm or SGA infants are well documented because these infants often have labile states and are difficult to interact with (Watt, 1990; Watt and Strongman, 1985), problems that will likely be compounded if the substance-abusing environment is chaotic and inconsistent.

Prenatal Exposure to Alcohol

Studies of the teratologic effects of prenatal alcohol exposure have been ongoing for many years since the initial reports of fetal alcohol syndrome (Jones, Smith, Ulleland, and Streissguth, 1973; Jones and Smith, 1973). Alcohol acts as a direct neuroteratogen affecting not only fetal facial morphology and growth but also brain growth, structure, and function through mechanisms not yet elucidated (Goodlett and West, 1992; Schenker et al., 1990). In infancy, fetal alcohol syndrome is characterized by (1) intrauterine growth retardation with persistent poor growth in weight and/or height, (2) a pattern of specific minor physical anomalies which include a characteristic facial appearance, and (3) central nervous system deficits including microcephaly, delayed development, hyperactivity, attention deficits, intellectual delays, learning disabilities, and, in some cases, seizures (Claren and Smith, 1978; Smith, 1982). Children with a history of in utero alcohol exposure who have either the characteristic physical appearance and/or central nervous system dysfunction are given the diagnostic label of fetal alcohol effects (Claren and Smith, 1978). Even in the absence of fetal alcohol syndrome, infants born to alcoholic mothers show an increased incidence of intellectual impairment, congenital anomalies, and decreased birthweight (Aronson, Kyllerman, Sabel, Sandin, and Olegard, 1985; Day, 1992; Sokol, Miller, and Reed, 1980). Partial expression of the fetal alcohol syndrome and the issue of fetal alcohol effects have led to a number of studies relating amount of exposure to the presence or absence of diagnostic criteria and to the severity of the central nervous system manifestations. In general, more severe effects on physical growth are associated with more severe intellectual impairments (Streissguth, 1992), and heavier alcohol use is associated with more severe physical effects.

A study of the effect of prenatal exposure of alcohol on preschool-age children demonstrated effects on psychomotor development, neurological state, growth, and facial features from 1.5 oz of alcohol or more per day (Larroque and Kaminski, 1998). However, no clear dose-response and/or minimum duration of exposure has been established in the study of prenatal alcohol exposure (Day, 1992; Streissguth, Barr, and Sampson, 1990). Other studies have suggested that the point at which prenatal exposure occurs may be an important predictor of outcome. Korkman, Autti-Raemoe, Koivulehto, and Granstroem (1998) found that school-age children between the ages of 5 and 9 who had been exposed to alcohol only during the first trimester of pregnancy did not significantly differ from controls on measures of attention, receptive language, and cognitive processing (naming tasks). However, children who were exposed for the duration of the pregnancy demonstrated lower function on these measures.

Hundreds of reports of children with fetal alcohol syndrome are now available detailing their delayed development in the first 2 to 3 years (e.g., Coles, Smith, Lancaster, and Falek, 1987; Gusella and Fried, 1984; O'Connor, Brill, and Sigman, 1986). However, significantly fewer studies describe follow-up findings through school age and adolescence (Streissguth, 1992). Streissguth (1976) reported on a 7-year follow-up of 23 children of alcoholic mothers compared to 46 nonalcoholic controls matched for socioeconomic status, age, education, race parity, and marital status. At 7 years of age, children of alcoholic mothers had significantly lower IQ scores and poorer performance on tests of reading, spelling, and arithmetic, and 44% of the children of alcoholic mothers compared to 9% in the control group had IQ scores in the borderline to retarded range. Significant differences in height, weight, and head circumference were also apparent. In a study of 21 children of alcoholic mothers compared to a matched control sample, Aronson and colleagues (1985) described significantly greater problems with distractibility, hyperactivity, and short attention spans in the alcohol exposed group. Coles and colleagues (1991), studying children at age 70 months who were exposed to alcohol throughout gestation, reported deficits in sequential processing and on some measures of academic skills, including reading and mathematics. Aronson and Hagberg (1998) found that one fourth of their sample of 24 prenatally exposed children were enrolled in schools for the mentally retarded and that 11 of the children received services for special education. Behavior problems have been described for other cohorts (e.g., Steinhausen, Nestler, and Spohr, 1982) and impairments in concentration and attention, social withdrawal and conduct problems continue to be described for adolescents and young adults exposed in utero to alcohol (Streissguth et al., 1991; Streissguth et al., 1999).

Prenatal Exposure to Opiates

In contrast to alcohol exposure, newborns who have been exposed prenatally to opiates (heroin or methadone) are born passively addicted to the drug and exhibit withdrawal symptoms in the first days to weeks after delivery (Desmond and Wilson, 1975). Numerous studies have now also replicated the finding that prenatal opioid exposure reduces birthweight and head circumference (Finnegan, 1976; Hans, 1992; Kaltenbach and Finnegan, 1987; Jeremy and Hans, 1985; Wilson, Desmond, and Wait, 1981). Similar findings in animal models that control for exposure to other drugs such as alcohol or tobacco and for poor maternal health support the finding of an effect of opiates on fetal growth (Zagon and McLaughlin, 1984). Prenatal exposure to opiates also contributes significantly to an increased incidence of sudden infant death syndrome (SIDS). In some studies, the incidence of SIDS is eight times that reported for non-opiate-exposed infants (Hans, 1992; Finnegan, 1979; Rosen and Johnson, 1988; Wilson, Desmond, and Wait, 1981).

On neurobehavioral assessments in the newborn period, opiate-exposed infants are more easily aroused and more irritable (Jeremy and Hans, 1985; Marcus and Hans, 1982; Strauss, Starr, Ostrea, Chavez, and Stryker, 1976). They exhibit proportionately less quiet, compared to active, sleep and show increased muscle tone and poor motor control (e.g., tremulousness and jerky movements). Opiate-exposed infants are less often in alert states and more difficult to bring to an alert state. For the majority of infants, the dramatic neurobehavioral abnormalities seen in the newborn period generally diminish over the first month of life (Jeremy and Hans, 1985) and are thus assumed to reflect the transitory symptoms of narcotic withdrawal rather than evidence of permanent neurological dysfunction (Hans, 1992).

Past the neonatal period, a number of studies have documented small, and not usually statistically significant, delays in the acquisition of developmental skills as measured by the Bayley (1969; Hans, 1989; Hans and Jeremy, 1984; Rosen and Johnson, 1982; Wilson et al., 1981; Strauss et al., 1977). However, much more consistent and significant across studies have been the findings of persistent problems in poor motor coordination, high activity level, and poor attention among opiate-exposed infants in the first year of life (Hans and Marcus, 1983; Hans, Marcus, Jeremy, and Auerbach, 1984). These state and motor regulatory difficulties make it difficult for a well-functioning adult in a relatively nonstressed environment to care for the infant and are significant problems for an opiate-addicted adult experiencing her or his own state and attentional regulatory problems (Hans, 1992).

Follow-up studies through early childhood of opiate-exposed compared to non-opiate-exposed children have continued to report few to no differences in cognitive performance (Kaltenbach and Finnegan, 1987; Strauss et al., 1977; Wilson, McCreary, Kean, and Baxter, 1979). However, opiate-exposed school-age children show higher activity levels, are often impulsive with poor self-control, show poor motor coordination, and have more difficulty with tasks requiring focused attention (Olofsson, Buckley, Andersen, and Friss-Hansen, 1983; Strauss et al., 1977). There is also an increased incidence of attention deficit disorder among opiate-exposed school-age children (Hans, 1992). Two studies have described altered sex-dimorphic behavior in opiate-exposed young children (Sandberg, Meyer-Bahlburg, Rosen, and Johnson, 1990; Ward, Kopertowski, Finnegan, and Sandberg, 1989). Opiate-exposed boys showed more stereotypically feminine behavior than nonexposed boys, and there were no differences between exposed and nonexposed girls. These findings are consistent with similar observations of male rats exposed to opioid drugs in utero (Ward, Orth, and Weisz, 1983).

Past the years of early childhood, there are few studies of the long-term effects of prenatal opiate exposure, and those available usually lack a nonexposed control group or are not based on a longitudinal design (Hans, 1992). The data from these studies suggest that by adolescence, opiate-exposed children exhibit an increased incidence of behavior and conduct problems including impulsivity, involvement in criminal activities or in early substance abuse, more antisocial behavior, and increased school dropout (Bauman and Levine, 1986; Sowder and Burt, 1980; Wilson, 1989). It is not altogether clear how much these problems in conduct and impulse regulation are attributable to persistent effects of prenatal opiate exposure and how much they are the consequence of cumulative exposure to the discord and dysfunction often characterizing substance-abusing households.

Prenatal Exposure to Cocaine

Prenatal cocaine exposure potentially affects developing brain in a variety of ways. In the pregnant animal, cocaine ingestion results in decreased uteroplacental blood flow, severe uteroplacental insufficiency (acute and chronic), maternal hypertension, and fetal vasoconstriction (Moore, Sorg, Miller, Key, and Resnick, 1986; Woods, Plessinger, and Clark, 1987); in humans, cocaine use has been associated with spontaneous abortion, premature labor, and abruptions (Bingol, Fuchs, Diaz, Stone, and Gromisch, 1987; Cherukuri, Minkoff, Feldman, Parekh, and Glass, 1988; Lindenberg, Alexander, Gendrop, Nencioli, and Williams, 1991). The effect of cocaine use on placental blood flow probably contributes to the relation between cocaine and fetal growth. Several investigators have reported that in utero cocaine use is associated with low-birthweight infants (MacGregor et al., 1987; Oro and Dixon, 1987; Ryan, Ehrlich, and Finnegan, 1987), and one report showed that crack-exposed infants were 3.6 times more likely to have intrauterine growth retardation than infants born to non-drug-using women matched for age, socioeconomic status, and alcohol use (Cherukuri, Minkoff, Feldman, Parekh, and Glass, 1988). Two studies have also reported microcephaly in addition to growth retardation (Fulroth, Phillips, and Durand, 1989; Hadeed and Siegel, 1989). A higher rate of congenital malformations in infants exposed to cocaine has been reported (Chasnoff, Chisum, and Kaplan, 1988; Isenberg, Spierer, and Inkelis, 1987; Teske and Trese, 1987).

In early reports, prenatal cocaine exposure was predictively linked to moderate to severe developmental delays across all domains. Subsequent studies have failed to confirm these findings and have reported mild to no impairments in overall developmental functioning in cocaine exposed children compared to non-cocaine-exposed groups (Held, Riggs, and Dorman, 1999; Lester, LaGasse, and Seifer, 1998; Richardson, Conroy, and Day, 1996; Wasserman et al., 1998). The developmental profiles of a group of 106 cocaine and/or alcohol exposed 24-month-old infants followed from birth were compared to the performance of 45 toddlers exposed to marijuana and/or alcohol but no cocaine and 77 non-drug-exposed children (Chasnoff, Griffith, Freier, and Murray, 1992). Mothers of infants in the two comparison groups were similar to the cocaine-using mothers on socioeconomic status, age, marital status, and tobacco use during pregnancy. On repeated developmental assessments using the Bayley Scales (1969) at 3, 6, 12, 18, and 24 months, albeit with a high rate of attrition from the original cohort, there were no mean differences in either the mental or motor domains, although the investigators cautioned that a higher percentage of cocaine-exposed infants scored two standard deviations below the mean (Chasnoff et al., 1992). A number of investigative groups have reported failures to find differences among cocaine-exposed children on general measures of developmental competency (e.g., Anisfeld, Cunningham, Ferrari, and Melendez, 1991; Arendt, Singer, and Minnes, 1993; Billman, Nemeth, Heimler, and Sasidharan, 1991).

Although the dire predictions of pervasive and global developmental impairments secondary to fetal cocaine exposure have not come to pass, there are several areas of function that do appear to be affected by prenatal exposure to cocaine. Evidence is beginning to accumulate about impairments in a range of specific functions such as neonatal habituation, attentional or arousal regulation, reactivity to novelty, and recognition memory. Impairments in these domains would potentially make normal parenting activities of contingent responsiveness and structuring attention more important for those prenatally cocaine-exposed infants who are more reactive and easily overaroused.

In a study of the effects of prenatal cocaine exposure on novelty preference and visual recognition memory in infants, exposed infants performed less well on visual expectancy tasks, and performed more poorly on memory recognition and information processing tasks than did controls (Jacobson, Jacobson, Sokol, Martier, and Chiodo, 1996). In a study examining neonatal outcomes, Delaney-Black et al. (1996) administered Brazelton Neonatal Behavioral Assessment Scales to both exposed and nonexposed infants within the first 48 hours of life. Children who had been prenatally exposed to cocaine had poorer state regulation than did controls; this difference appeared to be related to the level of cocaine concentration in the infant's meconium, suggesting a dose–response relation between cocaine and state regulation at birth.

A growing body of literature suggests that attention and arousal may be deleteriously affected by prenatal cocaine exposure. In a study of arousal regulation, Mayes, Bornstein, Chawarska, Haynes, and Granger (1996) found that 3-month-old children who were prenatally exposed to cocaine were more likely to respond negatively (display negative affect and cry) to the presentation of a novel stimulus than were nonexposed controls; this finding suggests that exposed infants were less able to modulate their arousal levels when presented with a novel stimulus. In a study examining the effects of drug use on mother–infant interaction, Mayes and colleagues (1997) found that mothers who were polydrug users including cocaine were less attentive and responsive to their 3- and 6-month old infants when compared both to nondrug-using controls, and polydrug using mothers who did not use cocaine. Bendersky and Lewis (1998) seated children in front of mothers who were asked to talk and touch their infants for 2 minutes, then turn away from the infant for 45 seconds, and then resume interaction for a final minute. The interaction was videotaped and coded for facial expressions (both mother and child). The authors found that cocaine exposed children were less able to recover after their mothers looked away from them during the session, suggesting that they were less able to modulate their arousal levels than were nonexposed children. Coles, Bard, Platzman, and Lynch (1999) studied 105 8-week-old infants' responses to auditory, visual, and social stimulation. The authors measured the infants' heart rates (HR), and children who had been exposed to cocaine had accelerations in HR in response to social stimulation, where controls had HR deceleration. The authors suggest that the increased HR represents a distressed overaroused state, where the deceleration in the controls indicates focused attention.

These findings are particularly troubling in that we might expect that attentional and arousal problems would likely be compounded by maternal interaction characterized by inattention and unresponsiveness. As we discuss below, it is conceivable that a developmental spiral emerges in which mothers who are prone to lower levels of prosocial interaction with their infants have children who are in the most need for maternal "help" with attentional and arousal regulation. As the infant's attentional and arousal deficits manifest over the developmental course, it follows that they become more difficult and less rewarding to parent, which then leads to further decrements in prosocial parental involvement with the child.

Although relatively few studies have followed cocaine exposed children past the first few years of life, there are several studies that indicate that prenatal cocaine exposure has longer term developmental effects in children. In a study of 6-year-old children, Richardson and colleagues (1996) found that performance on vigilance task appeared impaired by prenatal cocaine exposure; that is, prenatally exposed children were less able to sustain attention than were controls. In another study of 6-year-old children, Delaney-Black et al. (1998) had first-grade teachers who were blind to children's drug exposure status rate behavior. The authors found that the teachers rated cocaine exposed children as having more behavioral problems in the classroom than did controls.

Thus, prenatal exposure to alcohol, cocaine, or heroin may contribute to specific short- and long-term impairments or vulnerabilities in arousal modulation, activity level, or attentional regulation that may make it more difficult for an adult to parent the child. Moreover, when that adult is involved in substance abuse, her or his addiction, and the associated environmental, psychiatric, and neuropsychological effects may further impair the interactions between the child and parent as assessed through both indirect measures of the incidence of abuse and neglect and direct observational measures of parenting attitudes and behaviors.

EFFECTS OF SUBSTANCE ABUSE ON CONCEPTS OF PARENTING

Although it is clear that there is a range of problems that occur as the result of fetal insult secondary to teratologic exposure, the effects of parental substance abuse on children are not limited to fetal development during pregnancy and may occur after birth as well. Addiction to any substance points to personality characteristics, disabilities, or impairments, each of which may have significant implications for an adult's ability to parent a child. These characteristics may predispose an adult to adopt an authoritarian, overcontrolling, or underinvolved style of parenting. Moreover, all substances of abuse alter in varying degree an individual's state of consciousness, memory, affect regulation, and impulse control and may become so addictive that the adult's primary goal is to be able to supply her or his addiction to the exclusion of all else and all others in her or his life. These types of alterations likely influence markedly at any given moment the adult's capacity to sustain contingent, responsive interactions with an infant and young child. No studies have specifically examined whether or not the duration of an adult's substance abuse also impacts on the degree of parenting dysfunction. However, neuropsychological impairments in concentration and memory associated with, for example, chronic cocaine abuse (O'Malley, Adamse, Heaton, and Gawin, 1992) might be expected to influence certain parenting behaviors such as the capacity to sustain an interaction.

Numerous conceptual approaches to parenting seek to define functional domains that most describe those individual differences in childrearing (Macoby and Martin, 1983; Miller et al., 1999), with some predictive saliency for later child outcomes. From infant observations comes an emphasis on parental responsiveness, contingency, and reciprocity (Belsky, Rovine, and Taylor, 1984; Bornstein, in Vol. 1 of this *Handbook*), affective attunement (Stern, 1985), interactive synchrony or match and mismatch (Cohn and Tronick, 1988; Isabella, 1993; Tronick and Cohn, 1989). During contingent, reciprocal interactions, infants develop expectations for social engagement and responsiveness. A sense of contingency also provides infants and children with control over their environment and contributes to self-efficacy and self-regulation (Lewis and Goldberg, 1969; Tronick and Gianino, 1986). Impairments in early interactions in the form of diminished responsivity, poor synchrony, or increased maternal anxiety have been related to inadequate social adjustment and an increased risk for psychopathology in the preschool years (Barnett, Schaafsma, Gusman, and Parker, 1991; Sroufe, Fox, and Pancake, 1983).

Based on interactions with older children, two intersecting dimensions of parenting have been proposed: the degree of demandingness or authoritarian behavior and the level of parental responsiveness (Macoby and Martin, 1983). The intersection of these two dimensions describes four different patterns of parenting behavior, including "authoritarian and autocratic," "indulgent and permissive," "authoritative and reciprocal," and "indifferent and neglectful." Although there is much individual variation and mixing of these styles, behaviors that are generally authoritative and autocratic or indifferent are not responsive to the child's needs and represent the two styles described more commonly in substance-abusing families. Authoritative/autocratic styles place demands and conditions on children that may or may not match the child's expectations and wishes. Indifferent/neglectful styles do not attend to the child even to set expectations and conditions for behavior. Either style carries certain risks for later developmental and behavioral problems. Children reared in a predominantly authoritative and autocratic style tend more often to exhibit an external locus of control; that is, they look more often to others for guidance and tend to blame external events for their disappointments and frustrations (Loeb, Horst, and Horton, 1980). Moreover, although results vary, children from such environments respond more aggressively in a number of different situations and are overall more aggressive than children from less authoritative/autocratic homes (Patterson, 1982; Yarrow, Campbell, and Burton, 1968). The impact of indifferent or neglectful environments seems to rest more strongly in the domains of the capacity for social relatedness (Egeland and Sroufe, 1981a). Children of psychologically unavailable mothers show early disturbances in attachment as well as increasing deficits with age in cognitive and language functions (Egeland and Sroufe, 1981b).

SPECIFIC SUBSTANCES OF ABUSE AND EFFECTS ON PARENTING

There are differences in the behavioral and personality characteristics of substance-abusing adults, according to the specific substance of abuse. For example, substance abuse treatment programs find that treatment strategies successful for one drug do not necessarily translate to successful treatments for other drug addictions, and that a number of factors influence participation and treatment success, as the incidence of polydrug use, whether or not intravenous drug use is involved, comorbidity with HIV infection, and concomitant involvement in criminal activity all affect outcome (Kosten, 1991, 1992; Newcomb, 1992; Pickens and Fletcher, 1991). Systematic studies of psychopathology among substance abusers find, for example, that abuse of cocaine versus opiates is associated with a different spectrum of psychological disorders (Khantzian, 1985). Heroin addicts are generally considered a more psychiatrically deviant group than cocaine abusers (Rounsaville, Anton et al., 1991), but there are higher incidences of drug abuse and alcoholism among the relatives of cocaine abusers than heroin addicts (Rounsaville and Luthar, 1992). These types of factors that influence treatment issues according to the specified drug of abuse likely also affect the adult's parenting capacities beyond the issue of teratologic effects.

Abused drugs differ markedly in their psychological and physiological effects on the user, and these effects in turn differentially influence the adult's capacity to respond to a child. Agents such as alcohol, marijuana, heroin, or anxiolytic drugs such as valium tend to depress mood, whereas stimulants such as cocaine or amphetamines increase activity and contribute to a sense of euphoria and elation. In either case, the adult's moment-to-moment responsiveness to children's needs is impaired. In one case the impairment is toward depression and withdrawal, and in the other toward unpredictable activity and impulsivity. Although the distinctions are not absolute, the child's experience will differ depending on whether or not the parent is predominantly withdrawn or unpredictably agitated. Moreover, as cited earlier, for a proportion of substance-abusing adults, the individual's drug of choice may also in part indirectly reflect different preexisting conditions (Clure et al., 1999) that the drug use may be intended to self-medicate (Khantzian, 1985; Khantzian and Khantzian, 1984). These conditions, such as depression or anxiety disorders, do not only carry potential genetic risks for the child but will also surely influence parenting in the domains of affective availability, capacity to foster the child's independence, and parent's tolerance for the child's aggression.

The social context of the particular abused substance varies markedly and these factors also indirectly influence parenting. Alcohol, although when abused poses major health and psychological problems, is legally available, and its use is more socially acceptable than cocaine and heroin abuse. Similar differences in perceived social acceptance are found between cocaine and heroin. In a national survey of female arrestees, there was a much greater agreement between self-report of marijuana or heroin use and results of urine testing. In contrast, arrestees much more often failed to disclose their cocaine use despite positive urine screens (National Institute of Justice, 1990). Abuse of cocaine far more often involves the user directly or indirectly in criminal activities such as prostitution, theft, or actual drug dealing (Boyd and Mieczkowski, 1990) and exposes the user as well as her or his children to personal and property violence. Because of these activities, cocaine-abusing adults are more likely to be arrested and incarcerated repeatedly, exposing their children to multiple episodes of parental separation and placements usually with different foster families (Haugaard and Hazan, in Vol. 1 of this *Handbook*) or with other (often substance-abusing) neighbors or relatives (Lawson and Wilson, 1980). Additionally, substance-abusing parents often report feeling more isolated and lonely, with few friends or relatives in their neighborhoods or immediate communities whom they identify as supportive and helpful (Tucker, 1979). Feelings of isolation and self-denigration may reflect both pre- and postmorbid states related to the adult's substance abuse, but in any case parents who experience isolation and separateness may be at greater risk for problems in caring for their children especially when their isolation is compounded by the psychological effects of their addiction.

Research studies have repeatedly documented the markedly increased occurrence of severe, often multigenerational, impairments in parenting among substance-abusing families as measured by the incidences of physical and sexual abuse, neglect, abandonment, and foster placement (Black and Mayer, 1980; Brookoff et al., 1997; Lawson and Wilson, 1980; Wasserman and Leventhal, 1993; Widom, Ireland, and Glynn, 1995; Widom and White, 1997). In a case-control study of all consecutive emergency room or hospital evaluations of injuries felt to be secondary to abuse, children who were abused were significantly more likely to come from cocaine-abusing households (Wasserman and Leventhal, 1993). Black and Mayer (1980) reported on a sample of 200 addicted parents, 92 of whom were alcoholics and 108 opiate addicts. In 22.5% of the families, a child was physically or sexually abused, and in 41%, neglect was felt to have occurred. There were no differences in the occurrence rates of abuse or neglect between alcohol or opiate-addicted individuals. However, mothers who abused their children were more likely to have greater difficulties tolerating frustration, more likely to be severely depressed, and often misinterpreted their children's needs.

Neglect and out-of-home placement are extremely common among the children of opiate-using adults. In a sample of heroin-exposed children followed through school age (Wilson, 1989), only 12% were living with their biological mother, 60% lived with extended family or friends, and 25% had been adopted. By their first birthday, nearly half (48%) of these children were living away from their biological mothers. Lawson and Wilson (1980) studied mothers both in and out of treatment, one of the few reports in the area of the relation between abuse and neglect and substance abuse to include these two groups. Sixty-four women addicted to opiates were followed from birth through their child's first year of life, and 35 of the 64 were in methadone treatment when their child was 1 year. At 1 year, 23 of the 64 children from substance-abusing families were no longer in the care of their mothers, including five who were abandoned prior to hospital discharge and four who were relinquished to friends within one month of hospital discharge. A number of risk factors appear to identify those women who are more likely to abandon their children. These include no prenatal care and no interest or participation in a drug treatment program, being homeless and without income, having little to no involvement in the infant's hospital course when the infant was premature or hospitalized for neonatal withdrawal, and having abandoned previous children (Lawson and Wilson, 1979). Of the 23 mothers not caring for their children at the end of a year, 70% had at least three of these characteristics, compared to 5% of the group who did not abandon their infants. Additionally, half of the affected children were in the care of a relative, usually the maternal grandmother. However, as others have noted (Deren, 1986), because of multigenerational patterns of abuse and substance-abuse, children of substance-abusing parents placed with relatives may continue to be at greater risk for abuse.

DIRECT ASSESSMENTS OF PARENTING ATTITUDES AND BEHAVIORS

Several studies have been conducted of the parenting attitudes and behaviors of addicted mothers. In a study of the parenting attitudes, expectations, and experiences of 170 women in drug treatment (methadone maintenance and therapeutic communities) compared to 175 drug-free women, few significant differences emerged between addicted and nonaddicted mothers (Colten, 1980). Specifically, there were no differences in the parents' expectations for their children or the descriptions given about their relationships with their children. Over 80% in both groups reported positive relationships. However, Kaltenbach, Leifer, and Finnegan (1982) as well as Lief (1985) described a significant lack of understanding about basic child development issues among substance-abusing women. In a study examining mother's assessments of their children's development, mothers who had substance-abuse problems were far less likely to be concerned about their children's physical and mental development, as they grossly overestimated their children's ability (Seagull et al., 1996). Additionally, opiate-addicted mothers were more likely to report feeling inadequate in their role as a parent and perceived that they had little control over their children. They report being especially concerned about their children becoming addicts themselves, dropping out of school, or becoming involved in criminal activity (Colten, 1982). Addicted mothers wanted better for their children than they perceived themselves as either having or providing.

On the other hand, studies among opiate addicts also point to the ambivalent feelings mothers have about keeping their children. Addicted mothers report their guilt about foster placements and their wish to be reunited with their children and to try again to constitute a family (Fanshel, 1975; Nichtern, 1973). Fanshel reported that children of opiate addicts who were in foster care had been placed at younger ages than those of nonopiate addicts, had more frequent placements, and were visited less by their parent than other children in placement. In a 3-year follow-up of 57 methadone maintained mothers and a group of 31 drug-free controls matched for ethnicity, socioeconomic status, infant sex, birthweight, and gestational age, opiate-addicted mothers were far less likely to have remained their child's primary parent and were significantly more likely to have been referred to child protective or special service agencies for neglect, abandonement, or abuse (Fiks, Johnson, and Rosen, 1985). It is important to note that few studies rely on more open-ended interview techniques to explore how mothers perceive the effects of their substance abuse on their parenting. Also, although a frequent clinical consideration, no study has examined how much maternal attitudes toward the child are also influence by her worries and guilt over potentially damaging her child through her addiction. Such worries may be sufficient to affect her participation in treatment programs for herself or for her child for fear that others will remind her of what she believes she has done through her addiction.

Reports of parenting behaviors among substance-abusing versus nonabusing parents reveal significant differences. When opiate addicted women were asked about their behaviors when they are upset or angry, they more often responded that they took their anger out on their children in a number of ways including harsh criticism and yelling (Tucker, 1979). Such a response occurred twice as often in opiate-addicted women compared to opiate-addicted men who were not fathers or nonaddicted women. Using the Parent Attitudes Research Instrument (PARI), Wellisch and Steinberg (1980) compared the responses of four groups of women: addicted mothers participating in a detoxification program, addicted women in a methadone maintenance program who were not themselves parents, mothers who were not addicted, and women who were neither parents nor addicted. Addicted mothers' responses were significantly higher on *authoritarian overinvolvement*—a factor describing a parent who is likely to exclude outside influences and help in her parenting and tries overly to control her child's development. It is similar to the authoritarian/autocratic style parenting cited earlier, which is associated with problems with aggressivity in the child's later development. Addicted mothers frequently reported relying on harsh, punitive responses (Lief, 1985; Miller et al., 1999) expressed through yelling and threatening and a tendency to rely on verbal rather than physical punishment (Colten, 1980). Of those few intervention programs working with both mothers and their children, changing these preferred or habitual modes of discipline has seemed the most difficult

(Lief, 1985), but these attitudes about control and perceived angry styles of interacting seem more prevalent among substance-abusing women when compared to non-drug-using parents.

There are surprisingly few direct observational studies of parent–child interactions among substance-abusing mothers and their children, and most of these have involved adults addicted to alcohol or opiates. In 1985, Lief presented a series of clinical descriptions of interactions between mothers in treatment and their infants and toddlers. Described as points for intervention were the impoverished use of language between substance-abusing mothers and their infants, restriction of exploration which was seen as the infant's "getting into things" (p. 76) and a diminished responsiveness to the infant's bids for social interaction. Fewer than 10 studies have systematically investigated the interactive behaviors between substance-abusing mothers and their infants. The measures employed have been quite variable both in the amount of interactive detail studied and in the aspects of interaction considered potentially impaired by substance abuse. In a study of immediately postpartum cocaine-using mothers, Neuspiel, Hamel, Hochberg, Greene, and Campbell (1991) compared to a socioeconomically similar comparison group reported no differences between the two groups in maternal interactive behavior around feeding the newborn. Mayes and colleagues (1997) examined mother–child interactions at 3 and 6 months for children who had been fetally exposed to polydrug use (with cocaine), polydrug use (without cocaine), and nonexposed community controls. Mothers who had used both cocaine and other drugs during pregnancy engaged in fewer interactions and were less responsive to their infants than both the noncocaine polydrug group and community controls. No significant differences emerged between the polydrug noncocaine group and the community controls on ratings of dyadic interaction. This finding has bearing on another study (Hagan and Myers, 1997) examining the effects of cocaine and/or polydrug exposure on mother and child play, which found no significant group differences. Given the Mayes et al. (1997) findings, these results should be interpreted with caution, as the study did not separate out subgroups of polydrug use. In another study of infant/maternal interactions, drug abusing mothers had poorer patterns of interaction with their children than did nonexposed controls, where mothers exhibited less pleasure, enthusiasm, and enjoyment during play with their infants (Burns, Chethik, Burns, and Clark, 1997).

Most research groups have reported impairments in a number of interactive domains. Householder (1980, cited in Hans, 1992), reporting on the interactions between opioid-using mothers and their 3-month-old infants, described more physical activity, less emotional involvement with the infant, and less direct gaze toward the infant than nonopioid using mothers. Opiate-addicted mothers tended either to withdraw completely from the interaction or to be persistently physically intrusive. In a study of 15 mothers in a methadone maintenance clinic compared to 15 non-opiate-addicted women interacting with their own 2- to 6-year-old children (Bauman and Dougherty, 1983), addicted women were more likely to use a threatening, commanding, or provoking approach to discipline and "to reinforce a disruptive method of attention seeking" (p. 301) in comparison to nonaddicted mothers who relied more on positive reinforcement. The 2- to 6-year-old children of the substance-abusing mothers in that study also were significantly more provocative and complaining with their mothers. Bernstein and colleagues (1984) reported that 17 mothers participating in a methadone maintenance clinic, when compared to 23 non-opiate-addicted group, reacted less often and less contingently to their 4-month-old infant's communicative bids and less often tried to elicit or encourage communicative play with their infant. Similar impairments in maternal responsiveness and reciprocity were reported by Burns, Chethik, Burns, and Clark (1991) in a group of 5 polydrug using mothers, two of whom primarily used cocaine.

In a study of the predictive validity of maternal behavior for infant developmental outcome, Bernstein and colleagues (1986) reported on maternal interactive behaviors at 4 and 12 months using the same cohort from their 1984 study of 16 methadone maintained mothers and their infants and 23 non-opioid-using controls recruited from similar socioeconomic circumstances. Mothers were asked to interact with their infants around everyday activities (e.g., at 4 months diapering, feeding, and playing with a rattle, and at 12 months interesting the infant in a toy). Maternal and infant behavior were rated as positive or negative along different domains. For the mothers, these domains included emotional tone, contingency or pacing, clarity of cues, availability, and apparent interest in communication. Raters were blind to group membership. Maternal responsiveness when the infant was 12 months was a significant positive predictor of infant performance on the Bayley Scales, and methadone-using mothers overall had less positive interactions.

Studies of attachment profiles among pre- and postnatally substance-exposed children are to date few. Goodman (1990, cited in Hans, 1992) studied attachment patterns in 35 methadone-exposed and 46 nonexposed 1-year-old infants. Methadone-exposed infants more often showed disorganized (Group D; Main and Solomon, 1986) or mixed, insecure attachment patterns. Similarly, Rodning, Beckwith, and Howard (1989, 1991), studying eighteen 13-month-old children prenatally exposed to cocaine, PCP, heroin, and/or methadone, compared to 41 matched preterm children matched by socioeconomic status (SES), showed that drug-exposed toddlers were more likely to be insecurely attached to their mothers, and most of the comparison group of non-drug-exposed premature infants were securely attached. In addition, the drug-exposed children showed higher rates of disorganized attachment behaviors. The first study from Rodning's group (1989) suggested that the high rate of insecure attachment was related more to postnatal environmental conditions than to the effects of prenatal drug exposure on infant behavior because drug-exposed children reared in foster care or by a relative were less likely to be insecurely attached than those living with their biological mothers. Similar differences among these three types of parenting subgroups were not found in the larger study of 39 infants (Rodning et al., 1991), but infants from drug-using homes continued to show more-disturbed attachment patterns. In a similar study of maternal alcohol use (O'Connor, Kasari, and Sigman, 1990; reported in Griffith and Freier, 1992), maternal interactions and maternal prenatal alcohol use significantly predicted infant attachment behaviors at 1 year of age.

Importantly, in two observational studies of mother–infant interaction, the investigators have pointed out that, although the substance-abusing mothers had apparently more impaired interactions than comparison groups, a number of associated (e.g., comorbid) factors in addition to, or instead of, their substance abuse seemed to predict poor parenting. In the 1984 study conducted by Bernstein and colleagues, 47% of the opiate-addicted women and 70% of the comparison group received adequate communication scores. Women with poor interaction scores showed lower IQs, lower SES (based on a combination of maternal education and family income), and had fewer contacts with their child's father (methods described in Marcus, Hans, Patterson, and Morris, 1984). Similarly, Jeremy and Bernstein (1984), reporting on the dyadic interactions of the same cohort of 17 methadone-maintained women and their 4-month-old infants, again compared to 23 non-opiate-using mothers (Bernstein, Jeremy, Hans, and Marcus, 1984; Bernstein, Jeremy, and Marcus, 1986), found that drug use status alone did not significantly predict maternal interactive behavior. Instead, maternal psychological and psychosocial resources as measured by assessments of maternal IQ and semistructured, diagnostic psychiatric interviews, were more predictive of the quality of the mother–infant interaction than was drug-use status. Indeed, maternal drug-use, when analyzed together with other maternal variables, was not a significant predictor of mothers' interactive performance. Similarly, Johnson and Rosen (1990), examining the maternal behaviors of a sample of 75 multirisk infants, half of whom were methadone exposed, found no relation between the severity of maternal drug abuse and the degree of maternal responsiveness toward the infant.

As discussed earlier, diverse infant characteristics and behavior may be related to the effects of prenatal drug exposure, as has been demonstrated in fetal alcohol effects, narcotic withdrawal, or the more general contributions of prenatal drug exposure to prematurity and intrauterine growth retardation (Watt, 1990; Zuckerman, Frank, Hingson, and Amaro, 1989). Each of these characteristics alone or in combination may make the infant more difficult to care for. Investigators of parenting among substance-abusing mothers now employ interactive models that examine how variations in infant characteristics also influence maternal behaviors (Griffith and Freier, 1992). For example, in a study of maternal alcohol use, mother–infant interaction, and infant cognitive development, O'Connor, Sigman, and Kasari (1992, 1993) reported that the direction of strongest association was between maternal prenatal alcohol use and the effects on infant affective regulation, which in turn influenced mother–infant interaction and subsequent infant cognitive outcome. Postnatal maternal alcohol consumption did not relate to maternal interactive characteristics. Additional studies examining these types of interrelations among pre- and postnatal drug exposure effects on maternal and infant behavior are required in order to move the field beyond the prevailing view that parental substance abuse uniformly impairs parenting, which in turn contributes significantly to impaired infant and child outcome.

From animal models come some very preliminary findings suggesting that cocaine use during pregnancy alters maternal behavior when caring for their own infants and that such alterations also influence the behavior of the offspring regardless of the prenatal exposure status. In a study of the effects of cocaine exposure on maternal behavior in rats, animals were administered cocaine directly to the medial preoptic area or the nucleus acumbens, both of which are known to play a role in maternal behavior. Rats who were administered cocaine to these area showed significant decrements in maternal behavior (Rosenblatt, in Vol. 2 of this *Handbook*; Vernotica, Rosenblatt, and Morrell, 1999). In another study of rat maternal behavior, pregnant rats were administered cocaine, and the quality of the nests that they built were evaluated and compared to controls that had not been exposed. The exposed animals built poorer quality nests (used less nesting material and did not fully enclose the nest) than did controls (Quinones-Jenab, Batel, Schlussman, Ho, and Kreek, 1997).

In another study using a rat model, cocaine treated mothers were significantly more aggressive to intruders when protecting their young than either non-cocaine-treated mothers or cocaine or non-cocaine-treated foster mothers (Heyser, Molina, and Spear, 1992). The infant behavior was also altered, in that regardless of the prenatal exposure conditions, infants reared by cocaine treated mothers were more quickly aggressive to challenge (Goodwin et al., 1992). Although animal models for parenting behavior in substance-abusing conditions are only recently being developed, their value may be in suggesting hypotheses for interactive effects between pre- and postnatal exposure conditions on both infant outcomes and parenting behaviors. Finally, animal model studies have made it clear that specific alterations in brain neurochemistry that occur with cocaine or opiate abuse directly alters maternal behaviors. How these brain related effects are expressed in human beings is yet to be studied.

DEVELOPING MODELS FOR SUBSTANCE ABUSE AND PARENTING

Given the complexity of the findings outlined in this chapter, it is clear that there is need for the development of models that are constructed from multiple factors, such as genetic predispositions for particular kinds of affective and behavioral disregulation, the teratologic effects of a substance on fetal development, parental dispositional qualities, the effects of drug use on parental sensitivity and responsiveness to their children, and the effects that drug use may have on parents and children in a larger social context (i.e., increased levels of chaos, violence, absence due to incarceration, and so forth). In order for such a model to have good descriptive and predictive utility, it must specify what types of deficits in parenting occur as a function of specific substance use and what impairments in parenting are not directly related to substance abuse, but rather to the other factors (such as psychopathology) that are often associated with addictions. These apparent deficits in parenting must, in turn, be linked to outcomes in children.

The model we propose below focuses on the ways in which arousal and attentional processes in parents and their children may be affected by cocaine exposure (see Figure 13.1). We present this model as one specifically focused on a narrow band of functions, but it is contextualized by other, less-specific variables that surely affect parenting and substance abuse. We do not assume that arousal and attention are the only (nor necessarily the central) variables worth examining in substance abuse and parenting. Rather, these are one set of capacities among many that may play an important role in the ways in which substance abuse affects parenting. The goal is not to provide

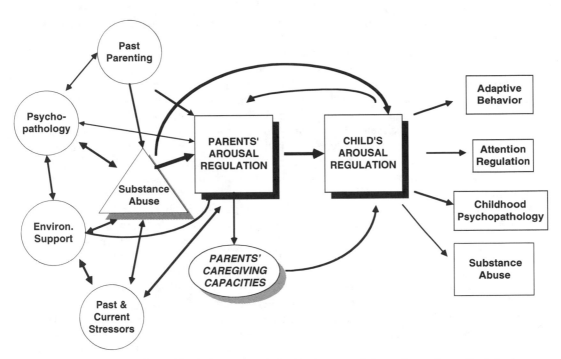

FIGURE 13.1. Theoretical model for the interactive relationships between substance abuse and parenting behavior.

a universal model for substance abuse and parenting. Rather, it points to one well established set of deficits in parenting that occur in the course of cocaine use, and projects how those deficits are thought to influence children in particular ways. The model also illustrates how the relation between cocaine abuse and deficits in attention and arousal regulation in adults may be mediated by a number of other co-occurring events and circumstances.

The ability to modulate arousal is central to many domains of other human neuropsychological function, and as such it is an important variable to account for in the development of a model of substance abuse in general, and cocaine abuse in particular. Individual differences in arousal regulation are both genetically and experientially based. Experiences include perinatal events such as substance exposure, postnatal parenting, and acute or chronic trauma. Each individual has a particular band or window of optimal arousal that is a "best fit" for that individual. In the event that the threshold is exceeded, individuals are thought to "overload" and are unable to efficiently and effectively function cognitively, socially, and emotionally. Some individuals who are tolerant of high levels of arousal have relatively wide bands, whereas individuals who are not tolerant of arousal have narrower bands of tolerance and are more liable to exceed their threshold and overload. Over the developmental course, parents play an important role in helping their children to develop functional control of their own internal processes (specifically arousal and attention), and children learn to modulate their own states so that they are able to function optimally both socially and cognitively.

How do parents modulate their children's arousal states and facilitate the development of such capacities in their children? Parents govern the intensity and duration of stimuli in their children's environment so that a range of optimal exposure to stimuli is maintained. Responsive parents recognize when their young children are becoming overstimulated and act to limit further stimulation so that the child does not become hyperaroused. This process allows children to develop increasingly greater tolerance for novel and stimulating environments over time, while maintaining levels within an acceptable and adaptive band of arousal. In the event that parents do a poor job helping their infants modulate attentional and arousal processes, the children exceed the threshold of adaptive stimulation and are more readily overloaded. As a result, these infants may be less able to learn to modulate their own arousal during the developmental course and are prone to arousal problems later on in their lives.

Substance abuse may also play a part in the way in which individuals modulate arousal states. As noted above, substance abuse may be an attempt to treat arousal and/or attentional deficits that are secondary to psychopathology resulting from genetic predispositions, environmental stressors, or a combination of both factors. Drug use alters arousal and attentional patterns and thresholds directly, and as such plays a potentially important role in an individual's experience of these processes.

The development of psychopathology such as anxiety and depression is an important factor in the ability to modulate arousal. Individuals with pathology (for example, anxiety disorders) are, by definition, less able to modulate their arousal levels than are "normal" individuals. When substance abuse is added to the environmental mix, individuals at risk for significant problems for arousal regulation by virtue of their psychopathology are further compromised, in that they use external substances either to stimulate or reduce arousal and attention. This likely leads to a recursive positive feedback loop, in which overstimulation elicits drug use, which over time erodes environmental stability, ultimately leading to progressively higher levels of stressors in the environment. This stimulation is dealt with by continued substance use.

Thus, parents' arousal regulation may affect their children's own regulation in two ways. First, predispositions for arousal regulation dysfunction may be due to genetic factors that are inherited. Second, parents are active participants in helping their children to develop tolerance for increasing levels of arousal over time in the manner outlined above. This type of responsive parenting depends in large part on the parent's ability to modulate their own arousal and attentional state. Parents are unlikely to adaptively intervene with their young children (i.e., alter the stimulation levels of the environment) if they are poorly regulated themselves. They are likely to be over or underaroused, and as such are not able to respond optimally to their children's cues. We would also expect that children who inherit a genetic predisposition for arousal disregulation problems are difficult to parent, as their band of optimal arousal is quite narrow. Parents of children who suffer from these deficits are not likely to be able to manage highly demanding, irritable, and overstimulated infants, as an overstimulated infant is arousing. This process initiates a spiral in which deficits in parenting lead to the erosion of a child's ability to manage arousal, which in turn leads to greater deficits in parenting.

Problems with arousal regulation are compounded if a child has been exposed to cocaine prenatally. In the event that there is exposure before birth, the teratologic effects of cocaine may compromise neurological development central to arousal, and as such may affect arousal modulation directly. If the mother herself has arousal regulation problems, then it follows that she may transmit a genetic susceptibility for arousal problems to her offspring. Finally, a mother with these arousal deficits herself would likely be unable to effectively help her child modulate arousal, as her own hyperaroused state would preclude responsive parenting. This would, in turn, lead to a child who develops severe arousal modulation problems secondary to genetic susceptibility, neurologic insult due to teratogenic exposure, and parenting that is not helpful to modulating the child's environment.

CONCLUSIONS

Many of the studies in the substance-abuse literature are based on a fairly narrow sample of the substance-abusing population. By and large, studies have been conducted on individuals who are disproportionately single, have low levels of formal education, high levels of comorbid psychopathology, are of low SES, and who come from urban communities. We do not dispute the findings that indicate that individuals addicted to drugs and alcohol are disproportionately affected by poverty, low social status, high exposure to trauma, and high levels of comorbid conditions. However, it may be that the samples used in many of the reported studies represent a subset of the drug and alcohol using population that is severely impaired. If this is the case, generalizing the findings from this extremely impaired sample to the population of drug and alcohol abusing parents as a whole might well be inappropriate. Individuals who share one central diagnostic feature (the overuse or misuse of substances), but share few if any of the other features commonly associated with drug abuse (i.e., are educated, financially stable, socially connected, and so forth) might well have a more diverse set of resources from which to draw, which we would expect would ameliorate the "pure" effects of substance abuse.

To extend this logic further, as the number of stressors increases (economic instability, poor social support, health problems, psychopathology, and so forth), we would expect that an individual's ability to effectively parent decreases in direct proportion to the number of stressors. In this context, substance abuse is no different from other stressors, in that the effects of the use on parenting are likely to be exacerbated or ameliorated by the presence or absence of multiple other factors in an individuals' life.

Considerations of the effects of substance abuse on infant outcome have traditionally focused on the teratologic effects of prenatal exposure to agents such as alcohol, opiates, or cocaine. It has been acknowledged that postnatal environmental conditions, such as parental discord and continued parental substance abuse, may exacerbate the effects related to the prenatal substance exposure. But little systematic research has been directed toward the effects of substance abuse on an adult's capacity to parent children and on the contributions of a postnatal substance-abusing environment to infant and child outcomes. Numerous correlative findings would suggest that substance abuse impairs parenting capacities. These include the association of parental substance abuse with (1) other psychiatric disorders including depression and antisocial personality, (2) multigenerational transmission of both substance abuse patterns and psychiatric disorders, (3) a high incidence of violence both between adults and toward children, (4) an increased risk for abandonment and neglect, and (5) a generally poor sense of competence as a parent and a poor understanding of the needs of children. How these various associated factors combine to influence an adult's interactive capacities with a child, and how child characteristics influence those patterns of adult interactiveness, are questions that are only now being studied systematically. It is likely that the impairments in parenting manifest as withdrawn or excessively intrusive behaviors seen in observational studies of substance-abusing adults are not related solely to substance abuse per se but are a cumulative reflection of the many risk factors that accompany substance abuse. However, until systematic studies of specific aspects parent–child interactions are conducted, it will remain unclear whether and how different substances of abuse impair parenting in specific and unique ways. These studies are also needed to design more effective and specifically targeted interventions for substance-abusing mothers and their children who are presenting in increasing numbers to substance abuse and child development clinics.

Given the heterogeneity of potential problems in parenting that flow from substance abuse, in some regards it is meaningless to speak in general terms about "the effect of drugs on parenting and children." Membership to the category "substance abuser" or "addict" in this context provides limited predictive and descriptive utility and provides little insight into understanding function or dysfunction in the role of parent. A more valuable, if more challenging, perspective is to attempt to link specific vulnerabilities in parenting to drug use of specific types, and then to link those vulnerabilities to outcomes in children. As stated above, this approach is not well represented in the literature, but the development of such integrative models may provide a more descriptive and predictive strategy for researchers and clinicians. Clearly, much work remains to be done. There is need for ongoing research that provides clear links between parental variables and developmental decrement that occurs as the result of parental behavior.

ACKNOWLEDGMENTS

This work was supported by National Institute on Drug Abuse grants RO1-DA-06025 (LCM) and KO2-DA00222 (LCM) and National Institute of Child Health: Human Development grant P01-HD03008. Additionally, the work was supported in part by the Children's Clinical Research Center grant MO1-RR06022, the General Clinical Research Centers Program, the National Center for Research Resources, the National Institute of Health, and the National Institute of Mental Health Research Training Grant in Neurobiological Childhood Disorders grant 5T32MH18268.

REFERENCES

Ackerman, R. J., and Michaels, J. A. (1990). *Children of alcoholics: A bibliography and resource guide.* Deerfield, FL: Health Communications.

Anisfeld, E., Cunningham, N., Ferrari, L., and Melendez, M. (1991). Infant development after prenatal cocaine exposure. *Society for Research in Child Development, 8,* 153.

Annis, H. M. (1974). Patterns of intra-familial drug use. *British Journal of Addictions, 69,* 361–369.

Arendt, R., Singer, L., and Minnes, S. (1993). Development of cocaine exposed infants. *Society for Research in Child Development.*

Aron, W. S. (1975). Family background and personal trauma among drug addicts in the United States: Implications for treatment. *British Journal of Addictions, 10,* 295–305.

Aronson, M., and Hagberg, B. (1998). Neuropsychological disorders in children exposed to alcohol during pregnancy: A follow-up study of 24 children to alcoholic mother in Goeteborg, Sweden. *Alcoholism: Clinical and Experimental Research, 22,* 321–324.

Aronson, M., Kyllerman, M., Sabel, K. G., Sandin, B., and Olegard, R. (1985). Children of alcoholic mothers: Developmental, perceptual, and behavioral characteristics as compared to matched controls. *Acta Psychiatrica Scandinavica, 74,* 27–35.

Barnett, B., Schaafsma, M. F., Gusman, A. M., and Parker, G. B. (1991). Maternal anxiety: A 5-year review of an intervention study. *Journal of Child Psychology and Psychiatry and Allied Disciplines, 32,* 423–438.

Bauman, P. S., and Dougherty, F. E. (1983). Drug-addicted mothers' parenting and their children's development. *International Journal of the Addictions, 18,* 291–302.

Bauman, P. S., and Levine, S. A. (1986). The development of children of drug addicts. *International Journal of the Addictions, 21,* 849–863.

Bayley, N. (1969). *Manual for the Bayley Scales of Infant Development.* New York: Psychological Corporation.

Beckwith, L., Howard, J., Espinosa, M., and Tyler, R. (1999). Psychopathology, mother–child interaction, and infant development: Substance-abusing mothers and their offspring. *Development and Psychopathology, 11,* 715–725.

Belsky, J., Rovine, M., and Taylor, D. C. (1984). The Pennsylvania infant and family development project III: The origins of individual differences in mother–infant attachment: Maternal and infant contributions. *Child Development, 48,* 182–194.

Bendersky, M., and Lewis, L. (1998). Arousal modulation in cocaine-exposed infants. *Developmental Psychology, 34,* 555–564.

Ben-Yehuda, N., and Schindell, B. J. (1981). The addict's family of origin: An empirical survey analysis. *International Journal of Addiction, 16,* 505–525.

Bernardi, E., Jones, M., and Tennant, C. (1989). Quality of parenting in alcoholics and narcotic addicts. *British Journal of Psychiatry, 154,* 677–682.

Bernstein, V., and Hans, S. (1994). Predicting the developmental outcome of two-year-old children born exposed to methadone: Impact of social-environmental risk factors. *Journal of Clinical Child Psychology, 23,* 349–359.

Bernstein, V., Jeremy, R. J., Hans, S., and Marcus, J. (1984). A longitudinal study of offspring born to methadone-maintained women: II. Dyadic interaction and infant behavior at four months. *American Journal of Drug and Alcohol Abuse, 10,* 161–193.

Bernstein, V., Jeremy, R. J., and Marcus, J. (1986). Mother–infant interaction in multiproblem families: Finding those at risk. *Journal of the American Academy of Child Psychiatry, 25,* 631–640.

Billman, D., Nemeth, P., Heimler, R., and Sasidharan, P. (1991). Prenatal cocaine exposure: Advanced Bayley Psychomotor Scores. *Clinical Research, 39,* 697A.

Bingol, N., Fuchs, M., Diaz, V., Stone, R. K., and Gromisch, D. S. (1987). Teratogenicity of cocaine in humans. *Journal of Pediatrics, 110,* 93–96.

Black, R., and Mayer, J. (1980). Parents with special problems: Alcoholism and opiate addiction. *Child Abuse and Neglect, 4,* 45–54.

Bornstein, M. H. (1989). Stability in early mental development: From attention and information processing in infancy and language and cognition in childhood. In M. H. Bornstein and N. A. Krasnegor (Eds.), *Stability and continuity in mental development: Behavioral and biological perspectives* (pp. 147–170). Hillsdale, NJ: Lawrence Erlbaum Associates.

Bornstein, M. H., Mayes, L. C., and Park, J. (1998). Language, play, emotional availability, and acceptance in cocaine-exposed and non-cocaine-exposed young children and their mothers. *Parole, 1,* 7–8.

Boyd, C. J., and Miecskowski, T. (1990). Drug use, health, family, and social support in "crack" cocaine users. *Addictive Behaviors, 15,* 481–485.

Brookoff, D., O'Brien, K., Cook, C. S., Thompson, T. D., and Williams, C. (1997). Characteristics of participants in domestic violence. *Journal of the American Medical Association, 277,* 1369–1373.

Burns, W. J. (1986). Psychopathology of mother–infant interaction. In I. Chasnoff (Ed.), *Drug use in pregnancy: Mother and child* (pp. 106–116). Lancaster, England: MTP.

Burns, W. J., and Burns, K. A. (1988). Parenting dysfunction in chemically dependent women. In I. Chasnoff (Ed.), *Drugs, alcohol, pregnancy, and parenting* (pp. 159–171). London: Kluwer.

Burns, K., Chethik, L., Burns, W. J., and Clark, R. (1991). Dyadic disturbances in cocaine-abusing mothers and their infants. *Journal of Clinical Psychology, 47,* 316–319.

Burns, K. A., Chethik, L., Burns W. J., and Clark, R. (1997). The early relationship of drug abusing mothers and their infants: An assessment at either to twelve months of age. *Journal of Clinical Psychology, 53,* 279–287.

Chambers, C. D., Hinesby, R. K., and Moldestad, M. (1970). Narcotic addiction in females: A race comparison. *International Journal of the Addictions, 5,* 257–278.

Chasnoff, I. J., Chisum, G. M., and Kaplan, W. E. (1988). Maternal cocaine use and genitourinary tract malformations. *Teratology, 37,* 201–204.

Chasnoff, I. J., Griffith, D. R., Freier, C., and Murray, J. (1992). Cocaine/polydrug use in pregnancy: Two-year follow-up. *Pediatrics, 89,* 284–289.

Chasnoff, I. J., Landress, H. J., and Barrett, M. E. (1990). Prevalence of illicit drugs or alcohol abuse during pregnancy and discrepancies in mandatory reporting in Pinellas County, Florida. *New England Journal of Medicine, 322,* 102–106.

Cherukuri, R., Minkoff, H., Feldman, J., Parekh, A., and Glass, L. (1988). A cohort study of alkaloidal cocaine ("crack") in pregnancy. *Obstetrics and Gynecology, 72,* 147–151.

Claren, S. K., and Smith, D. W. (1978). The fetal alcohol syndrome. *New England Journal of Medicine, 298,* 1063–1067.

Clure, C., Brady, K. T., Saladin, M. E., Johnson, D., Waid, R., and Rittenbury, M. (1999). Attention deficit/hyperactivity disorder and substance use: Symptoms pattern and drug choice. *American Journal of Drug and Alcohol Abuse, 25,* 441–448.

Cohn, J. F., and Tronick, E. Z. (1988). Mother–infant face-to-face interaction: Influence is bidirectional and unrelated to periodic cycles in either partner's behavior. *Developmental Psychology, 24,* 386–392.

Coles, C. D., Bard, K. A., Platzman, K. A., and Lynch, M. E. (1999). Attentional response at eight weeks in prenatally drug-exposed and preterm infants. *Neurotoxicology and Teratology, 21,* 527–537.

Coles, C., Brown, R., Smith, I., Platzman, K., Erikson, S., and Falek, A. (1991). Effects of prenatal alcohol exposure at school age. I. Physical and cognitive development. *Neurotoxicology and Teratology, 13,* 357–367.

Coles, C. D., Smith, I. E., Lancaster, J. S., and Falek, A. (1987). Persistence over the first months of neurobehavioral differences in infants exposed to alcohol prenatally. *Infant Behavior and Development, 10,* 23–37.

Colten, M. E (1980). A comparison of heroin-addicted and non-addicted mothers: Their attitudes, beliefs, and parenting experiences. (NIDA Services Research Report, Pub. No. 81-1028). *Heroin-addicted parents and their children.* DHHS, Washington, DC.

Colten, M. E. (1982). Attitudes, experiences, and self-perception of heroin addicted mothers. *Journal of Social Issues, 38,* 78–92.

Coppolillo, H. (1975). Drug impediments to mothering behavior. *Addictive Diseases, 2,* 201–208.

Courtwright, D. T. (1982). *Dark paradise.* Cambridge, MA: Harvard University Press.

Davis, S. K. (1990). Chemical dependency in women: A description of its effects and outcome on adequate parenting. *Journal of Substance Abuse Treatment, 7,* 225–232.

Dawson, G., Klinger, L. G., Panagiotides, H., and Spieker, S. (1992). Infants of mothers with depressive symptoms: Electroencephalographic and behavioral findings related to attachment status. *Development and Psychopathology, 4,* 67–80.

Day, N. L. (1992). Effects of prenatal alcohol exposure. In I. S. Zagon and T. A. Slotkin (Eds.), *Maternal substance abuse and the developing nervous system* (pp. 27–44). Boston: Academic Press.

Densen-Gerber, J., and Rohrs, C. C. (1975). Drug-addicted parents and child abuse. *Contemporary Drug Problems, 2,* 213–226.

Delaney-Black, V., Covington, C., Ostrea, E., Romero, A., Baker, D., Tagel, M., Nordstrom-Klee, B., Silvestre, M., Angelilli, M. L., Hack, C., and Long, J. (1996). Cocaine and neonatal outcome: Evaluation of dose–response relationship. *Pediatrics, 98,* 735–740.

Delaney-Black, V., Covington, C., Templin, T., Ager, J., Martier, S., and Sokol, R. (1998). Prenatal cocaine exposure and child behavior. *Pediatrics, 102,* 945–950.

Deren, S. (1986). Children of substance abusers. A review of the literature. *Journal of Substance Abuse Treatment, 3,* 7–94.

Desmond, M. M., and Wilson, G. S. (1975). Neonatal abstinence syndrome: Recognition and diagnosis. *Addictive Diseases, 2,* 113–121.

Egeland, B., and Sroufe, L. A. (1981a). Attachment and early maltreatment. *Child Development, 52,* 44–52.

Egeland, B., and Sroufe, L. A. (1981b). Developmental sequelae of maltreatment in infancy. *New Directions for Child Development, 11,* 77–92.

Ernhart, C. B., Wolf, A. W., Linn, P. L., Sokol, R., Kennard, M., and Filipovich, H. (1985). Alcohol-related birth defects: Syndromal anomalies intrauterine growth retardation and neonatal behavioral assessment. *Alcoholism, Clinical and Experimental Research, 9,* 506–511.

Escamilla-Mondanaro, J. (1977). Women: Pregnancy, Children and addiction. *Journal of Psychedelic drugs, 9,* 59–68.

Fanshel, D. (1975). Parental failure and consequences for children: The drug abusing mother whose children are in foster care. *American Journal of Public Health, 65,* 604–612.

Fawzy, F., Coombs, R., and Gerber, B. (1983). Generational continuity in the use of substances: The impact of parental substance use on adolescent substance use. *Addictive Behaviors, 8,* 109–114.

Fiks, K. B., Johnson, H. L., and Rosen, T. S. (1985). Methadone-maintained mothers: 3-year follow-up of parental functioning. *International Journal of the Addictions, 20,* 651–660.

Finnegan, L. P. (1976). Clinical effects of pharmacologic agents on pregnancy, the fetus, and the neonate. *Annals of the New York Academy of Science, 281,* 74–89.

Finnegan, L. P. (1979). In utero opiate dependence and sudden infant death syndrome. *Clinics in Perinatology, 6,* 163–180.

Frick, P. J., Lahey, B. B., Loeber, R., Stouthamer-Loeber, M., Christ, M. A., and Hanson, K. (1992). Familial risk factors to oppositional defiant disorder and conduct disorder: Parental psychopathology and maternal parenting. *Journal of Consulting and Clinical Psychology, 60,* 49–55.

Fried, P. (1992). Who is it going to be? Subject selection issues in prenatal drug exposure research. *NIDA Research Monograph, 117,* 121–136.

Friedman, A. S., Pomerance, E., Sanders, R., Santo, Y., and Utada, A. (1980, Fall). The structure and problems of the families of adolescent drug users. *Contemporary Drug Problems,* 327–356.

Fulroth, R., Phillips, B., and Durand, D. J. (1989). Perinatal outcome of infants exposed to cocaine and/or heroin in utero. *American Journal of Diseases in Children, 143,* 905–910.

Glantz, M. D. (1992). A developmental psychopathology model of drug abuse vulnerability. In M. D. Glantz and R. W. Pickens (Eds.), *Vulnerability to drug abuse* (pp. 389–418). Washington, DC: American Psychological Association.

Goodlet, C. R., and West, J. R. (1992). Alcohol exposure during brain growth spurt. In I. S. Zagon., and T. A. Slotkin (Eds.), *Maternal substance abuse and the developing nervous system* (pp. 45–75). Boston: Academic Press.

Goodman, G. A. (1990). *Identifying attachment patterns and their antecedents among opioid-exposed 12-month-old infants.* Unpublished doctoral dissertation, Northwestern University Medical School, Chicago.

Goodwin, G. A., Heyser, C. J., Moody, C. A., Rajachandran, C. (1992). A fostering study of the effects of prenatal cocaine exposure: II. Offspring behavioral measures. *Neurotoxicology and Teratology, 14,* 423–432.

Griffith, D., and Freier, C. (1992). Methodological issues in the assessment of the mother–child interactions of substance-abusing women and their children. *NIDA Research Monograph, 117,* 228–247.

Gusella, J., and Fried, P. (1984). Effects of maternal social drinking and smoking on offspring at 13 months. *Neurobehavioral Toxicology and Teratology, 6,* 13–17.

Hadeed, A. J., and Siegel, S. R. (1989). Maternal cocaine use during pregnancy: Effect on the newborn infant. *Pediatrics, 84,* 205–210.

Hagan, J. C., and Myers, B. J. (1997). Mother–toddler play interaction: A contrast of substance-exposed and nonexposed children. *Infant Mental Health Journal, 18,* 40–57.

Hans, S. L. (1989). Developmental consequences of prenatal exposure to methadone. *Annals of the New York Academy of Science, 562,* 195–207.

Hans, S. L. (1992). Maternal opioid use and child development. In I. S. Zagon and T. A. Slotkin (Eds.), *Maternal substance abuse and the developing nervous system* (pp. 177–214). Boston: Academic Press.

Hans, S. L., Bernstein, V. J., and Henson, L. G. (1990). *Interaction between drug-using mothers and their toddlers.* Paper presented at the Seventh International Conference on Infant Studies, Montreal, Quebec, Canada.

Hans, S. L., Bernstein, V. J., and Henson, L. G. (1999). The role of psychopathology in the parenting of drug-dependent women. *Development and Psychopathology, 11,* 957–977.

Hans, S. L., and Marcus, J. (1983). Motor and attentional behavior in infants of methadone maintained women. *National Institute on Drug Abuse Research Monograph, 43,* 287–293.

Hans, S. L., and Jeremy, R. J. (1984). Post-neonatal motoric signs in infants exposed in utero to methadone. *Infant Behavior and Development, 7,* 158.

Hans, S. L., Marcus, J., Jeremy, R. J., and Auerbach, J. G. (1984). Neurobehavioral development of children exposed in utero to opioid drugs. In J. Yanai, (Ed.), *Neurobehavioral teratology* (pp. 249–273). New York: Elsevier.

Hawley, T. L., and Disney, E. R. (1992). Crack's children: The consequences of maternal cocaine abuse. *Social Policy Report of the Society for Research in Child Development, 6,* 1–22.

Heath, D. B. (1991). Women and alcohol: Cross-cultural perspectives. *Journal of Substance Abuse, 3,* 175–185.

Held, J. R., Riggs, M. L., and Dorman, C. (1999). The effect of prenatal cocaine exposure on neurobehavioral outcome: A meta-analysis. *Neurotoxicology and Teratology, 21,* 619–625.

Heyser, C. J., Molina, V. A., and Spear, L. P. (1992). A fostering study of the effects of prenatal cocaine exposure: I. Maternal behaviors. *Neurotoxicology and Teratology, 14,* 415–421.

Householder, J. (1980). *An investigation of mother–infant interaction in a narcotic-addicted population.* Unpublished doctoral dissertation, Northwestern University, Evonston, IL.

Howard, J., Beckwith, L., Espinosa, M., and Tyler, R. (1995). Development of infants born to cocaine-abusing women: Biologic/maternal influences. *Neurotoxicology and Teratology, 17,* 403–411.

Isabella, R. A. (1993). Origins of attachment: Maternal interactive behavior across the first year. *Child Development, 64,* 605–621.

Isenberg, S. J., Spierer, A., and Inkelis, S. H. (1987). Ocular signs of cocaine intoxication in neonates. *American Journal of Ophthalmology, 103,* 211–214.

Jacobson, S. W., Jacobson, J. L., Sokol, R. J., Martier, S. S., and Chiodo, L. M. (1996). New evidence for neurobehavioral effects of in utero cocaine exposure. *Journal of Pediatrics, 129,* 581–590.

Jeremy, R. J., and Bernstein, V. (1984). Dyads at risk: Methadone-maintained women and their four-month-old infants. *Child Development, 55,* 1141–1154.

Jeremy, R. J., and Hans, S. L. (1985). Behavior of neonates exposed in utero to methadone as assessed on the Brazelton scale. *Infant Behavior and Development, 8,* 323–336.

Johnson, H. L., Glassman, M. B., Fiks, K. B., and Rosen, T. S. (1990). Resilient children: Individual differences in developmental outcome of children born to drug abusers. *Journal of Genetic Psychology, 151,* 523–539.

Johnson, H. L., and Rosen, T. S. (1990). Difficult mothers of difficult babies: Mother–infant interaction in a multi-risk population. *American Journal of Orthopsychiatry, 60,* 281–288.

Johnson, V., and Pandina, R. J. (1991). Effects of the family environment on adolescent substance use, delinquency, and coping styles. *American Journal of Drug and Alcohol Abuse, 17,* 71–88.

Jones, K. L., and Smith, D. W. (1973). Recognition of the fetal alcohol syndrome in early infancy. *Lancet, 2,* 999–1001.

Jones, K. L., Smith, D. W., Ulleland, C. N., and Streissguth, A. P. (1973). Pattern of malformation in the offspring of chronic alcoholic mothers. *Lancet, 1,* 1267–1271.

Kaltenbach, K., and Finnegan, L. P. (1987). Perinatal and developmental outcome of infants exposed to methadone in utero. *Neurotoxicology and Teratology, 9,* 311–313.

Kaltenbach, K., Leifer, B., and Finnegan, L. (1982). Knowledge of child development in drug dependent mothers. *Pediatric Research, 16,* 87.

Kessler, R. C., Crum, R. M., Warner, L. A., Nelson, C. B., Schulenberg, J., and Anthony, J. C. (1997). Lifetime co-occurrence of DSM-III-R alcohol abuse and dependence with other psychiatric disorders in the National Comorbidity Survey. *Archives of General Psychiatry, 54,* 313–321.

Kessler, R. C., Nelson, C. B., McGonagle, K. A., Edlund, M. J., Frank, R. G., and Leaf, P. J. (1996). The epidemiology of co-occurring addictive and mental disorders: Implications for prevention and service utilization. *American Journal of Orthopsychiatry, 66,* 17–31.

Khantzian, E. J. (1983). An extreme case of cocaine dependence and marked improvement with methylphenidate treatment. *American Journal of Psychiatry, 140,* 784–785.

Khantzian, E. J. (1985). The self-medication hypothesis of addictive disorders: Focus on heroin and cocaine dependence. *American Journal of Psychiatry, 142,* 1259–1264.

Khantzian, E. J., Gawin, F., Kleber, H. D., et al. (1984). Methylphenidate treatment of cocaine dependence—A preliminary report. *Journal of Substance Abuse Treatment, 1,* 107–112.

Khantzian, E. J., and Khantzian, N. J. (1984). Cocaine addiction: Is there a psychological predisposition? *Psychiatric Annals, 14,* 753–759.

Korkman, M., Autti-Raemoe, I., Koivulehto, H., and Granstroem, M. (1998). Neuropsychological effects at early school age of fetal alcohol exposure of varying duration. *Child Neuropsychology, 4,* 199–212.

Kosten, T. (1991). Client issues in drug abuse treatment: Addressing multiple drug use. *NIDA Research Monograph, 106,* 136–151.

Kosten, T. (1992). Matching patients to treatment. In T. R. Kosten and H. D. Kleber (Eds.), *Clinician's guide to cocaine addiction* (pp. 389–395). New York: Guilford.

Larroque, B., and Kaminski, M. (1998). Prenatal alcohol exposure and development at preschool age: Main results of a French study. *Alcoholism: Clinical and Experimental Research, 22,* 295–303.

Lawson, M., and Wilson, G. (1979). Addiction and pregnancy: Two lives in crisis. *Social Work in Health Care, 4,* 445–457.

Lawson, M., and Wilson, G. (1980). Parenting among women addicted to narcotics. *Child Welfare, 59,* 67–79.

Lester, B. M., LaGasse, L. L., and Seifer, R. (1998). Cocaine exposure and children: The meaning of subtle effects. *Science, 282,* 633–634.

Lester, B. M., Boukydis, C., Zachariah, and Twomey, J. (2000). Maternal substance abuse and child outcome. In C. H. Zeanah (Eds.), *Handbook of infant mental health* (2nd ed., pp. 161–175). New York: Guilford.

Lewis, M., and Goldberg, S. (1969). Perceptual-cognitive development in infancy: A generalized expectancy model as a function of mother–infant interaction. *Merrill-Palmer Quarterly, 15,* 81–100.

Lief, N. R. (1985). The drug user as parent. *International Journal of the Addictions, 20,* 63–97.

Lindenberg, C. S., Alexander, E. M., Gendrop, S. C., Nencioli, M., and Williams, D. G. (1991). A review of the literature on cocaine abuse in pregnancy. *Nursing Research*, *40*, 69–75.

Loeb, R. C., Horst, L., and Horton, P. J. (1980). Family interaction patterns associated with self-esteem in preadolescent girls and boys. *Merrill-Palmer Quarterly*, *26*, 203–217.

Lohr, M. J., Gillmore, M. R., Gilchrist, L. D., and Butler, S. S. (1992). Factors related to substance use by pregnant, school-age adolescents. *Journal of Adolescent Health*, *13*, 475–482.

Luthar, S., Anton, S. F., Merikangas, K. R., and Rounsaville, B. J. (1992). Vulnerability to substance abuse and psychopathology among siblings of opioid abusers. *Journal of Nervous and Mental Disorders*, *180*, 153–161.

Luthar, S. S., Cushing, G., Merikangas, K. R., and Rounsaville, B. J. (1998). Multiple jeopardy: Risk and protective factors among addicted mothers' offspring. *Development and Psychopathology*, *10*, 117–136.

Luthar, S., Merikangas, K. R., and Rounsaville, B. J. (1993). Parental psychopathology and disorders in offspring. *Journal of Nervous and Mental Disorders*, *181*, 351–357.

Luthar, S., and Zigler, E. (1991). Vulnerability and competence: A review of research on resilience in childhood. *American Journal of Orthopsychiatry*, *61*, 6–22.

Macoby, E. E., and Martin, J. A. (1983). Socialization in the context of the family: parent–child interaction. In E. M. Hetherington (Ed.), *Socialization, personality, and social development: Vol. 4. Handbook of child psychology* (pp. 1–102). New York: Wiley.

MacGregor, S. N., Keith, L. G., Bachicha, J. A., and Chasnoff, I. J. (1989). Cocaine use during pregnancy: Correlation between prenatal care and perinatal outcome. *Obstetrics and Gynecology*, *7*, 882–885.

Main, M., and Solomon, J. (1986). Discovery of an insecure-disorganized/disoriented attachment pattern. In T. B. Brazelton, and M. Yogman (Eds.), *Affective development in infancy*. Norwood, NJ: Ablex.

Marcus, J., and Hans, S. L. (1982). Electromyographic assessment of neonatal muscle tone. *Psychiatry Research*, *6*, 31–40.

Marcus, J., Hans, S. L., Patterson, C. B., and Morris, A. J. (1984). A longitudinal study of offspring born to methadone-maintained women. I. Design, methodology, and description of women's resources for functioning. *American Journal of Drug and Alcohol Abuse*, *10*, 135–160.

Mayes, L. C., Bornstein, M. H., Chawarska, K., Haynes, O. M., and Granger, R. H. (1996). Impaired regulation of arousal in 3-month-old infants exposed prenatally to cocaine and other drugs. *Development and Psychopathology*, *8*, 29–42.

Mayes, L. C., Feldman, R., Granger, R. H., Haynes, W. M., Bornstein, M. H., and Schottenfeld, R. (1997). The effects of polydrug use with and without cocaine on mother–infant interaction at 3 and 6 months. *Infant Behavior and Development*, *20*, 489–502.

McCall, R., and Carriger, M. (1993). A meta-analysis of infant habituation and recognition memory performance as predictors of later IQ. *Child Development*, *64*, 57–79.

McCord, W., and McCord, J. (1960). *The origins of alcoholism*. London: Tavistock.

Merikangas, K. R., Rounsaville, B. J., and Prusoff, B. A. (1992). Familial factors in vulnerability to substance abuse. In M. Glantz, and R. Pickens (Eds.), *Vulnerability to drug abuse* (pp. 75–98). Washington, DC: American Psychiatric Association.

Miller, B. A., Smyth, N. J., and Mudar, P. J. (1999). Mothers' alcohol and other drug problems and their punitiveness toward their children. *Journal of Studies on Alcohol*, *60*, 632–642.

Mirin, S. M., Weiss, R. D., Griffin, M. L., and Michael, J. L. (1991). Psychopathology in drug abusers and their families. *Comprehensive Psychiatry*, *32*, 36–51.

Mondanaro, J. E. (1977). Women, pregnancy, children, and addiction. *Journal of Psychedelic Drugs*, *9*, 59–67.

Moore, T. R., Sorg, J., Miller, L., Key, T., and Resnik, R. (1986). Hemodynamic effects of intravenous cocaine on the pregnant ewe and fetus. *American Journal of Obstetrics and Gynecology*, *155*, 883–888.

Musto, D. (1973). *The American disease: Origins of narcotic control*. New Haven, CT: Yale University Press.

Mutzell, S. (1993). Male offspring of alcoholic parents compared with men from the general population. *Early Child Development and Care*, *88*, 61–72.

National Institute of Justice. (1990). *Drug use forecasting annual report*. Washington, DC: Author.

Neuspiel, D. R., Hamel, S. C., Hochberg, E., Greene, J., and Campbell, D. (1991). Maternal cocaine use and infant behavior. *Neurotoxicology and Teratology*, *13*, 229–233.

Newcomb, M. D. (1992). Understanding the multidimensional nature of drug use and abuse: The role of consumption, risk factors, and protective factors. In M. Glantz and R. Pickens (Eds.), *Vulnerability to drug abuse* (pp. 255–297). Washington, DC: American Psychiatric Association.

Nichtern, S. (1973). The children of drug users. *Journal of the American Academy of Child Psychiatry*, *12*, 24–31.

O'Connor, M. J., Brill, N., and Sigman, M. (1986). Alcohol use in elderly primips: Relation to infant development. *Pediatrics*, *78*, 444–450.

O'Connor, M. J., Kasari, C., and Sigman, M. (1990). *The influence of mother–infant interaction on attachment behavior of infants exposed to alcohol prenatally*. Paper presented at the Seventh International Conference on Infant Studies, Montreal, Quebec, Canada.

O'Connor, M. J., Sigman, M., and Kasari, C. (1992). Attachment behavior of infants exposed prenatally to alcohol: Mediating effects of infant affect and mother–infant interaction. *Development and Psychopathology, 4*, 243–256.

O'Connor, M. J., Sigman, M., and Kasari, C. (1993). Maternal alcohol use and infant cognition. *Infant Behavior and Development, 16*, 177–193.

Oloffson, M., Buckley, W., Andersen, G. E., and Friss-Hansen, B. (1983). Investigation of 89 children born by drug-dependent mothers: Follow-up 1–19 years after birth. *Acta Paediatrica Scandinavica, 72*, 407–410.

Olson, H. C., and Toth, S. K. (1999). Samples in research on prenatal cocaine exposure: Vexing problems and practical solutions. *Journal of Drug Issues, 29*, 237–252.

O'Malley, S., Adamse, M., Heaton, R. K., and Gawin, F. H. (1992). Neuropsychological impairments in chronic cocaine abusers. *American Journal of Drug and Alcohol Abuse, 18*, 131–144.

Oro, A. S., and Dixon, S. D. (1987). Perinatal cocaine and methamphetamine exposure: Maternal and neonatal correlates. *Journal of Pediatrics, 111*, 571–578.

Parker, G., Tupling, H., and Brown, L. (1978). A parental bonding instrument. *British Journal of Psychiatry, 141*, 437–446.

Patterson, G. R. (1982). *Coercive family process.* Eugene, OR: Castalia.

Pickens, R. W., and Fletcher, B. W. (1991). Overview of treatment issues. *NIDA Research Monograph, 106*, 1–19.

Pihl, R. O., Peterson, J., and Finn, P. (1990). Inherited predisposition to alcoholism: Characteristics of sons of male alcoholics. *Journal of Abnormal Psychology, 99*, 291–301.

Prescott, C. A., and Kendler, K. S. (1999). Genetic and environmental contributions to alcohol abuse and dependence in a population based sample of male twins. *American Journal of Psychiatry, 156*, 34–40.

Quinones-Jenab, V., Batel, P., Schlussman, S. D., Ho, A., and Kreek, M. J. (1997). Cocaine impairs maternal nest building in pregnant rats. *Pharmacology, Biochemistry and Behavior, 58*, 1009–1013.

Raynes, A. E., Clement, C., Patch, V. D., and Ervin, F. (1974). Factors related to imprisonment in female heroin addicts. *International Journal of the Addictions, 9*, 145–150.

Regan, D., Leifer, B., and Finnegan, L. (1982). Generations at risk: Violence in the lives of pregnant drug abusing women. *Pediatric Research, 16*, 91.

Richardson, G. A., Conroy, M. L., and Day, N. L. (1996). Prenatal cocaine exposure: Effects on the development of school-aged children. *Neurotoxicology and Teratology, 18*, 627–634.

Robins, L. N. (1966). *Deviant children grown up.* Baltimore: Williams and Wilkins.

Rodning, C., Beckwith, L., and Howard, J. (1989). Characteristics of attachment organization and play organization in prenatally drug-exposed toddlers. *Development and Psychopathology, 1*, 277–289.

Rodning, C., Beckwith, and Howard, J. (1991). Quality of attachment and home environments in children prenatally exposed to PCP and cocaine. *Development and Psychopathology, 3*, 351–366.

Rohsenow, D. J., Corbett, R., and Devine, D. (1988). Molested as children: A hidden contribution to substance abuse? *Journal of Substance Abuse Treatment, 5*, 13–18.

Rosen, T. S., and Johnson, H. L. (1982). Children of methadone-maintained mothers: Follow-up to 18 months of age. *Journal of Pediatrics, 101*, 192–196.

Rosen, T. S., and Johnson, H. L. (1988). Drug-addicted mothers, their infants, and SIDS. *Annals of the New York Academy of Science, 533*, 89–95.

Rounsaville, B. J., Anton, S. F., Carroll, K., Budde, D., Prusoff, B. A., and Gawin, F. (1991). Psychiatric disorders of treatment-seeking cocaine abusers. *Archives of General Psychiatry, 48*, 43–51.

Rounsaville, B. J., Kosten, T. R., Weissman, M. M., and Kleber, H. D. (1985). *Evaluating and treating depressive disorders in opiate addicts.* Rockville, MD: National Institute on Drug Abuse.

Rounsaville, B. J., Kosten, T. R., Weissman, M. M., Prusoff, B., Pauls, D., Foley, S., and Merikangas, K. (1991). Psychiatric disorders in the relatives of probands with opiate addicts. *Archives of General Psychiatry, 48*, 33–42.

Rounsaville, B. J., and Luthar, S. S. (1992). Family/genetic studies of cocaine abusers and opioid addicts. In T. R. Kosten, and H. D. Kleber (Eds.), *Clinician's guide to cocaine addiction* (pp. 206–221). New York: Guilford.

Rounsaville, B. J., Weissman, M. M., Wilber, C. H., Kleber, H. D. (1982). Pathways of opiate addiction: An evaluation of differing antecedents. *British Journal of Psychiatry, 141*, 437–466.

Ryan, L., Ehrlich, S., and Finnegan, L. (1987). Cocaine abuse in pregnancy: Effects on the fetus and newborn. *Neurotoxicology and Teratology, 9*, 295–299.

Sandberg, D. E., Meyer-Bahlburg, H. F. L., Rosen, T. S., and Johnson, H. L. (1990). Effects of prenatal methadone exposure on sex-dimorphic behavior in early school-age children. *Psychoneuroendocrinology, 15*, 77–82.

Schenker, S., Becker, H. C., Randall, C. L., Phillips, D. K., Baskin, G. S., and Henderson, G. L. (1990). Fetal alcohol syndrome: Current status of pathogenesis. *Alcoholism, Clinical and Experimental Research, 14*, 635–647.

Schuckit, M. (1999). New findings on the genetics of alcoholism. *Journal of the American Medical Association, 281*, 1875–1876.

Seagull, F. N., Mowery, J. L., Simpson, P. M., Robinson, R. R., Martier, S. S., Sokol, R. J., and McGarver-May, D. G. (1996). Maternal assessment of infant development: Associations with alcohol and drug use in pregnancy. *Clinical Pediatrics, 35*, 621–628.

Smart, R. G., and Fejer, D. (1972). Drug use among adolescents and their parents: Closing the generation gap in mood modification. *Journal of Abnormal Child Psychology, 79,* 153–160.

Smith, D. W. (1982). *Recognizable patterns of human malformation: Genetic, embryologic, and clinical aspects* (3rd ed.). Philadelphia: Saunders.

Smith, I. E., Coles, C. D., Lancaster, J., Fernhoff, P., and Falek, A. (1986). The effect of volume and duration of prenatal ethanol exposure on neonatal physical and behavioral development. *Neurotoxicology and Teratolology, 8,* 375–381.

Sokol, R. J., Miller, S., and Reed, G. (1980). Alcohol abuse during pregnancy: An epidemiological study. *Alcoholism, Clinical and Experimental Research, 4,* 135–145.

Sowder, B. J., and Burt, M. R. (1980). *Children of heroin addicts: An assessment of health, learning, behavioral, and adjustment problems.* New York: Praeger.

Sroufe, L. A., Fox, N. E., and Pancake, V. R. (1983). Attachment and dependency in developmental perspective. *Child Development, 54,* 1615–1627.

Steinhausen, H. C., Nestler, V., and Spohr, H. L. (1982). Development and psychopathology of children with the fetal alcohol syndrome. *Developmental and Behavioral Pediatrics, 3,* 49–54.

Stern, D. N. (1985). *The interpersonal world of the infant.* New York: Basic Books.

Stout, R. L., Brown, P. J., Longabaugh, R., and Noel, N. (1996). Determinants of research follow-up participation in an alcohol treatment outcome trial. *Journal of Consulting and Clinical Psychology, 64,* 614–618.

Strauss, M. E., Starr, R. H., Ostrea, E. M., Jr., Chavez, C. J., and Stryker, J. C. (1977). Behavioral concomitants of prenatal addiction to narcotics. Annual Progress in Child Psychiatry: Child Development, 108–118.

Streissguth, A. P. (1976). Psychologic handicaps in children with fetal alcohol syndrome. *Work. Prog. Alcohol, 273,* 140–145.

Streissguth, A. P. (1992). Fetal alcohol syndrome and fetal alcohol effects: A clinical perspective on later developmental consequences. In I. S. Zagon and T. A. Slotkin (Eds.), *Maternal substance abuse and the developing nervous system* (pp. 5–26). Boston: Academic Press.

Streissguth, A. P., Aase, I. M., Clarren, S. K., Randels, S. P., LaDue, R. A., and Smith, D. F. (1991). Fetal alcohol syndrome in adolescents and adults. *JAMA, 265,* 1961–1967.

Streissguth, A. P., Barr, H. M., Bookstein, F. L., Sampson, P. D., and Olson, H. C. (1999). The long-term neurocognitive consequences of prenatal alcohol exposure: A 14-year study. *Psychological Science, 10,* 186–190.

Streissguth, A. P., Barr, H. M., and Sampson, P. D. (1990). Moderate prenatal alcohol exposure: Effects on child IQ and learning problems at age 71/2 years. *Alcoholism, Clinical and Experimental Research, 14,* 662–669.

Streissguth, A. P., Barr, H. M., Sampson, P. D., Darby, B. L., and Martin, D. C. (1989). IQ at age 4 in relation to maternal alcohol use and smoking during pregnancy. *Developmental Psychology, 25,* 3–11.

Suffet, F., and Brotman, R. (1976). Employment and social disability among opiate addicts. *American Journal of Drug and Alcohol Abuse, 3,* 387–395.

Teske, M. P., and Trese, M. T. (1987). Retinopathy of prematurity-like fundus and persistent hyperplastic primary vitreous associated with maternal cocaine use. *American Journal of Ophthalmology, 103,* 719–720.

Tesson, B. M. (1990). Who are they? Identifying and treating adult children of alcoholics. *Journal of Psychosocial Nursing and Mental Health Services, 28,* 16–21.

Tronick, E. Z., and Cohn, J. F. (1989). Infant–mother interaction: Age and gender differences in coordination and occurrence of miscoordination. *Child Development, 60,* 85–92.

Tronick, E. Z., and Gianino, A. F. (1986). The transmission of maternal disturbance to the infant. In E. Tronick and T. Field (Eds.), *Maternal depression and infant disturbance* (pp. 5–11). New York: Wiley.

Tucker, M. B. (1979). A descriptive and comparative analysis of the social support structure of heroin-addicted women. *Addicted women: Family dynamics, self-perceptions, and support systems* (pp. 37–76). Washington, DC: National Institute on Drug Abuse, Supt. of Docs., U.S. Government Printing Office.

Valliant, G. (1980). Natural history of male psychological health. VIII: Antecedent of alcoholism and orality. *American Journal of Psychiatry, 137,* 181–186.

Verheul, R., Kranzler, H. R., Poling, J., Tenne, H., Ball, S., and Rounsaville, B. J. (2000). Co-occurrence of Axis I and Axis II disorders in substance abusers. *Acta Psychiatrica Scandinavica, 101,* 110–118.

Vernotica, E. M., Rosenblatt, J. S., and Morrell, J. I. (1999). Microinfusion of cocaine into the medial preoptic area or nucleus acumbens transiently imparis maternal behavior in the rat. *Behavioral Neuroscience, 113,* 377–390.

Ward, O. B., Kopertowski, D. M., Finnegan, L. P., and Sandberg, D. E. (1989). Gender-identity variations in boys prenatally exposed to opiates. *Annals of the New York Academy of Science, 562,* 365–366.

Ward, O. B., Orth, T. M., and Weisz, J. (1983). A possible role of opiates in modifying sexual differentiation. In M. Schlumpf and W. Lichtensteinger (Eds.), *Monographs in neural science* (Vol. 9, pp. 194–200). Basel, Switzerland: Karger.

Wasserman, G. A., Kline, J. K., Bateman, D. A., Chiriboga, C., Lumey, L. H., Friedlander, H., Melton, L., and Heagarty, M. C. (1998). Prenatal cocaine exposure and school-age intellegence. *Drug and Alcohol Dependence, 50,* 203–210.

Wasserman, D. R., and Leventhal, J. M. (1993). Maltreatment of children born to cocaine-abusing mothers. *American Journal of Diseases of Children, 147,* 1324–1328.

Watt, J. E. (1990). Interaction, intervention, and development in small for gestational age infants. *Infant Behavior and Development, 13,* 273–286.

Watt, J. E., and Strongman, K. T. (1985). The organization and stability of sleep states in fullterm, preterm, and small-for-gestational age infants: A comparative study. *Developmental Psychobiology, 18,* 151–162.

Wellisch, D. K., and Steinberg, M. R. (1980). Parenting attitudes of addict mothers. *International Journal of the Addictions, 15,* 809–819.

Widom, C. S., Ireland, T., and Glynn, P. J. (1995). Alcohol abuse in abused and neglected children followed-up. Are they at increased risk? *Journal of Studies on Alcohol, 56,* 207–217.

Widom, C. S., and White, H. R. (1997). Problem behaviours in abused and neglected children grown up: Prevalence and co-occurrence of substance abuse, crime and violence. *Criminal Behaviour and Mental Health, 7,* 287–310.

Wilson, G. S. (1989). Clinical studies of infants and children exposed prenatally to heroin. *Annals of the New York Academy of Science, 562,* 183–194.

Wilson, G. S., Desmond, M. M., and Wait, R. B. (1981). Follow-up of methadone-treated and untreated narcotic-dependent women and their infants: Health, development, and social implications. *Journal of Pediatrics, 98,* 716–722.

Wilson, G. S., McCreary, R., Kean, J., and Baxter, J. C. (1979). The development of preschool children of heroin-addicted mothers: A controlled study. *Pediatrics, 63,* 135–141.

Wolock, I., and Magura, S. (1996). Paternal substance abuse as a predictor of child maltreatment re-reports. *Child Abuse and Neglect, 20,* 1183–1193.

Woods, J. R., Plessinger, M. A., and Clark, K. E. (1987). Effect of cocaine on uterine blood flow and fetal oxygenation. *Journal of the American Medical Association, 257,* 957–961.

Yarrow, M. R., Campbell, J. D., and Burton, R. (1968). *Child rearing, an inquiry into research and methods.* San Francisco: Jossey-Bass.

Yates, W. R., Cadoret, R. J., Troughton, E. D., and Stewart, M. A. (1996). An adoption study of *DSM-IIIR* alcohol and drug dependence severity. *Drug and Alcohol Dependence, 41,* 9–15.

Zagon, I. S., and McLaughlin, P. (1984). An overview of the neurobehavioral sequelae of perinatal opiod exposure. In J. Yanai (Ed.), *Neurobehavioral teratology* (pp. 197–233). Amsterdam: Elsevier.

Ziedonis, D. M. (1992). Comorbid psychopathology and cocaine addiction. In T. R. Kosten and H. D. Kleber (Eds.), *Clinician's guide to cocaine addiction* (pp. 335–358). New York: Guilford.

Zuckerman, B., Amaro, J., Bauchner, H., and Cabral, H. (1989). Depressive symptoms during pregnancy: Relationships to poor health behaviors. *American Journal of Obstetrics and Gynecology, 160,* 1107–1111.

Zuckerman, B., Frank, D. A., Hingson, R., and Amaro, H. (1989). Effects of maternal marijuana and cocaine use on fetal growth. *New England Journal of Medicine, 320,* 762–768.

14

Parenting and Child Maltreatment

Sandra T. Azar
Clark University

INTRODUCTION

Child maltreatment is seen as specific acts of omission or commission that are judged by a mixture of community values and professional expertise to be inappropriate or damaging (Garbarino and Giliam, 1980). Over 1 million children are affected by child maltreatment each year, with 2,000 children killed by their caregivers (National Center on Child Abuse and Neglect, 2000). Given underreporting occurs, actual figures may be twice these amounts. Although multiple forms of child maltreatment have been identified, this chapter focuses on two types, physical abuse and neglect. *Physical abuse* involves parental use of aversive or inappropriate control strategies (e.g., beatings, consistent use of coercive responses). *Neglect* is an omission of actions by parents that leads to harm or endangerment of children's health or well-being and includes a heterogenous set of events (e.g., from lack of supervision to poor hygiene). Contrary to popular belief, the latter constitute the largest group of cases (53.5% versus 22.7% for abuse). Because emotional abuse is often closely woven into physical abuse and seen by some as core to many forms of neglect, it will be included where appropriate in discussion.

The study of parents who physically abuse and neglect children is of interest to social scientists because of the risk they present to their offspring[1] and a desire to better understand when and how to intervene to reduce this risk (Azar, 1986, 1989, 1998; Cicchetti and Lynch, 1995, Wolfe, 1987). Society has also called on social science in the form of expert testimony to help determine when parents are so unable to parent that their legal bond to their children should be severed permanently (Azar, Lauretti, and Loding, 1998; Grisso, 1986). This chapter attempts to contextualize our understanding

---

[1]The focus of this text is on parenting, and therefore less attentions paid to children and their outcomes as a result of abuse and neglect. The reader is referred to Azar and Bober (1999) and Cicchetti and Lynch (1995) for discussions of child outcomes. It must be pointed out that the types of outcomes observed among such children are heterogenous in nature, and thus a broader focus on parental failures is needed to understand this heterogeneity.

of child maltreatment as a set of disturbances in one of the major tasks of adult development—parenting. This approach flies in the face of social science's typical approach of "splitting rather then lumping" (i.e., making sharp distinctions between narrowly defined clinical phenomena such as parenting problems in substance abusers and the more normative concerns of parents at the transition to parenthood). There is value to broadening our perspective in this way. Stopping abusive or neglectful behavior does not necessarily mean that parenting in such families is now occurring smoothly. Such behaviors are typically the tip of an iceberg of disturbed interpersonal responses, which produce distress for adults as well as place their offspring at risk.

Parents who are abusive and neglectful from this perspective are seen as being on a continuum with all parents. At one end is parenting that is complex and flexible enough to result both in a match of parental capacities with the multiple possible contexts that present themselves in this role (e.g., coping with limited resources, single parenthood, and a hyperactive child) and in optimal outcomes for parents themselves and their children, as well as society as a whole.[2] At the other end is parenting that is relatively less complex and more rigid, such that when varying levels and types of contextual obstacles occur, the quality of parenting is unequal to the task, and maladaptive responses occur. Child outcomes are likely to be poor and parents' own adjustment adversely affected. Inherent in this view is the idea that a certain level of parenting may be adequate given low stress, high economic resources, and an easy to care for child (e.g., one with qualities such as an easy temperament), but may lead to failures if context changes (e.g., a seriously ill child is born). This view stands in sharp contrast to those that envision maltreaters as a unique group of adults whose behavior represents an aberration (e.g., psychodynamic views and attachment approaches).

The perspective advocated here also contextualizes parenting itself. That is, the parenting function, as Palkovitz (1996) has said, is not simply "on" or "off," but rather is part of the flow of all tasks in adult life. Maladaptive parenting needs to be seen within this larger developmental context. To view it as a separate entity may be less productive. Under optimal conditions, parenting is an interpersonal context in which adult development can be facilitated and where both earlier failures in social, emotional, and cognitive development and current environmental supports and strains can alter an individual's trajectory (Azar, in press). Thus, challenges in the parenting role, if within adult's "zone of proximal development" (Vygotsky, 1934), can pull adults to higher levels of development in the same way that challenges in other life domains can. Factors restricting opportunities for adult growth generally will also restrict the use of the "opportunities" presented by parenting as well.

This view also does not see parenting as entirely instinctual such that the "right" behaviors are triggered once one enters the role. It carries a different set of assumptions. These will be outlined first to provide a background against which to consider the discussion that follows.

First, embedded in this approach is the idea that the parenting role is socially constructed and thus need not be "universal" in nature across ethnic, racial, or class lines: "The images of motherhood and fatherhood reveal our shared ideals, standards, beliefs, and expectations regarding men and women as parents" (Thompson and Walker, 1989, p. 859). Social groups differ in their constructions of the role and these constructions change over time (i.e., role demands are not stagnant). Yet images of parenting have been described as both enduring and emerging (Cusinato, 1994). Thus, in thinking about child abuse and neglect, it must be considered that what we define as maladaptive in parenting has varied with historical era. Older social constructions and newer ones coexist in today's society, resulting in disparities in some parents' views from those of the larger society (e.g., older views that saw children as the property of parents and that parents determine solely how children are to be treated coexist with current views that parents be "child centered" in their actions and that the state plays a role in determining their care (Mason, 1994; Zelizer, 1985)).

---

[2]One view is that society is most interested in parenting as it relates to the socialization of its new members and the costs it incurs (e.g., health care, special educational needs, and criminal behavior) if this role is not fulfilled well. This chapter will in part reflect on how this interest affects research, treatment, and policy in the area of child maltreatment.

Role demands are set by the group with which parents most identify, and it is this group that acts as the standard against which they judge "acceptable" social behavior (Azar and Benjet, 1994; Azar and Cote, in press). Sibling caregiving is valued as a part of socialization in some cultures, but in some situations is labeled as neglect in U.S. society. This may present problems for immigrant parents. Thus, unique group-based differences exist in the individual's internal construction of parenthood's demands. These differing constructions interact with context and can challenge or facilitate adult development and how parental role functioning is evaluated by the larger society (i.e., whether community standards label parents as abusive or neglectful).

Parenting is not divorced from social conditions that drive a host of social behaviors (Azar, 1986; Azar and Benjet, 1994; Goodnow and Collins, 1990; Kohn, 1963). If parents are ambivalent about their social group, or feel harassed by the demands that the group places on them or un-equal to these demands, there may be difficulties. For example, minority parents within the United States may see their role as preparing children for exposure to discrimination, which may lead to a unique set of parenting practices. Parents struggling economically within our society have contradictory demands placed on them. Single mothers living in urban poverty may choose to allow their children to walk to the store to do errands (encouraging autonomy) while to do so leaves their offspring vulnerable to environmental risks, which may be labeled as neglectful—lack of super-vision. They must balance needs for assistance in shopping (competing with needs of younger siblings and exhaustion from demanding jobs) against the safety needs of their children. Contex-tual risk may be so great that parents are doomed to failure or, in some cases, their capacities too limited to negotiate even the smallest of contradictory needs (e.g., some developmentally disabled parents).

Finally, meeting of these demands is voluntary. Ruddick (1989) argued that parents are labeled as such just because of and to the degree to which they are committed to meeting the demands that define parental work. When children demand care, the reality of their vulnerability and the necessity of a response seem "unshakable" in her words. The *perception* of vulnerability, however, is optional, as is the responding with care. Thus, interpretation may produce individual differences in motivation in the role and conflict with societal standards for level of child care.

These assumptions are not carried within the legal statutes that govern identification and "treatment" of abusing and neglectful parents, but must be considered by social scientists. Every parent must negotiate these issues and how well they do so may reflect a broad array of capacities with which they come to the role and new ones they develop, as well as contextual supports and obstacles they encounter along the way. These capacities are just now being articulated by social scientists and hold the most promise for understanding the origins of child abuse and neglect.

Keeping this larger picture in mind, this chapter begins its discussion of child maltreating parents with a historical overview of the nature of societally defined parental responsibilities to children and the identification of child maltreatment as a social concern and its definition. It then moves to a discussion of the major theories of etiology, both that posit child maltreaters are a separate category of parent and those that are more in line with a continuum perspective, although the latter will be given more attention. Finally, it will overview the research on factors that place a parent at risk for child abuse and current interventions and future directions for the field.

Where possible, attention is paid to the socially constructed nature of our views of acceptable parenting (elements open to debate in light of sociocultural perspectives). In discussing intervention, historical continuity will be highlighted in our approaches, and particular attention will be paid to whether society has perceived itself as playing a role in supporting parenting. In doing so, this chapter is not attempting to politicize the discussion, but to sharpen future research to better address with scientific data the debates that influence social policy, legal decision making, and the lives of parents and their families. This approach requires more refined data on the qualities of competent parenting, including differentiation of parenting practices that are truly harmful from those that just represent sociocultural disparities without affecting child outcomes. It also requires a deeper understanding of the development of adults as they undertake the role of parent and the contexts that support it.

Developing a science based on such a view may move our field forward and away from society's blaming stance toward such parents (Azar, 1996; Farber and Azar, 1999).

HISTORICAL CONSIDERATIONS IN PARENTING MALTREATMENT

Most historical accounts date society's major concern with child maltreatment in this country to the identification of the Battered Child Syndrome (Kempe, Silverman, Steele, Droegemueller, and Silver, 1962) and passage of mandated abuse reporting laws in the early 1960s. However, these events were the culmination of a long historical shift in the place of children in family and community life. They also reflect shifting schema regarding the value of children and parents' responsibilities to them (i.e., fundamental changes in role schema regarding the parenting function).

LeVine (1974), in considering cross-culturally the goals of families, highlights three basic goals: (1) promoting the physical survival and health of children, ensuring that they will live long enough to have children of their own (the *survival goal*), (2) fostering skills and behavioral capacities that children will need for economic self-maintenance in adulthood (the *economic goal*), and (3) fostering capabilities for maximizing other cultural values (e.g., morality and achievement) (the *self-actualization goal*). At other points in history within this country and in many societies even today, responsibility for these functions is distributed throughout the extended family and community rather than vested in just two adults. This narrowing of responsibility for the functions of parenting increases potential for failures to meet them in today's society. For example, a parent who often leaves her child with relatives may be viewed with suspicion (e.g., can this mother parent independently?). Also both family members and society may not feel the press to fulfill such functions as strongly.

Societal "protection" of children emerged historically around the goals of economic self-sufficiency and moral fitness before physical protection or developmental needs. That is, the issue of most concern was (and may still be) the economic contribution or drain of children to society. Only recently has children's self-actualization become of interest (i.e., rights to care and need satisfaction separate from those chosen by parents). This has also been part of the "sacralization" of children (a focus away from their economic value to their sentimental value; Zelizer, 1985).

The protection given to children gradually increased as the value of children changed. They were at first seen as household labor, and then, as lifespans lengthened, became a source of care in parents' old age. With industrialization and in agricultural communities, children were sources of added income for the family through their labor. Only recently, with improvements in the health and economic stability of families, did they come to have sentimental value.[3] The increase in rights accorded them also occurred as those of women began to increase.

Throughout history, however, society did make some efforts to protect children, many of which look similar to those of today. Some led to other kinds of caregiving "harm" (e.g., placement in poorly run orphanages and indenturing children to families where they were mistreated). Debates continue about potential harm when society takes such actions (Haugaard and Hazan, in Vol. 1 of this *Handbook*).

In ancient times, children's right to live was ritually bestowed upon them by their parents. They were nonpersons until given their first nourishment or a name (tenBensel, Rheinberger, and Radbill, 1997). They were seen as the property of their parents, or, more specifically, their fathers. Parents

---

[3]It needs to be kept in mind that until recently adults themselves were struggling for survival, and thus, even for an adult, self-actualization was not a priority. This needs to be considered in thinking about parents' priorities even today. The author has seen a failure in clinical practice to consider the idea that not all parents can make the same child-centered choices because of their economic status. For example, she has heard clinical colleagues say a mother was "obviously" not bonded to her children because she always worked the night shift and was not around when they were home. This was said despite the family's deep level of financial instability and the economic benefits of such a work schedule (e.g., a better pay scale and the fact that the father could care for the children while the mother worked reducing childcare costs).

could give them to others to work off parental debts (Kadushin, 1967). Children who had disabilities were put to death in Greece in the first century B.C. (tenBensel et al., 1997). Thus, the role of parent involved a high degree of power over children, with responsibilities for their care not articulated.

With the advent of Christianity, protection of children began to be legislated by the state. In 374 A.D., Roman law labeled infant killing by parents murder and established the state's responsibility to take care of the welfare of poor children (*parens patriae*[4]). However, the idea that parents were to insure children's basic physical or emotional needs did not come until much later.

The economic value of children emerged first. Unfortunately, it came from exploitation in the sixteenth and seventeenth centuries. By the Industrial Revolution (the eighteenth century), indenturing as servants to others and apprenticing children were common practices in cities and sources of income for parents. Indeed, southern colonies "imported" children for labor (Mason, 1994). In rural homes, the birth of children was welcomed because children provided labor on farms. With lengthening lifespans, they were also seen as security for parents in later life (Zelizer, 1985), a view still existing in countries without other forms of old age security (Kagitcibasi, 1982).

Consistent with children's labor value were the areas where the "state" took interest in their "care." The Puritans in colonial America wanted children to be reared morally and with training to be productive citizens (i.e., for males, in some sort of trade, or for females, in household skills). Parents could not assign them only menial work, such as tending livestock, but were to prepare them to perform skilled tasks. In an early form of child protective services, town selectman could enter the homes of and investigate fathers who were suspected of not meeting these standards. If the offence was repeated, they could remove children and apprentice them to another adult to provide the requisite moral and vocational education (Mason, 1994). Similarly, in colonial Virginia from 1631 to 1645, a series of acts was passed requiring fathers to provide compulsory religious education to all children. Here, community needs for order and productivity defined fit parenting.

Even then the meeting of parental role functions was more closely monitored for the poor, something that is still be true today. Workhouses were established in Virginia to place children whose parents were too poor "to give them good breeding" (Mason, 1994). Society provided assistance to support parents only in extreme cases and where they were not seen as at fault for their situation (e.g., widows). The level of this support, typically from private agencies, however, was such that mothers still needed to work to support their families and many had to give children up to the care of relatives or institutions either temporarily or permanently (Chase-Lansdale and Vinovskis, 1995). Thus, society did not see itself as in the business of supporting parenting.

A review of legal custody decisions around this period hinted at society's beginning to hold parents to at least minimal standards of care. At first this was around fathers' responsibility to provide religious education and training. In the mid-1800s, however, the *tender years doctrine* began to be applied in divorce, where custody of younger children was routinely awarded to women due to a new belief in their greater ability to provide care in the early years of life. This marked a change in the idea of children as fathers' "property" and attention to mothers' role in children's lives, and an emphasis on parents' providing for needs beyond moral and vocational ones and gross survival. Historical accounts attribute this change to the "cult of motherhood" promoted in ladies magazines and popular culture (a kind of idealization of maternal role functions) that influenced judges' custody decisions (Mason, 1994). With it, mothers began to be held responsible for children's welfare.

By the nineteenth century, other concerns emerged. At first, it involved the extremes (abandonment). Orphanages were established. As with other societal efforts to take over parental role functioning (indenturing systems), outcomes were not always positive. Public health concerns and poor treatment were publicized in the media (e.g., Dickens's *Oliver Twist*). Other efforts to remove children from parents occurred. The New York Children's Aid Society raised money to move immigrant children who were wandering the streets of poor neighborhoods, unsupervised and

---

[4]This was the beginning of the state seeing itself as having "parental" responsibilities for children over and above those of parents.

not being educated, to foster homes "out west" (Janko, 1994). Clearly, such "visuals" of the poor were problematic, as they were inconsistent with the American dream.

Gradually, larger scale public funding began for the "deserving" poor (e.g., workman's compensation to families of disabled workers, widows' pensions, the Social Security Act of 1935 with Aid to Dependent Children provisions for children of separated, divorced and never married mothers). Yet funding for children did not have the assumption of supporting adults while they cared for children. Despite this, often provisions were made for examining the qualities of the adult involved. Although intended to cover all children, states restricted funding by requiring that children live in "suitable homes," and thus made judgments regarding standards of adult behavior. One southern state even created policy definitions of "suitable" that excluded large numbers of African American children. Not until the mid 1900s were separate provisions for support to caregivers included (Aid to Dependent Children was retitled Aid to Families with Dependent Children [AFDC]). This formal supporting of caregiving marked a change in society's involvement in parenting, although it remains ambivalent (e.g., recent welfare reform has occurred to shorten mothers' stay on welfare and limit its lifetime use—the Personal Responsibility and Work Opportunity Reconciliation Act of 1996).

It is against this backdrop that the issue of child abuse arose. First to react were private agencies. In the late 1800s, the Society for the Prevention of Cruelty to Children (SPCC) was organized by the leadership of the Society for the Prevention of Cruelty to Animals in response to the beating and starvation of an 8-year-old child by her adoptive parents (tenBensel et al., 1997). The SPCC became the first investigator of cases of abuse, and it argued within courts for the protection of children. The rise of social work and juvenile courts also helped efforts here. Some argue that efforts were preventive in nature rather than legal and punitive, but placing children in foster care was still the most common response (Haugaard and Hazan, in Vol. 1 of this *Handbook*). Private agencies continued to dominate societal actions until the middle of the next century, when the legal approaches of today were instituted.

In the late 1940s, improvements in radiology allowed the identification of past fractures in children not possible earlier. Medical articles began to appear hinting that parents may be to blame for some childhood injuries (Caffey, 1946). It was not until a decade later, however, that a seminal paper by Kempe and his colleagues (Kempe, Silverman, Steele, Droegemueller, and Silver, 1962) was published that this idea that parents were doing serious harm to their children gained professional and societal acceptance. Amid public uproar, statutes were passed nationwide to mandate professional reporting of suspected physical abuse of children.

The speed with which statutes were passed was unprecedented (tenBensel et al., 1997). This may be due to a shift in the expectations society had of parents or to the fact it had begun to help some parents (AFDC, i.e., it felt greater freedom to act if parents failed in their role).

Initially, it was thought that child abuse was rare and that such parents were psychiatrically ill. However, it quickly became clear that large numbers of children were involved and that most maltreaters were not significantly psychiatrically disordered. Over time, other forms of maltreatment came to light (e.g., sexual and emotional abuse, and neglect) and became the object of mandated reporting. Recently new parental failures have been identified (e.g., exposure to domestic violence and in utero drug exposure), broadening where society has intervened.

Overall, this historical review highlights some of the global issues noted in the introduction. First, social conditions changed the nature of standards to which parents were held (e.g., as life standards improved and children's value changed, standards for parenting also changed). Second, interest in parents' meeting role requirements varied (e.g., which parent was responsible). Finally, interventions were often gross (replace parents with someone else—indenture a child; place children in orphanages), were more often directed at the poor, and, at times, failed to improve children's situation. Support to parents themselves was provided with ambivalence and only to those viewed as "deserving" and not to "blame" for their failures to provide for their children. These themes persist today.

The science surrounding child maltreatment has been influenced by the politics surrounding it. In developing science that is applied in decision making the field has been in a "react" rather than an initiating mode (Azar, Fantuzzo, and Twentyman, 1984). It too rapidly moved to developing interventions without adequate definition of the phenomenon, theory building, or understanding of abuse's origins. It accepted societal perspectives that such parents' behaviors had to be aberrations and placed less emphasis on the idea that there might be a complex interaction of causal factors.

Although this complexity has finally received acceptance by researchers, the prevailing societal bias of seeing such parents as different from others, imperatives of funding, and other pressures have kept the field mired in a categorical view (e.g., parents are seen as having attachment problems, as personality disordered, or substance abusers). This has led to definitional problems and colored theory building and intervention development, which are discussed below.

DEFINITION OF CHILD MALTREATMENT

Before developing theory or intervention in a social problem, definition of the relevant parameters of that problem is needed. The multidisciplinary nature of professional involvement in child abuse has made consensus as to how it should be defined difficult. Initial definitions were legal or medical, and aimed at identification and prosecution (determining intent or validating the occurrence of abuse). Although determination of culpability is useful for courts, it is not as helpful as a basis for science. Further, psychologically damaging acts may not leave any physical evidence.

With the shift to intervention, maltreatment came to be defined in the way noted in the introduction of this chapter—as specific acts judged by a mixture of community values and professional expertise to be inappropriate or damaging (Garbarino and Giliam, 1980). Such a definition is "socially mediated" and allows for a narrow versus a broad continuum in thinking about impact (e.g., demonstrable harm versus endangerment) and actions (e.g., from failure to supervise to threatening a child with knife). With more focus on child outcome, even broader definitions have emerged, including seeing maltreatment as part of a more general breakdown in caregiver capacities. Here, the focus is on parents, their repertoire of caregiving and life skills, and the parent–child relationship (Azar, 1986; Azar, Barnes, and Twentyman, 1988).

The legally identified categories of abuse and neglect are umbrellas for a heterogeneous set of events occurring to children. For example, Zuravin (1991) defined 13 types of behaviors included in neglect: supervisory neglect, refusal or delay in providing health or mental health care, custody refusal or related neglect, abandonment/desertion, failure to provide a home, personal hygiene neglect, housing hazards or sanitation problems, nutritional neglect, and educational neglect. Some definitions include emotional neglect (a marked indifference to children's need for affection, attention, and emotional support), as well as exposure to chronic or extreme spousal abuse. Emotional abuse has been seen as both central to all maltreatment and as a distinct entity. It includes acts that are psychologically damaging to chidlren's behavioral, cognitive, affective, or physical functioning (e.g., rejecting, terrorizing, or degrading; Brassard, Germain, and Hart, 1987). Clearly, this heterogeneity has been difficult to encompass in a single psychological theory of parenting.

Problematic also is the fact that there is no consensus regarding the level at which these difficulties become maltreatment, particularly neglect (e.g., what is adequate supervision?). The developmental stage of the child matters. Behaviors considered neglectful for infants may not be for the care of an adolescent. Also, children's special needs (e.g., chronic illness) may require some omissions of care to be labeled as problematic that would not be otherwise. The issue of how chronically an omission needs to occur before it is considered neglectful has also not been addressed well. The etiology of chronic abuse or neglect may be quite different from that which occurs over a limited time period and in response to a parental stress (e.g., a job loss).

Types of maltreatment often co-occur and over multiple reports, many cases appear to move from one type to another (English, Marshall, and Orme, 1999). Co-occurrence may mean greater parental dysfunction or stress. For instance, a parent whose home is chaotic and marked by poor hygiene and who leaves her child with an inappropriate baby-sitter who molests the child may have more general problems in adult functioning (e.g., problem-solving skill or poor judgment); whereas one who reacts one time with hitting a child for destroying a treasured object may suffer from a narrower band difficulty (e.g., anger management).

Other attributes may also be important (e.g., severity, and frequency of abuse, and age of child; Cicchetti and Barnett, 1991). For example, physical abuse that occurs at points of children's pushes for autonomy (e.g., the terrible twos) may have different parent-based antecedents than when it occurs across all of childhood. The latter may indicate anger-control deficits, and the former may mean more pervasive problems. The most severe forms (leading to long-term child disability) may need to be distinguished from less severe forms to better use societal resources (Emery and Laumann-Billings, 1998).

One last factor discussed recently is the meaning that children take from their experience (Azar and Bober, 1999). Children may incorporate into schema regarding the self, others, and the world elements of their maltreatment that influence their later functioning. The child's view may be the best predictor of outcome. Although suggesting a focus on children's views, the entire context of parenting may temper the meaning to the child. Harsh treatment (not extreme abuse) that is predictable and within a context of otherwise positive parenting may not have the same meaning than if it occurs at erratic moments and in the absence of other "saving graces" in the relationship.

Finally, as noted earlier, parenting practices are socioculturally situated, and in considering definitions there needs to be greater openness to diverse pathways to parental fitness and meeting children's needs. Our current theories of parenting are based on narrow samples (e.g., middle- and upper-income, European American parents; Azar and Cote, in press; Chao, 1997). Current frames for judging parenting capacities need not be abandoned, but care should be taken in accepting their universal utility, and a "functional" approach to judging practices may be required (i.e., distinguishing practices that are cultural universals from ones requiring more local definition; Korbin, 1994).

THEORY IN PARENTING AND CHILD MALTREATMENT

Although the earliest decades of the field of child maltreatment suffered from a lack of sophisticated theory (Azar, Fantuzzo, and Twentyman, 1984; Crittenden, 1998), the last two have seen a growth of more sophisticated attempts to explain the origins of physical abuse. Etiological theories specific to neglect, however, continue to lag behind, perhaps because of the heterogeneity of the behaviors under this label and the sociopolitical issues that surround behaviors so closely linked to poverty in the United States. This lack of progress is striking given the high prevalence of neglect.

Theories of child maltreatment have had very different starting points (Azar, 1991b; Azar, Povilaitis, Lauretti, and Pouquette, 1998; Gelles and Straus, 1979). First, theories have varied depending on the nature of the definition used (e.g., from a narrow focus on abuse as aggression to viewing it as part of a larger category of social relational problems). Second, some models have attempted to explain all types of maltreatment or other forms of interpersonal violence, whereas others have addressed only one type. Third, the locus of causality has also varied, from seeing maltreatment as stemming from a defect within the perpetrator to seeing it as resulting from larger societal values (e.g., condoning of violence). Finally, some theories have favored a categorical view (e.g., attachment formulations), and others have argued for a continuum. This complexity makes summarizing theory a daunting task. Examples of theories that focus on parents, the parent–child relationship, and family transactions that the parent may direct will be outlined. Where appropriate, references to broader theories are noted. These are sociological ones (Straus, 1973) or ones focused solely on explaining child outcomes (Cicchetti and Lynch, 1995).

Over the last four decades, theories have shifted from single cause models (e.g., stress leads to abuse) to complex lists of alternative possible causes, to more integrated perspectives (e.g., social ecological models of abuse). If specified well enough, these integrated approaches hold the most promise. A sampling of early theories and more recent ones is provided below.

Early models focused on single factors within (1) perpetrators (e.g., personality disorders, psychopathology; Lanyon, 1986; Melnick and Hurley, 1969); (2) children (e.g., heightened care needs such as prematurity or provocative behavior); (3) parent–child relationships (e.g., bonding failure or attachment views; Crittenden and Ainsworth, 1989; Klaus and Kennell, 1982), or (4) the sociological/sociocultural context (e.g., stress and societal values; Garbarino, 1976; Gil, 1970). Single factors, however, proved to be inadequate explanations and often were founded on faulty assumptions. For example, those that focused on parental psychopathology were based on case studies of severe or bizarre abuse. Only a small portion of maltreaters seem to have personality disorders or other psychiatric disorders, and no one form of disorder has been identified as characterizing this group of adults. Perpetrator symptoms may still increase risk for maltreating children, especially emotion-regulation problems (e.g., depression and anger regulation; Milner, 1998).

These early models did highlight factors that continue to be explored today. For example, Green (1976) posited an intergenerational transmission model that rests on identification processes. He argued that child abusers were subjected to abuse by their own caregivers and internalized two disparate identifications, one of the harsh, punitive parent and the other of unlovable, unworthy child. When confronted with frustrating caregiving situations in adulthood, these identifications emerge, with the parent reexperiencing the anxiety of being the "unworthy child." Because this anxiety is intolerable, it is projected onto the child and the identification with the punitive parent then emerges, allowing a cathartic experience (abuse) to be enacted. Intergenerational transmission is not inevitable (see discussion below), but this formulation is not inconsistent with more recent cognitive formulations that argue for adults entering parenting with disturbed parenting "scripts."

Other prominent single-factor perspectives for which more support has been found are that contextual strain and/or lack of resources produce maltreatment. Factors include low income (Garbarino, 1991), lack of social support, and high stress (Gaudin, Polansky, Kilpatrick, and Shilton, 1993). For example, economic hardship can have far-reaching impact both directly on parenting itself and the factors that act as buffers to risk for children (e.g., marital relationship, Hoff, Laursen, and Tardif, in Vol. 2 of this *Handbook*; McCloyd, 1990). Yet not all stressed and isolated parents become maltreaters. Some may be less able to balance their resources or the cadence with which stressors occur overwhelms their capacities.

Another sociological model focused on societal values. This view argued that as long as society condones the use of physical punishment, abuse will occur (Straus, 1994). Cross-cultural data are used as evidence to support this contention.

As the limitations of these single-factor models were felt, attempts were made to posit "menus" of these single factors, which then evolved into more integrated approaches. Most have focused on physical abuse and use elements of multiple theoretical orientations (cognitive, family systems, attachment, social ecological, and behavioral) to create hierarchical understandings of etiology. Social-situational models in which individual and social contextual factors combine to produce abuse were the first. The most comprehensive framework, Belsky's social ecological model (1980; Belsky and Vondra, 1989), posited that factors at four levels may influence the probability of abuse's occurrence. These include: individual characteristics (e.g., parental IQ), aspects of the family (e.g., marital satisfaction), forces within the community (e.g., poverty), and cultural factors (e.g., values). Cicchetti and Rizley (1981) further argued that whether these factors are enduring or more transient would affect children's outcome. These models are aimed at understanding the outcomes seen in children and specify a host of factors, many of which could lead to a variety of child risks, not just abuse, and that could act as both mediators (cause) and moderators of that risk (buffering or increasing). Thus, they are less useful in developing focused interventions for already abusive parents, but have more value for screening in broad spectrum general prevention efforts.

Recent developmental models focus exclusively on disturbances seen within the parent–child relationship. Attachment theory has been invoked. Maltreatment by a caregiver has been found to lead to an insecure attachment style in children and to affect their interpersonal responses. Working backward from this link and with an intergenerational focus, maltreating parents are seen as having disturbed attachment styles that negatively influence interpersonal responses, including those in parenting (Crittenden and Ainsworth, 1989). In a recent reformulation, this model has included neurobiological elements (early stress from abuse leading to an overresponsiveness to danger) that result in negative biases in processing information in the environment (Crittenden, 1998).

As social learning theorists entered the field, models implicating skill deficits in parents appeared. For example, Wolfe (1987) posited an escalation model of abuse where the abusive parent is seen as overrelying on coercion to elicit child compliance. Initially effective, children eventually habituate to such strategies and increasingly higher levels of coercion are required to produce an impact, culminating in physical abuse.

In another effort of this type, Azar and Twentyman (1986) posited five areas of deficit contributing to child maltreatment, including social cognitive disturbances, and skills deficits in parenting, stress management, social skills, and anger regulation. These disturbances may have their origins in parents' own childhood experiences (poor modeling provided by adult caregivers), but may also evolve under situational strain (e.g., mood disturbances, a high-crime neighborhood, marital violence, and substance abuse). Thus, no primacy is given to early experience, as in attachment theory. Each disturbance is seen as producing maladaptive parenting and an environment where children's development suffers more broadly. For example, poor social skills would lead to fewer friends, perceptions of low intimacy, poor marital relationships, greater distress, poorer adjustment, greater negative arousal, and a lower mood state, all of which are linked to child abuse, parent–child interaction problems, and poor child outcomes. Priority, however, is given to social-cognitive problems as specific precursors to physical abuse and neglect (i.e, the foundational disturbance in this approach is an information-processing one; see also Crittenden, 1993; and Milner, 1993). Cognitively based disturbances (e.g., expectancies, misattributions, problem solving deficits, lack of cognitive complexity/flexibility) drive the other disturbances and increase risk for child maltreatment.

In an elaboration of this model, maltreatment is further contextualized against the backdrop of adult development and tasks that all individuals face in becoming parents (Azar and Siegel, 1990; Azar, in press). Parenting is seen as requiring a foundation of general social cognitive capacities, as well as providing a unique environment for further adult social-cognitive development (Newman and Newman, 1988; Palkovitz, 1996). Social-cognitive theorizing argues that individuals develop cognitive structures to aid them in handling the thousands of pieces of information that bombard them each moment of each day, including those involved in making parenting decisions. Indeed, role-specific schema develop that ideally reflect societal social constructions. For example, in today's society adults need to have a "parent" role schema that defines it as requiring caregiving and protection where authority, resources, and responsibility are distributed unevenly and where, at least in the early years, a lot of the relationship "work" is done by the adult. (Reciprocally, the "young child" role schema is one of lower capacities.) The complexity, flexibility, and content of the adult's schema can either facilitate or destabilize their functioning both within the family and outside of it. Difficulties at this fundamental level would short-circuit all subsequent responses parents would make. That is, if one misperceives or misinterprets child or situational cues, then responses that follow would be maladaptive or asynchronous with children's needs and would lead to fewer opportunities for adults to "develop" into the role (i.e., they would be out of step with the transactions that occur, and thus out of their zone of proximal development).

Effective parents approach interactions with their children with developmentally sensitive schema (role expectations; Azar, 1986, 1989; Azar, Robinson, Hekimian, and Twentyman, 1984), including accurate perceptions of children's capabilities as well as what their own role is in moving them forward developmentally. The schema are flexible enough to act as frameworks for the variety of parenting tasks required across development and the special needs certain children may have. Such expectancies have been linked to more appropriate parenting responses, and inaccurate perceptions have characterized maltreaters (Azar, Robinson, et al., 1984; Azar and Rohrbeck, 1986; Barnes and Azar, 1990). Neglect may occur, for example, if parents expect that very young children will provide them with comfort and care rather than the other way around.

Effective parents also have an adequate enough repertoire of childrearing strategies (problem-solving skills) to adapt their responses to any given situation (e.g., verbal explanations regarding safety may be effective with an adolescent, but are not with a toddler). In contrast, abusive and neglectful parents possess a narrower and less discriminant repertoire of such responses (Azar, Robinson, et al., 1984; Hanson, Pallotta, Tishelman, and Conaway, 1989; Trickett and Kuczynski, 1986) and experience more failures and frustration in parenting. Parents who feel less in control show depression and less-effective interactions (Donovan and Leavitt, 1989).

Effective parents in today's terms also have a positive bias in their interpretations of events involving their children that, together with their sensitive schema and parenting skills, allows them to maintain a more positive affective state and to make adaptive and positive responses, even when children behave aversively or their needs are unclear. When their 3-year-old has spilled milk, they draw on their understanding that 3-year-old children have trouble holding onto objects and make attributions to developmental factors (e.g., "She's only 3") or to external factors outside both their own and their children's control, thus reducing stress and frustration. Parents who have "unrealistic" expectations of children attribute children's mishaps to spitefulness or their own inadequacy to get children to "mind" them (Azar, 1988; Larrance and Twentyman, 1983). Such attributions contribute to less persistence in childrearing efforts, finding childcare aversive, feeling ineffective in encounters with children, and, ultimately, may cause a withdrawal from the role or aversive responses. Lower efficacy has been linked to less parental involvement (Swick, 1988), and psychological unavailability has been linked to poor child outcomes (Egeland and Erickson, 1987).

Thus, appropriate schemas, adaptive attributions, and a wide repertoire of childrearing strategies and problem-solving skills combine to produce a situation in which parents are attuned to the developmental needs of their children, and can discriminate between situations when intervention is required and when it is not and at what level to respond (e.g., use distraction vs. a time-out), and are capable of meeting parenting tasks more calmly, flexibly, and successfully. Lack of such capacities may contribute to dissatisfaction in the role of parent and a failure to learn, resulting, at best, in inept parenting and, at worst, inappropriate responses such as abuse and neglect.

In this model, environmental stress (associated with maltreatment) may increase risk not only by making fewer options available to parents, but also by taxing parents' already troubled cognitive system. Cognitive processing narrows under stress and results in further decrements in learning capacities, the ability to maintain a positive mood state, and functioning. Parents who are effective have skills to cope with stress when it does occur, to develop buffers for themselves against its negative consequences, and, when possible, to anticipate and prevent stressors from occurring in the first place. They can marshall social supports to reduce strain and to provide new information, modeling, and feedback that act to fine-tune further their parenting schema and to introduce new behavioral strategies. Maltreating parents are more impulsive in their responses (Rohrbeck and Twentyman, 1986), which may lead to more stressors befalling them and interfere with social supports to help them (Salzinger, Kaplan, and Artemyeff, 1983).

Furthermore, as children develop, demands on parents shift, and the environmental supports needed also change. For example, the parent of an infant must have a high tolerance for crying and a capacity to problem solve and arrive at appropriate care solutions. The parent of a newly mobile toddler needs to be vigilant and monitor safety issues in the home. The ability to marshal a cadre of friends and/or relatives support both of these capacities (e.g., provides wider solutions or respite from stressors). The level and type of frustration tolerance and monitoring skills needed for infants and toddlers, however, are very different from that required for teenagers. At this later point in development, good communication skills and accurate understanding of adolescents' need for autonomy, as well as monitoring (e.g., rule setting), are required to provide an optimal environment for development. The *quality* of verbal communication skills (e.g., modeling of negotiation skills) required with teens may be crucial, whereas for infants it is the *amount* of communication (e.g., verbal stimulation) that is important. Children with special needs may also require unique types or levels of skills that the child without such needs (e.g., a hyperactive child requires a higher level of frustration tolerance, parent–child match; Blaher, 1984).

Thus, these schema and other cognitive processes (e.g., attributional style and problem solving) guide parenting responses and determine whether the family context does or does not promote children's development (i.e., producing one that is rich or devoid of economic, social, and emotional resources). Adults who show the kinds of deficits described above may be less able to master this phase of adulthood and to utilize it for personal growth. The deficits they have are in skill areas needed for "learning" in social relationships (i.e., they play a role in overall adult competence, well-being, self-efficacy, and life satisfaction). Instead of enhancing parents' sense of themselves, parenting would be a source of negative feedback and a sense of inadequacy. Also, since the skill requirements of the role straddle those of other roles in adult life (e.g., relationships with partners and employers, and overall work competence), other sources of such enhancement may also be restricted, and failures in these roles may further contribute to strain on the adult and may spill over into parenting. Abuse and neglect would thus arise in a context of both general failures in adult life and specific ones in parenting tasks.

Overall, this model provides explanations for processes nonconducive to adult learning and a downward trajectory of parent–child interactions with fewer self-corrective mechanisms. As the child reacts to these parenting failures (e.g., their development is negatively affected), further deterioration of parenting may occur (e.g., a delayed child may be more aversive, provide more violations of expectations, more difficult childrearing problems to solve, and validation of negative attributions). Indeed, the abused and neglected child has been shown to exhibit social, emotional, academic, and cognitive problems that mirror many of the same disturbances outlined in this model (Azar and Bober, 1999; Cicchetti and Lynch, 1995). The result will be a continuum of parenting incompetency from inept parenting to abusive and neglectful behavior, with the latter occurring as the level and number of these cognitive disturbances increase. When children's needs are violated to such an extent that poor outcome is likely, parenting incompetency might legitimately be viewed as of concern to society and targeted for intervention.

As can be seen from this brief overview, theories of the origins of child maltreatment have evolved as our knowledge base has improved. Current ones provide a better base for treatment development and preventive efforts. Evidence supporting these models will be described next.

CLASSICAL AND MODERN RESEARCH ON ABUSIVE AND NEGLECTFUL PARENTS

Relative to other social and health-related problems in our society (e.g., heart disease and delinquency), little research has occurred on child abusing and neglectful parents. That which is available has focused on physically abusive parents, and primarily mothers. Much less attention has been given to understanding the characteristics of neglectful parents. Studies of parents have also suffered from many methodological problems. These problems include a narrow focus on samples identified by social service agencies (restricting our understanding to extreme abuse or neglect), a lack of a theoretical base in their conception such that they were no more than "fishing expeditions," and a failure to control for important confounding factors (e.g., child age and social status; Azar, Fantuzzo, and Twentyman, 1984). With improvement in research, however, a picture is beginning to emerge of the characteristics of such parents.

First, demographic, historical, and contextual factors have been associated with child maltreatment. Most prominent are socioeconomic status (SES), parental history of maltreatment by their own caregivers, and life stress. The causal role of each of these is still, however, in question.

Low SES has long been seen as a risk factor for child maltreatment (Olsen and Holmes, 1986; Straus, Gelles, and Steinmetz, 1980). The majority of lower SES parents, however, do not maltreat their children. The lack of resources and role demands that characterize lower SES subcultures and contexts may thus be setting events for abuse and neglect and not be the sole cause in the majority of cases. Lack of resources makes it more difficult to meet children's needs, and coupled with intrapersonal deficits within parents make the other tasks of adult life more difficult. Also, lower SES environments are filled with risks that require better skills than contexts that are more benign. A useful metaphor is that life mimics a video game for such parents where dangers "pop out" at the family at an extremely fast pace and only the most "skilled" parent can respond successfully. Finally, lower SES status itself may be indicative of broader adult adjustment problems and/or be associated with difficulties in children that may make the tasks of rearing them harder (e.g., higher incidence of special needs children; see Hoff, Laursen, and Tardif, in Vol. 2 of this *Handbook*).

An intergenerational transmission of abuse has also been posited, although causality here also has been questioned. Recent estimates suggest that between 25% and 35% of maltreated children grow up to maltreat their own children (Kaufman and Zigler, 1987). Some reviews suggest that this is both an overestimate and an underestimate, or that it varies by type of maltreatment (e.g., lower rates for neglect; Starr, MacLean, and Keating, 1991). Because abuse and neglect in one's family of origin varies with other forms of family dysfunction, it may be that such histories are a marker variable rather than causal. For instance, studies of neglectful parents suggest a chaotic home life in their family of origins (Zuravin and Di Blasio, 1996), which fosters disturbed relationship patterns (e.g., "scripts" for parenting; Azar, 1991a; Gara, Rosenberg, and Herzog, 1996; Zeanah and Zeanah, 1989), placing the next generation at risk. For example, it has been found that abused mothers have less-complex schema's of their own children's negative behavior (Gara, Allen, Herzog, and Woolfolk, 2000).

Maltreaters also have significantly higher stress levels (Egeland, Breitenbucher, and Rosenberg, 1980). The nature of the stressors, however, also suggest broader spectrum difficulties around affect regulation and coping capacities in adult life (e.g., unemployment and domestic violence).

Beyond these demographic, historical, and contextual factors, psychological factors within the parent have been studied. Early case studies based in psychoanalytic theorizing described very disordered individuals (Steele, 1980). Neglectful mothers, for example, were described as having severe defects in ego and in general personality development (e.g., immaturity and narcissism). Studies, however, have failed to distinguish such parents as possessing any specific diagnoses.

More evidence has amassed regarding other problems. First, as many as one third of maltreating parents have IQs in the borderline or mentally retarded range, particularly those who are neglectful (Schilling and Schincke, 1984). Cognitive functioning may contribute to the interactive and other parenting problems seen in this population. Substance abuse has also been suggested as a correlate of abuse and neglect. Clearly, the familial disorganization that occurs in families affected by substance abuse may result in neglect of children, and such problems may facilitate parental impulse control problems. Yet the data supporting this relationship are circumstantial. Take, for example, evidence that substance abuse is correlated with removal of children from homes (Famularo, Stone, Barnum, and Wharton, 1986). Although substance abuse may produce problems requiring foster placement, courts may also be more willing to remove children when it is present.

Studies indicate cognitive, emotional, and behavioral disturbances in parents who abuse and neglect their children or who show risk for doing so. Most pervasive is a variety of parenting skill deficits. Abusive and neglectful parents engage in fewer positive interactions with children, less overall interaction, and more insensitive interactions (Bousha and Twentyman, 1984; Burgess and Conger, 1978; Oldershaw, Walters, and Hall, 1989). Physically abusive parents of preschool and school-age children also tend to use more coercive and rigid control tactics and to do so in an indiscriminant manner (Cerezo, D'Ocon, and Dolz, 1996). Modeling of coercive behavior may explain the behavioral and social problems seen in abused children (George and Main, 1979; Hoffman-Plotkin and Twentyman, 1984; Salzinger, Feldman, Hammer, and Rosario, 1993), whereas the lack of cognitive stimulation may explain such children's cognitive and academic problems (Eckenrode, Laird, and Doris, 1993).

Mothers who are at risk of physically abusing and/or neglecting their children also use explanation less when disciplining (Barnes and Azar, 1990; Trickett and Kuczynski, 1986). Crucial to children's social development (e.g., perspective taking), this may set in motion a cycle of child social failures that lead to further parenting problems (i.e., the child fails to acquire social rules as other children do and the parent, in turn, reacts with further frustration to the child's "unwillingness" to "behave," compared to other children). Also, in families with low interaction rates, children are rewarded for engaging in negative behavior because it may be the easiest way to produce a reaction from a withdrawn parent. Indeed, the studies cited above show that maltreated children exhibit high levels of noncompliance and aversive behavior. Unfortunately, such child behavior would lead to perceptions of ineffectiveness as a parent and further adult withdrawal from the very situations where they might achieve mastery. Abusive parents show lower self-esteem and low perceived control in parenting (Culp, Culp, Soulis, and Letts, 1989; Trickett and Susman, 1988). The latter has also been linked to more general negative adult outcomes (Bugenthal, Mantyla, and Lewis, 1989).

Social-cognitive problems have also been found (Azar, 1986, 1989; Milner, 1993). Physically abusive and neglectful parents have poorer problem-solving ability in childrearing and nonchildrearing situations (e.g., managing of finances and social problems, Azar, Robinson, et al., 1984; Hanson et al., 1989). Parents at risk for abuse show poorer cognitive flexibility (Nayak and Milner, 1996, cited in Milner, 1998). Problem-solving difficulties and rigid thinking are linked to many adult adjustment problems. Although not found consistently across studies, abusive parents and those at risk for abuse also have been shown to make more negative attributions to children (Larrance and Twentyman, 1983; Plotkin, 1983) and have biases in interpreting the behavior of other adults (Miller and Azar, 1996). They also fail to temper these attributions when provided with mitigating information (Milner and Froody, 1994) and judge child misbehavior more harshly, seeing more negative behavior than do outside observers (Chilamkurti and Milner, 1993; Mash, Johnson, and Kovitz, 1983; Reid, Kavanagh, and Baldwin, 1987). Also, they have more unrealistic expectations regarding what is appropriate child behavior (Azar, Robinson, et al., 1984; Azar and Rohrbeck, 1986) and have discrimination problems that result in poor "tracking" of child behavior (Wahler and Dumas, 1989) and indiscriminate coercive responses.

These difficulties have been linked to each other. That is, higher levels of unrealistic expectations of children are positively correlated with more negative intent attributions to children's misbehavior, poorer problem solving, and to greater use of physical punishment and other coercive responses (Azar, 1998; Barnes and Azar, 1990; Plotkin, 1983). A picture emerges of adults who have difficulty processing social information and who, when they interact with children, may not be able to respond in ways that support either their own or their children's development. Indeed, Trickett and Susman (1988) reported that such parents view childrearing as harder and less satisfying.

Contributing further to the negative environment are deficits prohibiting the smooth regulation of behavior both within and outside the family. Maltreaters have difficulties managing stress and experience some events as more stressful than nonabusive parents. For example, physical abusers and at-risk parents show greater physiological arousal in response to both child related and non-child-related stimuli (see Milner, 1998, for a review). Physical abusers also show poorer ability to regulate emotion and its expression, and as a result they may respond aggressively to behaviors that would not provoke such responses in others. Rohrbeck and Twentyman (1986) found evidence of heightened impulsivity in such parents. Parenting requires an ability to take measured steps to respond to difficult and confusing child behavior and to stay calm. Indeed, when any parent is angry, he or she is more likely to respond to negative child behavior (especially if ambiguous as to cause) with more negative attributions and more upset (Dix, Reinhold, and Zambarano, 1990).

Findings also suggest social skills deficits. Physical abusers have smaller social support networks (Salzinger, Kaplan, and Artemyeff, 1983), view themselves as more isolated (Newberger, Hampton, Marx, and White, 1986), and overattribute responsibility for aversive behavior to others (Miller and Azar, 1996). Lower levels of empathy have also been shown (Frodi and Lamb, 1980; Melnick and Hurley, 1969). The types of stress found in this population (e.g., marital problems) suggest that interpersonal difficulties may characterize many of these parents' social transactions.

These areas of disturbances may come together with contextual factors to disrupt the parent's capacity to master this stage of adulthood. To give a flavor of what this means, the phases of parenting are discussed briefly below, with examples of how these disturbances may result in distress and ultimately maltreatment. Factors that might facilitate adult development are identified.

The Parenting of Infants and Toddlers

How adults make the transition to parenthood is crucial. The demands of infants are great, and the birth of children may uncover preexisting interpersonal inadequacies that may be exacerbated by the birth of each subsequent child. All parents experience some level of violated expectancies during this transition, especially within the marital system (Kalmuss, Davidson, and Cushman, 1992). Those with more flexible expectancies, however, show less such distress. This may place parents with more unrealistic expectations at greater risk at this transition.

The tasks of parenting during this early period, even under ideal circumstances, may be overwhelming to adults' sense of autonomy. Indeed, in recent years, pressure in the role has increased, with a growing emphasis on being "child centered" and putting aside one's own needs for one's children. This mandate is incongruent with current definitions of young adulthood emphasizing having diversified interests, free exploration, and a focus on the self. Maltreating parents begin their parenting earlier (National Research Council, 1993) and thus may still be in a stage where the focus on self strongly competes with societal demands for a focus on the child.

Prematurity, poor nutrition, and inadequate prenatal care, which have been associated with the poverty common among maltreating parents, may increase children's caregiving needs during this period. Although consistent triggers for physical abuse have not been identified, common ones during this period include: prolonged crying, feeding and sleep problems, and soiling (Herrenkohl, Herrenkohl, and Egolf, 1983). Lack of knowledge of basic childcare common among maltreating parents (Feldman, 1998) can increase difficulties. For example, feeding infants solid foods too early can lead to stomach discomfort and a more colicky baby. In many cultures there is a prior period of slow apprenticeship in this role under the watchful eyes of experienced adults and, even after assuming parenthood, extended family is available for assistance. The younger parent is not left adrift on their own resources and given some time to develop the skills necessary.

Social support can alleviate some of the strain of this period, but is less common among maltreating parents. Many disturbances in family interaction have been documented in this age period (e.g., insensitive caregiving) that suggest an inadequate preparation for this transition and poor carrying out of the role. The social relationship disturbances found in some abused children may have their roots in this early period (i.e., attachment problems and poor modeling; Azar, Barnes, and Twentyman, 1988; Cicchetti, 1989). Infants and toddlers may come to experience their world as untrustworthy, further eroding the potential for harmonious parent–child interactions.

As toddlers become more mobile, environmental risks and lack of supervision may result in injuries. Again, cultures where parents live with extended family may provide resources for such supervision. Families living alone (either with a partner or as a single parent) and in subquality housing may have more difficulties as the environments themselves have more risk factors (e.g., no screens on windows and lead paint), and typical levels of parental monitoring may be inadequate (Crouter and Head, in Vol. 3 of this *Handbook*). In discussing factors that may lead to childhood injury, Peterson and Gable (1998) argued that parental expectancies that children can and will control their impulses may lead parents to believe children require less supervision (e.g., they will check before crossing the street). Such unrealistic expectations of children are prevalent in maltreating parents. With more adults around to provide feedback and information, such expectancies may be "corrected," and parenting may go on without incident. Without them, however, a context for risk evolves. Also, all parents' overrely on rules (e.g., he "knows" not to touch the stove) and underestimate how much supervision is required. Parents at risk for maltreating children may be outliers on this continuum.

The Preschool and School-Age Years

Increases in children's abilities to operate autonomously and desire to use these new capacities, which occur during this period, may result in behaviors that may be perceived by all parents as oppositional. Parents need fine-tuned child-management and social-cognitive capacities and good stress coping to prevent mislabeling such behavior as intentional–aversive child actions and to manage the stress involved. Both of these are areas of deficit for adults at risk for child maltreatment. For all parents, use of physical punishment generally peaks during the late preschool years. Parents with low frustration tolerance and negative biases may be particularly vulnerable to engaging in discipline that approaches physical abuse during this period. Again, a compensatory "other" who helps to generate solutions or provide self-soothing statements may decrease risk (e.g., "My two-year old was just like this"). Observing other parents operate with similar-age children may provide alternative modeling. Child abusers, however, spend less time with other adults with their children present (Salzinger et al., 1983).

Children's expressing greater desire for autonomy common in middle childhood may reinforce parents' expectations that they are able to care for themselves (e.g., being left home alone). All parents may not be immune from this. High stress and low resources may push parents to rely on their offspring more for assistance. Injuries due to house fires when children are unsupervised occur during this period (Dubowitz, 1991). Under economic strain, the child's appearance of less physical vulnerability may free parents to provide less resources to them (e.g., feeling they can fend for themselves). Parents' own caregiving history may also allow them to see this as normal.

As children mature, parents who are cognitively limited may have more difficulty taking the lead and may provide less structure and adequate care. Poor nutrition and fatigue due to a lack of a structured routine may influence child school performance and behavior and result in more parental stress (e.g., experiencing shame at being called into school due to a child's social or academic problems).

The Adolescent Years

This period has not received much attention in the maltreatment literature. Rates of *identified* maltreatment appear lower during this period, but in reality remain high in community samples. Indeed, aggressive parenting practices peak at age 4 and again in the early teen years (although the rate is much lower; Wauchope and Straus, 1987). Maltreated adolescents exhibit behavior that label them as troubled (running away, truancy, delinquency, and oppositional behavior). For parents with poor problem-solving skills, unrealistic expectations, and a negative attributional bias, much anger and frustration may occur.

Triggers for abuse during adolescence may have to do with shifting allegiance to peers and emerging sexuality. The latter may explain the higher use of aggressive parenting practices with females that occurs among all parents in the age period. Earlier failures in managing child behavior may herald more trouble during this period. Parents' success at developing a well-functioning relationship with their younger child has been shown to be a precursor to establishing a positive and less stressful relationship with them in the teen years (i.e., those with early histories of negative interactions show greater increases, and those with lower warmth are more are risk for declines in cohesion; Conger and Ge, 1999). Isolation, common among parents at risk for abuse and neglect, may result in greater risk. Parents who expect teenagers will continue to care for them and to give up peer interactions to keep them company may be disappointed and react negatively.

For all parents, the age at which they initially became parents may have a cascading effect across the lifespan. Early parenting, common in maltreaters, may lead to unique aspects of parent–child relationships (e.g., young single mothers may be dating—or want to be—alongside teenage daughters and may experience feelings of "competition" and/or jealousy).

Adolescents' focus on identity formation may make them particularly reactive to emotional abuse (e.g., belittling), increasing conflict. The combination of a parent less able to manage anger and a more reactive teenager may bode poorly for their transactions. Neglect may take different forms. Educational neglect, poor nutrition, and lack of supervision may be especially prominent and influence long-term health and adjustment. Lack of supervision increases vulnerability to sexual abuse and antisocial behavior. Neglect has been associated with heightened risk-taking behaviors (e.g., early sexual activity and teenage parenthood; Kaplan, Pelcovitz, and La Bruna, 1999; Wright, 1994).

In summary, available research findings suggest it is crucial to take a cognitive behavioral developmental view of families in thinking about child maltreatment. What occurs between parent and child is highly dependent on the interaction between the parent's stage of adult development and mastery of the parenting tasks, and the stage-salient tasks the child must accomplish.

TREATMENT AND PREVENTION OF CHILD MALTREATMENT

Interventions and preventive efforts in abusive and neglectful parenting have taken myriad forms: (1) temporary foster care placement of children or in some cases permanently severing their legal bonds to parents and placing them for adoption, (2) traditional psychotherapy, (3) self-help groups, (4) shotgun interventions that address combinations of almost every aspect of adult and parental functioning, and (5) interventions that target specific skills or parent–child relationships.

Foster care seems to go in and out of favor (e.g., in 1998, 520,000 children were placed in foster care compared to 280,000 in 1987; Adoptions and Foster Care Analysis and Reporting System, 2000), but it has been the most common form of intervention. Despite its high use, the assumptions of foster care have been questioned. There has been inconsistency in the factors that lead to placement, children have received poor care while in care, and rather than be temporary, children have been subject to multiple and lengthy placement. Most relevant is the fact that only limited treatment services are typically provided to parents while children are in care. Treatment deliverers also tend to be inadequately trained and carry heavy caseloads, making intervention spotty (Haugaard and Hazan, in Vol. 1 of this *Handbook*; Williams, 1983). In addition, parental contact with a child in foster care may be quite limited. Lack of contact may make return of the child home and unification of the family after foster placement a difficult transition for both parent and child. Kinship care (placement with members of the parent's family) is quite common. Putting aside the issue of whether such homes differ significantly from that of the parent, the utility of such placements in facilitating reunification may rest on the relationship the parent has with these other caregivers (e.g., such homes may provide continuity and maintain a link to parents, or, in the case of negative relationships, may lead to further deterioration of parent–child relationships due to the animosity involved). Transitions between foster care and home can be destabilizing for both parent and child. For example, with reunification can come disparities in resources available to children (e.g., in foster care they had their own room and nicer clothes) and may result in the child making overt comparisons between foster parents and biological parents, leading to distress for the parent who is attempting to resume her or his role (e.g., reinforcing their sense of inadequacy) and thus increase risk in the relationship.

Also, a portion of children placed in foster care never return home or go in and out of foster care, with detriment to their outcomes. Adoptions of such children, who tend to be older and have special needs, have high disruption rates (Barth and Berry, 1988). This has led to legislation that attempts to expedite the termination of parental rights, requiring permanency planning for children in a shorter space of time (Adoption and Safe Families Act, 1997). Parents must achieve better functioning more quickly. This legislation has mandated that services be provided to parents, but given the lack of service availability, it still may lead to more parents losing custody. Also, despite the unique needs of such children, there are limited postadoption services for adoptive parents to help them with the behaviors maltreated children bring into their care.

Evaluations of traditional psychotherapeutic approaches with maltreating parents have produced disappointing results (e.g., high recidivism rates; Berkeley Planning Associates, 1978; Daro, 1988).

Self-help groups such as Parent's Anonymous have been used that take a more holistic approach, address a range of adult and parenting issues, and establish natural support networks. In these groups, professionals initially act as *sponsors* and gradually decrease their facilitating role as parents from within the group emerge to lead themselves. Thus, they may increase self-efficacy and greater interpersonal control and foster adult development. Positive effects of such groups have been reported, but data are quite limited. Participants also may vary in systematic ways from court-referred parents seen by agencies (National Research Council, 1993).

The last two approaches (a broad spectrum and narrowly focused strategies) have more data showing effectiveness. Targeted interventions using cognitive and behavioral strategies have shown impact with already maltreating parents. Even these, however, appear less successful as parental difficulties become more extreme (e.g., multiple abuse reports, serious problems with employment, consistent problems with housing and transportation, and frequent fights between partners; Szykula and Fleischman, 1985). Broad interventions that target multiple aspects of adult, parenting, and family functioning and provide resources are more effective when applied in preventive interventions (Guterman, 1999). Examples of these last two approaches will be highlighted.

Interventions With Parents of Infants and Toddlers

Treatment during this phase of parenting target a variety of issues: decreasing cognitive distortions; increasing infant stimulation, knowledge of child care, and child development; and improving stress coping. Because attachment problems emerge during this period, it has been suggested that treatment should focus on changing parents' "representational models" of relationships (Egeland and Erickson, 1990), or in cognitive-behavioral terms, cognitive restructuring of their core relational schemas. Crittenden (1993) recommended using videotaped interactions with infants to identify and work with parents' maladaptive interpretations of infant behavior. The efficacy of such an approach within this developmental era, however, has not yet been assessed.

Increasing parent–infant interaction and childcare abilities using behavioral strategies has also been done. Feldman, Case, and Sparks (1992), for example, worked with mentally retarded mothers of newborns and infants and targeted responses required for children's basic survival (e.g., proper diapering, dressing, feeding, and protection). Mothers' baseline skills were observed using function-ally analytically derived observation measures (e.g., for bottle feeding, nine steps were assessed, such as props bottle and checks temperature). Interestingly, on average, nonmaltreating parents do not receive perfect scores on such measures, supporting the idea of a continuum perspective (Feldman, 1998; Greene and Kilili, 1998). Skills where these mothers showed deficits were then targeted. Training consisted of verbal instructions, specially designed picture books depicting each step in the task analysis, modeling each step by a trainer, and feedback on the mother's actual per-formance in training sessions. Mothers received coupons (exchangeable for small gifts) contingent on scoring 80% correct on the trained skills. Weekly sessions ranged from 2 to 29 weeks, depending upon the mothers' acquisition of skills (sessions lasted from 10 to 60 minutes, with some sessions devoted to one skill and others to training of a series of skills in succession). Child involvement was, typically, maximized during training. In some cases (e.g., training in dealing with a diaper rash), a doll was used for training skills. In home visits, time was also spent on advice, support, and problem solving on other life issues (e.g., finding an apartment). Thus, factors needed to ensure a context for adult development were also targeted. Trained mothers did significantly better than the nontreated control group on trained skills and did not differ significantly from community comparison mothers. Further, skills were maintained at follow-up (28 weeks). This study suggests that behaviorally based training in basic childcare skills may be useful.

Using similar methods, programs have been designed to increase parent–infant interaction (Lutkzer, Huynen, and Bigelow, 1998). Training takes place both in contrived activities and in natural moments such as mealtime on behaviors crucial to child development (e.g., smiling, verbal-izing to the infant, touch, and imitation). These are modeled and then practiced with feedback. Time is also spent discussing parents' concerns as they approach interaction, and goals are developed with parents. Thus, efforts are directed by the adult, and their unique concerns are a focus.

In such work generally, Tymchuk (1998) highlighted the importance of determining the best learning environment for parents' level of capacities and providing prosthetic materials to compensate for deficits where needed. This provides attention to parents developing a sense of efficacy in their role and keeps the work within their "zone of proximal development." Rewards to parents for progress are also important. Training in the home is important for generalization and may be more comfortable for parents than therapists' offices. Working with adults on issues as personal as parenting and hygiene also requires sensitivity on therapists' part (Azar, 1996).

Because stress reduction can be an important goal during this period, daycare is often provided to parents. It also provides a safe place for children. Therapeutic daycare programs go beyond just these limited goals and have supportive educational parent groups and have parents take part in class activities; Ayoub, 1991; Crittenden, 1983). With their permission, parents also can be videotaped while interacting with teachers and children for later group discussions. The modeling of nonviolent conflict resolution by staff is key. Although the child impact of such programs has been studied, little data are available on parents. To reduce negative reactions to infant crying or phobic-like responses to physical contact, relaxation training and systematic desensitization are also effective with parents (Gilbert, 1976; Sanders, 1978; Sandford and Tustin, 1974).

Because motivation for change is high at the transition to parenthood, prevention efforts often occur in this age period. Studies, many with teenage mothers, have found positive effects. With some exceptions, programs have been aimed at promoting infant development (e.g., increasing stimulation), improving parent–infant transactions, and increasing parental educational and vocational outcomes rather than reducing abuse. Some, however, have successfully targeted abuse (Bell, Casto, and Daniels, 1983; Olds, Henderson, Chamberlin, and Tatelbaum, 1986). Efforts that target parent adjustment as well as children's promote the best outcomes. Center-based approaches or those combining center based with home-based work have shown more impact on adults (e.g., reductions in second pregnancies, increased employment, less welfare dependence, and fewer referrals for child abuse (Bell et al., 1983; Field, Widmayer, Stringer, Greenburg, and Stoller, 1982).

Interventions With Parents of Preschool and School-Age Children

This age period has probably been the richest in terms of empirical work with already abusive and neglectful parents. Because inappropriate child management strategies and failure to supervise are common, child management training is often used with physically abusive parents to widen parents' repertoire of positive management strategies (e.g., use of reward) and provide them with alternatives to harsh and coercive punishment (e.g., use of distraction or time-out; Azar and Wolfe, 1998). Efforts to reduce parental anger are also important. Package approaches combining child management training, stress and anger management, education in child development with active instruction, modeling, role plays, and feedback by therapists have shown positive outcomes (Wolfe, Sandler, and Kaufman, 1981), as well as those that have added cognitive strategies (e.g., problem-solving training, and cognitive restructuring of distorted beliefs about children; Azar, 1989; Azar and Ferraro, 2000; Azar and Twentyman, 1984; Kolko, 1996). Other elements include films for modeling parenting responses, use of radio transmitters to coach parents through a one-way mirror, and group work. As with parents of infants, when parents' own basic needs are not met, their willingness and capacity to engage in parenting fully may be compromised. Other support services are often needed. Changes in interaction, child problems, and rates of child maltreatment have been shown.

Other areas targeted using cognitive and behavioral strategies include: safety concerns (Peterson and Gable, 1998; Tertinger, Greene, and Lutkzer, 1984); home hygiene (Greene and Kilili, 1998); nutrition, meal planning, and budgeting (Greene, Norman, Searle, Daniels, and Lubeck, 1995; Sarber, Halasz, Messmer, Bickett, and Lutzker, 1983); responding to children's medical illnesses (Delgado and Lutzker, 1988); handling emergencies (e.g., grease fires; Tymchuk, 1998); decision making (Tymchuk, 1998); adult health issues (migraines); and marital issues. All use instruction, modeling, role plays, and feedback. Adaptations for developmentally disabled parents and visual aids to combat literacy issues (e.g., pictorial prompts and use of board games) have been described. Children are directly involved where possible. Since depression and substance abuse may act as obstacles to parents' being aware of children's risky behavior (less attention and vigilance) and lead to parents' not using skills they do have, these problem areas may require intervention as well.

Systemic family therapy has also been successfully utilized (Becker et al., 1995; Kolko, 1996). For example, one study used multisystemic therapy where content varied depending on family needs (using reframing, joining, and prescribed tasks; Brunk, Henggler, and Whelan, 1987). Work was also done with parents' social network (e.g., extended family, peers, and agency personnel).

Interventions With Parents of Adolescents

One obstacle to undertaking treatment during this period is the difficulty engaging parents in treatment. Misinterpretations regarding child behavior, such as labeling the child as "bad," may be very firmly ingrained by the time adolescence arrives, and thus resistance to change may be strong. Also, patterns of family conflict and parental withdrawal from parenting may be firmly established. Parents' self-efficacy may also be so low that they may prefer to abdicate responsibility. Efforts to increase motivation may be crucial. Despite the high rates of abuse to adolescents, there is almost no empirical treatment literature in this age period. One clinical report by Schellenbach and Guerney (1987) outlined a 7-week group package approach that included developmental education; training in empathic and clear communication, using modeling, role plays and homework assignments; training in negotiation skills, goal setting, and problem solving; and also in the use of reinforcement and alternative discipline techniques (e.g., establishing rules, consequences, and constructing behavioral contracts). Incentives were provided for attendance (e.g., lottery tickets). Although evaluation data were not reported, these techniques have been effective with families showing problems similar to those of abused teenagers (DiGuiseppe, 1988). Because failure to monitor teenagers is a predictor of negative outcomes in this age group, supervision is also an important target (Dishion, Andrews, Kavanagh, and Soberman, 1996).

In this overview, some promising efforts at intervention and prevention have been highlighted. These have been aimed at improving parental skills and decreasing social cognitive obstacles to parenting (e.g., cognitive distortions and poor problem solving) and increasing parental motivation and efficacy. Work addressing environmental obstacles has also been combined with these efforts to increase parental resources and reduce stressors.

Issues in Dissemination of Treatments

Although interventions for already abusive and neglectful parents based in social learning theorizing seem promising, these approaches have not received widespread use. It is unclear as to why this has occurred. Some explanations are possible. First, there is generally a dearth of services (Berkowitz and Sedlak, 1993). Also, as the historical review noted, society is less willing to take over supporting parental role functions. There are still deeply held beliefs that difficulties in parenting are constitutional in nature (i.e., a belief that parenting comes naturally and is an instinct, therefore, those who do not have it are fundamentally damaged in some way or have had some moral lapse (Azar, 1996; Farber and Azar, 1999)). The idea that parenting is "learned" flies in the face of such beliefs. Thus, removing the child may be viewed as the best solution, rather than providing assistance to parents to remain in their role. This view may explain why adoptive parents are also provided with little assistance to deal with the unique problems maltreated children bring.

The idea of parental functions being shared throughout the community, common in some cultures, is also antithetical to the "American way," in which self-sufficiency is emphasized. Clearly, the limited services provided to many families makes sense in this light (i.e., if you are in trouble as a parent, it is your job to right yourself, and if not, we will provide another socialization agent who will better meet our standards). Recent shifts in welfare policy echo this view. Although permanency planning initiatives to place children whose parents may never be ready to have them return home may make sense in some situations, the vast majority of children will return home and/or will be in the revolving door of the foster care system. Stronger efforts to implement interventions with an empirical base that allow for careful baseline and outcome measures of progress, rather than interfere with permanency planning, may better document failures and identify faster those parents who will not benefit from treatment and may result in swifter decision making.

CONCLUSIONS

Over the last century increasing emphasis has been placed on parental influences on children's lives and on the psychological responsibilities of this role. The field of child maltreatment needs to be seen within this context. The emergence of protection for children came with a changed view of children. Society has begun to set socialization goals (e.g., mandatory education) and make decisions about some aspects of children's care (e.g., mandatory immunizations). With this transformation, it has also become punishing of parents who fail to fulfill the demands of this role. Scholars have heralded this change as enlightened social policy to protect our society's most vulnerable members, and it is part of a global effort in this direction (U.N. General Assembly, 1989). This attention to children's needs is positive. Yet, although society has demanded more from parents, it remains ambivalent regarding supporting them in their role (i.e., the increasing valuing of children has not led to an increasing valuing of parenting; Farber and Azar, 1999).

This ambivalence has played itself out in social policy directed at families (e.g., first providing supports for single, poor mothers, then pressing them to "take responsibility" for their families and pursuing "deadbeat" dads; Chase-Lansdale and Vinovskis, 1995). We have seen pendulum swings in child protection policy—at one point focusing on removing children, then keeping families together, and again, pushing for speedy permanency planning and shorter time frames to terminate parental rights (Adoption and Safe Families Act, 1997).

Over the last four decades, social scientists have begun to play a more active role in policy making regarding nurturing and protection of children both on the individual family level (e.g., testifying in divorce cases) and national policy (e.g., participation in the development of Head Start). In child maltreatment, with some exceptions, it has also participated in society's emphasis on seeing parents as the sole villains. We have let society set the emphasis of our agenda. That is, to date it has been driven by the strong emotional reaction to the extreme cases of maltreatment that make their way into the media (e.g., work was done on children's memory when court issues emerged here). Although our field's initial reactions were appropriate as legislation was drafted and procedures and programs are put into place to protect children, and were a necessary first step for our field to establish its utility to policy makers (child welfare initiatives have been dominated by other disciplines), it did not foster a careful development of science. Basic research and funding have lagged behind in this area (e.g., compared to that for schizophrenia and depression; Thompson and Wilcox, 1995).

Over the last two decades, research in child maltreatment has begun to improve. Our understanding of child outcomes has increased, but our theory-driven understanding of maltreating parents has progressed more slowly. Societal assumptions that parenting is an automatized set of responses that gets activated once one is placed in the role, as opposed to socially constructed ones whose nature has to be understood and mastered by the adult undertaking them, may be at fault. The sophistication required for today's parenting belies such a belief and it has not led us far.

It is not openly acknowledged that today parenting requires extensive cognitive, social, and emotional capacities, especially if carried out in a low-resourced and high-stress environment. Most parents feel the pressure of the violated expectancies as they transition into parenting (i.e., it does not come "naturally"). The extent to which they experience this sense of violated expectancies can lead to problems in this transition. Although the tension produced by the unevenness of the responsibilities involved has been posited to move adults to higher levels of cognitive, social, and emotional development, for unskilled and socially and economically under-resourced adults, the level of tension may not be optimal for their own continued growth and for the "growing" into the role that is required. For those who had poor parental role models, their very understanding of this role's requirements may be inadequate, and this may add to their strain. For those who are faltering in their adult adjustment, the added responsibility and the experienced "vulnerability" of their child may exacerbate their own sense of vulnerability and be detrimental to behaviors that are necessary to ensure their offspring's survival. For example, one maltreating mother described herself as immobilized when her daughter caught her hand in a fence. Not knowing what to do, she just left her child there, and her daughter's struggles left a bruise. Other mothers talk of fear of bringing babies home from the hospital and checking every 10 minutes to make sure they are still breathing. This is not unlike fear described by mothers with seriously ill babies who bring them home without the medical supports of the hospital. Both groups feel unprepared for a role where task demands feel beyond their capacities.

The field needs to articulate better the *psychological problem* that is child abuse and neglect—the psychological factors within a parent and a parent–child dyad that would lead to a mismatch between parental capacities and child needs. This articulation may not cover all who are identified by the child protection system (extreme substance abuse), but would capture the end of this continuum where psychological interventions may have the most impact. This conclusion may seem contradictory to the original premise that child maltreaters need not be conceived of as a separate category of individuals. Yet even a continuum perspective may foster points on the continuum where a "diagnosis" is in order. To pose an analogy, our field's interest in delinquency (a legal problem) resulted in many early attempts to understand the behavior and to intervene. Yet it was not until researchers were able to carve out the core psychological characteristics of those that engage in delinquent behavior (i.e., defined conduct disorder) that a concerted effort at identifying affected individuals and studying the trajectory of the development of such behavior could occur. Similarly, in depression, the study of mild and/or transient levels of well-specified symptoms have led to a better understanding than just studying those who have attempted to suicide. A similar effort is needed within child maltreatment.

Core characteristics of individuals who engage in child maltreatment that lead to failures in this adult developmental task have begun to be articulated. The field of parenting needs to better define these characteristics and study those individuals who possess them to track the trajectory of the development of maltreating behavior and the actions and contextual factors that decrease its occurrence. This chapter offers a cognitive behavioral and developmental approach to defining child maltreatment and ways to intervene based in this view that have shown some promise. Other views might be developed as well, and their premises examined.

We must approach articulation of these core characteristics carefully. Racial, class, and ethnic differences exist in parenting practices. In defining the core characteristics, we need to select those that are really "core" as opposed to epiphenomena of membership in a diverse group. For example, it is too easy to say that parenting practices that result from poverty (e.g., controlling behavior in the face of danger in neighborhoods) are evidence of problems when they may actually be functional for this context and actually predict better child outcomes. Baldwin, Baldwin, and Cole (1990) found that controlling behavior in parents in low-income, urban settings may not lead to negative outcomes, as it does in suburban ones. This suggests work is needed to provide more specified norms against which to measure effectiveness of parenting practices in different levels of contextual strain and resources. This is a tall order given the poor state of the field in understanding parenting practices in a socioculturally and contextually sensitive manner, but should serve as an ideal. If we do not do this, when our field's expertise is accessed in developing the content for interventions and in custody decision-making regarding parental fitness, inaccurate responses may be given to the detriment of parents', children's, and families' well-being.

Finally, as discussed throughout this chapter, the tasks of parenthood, their successful completion, and the nature of children's needs, although seeming self-evident, change with the state of our scientific knowledge about child development and majority community standards for adequate parenting. For example, there was a period in U.S. society when bottle feeding a baby was considered "enlightened" parenting, and today breast feeding is encouraged as better for children. Although this idea cannot be fully developed within the space limitations of this chapter, the historically situated nature of our definitions of adaptive and maladaptive parenting is a "lurking" issue in this field and one worthy of further consideration.

ACKNOWLEDGMENTS

This chapter was written while the author was on sabbatical and had a Liberal Arts Fellowship at Harvard Law School, in Boston, Massachusetts. The material presented in this chapter was also in part supported by a National Institute of Mental Health (NIMH) FIRST Award (NIMH grant no. MH46940) to the author.

REFERENCES

Adoption and Safe Families Act, U.S. Public Law, 105–189 (1997).

Adoptions and Foster Care Analysis and Reporting System. (2000). *Current placement setting of children in foster care on March 31, 1999* [online]. Available: http/www.acf.dhhs.gov/programs/cb/statstarreport/rpt0100/ar0110c.htm

Ayoub, C. (1991). Physical violence and preschoolers: The use of therapeutic day care in treatment of physically abused children and children from violent families. *The Advisor, 4,* 1–18.

Azar, S. T. (1986). A framework for understanding child maltreatment: An integration of cognitive behavioral and developmental perspectives. *Canadian Journal of Behavioral Science, 18,* 340–355.

Azar, S. T. (1988, November). *Childrearing stress and attributional processes.* Paper presented at the meeting of the Association for the Advancement of Behavioral Therapy, New York.

Azar, S. T. (1989). Training parents of abused children. In C. E. Schaefer and J. M. Briesmeister (Eds.), *Handbook of parent training* (pp. 414–444). New York: Wiley.

Azar, S. T. (1991a, April). *Concern about the physical abuse of adolescents: A case of neglect.* Paper presented at the annual meeting of the Eastern Psychological Association, New York.

Azar, S. T. (1991b). Models of physical child abuse: A metatheoretical analysis. *Criminal Justice and Behavior, 18,* 30–46.

Azar, S. T. (1996). Cognitive restructuring of professionals' schema regarding women parenting in poverty. *Women and Therapy, 18,* 147–161.

Azar, S. T. (1998). A cognitive behavioral approach to understanding and treating parents who physically abuse their children. In D. Wolfe and R. McMahon (Eds.), *Child abuse: New directions in prevention and treatment across the life span* (pp. 78–100). New York: Sage.

Azar, S. T. (in press). Adult development and parenting. In J. Demick (Ed.), *Adult development.* New York: Sage.

Azar, S. T., Barnes, K. T., and Twentyman, C. T. (1988). Developmental outcomes in physically abused children: Consequences of parental abuse or the effects of a more general breakdown in caregiving behaviors? *Behavior Therapist, 11,* 27–32.

Azar, S. T., and Benjet, C. L. (1994). A cognitive perspective on ethnicity, race, and termination of parental rights. *Law and Human Behavior, 18,* 249–268.

Azar, S. T., and Bober, S. (1999). Children of abusive families. In W. K. Silverman and T. H. Ollendick (Eds.), *Developmental issues in the clinical treatment of children and adolescents* (pp. 371–392). Boston: Allyn & Bacon.

Azar, S. T., and Cote, L. (in press). Sociocultural issues in the evaluation of the needs of children in custody decision-making: What do our current frameworks for evaluating parenting practices have to offer? *International Journal of Law and Psychiatry.*

Azar, S. T., Fantuzzo, J., and Twentyman, C. T. (1984). An applied behavioral approach to child maltreatment: Back to basics. *Advances in Behavior Research and Therapy, 6,* 3–11.

Azar, S. T., and Ferraro, M. H. (2000). How can parenting be enhanced? In H. Dubowitz and D. Depanfilis (Eds.), *Handbook of child protection practice* (pp. 437–446). Thousand Oaks, CA: Sage.

Azar, S. T., Lauretti, A., and Loding, B. (1998). The evaluation of parental fitness in termination of parental rights cases: A functional-contextual perspective. *Clinical Child and Family Psychology Review, 1,* 77–99.

Azar, S. T., Povilaitis, T., Lauretti, A., and Pouquette, C. (1998). Theory in child abuse. In J. Lutzker (Ed.), *Handbook of child abuse research and treatment* (pp. 3–30). New York: Plenum.

Azar, S. T., Robinson, D. R., Hekimian, E., and Twentyman, C. T. (1984). Unrealistic expectations and problem solving ability in maltreating and comparison mothers. *Journal of Consulting and Clinical Psychology, 52*, 687–691.

Azar, S. T., and Rohrbeck, C. A. (1986). Child abuse and unrealistic expectations: Further validation of the Parent Opinion Questionnaire. *Journal of Consulting and Clinical Psychology, 54*, 867–868.

Azar, S. T., and Siegel, B. (1990). Behavioral treatment of child abuse: A developmental perspective. *Behavior Modification, 14*, 279–300.

Azar, S. T., and Twentyman, C. T. (1984, November). *An evaluation of the effectiveness of behaviorally versus insight oriented group treatments with maltreating mothers.* Paper presented at the annual meeting of the Association for Advancement of Behavior Therapy, Philadelphia.

Azar, S. T., and Twentyman, C. T. (1986). Cognitive behavioral perspectives on the assessment and treatment of child abuse. In P. C. Kendall (Ed.), *Advances in cognitive behavioral research and therapy* (Vol. 5, pp. 237–267). New York: Academic Press.

Azar, S. T., and Wolfe, D. A. (1998). Child abuse and neglect. In E. G. Mash and R. A. Barkley (Eds.), *Behavioral treatment of childhood disorders* (2nd ed.). New York: Guilford.

Baldwin, A., Baldwin, C., and Cole, R. E. (1990). Stress-resistant families and stress-resistant children. In J. E. Rolf, A. S. Masten, D. Cicchetti, K. N. Wechterlein, and S. Weintraub (Eds.), *Risk and protective factors in the development of psychopathology* (pp. 257–280). New York: Cambridge University Press.

Barnes, K. T., and Azar, S. T. (1990, August). *Maternal expectations and attributions in discipline situations: A test of a cognitive model of parenting.* Paper presented at the annual meeting of the American Psychological Association, Boston.

Barth, R. P., and Berry, M. (1988). *Adoption and disruption: Rates, risk, and responses.* New York: De Gruyter.

Becker, J. V., Alpert, J., BigFoot, D. S., Bonner, B. L., Geddie, L. F., Henggler, S. W., Kaufman, K. L., and Walker, C. E. (1995). Empirical research on child abuse treatment: Report of the child abuse and neglect treatment working group, American Psychological Association. *Journal of Child Clinical Psychology, 24*, 23–46.

Bell, C. A., Casto, G., and Daniels, D. (1983). Ameliorating the impact of teen-age pregnancy on parent and child. *Child Welfare, 62*, 167–173.

Belsky, J. (1980). Child maltreatment: An ecological integration. *American Psychologist, 35*, 320–335.

Belsky, J., and Vondra, J. (1989). Lessons from child abuse: The determinants of parenting. In D. Cicchetti and V. Carlson (Eds.), *Child maltreatment* (pp. 153–202). New York: Cambridge University Press.

Berkeley Planning Associates. (1978). *Evaluation of child abuse demonstration projects, 1974–1977.* Washington, DC: U.S. Department of Health, Education and Welfare.

Berkowitz, S., and Sedlak, A. J. (1993). *Study of high risk: Child abuse and neglect groups. State survey report.* Washington, DC: National Center on Child Abuse and Neglect.

Blaher, J. (1984). *Severely handicapped young children and their families* (pp. 3–50). New York: Academic Press.

Bousha, D., and Twentyman, C. T. (1984). Abusing, neglectful and comparison mother–child interactional style. *Journal of Abnormal Psychology, 93*, 106–114.

Brassard, M. R., Germain, R., and Hart, S. N. (1987). *Psychological maltreatment of children and youth.* New York : Pergamon.

Brunk, M., Henggeler, S. W., and Whelan, J. P. (1987). Comparison of multisystemic therapy and parent training in the brief treatment of child abuse and neglect. *Journal of Consulting and Clinical Psychology, 55*, 171–178.

Bugenthal, D. B., Mantyla, S. M., and Lewis, J. (1989). Parental attributions as moderators of affective communication to children at risk for physical abuse. In D. Cicchetti and V. Carlson (Eds.), *Child maltreatment* (pp. 254–279). New York: Cambridge University Press.

Burgess, R. L., and Conger, R. D. (1978). Family interaction in abusive, neglectful and normal families. *Child Development, 49*, 1163–1173.

Caffey, J. (1946). Multiple fractures in the long bones of infants suffering from chronic subdural hematoma. *American Journal of Roentgenology, 56*, 163–173.

Cerezo, M. A., D'Ocon, A., and Dolz, L. (1996). Mother–child interactive patterns in abusive familes versus non-abusive families. *Child Abuse and Neglect, 20*, 573–587.

Chao, R. (1997, April). *The "meaningfulness" of our most familiar constructs: Research on parenting for ethnically diverse populations.* Paper presented at the biennial meeting of the Society for Research in Child Development, Washington, DC.

Chase-Lansdale, P. L., and Vinovskis, M. S. (1995). Whose responsibility? An historical analysis of the changing roles of mothers, fathers, and society. In P. L. Chase-Lansdale and J. Brooks-Gunn (Eds.), *Escape from poverty. What differences does it make?* (pp. 11–37). New York: Cambridge University Press.

Chilamkurti, C., and Milner, J. S. (1993). Perceptions and evaluations of child transgressions and disciplinary techniques in high- and low-risk mothers and their children. *Child Development, 64*, 31–44.

Cicchetti, D. (1989). How research on child maltreatment has informed the study of child development. In D. Cicchetti and V. Carlson (Eds.), *Child maltreatment* (pp. 377–431). Cambridge: Cambridge University Press.

Cicchetti, D., and Barnett, D. (1991). Toward the development of a scientific nosology of child maltreatment. In D. Cicchetti and W. Grove (Eds.), *Thinking clearly about psychology* (pp. 346–377). Minneapolis: University of Minnesota Press.

Cicchetti, D., and Lynch, M. (1995). Failures in the expectable environment and their impact on individual development: The case of child maltreatment. In D. Cicchetti and D. Cohen (Eds.), *Developmental psychopathology: Risk, disorder, and adaptation* (pp. 32–71). New York: Wiley.

Cicchetti, D., and Rizley, R. (1981). Developmental perspectives on the etiology, intergenerational transmission, and sequelae of child maltreatment. *New Directions for Child Development, 11*, 31–56.

Conger, R. D., and Ge, X. (1999). Conflict and cohesion in parent-adolescent relations: Changes in emotional expression from early to midadolescence. In M. Cox and J. Brook-Gunn (Eds.), *Conflict and cohesion in families* (pp. 185–206). Mahwah, NJ: Lawrence Erlbaum Associates.

Crittenden, P. M. (1983). The effects of mandatory protective daycare on mutual attachment in maltreating mother–infant dyads. *Child Abuse and Neglect, 3*, 297–300.

Crittenden, P. M. (1993). An information processing perspective on the behavior of neglectful parents. *Criminal Justice and Behavior, 20*, 27–48.

Crittenden, P. M. (1998). Dangerous behavior and dangerous contexts. In P. K. Trickett and C. J. Shellenbach (Eds.), *Violence against children and the family and the community* (pp. 11–38). Washington, DC: American Psychological Association.

Crittenden, P. M., and Ainsworth, M. D. S. (1989). Child maltreatment and attachment theory. In D. Cicchetti and V. Carlson (Eds.), *Child maltreatment* (pp. 432–463). Cambridge: Cambridge University Press.

Culp, R. E., Culp, A. M., Soulis, and Letts, D. (1989). Self esteem and depression in abusive, neglecting, and nonmaltreating mothers. *Infant Mental Health Journal, 10*, 243–251.

Cusinato, M. (1994). Parenting over the family life cycle. In L. L'Abate (Ed.), *Handbook of developmental family psychology and psychopathology* (pp. 83–115). New York: Wiley.

Daro, D. (1988). *Confronting child abuse: Research for effective program design.* New York: Free Press.

Delgado, A. E., and Lutzker, J. R. (1988). Training young parents to identify and report their children's illnesses. *Journal of Applied Behavioral Analysis, 21*, 311–319.

DiGiuseppe, R. (1988). A cognitive-behavioral approach to the treatment of conduct disorder children and adolescents. In N. Epstein, S. F. Schlesinger, and W. Dryden (Eds.), *Cognitive-behavioral therapy with families* (pp. 183–214). New York: Brunner/Mazel.

Dishion, T. J., Andrews, D. W., Kavanagh, K., and Soberman, L. H. (1996). Preventive interventions for high-risk youth. In R. D. Peters and R. J. McMahon (Eds.), *Preventing childhood disorders, substance abuse, and delinquency* (pp. 184–214). Thousand Oaks, CA: Sage.

Dix, T., Rheinhold, D. P., and Zambarano, R. J. (1990). Mothers' judgments in moments of anger. *Merrill-Palmer Quarterly, 36*, 465–486.

Donovan, W. L., and Leavitt, L. A. (1989). Maternal self-efficacy and infant attachment: integrating physiology, perception, and behavior. *Child Development, 60*, 460–472.

Dubowitz, H. (1991). The impact of child maltreatment on health. In R. H. Starr and D. A. Wolfe (Eds.), *The effects of child abuse and neglect* (pp. 278–294). New York: Guilford.

Eckenrode, J., Laird, M., and Doris, J. (1993). School performance and disciplinary problems among abused and neglected children. *Developmental Psychology, 29*, 53–62.

Egeland, B., Breitenbucher, M., and Rosenberg. D. (1980). Prospective study of the significance of life stress in the etiology of child abuse. *Journal of Consulting and Clinical Psychology, 48*, 194–205.

Egeland, B., and Erickson, M. F. (1987). Psychologically unavailable caregiving. In M. Brassard, R. Germain, and S. Hart (Eds.), *Psychological maltreatment of children and youth* (pp. 110–120). New York: Pergamon.

Egeland, B., and Erickson, M. F. (1990). Rising above the past: Strategies for helping new mothers break the cycle of abuse and neglect. *Zero to Three, 11*, 29–35.

Emery, R. E., and Laumann-Billings, L. (1998). An overview of the nature, causes, and consequences of abusive family relationships. *American Psychologist, 53*, 121–135.

English, D. J., Marshall, D. B., and Orme, M. (1999). Characteristics of repeated referrals to child protective services in Washington State, WA, US. *Child Maltreatment, 4*, 297–307.

Famularo, R., Stone, I., Barnum, R., and Wharton, R. (1986). Alcoholism and severe child maltreatment. *American Journal of Orthopsychiatry, 56*, 481–485.

Farber, B., and Azar, S. T. (1999). Blaming the helper. The marginalization of teachers and parents of the urban poor. *Journal of Orthopsychiatry, 69*, 515–528.

Feldman, M. A. (1998). Parents with intellectual disabilities. In J. R. Jutzker (Ed.), *Handbook of child abuse research and treatment* (pp. 401–420). New York: Plenum.

Feldman, M. A., Case, L., and Sparks, B. (1992). Effectiveness of home based early intervention on the language development of children of mothers with mental retardation. *Research in Developmental Disabilities, 14*, 387–408.

Field, T. M., Widmayer, S., Stringer, S., Greenburg, R., and Stoller, S. (1982). Effects of parent training on teenage mothers and their infants. *Pediatrics, 69*, 703–707.

Frodi, A. M., and Lamb, M. (1980). Child abuser's responses to infant smiles and cries. *Child Development, 51*, 238–241.

Gara, M. A., Allen, L. A., Herzog, E. P., and Woolfolk, R. L. (2000). The abused child as parent: The structure and content of physically abused mothers' perceptions of their babies. *Child Abuse and Neglect, 24*, 627–639.

Gara, M. A., Rosenberg, S., and Herzog, E. P. (1996). The abused child as parent. *Child Abuse and Neglect, 20*, 797–807.

Garbarino, J. (1976). A preliminary study of some ecological correlates of child abuse: The impact of socioeconomic stress on mothers. *Child Development, 47*, 178–185.

Garbarino, J. (1991). Not all bad developmental outcomes are the result of child abuse. *Development and Psychopathology, 3*, 45–50.

Garbarino, J., and Giliam, G. (1980). *Understanding abusive families.* Lexington, MA: Lexington Books.

Gaudin, J. M., Polansky, N. A., Kilpatrick, A. C., and Shilton, P. (1993). Loneliness, depression, stress and social supports in neglectful families. *American Journal of Orthopsychiatry, 63*, 597–605.

Gelles, R. J., and Straus, M. A. (1979). Determinants of violence in the family: Toward a theoretical integration. In W. R. Burr, R. Hill, F. I. Nye, and I. L. Reiss (Eds.), *Contemporary theories about the family* (pp. 549–581). New York:

George, C., and Main, M. (1979). Social interactions of young abused children: Approach, avoidance and aggression. *Child Development, 35*, 306–318.

Gil, D. (1970). *Violence against children: Physical child abuse in the United States.* Cambridge, MA: Harvard University Press.

Gilbert, M. R. (1976). Behavioral approach to the treatment of child abuse. *Nursing Times, 72*, 140–143.

Goodnow, J. J., and Collins, W. A. (1990). *Development according to parents: The nature, source, and consequences of parents' ideas.* Hillsdale, NJ: Lawrence Erlbaum Associates.

Green, A. (1976). A psychodynamic approach to the study and treatment of child abusing parents. *American Academy of Child Psychiatry, 15*, 414–429.

Greene, B. F., and Kilili, S. (1998). How good does a parent have to be? In J. R. Jutzker (Ed.), *Handbook of child abuse research and treatment* (pp. 53–74). New York: Plenum.

Greene, B. F., Norman, K. R., Searle, M. S., Daniels, M., and Lubeck, R. C. (1995). Child abuse and neglect by parents with disabilities. *Journal of Applied Behavior Analysis, 28*, 417–434.

Grisso, T. (1986). *Evaluating competencies.* New York: Plenum.

Guterman, N. B. (1999). Enrollment strategies in early home visitation to prevent physical child abuse and neglect and the "universal versus targeted" debate: A meta-analysis of populaton based and screening based programs. *Child Abuse and Neglect, 23*, 863–890.

Hansen, D. J., Pallotta, G. M., Tishelman, A. C., and Conaway, L. P. (1989). Parental problem-solving skills and child behavior problems: A comparison of physically abusive, neglectful, clinic, and community families. *Journal of Family Violence, 4*, 353–368.

Herrenkohl, R. C., Herrenkohl, E. C., and Egolf, B. P. (1983). Circumstances surrounding the occurrence of child maltreatment. *Journal of Consulting and Clinical Psychology, 51*, 424–431.

Hoffman-Plotkin, D., and Twentyman, C. T. (1984). A multimodal assessment of behavioral and cognitive deficits in abused and neglected preschoolers. *Child Development, 55*, 794–802.

Janko, S. (1994). *Vulnerable children, vulnerable families.* New York: Teachers College Press.

Kadushin, A. (1967). *Child welfare services.* New York: Macmillian.

Kagitcibasi, C. (1982). Old-age security value of children. Cross-national socioeconomic factors. *Journal of Cross Cultural Psychology, 13*, 29–42.

Kalmuss, D., Davidson, A., and Cushman, L. (1992). Parenting expectations, experiences, and adjustment to parenthood: A test of the violated expectations framework. *Journal of Marriage and the Family, 54*, 516–526.

Kaplan, S. J., Pelcovitz, D., and La Bruna, V. (1999). Child and adolescent abuse and neglect research: A review of the past 10 years. *Journal of the American Academy of Child and Adolescent Psychiatry, 38*, 1214–1222.

Kaufman, J., and Zigler, E. (1987). Do abused children become abusive parents? *American Journal of Orthopsychiatry, 57*, 186–192.

Kempe, C. H., Silverman, F., Steele, B., Droegemueller, W., and Silver, H. (1962). The battered child syndrome. *Journal of the American Medical Association, 181*, 17–24.

Klaus, M. H., and Kennell, M. (1982). *Maternal–infant bonding* (2nd ed.). Cambridge: Cambridge University Press.

Kohn, M. L. (1963). Social class and parent–child relationships: An interpretation. *American Journal of Sociology, 108*, 471–480.

Kolko, D. J. (1996). Individual cognitive behavioral treatment and family therapy for physically abused children and their offending parents: A comparison of clinical outcomes. *Child Maltreatment, 1*, 322–342.

Korbin, J. E. (1994). Sociocultural factors in child maltreatment. In G. B. Melton and F. D. Barry (Eds.), *Protecting children from abuse and neglect* (pp. 182–223). New York: Guilford.

Lanyon, R. I. (1986). Theory and treatment in child molestation. *Journal of Consulting and Clinical Psychology, 54*, 176–182.

Larrance, D. T., and Twentyman, C. T. (1983). Maternal attributions in child abuse. *Journal of Abnormal Psychology, 92*, 449–457.

LeVine, R. A. (1974). Parental goals: A cross-cultural view. *Teachers College Record, 76,* 226–239.

Lutzker, J. R., Huynen, K. B., and Bigelow, K. M. (1998). Child neglect. In V. B. Van Hasselt and M. Hersen (Eds.), *Handbook of psychological treatment protocols for children and adolescents* (pp. 467–500). Hillsdale, NJ: Lawrence Erlbaum Associates.

Mash, E. J., Johnston, C., and Kovitz, K. (1983). A comparison of the mother–child interactions of physically abused and non-abused children during play and task situations. *Journal of Clinical Child Psychology, 12,* 337–346.

Mason, M. (1994). *From father's property to children's rights.* New York: Columbia Unversity Press.

McCloyd, V. C. (1990). The impact of economic hardship on Black families and children: Psychological distress, parenting, and socioemotional development. *Child Development, 61,* 311–346.

Melnick, B., and Hurley, J. R. (1969). Distinctive personality attributes of child-abusing mothers. *Journal of Consulting and Clinical Psychology, 33,* 746–749.

Miller, L. R., and Azar, S. T. (1996). The pervasiveness of maladaptive attributions in mothers at-risk for child abuse. *Family Violence and Sexual Abuse Bulletin, 12,* 31–37.

Milner, J. S. (1993). Social information processing and physical child abuse. *Clinical Psychology Review, 13,* 275–294.

Milner, J. S. (1998). Individual and family characteristics associated with intrafamilial child physical and sexual abuse. In P. K. Trickett and C. J. Shellenbach (Eds.), *Violence against children and the family and the community* (pp. 141–170). Washington, DC: American Psychological Association.

Milner, J. S., and Froody, R. (1994). The impact of mitigating information on attributions for positive and negative child behavior by adults at low- and high-risk of child abusive behavior. *Journal of Social and Clinical Psychology, 13,* 335–351.

National Center on Child Abuse and Neglect. (2000). *Child maltreatment 1998. Reports from the states to the National Center on Child Abuse and Neglect.* Washington, DC: U.S. Department of Health and Human Services.

National Research Council. (1993). *Understanding child abuse and neglect.* Washington, DC: National Academy Press.

Nayak, M., and Milner, J. S. (1996). *Neuropsychological functioning: Comparison of parents at high- and low-risk for child physical abuse.* Unpublished manuscript.

Newberger, E. H., Hampton, R. L., Marx, T. J., and White, K. M. (1986). Child abuse and pediatric social illness. *American Journal of Orthopsychiatry, 56,* 589–601.

Newman, P. R., and Newman, B. M. (1988). Parenthood and adult development. In R. Palkovitz and M. B. Sussman (Eds.), *Transitions to parenthood* (pp. 313–337). New York: Haworth.

Oldershaw, L., Walters, G. C., and Hall, D. K. (1989). A behavioral approach to the classification of different types of abusive mothers. *Merrill-Palmer Quarterly, 35,* 255–279.

Olds, D. L., Henderson, C. R., Chamberlin, R., and Tatelbaum, R. (1986). Preventing child abuse and neglect: A randomized trial of nurse home visitation. *Pediatrics, 78,* 65–78.

Olsen, L. J., and Holmes, W. M. (1986). Youth at risk: Adolescents and maltreatment. *Child and Youth Services Review, 8,* 13–35.

Palkovitz, R. (1996). Parenting as a generator of adult development: Conceptual issues and implications. *Journal of Social and Personal Relationships, 13,* 571–592.

Peterson, L., and Gable, S. (1998). Holistic injury and prevention. In J. R. Lutzker (Ed.), *Handbook of child abuse research and treatment* (pp. 291–318). New York: Plenum.

Plotkin, R. (1983). *Cognitive mediation in disciplinary actions among mothers who have abused or neglected their children: Dispositional and environmental factors.* Unpublished doctoral dissertation, University of Rochester, NY.

Reid, J. B., Kavanagh, K., and Baldwin, D. V. (1987). Abusive parents' perceptions of child problem behaviors. *Journal of Abnormal Child Psychology, 15,* 457–466.

Rohrbeck, C. A., and Twentyman, C. T. (1986). A multimodal assessment of impuisiveness in abusing, neglectful, and nonmaltreating mothers and their preschool children. *Journal of Consulting and Clinical Psychology, 54,* 231–236.

Ruddick, S. (1989). *Maternal thinking. Toward a politics of peace.* New York: Beacon.

Salzinger, S., Feldman, R., Hammer, M., and Rosario, M. (1993). The effects of physical abuse on children's social relationships. *Child Development, 64,* 169–187.

Salzinger, S., Kaplan, S., and Artemyeff, C. (1983). Mother's personal social networks and child maltreatment. *Journal of Abnormal Psychology, 92,* 68–72.

Sanders, W. (1978). Systematic desensitization in the treatment of child abuse. *American Journal of Psychiatry, 135,* 483–484.

Sandford, D. A., and Tustin, R. D. (1974). Behavioral treatment of parental assault on a child. *New Zealand Psychologist, 2,* 76–82.

Sarber, R. E., Halasz, M. M., Messmer, M. C., Bickett, A. D., and Lutzker, J. R. (1983). Teaching menu planning and grocery shopping skills to a mentally retarded mother. *Mental Retardation, 21,* 101–106.

Schellenbach, C. J., and Guerney, I. F. (1987). Identification of adolescent abuse and future intervention. *Journal of Adolescence, 10,* 1–12.

Schilling, R. F., and Schinke, S. P. (1984). Maltreatment and mental retardation. *Perspectives and Progress in Mental Retardation, 1,* 11–22.

Starr, R. H., MacLean, D. J., and Keating, D. P. (1991). Life span developmental outcomes of child maltreatment. In R. Starr and D. A. Wolfe (Eds.), *The effects of child abuse and neglect* (pp. 1–32). New York: Guilford.

Steele, B. F. (1980). Psychodynamic factors in child abuse. In R. E. Helfer and C. H. Kempe (Eds.), *The battered child* (86–103). Chicago: University of Chicago Press.

Straus, M. A. (1973). A general systems theory approach to a theory of violence between family members. *Social Science Information, 12*, 105–125.

Straus, M. A. (1994). *Beating the devil out of them: Corporal punishment in America.* New York: Lexington Books.

Straus, M. A., Gelles, R. J., and Steinmetz, S. K. (1980). *Behind closed doors: Violence in the American family.* New York: Doubleday/Anchor.

Swick, K. J. (1988). Parental efficacy and involvement. *Childhood Education, 64*, 37–42.

Szykula, S. A., and Fleischman, M. J. (1985). Reducing out-of-home-placements of abused children: Two controlled studies. *Child Abuse and Neglect, 9*, 277–284.

tenBensel, R. W., Rheinberger, M. M., and Radbill, S. X. (1997). Children in a world of violence: The roots of child maltreatment. In M. E. Helfer, R. S. Kempe, and R. D. Krugman (Eds.), *The battered child* (pp. 3–28). Chicago: University of Chicago Press.

Tertinger, D. A., Greene, B. F., and Lutzker, J. R. (1984). Home safety: Development and validation of one component of an ecobehavioral treatment program for abused and neglected children. *Journal of Applied Behavior Analysis, 17*, 150–174.

Thompson, F. A., and Wilcox, B. L. (1995). Child maltreatment research. Federal support and policy issues. *American Psychologist, 50*, 789–793.

Thompson, L., and Walker, A. J. (1989). Gender in families: Women and men in marriage, work, and parenthood. *Journal of Marriage and the Family, 51*, 845–871.

Trickett, P. K., and Kuczynski, L. (1986). Children's misbehaviors and parental discipline strategies in abusive and nonabusive families. *Developmental Psychology, 22*, 115–123.

Trickett, P. K., and Susman, E. J. (1988). Parental perceptions of child-rearing practices in physically abusive and nonabusive families. *Developmental Psychology, 24*, 270–276.

Tymchuk, A. J. (1998). The importance of matching educational interventions to parent needs in child maltreatment. In J. R. Lutzker (Ed.), *Handbook of child abuse research and treatment* (pp. 421–448). New York: Plenum.

U.N. General Assembly (1989, November). *Adoption of the convention on the rights of the child* (U.N. Doc. A/Res/44/25). New York: Author.

Vygotsky, L. S. (1934). *Thought and language.* Cambridge, MA: MIT Press.

Wahler, R. G., and Dumas, J. E. (1989). Attentional problems in dysfunctional mother–child interactions: An interbehavioral model. *Psychological Bulletin, 105*, 116–130.

Wauchope, B. A., and Straus, M. A. (1987, July). *Age, class, and gender differences in physical punishment and physical abuse of American children.* Paper presented at the National Conference of Family Violence Research, Durham, NH.

Williams, G. (1983). The urgency of authentic prevention. *Journal of Clinical Child Psychology, 12*, 312–319.

Wolfe, D. A. (1987). *Child abuse: Implications for child development and psychopathology.* Newbury Park, CA: Sage.

Wolfe, D. A., Sandler, J., and Kaufman, K. (1981). A competency-based parent training program for abusive parents. *Journal of Consulting and Clinical Psychology, 49*, 633–640.

Wright, S. A. (1994). Physical and emotional abuse and neglect of preschool children: A literature review. *Australian Occupational Therapy Journal, 41*, 55–63.

Zeanah, C. J., and Zeanah, P. D. (1989). Intergenerational transmission of maltreatment: Insights from attachment theory and research. *Psychiatry, 52*, 177–196.

Zelizer, V. A. (1985). *Pricing the priceless children.* New York: Basic Books.

Zuravin, S. J. (1991). Research definitions of child physical abuse and neglect: Current problems. In R. H. Starr and D. A. Wolfe (Eds.), *The effects of child abuse and neglect: Issues and research* (pp. 100–128). New York: Guilford.

Zuravin, S. J., and Di Blasio, F. A. (1996). The correlates of child physical abuse and neglect by adolescent mothers. *Journal of Family Violence, 11*, 149–166.

15

Parent Education

Camille Smith
Ruth Perou
Catherine Lesesne
Centers for Disease Control and Prevention

INTRODUCTION

Parent education is an organized effort with clear content, target population, and goals aimed at enhancing or changing parental role performance (Harman and Brim, 1980). Parent education as presented in this chapter is directed at educational efforts that attempt to enhance or facilitate parent behaviors that will influence positive developmental outcomes in their children.

Three important contributions to the widespread interest in parenting education have occurred in the United States over the last century. As a nation, we realize and acknowledge that there is no job as important as parenting to the welfare of our society; there have been dramatic cultural and social changes in the Unites States, and the last 40 years have brought an increase in the knowledge of child development and the importance of effective parenting practices on positive outcomes for children.

There is no greater responsibility than rearing a child, and no job more important to the future of our society than parenting. Parents prepare the next generation for the physical, economic, and psychosocial situations such that it will survive and flourish (Pew Charitable Trust, 1996). A child depends on parents for the essential ingredients of life: food, clothing, shelter, health care, nurturance, and love. Parents help shape a child's attitude, confidence, and skills in engaging the world. Being a parent is most often considered a desirable role, and parents usually view parenting as a meaningful and satisfying activity. However, it is arguably the single most demanding and time-consuming role encountered in young and middle adulthood. Effective parenting requires a significant and sustained investment of time and energy on the part of the parent. Ineffective parenting is one of, if not the most, serious risks for childhood behavior problems confronting families during a child's early years of life (Swick and Graves, 1993). Parenting competencies figure prominently in the etiology of child and adolescent problem behaviors (Dishion, Patterson, Stoolmiller, and Skinner, 1991).

Parent education is based on the principles that parenthood is an extremely complex, demanding, and, however, rewarding job, and that education can help parents perform their job more effectively.

For generations our society has assumed that the capacity to rear a child was instinctive, especially for women. However, many parents had questions about their parenting and wanted to know if what they were doing was "right." Fortunately for most parents in years past, there has been a wide array of supports and resources available through their own parents, extended families, churches, synagogues and the communities. Common experiences, practical advice, and homespun wisdom were shared with mothers and fathers seeking advice. In the last generation, however, America changed in terms of family lifestyles, and these traditional supports are not as readily available. Family life changed as workforce participation, mobility, absent fathers, and teen parents increased.

Forty years ago the majority of families in the United States were composed of two parents, one of whom stayed home to care for the children while the other went to work. In 1999, 64% of mothers with children under age 6 , and 78% of mothers with children ages 6 to13 were working. Almost 60% of mothers with infants (under age 1) are in the labor force. Everyday 13 million preschoolers, including 6 million infants and toddlers, are in out-of-home childcare (Children's Defense Fund, 1999).

America is a highly mobile society, with 43 million people changing addresses each year. In 1999, almost a quarter (23%) of children lived with only their mother, 4% lived with only their father, and 4% lived with neither of their parents (Children's Defense Fund, 1999). These family life changes have dramatically altered the informal support networks that parents use to gain information about childrearing, leading parents to seek out formal parenting education classes and resources.

Extensive workforce participation by parents results in less time and energy to devote to individual children. Consequently, children are spending more hours in front of televisions, computers, video games, and other technological machines. Children ages 2 to 4 spend over 4 hours everyday, on average, exposed to the media, and over a quarter have TVs in their bedrooms (Roberts, Foehr, Rideout, and Brodie, 1999). This initially led to an emphasis on "quality time" (versus quantity) with respect to parenting. However, the pendulum seems to be swinging back toward the middle to emphasize the importance of both the amount of time spent by parents with their children and how they spend that time together.

The research on child development over the last 40 years has also influenced the numbers of parents taking part in a variety of parent education programs that are focused on child outcomes. These programs address topics such as child development, social and emotional growth as well as positive discipline. Elements of the programs may include parent group meetings and or home visits. This research has shed light on the importance of early environmental experiences and especially those between parent and child that can have an inhibiting or facilitating effect on all areas of child development. Parenting that is attuned to children's abilities and to the developmental tasks they face has historically promoted a variety of positive developmental outcomes including emotional security, behavioral independence, social competence, and intellectual achievement (Belsky, Taylor, and Rovine, 1984). As a result of the proliferation of research that has addressed the positive outcomes of warm, nurturing, and responsive parenting, as well as the serious risks of ineffective parenting, parent education programs have been developed in virtually every community in the United States.

The notion of parent education has evolved and taken many forms over the last 100 years. There have been literally hundreds of books devoted to the topic aimed at different audiences: parents, researchers, advocates, policy makers, and others. This chapter will attempt to address the topic of parent education, first from a definitional, theoretical, and historical perspective, and then take a look at some of the limitations in parenting education knowledge. A sample of nationally known and replicated models of parent education programs and materials, will be discussed. The programs selected to be presented here are those which have had an extensive evaluation completed. We will address these programs from two perspectives: universal access, or programs that are available to all families; and targeted access, or programs whose participants meet a certain set of criteria that place them at risk of developing problems if some kind of intervention is not undertaken. More specifically, in the targeted section we will look at parent education in the following areas: parents of low income or low education, the prevention of child abuse and neglect, preventing or reducing juvenile delinquency and youth violence, rearing children with disabilities and/or behavioral problems, and teenage mothers. We will conclude with a discussion on parent education research and evaluation, and what we believe every parent education program should emphasize.

DEFINING PARENT EDUCATION

A relevant British researcher defined parenting education saying, "Parenting education describes a range of teaching and support programmes which focus on the skills, feelings, and tasks of being a parent" (Einzig, 1996, p. 222). Parent education incorporates experiences that give parents added knowledge and understanding. Parent education can positively affect the satisfaction and functioning of families by communicating knowledge about child development and relationships that increases understanding, providing alternative models of parenting that widen parents' choices, teaching new skills, and facilitating access to community services (Hammer and Turner, 1985).

Einzig (1996) reviewed parenting education in the United Kingdom and noted parenting education is multifaceted not just for expecting parents, and both universal and targeted in nature. However, Einzig also recognized that parenting education in the United Kingdom, although diverse in goals, often has objectives that are met using similar or common components in modern parenting programs. These include increasing the confidence of parents in their role as parents, emphasizing the importance and power of parenting skills when maximized, recognizing the uniqueness or temperament of each child, allowing parents to explore their own parenting with other parents, and encouraging parents to consider different parenting practices that may increase their effectiveness as they rear their child.

Parent education is distinguished from clinical or counseling approaches to helping parents by its focus on building strengths in families in order to prevent subsequent problems. Parent education and clinical approaches may use similar techniques and types of programs, for example, behavior management skills training (Dangel and Polster, 1984) or communication training (Gordon, 1975). However, parent education differs from therapy in its emphasis on family and developmental issues rather than psychopathology.

Parent education is one strategy within a larger array of support services that can be offered to families and that in many cases is integrated with those services. Weissbourd and Kagan (1994) detailed the history and scope of family support in the United States. They pointed out that families have always needed support and that there is a long tradition of providing that support. Family support programs see parent education as one component of their services. They have been strongly influenced by Bronfenbrenner's ecological model Bronfenbrenner (1986). Family support programs acknowledge that families are complex systems and that each functions as part of a larger community. Dunst (1995) defines family support as follows: "Family support programs place primary emphasis on the strengthening of individual and family functioning in ways that empower people to act on their own behalf, and especially efforts that strengthen and support parental child-rearing capabilities. This emphasis is reflected in the careful selection of terms like enhance, promote, nurture and enable to describe the processes of program efforts, and terms like strengthen and empower to describe the outcomes of these efforts" (Pew Charitable Trust, 1996).

There is no single model of parent education. It involves a wide range of strategies including handbooks and manuals; television, video, and audio series; group-based parenting and child development classes, home-visiting programs; and a combination of the above. Parent education may be designed as universal access programs for all parents or targeted for parents with known or identified risk factors. See Table 15.1 for a list of attributes of several parent education programs.

THEORY IN PARENTING EDUCATION

Although there is no single model of parenting education, an important factor that may be considered when looking at parent education is the philosophical or theoretical foundation of the program. There are various theoretical perspectives in parent education, the universal programs discussed in

TABLE 15.1
The Myriad of Parent Education

Target Population	Program Goals	Delivery Method/Location	Tools	Evaluation Methods	Numbers
All parents	Parent focused	Group meetings	Standardize	Experimental	MELD: 30,000
New parents	Parenting knowledge,	Home visit	curriculum	Quasi-	parents
At-risk	skills, and abilities	Child	Program	experimental	PAT: 1450
Low-income	Academic	development	developed	Process	programs
Low-	Economic	classes	curriculum	evaluation	SCFE: 398 school
education	self-sufficiency	School	Videos	Cost Analysis	districts;
Abuse and	Interpersonal	Specialized	Handbooks	Participant	230,000 families
neglect	Family planning	school	Manuals	satisfaction	Even Start: 732
Violence	Child focused health	Combination of	Television	Survey	sites nationally
prevention	behavioral	the above	Audio series	Exit interview	Head Start 793,809
Children	socioemotional		Parenting books	Rate (e.g.,	children served
with	cognitive		Parenting	graduation; #	(FY 98)
disabilities	Parent-child quality of		magazines	re-pregnancy)	HIPPY: 120 sites
Teenagers	interaction abuse		Internet sites		nationally;
	and neglect				15,000 families
	communication				
	Family economic				
	functioning				

this chapter can be grouped into three broad theories, reflective (active listening), Adlerian, and behavioral.

Reflective programs are based on the philosophy of Carl Rogers. The focus here is on the nonjudgmental communication of feelings and resolution of conflicts. In this therapeutic approach, parents learn to recognize, understand, and accept their children's feelings and resolve conflicts using a democratic, no-blame approach. Parents learn three basic techniques: active listening (nonjudgmental, accepting listening), I-messages (feelings expressed without blame), and the no-lose method (a six-step conflict-resolution approach; Todres and Bunston, 1993). This model emphasizes the important mediating role of a child's feelings on a child's behaviors and on parent–child interactions (Medway, 1989).

Adlerian parenting programs are based on the theories of Alfred Adler. In developing their parenting programs, Dreikus and Dinkmeyer applied Adlerian theories to childrearing (Medway, 1989). With respect to behavior, Adler believed that individuals "have choices and are not helpless victims of inner drives" (Todres and Bunston, 1993, p. 226). Human behavior is seen in a social context and having a social purpose. In Adlerian programs, parents are encouraged to establish democratic households with firm, clear, consistent family rules (Cheng Gorham and Balter, 1997).

Behavioral parenting programs are based on the theories of B. F. Skinner. "Behavioral parent education focuses on observable child behavior and the environmental circumstances that maintain behavior patterns" (Cheng Gorham and Balter, 1997, p. 341). These programs utilize behaviorists theories and practices to modify child behaviors. Parents are taught how to eliminate unwanted behaviors and promote desired behaviors in their children.

Regardless of theoretical foundation, parent education must be geared to the strengths, styles, and needs of individual families. However, parent education has been criticized at times for not being supportive of the uniqueness of families (Pew Charitable Trust, 1996). Parenting "cookbooks" and courses with "the answers" to every parenting dilemma may be detrimental to families if they find the approach difficult to tailor to their unique situations, or to their moral and religious beliefs, some may actually hinder a parent's feelings of self-efficacy. Some programs have been accused of being insensitive to the strengths and values of minority families while attempting to impose values of middle socioeconomic status (SES).

Current research has shown that succinct formulas for good parenting have been replaced by an appreciation for the many ways in which parents adjust what they do in response to the needs and characteristics of their children, the conditions in which they live, and the circumstances of their own lives (Cowan and Cowan, 1992; Elder, 1991).

HISTORICAL CONSIDERATIONS IN PARENT EDUCATION

The history of parent education reflects the political and economic state of the country, the prevailing ideas of the leading thinkers in child psychology and development, who were influenced by the tenor of the times, and the current attitudes toward women and the family (Weissbourd, 1987). Childrearing suggestions in print date back over 2,000 years (Dangel and Polster, 1984), and handbooks for parents appeared as early as 1633 (Fein, 1980). From the beginning of civilization, parents have been "educated" in one way or another to accept certain principles of childrearing. Every period of history has had its beliefs about children and how parents should train, discipline, and prepare them for good citizenship in the society with which they live (Kagan, Powell, Weissbourd, and Zigler, 1987). Older manuscripts suggest such techniques as submerging babies in freezing water to increase their strength or using opium to quiet a cranky baby (Dangel and Polster, 1984). In the earliest days of our country, childrearing practices were based on moral principles of religious beliefs, with the church acting as a major source of parent education.

Formal parenting education had its roots in the Maternal Associations of the early 1800s (Schlossman, 1983). They began in Portland, Maine, and had as their purpose discovering the most effective method of "breaking the will of the child." Formal parenting education escalated with the formation of the Charity Organization Societies of the 1890s the National Congress of Mothers of 1897 (which became the national Parent–Teacher Association), and the Child Study Associations of the early 1900s. These were primarily groups of mothers who joined together to share common parental concerns. Although different in their audiences and preferred strategies (Halpern, 1991), each of these efforts recognized the importance of the parenting role and the needs for parents with young children to have special knowledge regarding childrearing. Soon thereafter the "friendly visitors" to poor families began, and then the settlement house movement for new immigrants. The settlement house movement built on notions of home visiting, and parent education added an emphasis on community strengths (Kagan et al., 1987). For an interesting discussion on the history of parenting education from 1897 to 1929, see Schlossman (1976).

At the end of World War II, American society was changing dramatically (Pew Charitable Trust, 1996), and in 1946 a book was published that changed the way many Americans reared their children: *Baby and Child Care*, by Benjamin Spock. It was a best-seller for nearly 25 years. Although there was a practical need for specific information that can come from a book, parents were still feeling a need to be with other parents for emotional support and "experienced" advice. The big questions at this time were "How permissive should I be with my child?" and "What is the best way to raise my child?" (Pew Charitable Trust, 1996)

In the 1950s and 1960s many clinical and academic professionals were thinking about and writing on the importance of parenting and parent education: Arnold Gesell, Alfred Adler, Carl Rogers, Selma Freiberg, Erik Erikson, Haim Ginott, John Holt, and John Bowlby, to name a few (Pew Charitable Trust, 1996). In the 1960s, new research (Bloom, 1964; Gordon, 1966; Hunt, 1961) appeared pointing to the critical importance of the early years of life, which resulted in increasing pressure on the federal government to take an unprecedented role in child welfare. The focus of parent education began to shift from middle-SES self-improvement to the disadvantaged. As part of the War on Poverty, the federal government funded a variety of comprehensive programs that were aimed at reducing educational inequality and eventually poverty. Head Start was established to provide intervention in the early years for "disadvantaged" children, with hopes of improving their chances for success in school and therefore for success in American life. Through Head Start, parents became partners in their child's education.

Then in the 1970s, a new technology for educating parents emerged: parenting skill-building programs. These programs were designed to improve parenting effectiveness by providing a clear parenting philosophy and a set of skills and strategies. Example of some of these programs are: Parent Effectiveness Training (P.E.T.), created by Gordon (1970, 1975); Systematic Training for Effective Parenting (STEP), created by Dinkmeyer and McKay (1976); and Confident Parenting, created by Aitchison (1976).

Earlier research (Bloom, 1964; Gordon, 1966; Hunt, 1961) that provided the impetus for government programs to enhance the chances for disadvantaged children now provided middle-SES parents with a new perspective on child development that created possibilities for giving their own children a head start (Kagan et al., 1987). As a result of these activities, parent education's emphasis shifted from personality development toward an emphasis on cognitive growth. Information for parents on how to teach their children the basic skills of reading and mathematics at an early age was eagerly received by parents, and "infant stimulation" classes started developing (Dowley, 1971).

By the 1980s and 1990s there seemed to be a parenting education program in virtually every community in the United States. Some of these classes focused on the immediate concerns of birthing and the biological caregiving tasks of early parenting, others focused on the developmental nature of parenting (nurturing, teaching, socializing, and modeling) and the importance of early learning experiences (Galinsky, 1994; Schaefer, 1991; Swick, 1984).

During this time there was also an increased awareness of the impact of culture on family life. This led to efforts to make programs more responsive to the changing needs and characteristics of families. Several methods were employed, including developing culturally specific programs or tailoring existing programs to the families being served (Cheng Gorham and Balter, 1997; Powell, 1989). Parenting programs such as AVANCE, Effective Black Parenting, and Honoring Our Children by Honoring Our Traditions, became more widely available and implemented (Alvy, 1994; Cheng Gorham, and Balter, 1997). We also see a changing role for the parent educator from expert to partner (Powell, 1989).

In the 1990s, emphasis renewed on responsibility and accountability in the social and political realm. On the policy side, the Government Performance and Results Act of 1993 (GPRA) and the Personal Responsibility and Work Reconciliation Act of 1996 (i.e., "welfare reform") were passed. The GPRA required federal programs (e.g., Head Start) to document effectiveness (GAO, 1998a). Welfare reform mandated a reduction of the number of people on welfare and an increased need for self-sufficiency training. On the social side, the national fatherhood initiative was launched in 1994 to "restore responsible fatherhood as a national priority" (National Fatherhood Initiative, 2001). On the social service side, a number of national models expanded efforts to document their effectiveness. Among them are Missouri's Parents as Teachers, Parent Effectiveness Training, Minnesota's Early Learning Design (MELD) and Early Childhood Family Education (ECFE), HIPPY (Home Instruction Program for Preschool Youngsters), and Hawaii's Healthy Start.

The 1990s also saw an increased impact of media and technology on parenting education. Parenting was the topic of focus on television shows (e.g., *The Oprah Winfrey Show*) and television specials (e.g., *I Am Your Child*). There was an exponential proliferation of parenting books, magazines, and Internet Web sites. A search for the term *parenting* yielded over 2 million "hits," with the results ranging from sites with broad, overall information on parenting (e.g., Parenting.com) to a very specific focus (e.g., Tucson Family).

LIMITATIONS IN PARENTING EDUCATION KNOWLEDGE

There has been significant research conducted in the field of parenting education. However, methodologically sound, well-documented research projects are still lacking. There have been hundreds of individual research projects on the dynamics of healthy parenting. This research has shown that there is solid evidence on the critical role parents play in rearing healthy children and that well-designed, controlled programs can have positive impacts on children's outcomes. However, research on various parenting programs must be viewed somewhat cautiously. Many studies did not use an experimental design with control groups, nor did they attempt to control the range of statistical variables and external factors. The connection between parent behavior change to positive child outcomes has been inferred rather than proven. The number of these studies that have followed cohorts longitudinally is very small (Pew Charitable Trust, 1996).

The growing diversity of families with young children also raises profoundly important questions about how best to match programs to the needs, values, and goals of various ethnic and cultural groups. Another challenge to parenting education interventions is posed by the demographics and circumstances of working parents, for whom finding the time to participate in these programs is exceedingly difficult.

Despite the limitations of parenting education as a science, this field seems to evolve and grow as time goes on. The purpose of parenting education and the methods by which parenting programs are embarked on also continue to grow.

UNIVERSAL ACCESS PARENT EDUCATION PROGRAMS

In recent history, parent education has been broadly administered in one of two ways: universal access programs or targeted (at-risk) programs. Universal access parenting education programs are designed to inform and prepare parents for the duties and responsibilities of parenthood and are offered to all parents. Oftentimes, universal programs have health and safety foci, occur early in the child's life, and at times more generally serve as parental support. Conversely, targeted parenting education programs are offered to a select group of parents whose child is "at risk" for a particular poor outcome or who are themselves "at risk" for negative parenting behaviors, such as parents who have been involved with child protective services. This section attempts to describe the commonalities and differences between universal parenting education programs that are available to all parents, and the next section addresses targeted parent education programs for parents with children who are at risk for or have developmental delays.

Herein we provide a brief overview of some of the leading universally available parenting programs in the United States. Where possible, we focus on programs that have been reviewed and evaluated. This review is not meant to be exhaustive or reflective of the many programs in the United States, but offers a sample of national-level programs currently in existence or programs whose core reflects the components previously noted as common among many parenting education programs. Universal access programs may focus on enrolling families with a "target"-age child (e.g., infant or preschool age); however, the programs are open to all families, not only those who are considered at risk for developmental or other problems. From a public health perspective, universal access programs may be thought of as primary prevention activities. The intent is to provide services to the broadest group of individuals in order to prevent developmental delays or a health-threatening condition from occurring or to promote an optimal condition. A program to provide prenatal care and education classes to all first-time mothers in an effort to reduce birth complications that place infants at risk for later developmental problems would be an example of a universal access program or primary prevention program.

Some states such as Minnesota and Missouri have initiated universal access parent education programs that have as a primary goal the enhancement of early child development. For instance, Missouri's Parents as Teachers (PAT) program began in 1981 to demonstrate the value of high-quality parenting and its effects on the ability of first-time parents to enhance the development of their child from birth to age 3. The basic premise of PAT is "that babies are born learning and that parents are their first and most influential teachers." (Winter and Rouse, 1991). The major goals of the program are to assist parents in gaining knowledge of child development in order to give their children a solid foundation for school success and to increase parents' feelings of self confidence and competence. Elements of the program typically include monthly home visits by credentialed para-professional parent educators who provide information on the child's development, model and involve parents in age-appropriate activities, and respond to concerns or issues that parents may have regarding their children. Also included are monthly group meetings in which parents share insights and develop a support network, and periodic screening of the child's physical and intellectual development. In 1996, the Parents as Teachers National Center revised the PAT curriculum to reflect the latest understanding about brain development and improved outcomes for children. The title of this new curriculum is Born to Learn, and it is in the process of being evaluated.

In 1985, the program was open to all parents of children from birth to 3, and starting in 1993, some school districts offered services to parents of children up to age 5. In addition, the PAT program is being implemented on a smaller scale in many states around the country.

The Minnesota Department of Education implemented the Early Childhood Family Education (ECFE) Program in 1975. It was designed for all Minnesota families with children from birth through kindergarten. Children and their parents participate in weekly sessions that promote creative play activities, special events, and parental problem solving. The goal of the program is to enhance and support the competence of parents in providing the best possible environment (i.e., the most developmentally appropriate) for the healthy growth of their children.

Minnesota Early Learning Design (MELD) was founded in 1973 by Ellwood. MELD is a primary prevention program that brings together groups of parents during pregnancy and the first two years of their child's life. MELD aims to address the "universal needs" of parents through providing information in five subject areas: health, child development, child guidance, family management, and parental personal growth. Services are intended to be flexible and are designed to meet the needs of specific populations including new parents, parents with children up to age 3 that are chronically ill or disabled; young mothers, ages 13 to 20, with new babies; and single mothers with children.

In addition to this sample of national universal access parenting education programs, numerous skill-based training materials have developed over the last 30 years. They have been adapted and modified over time to reflect the tenor of the times and their current thinking about childrearing. Described below is a small sample of parent education curriculum materials that have been developed. The ones described here are materials that have been used extensively and many principles infused into other programs over the years. One example of such a program is Parent Effectiveness Training. P.E.T. was created in the 1960s by Thomas Gordon (a disciple of Carl Rogers). This was one of the original parenting education programs in the United States. P.E.T. is a formally structured course of eight 3-hour training sessions. It imparts a philosophy of human relationships and a set of childrearing skills that are intended to assist parents in building a warm, close, and enjoyable relationship with their child while fostering a family environment that is supportive of the needs of each family member. P.E.T. grew out of the ideas of Carl Rogers. He believed that maximum growth occurs within relationships that are characterized by high degrees of acceptance and genuineness. According to P.E.T., an effective parent would be genuine, self-disclosing, fallible, accepting and respectful of the feelings, ideas, and values of spouses and children, and fair, using influence or persuasion rather than power (rewards and punishments) to meet personal needs (Alvy, 1994).

The P.E.T. program begins by teaching parents to understand their children's behavior as being either acceptable or unacceptable, and emphasizes therapeutic or active listening skills. In order to actively listen, parents need to be sensitive and articulate about what their child is feeling. They also need to empathize with their children's problems as they actively listen. An example would be when a child comments that no one picks him to be on their kickball team, and the parent actively listens and responds with "You want to play kickball too, and when no one picks you to be on their team you feel left out and disappointed." This type of a response, according to P.E.T. training, encourages further discussion between the parent and child about what the child is thinking and feeling. P.E.T. teaches parents to use I-messages when spontaneously expressing positive feelings to the child. An example of a positive I-message would be: When a child puts away all his toys after playing with them and the parent says, "When you put away your toys, I really appreciated it, because I didn't have to spend the time cleaning up and was able to start dinner."

Another example of a skill-building parent education program is Systematic Training for Effective Parenting. This program is based on the philosophy and childrearing ideas of Alfred Adler and Rudolph Dreikurs. It is a formally structured course of nine 2-hour sessions. It teaches a philosophy of family life and a set of childrearing skills that are intended to promote cooperation in the family, positive relationships, and self-confidence and independence in children. It was created in 1976 by Adlerian psychologists Dinkmeyer and McKay (Alvy, 1994) The STEP program is based on fundamental assumptions from Adlerian Psychology that all behavior occurs for a social purpose and that people are decision-making social beings whose main goal in life is to belong. These assumptions get translated into viewing a child's behavior as always reflecting the need to belong, regardless of how negative the behaviors may seem to adults. The program is based on four basic ingredients to building positive relationships with children (Alvy, 1994):

(1) Demonstrating mutual respect: Parental respect is earned by showing respect for the child's feelings, thoughts, and privacy;
(2) Taking time for fun: insuring regular enjoyable times with children and the whole family;
(3) Encouragement: To feel adequate, children need frequent encouragement through minimizing the importance of children's mistakes while recognizing their assets and strengths;
(4) Communicating love: spontaneous verbal expressions and nonverbal signs such as pats, hugs, and kisses.

Confident Parenting was created in the early 1970s by behavioral psychologist Aitchison. The Confident Parenting Program represents a social conditioning or social learning theory approach to parent training, and therefore is grounded in the learning theories and principles associated with B.F. Skinner (1953). This is a formally structured course of ten 2-hour sessions. It was primarily designed for parents of preschool and elementary school-age children. It teaches a philosophy of social behavior and a set of parenting skills to decrease negative and disturbing interactions between parents and children and to increase positive interactions. In so doing, it intends to promote warm and loving relationships in the family (Alvy, 1994). The program begins by teaching the parents that behavior is shaped by consequences. It is implicit in the program that an effective parent is one who is successful at managing the consequences of their children's behaviors. A great deal of emphasis is placed on helping parents use more specific rather than global descriptions of their child's behavior. For example, instead of saying "he is so selfish and such a bad boy," a parent may say, "(He doesn't share his toys with his friend.)" They are then taught how to pinpoint the specific behaviors that they would like to see their children engage in more frequently and which behaviors they would like to see less of. They are taught methods for managing the consequences of those behaviors and which behaviors are most likely to be increased or decreased by the use of each method (Alvy, 1994). The thrust of the entire program is to enhance the parent's behavior management skills. In so doing, the program intends to train parents to be (what it considers) appropriate role models: parents who are positive, consistent, efficient and nonviolent.

Finally, Active Parenting was founded in 1983 by Popkin. It is a video-based psychoeducational parenting education program. Active Parenting teaches a variety of discipline and communication skills, many of which are similar to those that are also taught in the P.E.T. and STEP programs. These skills can help parents learn how to guide their children's development through the provision of freedom within limits. Freedom within limits means that, in a democratic household, freedom is ideal, but so are the rights of others and the responsibilities of all. The parent is the leader, one who encourages cooperation and stimulates learning. There is order and routine, and everyone in the family is an important member of it. The major purpose for parents is to assume the democratic approach and to utilize the related skills that enable their children to develop and thrive in a democratic society: courage, responsibility, and cooperation (Alvy, 1994).

Not all parent education programs in the United States adhere to the theoretical orientation of the above-mentioned programs. Many parent education programs have started locally in communities and were designed to meet specific community needs, cultural identities, or religious perspectives.

TARGETED PARENT EDUCATION PROGRAMS

It is not the intent of this chapter to address the empirical knowledge base on the efficacy of early intervention, but rather to address parent education as one component of early intervention for children with or at risk for developmental delays. As in the section on universal programs, we will provide an overview of some of the leading targeted parenting education programs that have been reviewed and replicated. Targeted programs, for this review, are defined as those whose participants meet a certain set of criteria that place them "at risk" of developing problems if some kind of intervention is not undertaken.

The focus of the next section is to explore the goals and methods of targeted programs as compared to universal programs. Again, we will focus on a few nationally recognized, targeted parenting education programs as well as those with completed evaluations where appropriate. Although targeted parenting education is a massive literature, we have selected six primary areas for review, and they are parenting education programs targeting:

(1) Parents of low income or low education;
(2) The prevention of child abuse and neglect;
(3) Preventing or reducing juvenile delinquency and youth violence;
(4) Rearing children with disabilities and/or behavior problems;
(5) Teenage mothers.

Parents of Low Income or Low Education

In 1964, the U.S. Council of Economic Advisors reported that much of the country's poverty was contained in physically or culturally isolated enclaves in rural and urban areas, and half of the nation's 30 million poor people were children (Zigler and Muenchow, 1992), and a large percentage of poor families were headed by a person with only a grade school education (Johnson, 1965). These statistics were thought at the time to be the reason for the rising crime rate and decline in the number of individuals physically and intellectually capable of assuming productive roles in the military service or private industry. Political and economic conditions at the time gave both the desire and the means to attack the problems associated with socioeconomic disadvantage. Through education and self-help programs, it was hoped, the War on Poverty could succeed in transforming the lives of poor Americans.

A large body of literature suggests that low levels of maternal education are strongly associated with several indicators of poor child development, including impaired play behavior, mild mental retardation, behavior problems, and poor academic achievement and cognitive and communicative outcome (Fewell, Casal, Glick, Wheeden, and Spiker, 1996; Jordan, 1978; Kopp and McCall, 1982; Victora, Huttly, Barros, Lombardi, and Vaughan, 1992; Wallace, Roberts, and Lodder, 1998; Yeargin-Allsopp, Drews, Decoufle, and Murphy, 1995). As articulated by Brooks-Gunn, Gross, Kraemer, Spiker, and Shapiro (1992), low maternal education is associated with multiple factors that have a negative effect on the outcome of the child, such as low birth weight, poverty, poorly organized home environment, and less facilitative childrearing characteristics. Level of maternal education also appears to be related to a number of parenting behaviors which are associated with the child's behavioral and socioemotional performance and competence (Altman, 1987; Goodman, 1990; Laosa, 1982; Richman, Miller, and LeVine, 1992; Strom, Hathaway, and Slaughter, 1981).

No one environmental factor can explain the differences in a child's developmental outcome, but socioeconomic factors clearly play a role. Parental income has consistently been cited as a positive correlate of early childhood development in areas such as cognitive and speech/language development (Duncan, Yeung, Brooks-Gunn, and Smith, 1998; Oller, Eilers, Steffens, and Lynch, 1994). Parent–child interaction in play or educational activities during the early developmental years appear to be qualitatively different for varying levels of family SES (Oller et al., 1994; Peralta de Mendoza, 1995). When compared to middle-SES dyads, low-SES dyads did not exhibit the same level of responsiveness, vocalization, language interactions, and early literacy skills (Oller et al, 1994; Peralta de Mendoza, 1995; Rush, 1999). Socioeconomic status has been associated with parenting styles as well; lower SES is associated with a higher likelihood of authoritarian-style parenting behaviors (Radziszewska, Richardson, Dent, and Flay, 1997).

Although low-income and low-education families are at greater risk for less than optimal parenting practices and less than optimal child development, there are interventions that can help to ameliorate those risks and outcomes. A few parenting education programs have been designed to address these needs.

Head Start was conceived in the 1960s and was designed to address the significant problem of poor children who failed to arrive at kindergarten and first grade on a par with other children. Head Start and Early Head Start are comprehensive child development programs that serve children from birth to age 5, pregnant women, and their families. They are child-focused programs and have the overall goal of increasing the school readiness of young children in low-income families. Head Start provides a range of individualized services in the areas of education and early childhood development: medical, dental, and mental health; nutrition; and parent involvement. Although initial studies showed positive results, current evaluations of the effectiveness of Head Start programs are inconclusive (GAO, 1998a). However, the Health and Human Services Agent (HHS) has implemented initiatives to assess the impact of the program. These include new performance measures, the Family and Child Experiences Survey (FACES, a nationally representative longitudinal study), and utilizing the National Center for Education Statistics data (GAO, 1998a).

Even Start Family Literacy Programs (Title 1, Part B of the Elementary and Secondary Education Act) support local family-centered education projects intended to help families with young children—including infants and toddlers—break the cycle of poverty and illiteracy. Even Start programs integrate early childhood education, adult basic and literacy education, and parenting education to involve parents and children, from birth through age 7, in learning. Many of the Even Start programs provide parenting education for parents of infants and toddlers in multiple formats to accommodate different learning styles. The formats may include: parenting education classes, support groups, home visits, parent–child instruction, and one-on-one communication between project staff and parents. As with Head Start, the effectiveness of Even Start is inconclusive (GAO, 2000). Even Start has also implemented performance measures to address the issue of program effectiveness (GAO, 2000).

Home Instruction Program for Preschool Youngsters (HIPPY) was developed in 1969 in Israel. The first HIPPY programs in the United States began in 1984. It is designed to help parents who have limited formal schooling to be better first teachers of their 3- to 5-year old children. HIPPY programs are delivered in the home by para-professionals who are themselves parents and who have been trained by HIPPY staff members. The original curriculum is highly structured; however, local programs are encouraged to tailor the program to the characteristics of their population. On alternate weeks, small groups of parents meet to share their experiences, which assists in the promotion of community building. It has been widely replicated around the United States. Evaluations of the HIPPY programs have yielded mixed results (Baker Piotrikowski, and Brooks-Gunn, 1999). Although one study showed positive gains in measures of school success for program children, these results have not been replicated in other studies (Baker et al., 1999). One possible reason for the mixed results may be due to the level parent participation in the program. This points to the importance of employing qualitative and process evaluation methods in the evaluation of program effectiveness.

The Nurse Home Visitation Program (NHVP) was started in Elmira, New York, in 1977 (Olds et al., 1999). As the name implies, the program is delivered at participants' home by nurses. The recipients are first-time, low-income mothers and their families. The program starts during pregnancy and lasts through the first 2 years of the child's life. The program's three goals are to improve pregnancy outcomes, child health and development, and families' economic self-sufficiency. The weekly (later monthly) home visits last about 75 to 90 minutes and focus on changing the mother's behavior in areas that affect the three program goals. An important aspect about the Nurse Home Visitation Program is the use of research in program development, implementation, and evaluation. The NHVP is one of a few parenting programs with longitudinal follow-up of participants (e.g., in Elmira, New York, Memphis, Tennessee and Denver, Colorado, children are being followed through age 15, Olds et al., 1999). Although not a primary goal of the program, the NHVP has been shown to be effective in reducing child abuse and neglect.

THE PREVENTION OF CHILD ABUSE AND NEGLECT

Child abuse and neglect are serious problems in U.S. communities. Federal and state governments annually spend over $44 million on child protective services. Although these efforts are necessary for the protection of children, they are reactive to crises in homes or allegations of abuse or neglect based on physical evidence in the affected child. In an effort to lessen the impact of this social problem, prevention programs have surfaced in the last 2 decades. Programs with the goal of preventing child abuse and neglect often target two groups: parents and service providers (educators, social workers, health care workers, and childcare providers). Parenting education and support have been the mechanisms employed in most secondary prevention efforts related to child abuse and neglect. Prevention programs have also been aimed at increasing awareness, knowledge, and skills of identifying suspicious behaviors or evidence of child abuse and neglect in service providers working with children and families. Although we do not discuss these efforts here as our focus remains on parenting education, prevention programs targeting service providers are equally important and represent critical elements to preventing the severe or deadly abuse of children.

Parent or parenting characteristics known to be associated with child abuse and neglect are well studied. Of course, prediction of child abuse is not a perfect science, but nor is the prediction of human behavior. Both are similarly plagued by an inability to predict reliably the outcomes of children whose parents share known risk factors. Despite the limitations of prevention programs and science, particularly secondary prevention efforts, targeted parenting education efforts exist in large-scale proportions. One such program designed to prevent child abuse and neglect is Healthy Start Hawaii. Adaptations of this program can now be found in many states.

Healthy Start began in Hawaii in 1988. This program is a child abuse and neglect prevention program originally conceived to improve family coping skills and functioning, promote parenting skills and parent–child interaction, and promote optimal child development, and as a result to prevent child abuse and neglect. The model was adapted by the National Committee to Prevent Child Abuse and became Healthy Families America. Participants are identified by a hospital-based screen as those families with newborns that are at risk for abuse. Initial nonexperimental evaluations (lack of control group) of the program showed a lower than average rate of abuse and neglect in intervention families after one year in the program (Duggan et al., 1999). However, later experimental evalutaion showed no significant difference in abuse and neglect between intervention and control families at the year two follow-up (Duggan et al., 1999). The evaluation did yeild some other interesting findings, for example, differences in outcomes among subgroups, variations in program quality, and potential impact of rate of attrition on program success (Duggan et al., 1999).

Prevention of Youth Violence and Delinquency Through Parenting Education

The prevention of youth violence has been a hot-button topic in recent years as incidents of school violence and extreme bullying became the subject of nightly news across the United States Prevention efforts in this regard have been quite varied and, especially among younger children, parenting education has been a key component in these programs.

The Centers for Disease Control and Prevention supports activities to evaluate violence prevention programs in school-age populations as part of its school violence prevention efforts. One such program is the Early Alliance program in South Carolina (Dumas, Prinz, Smith, and Laughlin, 1999). Early Alliance targets children ages 6 to 8 years old and their parents. The program emphasizes skill building and establishing beneficial links between the child's home and school using home-based meetings with parents, and other care providers, as well as key caregivers and teachers. One of Early Alliance's goals is to determine if the intervention affects parenting difficulties and family social support positively using rigorous program evaluation techniques. Early recruitment and process data have been released showing that community interventions will be participated in, can receive parental investment, and substantively be informed by early child development literature (Prinz et al., 2001). Programs such as Early Alliance are multifaceted, drawing on families, schools, and community resources to alter the outcomes of at-risk children, and involve parents in the process through parenting education and training in targeted areas such as contingency management and behavior modification/reinforcement.

As youth get older, prevention activities mold themselves more readily to the whole gamut of factors exerting influence over adolescent life. Parenting education is often a part of violence and delinquency prevention activities, but other influences such as peers, school, and psychopathology, if relevant, are given equal or more weight in such efforts. It is notable that parenting education programs appear to acknowledge the dwindling influence parents have on their children as they get older, but still include parenting as a component despite studies that have shown that children with chronic behavior problems do not reap long-term benefits from their parents (Dodge, 1993; Kazdin, 1993). By doing so, prevention efforts focus less on parenting factors and more on other related factors as well as adolescents growing autonomy.

Multisystemic Therapy, or MST, is an example of a delinquency prevention and intervention program that has been evaluating with many populations of adolescents presenting with truancy, delinquency, violence, and even sexual offending (Borduin and Henggeler, 1990; Borduin, Henggeler, Blaske, and Stein, 1990; Shoenwald, Ward, Henggeler, Pickrel, and Patel, 1996). It is important to note that such intensive therapeutic interventions incorporate parenting education as part of a comprehensive approach to addressing delinquency or behavioral issues in adolescents. However, these efforts are much more treatment oriented but necessarily so, given the nature of the problems it is meant to address. Evaluation of MST models has been carefully carried out for different target populations with notable success (Henggeler, 1996); however, these interventions are time and labor intensive and do not reach community-level implementation. Consequently, efforts to prevent or reduce teen violence are lacking in implementation and evaluation at the community level.

Community and school-based violence prevention programs utilizing parenting education as a central mechanism for healthy child development are increasingly being funded at the state and federal levels as school violence has escalated in seriousness and seemingly in frequency. With the growth of prevention efforts in this area, programmatic evaluation is likely to grow as well. Systematic understanding of the effectiveness of parenting education components to violence prevention programs targeting young children is critical to furthering such prevention goals. Similar issues arise when examining parenting training and education targeted toward parents of children with disabilities, behavior problems, or other special needs.

Rearing Children With Disabilities and Behavior Problems

Early intervention services for young children with developmental disabilities are guided by a federal entitlement to services for all children with a diagnosed impairment or a documented delay (with the option for states to serve infants at risk for subsequent developmental problems). This entitlement was first established in 1986 under Part H of Public Law 99-457 and reauthorized in 1997, under Part C of the Individuals with Disabilities Education Act. Although the mandate for individualized family service plans provides room for individuality based on the needs, resources, and concerns of the families, it is imperative that a family-centered model is employed. This model combines child therapies and educational instruction with an array of parent services, one of which is parent education. Parent education for children with disabilities may take it's form in support groups, individual counseling, educational information and guidance, as well as assistance in accessing needed resources and services for the child and/or family.

Parenting interventions are often first-line, nonmedical interventions offered to parents of a child with behavioral problems. Behavior problems are broadly defined for the purposes of this section, however, they refer mainly to externalizing behavior problems and disorders such as oppositional defiant disorder, attention deficit hyperactivity disorder (ADHD), and conduct disorder (American Psychiatric Association, 1994). The most common behavioral disorder in children is ADHD (American Psychiatric Association, 1994), and behavior disorders are amenable to behavior management and organizational structure to alter negative behavior patterns (MTA Cooperative Group, 1999a, 1999b). Across the United States, many parent-organized support groups have emerged in an effort to deal collectively with the issues common to parenting ADHD youth. Children and adults with attention deficit hyperactivity disorder (CHADD) is the national-level organization representing all the local chapters of CHADD and providing resources to parents with an ADHD child and parent leaders of local groups (CHADD, 2000).

Parents of children with behavioral disorders face significant stressors that parents without such children face but in less concentration. Such stressors are marital conflict, complaints from teachers, high incidents of sibling disagreements, and failed discipline techniques (Anastopoulos, Smith, and Wien, 1998; Suarez and Baker, 1997), and these may result in negative parenting styles over time (Barkley, 1998).

More formal parenting education programs targeting parents of children with behavioral disorders are varied in format, content, length, and leadership (Webster-Straton, 1994). A common model of parenting education or training for parents of children with behavior disorders is focused on teaching parents behavioral modification (Kazdin, 1997) techniques and ways to manage parenting frustrations in rearing a child with attentional and behavioral problems. One such parent-training program was developed by Barkley and colleagues and operates in Worchester, Massachusetts (Barkley, 1998). Many components or variations of behavior modification training were incorporated into this clinic-based program and have since informed other nonclinical parent training programs. The Barkley model, an ADHD parent-training program, includes a cognitive-behavioral theoretical perspective and has as its goal to effect behavior change in parents and children over the course of 8 to12 individualized sessions. This clinic model is intensive, highly structured, and has specific goals for successful completion.

From the clinic-based model, a community parenting program named COPE (Community Parent Education) was developed specifically to work with groups of parents struggling to rear a child with a behavioral problem (Barkley, 1998). The COPE program uses similar techniques but in a group setting. The program is designed for parents of children ages 4 to12, as parent training is not thought to be as effective in later years. Because this program and most others focusing on behavioral problems are social learning and cognitive-behavioral in nature, the parent training sessions are loosely structured, in a group format, and often include specific didactic videos of parenting skills (effective and ineffective) as well as group problem-solving or homework assignments between sessions to utilize new skills. Social learning theory (SLT; Bandura, 1977) maintains that the potential or likelihood of a person exhibiting a behavior is the result of specific reinforcement values and reward expectancies that are situation-specific. SLT, which was a precursor to cognitive behavioral theories (CBT), places emphasis on the role of modeling and informs newer, related theories, such as CBT. Cognitive behavioral theories have as their goal to reduce cognitive distortions and regulate emotional arousal. Using principles of SLT as well as behavioral research on self-regulation, CBTs have become a very popular technique for changing maladaptive behaviors of children and youth. The COPE model is focused on teaching parents management skills and how to use reinforcement and behavior modification to change their child's behavior in home and school environments, while addressing issues and stress parents face rearing a child with this type of problem. To reinforce the acquisition of effective parenting behaviors, COPE hosts monthly booster sessions after the 12-week formal program to reinforce techniques previously taught.

COPE is just one of many parenting education and training efforts for those struggling with rearing a child with behavioral problems. Similarly, programs targeting parents of children with specific problems such as developmental delays (Lutzker and Steed, 1998), parent-centered research of out-of-home placements of children with mental retardation (Bromley and Blacher, 1991), and parenting intervention in families dealing with autism (Schreibman and Koegel, 1996) are all common efforts to gain critical parenting knowledge through research and to increase specialized parenting skills, decrease parental stress, and improve the outcomes of children through intervention. These community-based programs, like others, are growing, but evaluation of such parent-training programs is limited (Todres and Bunston, 1993; Tramontana, Sherrets, and Authier, 1980). However, the effectiveness of consistently administered behavior modification techniques with disruptive children in classrooms, for instance, has had as great an effect on the behavior of disruptive children as psychopharmacological interventions alone (O'Leary, Pelham, Rosenbaum, and Price, 1976). COPE conducted an evaluation using community samples of COPE-enrolled parents, parents receiving individual clinic-based parent training, and a wait-list control group for comparison, and found COPE to be most beneficial at the 6-month follow-up (Cunningham et al., 1979). However, both formal and informal training for parents of children with behavioral problems have not usually been rigorously evaluated or evaluated for long-term benefits. Without careful evaluation, it is difficult to know if parents actually are consistent in their implementation of new skills, for how long, and if parenting changes make for improved outcomes in their child's functioning.

Parenting Education for Teenage Mothers

Although its rate is currently on the decline, teen pregnancy is still a problem of national concern. In 1998 there were about 900,000 teen pregnancies, and 78.8% of pregnant teens were unmarried (Ventura, Matthews, and Curtin, 1999). Teen pregnancy detrimentally affects the teen mother, her child, and society. The impact on the teen mother runs from educational (less likely to complete high school) to economic (lower earnings) to social (increased dependency on welfare). Children born to adolescent mothers are at greater risk for lower birth weights and more health problems, child abuse and neglect, living in poverty, and poor school outcomes (GAO, 1998b). Additionally, these children are later more likely to become teenage parents, thus potentially continuing the risk cycle.

Teen programs range from targeted goals (e.g., high school diploma and better parenting skills) to comprehensive goals (e.g., promoting the development of human capital). Given the nature of the target population, most of these programs take place in school settings or in specialized schools for new and expectant teen parents (Pew Charitable Trust, 1996).

Although there are various programs across the United States to address the issue of teen parenting, few of these programs have methodologically sound evaluations. Overall, teen parenting programs have had mixed results. Some have been moderately successful, but only with respect to certain variables (e.g., delay in onset of next pregnancy). Of those with evaluation data, one major challenge that many programs face is participant attendance. What follows are some examples of teen programs that have been evaluated.

The Adolescent Parents Project was developed by the Child Welfare League in collaboration with MELD and MELD's Young Moms program. The goals are to promote economic self-sufficiency and long-term success in rearing healthy children. Group meetings are held on a weekly basis and start during the third trimester and last until the child reaches age 2 years. In a quasi-experimental evaluation of two implementation sites (Atlanta, Georgia, and Toledo, Ohio), results showed no significant differences between program and control mothers, except for better infant health care in Atlanta. As with many teen parenting programs, a potential source for the lack of significant result may be subject participation. Although the program is designed to last 100 weeks, participants only attended 20 to 29 weeks.

The Family Growth Center (FGC) is a community-based family support center in an area of Pittsburgh with high rates of poverty and teen pregnancy. The program provides social support, medical intervention, and community support. Social workers provide general support, parenting advice, and crisis intervention through home visits during the child's first 6 months. At the center, mothers have access to comprehensive services including parenting and birth control classes, school advocacy, and case management. A study of 88 pairs of teen mothers and their infants showed reduced dropout rates (10% vs. 42%) and repregnancy rate (12% vs. 63%) for program mothers. There were no differences in family and community support and attitudes toward rearing children between program and comparison mothers. However, the evaluation had methodological problems (i.e., lack of random assignment and high attrition rate).

The Learning, Earning and Parenting Program (LEAP) is sponsored by the Ohio Department of Human Services and is mandatory for all Ohio pregnant teens and teen mothers who receive AFDC and do not have a high school diploma. The primary goal of the program is to keep mothers in school in order to promote graduation, employment, and (hopefully) leaving welfare. The program does this by providing financial incentives and penalties for school attendance and absences, respectively. In a randomized trial of 1,188 teens, LEAP participants who were enrolled in school were more likely to complete high school (61.3% vs. 51.1%) than controls. Compared to a control group, LEAP participants who had dropped out were more likely to be back in school (46.8% vs. 33.4%). A quasi-experimental study had similar results (22.0% of the LEAP group complete high school compared to a statewide control group in which only 13.5% graduated).

The Teenage Parent Demonstration Project was funded by the Administration for Children and Families and implemented in three sites. One site was Project Advance in Illinois, and the other two, Teen Progress, were in New Jersey. The program's philosophy is that mothers are personally responsible for their and their child's health and welfare, and the government is responsible for providing assistance toward self-sufficiency when needed and to intervene early to deter the onset of dependency patterns. The two program goals are economic self-sufficiency and improved parenting skills. All teen mothers of a single child who were new recipients of Aid to Families with Dependent Children (AFDC) were eligible. The program followed a case management approach to achieve program goals. These included identifying education needs, referral to appropriate services, and counseling. The program also offered workshops on personal skills and coping with parenting, General Educational Development (GED) courses, and childcare and transportation. A randomized, experimental study showed no significant differences in welfare status or number of subsequent births. However, in a substudy, program mothers were less authoritarian in interactions with their children.

New Chance was a research study evaluating the effectiveness of a comprehensive two-generational approach with teen mothers. The goal was to prevent the potential poor outcomes for teen mothers and their children. Sixteen communities utilized existing community services to provide teen mothers with academic, vocational, parenting, interpersonal, and family planning skills. Program children received pediatric health services and good-quality childcare. Women who were ages 16 to 22 became mothers in their teens and head of household, were high school dropouts, and receiving AFDC were eligible to participate in the program. Although program mothers showed gains in most areas, there were no significant differences between the program and control mothers. The lack of differences were attributed to the fact that control mothers were not true controls because they were receiving existing services.

RESEARCH AND EVALUATION IN PARENTING EDUCATION

There have been numerous reviews on parenting interventions (Brooks-Gunn, Barlin, and Fuligni, 2000; Cowan et al., 1998), and what has come out of these reviews is that we know a lot about child development and parenting but still little about how to "influence" parenting (beliefs, attitudes, behaviors, and practices) to benefit child outcomes, and what specific aspects of these programs work. What these reviews have shown us is that parenting is open to change, but it is not easy to change (Shonkoff and Phillips, 2000). A number of carefully evaluated interventions have successfully improved various dimensions of parenting, and for some have linked these changes to improved child outcomes; however, there are few studies of efforts to improve parenting that have at the same time looked at the causal influences of changes in parental behavior on child outcomes (Shonkoff and Phillips, 2000). The exceptions have, however, provided compelling evidence that by applying what we know about good parenting practices from the correlational literature to intervention efforts can have beneficial impact on child developmental outcomes.

What has become clear from the research over many years is that the fundamental principle that parenting education programs (both universal and targeted) must stress is the importance of relationships. Relationships are among the most significant influences on healthy growth and psychological well-being. The quality of the parent–child relationship has long been acknowledged to be one of the most powerful predictors of optimal child development. Warm, responsive parenting is associated with later child language development (Bee et al., 1982; Clarke-Stewart, 1973; Eladro, Bradley, and Caldwell, 1977), cognitive development (Bakeman and Brown, 1980; Bee et al., 1982; Escalona, 1987; Lyons-Ruth, Connell, Zoll, and Stahl 1989), school success (Werner and Smith, 1982), and behavioral adjustment (Escalona, 1987; Maccoby and Martin, 1983, Pettit and Bates, 1989). Conversely, parents who are less involved and affectionate with their children are more likely to experience many more academic and behavioral problems with those children as they grow in years (Olweus, 1980). Research on children's resilience in the face of environmental risk suggests that, throughout childhood, having just one warm, supportive relationship with a caring adult is consistently related to lower risk that a child will turn to delinquency, substance abuse, or other maladaptive behavior (Rutter, 1979). It is not within the scope of this chapter to discuss the many specific parental behaviors that are correlated with good child developmental outcomes; however, it is imperative that we stress the key component that should be a part of every parent education program: the importance and significance of the parent–child relationship.

There are significant limitations to evaluating of parenting programs across disciplines, theoretically driven programs, universal access, and targeted programs. These limitations are not necessarily due to poor science, although that can often be the case, but rather due to the nature of the beast. Program evaluation is complicated methodologically and theoretically. For instance, one critical question for parenting education program evaluation is "What is the goal of the program?" Similarly, "What is the desired outcome?" and "For whom are these outcomes anticipated?" Do we define success in terms of parental change in behavior and/or attitudes, or is success a function of improved functioning for the child of enrolled parents?

Traditionally, only quantitative outcome data have been utilized to assess the success of a program. Outcome evaluation requires data on the individual parents, and sometimes their children. These data examine parental behavior change, attitude change, child behavior or performance change, or the absence of negative outcomes such as child abuse. Outcome evaluations might also include information on access to the program, parents' willingness to participate, and their level of participation or engagement as mediating outcomes. However, when the outcome data show no effect or an effect only for a subgroup of program participants, researchers are left with the question, "Why?" One way to address this shortcoming is to include a process evaluation and employ qualitative methods in addition to quantitative methods.

Process evaluation requires data on the mechanisms by which a program establishes itself, trains its staff, and generally operates on a day-to-day basis. More and more programs are employing process evaluation to better understand their functioning and impact. For example, many programs have identified participant attendance and engagement as a key component to program success (e.g., HIPPY, the NHVP, teen programs, and others). Using process data, program administrators are able to identify promoters and barriers to attendance and engagement and use this information to make program improvements.

Qualitative methods are increasingly used in program evaluation and have specific strengths and weaknesses for psychological research. Qualitative methods can be valuable for parent education programs, community-level research, and empowerment because they are meaningful to the participants, empower the population, and increase the likelihood that substantive changes, initiatives, and even interventions will have lasting effects. Their strength is in examining the "why" from the perspective of the people who know "why." Qualitative studies may be less ideal when researching questions that require both external validity and strong internal validity. Studies that are not foundation building (e.g., exploring theoretical phenomena or charting new territory), should utilize both quantitative and qualitative methods. (For a review of theory and methods of program evaluation, see Guba and Lincoln, 1989).

We know a great deal about parenting and what is related to good outcomes in children generally, but not in all individual cases. We still do not completely understand all the hows and whys. Researchers are still working on identifying everything that goes into the "magic" of parenting. However, with concerted efforts to examine how and when parenting education programs change behavior and provide beneficial effects to the children of parents being served, science can better inform the field.

CONCLUSIONS

The evolution of the notion of parent education has evolved and taken many forms over the last 100 years. It has grown from sharing information on the front porch of the general store and at church gatherings, to small informal groups of parents getting together, to national multimillion-dollar programs. Parent-education programs have always seemed to reflect the current political climate and tenor of the times as well as the ideas of leading thinkers of the day. Parent education has been marked by a diversity in program design and implementation, materials used, and preferred audiences and evaluation measures. Despite the considerable diversity of designs, parent-education programs have been based on the common assumption that parents play a central role in their children's development and that additional information and support can assist them in this role. There is no single model of parent education, and there is no one curriculum that meets the unique and individualized needs of all parents. However, we conclude that a parent-education program should emphasize what is essential for a child's well-being: stable loving relationships with parents who provide nurturing, reciprocal interactions; safety from harm; consistent discipline; and a stimulating, encouraging learning environment. In addition, the transmission of cultural and moral values and virtues is one of a parent's most important and fundamental jobs.

In this chapter, we have addressed parent education in the broadest sense. We attempted to highlight a few of the nationally recognized, evaluated, and replicated models and curricula that have influenced parent education programs in this country. We have discussed some of the limitations in research as well as problems with evaluation of parent-education programs.

We have learned a great deal from the many parent education programs over the years, and it is our hope that as parent education continues to evolve several features will hallmark progress: first, that attention will be paid to the unique and individual needs of parents in the design and implementation of service delivery; second, that parent educators will have an exceptional knowledge base and be adequately trained; and third, that appropriate process evaluation measures will be a part of every parent-education program.

REFERENCES

Aitchison, R. (1976). *Confident parenting*. Studio City, CA: Center for the Improvement of Child Caring.
Altman, J. S. (1987). The effects of selected caregiver behaviors on adaptive behavior development: Daycare vs. home/mother care. *Dissertation Abstracts International, 48*, 1110A.

Alvy, K. T. (1994). *Parent training today*. Studio City, CA: Center for the Improvement of Child Caring.

American Psychiatric Association. (1994). *Diagnostic and statistical manual of mental disorders* (4th ed.). Washington, DC: Author.

Anastopoulos, A. D. (1998). A training program for parents of children with attention-deficit/hyperactivity disorder. In J. M. Briesmeister and C. E. Schaefer, (Eds.), *Handbook of parent training: Parents as co-therapists for children's behavior problems* (2nd ed., pp. 27–60). New York: Wiley.

Anastopoulos, A. D., Smith, J. M., and Wien, E. E. (1998). Counseling and training parents. In R. A. Barkley (Ed.), *Attention-deficit hyperactivity disorder: A handbook for diagnosis and treatment* (2nd ed., pp. 373–393). New York: Guilford.

Baker, A. J. L., Piotrikowski, C. S., and Brooks-Gunn, J. (1999). The home instruction program for preschool youngsters (HIPPY). *The Future of Children: Home Visiting: Recent Program Evaluations, 9*, 116–133.

Bakeman, R., and Brown, J. V. (1980). Early interaction: Consequences for social and mental development. *Child Development, 51*, 437–447.

Bandura, A. (1977). *Social learning theory*. Englewood Cliffs, NJ: Prentice-Hall.

Barkley, R. A. (1998). *Attention-deficit hyperactivity disorder: a handbook for diagnosis and treatment* (2nd ed.). New York: Guilford.

Bee, H. L., Barnard, K. E., Eyres, S. J., Gray, C. A., Hammond, M. A., Spietz, A. L., Snyder, C., and Clark, B. (1982). Prediction of IQ and language skill from perinatal status, child performance, family characteristics, and mother–infant interaction. *Child Development, 53*, 1134–1156.

Belsky, J., Taylor, D. G., and Rovine, M. (1984). The Pennsylvania infant and family development project, II: The development of reciprocal interaction in the mother–infant dyad. *Child Development, 55*, 706–717.

Bloom, B. S. (1964). *Stability and change in human characteristics*. New York: Wiley.

Booth, C. L., Spieker, S. J., Barnard, K. E., and Morisset, C. E. (1992). Infants at risk: The role of preventive intervention in deflecting a maladaptive developmental trajectory. In J. McCord and R. E. Tremblay (Eds.), *Preventing antisocial behavior: Interventions from birth through adolescence* (pp. 21–42). New York: Guilford.

Borduin, C. M., and Henggeler, S. W. (1990). Multisystemic approach to the treatment of serious delinquent behavior. In R. J. McMahon and R. DeV. Peters (Eds.), *Behavior disorders of adolescence*. New York: Plenum.

Borduin, C. M., Henggeler, S. W., Blaske, D. M., and Stein, R. (1990). Multisystemic treatment of adolescent sexual offenders. *International Journal of Offender Therapy and Comparative Criminology, 35*, 105–114.

Bromley, B. E., and Blacher, J. (1991). Parental reasons for out-of-home placement of children with severe handicaps. *Mental Retardation, 29*, 275–280.

Bronfenbrenner, U. (1986). Ecology of the family as a context for human development. *Developmental Psychology, 22*, 723–742.

Brooks-Gunn, J., Berlin, L. J., and Fuligni, A. S. (2000). Early childhood intervention programs: What about the family? In J. P. Shonkoff and S. J. Mcisels (Eds.), *Handbook of early childhood intervention* (2nd ed., pp. 549–587). New York: Cambridge University Press.

Brooks-Gunn, J., Gross, R. T., Kraemer, H. C., Spiker, D., and Shapiro, S. (1992). Enhancing the cognitive outcomes of low- birth-weight, premature infants: For whom is the intervention most effective? *Pediatrics, 89*, 1209–1215.

Cheng Gorham, J., and Balter, L. (1997). Culturally sensitive parent education: A critical review of quantitative research. *Review of Educational Research, 67*, 339–369.

Children and Adults with Attention Deficit/Hyperactivity Disorder. (2000). *CHADD facts 8*. Landover, MD: Author.

Children's Defense Fund. (1999). The state of America's children. (1999, Yearbook). Washington, DC.

Clarke-Stewart, K. A. (1973). Interactions between mothers and their young children: Characteristics and consequences. *Monographs of the Society for Research in Child Development, 38* (Serial No. 153).

Cowan, P. A., and Cowan, C. P. (1992). *When partners become parents*. New York: Basic Books.

Cunningham, C. E., and Barkley, R. A. (1979). The interactions of hyperactive and normal children with their mothers during free play and structured task. *Child Development, 50*, 217–224.

Dangel, R. E., and Polster, R. A. (Eds.). (1984). *Parent training*. New York: Guilford.

Dinkmeyer, D., and McKay, G. D. (1976). *Systematic training for effective parenting*. Circle Pines, MN: American Guidance Service.

Dishion, T. J., Patterson, G. R., Stoolmiller, M., and Skinner, M. L. (1991). Family, school, and behavioral antecedents to early adolescent involvement with antisocial peers. *Developmental Psychology, 27*, 172–180.

Dodge, K. A. (1993). The future of research on the treatment of conduct disorder. *Development and psychopathology, 5*, 311–319.

Dowley, E. (1971). Perspectives on early childhood education. In R. H. Anderson and H. G. Shane (Eds.), *As the twig is bent*. Boston: Houghton Mifflin.

Duggan, Anne, K., McFarlane, Elizabeth, C., Windham, Amy, M., Rohde, Charles, A., Salkever, David, S., Fuddy, Loretta, Rosenberg, Leon, A., Buchbinder, Sharon, B., Sia, Calvin, C. J. (1999). Evalution Hawaii's Healthy Start Program. Future of Children. Vol 9(1), 66–90. The David and Lucie Packard Foundation, US Virgin, Islands.

Dumas, J. E., Prinz, R. J., Smith, E. O., and Laughlin, J. (1999). The Early Alliance prevention trial: An integrated set of interventions to promote competence and reduce risk for conduct disorder, substance abuse, and school failure. *Clinical Child and Family Psychology Review, 2,* 37–53.

Duncan, G. J., Yeung, W. J., Brooks-Gunn, J., and Smith, J. R. (1998). How much does childhood poverty affect the life chances of children? *American Sociological Review, 63,* 406–423.

Dunst, C. (1995). *Enabling and empowering families: Principles and guidelines for practice.* Cambridge, MA: Brookline.

Eladro, R., Bradley, R., and Caldwell, B. M. (1977). A longitudinal study of the relation of infants' home environments to language development at age three. *Child Development, 48,* 595–603.

Elder, G. H. (1995). Life trajectories in changing societies. In A. Bandura (Ed.), *Self-efficacy in changing societies* (pp. 46–68). New York: Cambridge University Press.

Einzig, H. (1996). Parenting education and support. In R. Bayne and I. Horton (Eds.), *New directions in counseling* (pp. 220–234); London: Routledge.

Escalona, S. K. (1987). *Critical issues in the early development of premature infants.* New Haven, CT: Yale University Press.

Fein, G. (1980). The informed parent. In S. Kilmer (Ed.), *Advances in early education and day care* (pp. 155–185); Greenwich, CT: JAI.

Fewell, R. R., Casal, S. G., Glick, M. P., Wheeden, C. A., and Spiker, D. (1996). Maternal education and maternal responsiveness as predictors of play competence in low-birth-weight, premature infants: A preliminary report. *Journal of Developmental and Behavioral Pediatrics, 17,* 100–104.

Galinsky, E. (1994). Families and work: The importance of the quality of the work environment. In S. L. Kagan and B. Weissbourd (Eds.), *Putting families first: America's family support movement and the challenges of change* (pp. 112–136); San Francisco: Jossey-Boss.

GAO/T-HEHS-98-183. (1998a). *Head Start: Challenges faced in demonstrating program results and responding to societal changes:* Author.

GAO/HEHS-99-4. (1998b). *Teen pregnancy: State and federal efforts to implement prevention programs and measure their effectiveness:* Author.

GAO/T-HEHS-00-83. (2000). *Preschool education: Federal investment for low-income children significant but effectiveness unclear:* Author.

Goodman, P. S. (1990). Factors affecting the development of social competence in the four-year-old child. *Dissertation Abstracts International, 51,* 662–663.

Gordon, I. J. (1966). New conception of children's learning and development. In W.B. Waltjen (Ed.), *Learning and mental health in the schools* (pp. 49–73); Washington, DC: Association for Supervision and Curriculum Development.

Gordon, T. (1970). *Parent effectiveness training.* New York: Wyden.

Gordon, T. (1975). *Parent effectiveness training.* New York: New American Library.

Guba, E. G., and Lincoln, Y. S. (1989). *Fourth generation evaluation* (pp. 294). Newbury Park, CA: Sage.

Halpern, R. (1991). Supportive services for families in poverty. Dilemmas of reform. *Social Service Review, 65,* 343–364.

Harman, D., and Brim, O. G., Jr. (1980). *Learning to be parents: Principles, programs and methods.* Beverly Hills, CA: Sage.

Hammer, T. J., and Turner P. H. (1985). *Parenting in contemporary society.* Englewood Cliff, NJ: Prentice-Hall.

Henggeler, S. W. (1996). Treatment of violent juvenile offenders: We have the knowledge. *Journal of Family Psychology, 10,* 137–141.

Hunt, J. M. (1961). *Intelligence and experience.* New York: Ronald.

Johnson, L. B. (1965). *The american promise.*

Jordan, T. E. (1978). Influences on vocabulary attainment: A five-year prospective study. *Child Development, 49,* 1096–1106.

Kagan, S. L., Powell, D. R., Weissbourd, B., and Zigler, E. F. (1987). *America's family support programs: Perspectives and prospects.* New Haven, CT: Yale University Press.

Kazdin, A. E. (1993). Treatment of conduct disorder: Progress and directions in psychotherapy research. *Development and Psychopathology, 5,* 277–310.

Kazdin, A. E. (1997). Parent management training: Evidence, outcomes, and issues. *Journal of the American Academy of Child and Adolescent Psychology, 36,* 1349–1356.

Kopp, C. B., and McCall, R. B. (1982). Predicting later mental performance for normal, at-risk, and handicapped infants. In P. Baltes and O. Brim (Eds.), *Life span development and behavior* (pp. 33–36); New York: Academic Press.

Laosa, L. M. (1982). Families as facilitators of children's intellectual development at 3 years of age: A causal analysis. In L. M. Laosa and I. M. Sigel (Eds.), *Families as learning environments for children* (pp. 1–46); New York: Plenum.

Lutzker, J. R., and Steed, S. E. (1998). Parent training for families of children with developmental disabilities. In J. M. Briesmeister and C. E. Schaefer (Eds.), *Handbook of parent training: Parents as co-therapists for children's behavior problems* (2nd ed., pp. 281–307). New York: Wiley.

Lyons-Ruth, K., Connell D. B., Zoll, D., and Stahl, J. (1987). Infants at social risk: Relations among infant maltreatment, maternal behavior, and infant attachment behavior. *Developmental Psychology, 23,* 223–232.

Maccoby E. E., and Martin, J. A. (1983). Socialization in the context of the family: Parent–child interaction. In P. H. Mussen and E. M. Hetherington (Eds.), *Handbook of child psychology: Vol. 4. Socialization, personality, and social development* (4th ed., pp. 1–102). New York: Wiley.

Medway, F. J. (1989). Measuring the effectiveness of parent education. In M. J. Finel (Ed.), *The second handbook on parent education: Contemporary perspectives* (pp. 237–255). San Diego, CA: Academic Press.

MTA Cooperative Group. (1999a). Moderators and mediators of treatment response for children with attention-deficit/hyperactivity disorder: Multimodal treatment study of children with attention-deficit/hyperactivity disorder. *Archives of General Psychiatry, 56*, 1088–1096.

MTA Cooperative Group. (1999b). A 14-month randomized clinical trial of treatment strategies for attention-deficit/hyperactivity disorder. Multimodal treatment study of children with ADHD. *Archives of General Psychiatry, 56*, 1073–86.

National Fatherhood Initiative. (2001). Available: *www.fatherhood.org/about-us.html*

O'Leary, K. D., Pelham, W. E., Rosenbaum, A., and Price, G. H. (1976). Behavioral treatment of hyperkinetic children: An experimental evaluation of its usefulness. *Clinical Pediatrics, 15*, 510–515.

Olds, D. L., Henderson, Jr., C. R., Kitzman, H. J., Eckenrode, J. J., Cole, R. E., and Tatelbaum, R. C. (1999). Prenatal and infancy home visitation by nurses: Recent findings. *The Future of Children: Home Visiting: Recent Program Evaluations, 9*, 44–65.

Oller, D. K., Eilers, R. E., Steffens, M. L., and Lynch, M. P. (1994). Speech-like vocalizations in infancy: An evaluation of potential risk factors. *Journal of Child Language, 21*, 33–58.

Olweus, D. (1980). The consistency issue in personality psychology revisited with special reference to aggression. *British Journal of Social and Clinical Psychology, 19*, 377–390.

Peralta de Mendoza, O. A. (1995). Developmental changes and socioeconomic differences in mother–infant picture book reading. *European Journal of Psychology of Education, 10*, 261–272.

Pettit, G. S., and Bates, J. E. (1989). Family interaction patterns and children's behavior problems from infancy to four years. *Developmental Psychology, 25*, 413–420.

Pew Charitable Trust. (1996). *See how we grow: A report on the status of parenting education in the U.S.* Philadelphia, PA: Author.

Powell, D. R. (1989). *Families and early childhood programs.* Washington, DC: National Association for the Education of Young Children.

Prinz, R. J., Smith, E. P., Dumas, J. E., Laughlin, J. E., White, D. W., and Barron, R. (2001). Recruitment and retention of participants in prevention trials involving family-based interventions. *American Journal of Preventive Medicine, 20*, 31–37.

Radziszewska, B., Richardson, J. L., Dent, C. W., and Flay, B. R. (1996). Parenting style and adolescent depressive symptoms, smoking, and academic achievement: Ethnic, gender, and SES differences. *Journal of Behavioral Medicine, 19*, 289–305.

Richman, A. L. Miller, P. M., and LeVine, R. A. (1992). Cultural and educational variations in maternal responsiveness. *Developmental Psychology, 28*, 614–621.

Roberts, D. F., Foehr, U. G., Rideout, V. J. and Brodie, M. (1999). *Kids and media at the new millennium.* Menlo Park, CA: Kaiser Family Foundation.

Rush, K. L. (1999). Caregiver–child interactions and early literacy development of preschool children from low-income environments. *Topics in Early Childhood Special Education, 19*, 3–14.

Rutter, M. (1979). Protective factors in children's response to stress and disadvantage. In M. W. Kent and J. E. Rolf (Eds.), *Primary prevention of psychopathology: Vol. 3. Promoting social competence and coping in children* (pp. 49–74). Hanover, NH: University Press of New England.

Schaefer, E. S. (1991). Goals for parent and future-parent education: Research on parental beliefs and behavior. *Elementary School Journal, 91*, 239–247.

Schlossman, S. L. (1976). Before home start: Notes toward a history of parent education in America, 1897–1929. *Havard Educational Review, 46*, 436–467.

Schlossman, S. L. (1983). The formative era in American parent education: Overview and interpretation. In R. Haskins and D. Adams (Eds.), *Parent education and public policy* (pp. 7–39); Norwood, NJ: Ablex.

Schreibman, L., and Koegel, R. L. (1996). Fostering self-management: Parent-delivered pivotal response training for children with autistic disorder. In E. D. Hibbs and P. S. Jensen (Eds.), *Psychosocial treatments for child and adolescent disorders: Empirically based strategies for clinical practice* (pp. 525–552); Washington, DC: Amarican Psychratric Association.

Shoenwald, S. K., Ward, D. M., Henggeler, S. W., Pickrel, S. G., and Patel, H. (1996). Multisystemic therapy treatment of substance abusing or dependent adolescent offenders: cost of reducing incarceration, inpatient and residential placement. *Journal of Child and Family Studies, 4*, 431–444.

Shonkoff, J., and Phillips, D. (Eds.). (2000). *From neurons to neighborhoods.* Committee on integrating the science of early childhood development.

Skinner, B. F. (1953). *Science and human behavior.* New York: Macmillan.

Strom R., Hathaway, C., and Slaughter, H. (1981). The correlation of maternal attitudes and preschool children's performance on the McCarthy scales of children's abilities. *Journal of Instructional Psychology, 8*, 139–145.

Suarez, L. M., and Baker, B. L. (1997). Child externalizing behavior and parents' stress: The role of social support. *Family Relations*, *47*, 373–381.

Swick, K. (1984). *Inviting parents into the young child's world*. Champaign, IL: Stipes.

Swick, K., and Graves, S. (1993). *Empowering at-risk families during the early childhood years*. Washington, DC: National Education Association.

Todres, R., and Bunston, T. (1993). Parent education program evaluation: A review of the literature. *Canadian Journal of Community Mental Health*, *12*, 225–257.

Tramontana, M. G., Sherrets, S. D., and Authier, K. J. (1980). Evaluation of parent education programs. *Journal of Clinical Child Psychology*, *9*, 40–43.

Ventura, S. J., Matthews, T. J., and Curtin, S. C. (1999). Declines in teenage birth rates, 1991–98: Update of national and state trends. *National Vital Statistics Reports*, *47*.

Victora, C. G., Huttly, S. R. A., Barros, F. C., Lombardi, C., and Vaughan, J. P. (1992). Maternal education in relation to early and late child health outcomes: Finds from a Brazilian cohort study. *Social Science Medicine*, *34*, 899–905.

Wallace, I. F., Roberts, J. E., and Lodder, D. E. (1998). Interactions of african american infants and their mothers: Relations with development at 1 year of age. *Journal of Speech, Language, and Hearing Research*, *41*, 900–912.

Webster-Stratton, C. (1994). Advancing videotape parent training: A comparison study. *Journal of Consulting and Clinical Psychology*, *62*, 583–593.

Weissbourd, B. (1987). A brief history of family support programs. In S. Kagan, D. Powell, B.Weissbourd, and G. Zigler (Eds.), *American family support programs* (pp. 38–56). New Haven, CT: Yale University Press.

Weissbourd, B., and Kagan, S. L. (Eds.). (1994). *Putting families first: America's family support movement and the challenge of change*. San Francisco: Jossey-Bass.

Werner, E. E., and Smith, R. S. (1982). *Vulnerable but invincible: A longitudinal study of resilient children and youth*. NewYork: McGraw-Hill.

Winter, M., and Rouse, J. M. (1991). Parents as teachers: *Nurturing literacy in the very young. Zero to Three*, *12*, 80–83.

Yeargin-Allsopp, M., Drews, C. D., Decoufle, P., and Murphy, C. C. (1995). Mild mental retardation in black and white children in metropolitan Atlanta: A case-control study. *American Journal of Public Health*, *85*, 324–328.

Zigler, E. F., and Muenchow, S. (1992). *Headstart: The inside story of America's most successful educational experiment*. New York: Basic Books.

Author Index

Chen, L., **I**, 300, *308*; **III**, 441, *458*;
 IV, 2, 10, 11, *18*; **V**, 155, *165*
Chen, S. J., **IV**, 61, 62, 80, *88*
Chen, X., **I**, 259, 260, 262, 265, 266, *273*,
 276, 385, 386, 396, 398, 400, 401,
 405, 406, *411*, *416*; **II**, 238, *248*,
 275, *277*; **III**, 158, *171*, 493, *506*;
 IV, 74, 79, *88*; **V**, 71, *87*, 106, *107*,
 130, *141*, 160, *164*, 274, 278, *308*
Chen, Z., **I**, 49, *66*
Chen, Z.-Y., **I**, 122, *127*
Cheney, D. L., **II**, 100, *138*, 186, 187, *202*
Cheng Gorham, J., **IV**, 392, 394, *407*
Cherlin, A. C., **III**, 180, *206*
Cherlin, A. J., **III**, 43, *66*, 113, 114, 115,
 117, 122, *136*, 143, 147, 150, 152,
 166, 179, 191, 200, 202, *205*, *206*,
 287, 289, 290, 291, 292, 295, 300,
 301, 302, 306, 307, *311*, *312*, *314*;
 IV, 61, *88*
Chernow, R., **V**, 213, *215*
Cherry, F. F., **II**, 221, *226*
Cherukuri, R., **IV**, 340, *353*
Chesler, M., **V**, *344*
Chesley, S., **II**, 67, *90*
Chesney, M., **V**, 448, *458*
Chess, S., **I**, 16, *42*, 175, *188*, 255, 256, *273*,
 276, 408, *417*; **II**, 258, *279*, 318,
 321, 322, 323, 324, *340*, *343*, *344*;
 IV, 166, 167, *176*, *180*, 268, *285*
Chestang, L., **I**, 299, *306*
Chester, N. L., **III**, 187, 188, *212*
Chethik, L., **IV**, 346, *353*
Cheung, C., **IV**, 66, 80, *88*
Cheung, P. C., **II**, 331, *342*; **IV**, 73, 74, 76,
 77, 79, *87*, *88*, *90*
Cheung, U., **II**, 65, 66, 67, 75, *89*
Cheung, U. S., **II**, 78, *89*
Chevalier, J. A., **II**, 288, *310*
Chevron, E., **III**, 420, *434*
Chiba, T., **II**, 78, *88*
Chicago Health Connection, **III**, 20, *23*
Chiesa, J., **III**, 443, 445, *458*; **V**, 60, *85*
Chih-Mei, C., **IV**, 81, *89*
Chilamkurti, C., **IV**, 374, *384*
Chilcoat, H. D., **III**, 463, 469, *482*; **IV**,
 308, *321*; **V**, 75, *84*
Child Care Bureau, **V**, 375, *401*
Child Trends, **III**, 121, *136*
Child Welfare League, **I**, 315, 316, *326*
Child, I. L., **II**, 232, *252*, 260, 261, 262,
 263, 264, 271, *276*, *280*; **IV**, 62, *92*
Childers v. Childers, **V**, 472, *482*
Childers, K. W., **V**, 355, 361, 362,
 363, *369*
Children and Adults with Attention
 Deficit/Hyperactivity Disorder, **IV**,
 402, *407*
Children's Advertising Review Unit and
 International Food Information
 Council, **V**, 366, *369*
Children's Defense Fund, **I**, *326*; **IV**, 390,
 407; **V**, 312, *325*, 444, *457*
Children's Foundation, **V**, 394, *401*
Childs, C. P., **I**, 52, *68*; **III**, 267, *280*

Chimezie, A., **I**, 299, *306*
Chin, M., **I**, 144, *157*
Chinapen, S., **II**, 5, 39, *57*, 76, *92*
Ching, W.-D., **I**, 90, *98*; **IV**, 83, *89*
Chin-Quee, D., **III**, 231, *245*
Chiodo, L. M., **IV**, 341, *355*
Chipungu, S. S., **III**, 153, 157, *172*
Chiriboga, C., **IV**, 340, *358*
Chirino, R., **II**, 44, *56*, 70, *90*
Chirkov, V. I., **V**, 106, *107*
Chisholm J. S., **II**, 23, *27*
Chisholm, K., **I**, 288, 302, *306*, *307*;
 IV, 185, 189, 190, *198*
Chism, J., **II**, 124, 131, *134*
Chistovich, I. A., **IV**, 194, *199*
Chisum, G. M., **IV**, 340, *353*
Chiu, L. H., **IV**, 73, *88*
Chiu, M. L., **IV**, 73, *88*
Chivers, D. J., **II**, 111, *137*
Chmielewski, D., **V**, 333, *345*
Cho, S. N., **IV**, 71, *87*
Chodorow, N., **I**, 191, 200, 213, *218*;
 III, 390, *409*, 564, 567, 571, 572,
 586, *593*
Choi, E., **IV**, 83, *88*
Choi, S., **IV**, 64, *90*
Chorpita, B. F., **IV**, 309, *321*
Chow, E., **I**, 193, *218*
Chowdhury, A., **I**, 124, *127*; **II**, 222, *226*
Chriki, M., **II**, 161, *177*
Christ, M. A., **IV**, 334, *354*
Christ, M. G., **IV**, 310, 312, *322*;
 V, 132, *137*
Christal, R. C., **III**, 418, *437*
Christensen, A., **III**, 79, 85, *101*; **IV**, 207,
 210, *223*
Christensen, K., **V**, 448, *458*
Christensen, M., **I**, 283, 284, 285, *309*;
 III, 350, *359*
Christenson, P., **V**, 355, 356, 357, 361,
 364, *369*
Christerphersen, E. R., **II**, 292, *308*
Christian, C. L., **I**, 303, *306*
Christian, M. D., **IV**, 10, *17*
Christian, R. E., **V**, 129, *137*
Christman, J. V., **II**, 301, *312*
Christoffersen, M. N., **III**, 117, *136*
Christopher, F. S., **V**, 127, *137*, 362,
 370
Christophersen, E. R., **V**, 11, *31*
Christopoulos, C., **V**, 277, *302*
Chryssoula, S., **I**, 282, 283, *308*
Chu, C., **IV**, 317, *321*
Chung, S. F., **IV**, 73, *92*
Chung, T., **I**, 177, *186*
Church, E., **III**, 301, *311*
Church, J., **I**, 6, *35*, 45, *70*; **III**, 4, 5, *25*
Churcher, J., **I**, 11, *35*
Churchill, A., **IV**, 264, *290*
Churchill, S. L., **II**, 291, *313*
Chute, P. M., **IV**, 278, *290*
Chyi-In, W., **II**, 239, 241, 243, 244, *252*;
 III, *212*
Cialdini, R. B., **V**, 126, *136*
Cibelli, C. D., **I**, 390, *414*

Cicchetti, D., **I**, 321, 322, *326*, *327*, 363,
 377, 393, *411*; **II**, 169, *176*; **III**,
 501, *507*; **IV**, 163, *175*, 191, *199*,
 296, *321*, 361, 368, 369, 370, 372,
 375, *384*, *385*; **V**, 36, 38, 46, *55*, *56*,
 284, 285, *302*
Cicirelli, V. G., **III**, 273, *280*
Cicognani, E., **I**, 214, *220*
Cielinski, K. L., **V**, 272, 273, *301*
Cirrito, J., **II**, 39, 51, *59*
Citro, C., **IV**, 96, *117*
City of Akron v. Akron Center for
 Reproductive Health, Inc., **V**,
 474, *482*
City of Ladue v. Horn, **V**, 468, *482*
Clamar, A., **III**, 348, *357*
Clancy, P. M., **IV**, 65, 72, *88*
Clancy, S., **II**, 72, 77, *92*
Claren, S. K., **IV**, 338, *353*
Clark, A., **IV**, 268, 275, 282, *285*
Clark, A. M., **III**, 340, *360*
Clark, B., **III**, 17, *23*; **IV**, 405, *407*; **V**, 202,
 215
Clark, C. B., **II**, 106, 109, *134*
Clark, C. M., **V**, 471, *482*
Clark, D. B., **IV**, 310, *321*
Clark, D. L., **IV**, 276, *290*
Clark, K. E., **IV**, 340, *359*; **V**, 274, *302*
Clark, L., **III**, 426, 428, 429, 432, *435*, *436*,
 437, *438*
Clark, L. A., **I**, 261, *273*; **III**, 420, 426,
 437, *438*
Clark, M. C., **II**, 44, *59*; **V**, 290, *305*
Clark, P. M., **I**, 232, *251*
Clark, R., **II**, 155, *178*, 215, 216, *227*;
 III, 49, *66*; **IV**, 209, *224*, 346, *353*;
 V, 105, *109*, 200, *215*
Clark, W., **III**, 400, *409*
Clarke, A. D. B., **I**, 24, *35*; **IV**, 192, *198*
Clarke, A. M., **I**, 24, *35*; **IV**, 192, *198*
Clarke, C., **I**, 408, *413*
Clarke, G., **II**, 68, *96*, 159, *181*
Clarke, L., **III**, 129, *138*
Clarke, M. C., **I**, 263, *277*
Clarke-Stewart, K. A., **I**, 22, *35*, 201, *218*;
 II, 239, *248*; **III**, 17, *23*, 34, 55, *64*,
 221, 225, 226, 227, 228, 229, 230,
 231, 232, 233, 234, 235, 237, 239,
 245, 294, *311*, 450, *457*, 486, *506*;
 563, *593*; **IV**, 149, *175*, 405, *407*;
 V, 43, 53, *55*, 223, *237*, 376, *401*
Clark-Lempers, D., **I**, 119, *131*, 400, 403,
 405, *414*; **II**, 242, *250*
Clarren, S. K., **IV**, 330, 339, *358*
Clatfelter, D., **IV**, 229, 234, *255*; **V**, 275,
 304
Clausen, J. A., **III**, 417, *435*
Clausen, S.-E., **IV**, 166, *175*
Clauson, J., **III**, 95, *101*
Claussen, A., **I**, 124, *128*
Clawson, M., **V**, 275, 283, *307*
Clawson, M. A., **IV**, 161, *179*
Clay, D., **V**, 339, *345*
Clayton, E. W., **V**, 445, 451, 454, 455,
 458, *459*

Ievers, C., **V**, 343, *345*
Iglehart, J. K., **V**, 447, *459*
Ignatoff, E., **I**, 347, *351*; **II**, 124, *134*, 236, *249*
Ihinger-Tallman, M., **III**, 294, 295, 305, *313*, *314*
Ikemoto, S., **II**, 77, 80, *91*
Iker, H., **V**, 441, *457*
Ikhlas, M., **IV**, 28, *40*
Ilan, T., **II**, 355, 356, *375*
Ill. Rev. Stat. ch., 750, 472, *483*
Illick, J. E., **IV**, 154, *177*
Imaizumi, Y., **I**, 228, *252*
Imamichi, T., **II**, 42, *59*
Imbesi, L., **IV**, 312, *322*
Impicciciatore, P., **V**, 445, *459*
In re Ackenhausen, **V**, 465, *483*
In re Adoption of Baby A and Baby B, **V**, 466, *483*
In re Adoption of J. J. B., **V**, 465, *483*
In re Adoption of Paul, **V**, 466, *483*
In re Adoption of Tachick, **V**, 465, *483*
In re Gault, **V**, 479, *483*
In re Phillip B., **V**, 467, *483*
In re Raquel Marie X., **V**, 466, *483*
In re Roger S., **V**, 475, *483*
Inch, L. J., **I**, 316, 317, 321, *326*
Inclan, J., **IV**, 36, *42*
Indelicato, S., **III**, 46, *65*
Individuals with Disabilities Education Act, Pub. L. No. 101-476, **V**, 477, *483*
Ingegneri, D. G., **I**, 146, *157*
Ingersoll, B. D., **I**, 282, *308*
Ingersoll, E. W., **I**, 9, *38*, 345, *354*
Ingersoll-Dayton, B., **III**, 163, *168*; **V**, 252, *265*
Inglis, W., **II**, 85, *90*
Ingman, M., **II**, 11, *28*
Ingoldsby, B. B., **IV**, 31, *42*
Ingoldsby, E. M., **V**, 131, *138*
Ingraham v. Wright, **V**, 478, *483*
Ingram, C. D., **II**, 65, *97*
Ingram, D. L., **V**, 447, *460*
Ingrassia, M., **IV**, 51, *57*
Ingulli, E. D., **V**, 24, *32*
Inhelder, B., **IV**, 251, *257*
Inkelis, S. H., **IV**, 340, *355*
Innis, R. B., **II**, 169, *173*
Inoue, W., **III**, 403, *410*
Inouye, E., **I**, 228, *252*
Insabella, G. M., **I**, 82, *97*; **III**, 89, *104*, 288, 289, 290, 298, 300, 304, 309, *312*, *313*
Insel, R. T., **II**, 41, *60*
Insel, T. R., **II**, 41, 43, *56*, *57*, *60*, 64, 65, 69, 74, 81, 85, *91*, *97*, 115, 116, *139*, 148, 159, 162, 164, 170, *177*, *181*
Inui, T. S., **V**, 451, *461*
Ionnotti, R., **V**, 332, *344*
Ippolito, M. F., **I**, 77, *96*
Irel, M., **I**, 120, *132*
Ireland, T., **IV**, 344, *359*
Ireys, H.T., **IV**, 266, 269, *288*; **V**, 337, *344*
Irizarry, N. L., **I**, 17, *37*
Ironsmith, M., **III**, 238, *250*

Irvin, N., **I**, 357, *378*
Irvine, A., **I**, 75, *95*
Irvine, A. B., **IV**, 171, *177*
Irving, H. H., **III**, 296, *310*
Isaacs, M. R., **III**, 451, *458*
Isabella, R. A., **II**, 23, *28*; **III**, 52, *63*, 374, 376, *386*, *388*; **IV**, 149, 163, *177*, 180, 214, 224, 342, *355*; **V**, 252, *263*
Isay, R., **III**, 589, *596*
Isenberg, S. J., **IV**, 340, *355*
Ishii, S., **III**, 403, *410*, *413*
Ishii-Kuntz, M., **III**, 32, 46, 60, *64*, *67*
Ishi-Kunta, M., **IV**, 4, *18*
Ishino, F., **II**, 81, *92*
Isley, S., **I**, 212, *223*; **III**, 56, *67*; **IV**, 229, 234, 239, *255*
Isley, S. L., **V**, 275, *304*
Ispa, J. M., **III**, 229, 230, *251*; **V**, 384, *402*
Israel, J., **IV**, 261, *288*
Israelashvili, R., **III**, 41, *68*, 427, 429, *436*
Itani, J., **II**, 99, 113, *135*
Ito, Y., **II**, 169, *177*
Itskovitz, J., **II**, 65, *91*
Iverson, S., **I**, 301, *305*
Ivey, P. K., **II**, 144, *181*, 299, *313*
Ivy, G. O., **II**, 78, *89*
Iwawaki, S., **IV**, 74, 76, *92*
Iyengar, S., **V**, 334, *346*
Izard, C., **I**, 403, *409*; **II**, 297, *307*
Izenson, N., **I**, 196, 198, *217*
Izquierdo, I., **II**, 79, *91*
Izquierdo, L. A., **II**, 79, *91*

J

Jablonka, K., **I**, 316, 317, 319, 320, 323, *327*
Jaccard, J., **I**, 76, *99*; **V**, 320, *326*
Jacklin, C. N., **I**, 198, 201, 202, 204, 214, *222*, *224*, 249, *253*, 260, 269, *275*; **III**, 519, *533*
Jackson, A., **I**, 333, *351*; **IV**, 104, *119*
Jackson, A. E., **I**, 214, *220*
Jackson, B., **III**, 444, 450, *458*
Jackson, D., **III**, 420, *437*
Jackson, D. D., **IV**, 236, *253*
Jackson, J. F., **II**, 22, *28*; **IV**, 22, 23, 33, *41*
Jackson, J. S., **IV**, 10, *19*, 49, 54, *57*
Jackson, K. M., **V**, 129, *136*
Jackson, L., **V**, 355, 357, *371*
Jackson, N., **V**, 204, *217*
Jackson, P. B., **III**, 547, *560*
Jackson, R. L., **V**, 261, *267*
Jackson-Beeck, M., **V**, 475, *483*
Jacob, E., **III**, 163, *168*
Jacob, M., **III**, 349, *358*
Jacob, M. C., **III**, 353, *358*
Jacob, T., **I**, 113, 117, *132*; **II**, 238, *250*; **IV**, 240, *255*
Jacobs, A., **IV**, 163, *179*
Jacobs, B. S., **I**, 334, *351*
Jacobs, E., **III**, 230, 240, *251*
Jacobs, F., **II**, 336, *340*

Jacobs, F. H., **II**, 338, *342*
Jacobs, J., **I**, 209, *218*; **III**, 525, *532*; **V**, 25, *34*, 452, *459*
Jacobs, J. E., **III**, 488, *507*
Jacobs, S. M., **I**, 169, 180, *186*
JacobsCarter, S., **IV**, 37, *41*
Jacobsen, C. F., **II**, 99, *135*
Jacobsen, M. M., **II**, 99, *135*
Jacobsen, P., **V**, 342, *346*
Jacobsen, R., **III**, 589, *593*
Jacobsen, R. B., **III**, 322, 323, *335*, *337*
Jacobsen, T., **II**, 23, *28*
Jacobson, A. M., **I**, 117, *129*, 202, 203, 213, 215, *221*; **III**, 183, *208*, 424, *436*; **V**, 337, 338, 343, *345*
Jacobson, D., **V**, 338, 341, *345*
Jacobson, D. S., **IV**, 255, 275, *288*
Jacobson, J. L., **I**, 26, *38*; **II**, 195, *200*, 285, 288, *310*; **III**, 229, 230, *252*; **IV**, 341, *355*; **V**, 228, *238*
Jacobson, K. C., **I**, 212, 213, *221*; **II**, 240, 244, *250*, *251*; **V**, 129, *138*
Jacobson, L., **III**, 429, *437*; **V**, 174, *193*
Jacobson, L. J., **III**, 199, *207*
Jacobson, S. W., **II**, 285, 288, *310*; **IV**, 341, *355*
Jacobvitz, D. B., **III**, 79, *106*, 195, *207*; **IV**, 163, *178*, 233, *255*; **V**, 44, *56*
Jacques, T. Y., **IV**, 167, *177*
Jaeger, E., **III**, 227, *252*
Jaeger, S., **I**, 6, *38*
Jaffe, J., **II**, 193, *199*
Jaffe, M. L., **III**, 396, *411*
Jaffe, S., **II**, 44, *54*
Jagers, R., **II**, 292, *310*
Jahoda, G., **II**, 258, 259, 260, 262, *278*
Jain, A., **III**, 31, 38, 39, 59, *67*; **V**, 257, *265*
Jain, D., **I**, 204, *224*; **III**, 97, *102*; **V**, 223, *240*
Jakobson, M., **IV**, 277, *291*
Jakobson, R., 3, *38*
Jakub, D. K., **III**, 155, *167*
Jakubowski, M., **II**, 71, *91*
Jalling, B., **II**, 197, *200*
James Bell Associates, 317, *326*
James, B., **V**, 81, *85*
James, C., **III**, 369, *388*
James, L. R., **I**, 173, *186*; **III**, 385, *388*
James, M. E., **II**, 169, *177*
James, W., **II**, 189, *200*
Jan, J. E., **IV**, 261, 268, 273, *288*
Janelli, L. M., **III**, 153, *168*
Janes, H. A., **IV**, 30, *43*
Janis, I. L., **V**, 443, *461*
Janko, S., **IV**, 366, *386*
Jankowiak, W., **IV**, 63, 65, 74, *89*
Janoski, T., **V**, 126, *139*
Janovetz, V. A., **III**, 46, *66*
Jans, J. E., **II**, 52, *60*, 69, *91*
Jansen, J., **III**, 343, *357*
Janson, C. H., **II**, 116, *138*
Janssen, A. W. H., **V**, 118, *138*
Janssens, J., **III**, 424, *436*
Janssens, J. M. A. M., **I**, 82, 86, *95*; **II**, 213, *226*; **III**, 522, *533*; **IV**, 157, *175*,

Subject Index

Weschler Pre-School Test of Intelligence,
    III, 371
West Indian/Caribbean Americans, IV, 12
West Virginia, V, 472–473
Western society
    childcare trends, III, 215
        teenage pregnancy, III, 174
    cross-cultural perspectives on
        attachment, V, 44
    cultural variability, II, 269
    effective parenting, V, 161–162
    ethics of parenting, V, 18
    object play, V, 224, 233
    parental attributions, III, 525
    parental investment theory, II, 8
    parental responsibilities in shaping
        children's character, V, 13,
        14–15, 17
    parenting competence, IV, 153–154
    sibling caregiving, III, 256, 258
Wet nursing, II, 363; IV, 152, 153
White Conference, II, 232
White House Conference on Children, I,
    315
White-collar families, IV, 138, 139–140
White-collar occupations, II, 233, see also
    Occupation
WHO, see World Health Organization
Why questions, III, 513–514
Widowhood, I, 143, 146; III, 112
Williams syndrome, I, 361–362, 363, 367
Wisconsin, V, 477
Wish, see Nuclear wish
Wish/intent, III, 564, 565

Withdrawal, IV, 210, 214, 339
Withdrawn behavior, III, 490
Within-group heterogeneity, IV, 260–261
Wives, IV, 243
Wobble, V, 198
Women
    control and patriarchal state, II, 348
    father involvement in families, III, 43
    parenthood as developmental stage, III,
        390–391
    parenting with sensory/physical
        disabilities, IV, 262
    patterns of employment and parental
        role, III, 47
    power and history of parenting, II, 357
    status in Western societies, I, 191
Women's Movement, III, 76–77, 79, 98
Women's rights, IV, 262
Work
    adolescent parenthood effects, III, 176,
        178–179
    childcare choice, V, 394
    conflicts of custodial parents, III, 118,
        119, 120–121
    cultural context of Greek parenting, II,
        359
    experiences and middle childhood, I, 85
    maternal/dual-earner employment, II,
        220, 221, 222–223
    parental monitoring/knowledge, III,
        476, 477–478
    quality of father involvement in
        families, III, 49–51
    sibling caregiving, III, 259

socioemotional adjustment of children,
    III, 49
Work Project Administration, III, 219
Workforce, IV, 390
Workhouses, IV, 365
Workmates, IV, 140
Workshops, III, 329–330
World Health Organization (WHO),
    III, 6
World wars, IV, 280, 393
Worry, V, 337
Worth, II, 289
Wright, Frank Lloyd, V, 210

X

X chromosomes, II, 12, see also Genetics;
    Heredity

Y

Yard child, I, 52–53
Yawning, II, 157
Yoruba society, III, 492
Young Moms program, IV, 403

Z

Zaire, II, 299
Zimbabawean mothers, V, 384
Zinacantan society, I, 52
Zone of proximal development, IV, 362;
    V, 488, 172
Zoo, II, 287